D1603682

PHASE TRANSITIONS IN SOLIDS

McGRAW-HILL INTERNATIONAL BOOK COMPANY

New York
St. Louis
San Francisco
Auckland
Beirut
Bogota
Düsseldorf
Johannesburg
Lisbon
London
Lucerne
Madrid
Mexico
Montreal
New Delhi
Panama
Paris
San Juan
São Paulo
Singapore
Sydney
Tokyo
Toronto

C. N. R. RAO
Solid State and Structural Chemistry Unit
Indian Institute of Science, Bangalore-560012, India

K. J. RAO
Materials Science Division
National Aeronautical Laboratory, Bangalore-560017, India

Phase Transitions in Solids

AN APPROACH TO THE STUDY OF THE CHEMISTRY AND PHYSICS OF SOLIDS

This book was set in Times New Roman 327

British Library Cataloguing in Publication Data

Rao, Chintamani Nagesa Ramachandra
Phase transitions in solids: an approach to the study of the chemistry and physics of solids.
1. Phase transformations (Statistical physics)
2. Solids
I. Title II. Rao, K J
530.4′1 QC176.8.P/ 77-30045

ISBN 0-07-051185-3

PHASE TRANSITIONS IN SOLIDS

1 2 3 4 MHMH 7 9 8 7

Printed litho in Great Britain by W & J Mackay Ltd, Chatham

स यो हैतानन्तवत उपास्तेऽन्तवन्तं स लोकं जयत्यथ
या हैताननन्तानुपास्तेऽनन्तं स लोकं जयति ॥ १३ ॥

And he who worships them as finite, obtains a finite world, but he who worships them as infinite, obtains an infinite world.

तदेतन्मूर्तं यदन्यद्वायोश्चान्तरिक्षाच्चैतन्मर्त्यमेतत्स्थितमेतत्सत्त-
स्यैतस्य मूर्तस्यैतस्य मर्त्यस्यैतस्य स्थितस्यैतस्य सत एष रसो य
एष तपति सतो ह्येष रसः ॥ २ ॥

Everything except air and sky is material, is mortal, is solid, is definite. The essence of that which is material, which is mortal, which is solid, which is definite is the sun that shines, for he is the essence of Saṭ (the definite).

—Brihadaranyakopanisaṭ

CONTENTS

PREFACE

The subject of phase transitions is of vital interest to physicists, chemists, metallurgists, ceramists, and others involved in the study of solids. This cross-disciplinary subject is not only of academic importance, but also of technological relevance. The literature abounds in experimental and theoretical studies of phase transitions in solids, and the subject is continually growing. Newer systems undergoing transitions and newer kinds of transitions are being constantly reported. At the same time, many unifying concepts have emerged in recent years which provide a better understanding of the nature of phase transitions. Although books and reviews devoted to specific aspects of phase transitions, like critical phenomena, ferroelectricity, soft modes, or metal–insulator transitions, have been appearing from time to time, most texts of solid state physics and chemistry deal with this subject cursorily. Metallurgists generally pay a lot more attention to this topic, but their treatment is by necessity confined to metals and alloys. Phase transitions, on the other hand, are of significance to a much wider spectrum of materials. We therefore considered it worth while to write a book which provides a unified presentation of phase transitions in solids and covers the many facets of a fascinating subject. This book is the result of such an effort.

The introductory chapter, besides describing the scope of the book, serves as a brief essay on phase transitions. There are separate chapters devoted to thermodynamics, crystal chemistry, statistical mechanics, soft mode theory, as well as kinetics and mechanisms of phase transitions; in addition, there is a chapter on properties of solid materials and phase transitions. Under thermodynamics (Chap. 2), due attention has been paid to the treatments of second-order transitions by Landau, Pippard, and Tizza. Landau's theory has been discussed again in relation to soft modes (Chap. 6), symmetry, and ferroelectricity (Chap. 7). In the chapter on crystal chemistry (Chap. 3), Born treatment of ionic crystals, ionicity of covalent crystals, Buerger's structural classification of phase transitions, and orientational relations in phase transitions have been discussed; polytypism and the role of defects in phase transitions are also examined in that chapter.

Various kinds of phase transitions including nucleation–growth, order–disorder and martensitic transitions, spinodal and eutectoid decompositions, and transitions in glasses and liquid crystals form the subject matter of Chap. 4. In the chapter on statistical mechanics (Chap. 5), the Ising model is discussed; the universality of critical exponents and their dependence on dimensionality is considered and a brief introduction to the renormalization group given.

We had particular difficulty in deciding the extent of coverage of the theory, experimental techniques, and case studies in Chap. 7 dealing with properties of solids and phase transitions. The main emphasis in this chapter is on magnetic, electrical, and dielectric properties of solids, and we have given what we consider to be a useful summary of investigations of transitions in a variety of materials employing a number of experimental techniques. The transitions discussed in this chapter include metal–insulator transitions, Peierls transitions in one-dimensional systems, and the cooperative Jahn–Teller effect.

We have cited a large number of examples and case studies of phase transitions throughout the text. While they are chosen mainly from inorganic materials, we have also given several examples from metal and organic systems. We have pointed out how the order parameter and the soft-mode concepts, as well as martensitic or deformational mechanisms, are of wide applicability in the study of phase transitions. We have listed a number of leading references to original papers and reviews in all the chapters, and they should prove useful to those interested in a more detailed study of the subject.

Considering that any of the chapters or sections of the book could easily form the subject matter of a book by itself, we had to make certain deliberate (probably subjective) choices in deciding the breadth and depth of coverage. We have aimed to bring out a sufficiently broad-based book containing one aspect or another of value to both experimentalists and theoreticians. To the beginner, the book should serve as a good introduction to phase transitions in solids and give glimpses of many of their physical manifestations.

A comment or two on the usefulness of this book in teaching would be in order. The book, in principle, can either form the basis of a course in solid state or materials science or be used as a reference or additional text. We feel that it is most instructive to understand the nature and properties of solids through phase transitions. We believe that graduate students with a moderate background in physics and chemistry or materials science should be able to follow most parts, although they may have to consult other texts to find out details of some of the experimental techniques or theories referred to in the book.

Much of the planning and drafting of the book were done when the senior author (C. N. R. R.) was a Commonwealth Visiting Professor at the University of Oxford. His special thanks are due to Professor J. S. Anderson and other colleagues of the Inorganic Chemistry Laboratory for their kindness and encouragement. His stay at Oxford was made most pleasant through his association with St.

Catherine's College as a Fellow, and his thanks are due to the Master and Fellows of the College for their courtesy and hospitality. The manuscript of the book was completed during the tenure of the senior author as a Jawaharlal Nehru Fellow, and his thanks are due to the Jawaharlal Nehru Memorial Fund for support.

The authors are thankful to Dr. S. Dhawan of the Indian Institute of Science, and Dr. S. Ramaseshan and Dr. S. R. Valluri of the National Aeronautical Laboratory, Bangalore, for their encouragement. The authors acknowledge the help of Messrs. A. Giridhar and P. S. Lakshminarasimham, and Drs. S. Ramasesha, P. Ganguly and A. K. Shukla, for their assistance in writing the text, and to Mr. Nihal Ahmad and Mr. Vijay Kumar for typing the manuscript. Their thanks are due to the Educational Development Centre, Indian Institute of Technology, Kanpur, for financial assistance toward the preparation of the manuscript.

CHAPTER

ONE

INTRODUCTION

A given assembly of atoms or molecules may be homogeneous or nonhomogeneous. The homogeneous parts of such an assembly, called phases, are characterized by thermodynamic properties like volume, pressure, temperature, and energy. An isolated phase is stable only when its energy—or more generally, its free energy—is a minimum for the specified thermodynamic conditions. If the phase is present in a local minimum of free energy instead of in a unique minimum, and is separated from still lower minima (under the same thermodynamic conditions) by energy barriers, the system is then said to be in a metastable state. If barriers do not exist, the state of the system becomes unstable and the system moves into a stable or equilibrium state, characterized by the lowest possible free energy. As the temperature, pressure, or any other variable like an electric or a magnetic field acting on a system is varied, the free energy of the system changes smoothly and continuously. Whenever such variations of free energy are associated with changes in structural details of the phase (atomic or electronic configurations), a *phase transformation* or *phase transition** is said to occur. In this book, our main concern is with the phase transitions of solids.

Thermodynamic Considerations

The classical Clapeyron equation satisfactorily predicts the features of first-order phase transitions involving discontinuous changes in the first derivatives of Gibbs

* We shall treat the terms "transformation" and "transition" as synonymous.

free energy such as entropy and volume. A number of examples of first-order transitions brought out by variation of temperature or pressure are known.[1-4] Although one often classifies second or higher-order transitions depending on the relation between the thermodynamic property undergoing discontinuity and the Gibbs free energy function,[5] these transitions are not readily explained by classical thermodynamics. Unlike the case of first-order transitions, where the free-energy surfaces, $G(P, T)$, of the two phases intersect sharply at the transition temperature,[5] it is difficult to visualize the nature of the free-energy surfaces in second or higher-order transitions. In second-order transitions, changes in heat capacity as well as compressibility and thermal expansivity are noticed at the transition temperature, while in the so-called λ-transitions (often grouped with second-order transitions), the heat capacity tends toward infinity at the transition temperature. Landau[6] made a monumental contribution to our understanding of structural phase transitions by expanding the free energy in terms of the long-range order parameter, ξ; ξ decreases with increase in temperature and goes to zero at the transition temperature. The concept of an order parameter today provides a very general way of examining phase transitions and related physical phenomena.

The analog of the Clapeyron relation for λ-transitions has been derived by Pippard[7] by employing a cylindrical approximation to the $S(T, P)$ surface. Tizza[8] has attempted to find the thermodynamic conditions for the borderline stability (characterized by fluctuations in thermodynamic properties) associated with λ-transitions; the treatment does indeed show how C_p tends to infinity at the transition temperature. Chapter 2 of this book deals with various aspects of thermodynamics of phase transitions in some detail, including hysteresis effects.

Although it is convenient to classify phase transitions as first or second-order, many real transformations are truly of mixed order, exhibiting features of both. Generally, in thermal transformations, the high-temperature form is of higher symmetry as well as higher disorder. It is indeed instructive to examine transitions in terms of changes in order or disorder. While discussing thermodynamics of phase transitions, it is often difficult to strictly assign relative thermodynamic stabilities to polymorphs, since stabilities are affected by the presence of impurities, deviations from stoichiometry, surface area, particle size, and so on.

Yang–Lee Theorems

From the point of view of statistical mechanics, a grand partition function, Z_G, as given by

$$Z_G(z, V, T) = \sum_{N=0}^{\infty} z^N Z_N(V, T) \qquad (1\text{-}1)$$

should contain all the information necessary to reflect the occurrence of a transition as a function of volume V, temperature T, or the activity of particles constituting the system, z. In Eq. (1-1), Z_N is the classical canonical partition function, and

z is equal to $\exp(\mu/kT)$, where μ is its chemical potential. That Z_G does indeed contain such information was proved by Yang and Lee.[9,10]

The partition function $Z_N(V, T)$ is given by

$$Z_N(V, T) = \frac{1}{N!\,\lambda^{3N}} \int \exp\left[-\frac{\Omega(r_1 \ldots r_N)}{kT}\right] d^{3N}r \tag{1-2}$$

where λ, the thermal wavelength, is given by $\sqrt{2\pi\hbar^2/mkT}$, and $\Omega(r_1 \ldots r_N)$ is the potential energy of the system. For finite values of V and T, the function in Eq. (1-2) is completely analytical, and nothing unusual would be expected to happen to the system. It is necessary therefore to discuss the behavior of the system in the limit $N, V \to \infty$ and $N/V = \rho$, remaining constant.[11] The phase transition may then be defined as any nonanalytic point of the grand canonical potential, p/kT, where

$$p/kT = \lim_{V \to \infty} \frac{1}{V} \ln Z_G(z, V, T) \tag{1-3}$$

Nonanalyticity only means that the function cannot be expanded by a Taylor's series at that point. Therefore a transition need not have to correspond to a discontinuity in p or any particular derivative.

In order to really see whether a transition occurs, one has to calculate appropriate quantities like p and v (for condensation, where v is the specific volume), and this is a very difficult problem. Yang and Lee, however, showed without recourse to actual calculation that Eq. (1-1) leads to a phase transition in the limit $V, N \to \infty$ and $V/N = 1/\rho$ remaining constant. The two assumptions made in the Yang–Lee theory relate to the nature of interparticle interactions: (*a*) interactions are pairwise additive, and (*b*) $\Omega(r) = \infty$ for $r < a$ and $\Omega(r) = 0$ for $r > b$. With this kind of potential it becomes obvious that when the number of particles exceeds the close-packing limit, no further terms appear in the partition function, because $\exp(-\Omega(r)/kT)$ becomes zero. Equation (1-1) therefore becomes

$$Z_G(z, V, T) = \sum_{N=0}^{B} z^N Z_N(V, T) \tag{1-4}$$

where B is the maximum number of particles which could be close-packed into volume V. The coefficients of z^N, namely Z_N, are all positive, and hence $Z_G(V, z, T)$ is completely analytical over the entire region for any finite volume V. There cannot be any transition occurring for real positive values of z, because $Z_G(V, z, T)$ does not become zero, and hence Eq. (1-3) (or any of its derivatives) does not show any singularity. However, there could be complex roots z_k and z_k^* (always appearing in conjugate pairs), or negative roots, such that $Z_G(V, z, T)$ becomes zero. With these zeros of the partition function, as they are often called, one can write Eq. (1-4) in its equivalent form

$$Z_G(z, V, T) = \prod_{k=1}^{B} \left(1 - \frac{z}{z_k}\right) \tag{1-5}$$

Roots z_k are distributed in the complex plane which also contains the positive real axis. But no z_k is present in a region R that surrounds the real positive axis. In the region R, $Z_G(z, V, T)$ is completely analytical. However, as the volume V tends to infinity the polynomial (1-4) grows in size and there will be a very large number of roots. With the increase in their density, z_ks "close in" on region R and at places begin to pinch the real axis. In order to see how a transition comes about in such a situation, we need the two theorems of Yang and Lee, and we state them here without proof:

(a) The $\lim_{V \to \infty} \left[\frac{1}{V} \ln Z_G(z, V, T) \right]$ exists for all positive real values of z. It is independent of the shape of V and is a continuous nondecreasing function of z.

(b) If there is a region R which contains a segment of real positive axis, then the grand canonical potential $(1/V) \ln Z_G(z, V, T)$ converges uniformly to a limit as $V \to \infty$, and this limit is an analytical function of z for all values of z in R.

If the segment of the real positive axis corresponds to the entire length of positive axis, then R is such that the system exists in a single phase. However, as shown in Fig. 1-1a, if z_k values close in on the real axis as $V \to \infty$ such that a segment of real axis is enclosed, then the grand canonical potential or the pressure p converges to a limit as a function of z. Let z_0 be the value on the real axis corresponding to a zero of $Z_G(z, V, T)$ which separates two regions R_1 and R_2 (see Fig. 1.1b). Then, in regions R_1 and R_2, the pressure p converges uniformly and separately to a limit according to the second theorem. The first theorem requires that this limit be continuous through z_0, as the system moves from region R_1 to region R_2 thereby requiring p to be continuous. However, the derivatives of p may be discontinuous, as shown in Fig. 1-1c. From the grand partition function, $Z_G(z, V, T)$, the specific volume, v, may be obtained as

$$\frac{1}{v} = \frac{1}{V} z \frac{\partial}{\partial z} [\ln Z_G(z, V, T)] \tag{1-6}$$

In the limit $V \to \infty$, the operations of taking the limit, $V \to \infty$, and $z(\partial/\partial z)$ may be interchanged, and hence

$$\begin{aligned} \frac{1}{v} &= \lim_{V \to \infty} \frac{1}{V} z \frac{\partial}{\partial z} [\ln Z_G(z, V, T)] \\ &= z \frac{\partial}{\partial z} \left\{ \lim_{V \to \infty} \frac{1}{V} [\ln Z_G(z, V, T)] \right\} \\ &= z \frac{\partial}{\partial z} \frac{p}{kT} = \frac{z}{kT} \left(\frac{\partial p}{\partial z} \right) \end{aligned} \tag{1-7}$$

Therefore, during the phase transition, v, the specific volume may show a discontinuity at z_0 and thus lead to a first-order phase transition. However, the

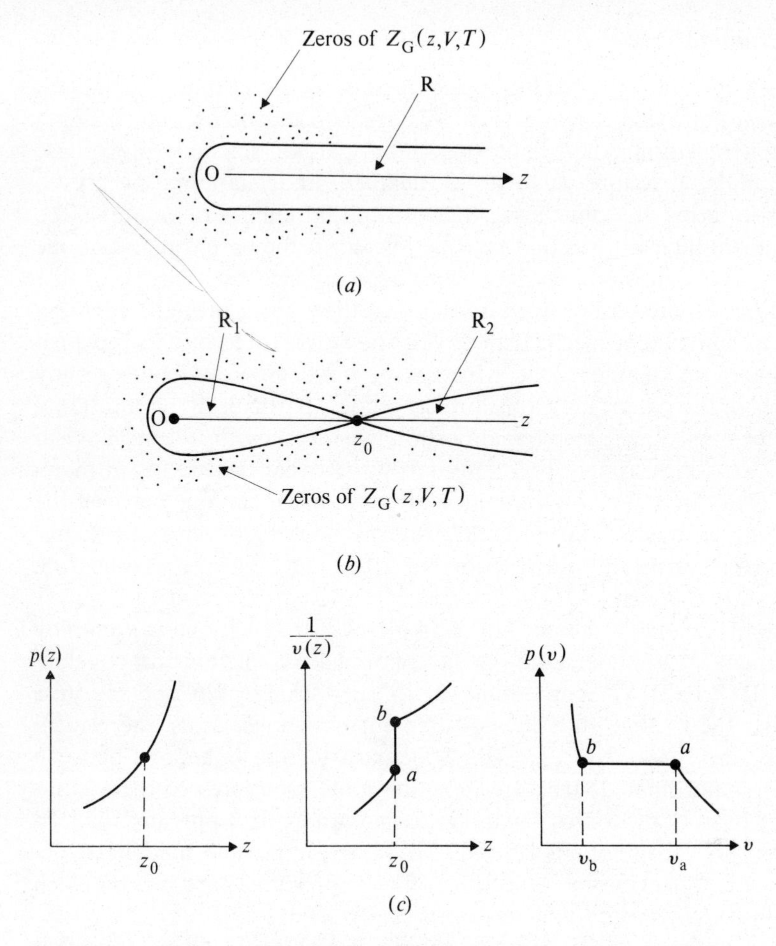

Figure 1-1 (*a*) Roots of grand partition function, $Z_G(z, V, T)$, surrounding the real positive axis. (*b*) Roots, z_k, closing in on the real positive axis creating regions R_1 and R_2. (*c*) Occurrence of a first-order transition in condensation phenomenon. (*From Huang.*[10])

discontinuity may occur in higher derivatives, leading to higher-order transitions, as stated earlier.

The possibility that z_k, a zero of the partition function, approaches the positive real axis and the convergence of the grand canonical potential in the limit $V \to \infty$ (Yang–Lee theorems), provides a purely statistical mechanical basis for explaining the occurrence of phase transitions. However, rigorous proofs are not available to show that z_k really approaches the positive real axis, and that too at one point. Various other potentials have been used in the literature to extend this purely statistical approach of Yang and Lee while discussing the convergence of thermodynamic properties of various ensembles.

Structural Considerations

While the thermodynamic treatment of phase transitions is very fundamental and useful, it does not provide a geometrical picture of the microscopic changes accompanying a transition. Another most essential part of the study of a phase transition in solids, therefore, involves a detailed understanding of crystal chemistry[3,4,12] in terms of atomic arrangements and bonding. For example, the new phase obtained after a transition may be related to the parent phase in one of several ways. The transition may have been accompanied by a change in the primary coordination or secondary coordination, either being brought out by a reconstructive or some other mechanism.[13] The transition could be accompanied by a major change in the electronic structure or bond type. A detailed study of the structures of the parent and transformed phases, particularly orientational relations between them, if any, becomes important in understanding the mechanism of a transition. It is increasingly becoming recognized that transitions in many solids may involve simple deformational (or orientational) relations between the two phases similar to those in martensitic transitions[14] common to metal systems. Topotaxy in phase transitions and reactions of solids indeed forms a fascinating aspect of solid state chemistry.[4,15]

In the case of the simplest ionic solids like NaCl or CsCl, one can employ the Born treatment[4,16] to understand the nature of phase transitions. In covalent solids like the III–V or II–VI compounds, the ionicity scale of Phillips[17] is quite useful to predict the relative stabilities of different structures. Thus, the critical value of the ionicity parameter ($f_i = 0.785$) demarcates the boundary between the tetrahedrally coordinated structures and the ionic structures of these compounds. On the basis of the ionicity parameter, one can explain pressure-induced transitions in $A^N B^{8-N}$ compounds involving covalent, ionic, and metallic structures. All these crystal chemical aspects of phase transitions are examined in Chap. 3, along with polytypism and some aspects of defect solids.

Polytypism (which is often referred to as one-dimensional polymorphism) is exhibited by a number of solids, where they occur in a variety of polytypic forms differing only in the *c*-parameter of the unit cell.[18,19] The origin of long periodicities (going up to hundreds or thousands of angstroms) in polytypes and other intergrowth compounds is of vital interest. While stacking faults and other defects may play an important role, there is no clear explanation for such long periodicities. Undoubtedly, there is a subtle interplay between long-range and short-range order forces in these systems. Polytypes exhibit both intra- and inter-polytypic transitions. The nature of these transitions is not very clear, particularly since the energy differences among the polytypes of a substance are very small indeed.

Generally it appears that native *point defects*, unlike plane or line defects, do not play a major role in phase transitions. Isolated point defects like anion vacancies normally exist in solids in very low concentrations. When their concentration is appreciable, they order themselves, often by forming clusters or complexes.[20,21] In many systems, as in Magneli phases or niobium oxide block structures, point defects are eliminated by *crystallographic shear*.[20–22] Phase transitions involving shear and block structures are quite interesting.

Mechanistic Considerations and Various Kinds of Phase Transitions

Thermodynamics alone cannot account for the different rates at which phase transitions take place. Phase transitions in many solids occur through the process of nucleation and propagation, each of these processes being associated with a specific activation energy. Generally, the nucleation process[23,24] involving the formation of nuclei of critical size of the transformed phase in the matrix of the parent phase requires higher activation energy than the propagation step. The theory of nucleation has been employed fairly satisfactorily to understand phase transition kinetics. Several types of kinetic expressions have been developed to interpret rate data, a particularly notable contribution being that of Avrami.[25] There are many examples of nucleation–growth transformations in metallic and non-metallic solids, and many of the transformations from metastable states to stable states proceed by this mechanism.

Many phase transitions in metallic and nonmetallic solids occur by the martensitic mechanism. *Martensitic transitions* exhibit some characteristic features in their thermodynamics, kinetics, and so on, but the more interesting features are those associated with the crystallography.[14,26–29] These transformations are diffusionless and occur at a very rapid rate through a shearing of discrete volumes of the material. The two phases are related by a deformational mechanism and hence show orientational relations. The lattice deformation can be understood following Bain.[30] By and large, martensitic transitions are athermal, although there are instances of isothermal transitions. In Chap. 4, various kinds of transitions involving different mechanisms are reviewed at length; the discussion includes nucleation-growth, martensitic, and order–disorder transformations, spinodal and eutectoid decompositions, glass and liquid crystal transitions, and so on.

Perfect order in solids is not realized at any temperature other than 0 K, and it is pertinent to talk of the extent of order or disorder as mentioned earlier. Three principal kinds of disordering transitions are generally found: positional disordering, orientational disordering, and disordering of electronic or nuclear spins. The entropy change in an *order–disorder transition* is mainly configurational in origin, and is given by $R \ln (\omega_2/\omega_1)$, where ω_2 and ω_1 are the number of configurations in the disordered and the ordered states. A large number of systems exhibit positional or orientational order–disorder transitions, and they have been investigated by a variety of experimental methods. Magnetic transitions (like ferromagnetic–paramagnetic) or dielectric transitions (like ferroelectric–paraelectric) are also cases of order–disorder transitions. There are also transitions involving disordering of defects like vacancies. The subject of order–disorder transitions is indeed vast.[31,32] Order parameters can obviously be employed to examine these transitions, and we shall discuss this aspect shortly.

Spinodal decompositions result from thermodynamic instabilities caused by composition.[29] These occur without any nucleation barrier, and are commonly found in binary solid solutions of metals as well as in glasses. There are other transformations in glasses which are of value in understanding the physics and chemistry of glasses or, in general, of amorphous materials.[33–35] *Glass transitions*, which are sometimes referred to as second-order transitions, crystallization of glasses (and melts), and switching transitions are some such transitions of interest.

Other than the glassy state, there is yet another state of matter with properties somewhere between those of crystals and liquids, namely the *mesophase*[36] (liquid crystalline state), which exhibits interesting phase transitions of both academic and technological interest. The plastic crystalline state, often found in organic solids, could also be considered a mesophase.

All through the discussion of various kinds of phase transitions, we have given a number of examples of inorganic compounds and, to a lesser extent, of metal systems and organic solids. The literature abounds in information on phase transitions in metal systems. It would be instructive to briefly examine the relations between various transformations in metal systems. Christian[37] has schematically shown relations among different transformations based on similarities and differences in the atomic processes involved (Fig. 1-2). Christian has regarded transformations characterized by a lattice correspondence (such as the martensite transformations) as *military* transformations and those without any correspondence as *civilian* transformations. In military transformations, the structures are always coherent or semicoherent, and the experimental criterion which distinguishes these from other transformations should be based on whether there is a change of shape in the transformed region. We should note that Fig. 1-2 also includes a few transformations which are quasi-homogeneous and do not involve nucleation in the normal sense.

Statistical Mechanics and Order Parameters

It was mentioned earlier how the long-range order parameter in second-order transitions decreases to zero as the critical temperature is approached. We can also define a *short-range order parameter* in such a way that $\xi_1 > \xi_2 \ldots \xi_i > \xi_{i+k}$, where ξ_i corresponds to the pair correlation coefficient at the nearest-neighbor distance. As ξ_i gets larger, ξ_i approaches a limiting value defined by the long-range order parameter. In real situations, any physically observable quantity which varies with temperature can be taken as an experimental order parameter. Thus, polarization in a ferroelectric material, magnetization or hyperfine field in a ferromagnetic material, line-width or anisotropic "g" value in an ESR experiment, and the intensity of diffuse electron scattering in the presence of charge-density wave instability, have been taken as order parameters. The most general order parameter would, however, be that due to *off-diagonal long-range order*.[38] In the case of lattice vibrations, this order parameter is the non-vanishing displacement amplitude, while in superconductors it is the non-vanishing expectation value of the pair-annihilation or pair-creation operators (in the BCS ground state).

One of the most interesting features of phase transitions is the similarity in behavior encountered in the variation of physical properties near the critical temperature. The dimensionless quantity, $\varepsilon = (T - T_c)/T_c$, is related to the long-range order parameter by the equation

$$p, M = A(-\varepsilon)^{\lambda} \tag{1-8}$$

where p and M refer to the order parameters in order–disorder and magnetic

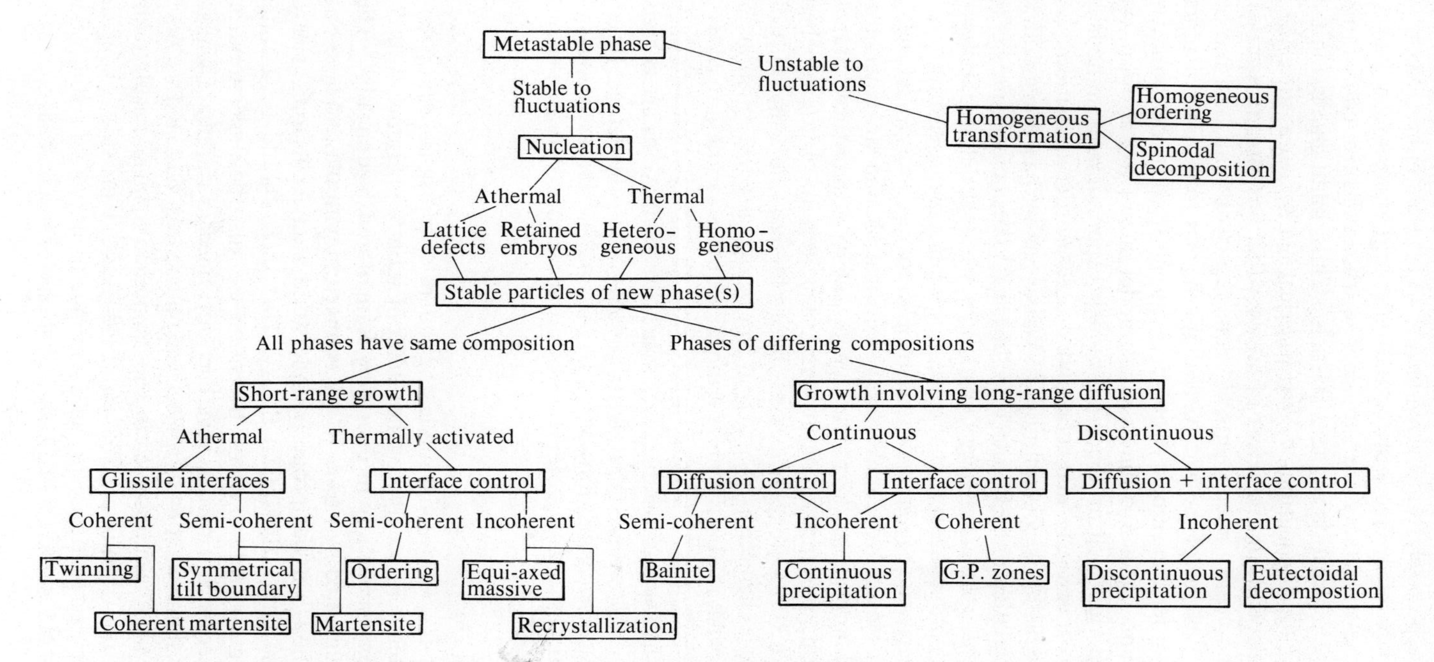

Figure 1-2 Relations between various transformations in metal systems. (*After Christian.*[37])

transitions respectively, and the exponent λ is always about $\frac{1}{3}$. Such a similarity in the behavior of diverse systems indicates that the basic physical processes leading to the transitions are similar. The transitions are cooperative and are caused by the interaction of many particles. Thus, small changes in temperature give rise to large fluctuations near the critical temperature, since the energy of disordering depends on the extent of disorder that has already accrued. In order to understand critical phenomena,[39,40] one resorts to statistical mechanics. The Ising model[41] is one of the widely-used approaches to examine magnetic as well as order–disorder transitions. A one-dimensional Ising model does not give rise to a transition, but a two-dimensional model shows a transition. Apart from rigorous methods such as the Ising models, approximate methods have been employed to investigate magnetic and order–disorder transitions; among the approximate methods, contributions of Weiss[42] as well as Bragg and Williams[43] deserve special mention. Effective field theories[44] satisfactorily predict the general behavior of three-dimensional systems, although not the details of critical behavior.

It was mentioned earlier that critical exponents are insensitive to the detailed nature of interparticle interactions. Critical behavior, however, depends on dimensionality. This leads to the universality of critical phenomena wherein transitions are classified simply according to the dimensionality of the lattice and the symmetry of the ordering parameter. Another important feature of critical phenomena is that the various critical exponents one obtains, for example in the study of magnetic transitions, are themselves related and can be expressed as functions of just two parameters. Such relations among critical exponents can be proved by the use of the *scaling hypothesis*;[45] here, one considers the correlation length, which is a measure of the average distance over which the fluctuations are correlated. Both the universality and the scaling hypotheses are best understood in terms of the *renormalization group* first introduced by Wilson.[46,47] In Chap. 5, various aspects of the statistical mechanics of phase transitions are briefly presented.

Soft Modes

A soft mode is a vibrational mode, the square of whose frequency tends toward zero as the temperature approaches the transition temperature. Soft modes were first found experimentally in quartz by Raman and Nedungadi.[48] Theoretically it was first suggested by Frohlich[49] in connection with the Lyddane–Sachs–Teller relation, although it was properly understood after Anderson[50] and Cochran[51] proposed the lattice dynamical theory. That there should be a softening of a mode during a structural phase transition can also be understood in terms of Landau's theory. Soft modes have been identified in the phase transitions of a variety of systems such as ferroelectrics, magnetic solids, and so on.[52–54] Soft modes have also been observed in superconductors, metal–insulator transitions, and martensitic transitions. Soft modes do indeed provide a unifying way of understanding phase transitions and continue to provide a fertile field of study. A discussion of soft modes in phase transitions forms Chap. 6.

Material Properties and Phase Transitions

Phase transitions in solids are accompanied by interesting changes in many of the material properties. Measurement of any sensitive property across the phase transition, in principle, provides a means of investigating the transition. Accordingly, several techniques of varying degrees of sophistication have been employed to study phase transitions of solids. Changes in properties at the phase transition are often of technological interest, and several materials applications have been discovered. In Chap. 7, three properties of solids are examined in some detail: magnetic, electrical, and dielectric; phase transitions associated with changes in these properties have been discussed with several illustrative examples.

In magnetic properties, in addition to the transitions from a magnetically ordered (ferro-, antiferro- or ferrimagnetic) state to the paramagnetic state,[55] Jahn–Teller distortions and spin–state transitions are also quite interesting. Under electrical properties, insulator–metal transitions[56] (including Mott transitions) are of great interest; a number of oxides and sulfides are known to exhibit these transitions. Other aspects of interest are the cooperative Jahn–Teller effect,[57] the Peierls transition[58] found in one-dimensional conductors like TTF-TCNQ or $K_2Pt(CN)_4Br_{0.3}\cdot 2\text{–}3H_2O$, the Anderson transition[56,59] associated with electron localization in disordered materials, and charge density waves[60] found in some polytypic tantalum sulfides[61] and other materials. An interesting system showing a transition from localized "*d*" electron behavior to itinerant behavior is that of rare earth cobaltites;[62,63] these solids also show spin–state transitions. Under dielectric properties, transitions from a ferro- or antiferroelectric state to a paraelectric state have formed the subject of intensive study for a number of years;[64,65] some highlights of these transitions are briefly described in Chap. 7. Devonshire's thermodynamic treatment based on Landau's theory, as well as group theoretical aspects of Landau's theory, are briefly discussed here.

While a number of examples have been cited for various kinds of phase transitions throughout this book, it has not been possible to provide complete lists of materials or literature references on all solids undergoing transitions. Such compilations and case histories may be found in the literature, typical ones being the reviews on binary halides,[66] inorganic nitrites, nitrates, and carbonates,[67] inorganic sulfates, phosfates, chromates, and perchlorates,[68] transition metal oxides[69] and sulfides,[70] perovskites,[71] spinels and other magnetic materials,[55,72] ferroelectrics,[65] and superconducting materials.[73,74] Interested readers are referred to these reviews for further information.

Applications of Phase Transitions

Following Goodenough,[75] applications of phase transitions may be classified into groups: those utilizing (i) the formation and/or motion of mobile boundaries between two or more phases coexisting below a critical temperature T_c, (ii) changes in physical properties as the temperature approaches T_c, (iii) changes in properties at T_c, and (iv) metastable phases obtained by control of the kinetics of nucleation or diffusion required for the transformation to stable phases. We shall briefly deal with materials applications, closely following Goodenough.[75]

Under the first category (phase transitions at $T < T_c$), where one makes use of changes in the net material properties by control of nucleation or movement of domain boundaries, we have large classes of materials like ferroelectrics, ferroelastics, ferromagnets, liquid crystals, and superconductors. In ferromagnets, long-range magnetic order below the Curie temperature induces a spontaneous magnetization, M_s, and many magnetic domains would be present each with an M_s vector oriented in a direction different from that in adjacent domains. The adjacent domains are separated by domain walls within which the M_s vector rotates from the orientation in one domain to that in the other. The net magnetization is determined by an external magnetic field. Ferroelectrics are characterized by different orientational states below T_c, but the spontaneous polarization is induced by a cooperative crystallographic distortion. The domain boundaries in ferroelectrics can be controlled by an external electric field. In ferroelastics, a cooperative crystal distortion induces a spontaneous strain below T_c. An externally applied stress controls the domain boundaries of a ferroelastic. Magnetic (or electric) and elastic long-range order coexist in many materials, so that spontaneous magnetization (or polarization) is controlled by an applied stress or a spontaneous strain by an applied magnetic or electric field. Coexistence of magnetic and electric long-range order is known in substances like $BiFeO_3$ ($BiFeO_3$ is an antiferromagnetic ferroelectric). Magnetoelectric phenomena have been investigated and exploited in recent years.[76] Optical properties of ferroelectrics, ferroelastics, and ferromagnets have found many applications, a typical example being the ferroelectric–ferroelastic $Gd_2(MoO_4)_3$, with a T_c of 433 K, which is transparent in the visible region.

Liquid crystals have been found useful for optical display, detection of temperature uniformity and impurities. These properties are related to the orientational order of molecules in the temperature region between T_c and the melting point. Superconductors (Type II) can be used to create high magnetic fields at low power; the ability of Type I superconductors to trap magnetic flux within the domains of the normal material may also have applications.

Two of the important properties which change near T_c are softening of an optical vibration mode before a displacive transition, and temperature-dependence of spontaneous magnetization in ferromagnets below T_c. These properties are used in dielectric and pyromagnetic detectors respectively. Invar alloys have lattice parameters which are essentially temperature-independent below the ferromagnetic Curie temperature, since a magnetically induced lattice expansion is superimposed on the usual thermal expansion in this system. In metallic $Bi_2Ru_2O_7$ (defect pyrochlore structure), resistivity is nearly temperature-independent in the range $150 < T < 500$ K. This is apparently due to electron coupling to soft vibrational modes above the T_c (150 K), where a phase change occurs. Electron–phonon coupling to soft modes in materials will probably afford some significant applications. Device applications of soft-mode anomalies have been discussed by Fleury.[77]

Coming to properties at T_c, we can conceive of uses being made of the latent heat of a first-order transition for storing energy and regulating temperature. First-order magnetic transitions could be used for switching. Semiconductor–metal transitions can be employed as circuit breakers, voltage dividers, or optical switches.

The importance of metastable stable states which persist at ambient pressure and temperature need not be emphasized. Control of the eutectoidal decomposition of the metastable bcc iron–carbon phase, austenite, below 996 K is of value to the steel industry. Austenite is made by quenching an fcc phase, but the transformation is diffusionless. When the carbon content is greater than 0.2 wt percent, cubic austenite transforms to tetragonal martensite by a diffusionless mechanism. Many high-pressure phases can be retained at atmospheric pressure if the forming pressure is released at room temperature. Diamond and boron nitride (zinc blende structure) are examples of such metastable phases. Impurities often stabilize metastable phases. Crystals of metastable phases can often be grown from solution or other means. Cubic $NaSbO_3$ with fast Na^+ conduction is a metastable phase prepared from $KSbO_3$ by ion exchange. The best-known examples of metastable materials are glasses and other amorphous materials. Switching properties and other application of such materials are well documented. Magnetic properties of materials like Heusler alloys depend on atomic ordering within a crystallographic phase. Local atomic order may affect magnetic properties, as in ferrospinels and ferrogarnets. Control of chemical inhomogeneities is quite useful, as in Mg–Mn ferrospinels used in computer memory cores, where the Jahn–Teller Mn^{3+} ions are segregated into Mn-rich regions by annealing.

Reactivity at Phase Transitions

The reactivity of many solids has been found to be high in the neighborhood of phase transitions.[3,78,79] This was first suggested by Hedvall[77] and is often referred to as the *Hedvall effect*. Thus, the reaction of BaO, SrO, and CaO with $AgNO_3$ sets in at the transition temperature of $AgNO_3$ (433 K). The reaction of BaO with AgI has a maximum rate near the α–β transformation of AgI (418 K). The reaction between SiO_2 and Fe_2O_3 is found at the α–β transformation temperature of SiO_2 (843 K). The reaction of Fe_2O_3 with ZnO to form zinc ferrite shows maximum rate when Fe_2O_3 has been heated beyond the Neél temperature (950 K). The self-diffusion of Pb in $PbSiO_3$ is at a maximum at the transition temperature (858 K). Synthesis of zircon is accelerated at the phase transition temperatures of zirconia.[80]

REFERENCES

1. A. R. Ubbelohde, *Quart. Rev.* (*London*), **11,** 246, 1957.
2. A. R. Ubbelohde, in "Reactivity of Solids," ed. J. H. de Boer, Elsevier, Amsterdam, 1961.
3. C. N. R. Rao and K. J. Rao, "Progress in Solid State Chemistry," ed. H. Reiss, vol. 4, Pergamon Press, Oxford, 1967.
4. C. N. R. Rao, in "Modern Aspects of Solid State Chemistry," ed. C. N. R. Rao, Plenum Press, New York, 1970; see also C. N. R. Rao, "Solid State Chemistry," Marcel Dekker, New York, 1974.
5. P. Ehrenfest, *Proc. Amsterdam Acad.*, **36,** 153, 1933.
6. L. D. Landau and E. M. Lifshitz, "Statistical Physics," Pergamon Press, Oxford, 1959.
7. A. B. Pippard, "Elements of Classical Thermodynamics," Cambridge University Press, 1966.
8. L. Tizza, in "Phase Transformations in Solids," ed. R. Smoluchowski, John Wiley, New York, 1957.
9. C. N. Yang and T. D. Lee, *Phys. Rev.* **87,** 404, 410, 1952.
10. K. Huang, "Statistical Mechanics," John Wiley, London, 1963.
11. C. J. Thompson, "Mathematical Statistical Mechanics," Macmillan, New York, 1972.
12. H. Krebs, "Fundamentals of Inorganic Crystal Chemistry," McGraw-Hill, London, 1968.
13. M. J. Buerger, in "Phase Transformations in Solids," ed. R. Smoluchowski, John Wiley, New York, 1957; see also *Fortschr. Miner.*, **39,** 9, 1961.
14. J. W. Christian, "The Theory of Transformations in Metals and Alloys," Pergamon Press, Oxford, 1965.
15. J. M. Thomas, *Phil. Trans. Roy. Soc.*, **277,** 251, 1974.
16. M. Born and K. Huang, "Dynamical Theory of Crystal Lattices," Oxford University Press, 1956; see also M. P. Tosi, "Solid State Physics," ed. F. Seitz and D. Turnbull, vol. 16, Academic Press, New York, 1964.
17. J. C. Phillips, "Bonds and Bands in Semiconductors," Academic Press, New York, 1973.
18. A. R. Verma and P. Krishna, "Polymorphism and Polytypism," John Wiley, New York, 1966.
19. A. R. Verma and G. C. Trigunayat, in "Solid State Chemistry," ed. C. N. R. Rao, Marcel Dekker, New York, 1974.
20. J. S. Anderson, in "Defects and Transport in Oxides," ed. M. S. Seltzer and R. I. Jaffee, Plenum Press, New York, 1974.
21. J. S. Anderson and R. J. D. Tilley, in "Surface and Defect Properties of Solids," *Chem. Soc. Specialist Periodical Report*, **3,** 1, 1974.
22. A. D. Wadsley and S. Andersson, in "Perspectives in Structural Chemistry," ed. J. D. Dunitz and J. A. Ibers, vol. 3, John Wiley, New York, 1970.
23. D. Turnbull, "Solid State Physics," ed. F. Seitz and D. Turnbull, vol. 3, Academic Press, New York, 1956.
24. J. Burke, "The Kinetics of Phase Transformations in Metals," Pergamon Press, Oxford, 1965.
25. M. Avrami, *J. Chem. Phys.*, **9,** 177, 1941.
26. L. Kauffman and M. Cohen, *Progress in Metal Physics*, ed. B. Chalmers and R. King, **7,** 165, 1958.
27. C. M. Wayman, "Introduction to the Crystallography of Martensitic Transformations," Macmillan, New York, 1964.
28. G. Meyrick and G. W. Powell, *Ann. Rev. Materials Sci.*, ed. R. A. Huggins, R. W. Bube, and R. W. Roberts, **3,** 327, 1973.
29. P. G. Shewman, "Transformations in Metals," McGraw-Hill, New York, 1969.
30. E. C. Bain, *Trans. AIME*, **70,** 25, 1954.
31. H. Warlimont (ed.), "Order–Disorder Transformations in Alloys," Springer-Verlag, Berlin, 1974.
32. N. G. Parsonage and L. A. K. Staveley, "Disorder in Crystals," Oxford University Press, 1977.
33. L. D. Pye, H. J. Stevens, and W. C. Lacourse (eds.), "Introduction to Glass Science," Plenum Press, New York, 1972.
34. R. W. Douglas and B. Ellis, "Amorphous Materials," Wiley-Interscience, New York, 1972.
35. H. Rawson, "Inorganic Glass Forming Systems," Academic Press, New York, 1967.
36. S. Chandrasekhar (ed.), "Liquid Crystals," Indian Academy of Sciences, Bangalore, 1975.

37. J. W. Christian, in "Physical Properties of Martensite and Bainite," *Special Report* 93, The Iron and Steel Institute, 1965.
38. W. R. Harrison, "Solid State Theory," McGraw-Hill, New York, 1970.
39. H. E. Stanley, "Introduction to Phase Transitions and Critical Phenomena," Clarendon Press, Oxford, 1971.
40. C. Domb and M. S. Green (eds.), "Phase Transitions and Critical Phenomena," Academic Press, New York, 1972.
41. E. Ising, *Z. Phys.*, **31,** 253, 1925.
42. P. Weiss, *J. Phys. Paris*, **6,** 661, 1907.
43. W. L. Bragg and E. J. Williams, *Proc. Roy. Soc.* (*Lond.*), **A145,** 699, 1934.
44. L. J. de Jongh and A. R. Miedema, *Adv. Phys.*, **23,** 1, 1974.
45. L. P. Kandanoff, W. Godze, D. Hamblen, R. Hecht, E. Lewis, V. V. Palciauskas, M. Rayl, J. Swift, D. Arpnes, and J. Kane, *Rev. Mod. Phys.*, **39,** 395, 1967.
46. K. G. Wilson and J. Kogut, *Phys. Repts.*, **12C,** 77, 1974.
47. M. E. Fisher, *Rev. Mod. Phys.*, **46,** 587, 1974.
48. C. V. Raman and T. M. K. Nedungadi, *Nature*, **145,** 147, 1940.
49. H. Frohlich, "Theory of Dielectrics," Clarendon Press, Oxford, 1949.
50. P. W. Anderson, "Fizika dielektrikov," ed. G. I. Skanavi, Akad Nauk SSR, Moscow, 1959.
51. W. Cochran, *Phys. Rev. Letts.*, **3,** 412, 1957; *Adv. Phys.*, **9,** 387, 1960.
52. J. F. Scott, *Rev. Mod. Phys.*, **46,** 83, 1974.
53. E. J. Samuelsen, E. Andersen, and J. Feder (eds.), "Structural Phase Transitions and Soft Modes," Universitets forlaget, Oslo, 1971.
54. R. Blinc and B. Zeks, "Soft Modes in Ferroelectrics and Antiferroelectrics," North-Holland, Amsterdam, 1974.
55. J. B. Goodenough, "Magnetism and the Chemical Bond," John Wiley, New York, 1963.
56. N. F. Mott, "Metal–Insulator Transitions," Taylor and Francis, London, 1974.
57. G. A. Gehring and K. A. Gehring, *Repts. Progress in Phys.*, **38,** 1, 1975.
58. R. E. Peierls, "Quantum Theory of Solids," Clarendon Press, Oxford, 1955.
59. P. W. Anderson, *Phys. Rev.*, **109,** 1492, 1958.
60. A. W. Overhauser, *Phys. Rev.*, **B3,** 3173, 1971; **167,** 691, 1969.
61. J. A. Wilson, F. J. DiSalvo, and S. Mahajan, *Adv. Phys.*, **24,** 117, 1975.
62. P. M. Raccah and J. B. Goodenough, *Phys. Rev.*, **155,** 932, 1967.
63. C. N. R. Rao and V. G. Bhide, *Proceedings of the 19th Conference on Magnetism and Magnetic Materials*, American Institute of Physics, 1974.
64. F. Jona and G. Shirane, "Ferroelectric Crystals," Pergamon Press, Oxford, 1962.
65. E. C. Subbarao, in "Solid State Chemistry," ed. C. N. R. Rao, Marcel Dekker, New York, 1974.
66. C. N. R. Rao and M. Natarajan, "Crystal Structure Transformations in Binary Halides," *NSRDS-NBS Monograph* 41, National Bureau of Standards, Washington, D.C., 1972.
67. C. N. R. Rao, B. Prakash and M. Natarajan, "Crystal Structure Transformations in Inorganic Nitrites, Carbonates, and Nitrates," *NSRDS-NBS Monograph* 53, National Bureau of Standards, Washington, D.C., 1975.
68. C. N. R. Rao and B. Prakash, "Crystal Structure Transformations in Inorganic Sulfates, Phosphates, Chromates, and Perchlorates," *NSRDS-NBS Monograph* 56, National Bureau of Standards, Washington, D.C., 1975.
69. C. N. R. Rao and G. V. Subbarao, "Transition Metal Oxides," *NSRDS-NBS Monograph* 49, National Bureau of Standards, Washington, D.C., 1974.
70. C. N. R. Rao and K. P. R. Pisharody, *Progress in Solid State Chemistry*, **10,** 207, 1975.
71. J. B. Goodenough and J. M. Longo, *Landolt-Bornstein, New Series, Group III*, vol. 4a, Springer-Verlag, New York, 1970.
72. T. F. Connolly and E. D. Copenhaver, *ORNL-RMIC-7*, Materials Information Centre, Oak Ridge National Laboratory, 1970.
73. B. W. Roberts, *NBS Technical Notes*, 408, 482, 724, 825, National Bureau of Standards, Washington, D.C.; see also *J. Phys. Chem., Ref. Data*, 1976.
74. E. M. Savitskii and V. V. Baron, "Physics and Metallurgy of Superconductors," Consultants Bureau, New York, 1970.

75. J. B. Goodenough, in "Phase Transitions," eds. H. Henisch, R. Roy, and L. E. Cross, Pergamon Press, New York, 1973.
76. A. J. Freeman and H. Schmid (eds.), "Magnetoelectric Interaction Phenomena in Crystals," Gordon and Breach, New York, 1975.
77. P. A. Fleury, in "Phase Transitions," eds. H. Henisch, R. Roy, and L. E. Cross, Pergamon Press, New York, 1973.
78. J. A. Hedvall, "Reacktionsfaehigkeit fester stoffe," Verlag Johann Ambrosium Barth, Leipzig, 1938.
79. F. A. Kroger, "The Chemistry of Imperfect Crystals," John Wiley, New York, 1964.
80. K. V. G. K. Gokhale, S. V. Ramañi, and E. C. Subbarao, *J. Mat. Sci.*, **4**, 469, 1969.

CHAPTER

TWO

THERMODYNAMICS OF PHASE TRANSITIONS

A solid phase has a uniform structure and composition throughout and is separated from other phases by sharp boundaries.[1] At these boundaries discontinuous changes occur in structure and/or composition. A solid undergoes a phase transition[2] when a particular phase of the solid becomes unstable under a given set of thermodynamic conditions. The variation in free energy at the transition is associated with structural or compositional changes.* Classical thermodynamics provides a general and sound basis for understanding phase transitions in solids. In this chapter we shall be discussing the thermodynamic classification of phase transitions, thermodynamic relations between phases at the phase transformations, and thermodynamic theories of phase transformations. We shall then discuss some aspects of temperature and pressure hysteresis in transformations and conclude with a brief reference to metastable phases and irreversible phase transitions.

2-1 THERMODYNAMIC CLASSIFICATION OF PHASE TRANSITIONS

During a phase transition, whereas the free energy of the system remains continuous, thermodynamic quantities like entropy, volume, heat capacity, and so on, undergo discontinuous changes. Depending on the relation between the thermodynamic quantity undergoing discontinuity and the Gibbs free energy function, Ehrenfest[3] classified phase transitions. In this simple scheme, a transition is said

* We shall mainly be concerned with changes in structure (atomic and electronic configuration) and related properties accompanying phase transitions.

to be of the same order as the derivative of the Gibbs free energy which shows a discontinuous change at the transition. Gibbs free energy is given by

$$G = H - TS = E + PV - TS \tag{2-1}$$

Hence

$$\begin{aligned} dG &= dE + P\,dV + V\,dP - T\,dS - S\,dT \\ &= V\,dP - S\,dT \end{aligned} \tag{2-2}$$

The first and second derivatives of the free energy may be written as

$$\left(\frac{\partial G}{\partial P}\right)_T = V \qquad \left(\frac{\partial G}{\partial T}\right)_P = -S \tag{2-3}$$

$$\left(\frac{\partial^2 G}{\partial P^2}\right)_T = \left(\frac{\partial V}{\partial P}\right)_T = -V\beta \qquad \left(\frac{\partial^2 G}{\partial P\,\partial T}\right) = \left(\frac{\partial V}{\partial T}\right)_P = V\alpha$$

$$\left(\frac{\partial^2 G}{\partial T^2}\right)_P = -\left(\frac{\partial S}{\partial T}\right)_P = -\frac{C_P}{T} \tag{2-4}$$

Here, C_P, α, and β are the heat capacity, volume thermal expansivity, and compressibility respectively. We readily see that transformations in which a discontinuous change occurs in volume and entropy (that is, when there is a latent heat of transformation) belong to the first order, and those in which discontinuous change occurs in heat capacity, thermal expansivity, and compressibility belong to the second order. Third and higher-order transformations will involve further differential quantities.

A first-order transition involving discontinuous change in entropy is represented graphically in Fig. 2-1*a*. Curves G_{I}, G_{II} and H_{I}, H_{II} represent the variations in free energies and enthalpies respectively of phases I and II at constant pressure. The free-energy curves intersect at T_t where the transition II → I occurs. For

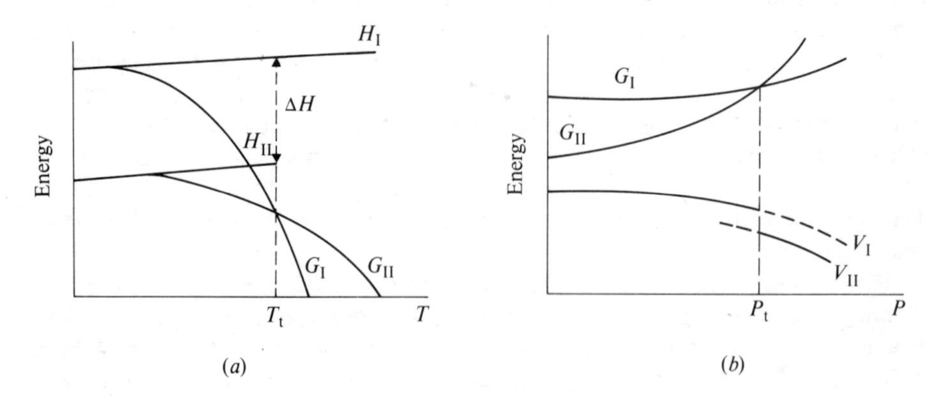

Figure 2-1 Variation of enthalpy and free energy with (*a*) temperature and (*b*) pressure in a first-order phase transition.

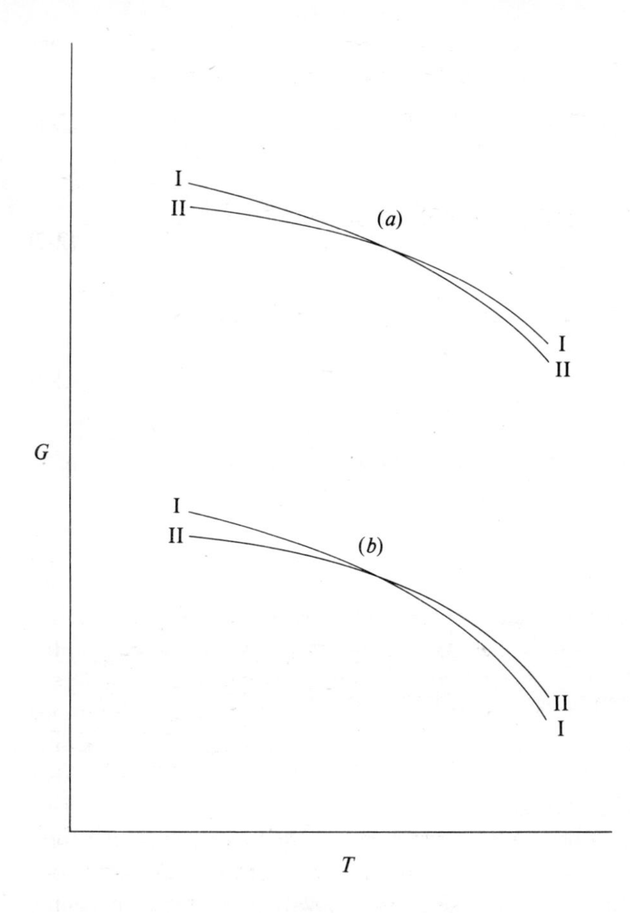

Figure 2-2 Free energy–temperature relations in a second-order phase transition.

temperatures greater than T_t, the variation in free energy will be represented by the G_I curve. The two phases coexist at T_t and are distinguishable by the different enthalpies (and hence different structural details) at the transition temperature. The G_I and G_{II} lines may be extrapolated meaningfully, though to limited extents, on either side of the transition temperature. They correspond to superheated and supercooled states respectively. In Fig. 2-1*b*, a similar first-order pressure transition[4,5] involving discontinuous change in volume at constant temperature ($T\Delta S \sim 0$) is represented schematically. Here, ΔV is the discontinuous volume change and P_t is the transition pressure. The extensions of G_I and G_{II} lines in Fig. 2-1*b* would correspond to supercompressed and superexpanded states respectively.

The nature of the G–T curve in a second-order transition is shown in Fig. 2-2. At the transition temperature we do not expect a real intersection of the curves, because the slopes of the $G(T)$ curves are equal. However, there could be a difference in the curvatures of $G(T)$. Since volume and entropy are continuous, there is no conceivable equilibrium of two phases. The question arises as to whether (*a*) or (*b*) in Fig. 2-2 gives a proper representation of such transitions.

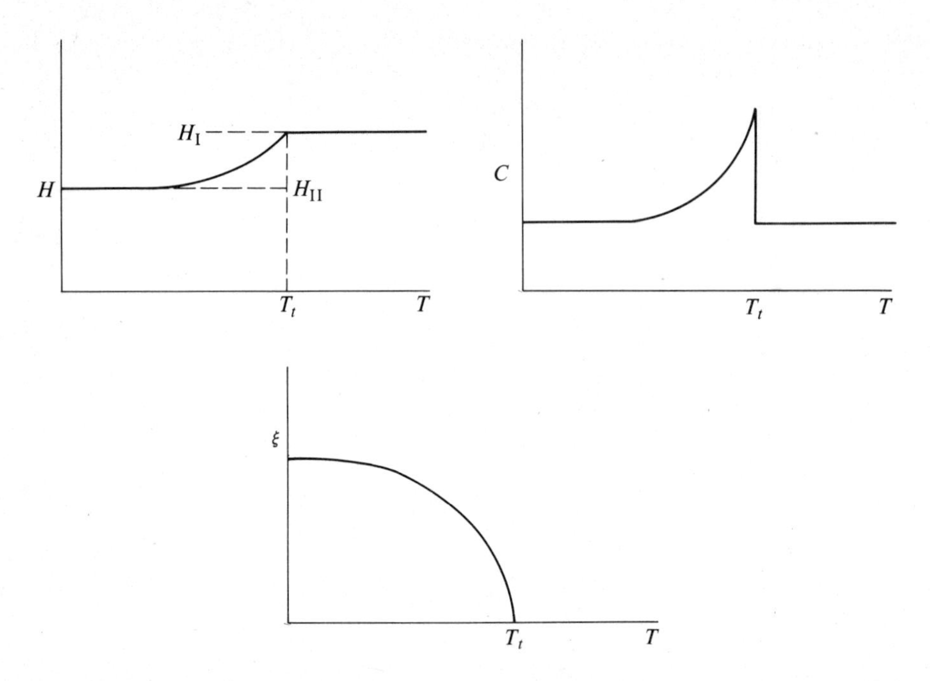

Figure 2-3 Variation of enthalpy, specific heat, and order parameter in a second-order transition.

If (*a*) were the proper representation, it would mean that the two $G(T)$ curves osculate at the transition point and G_{II} would always be lower than G_I. How can a transition then occur? On the other hand, if (*b*) is the proper representation, there could only be a discontinuity in the third derivatives of the free energy and hence a third-order transition. It would therefore appear that, either way, there cannot be a true second-order transition.[6] However, by elegant reasoning, Pippard[7] has shown that the classification scheme of Ehrenfest is essentially correct and that the continuation of two separate $G(T)$ curves beyond the transition temperature is unwarranted. It is nevertheless theoretically possible to have two $G(T)$ curves slightly below the transition temperature, and in such a case the G_I curve corresponds to a supercooled state.

Transformations belonging to the second order are almost always associated with some kind of disordering process.[8] In Fig. 2-3, variations of enthalpy, heat capacity, and the "order parameter," ξ, with temperature during a second-order transformation are depicted. In a second-order transition caused by pressure (at constant temperature), the variation of compressibility may be represented similarly.

There are a large number of examples of both thermal and pressure transformations in inorganic solids belonging to the first order.[5,9-11] Data on a few typical transitions may be found in Tables 2-1 and 2-2. Transitions which have finite discontinuities in specific heat and so on are virtually unknown except for

Table 2-1 Typical reversible thermal transitions[9]

Compound	Transition	T_t (°C)	ΔV_t (cc)	ΔH_t (cal-mol^{-1})	Width of hysteresis*
Quartz (SiO_2)	hexagonal α-β	575	1.33	86	0.7
CsCl	CsCl structure to NaCl structure	479	10.3	580	33
AgI	hexagonal to cubic	154	−2.2	1470	24
NH_4Cl	CsCl structure to NaCl structure	196	7.1	1070	35
NH_4Br	CsCl structure to NaCl structure	179	9.5	880	24
$NaNO_2$	orthorhombic to orthorhombic	166	1.66	250	<1
$AgNO_3$	orthorhombic to hexagonal	167	−0.50	920	16
K_2SO_4	orthorhombic to hexagonal	579	1.55	2140	1
Li_2SO_4	monoclinic to cubic	590	3.81	6900	35
$RbNO_3$	trigonal structure to CsCl structure	166	6.0	950	13
	CsCl structure to hexagonal structure	228	3.12	650	26
	hexagonal structure to NaCl structure	278	3.13	350	12
$CsNO_3$	hexagonal to cubic (CsCl)	161	3.13	350	12

* Hysteresis widths (in deg) were obtained from DTA peaks as differences between transformation temperatures while heating and cooling the solid.

Table 2-2 Typical reversible pressure transitions*

Compound	Transitions	P_t (k bars)	ΔV (cc)	ΔH_t (kcal mol^{-1})
KCl	NaCl structure to CsCl structure	19.6	−4.11	1.92
KBr	NaCl structure to CsCl structure	18.0	−4.17	1.83
RbCl	NaCl structure to CsCl structure	5.7	−6.95	0.81
SiO_2	quartz to coesite	18.8	−2.0	0.7
SiO_2	coesite to stishovite	93.1	−6.6	13.7
ZnO	wurtzite to NaCl structure	88.6	−2.55	4.6
$CdTiO_3$	ilmenite to perovskite	40.4	−2.9	3.8
CdS	wurtzite to rocksalt	17.4	−7.2	−2.5
$FeCr_2O_4$	spinel to Cr_3S_4 type	36.0	−6.5	−7.3

* Data from ref. 10. The shock method involving strong pressure pulses has been employed to study pressure transitions.[5] Grinding powders often induce pressure transitions[11] (e.g., $CaCO_3$ calcite → aragonite).

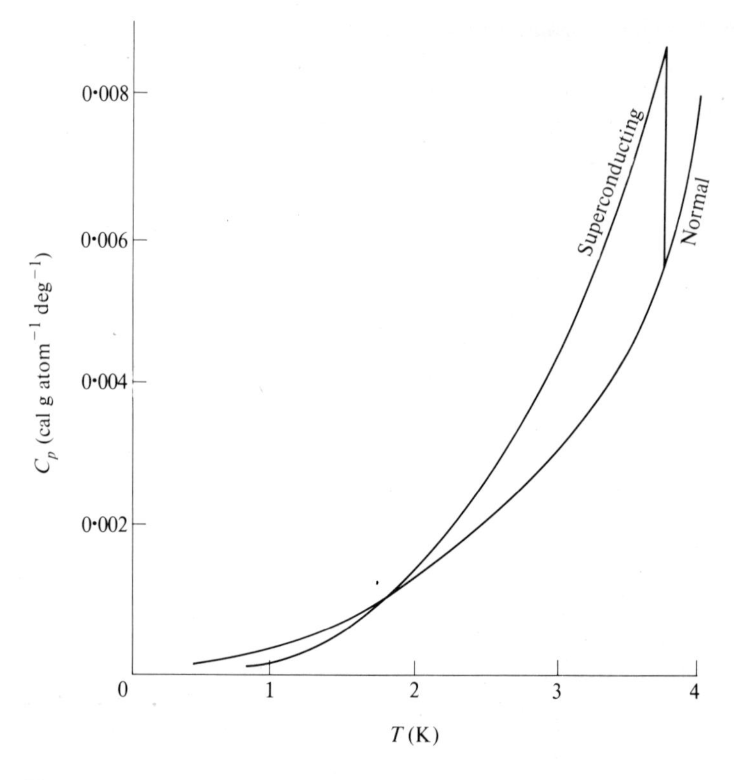

Figure 2-4 Specific heat of normal and superconducting tin. (*After Keesom and van Laer.*[12])

the case of the superconducting transition in tin at zero field[12] (Fig. 2-4). The Curie points in many ferromagnetics could be considered as examples of third-order transitions.[7]

A large number of transitions which are often incorrectly referred to as second-order transitions are actually lambda (λ) transitions. In these transitions, the heat capacity, when plotted as a function of temperature, tends toward infinity at T_t (which is more usually termed the critical temperature, T_c). The name "lambda transition" is actually derived from the lambda shape of the heat capacity curve. Transformation of crystalline quartz[13] (Fig. 2-5) and the order–disorder transition in β-brass are examples of λ-transitions. In simple λ-transformations, the approach to infinity is not symmetrical around the transformation (or critical) temperature. But there are transformations like the one in manganese bromide[7] which are symmetrical around T_c (Fig. 2-6) and are known as symmetrical λ-transitions. Lambda specific heat anomalies are lowered if one considers the variation of C_v rather than C_p, because of the increase in volume that may accompany the transitions.

Several of the known transformations do not strictly belong to any one kind described above.[9,11] For example, the phase transition of $BaTiO_3$, which has

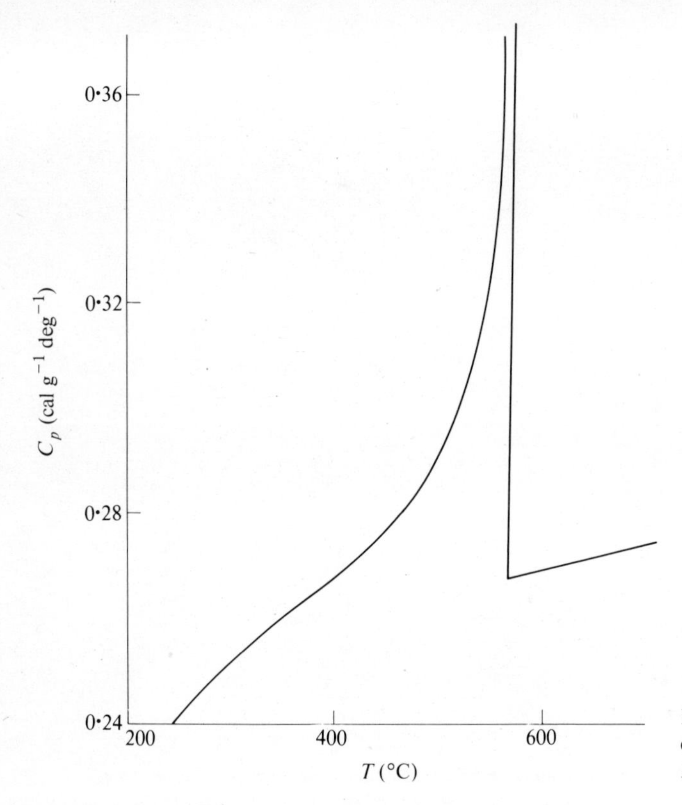

Figure 2-5 Specific heat of crystalline quartz. (*After Moser.*[13])

second-order character, also shows a small latent heat effect. The ferroelectric transition of KH_2PO_4 should theoretically be of the first order, but conforms more closely to the second order. There is superposition of second-order behavior in many first-order transitions, as in the case of alkali sulfates. It often happens that transitions have observable heat effects, and yet the approach to the transitions is marked by a gradual change of properties. It is possible that many transformations are really "mixed." Thus, even order–disorder changes in some instances are seen as abrupt changes toward the termination.

Ubbelohde[8] has preferred to classify transformations simply as thermodynamically continuous (or gradual) and thermodynamically discontinuous transformations. A systematic classification of phase transitions is desirable for clarity and a better appreciation of the phenomena. Existence of a measurable latent heat or a discontinuous volume change or, more precisely, formation of an interface with positive surface energy at the transformation may be taken as characteristics of a first-order transformation. Phase transitions of the first order generally exhibit hysteresis which may also be taken as a characteristic of these transitions.

A few comments on the entropy increase in thermal phase transitions would be in order. In first-order transitions, the high-temperature phases having high

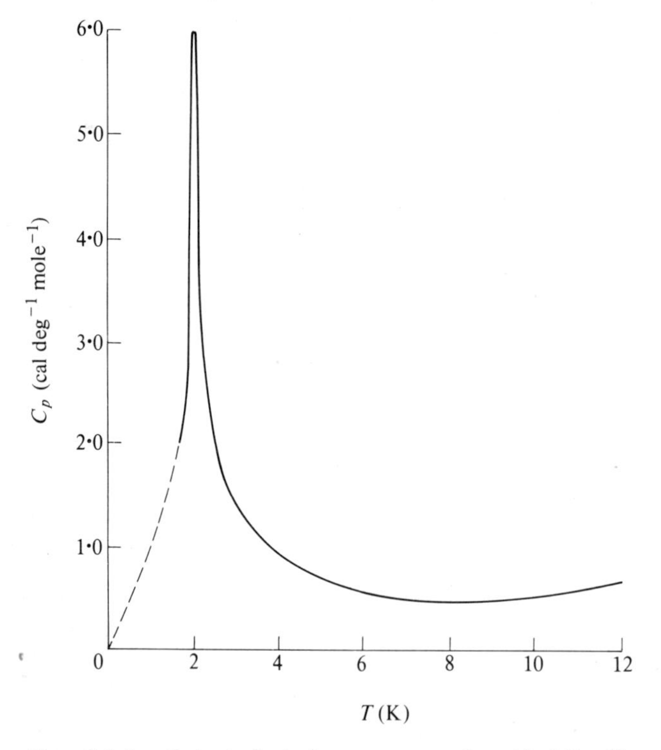

Figure 2-6 Specific heat of anhydrous manganese bromide. (*After Pippard.*[7])

internal energy and low density will also have higher entropy. In fact, the high-temperature structures are generally of higher symmetry and higher disorder than the low-temperature structures. In second-order transformations, there is always some randomization in the structure. Randomization can be in position or orientation. In NH_4Cl, $C_v \approx 9R$ above T_t, the contribution from the lattice being $6R$; the orientational contribution of $3R$ to C_v suggests the absence of free rotation above T_t (free rotation would require $C_v = 3R/2$). In hydrogen halides, the number of orientations, n, is found to be 6 from the entropy of the transition ($\Delta S = R \ln n$). Orientational and positional disorder in several systems are discussed later in Chap. 4.

2-2 THERMODYNAMIC RELATIONS AT THE PHASE TRANSITION

In a single-component system, free energies of two phases may be described in terms of surfaces of two variables, P and T. First-order transitions occur on the line of intersection of two surfaces. The slope of such a line describes the well-known Clapeyron–Clausius relation. Since the free energies G_I and G_II of the two phases are equal along this line for a first-order transition,

$$G_{II} - G_I = \Delta G = (V_2 - V_1)\,dP - (S_2 - S_1)\,dT$$
$$= \Delta V\,dP - \Delta S\,dT = 0$$

Therefore
$$\frac{dP}{dT} = \frac{\Delta S}{\Delta V} = \frac{\Delta H}{T\Delta V} \tag{2-5}$$

Transformations of the second and higher orders have zero values of ΔV and ΔS, and therefore Eq. (2-5) will have 0/0 indeterminacy. However, analogs of the Clapeyron equation which describe the relation of transition temperature to pressure may be obtained, since S and V are continuous through the transition. If S_{II} and S_I are the entropies of two (fictitious) phases, we have $S_{II} - S_I = \Delta S = 0$. Since S is a function of T and P, we have

$$\left(\frac{\partial \Delta S}{\partial T}\right)_P \cdot dT + \left(\frac{\partial \Delta S}{\partial P}\right)_T \cdot dP = 0$$

or
$$\frac{dP}{dT} = \frac{\Delta C_p}{VT\Delta\alpha} \tag{2-6}$$

$$\left(\frac{\partial S}{\partial T}\right)_P = \frac{C_p}{T} \quad \text{and} \quad \left(\frac{\partial S}{\partial P}\right)_T = -\left(\frac{\partial V}{\partial T}\right)_P = -V\alpha$$

Since V is continuous, we can show that

$$\frac{dP}{dT} = \frac{\Delta\alpha}{\Delta\beta} \tag{2-7}$$

where α and β are the coefficients of volume thermal expansion and isothermal compressibility respectively. It is possible to derive similar expressions for higher-order transitions as well. Equations (2-5), (2-6), and (2-7) and their analogs may be considered as Ehrenfest's equations for different orders of transitions. They provide the thermodynamic basis for the verification of the nature of transitions.[8,11,14] While Eq. (2-5) is generally satisfied by first-order transitions, the only cases where Eqs. (2-6) and (2-7) seem to be verified experimentally are in superconducting transitions[7] where a finite discontinuity of specific heat occurs.

For transformations of the λ type, a definition of ΔC_p and similar quantities becomes meaningless since the values approach infinity and indeterminacies of the type ∞/∞ occur. In these transitions, the analysis due to Pippard[7] is applicable. In Fig. 2-7 we have represented variations of entropy with temperatures for simple and symmetrical λ-transitions. For the symmetrical λ-transitions there is no sharp inflection at the transition temperature. Normally, the entropy, S, is a smoothly varying function of pressure, and it can be assumed that there is a regular fold in the $S(T, P)$ surface over a short range of pressure around the transition temperature. One can therefore employ a cylindrical approximation to the $S(T, P)$ surface, and write

$$S_\lambda = S(P) + f(P - aT) \tag{2-8}$$

where $a = (dP/dT)_\lambda$ and f represents some function describing the nature of the

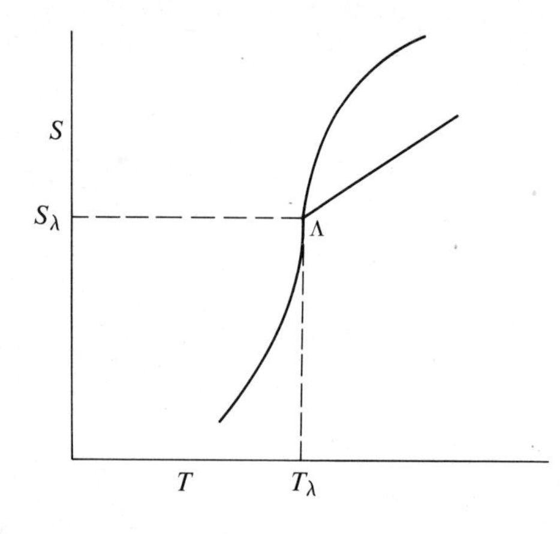

Figure 2-7 Variation of entropy with temperature at the lambda point.

curve in Fig. 2-6. Taking the second derivatives of S in Eq. (2-8) with respect to T and P, we have

$$\left(\frac{\partial^2 S}{\partial T^2}\right)_P = a^2 f'' \qquad \left(\frac{\partial^2 S}{\partial P^2}\right)_T = f'' \qquad \left(\frac{\partial^2 S}{\partial P\,\partial T}\right) = -af'' \tag{2-9}$$

where the double prime stands for the second derivative. We can thus write $a = (dP/dT)_\lambda$ as

$$a = \left(\frac{dP}{dT}\right)_\lambda = -\left(\frac{\partial^2 S}{\partial T^2}\right)_P \Bigg/ \left(\frac{\partial^2 S}{\partial T\,\partial P}\right) = -\left(\frac{\partial^2 S}{\partial T\,\partial P}\right) \Bigg/ \left(\frac{\partial^2 S}{\partial P^2}\right)_T \tag{2-10}$$

$$\frac{\partial}{\partial T}\left(\frac{\partial S}{\partial T}\right)_P = -a\,\frac{\partial}{\partial T}\left(\frac{\partial S}{\partial P}\right)_T = a\,\frac{\partial}{\partial T}\left(\frac{\partial V}{\partial T}\right)_P \tag{2-11}$$

and

$$\frac{\partial}{\partial P}\left(\frac{\partial S}{\partial T}\right)_P = -a\,\frac{\partial}{\partial P}\left(\frac{\partial S}{\partial P}\right)_T = a\,\frac{\partial}{\partial P}\left(\frac{\partial V}{\partial T}\right)_P \tag{2-12}$$

Equations (2-11) and (2-12) imply that

$$C_p/T_\lambda = aV\alpha + \text{constant}$$

or

$$C_p = aT_\lambda V\alpha + \text{constant} \tag{2-13}$$

This analog of the Clapeyron relation applicable to λ-transitions establishes a proportionality between C_p and α close to the transition temperature. By a similar cylindrical approximation to the $V(T, P)$ surface around T_λ, it is possible to infer a proportionality between α and β:

$$\alpha = a\beta + \text{constant} \tag{2-14}$$

Equations (2-13) and (2-14) are known as Pippard relations, and several λ-transitions have been analyzed in the light of these relations.[15-19] The case of the alpha–beta transition in quartz[18] where the validity of Pippard relations has been verified is illustrated in Fig. 2-8. Pippard relations are found to be valid

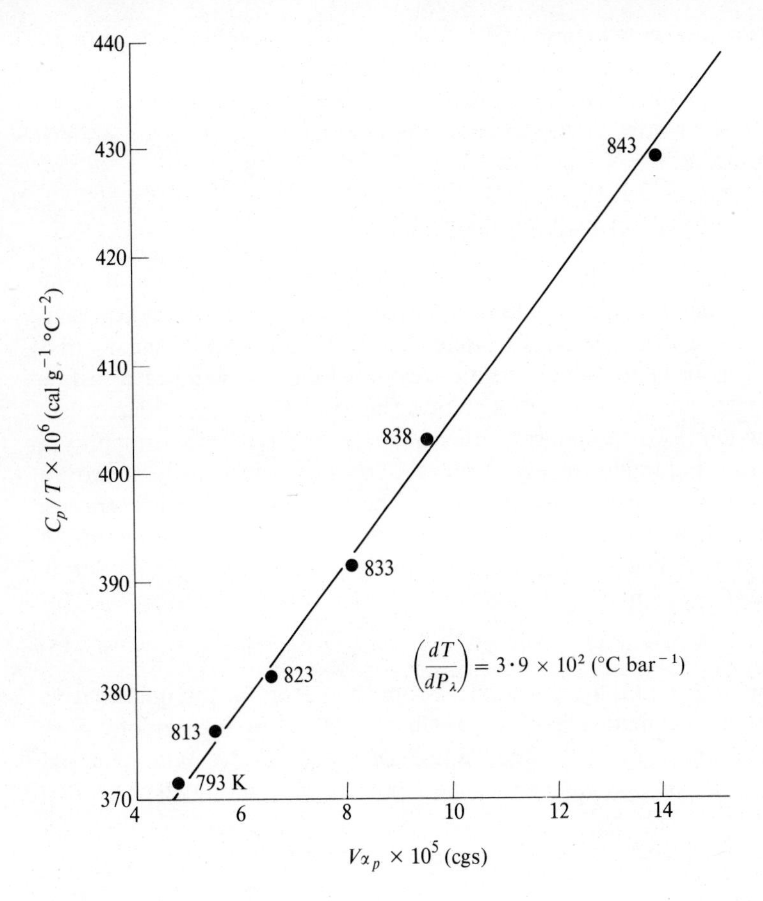

Figure 2-8 Plot of C_p/T vs $V\alpha$ near the transition temperature in quartz. (*After Hughes and Lawson.*[18])

even in the case of stress-broadened first-order phase transformations.[20] Caution is therefore necessary when characterizing transitions as λ-type on the basis of Pippard relations alone.

2-3 THERMODYNAMIC THEORIES OF PHASE TRANSITIONS

First-order phase transitions in solids are associated with latent heats, discontinuities in volume, and drastic structural changes* at the transition. For these transitions, $\Delta G = 0$ at the transition point where the phases are in equilibrium, leading directly to the Clapeyron–Clausius equation. The latent heats of trans-

* Change in crystal symmetry along with latent heat effects could be taken as a necessary criterion for a first-order transition. The symmetries of the two phases are not related in a first-order transition, while they are related in a second-order transition. (See Chap. 7 and Sec. 7-5 for a discussion of symmetry and phase transition.)

formations are generally small compared to the lattice energies. Theoretical treatments to predict the position of the equilibrium line become tedious.[21] We therefore have to content ourselves with the conceptual graphical descriptions given earlier. We shall now briefly discuss thermodynamic theories of second-order and λ-transitions.

Landau's Theory of Second-Order Transitions

It was pointed out earlier that during a second-order phase transition, the entropy and volume of the system remain continuous while the heat capacity and thermal expansivity undergo a discontinuous change. Landau[22] proposed a theory that can account for this behavior. The transition from a high temperature to a low temperature corresponds to the onset of an ordering process. In the ordered, less symmetrical (low-temperature) phase of the material, it is possible to identify a long-range ordering parameter, which decreases continuously with temperature and becomes zero at the transition temperature. The disordered high-temperature phase would have high symmetry.* The free energy can be written in terms of the order parameter, ξ. For small values of ξ (near the transition temperature), the free energy, $\phi(P, T, \xi)$, may be written as

$$\phi(P, T, \xi) = \phi_0(P, T) + a\xi + b\xi^2 + c\xi^3 + d\xi^4 + \cdots \tag{2-15}$$

where $\phi_0(P, T)$, a, b, c, and d are constants. From the nature of the quantitative description which will be made clear later in Chap. 5, changing the sign of ξ does not alter the state of the body.[23,24] If the value of $\phi(P, T, \xi)$ is to remain unaltered by the change of sign of ξ, coefficients of odd powers of ξ should be equal to zero. Therefore

$$\phi(P, T, \xi) = \phi_0(P, T) + b\xi^2 + d\xi^4 + \cdots \tag{2-16}$$

The equilibrium value of the long-range order parameter is obtained by the following conditions:

$$\left(\frac{\partial \phi}{\partial \xi}\right)_{P,T} = \xi(b + 2d\xi^2) = 0 \tag{2-17}$$

$$\left(\frac{\partial^2 \phi}{\partial \xi^2}\right)_{P,T} = (b + 6d\xi^2) > 0 \tag{2-18}$$

From Eq. (2-17), we obtain the solutions $\xi = 0$ and $\xi^2 = -b/2d$. Since $\xi = 0$ corresponds to the disordered state, it follows from Eq. (2-18) that $b > 0$ on one side of the transition temperature. Similarly, using the value $\xi^2 = -b/2d$ in Eq. (2.18), we find that $b < 0$ for the ordered phase. Thus, b should change sign through a second-order transition. Since b is negative for the ordered phase in the vicinity of the transition, d should be positive ($-b/2d = \xi^2 > 0$). Assuming b to vary linearly with temperature, we find that near the transition point

$$b(P, T) = B(T - T_c) \tag{2-19}$$

* See footnote on page 27.

where T_c is the "critical" or transition temperature; ξ^2 now becomes

$$\xi^2 = -b/2d = -B(T - T_c)/2d \tag{2-20}$$

It is interesting to derive the values of entropy and heat capacity of a system using Eqs. (2-16) and (2-20). Neglecting higher-order terms, we have

$$S = -\left(\frac{\partial \phi}{\partial T}\right)_{P,\xi} = S_0 - \xi^2\left(\frac{\partial b(P, T)}{\partial T}\right)_{P,\xi} \tag{2-21}$$

In the symmetrical phase (above the transition temperature), $\xi = 0$ and $S = S_0$. Below the transition temperature, making use of Eq. (2-20),

$$S = S_0 + \frac{b(P, T)}{2d}\left(\frac{\partial b(P, T)}{\partial T}\right)_{P,\xi} = S_0 + \frac{B^2}{2d}(T - T_c) \tag{2-22}$$

Equations (2-21) and (2-22) together guarantee the continuous nature of entropy through the transition. Since $C_p = T(\partial S/\partial T)_{P,\xi}$, we have for the two phases at the transition

$$C_p = (\partial S_0/\partial T)_P = C_{p_0} \qquad \text{and} \qquad C_p = C_{p_0} + B^2 T_c/2d \tag{2-23}$$

on either side of the transformation. ΔC_p will have a finite value given by

$$\Delta C_p = B^2 T_c/2d \tag{2-24}$$

We thus see that Landau's theory provides the basis for Ehrenfest's second-order transition. Similar relations for $\Delta\alpha$ and $\Delta\beta$ could be derived by considering expressions for volume instead of entropy. Extension of Landau's treatment has been attempted by various workers in conjunction with fluctuation theory.[25]

Tizza's Theory of Lambda Transitions

It was pointed out earlier that, except for the superconducting transitions, there are no instances of a finite discontinuity in derivative properties. The theory of Landau is not entirely adequate to account for the so-called λ-transitions. A strict thermodynamic theory to explain infinities in heat capacity, expansivity, and compressibility at the λ-point was developed by Tizza.[26] Tizza assumes that the λ-point is analogous to the critical point and that it marks a state of incipient instability. We know that in the case of fluid phases (liquid–gas equilibria) there is an equilibrium line terminating in a critical point. Above this point the material can be transformed from the liquid to the gaseous phase continuously. The critical point forms a boundary between the stable and the unstable states and is characterized by large values of fluctuations of thermodynamic properties. Tizza's theory of λ-transitions is directed toward finding the thermodynamic conditions for this special kind of borderline stability. We shall briefly examine Tizza's theory for a single-component system whose internal energy is entirely described by two variables P and V, and show how the heat capacity or thermal expansivity tends to infinity at the λ-transition.

The internal energy of a single-component solid system may be described in terms of its two natural coordinates, S and V. For small variations in coordinates, E may be expanded as

$$\begin{aligned} E &= E_0 + \delta E + \delta^2 E + \cdots \\ &= E_0 + (E_v\,dV + E_s\,dS) + \tfrac{1}{2}[E_{vv}(dV)^2 + 2E_{vs}\,dV\,dS + E_{ss}(ds)^2] + \cdots \end{aligned} \tag{2-25}$$

Thermodynamic stability requires that the term in parentheses should go to zero and the terms in square brackets should be "positive definite." This quantity is known as the stability quadratic. The terms E_s and E_v are $(\partial E/\partial S)_v = T$ and $(\partial E/\partial V)_s = -P$, and are the "thermodynamic forces." E_{ss}, E_{vv}, and E_{vs} are similarly the second derivatives, being equal to

$$\begin{aligned} E_{ss} &= \left(\frac{\partial^2 E}{\partial S^2}\right)_v = \left(\frac{\partial T}{\partial S}\right)_v \\ E_{vs} = E_{sv} &= \left(\frac{\partial^2 E}{\partial S\,\partial V}\right) = \left(\frac{\partial T}{\partial V}\right)_s = -\left(\frac{\partial P}{\partial S}\right)_v \\ E_{vv} &= \left(\frac{\partial^2 E}{\partial V^2}\right)_s = -\left(\frac{\partial P}{\partial V}\right)_s \end{aligned} \tag{2-26}$$

A negative stability quadratic indicates an unstable system.

A second-order transition in Tizza's theory corresponds to an "incipient instability" which implies that the stability quadratic becomes "positive semi-definite." That is, the value of the stability quadratic would be either zero or positive. In order to establish the conditions under which stability quadratic becomes positive semidefinite, the quadratic may be suitably transformed to contain only square terms,

$$\begin{aligned} \delta^2 E &= \tfrac{1}{2}[E_{vv}(dV)^2 + 2E_{vs}\,dV\,dS + E_{ss}(dS)^2] \\ &= \tfrac{1}{2}[\lambda_1\eta_1^2 + \lambda_2\eta_2^2] \end{aligned} \tag{2-27}$$

The stability quadratic becomes zero when each of the coefficients λ becomes zero. The transformation is brought about by a general procedure which is easy to follow, if we redesignate E_{vv} etc. as $E_{vv} = E_{11}$, $E_{vs} = E_{12}$, $E_{ss} = E_{22}$, $dV = x_1$, and $ds = x_2$. Defining a new variable η_1 as

$$\eta_1 = \left[x_1 + \frac{1}{E_{11}}(E_{12}x_2)\right] \tag{2-28}$$

we have

$$\eta_1^2 = \left[x_1^2 + \frac{1}{E_{11}^2}(E_{12}^2 x_2^2) + 2E_{12}x_1x_2/E_{11}\right]$$

Equation (2-27) can be written as

$$\delta^2 E = \tfrac{1}{2}[E_{11}x_1^2 + 2E_{12}x_1x_2 + E_{22}x_2^2]$$

If we introduce η_1 in the above expression, we get

$$\delta^2 E = \frac{1}{2}\left[E_{11}\eta_1^2 + \frac{1}{E_{11}}(E_{11}E_{22} - E_{12}^2)x_2^2\right]$$
$$= \tfrac{1}{2}[\lambda_1\eta_1^2 + \lambda_2\eta_2^2] \quad (2\text{-}29)$$

Here we have identified x_2 as η_2. We can now write λ_1 and λ_2 as

$$\lambda_1 = E_{11} = E_{vv} = -\left(\frac{\partial P}{\partial V}\right)_s$$
$$\lambda_2 = \frac{1}{E_{11}}(E_{11}E_{22} - E_{12}^2) = \frac{1}{E_{vv}}(E_{vv}E_{ss} - E_{vs}^2) \quad (2\text{-}30)$$
$$= \left(\frac{\partial T}{\partial S}\right)_P$$

Tizza's theory predicts that for the occurrence of a critical point it is enough that one of the λs becomes zero. Since the transformation involved in Eq. (2-29) requires E_{11} to be finite, it is meaningful to say that λ_2 becomes zero. This would mean that

$$\frac{T}{C_p} \to 0 \quad \text{or} \quad C_p \to \infty \quad (2\text{-}31)$$

The elegance of Tizza's theory would not be illustrated if some of the generalities implied in the above treatment are not mentioned. For example, E_{ss}, E_{sv}, and E_{vv} are the elements of a matrix

$$\begin{bmatrix} E_{ss} & E_{sv} \\ E_{vs} & E_{vv} \end{bmatrix} = [D]$$

whose elements relate the forces T and $-P$ to the coordinates V and S. The matrix is appropriately known as the "stiffness matrix." In matrix notation

$$[dT\ d(-P)] = \begin{bmatrix} E_{ss} & E_{sv} \\ E_{vs} & E_{vv} \end{bmatrix}\begin{bmatrix} ds \\ dv \end{bmatrix} \quad (2\text{-}32)$$

The role of forces and coordinates may be partially or completely changed by appropriate inversion.[27] On complete inversion we get

$$[dS\ d(-V)] = \begin{bmatrix} \dfrac{E_{vv}}{|D|} & -\dfrac{E_{vs}}{|D|} \\ -\dfrac{E_{vs}}{|D|} & \dfrac{E_{ss}}{|D|} \end{bmatrix}\begin{bmatrix} dT \\ d(-P) \end{bmatrix} \quad (2\text{-}33)$$

in which $|D|$ is the determinent of $[D]$. The elements of the square matrix in Eq. (2-33) represent generalized compliances, and the matrix is the "compliance matrix." The product of the coefficients λ_1 and λ_2 is actually equal to

$$\lambda_1\lambda_2 = E_{11}\frac{1}{E_{11}}[E_{11}E_{22} - E_{12}^2] = |D| \tag{2-34}$$

Therefore, even when one of the λs goes to zero, the determinant of the stiffness matrix goes to zero or more appropriately, all the elements of the compliance matrix go to infinity.[27] The compliance matrix in Eq. (2-33) is actually equal to

$$\begin{bmatrix} \dfrac{E_{vv}}{|D|} & -\dfrac{E_{vs}}{|D|} \\ -\dfrac{E_{vs}}{|D|} & \dfrac{E_{ss}}{|D|} \end{bmatrix} = \begin{bmatrix} \left(\dfrac{\partial S}{\partial T}\right)_P & -\left(\dfrac{\partial S}{\partial P}\right)_T \\ \left(\dfrac{\partial V}{\partial T}\right)_P & \left(\dfrac{\partial V}{\partial P}\right)_T \end{bmatrix} = \begin{bmatrix} \dfrac{C_p}{T} & \alpha \\ \alpha & V\beta \end{bmatrix} \tag{2-35}$$

Therefore C_p, α, and β all tend to infinity.

For the general case, where $\delta^2 E = \sum_{i,j} E_{ij}x_i x_j$, one can find a general transformation, $\delta^2 E = \sum_k \lambda_k \eta_k^2$, and according to Tizza's theory, it is sufficient that one of the λ_ks becomes zero. The determinant $|D_k|$ will then be identically zero and hence all the associated compliances go to infinity. Tizza's theory has been recently discussed in relation to the transformation in quartz.[28]

2-4 HYSTERESIS IN PHASE TRANSFORMATIONS

It was stated earlier that hysteresis is a common feature of both thermal and pressure transitions of the first order. It manifests itself as a difference in the

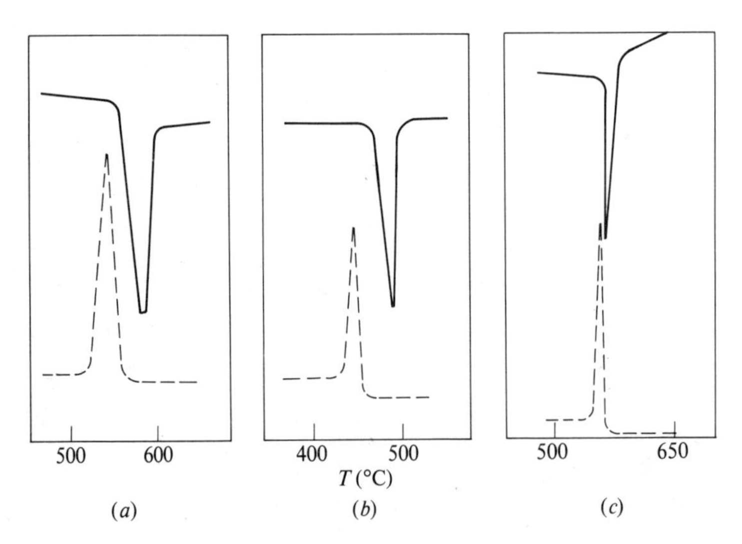

Figure 2-9 Typical differential thermal analysis curves of reversible thermal transitions showing hysteresis: (*a*) Li_2SO_4, (*b*) CsCl, (*c*) quartz. Full lines are heating curves and broken lines are cooling curves (temperature, °C). (*After Rao and Rao.*[9])

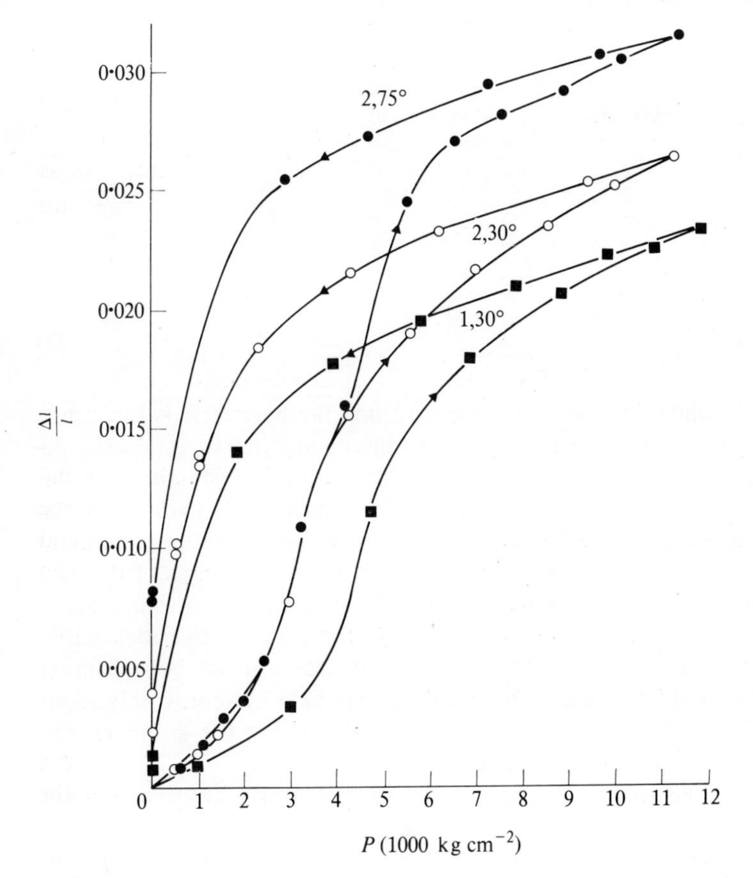

Figure 2-10 Fractional change of length of Ag_2O as a function of pressure showing very large pressure hysteresis. Sample 1 at 30°C, Sample 2 at 30°C and 75°C. (*After Bridgman.*[30])

transformation temperatures or pressures in the forward and reverse directions[9,29,30] (Figs. 2-9 and 2-10). Observation of hysteresis suggests that the transformation does not occur at the point where the free energies are exactly equal as represented by Eq. (2-5). Such a situation could arise through two possible causes.

One is the formation of a hybrid single crystal[8,31,32] wherein the two phases coexist within a general pattern of orientation. In such a case, additional terms representing the strain energy (ε) and the interfacial energy (η) would have to be included in the free energy expression as suggested by Ubbelohde.[8] The Gibbs functions for the two phases that coexist in the region of transformation temperature may be written as

$$\begin{aligned} G_{\mathrm{I}} &= G(P, T, \varepsilon_{12}, \eta_{12}) \\ G_{\mathrm{II}} &= G(P, T, \varepsilon_{21}, \eta_{21}) \end{aligned} \tag{2-36}$$

Table 2-3 Hysteresis in ammonium salts[14,33]

T_t(K)	Salt	ΔV (cc mol^{-1})	Width of hysteresis loop (deg)
234.4	NH_4Br	0.03	0.06
247.95	NHD_3Cl	0.07	0.07
214.9	ND_4Br	0.08	0.11
244.6	NH_3DCl	0.11	0.12
242.6	NH_4Cl	0.15	0.35
223.4	$(NH_4)_2SO_4$	0.35	1.2
168.1	ND_4Br	0.6	9.0

According to Ubbelohde, the main factor controlling the hysteresis is the strain energy, ε, stored in the hybrid crystal. The strain energy in either direction should not be greater than the breaking strength of the hybrid crystal or otherwise the new structure will result. In the neighborhood of T_t, the $G(P, T)$ surfaces of the two phases are supposed to get "thicker," their intersection being indeterminate over a narrow range of temperature. The state in which the domains of the two phases coexist at a temperature different from the true transition temperature T_t is likely to be a metastable equilibrium. The termination of this metastable region in the two directions marks the width of hysteresis. It has been pointed out by Ubbelohde[8] that lambda transitions show negligible hysteresis only when the volume differences between two phases is small, so that the strain energy greater than kT_t is not stored in the crystal.

Hysteresis could also occur for kinetic reasons. Though the free energies become equal for the two phases at T_t, the new phase cannot nucleate because of the existence of kinetic barriers. The nucleation barriers should be higher, and hence ΔT greater, for transitions involving larger values of ΔV. Indeed, this is found to be true in the transitions of ammonium halides investigated by Thomas and Staveley[33] (Table 2-3) and in several other transitions examined by Rao and Rao[9] (Table 2-1). The barriers include, in addition to strains, interfacial energies. Based on simple considerations of the theory of elasticity, it has been shown[9] that the strain energy is a function of ΔV. For transformations involving a positive ΔV, the nucleation of the new phase takes place under compression in the forward direction and under tension in the reverse direction. One would therefore expect the nucleation barriers, and hence the transition temperatures, to be different in the two directions.

In the absence of methods by which these barrier heights may be reliably calculated, quantitative prediction of hysteresis is not possible. However, with the notion of hybrid single crystal formation, the width of hysteresis has been calculated theoretically for the transition of solid methane,[34] and agreement with experimental values is satisfactory. Transformations in which metastable phases are formed while cooling high-temperature phases may also be considered as hysteresis effects.[9,35] Typical of such transformations are those found in KNO_3 and Bi_2O_3 (Fig. 2-11). The metastable phases (the rhombohedral (III) phase of

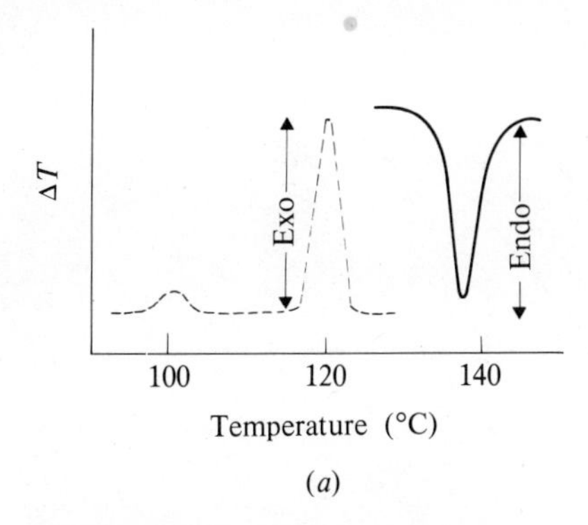

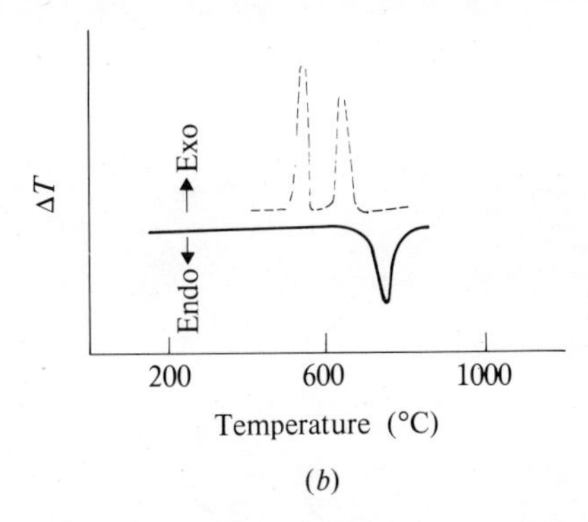

Figure 2-11 DTA curves of (*a*) KNO_3 and (*b*) Bi_2O_3 showing hysteresis occurring in the form of metastable phases. Full lines are heating curves and broken lines are cooling curves. (*From the laboratory of C. N. R. Rao.*)

KNO_3, which is ferroelectric, and tetragonal Bi_2O_3) occur only in the cooling parts of the cycle. The appearance of the new metastable phases could be manifestations of different magnitudes of strain in forward and reverse transformations.

Pressure hysteresis appears to be less understood than the thermal hysteresis. Generally, the width of the hysteresis increases with decreasing temperature,[29] as in the case of KCl or RbCl. The opposite form of behavior, namely increasing hysteresis width with increasing temperature, has also been reported[36] (e.g., CdS). Factors like particle size, rate of heating, and impurities also appear to affect the magnitude of thermal hysteresis.[9,37]

2-5 IRREVERSIBLE PHASE TRANSFORMATIONS AND STABILITIES OF POLYMORPHS

The thermodynamics of phase transitions discussed so far has assumed that the transformations are completely reversible, although often associated with hysteresis. Such an assumption is valid only if, during the variation of temperature or pressure, the system always traverses in its minimum free energy path. It is possible, however, that during the variation of pressure or temperature, the system ends up in a metastable state. More often than not, such situations arise because of kinetic reasons. It may sometimes be due to the method of preparation (as in thin amorphous films) whereby the system would not have sufficient energy to fluctuate and settle down with a unique minimum free energy. Metastable states transform to stable states with unique minimum free energy when sufficient energy is made available to them. Such transformations would be irreversible. It is not possible to assign any critical transformation temperature for an irreversible transformation. Because of kinetic factors, such transformations will be functions of both time and temperature. One can define a temperature below which an irreversible transformation does not take place, as in the case of TiO_2 (anatase),[38] illustrated in Fig. 2-12. Typical examples of irreversible transformations[11] are

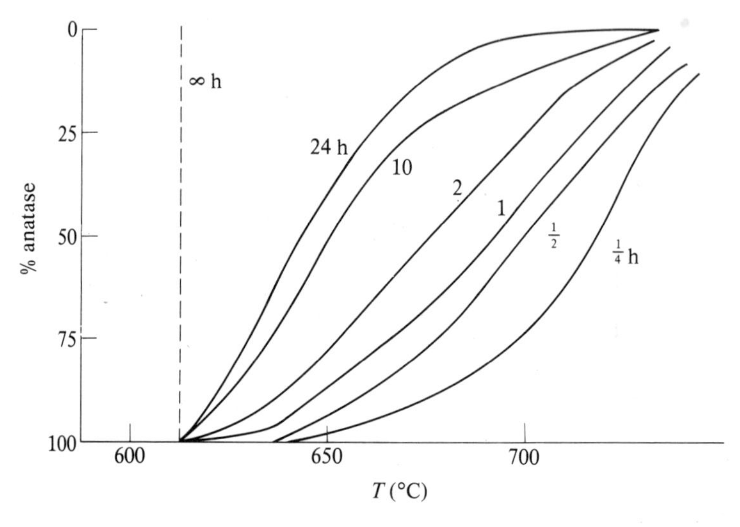

Figure 2-12 Conversion of anatase to rutile as a function of temperature for different times. (*After Czanderna, Rao, and Honig.*[38])

anatase–rutile or brookite–rutile in TiO_2, aragonite–calcite in $CaCO_3$, cubic–hexagonal or cubic–monoclinic transitions in rare-earth sesquioxides; crystallization of glasses and thin films would also belong to this category.[39] For such irreversible transformations, kinetics are investigated at different temperatures to derive activation energies.

From thermodynamic considerations we expect one of the polymorphs of a substance to be more stable than the others under a specified set of conditions. We should note, however, that this is strictly true for a solid of a specific composition (stoichiometry, impurity content, etc.). The presence of impurities and other defects, or a change in stoichiometry, may alter the relative thermodynamic stabilities of polymorphs.[11,35] Thus, in the presence of Sr^{2+}, the aragonite phase of $CaCO_3$ becomes more stable relative to the calcite phase, just as in the presence of SO_4^{2-}, the anatase phase of TiO_2 becomes more stable relative to the rutile phase. ZrO_2 becomes cubic at high temperatures (2470 K), but under the conditions of the experiment the solid is anion-deficient (and not stoichiometric).

Strictly speaking, it would be necessary to specify the particle size and surface area of a substance while defining the thermodynamic stabilities of its polymorphs. When particle size is small or surface area is large, we shall have additional degrees of freedom. Although these factors may not ordinarily have large effects on stability, there are instances where high surface area or small particle size stabilizes the high-temperature metastable phases at ordinary temperatures.[9,11,35,37] Thus, the tetragonal phase of ZrO_2 is stabilized at room temperature by small particle size; normally the tetragonal phase is formed around 1420 K. There are other instances where particle-size effects on phase transformations have been reported. It appears that the effects observed depend on the nature of the transformation.

REFERENCES

1. J. E. Ricci, "The Phase Rule and Heterogeneous Equilibria," Van Nostrand, New York, 1951.
2. R. Roy, in "Phase Transitions," ed. H. K. Henisch, R. Roy, and L. E. Cross, Pergamon Press, New York, 1973.
3. P. Ehrenfest, *Proc. Amsterdam Acad.*, **36,** 153, 1933.
4. W. Klement and A. Jayaraman, "Progress in Solid State Chemistry," ed. H. Reiss, vol. 3, Pergamon Press, Oxford, 1967.
5. W. Paul and M. Warschauer (eds.), "Solids Under Pressure," McGraw-Hill, New York, 1963.
6. E. Justi and M. von Laue, *Phys. Z.*, **35,** 945, 1934.
7. A. B. Pippard, "Elements of Classical Thermodynamics," Cambridge University Press, 1966.
8. A. R. Ubbelohde, *Quart. Rev.* (*London*), **11,** 246, 1957; see also "Reactivity of Solids," ed. J. H. de Boer, Elsevier, Amsterdam, 1961.
9. K. J. Rao and C. N. R. Rao, *J. Materials Sci.*, **1,** 238, 1966.
10. C. J. M. Rooymans, *Philips Research Reports Supplement*, no. 5, 1968.
11. C. N. R. Rao and K. J. Rao, "Progress in Solid State Chemistry," ed. H. Reiss, vol. 4, Pergamon Press, Oxford, 1967.
12. W. H. Keesom and P. H. van Laer, *Physica*, **5,** 193, 1938.
13. H. Moser, *Phys. Z.*, **37,** 737, 1936.
14. L. A. K. Staveley, *Quart. Rev.* (*London*), **3,** 64, 1949.
15. A. B. Pippard, *Phil. Mag.*, **1,** 473, 1956.
16. M. J. Buckingham and W. M. Fairbank, "Progress in Low Temperature Physics," ed. C. J. Garter, vol. 3, North-Holland, Amsterdam, 1961.
17. C. W. Garland and J. S. Jones, *J. Chem. Phys.*, **39,** 2874, 1963.
18. A. J. Hughes and A. W. Lawson, *J. Chem. Phys.*, **36,** 2098, 1962.
19. B. Viswanathan, S. N. Vaidya, and E. S. R. Gopal, *J. Indian Inst. Sci.*, **50,** 83, 1968.
20. F. J. Bartis, *J. Chem. Phys.*, **51,** 5176, 1969.
21. J. E. Mayer, in "Phase Transitions," *14th Chemistry Conference, Solvay Institute*, Interscience, New York, 1971.
22. L. D. Landau and E. M. Lifshitz, "Statistical Physics," Pergamon Press, Oxford, 1959.
23. M. A. Krivoglaz and A. A. Smirnov, "The Theory of Order–Disorder in Alloys," Macdonald, London, 1964.
24. H. Sato, in "Physical Chemistry, An Advanced Treatise," vol. 10, Academic Press, New York, 1970.
25. See, for example, A. Richard, *Am. J. Phys.*, **40,** 3, 1972; M. I. Salakhutdinov and A. A. Adkhamov, *Dokl. Akad. Nauk Tadzah. SSR*, **15,** 23, 1972.
26. L. Tizza, in "Phase Transformations in Solids," eds. R. Smoluchowski, J. E. Mayer, and W. A. Weyl, John Wiley, New York, 1951.
27. H. B. Callen, "Thermodynamics," John Wiley, London, 1960.
28. A. G. McLennan, *Phil. Mag.*, **28,** 1077, 1973.
29. A. J. Dornell and W. A. McCollum, *High Temp. Sci.*, **2,** 331, 1970.
30. P. W. Bridgman, *Rec. Trav. Chem.*, **51,** 627 (1932).
31. A. R. Ubbelohde, *Carsi. Semin. Chim.*, no. 5, 85, 1967.
32. A. R. Ubbelohde, *Brit. J. Appl. Phys.*, **7,** 313, 1956.
33. D. G. Thomas and L. A. K. Staveley, *J. Chem. Soc.*, 1420, 2572, 1951.
34. A. Guha and S. H. Lin, in "Extended Defects in Nonmetallic Solids," eds. L. Eyring and M. O'Keeffe, North-Holland, Amsterdam, 1970.
35. C. N. R. Rao, "Modern Aspects of Solid State Chemistry," Plenum Press, New York, 1970.
36. E. L. Kaminski, A. E. Omelchenko, and E. I. Estrin, *Fiz. Tverd. Tela.*, **12,** 3329, 1970.
37. M. Natarajan, A. R. Das, and C. N. R. Rao, *Trans. Faraday Soc.*, **65,** 3081, 1969.
38. A. W. Czanderna, C. N. R. Rao, and J. M. Honig, *Trans. Faraday Soc.*, **54,** 1069, 1958.
39. A. I. Berezhnoi, "Glass-Ceramics and Photo-Sitalls," Plenum Press, New York, 1970.

CHAPTER

THREE

CRYSTAL CHEMISTRY AND PHASE TRANSITIONS

The thermodynamic treatment discussed in Chap. 2 gives only a macroscopic picture of phase transitions. While the thermodynamics of phase transitions can be correlated with structural changes accompanying phase transitions, it does not provide information on specific structural features of the transitions. It is indeed instructive to examine phase transitions from the structural viewpoint. The importance of the structural approach need not be overemphasized. It is well recognized today that a knowledge of crystal chemistry in terms of atomic arrangements and bonding in crystals is essential for understanding properties of solids. Although most phase transitions are first identified by means of changes in crystal structure, detailed structural implications are not often examined. However, if crystal-chemical principles are borne in mind, the study of phase transitions becomes more interesting. Crystal chemistry can provide a basis for classification and prediction of the nature of phase transitions. Relations between the structures of the initial and transformed phases yield valuable information on the mechanism of transformations. In this chapter, we shall discuss the crystal chemistry of phase transitions, including orientational relations and topotaxy, polytypism, and shear structures, assuming an elementary knowledge of crystal chemistry[1-4] on the part of the reader. Importance of the nature of bonding, and the role of stacking faults and other defects, are pointed out. The origin of long periodicities in crystals is examined briefly.

3-1 STRUCTURAL BASIS FOR CLASSIFICATION AND PREDICTION OF PHASE TRANSITIONS

When a solid undergoes a phase transition by absorbing thermal energy, the transformed phase will possess higher internal energy. In the high-temperature phase, therefore, bonding between neighboring atoms or units would be weaker than in the low-temperature phase. This results in a change in the nature of the first-nearest neighbors (primary coordination) or of the second-nearest neighbors (secondary coordination). Buerger[5,6] has classified phase transitions on the basis of structural changes involving primary or higher coordination. He also relates the potential barriers for the transitions (or the transition speeds) to structural changes. Transformations where there are changes in primary coordination will involve more drastic changes in energy compared to those where only second or higher coordination changes. This can be easily visualized in the case of ionic crystals, where energies of ionic bonds vary inversely as the distance while the energies of van der Waals interaction vary inversely as the sixth power of distance.

Buerger's Structural Classification

According to Buerger, phase transitions in solids may be classified into the following categories:[5-7]

(i) Transformations involving first coordination
  (*a*) reconstructive (sluggish)
  (*b*) dilatational (rapid)
(ii) Transformations involving second coordination
  (*a*) reconstructive (sluggish)
  (*b*) displacive (rapid)
(iii) Transformations involving disorder
  (*a*) substitutional (sluggish)
  (*b*) rotational (rapid)
(iv) Transformations of bond type (sluggish)

Changes in primary coordination can take place by a *reconstructive transformation*, where the first-coordination bonds are broken and reformed. Such transformation may generally involve high energies of activation and may therefore be sluggish. Further, there may be no symmetry relation between the two phases. Reconstructive transformations give rise to large discontinuities in cell dimensions, symmetry, internal energy, and so on. Typical of these transformations is the transformation of aragonite (*Pnma*) to calcite (*R*3*c*) in $CaCO_3$ (723 K), where the coordination number of Ca changes from 9 to 6. Other examples are the transformations of HgI_2 (yellow to red, 6:3 to 4:2 at 400 K) and of HgS (4:4 to 2:2 around 600 K).

Changes in primary coordination may also take place through a dilatational mechanism, as in the thermal transformation of cesium chloride (752 K) or ammonium chloride (453 K) from CsCl structure to NaCl structure. The

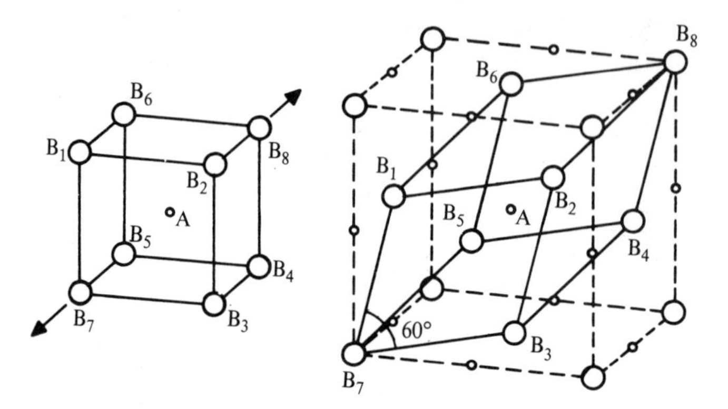

Figure 3-1 Mechanism of a dilatational transformation from CsCl structure to NaCl structure in an AB-type compound. (*After Buerger.*[5,6])

mechanism of dilatation from CsCl-type to NaCl-type structure is shown in Fig. 3-1. Dilatational transformations would be rapid compared to reconstructive transformations. In such transformations, the symmetry about the unique axis of dilatation tends to be preserved; in CsCl the symmetry $3m$ is preserved along the axis.

There are some transformations where only a part of the structure may undergo a change in the primary coordination. The ferroelectric transformations of barium titanate and lead titanate are likely to belong to this category, since the coordination of titanium goes from 6 to 5 because of the shifting of the position of titanium from the centre of the octahedron toward the vertex.

Many transformations involving changes in higher coordination may also have to proceed through the breaking of the primary bonds, and for this reason several of the features of reconstructive transformations involving higher coordination may resemble those of the reconstructive first-coordination transformations. Typical examples of these transformations are sphalerite–wurtzite (ZnS), cristobalite–tridymite–quartz (SiO_2), pyrite–marcasite (FeS_2), senarmonite–valentinite (Sb_2O_3), and arsenolite–clandetite (As_2O_3). Transformation of the anatase or brookite form of TiO_2 to the rutile form also appears to belong to this class.

In some transformations, changes in higher coordination can be effected by a distortion of the primary bond (Fig. 3-2). Such transformations may be called *distortional* or *displacive transformations.* These transformations will involve considerably smaller changes in energy and are usually fast. In displacive transformations, the high-temperature form is usually more open and has higher specific volume, specific heat, and symmetry. Examples of displacive transformations include the high–low transformations of quartz (843 K), tridymite (433 K and 378 K) and cristobalite (523 K). TiO_2 (anatase) appears to show a displacive transformation prior to its transformation to rutile by a reconstructive mechanism. Phase transformation of $SrTiO_3$ appears to be truly displacive; while transitions

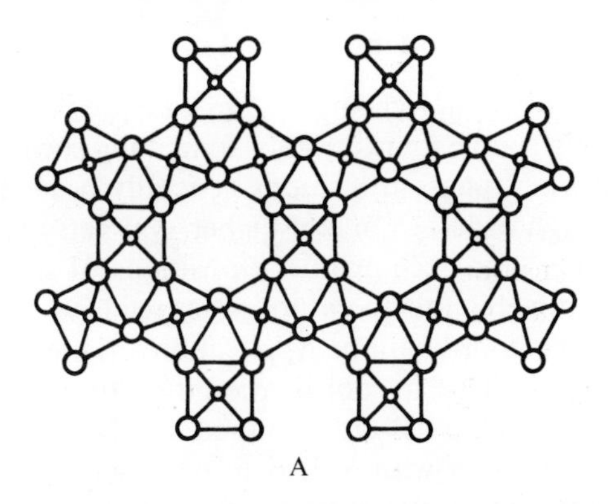

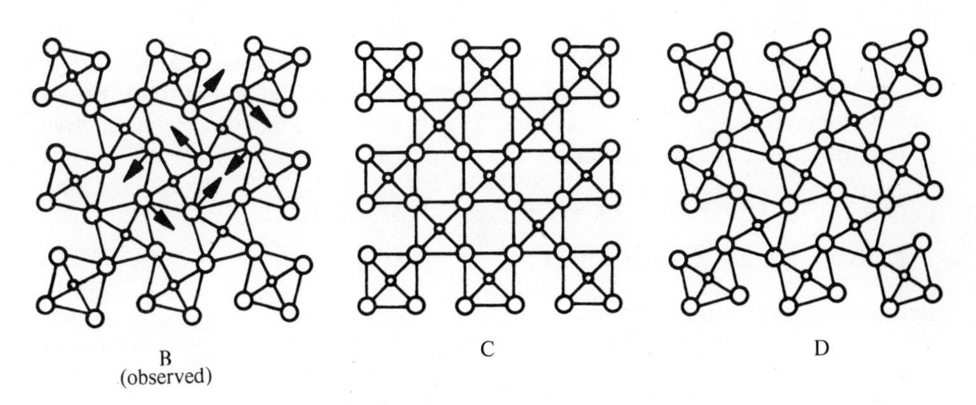

Figure 3-2 Transformation from the structure A to any of the other structures requires breaking of first-coordination bonds. Transformations among B, C, and D are only distortional. (*After Buerger.*[5,6])

of $BaTiO_3$ and $PbTiO_3$ are also often considered to be displacive, they can be described in terms of an order–disorder transition as well.

Buerger discusses disorder transformations of two types: rotational and substitutional. Disorder transformations are thermodynamically of second or higher order, and many of them also display first-order characteristics. Rotational transformations have some characteristics of displacive transformations. Substitutional transformations are commonly found in metals and alloys. Buerger also points out how many transformations are really "mixed" and how difficult it is to place them under any single category.

Buerger has defined transformations of the bond type where two polymorphs differ greatly in the nature of bonding. Examples of this kind are polymorphs of tin (grey and white), carbon (diamond and graphite), and phosphorus (yellow and black). One could probably classify these bond-type transformations under first-order discontinuous transformations as well.

Structural Changes Accompanying Phase Transitions in Simple Systems

From our knowledge of crystal chemistry, we can predict the nature of phase transitions in relatively simple ionic crystals. In making such predictions, we take into account that thermal phase transitions generally occur from a structure of low symmetry (and high order) to one of higher symmetry (and lower order). A positive volume change also accompanies transitions of the first order. This is related to the fact that the high-temperature phase tends to have greater openness of structure and lower coordination. Application of pressure will facilitate a transition involving an increase in coordination (negative volume change).

Let us first consider cubic AB-type compounds. These compounds can have CsCl, NaCl, or ZnS structure with 8:8, 6:6, or 4:4 coordination respectively, depending on the radius ratio. We can predict the following types of transitions in AB compounds.

	Examples
NaCl structure $\xrightarrow{\text{pressure}}$ CsCl structure	NaCl, KCl, RbCl, NaBr, KBr; monoxides and monosulfides of some metals
CsCl structure $\xrightarrow{\text{heat}}$ NaCl structure	CsCl, NH_4Cl, NH_4Br
ZnS structure $\xrightarrow{\text{pressure}}$ NaCl structure	AgI, NH_4F
NaCl structure $\xrightarrow{\text{heat}}$ wurtzite structure	MnS
ZnS structure $\xrightarrow{\text{heat}}$ B23 structure	AgI
NaCl structure $\xrightarrow{\text{pressure}}$ B9 structure	AgCl
CsCl $\rightarrow$ (distorted NaCl) $\rightarrow$ NaCl	$RbNO_3$

AB_2-type compounds generally possess the fluorite, tetragonal (e.g. rutile), distorted rutile, or some other low-symmetry structure. One possible mode of transformation can be

$$\text{Low-symmetry or distorted rutile structure} \xrightarrow{\text{heat}} \text{tetragonal (e.g. rutile)} \xrightarrow{\text{heat}} \text{fluorite structure}$$

Typical examples of such transformations are:

VO_2 (monoclinic) $\rightarrow$ VO_2 (rutile)
NbO_2 (distorted rutile) $\rightarrow$ NbO_2 (rutile)
TiO_2 (anatase, tetragonal) $\rightarrow$ TiO_2 (rutile)
TiO_2 (brookite, orthorhombic) $\rightarrow$ TiO_2 (rutile)
ZrO_2 (monoclinic) $\rightarrow$ ZrO_2 (tetragonal) $\rightarrow$ ZrO_2 (fluorite)

Many of the A_2B_3 compounds have the rare-earth oxide (C-type) structure or the corundum structure. Typical transformations of such compounds would be the following:

C-type oxide → hexagonal or monoclinic; e.g. rare-earth sesquioxides (defect structure)
Distorted corundum → corundum; e.g. V_2O_3, Ti_2O_3
or corundum

Turning to slightly more complex ionic solids, the aragonite–calcite transformation (e.g. $CaCO_3$) is an example of a thermal transformation from high to low coordination number; the reverse transformation is favored by the application of pressure. Perovskites of the general formula ABX_3 possess the ideal cubic structure if the tolerance factor $t = (r_A + r_X)/\sqrt{2}(r_B + r_X)$, is unity. Depending on the relative ionic sizes, perovskites show tetragonal, rhombohedral, orthorhombic, and other types of distortions. Both the A and the B ions play a role in determining the nature of distortion. Generally, the smaller the A cation, the greater is the tendency for distortion to orthorhombic symmetry. The high-temperature structure of many of these perovskites is cubic. Thus, $BaTiO_3$ and other titanates as well as many other ABX_3 compounds which have rhombohedral, orthorhombic, or some other low-symmetry structure at low temperatures, transform to the cubic phase at high temperatures. Similarly, spinels which have tetragonal distortion ($c/a \neq 1$) become cubic at high temperatures. Such predictions can be made, although grossly, in the case of simple solids which are fairly ionic. In the simplest of ionic crystals, it is possible to employ Born theory to predict the nature of phase transitions.

3-2 BORN TREATMENT AND PHASE TRANSITIONS IN IONIC SOLIDS

Cohesive energies of ionic solids can be satisfactorily calculated on the basis of the simple model originally proposed by Born.[9] We would therefore expect such a model to be able to predict the relative stabilities of two structures of an ionic solid connected through a transition. The Born model is briefly as follows.[10,11] The total energy of an ionic solid is made up of two parts: (i) the attractive part arising principally from Coulombic interaction, written as $\sum'_{i,j} Z_i Z_j e_i e_j / r_{ij}$, and (ii) the repulsive energy, which is taken as proportional to the inverse nth power of distance, $(r_{ij})^{-n}$. Since, in a periodic lattice, the distances r_{ij} can all be expressed in terms of basic vectors $\mathbf{a}_1$, $\mathbf{a}_2$, and $\mathbf{a}_3$ as

$$\mathbf{r}_{ij} = r_{ij}(1_1\mathbf{a}_1 + 1_2\mathbf{a}_2 + 1_3\mathbf{a}_3)$$

where 1_1, 1_2, and 1_3 are integers, we can write,

$$|\mathbf{r}_{ij}| = r_0(1_1^2 a_1^2 + 1_2^2 a_2^2 + 1_3^2 a_3^2)^{1/2}.$$

The energy U of the lattice is given by

$$U = -\frac{\alpha Z_1 Z_2 e^2}{r_0} + \frac{B}{r_0^n} \tag{3-1}$$

In Eq. (3-1), α is the Madelung constant which depends only on the structure, Z_1 and Z_2 are the charges on the ions, B is the repulsive constant, and n is the repulsive exponent. Equation (3-1) has undergone many changes since it was proposed originally. In its improved form, it includes attractive terms arising from van der Waals attraction and exponential repulsive terms. This model[12] gives U as

$$U = -\frac{\alpha Z_1 Z_2 e^2}{r_0} - \frac{C}{r_0^6} - \frac{D}{r_0^8} + B(r_0) - \phi_0 \tag{3-2}$$

and

$$B(r_0) = M_1 b_{+-} p_{+-} \exp(-r_0/\rho) + M_2\left(\frac{b_{++}p_{++} + b_{--}p_{--}}{2}\right)\exp(-ar_0/\rho) \tag{3-3}$$

C and D are, respectively,

$$\begin{aligned} C &= S_1^6 C_{+-} + S_2^6\left(\frac{C_{++} + C_{--}}{2}\right) \\ D &= S_1^8 d_{+-} + S_2^8\left(\frac{d_{++} + d_{--}}{2}\right) \end{aligned} \tag{3-4}$$

In the above expressions, M_1 and M_2 are the number of nearest and next-nearest neighbors respectively, b_{+-} etc. are the strength parameters characterizing repulsions between cations (+) and anions (−) and so on, p_{+-} etc. are Pauling overlap correction[12] constants given by, $p_{ij} = 1 + Z_i/n_i + Z_j/n_j$. Here, Z_i and Z_j are charges and n_i, n_j the number of valence shell electrons. The repulsive exponent, ρ, in Eq. (3-3) is referred to as the hardness parameter. The van der Waals constants C and D arise from dipole–dipole and dipole–quadrupole interactions respectively; ϕ_0 is the zero point vibrational energy. In the expressions for C and D, S_1^6, S_1^8, etc., are the lattice sums,[13] c_{+-}, etc., are the constants for dipole–dipole interactions, and d_{+-}, etc., are similar constants for dipole–quadrupole interactions. The constant a in the second exponent term in Eq. (3-3) is the ratio

$$a = \frac{r(\text{next-nearest neighbor})}{r(\text{nearest neighbor})}$$

The repulsive energy term in Eq. (3-3) accounts for the interactions only up to the second shell of ions. This is justified since the interactions fall off rapidly with distance.[10] Usually, the Madelung energy of an ionic compound like NaCl forms most part of the lattice energy and the repulsive energy is considerably small. Since at equilibrium the attractive and repulsive forces balance, the repulsive interactions should rise steeply below the equilibrium distance. Therefore, compressibilities are influenced more by the repulsive terms than by coulombic interactions.

Born and coworkers applied this ionic model to account for the relative stabilities of simple structures and to predict transition pressures. For a simple ionic salt like $A^{Z+}B^{Z-}$, Eq. (3-1) may be rewritten as

$$U = -\frac{\alpha(Ze)^2}{r} + \frac{M\lambda_{+-}}{r^n} \tag{3-5}$$

where Ze is the charge on either ion, M the first coordination number, λ_{+-} the repulsion constant, and n the repulsive exponent. By the condition that the lattice is in stable equilibrium, we have

$$\left(\frac{\partial U}{\partial r}\right)_{r=r_0} = 0 = \frac{\alpha(Ze)^2}{r^2} - \frac{nM\lambda_{+-}}{r^{n+1}}$$

or

$$\frac{\alpha(Ze)^2}{r} = \frac{nM\lambda_{+-}}{r^n}$$

Therefore

$$r^{n-1} = \frac{nM\lambda_{+-}}{\alpha(Ze)^2} \tag{3-6}$$

or

$$r = \left[\frac{nM\lambda_{+-}}{\alpha(Ze)^2}\right]^{1/(n-1)} \tag{3-7}$$

The equilibrium energy may now be written in a form which does not contain r explicitly:

$$\begin{aligned} U(r) &= -\frac{nM\lambda_{+-}}{r^n} + \frac{M\lambda_{+-}}{r^n} \\ &= -\frac{M\lambda_{+-}}{r^n}[n-1] \\ &= -\left[\frac{M\lambda_{+-}}{(nM\lambda_{+-})^{n/(n-1)}}\right][\alpha(Ze)^2]^{n/(n-1)}(n-1) \\ &= \left(\frac{\alpha^n}{M}\right)^{1/(n-1)}\left\{\left[\frac{(Ze)^{2n}}{n\lambda_{+-}}\right]^{1/(n-1)}\left(\frac{n-1}{n}\right)\right\} \end{aligned} \tag{3-8}$$

Equation (3-8) is so written that the terms in the curly brackets are independent of structure. The stability of a given structure is dependent only on the term α^n/M. The structure having the highest value of α^n/M will be the stablest for a given material. With this criterion, Born and coworkers showed that, for low values of n, the order of stability of structures is ZnS, NaCl, CsCl. Supposing for some value of $n = n_0$, two structures are equally stable; then

$$\frac{\alpha_1^{n_0}}{M_1} = \frac{\alpha_2^{n_0}}{M_2} \tag{3-9}$$

or

$$n_0 = \frac{\ln (M_1/M_2)}{\ln (\alpha_1/\alpha_2)} \tag{3-10}$$

For ZnS, NaCl, and CsCl structures, the values of n_0 are: ZnS–NaCl, 6.3; ZnS–CsCl, 9.5; NaCl–CsCl, 3.3. For low values of n_0, the ZnS structure is preferred, while for very high values of n_0, the CsCl structure is preferred. The following order of stability of structures which depend on the value of n_0 may thus be written:

$n_0 < 6.3$	ZnS, NaCl, CsCl
$6.3 < n_0 < 9.5$	NaCl, ZnS, CsCl
$9.5 < n_0 < 33$	NaCl, CsCl, ZnS
$33 < n_0$	CsCl, NaCl, ZnS

The preponderance of the NaCl structure is associated with the fact that n_0 generally lies in the neighborhood of 10. Although this approach is rather naive, it gives us a notion of the importance of the repulsive constant, n, which measures the steepness with which the repulsive energy rises with decrease in distance, because n is the slope of the curve of $\ln B(r)$ vs $\ln r$. It is the equivalent of $1/\rho$ in the more accurate description of repulsive energy.[14] The higher the n, the lower is the compressibility of an ionic solid.

We can now consider the conditions for pressure transformation in this model. This is achieved at absolute zero of temperature because the energy description is not sufficiently sophisticated to take care of the vibrational contribution to entropy at other temperatures. At absolute zero, the Gibbs free energy is the enthalpy itself. For any two structures 1 and 2 to be in equilibrium at a pressure P, we have

$$G_1 = G_2$$

Therefore at $T = 0$ K,

$$U_1 + PV_1 = U_2 + PV_2$$

$$P = \frac{U_2 - U_1}{V_1 - V_2} \tag{3-11}$$

The right-hand side of Eq. (3-11) contains terms which are pressure-dependent, but if we ignore the small pressure-dependence, the transition pressure may be calculated as

$$P \approx \frac{U_1^0 - U_2^0}{V_2^0 - V_1^0} \tag{3-12}$$

Using relation (3-5), $U^0(r)$ becomes equal to

$$U^0(r) = -[\alpha(Ze)^2/r][(n-1)/n] \tag{3-13}$$

Since $V_1 = s_1 r_1^3$ and $V_2 = s_2 r_2^3$, using the expression for r in Eq. (3-7) we can make a rough estimate of P.

$$P \approx \frac{\alpha(Ze)^2}{s_1 r_1^4} F_n \tag{3-14}$$

$$F_n = \left(\frac{n-1}{n}\right) \frac{1 - \left(\dfrac{\alpha_2}{\alpha_1}\right)^{n/(n-1)} \left(\dfrac{M_1}{M_2}\right)^{1/(n-1)}}{1 - \dfrac{s_2}{s_1} \left(\dfrac{M_2 \alpha_1}{M_1 \alpha_2}\right)^{3/(n-1)}} \tag{3-15}$$

The values so evaluated for transitions are only qualitatively correct. This is not surprising in view of the limitations of the model employed. What should be considered as a fascinating result of this approach is that F_n is negative for a transition from the NaCl to the ZnS structure (decrease in coordination). That is, such a transition can occur only under tension, while for a NaCl → CsCl transition involving increase in coordination, F_n is positive, indicating that the transition should occur under pressure. Thus we see that the Born model for ionic solids, though empirical, leads to a qualitative understanding of phase transitions under pressure.

For lack of accurate knowledge of entropies, as mentioned earlier, it is not profitable to apply the Born model to predict transition temperatures. However, the Born model has been used to find out whether energies predicted by this simple model for the two structures are consistent with experimental observations on the phase transition concerned. Let us consider the transition of cesium chloride.[7,10,15] At room temperature, cesium chloride has the cubic *Pm*3*m* structure with Cl at the center of the unit cell and Cs at the corners. This structure transforms to the NaCl structure (*Fm*3*m*) around 750 K at normal pressure. The transition is reversible and endothermic ($\Delta H \approx 600$ cal mol^{-1}). If the Born model is applied to calculate the lattice energies of the two structures of CsCl employing experimentally determined lattice parameters we should find that the lattice energy difference between the two structures is 600 cal mol^{-1}. If the values of various constants involved in the evaluation of lattice energy are taken from the early literature,[12] one finds that the *Fm*3*m* structure is more stable for cesium chloride at all temperatures. Attempts have been made to modify the Born model in order to obtain agreement with experiment on this transition. One such attempt is due to May,[16] who used the expression

$$-U = \frac{\alpha e^2}{r} + K\left(\frac{C}{r^6} + \frac{D}{r^8}\right) - B(r) + \phi_0 \tag{3-16}$$

where
$$B(r) = M_1 b_1 \exp(-r/\rho) + M_2 b_2 \exp(-ar/\rho) \tag{3-17}$$

Here, K is an arbitrary multiplicant of the van der Waals energy. It was necessary to use $K = 3.6$ in Eq. (3-16) in order to render the *Pm*3*m* structure of CsCl more stable than the *Fm*3*m* structure. However, the absolute value of the lattice energy also became too high compared to the experimental value.

It is possible to eliminate the enhancement of lattice energy and still use the van der Waals multiplicant K as in May's expression if the repulsive term is modified. Rao and coworkers[15,17] have calculated the lattice energies of the two phases of CsCl at the transition temperature making use of the available thermochemical data and heat of the transition along with a four-parameter repulsive energy term. The four relations used in order to solve for b_1, b_2, ρ_1, and ρ_2 were as follows:

$$-U_P = \frac{\alpha_P e^2}{r_P} + K\left(\frac{C_P}{r_P^6} + \frac{D_P}{r_P^8}\right) - B_P(r_P) + \phi_P \tag{3-18a}$$

$$-U_F = \frac{\alpha_F e^2}{r_F} + K\left(\frac{C_F}{r_F^6} + \frac{D_F}{r_F^8}\right) - B_F(r_F) + \phi_F \tag{3-18b}$$

$$r\left(\frac{\partial U_P}{\partial r_P}\right) = \frac{3TV_P\eta_P}{Nk_P} \tag{3-18c}$$

$$r^2\left(\frac{\partial^2 U_P}{\partial r_P^2}\right) = \frac{9V_P}{Nk_P}(1 + \psi) \tag{3-18d}$$

where ψ is a function involving η_P, pressure, and temperature derivatives of k_P; η_P and k_P are the volume thermal expansivity and compressibility respectively. It is usually a very small quantity ($\ll 1$). The subscripts P and F in Eqs. (3-18) refer to the *Pm3m* and *Fm3m* phases. By using additional experimental information on the transformation behavior of solid solutions[15,18] of CsCl with RbCl and KCl, the repulsive parameters and the appropriate K values (substantially greater than unity) have been calculated.*

Pressure transitions in potassium and rubidium halides have also been examined by Rao and Rao,[17] by employing increased van der Wals terms and a four-parameter repulsive term. Indeed, the recently evaluated van der Waals constants[20,21] support the use of such high van der Waals terms in transition calculations. If the recent values are employed in the expression for lattice energy, one can eliminate the use of the multiplicant K as a parameter[18,22] (i.e., $K = 1$ would suffice). The Born model has also been employed for studying the relative stabilities of various structures of silver halides which exhibit both pressure and thermal transitions.[23,24]

The Born treatment outlined above has assumed that the repulsive parameters are structure-independent. That is, b and ρ have the same value in both the *Pm3m* and *Fm3m* structures. Tosi and Fumi[25] have accounted for the phase transitions in alkali halides on the basis of structure-dependent two-parameter repulsive potentials. The Born–Mayer repulsive term, in the form of an exponential function, represents all the contributions, including many-body interactions.[10,25] Such contributions are in general structure-dependent. Tosi and Fumi argue that the repulsive parameters should be independently determined for the two structures. Direct evidence for the existence of many-body interactions which depend on the structure comes from quantum mechanical calculations.[26–28] Unfortunately, lattice energies in quantum mechanical calculations are themselves obtained as differences between two large terms (energies of ions in the free state and in the lattice positions), and uncertainties in such values are large. Such calculations cannot therefore be expected to accurately give small differences in energies

* It is found that the *Fm3m* structure gets stabilized at a specific composition in $Cs_{1-x}K_xCl$ ($x \approx 0.25$) and $Cs_{1-x}Rb_xCl$ ($x \approx 0.5$); $CsCl_{1-x}Br_x$, on the other hand, always has the *Pm3m* structure.[19]

between two structures. However, Colwell[27] has successfully examined the problem of relative stabilities of the two structures of CsCl quantum mechanically. Transition pressures in NaF and NaCl have been calculated quantum mechanically by Mansikka.[29] A somewhat semiempirical approach to estimate three-body contributions to lattice energies, and hence the stabilities of alkali halide structures, has been attempted by Jansen and Lombardi.[28,30]

The simplicity of the Born model has tempted workers to modify it marginally and account for phase stabilities. Unfortunately, there is at present no procedure to modify it such that many-body interactions are accounted for. Furthermore, it is important to remember that there are two important assumptions built into the Born model: (i) ions are point charges, and (ii) the interionic forces are central in character. Both these assumptions cause serious difficulties when small energy differences between structures are to be evaluated. Also, in many of the ionic solids including alkali halides, covalent contributions are not negligible and their presence seriously limits the validity of the Born model.

3-3 IONICITY AND COVALENCE IN CRYSTALS

The ionicity of bonds is generally defined in terms of the electronegativities of atoms. The most popular scale of electronegativities is due to Pauling,[31] who defined electronegativities X_A and X_B of atoms A and B, forming the molecule AB, as $\Delta_{AB} = 23M(X_A - X_B)^2$, where Δ_{AB} is the ionic contribution to the heat of formation in kcal/mole, and M the number of resonating bonds per molecule. If $(X_A - X_B)$ is large, the bond AB will tend to be ionic. The ionicity of bonds is given by $f_i = 1 - \exp[-(X_A - X_B)^2/4]$. We see that f_i can vary smoothly from zero $(X_A = X_B)$ to unity $((X_A - X_B) \gg 1)$. This is one of the definitions of ionicity employed to describe polar properties of chemical bonds. While this approach is very successful for discussing properties of bonds in molecules, the situation becomes different in crystals. Properties of many of the partially ionic crystals cannot be interpreted in terms of X_A, X_B, and f_i determined from molecular properties. In the last few years, Phillips[32,33] has developed a theory of covalence and ionicity in crystals which is found to be satisfactory in explaining a number of properties of $A^N B^{8-N}$ crystals (where neither A nor B is a transition-group element) with quantitative accuracy. We shall briefly describe Phillips's method and show how it explains relative stabilities of structures of I–VII, II–VI, and III–V compounds.

Phillips's Approach

The binary compounds $A^N B^{8-N}$ (N is the group in the periodic table) generally crystallize in interpenetrating cubic lattices with atoms A on one cubic lattice and atoms B on the other. The periodic potential on a valence electron can be broken up into symmetric (average potential) and antisymmetric (arising from difference $V_A - V_B$) parts with respect to A and B. The symmetric part is related to homopolar bonding and the antisymmetric part to the heteropolar bonding. In calculating band structures and physical properties of such solids, one normally employs ionic pseudopotentials or expresses the band structure in terms of empirical parameters. These are fixed by fitting them to experimental data like singularities in the optical absorption coefficient, $\varepsilon_2(\omega)$. A reliability of 0.1 eV is found for calculations of the band structure in a 10-eV range of energies. Only a few parameters (like the screened pseudopotential matrix elements $V(\mathbf{G})$ for wave vector $\mathbf{G}$) are sufficient to describe the band structure in this energy region. Information on ionicity is contained in six parameters, three for A and three for B, and in their relation to observed properties of the solids.

Phillips assumes that the gap between conduction and valence band states can be replaced by an average energy gap, E_g, between them. The average energy gap can be written as

$$E_g^2 = E_h^2 + E_i^2 \tag{3-19}$$

where h and i stand for homopolar and ionic parts. Such a relation between homopolar and ionic energies appears to be appropriate for this class of compounds. The assumption of a single energy gap E_g can be justified as follows. The occupied electronic states in $A^N B^{8-N}$ crystals occupy a certain region in **k**-space (the first four Brillouin zones) called the Jones zone, which is a dodecahedron. An energy gap separates this zone from the conduction band. Detailed calculations[34] on Group IV semiconductors have shown that the energy gap across the Jones zone face is indeed nearly equal to the average energy gap E_g defined by Phillips. The calculation can be extended to isomorphous $A^N B^{8-N}$ compounds.

In order to relate the observed properties of $A^N B^{8-N}$ compounds to the average gap E_g, Phillips uses Penn's one-gap model.[35] Penn calculated dielectric properties of a model isotropic semiconductor with a single band gap ($V_G = E_g/2$) to be the same for all directions of **G**, and to be nonzero only for a particular length **G**. The static dielectric constant is given by

$$\varepsilon(0) = 1 + \left(\frac{\hbar\omega_p}{E_g}\right)^2 \left(1 - \frac{E_g}{4E_f}\right) \tag{3-20}$$

In Eq. (3-20), E_f is the Fermi energy, ω_p is the plasma frequency and $\omega_p^2 = 4\pi n e^2/m$, where n is the electron density. For the solids being discussed here, $(E_g/4E_f) \approx 0.1$, and Eq. (3-20) can be used to find the gap E_g in terms of $\varepsilon(0)$.

Phillips[32] and Van Vechten[36] have assumed that the homopolar gap E_h depends only on density or, more specifically, on the cubic lattice constant. On the basis of comparison of E_g obtained from Eq. (3-20) for diamond and Si, they find (since $E_g = E_h$ for such monatomic crystals) that

$$E_h \propto a^{-2.5} \tag{3-21}$$

In Eq. (3-21), a is the lattice constant and the exponent was determined by fitting to C and Si. This relation is assumed to be universally applicable for this class of compounds. Having known E_h and E_g (from Eq. (3-20)), the ionic contribution E_i is calculated from the relation $E_g^2 = E_h^2 + E_i^2$.

For crystals containing atoms of groups III and IV, the observed dielectric constant has to be corrected for *sp–d* mixing. For Ge and α-Sn, this is done by using E_h from Eq. (3-21) and the observed $\varepsilon(0)$, and by assuming that the correction enters as $u_{eff} = D^{1/2}n$:

$$\varepsilon(0) = 1 + \frac{D(h\omega_p)^2}{E_g^2} \tag{3-22}$$

Van Vechten[36] has discussed the determination of D in other heteropolar crystals containing filled *d*-shell atoms, and has devised a meaningful semiempirical formula. With the knowledge of D (1.25 for Ge), Eq. (3-22) can be used to calculate E_g and Eq. (3-21) to find E_i. Typical values of E_h and E_i for a few compounds are given in Table 3-1. The values of the ionicity parameter of Phillips, defined as

$$f_i = \frac{E_i^2}{E_g^2} \tag{3-23}$$

are also given in Table 3-1. Phillips[32,33] has tabulated f_i for a large number of compounds.

We note here that Phillips's ionicity parameter has been obtained by relating an observed solid-state property, $\varepsilon(0)$, to the average energy gap. The relation is corrected for *d*-electron admixture effects and so on, but is assumed to be independent of structure. Ionicity thus derived is associated with each $A^N B^{8-N}$ crystal and does not make use of atomic or thermochemical data.

In covalently bonded compounds like diamond, Si, and Ge, the atoms are tetrahedrally coordinated through sp^3 hybridized orbitals. In ionic crystals like

Table 3-1 Parameters for some $A^N B^{8-N}$ crystals

Crystal	Structure*	Static dielectric constant $\varepsilon(0)$	E_h (eV)	E_i (eV)	f_i (Pauling)	f_i (Phillips)
C	D	5.7	13.6	0	0	0
BN	Z	4.5	13.1	7.8	0.42	0.22
GaAs	Z	10.9	4.3	2.9	0.26	0.31
AlN	W	4.8	8.2	7.3	0.56	0.45
ZnO	W	4.0	7.3	9.3	0.80	0.616
ZnSe	Z, W	5.9	4.3	5.6	0.57	0.676
CuBr	Z, W	4.4	4.1	6.9	0.80	0.735
MgS	W, R	5.1	3.7	7.1	0.67, 0.78	0.786
NaCl	R	2.3	3.1	11.8	0.94	0.935
RbI	R	2.7	1.6	7.1	0.92	0.951

* D—diamond; Z—zinc blende; W—wurtzite; R—rock salt.

NaCl, the ions have closed-shell configurations and the s–p energy difference is large compared with the width of the sp bands; the forces are mainly coulombic and nondirectional, and there is sixfold coordination. The $A^{III}B^{V}$ and $A^{II}B^{VI}$ compounds represent intermediate cases. An inspection of the periodic table shows that IV and III–V compounds have tetrahedral coordination; the same is true when A is IB or IIB. Sixfold coordination occurs if A is IA or IIA. Only nine compounds do not obey this generalization out of eighty such compounds examined. Phillips has shown that all crystals with $f_i \leq 0.785 \pm 0.01$ are tetrahedrally coordinated (diamond, ZnS, or wurtzite structure) and all crystals with $f_i \geq 0.785 \pm 0.01$ have sixfold coordination (rock salt structure). MgS ($f_i = 0.786$) and MgSe ($f_i = 0.790$) are two crystals which are on the borderline, and both the ZnS and rock salt structures are about equally stable in these compounds. Since tetrahedrally coordinated covalent structures of $A^{N}B^{8-N}$ compounds are of low density, they transform under pressure to octahedrally coordinated metallic or ionic structures of higher density. An interesting phase diagram of pressure versus f_i involving the metallic and ionic structures along with the covalent structure has been suggested by Phillips.[33] According to this, if $f_i \lesssim 0.35$, semiconductors transform to metals, while for $0.35 \lesssim f_i \leq 0.785$, semiconductors transform to metals through the intermediate insulating NaCl phase (e.g., CdTe). We thus see that Phillips's ionicity scale provides a quantitative and rational approach to predict structure of such binary solids.

This is an impressive achievement. The only systematic method of calculating the cohesive energy of structures is the Born–Mayer model for ionic crystals discussed in the previous section (3-2). Cohesive-energy differences between two structures of a compound are often as little as 1 kcal/mol, and it would be difficult to make structural predictions on the basis of the Born–Mayer model; the problem becomes particularly severe when there is appreciable covalency. The pseudopotential method is also not particularly convenient for calculating such properties of semiconductors.

Bond-charge calculations based on pseudopotentials on Si and diamond give results which agree well with the results of Phillips's ionicity scale. It has been found that in a series of selenides, bond charge decreases as f_i increases,[37] bond charge becoming zero when $f_i \approx 0.8$. This value of f_i is close to the critical value separating fourfold and sixfold coordinated structures. Apparently, the transverse acoustic mode becomes less and less stable as the bond charge decreases, and hence, as the bond charge approaches zero ($f_i \to 0.8$), the diamond or ZnS structure becomes unstable relative to wurtzite structure and the wurtzite structure with respect to the NaCl structure.[38] It has been found[32] that the ratio of force constants in cubic crystals (obtained from elastic constants) also varies linearly with f_i. The ionicity scale of Phillips has been applied to understand a number of properties of semiconductors. Particular mention must be made of the success in calculating cohesive energies of tetrahedrally coordinated semiconductors,[39] where it is shown that $\Delta H \propto f_i$. Undoubtedly, Phillips's ionicity ideas are useful in a number of solid state problems including the description of diamond versus graphite structures, the effect of d electrons, and so on.[33,38]

3-4 STRUCTURAL RELATIONS BETWEEN PHASES AND TOPOTAXY IN PHASE TRANSITIONS

Structural and orientational relations between the parent and transformed phases in phase transitions provide an insight into the mechanism of transitions. The term topotaxy is often used to describe three-dimensional relations between the crystal structures of the product and initial phases, just as the term epitaxy is used to describe two-dimensional orientational relations when a new phase is formed on the surface of another.[40,41] A reaction is considered to be topotactic if the lattice of the product phase shows one or a number of crystallographically equivalent, definite orientations relative to the initial parent lattice and the reaction has proceeded throughout the bulk of the initial phase. *Topochemical* reactions, on the other hand, are those where the nature and properties of the products are determined by the chemical changes proceeding within the crystal.

Topotaxy in organic solids was recognized as early as 1938 by Robertson and Ubbelohde.[42] Kitaigorodsky and others[40,43] found no special orientational relations between parent and product phases in single crystal–single crystal transformations of organic solids, and suggested that laws governing such phase transitions may indeed be the same as those applicable for growth of crystals from melts. While this may be true of transformations of many of the organic solids, it is noteworthy that Thomas and coworkers[40] find orientational relations in the phase transition of 1,8-dichloro-10-methylanthracene similar to those in stress-induced martensitic transformations. In martensite transformations of metallic systems, the plane of the martensite plate has a definite orientation with respect to the parent phase, the plane in the latter, parallel to the martensite plate, being the habit plane. The parent phase undergoes shear displacement along the habit plane during a martensite transition. We shall be discussing martensite transformations of solids at some length in Chap. 4, and it will suffice at this stage to note that features of martensite transitions and consequent orientational relations are found in phase transitions of many inorganic solids. Several topotactic and topochemical reactions of inorganic systems have been discussed in the literature.[40,41,44] We shall examine orientational relations in phase transitions of a few simple inorganic solids in this section.

In Sec. 3-1, it was mentioned how Buerger[5,6] viewed the CsCl–NaCl structural transition as one involving a dilatation mechanism. According to this mechanism, there is a 40 percent contraction along the $\langle 111 \rangle$ direction of the fcc lattice. Chatterji et al.[47] found one of the orientation relations in the transition of CsCl from NaCl structure (I) to CsCl structure (II) to be $(001)_{\mathrm{I}} \parallel (001)_{\mathrm{II}}$, $[110]_{\mathrm{I}} \parallel [001]_{\mathrm{II}}$. Fraser and Kennedy[48] have studied the NaCl(I) → CsCl(II) transition in NH_4Br in some detail, and found the following additional relations (stated in the nearest rational indices) within a few degrees:

A $\quad (001)_{\mathrm{I}} \parallel (1\bar{1}\bar{1})_{\mathrm{II}}, [010]_{\mathrm{I}} \parallel [\bar{1}01]_{\mathrm{II}}$

B $\quad (100)_{\mathrm{I}} \parallel (23\bar{3})_{\mathrm{II}}, [010]_{\mathrm{I}} \parallel [\bar{6}51]_{\mathrm{II}}$

C $\quad (001)_{\mathrm{I}} \parallel (023)_{\mathrm{II}}, [010]_{\mathrm{I}} \parallel [100]_{\mathrm{II}}$

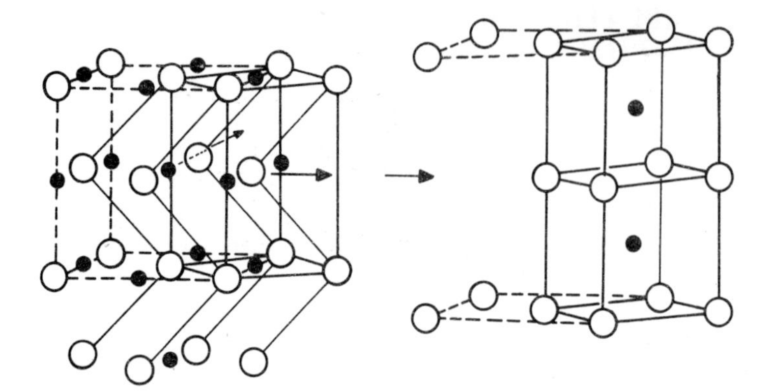

Figure 3-3 Transformation of NaCl structure to CsCl structure by unfolding of the packing and separation of cation and anion layers parallel to (001). Alternate (001) layers translate as shown and the interlayer spacing of like ions increases. The tetragonal cell (outlined) becomes two CsCl cells. (*After Kennedy.*[49])

In all these, a ⟨111⟩ direction had rotated by 14–25°. A similar mechanism seems to hold for the reverse II → I transition, and the product I was oriented with $[110]_{\mathrm{I}} \parallel [100]_{\mathrm{II}}$. In addition to contraction along ⟨111⟩, a 19 percent uniform expansion of I normal to ⟨111⟩ was also found necessary. Fraser and Kennedy[48] have carried out a martensite analysis (see Chap. 4) of the I → II transition, based on the ⟨111⟩ strain, which shows the habit planes to be close to $\{\bar{1}11\}_{\mathrm{I}}$, $\{210\}_{\mathrm{I}}$, and $\{310\}_{\mathrm{I}}$. The analysis agrees reasonably with the orientations mentioned above. Such transitions are also accompanied by large changes in shape (morphology) which can be accounted for by the martensite analysis. The effect of shape change on orientation relation has been discussed by Kennedy.[49]

The orientation relation $[110]_{\mathrm{I}} \parallel [110]_{\mathrm{II}}$ in NaCl–CsCl-type transitions in alkali and ammonium halides as well as in $RbNO_3$ is not readily accounted for by the ⟨111⟩ strain; even successive twinning involving several different ⟨111⟩ options yields this orientation as a secondary effect. Kennedy[49] has suggested a structural correspondence (Fig. 3-3) which leads directly to this orientation relation. Just as in the ⟨111⟩ strain, the deformation shown in Fig. 3-3 also requires no activated movement of ions. The principal distortions (length in product/length in parent) for I → II transitions are: [001] strain, $\eta_3 = 1.19$, $\eta_1 = \eta_2 = 0.84$; [111] strain, $\eta_3 = 0.59$, $\eta_1 = \eta_2 = 1.19$. The [001] strain requires smaller deformations. Pairs of options for the unique strain axis parallel to the cube axis can produce transformation twinning on $\{111\}_{\mathrm{II}}$ derived from $\{110\}_{\mathrm{I}}$.

The polymorphic transformation of PbO provides an interesting example of topotaxy.[50] The red tetragonal form of PbO transforms to the yellow orthorhombic form around 764 K. Both these forms have layer structures parallel to (001) with the oxygens sandwiched between the lead atoms. Projections along [001] of the two structures are shown in Fig. 3-4. The high-temperature orthorhombic form can be prepared at room temperature as a metastable phase which slowly trans-

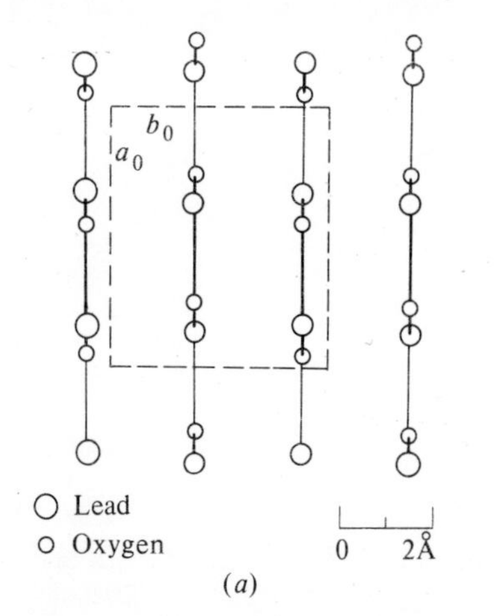

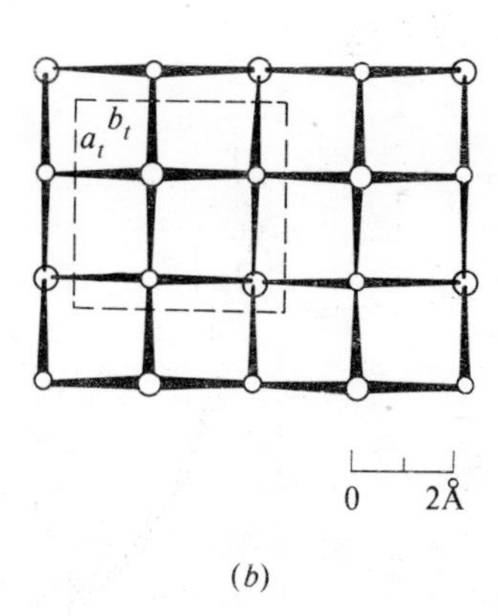

Figure 3-4 Projection along [001] of a layer of (*a*) orthorhombic and (*b*) tetragonal PbO. (*After Söderquist and Dickens.*[50])

forms back to the tetragonal form. It has been possible to carry out a single-crystal study of such a transformation. The main orientation relations are found to be $[001]_t \parallel [001]_0$ and $[110]_t \parallel [100]_0$. The mechanism of transformation becomes evident from the projection along the common axis [001] of the hybrid crystal (Fig. 3-5). Other examples of topotactic transitions[41] are the transformations of γ-AlOOH to α-Al_2O_3 (through γ, δ, and θ-phases) and γ-FeOOH to α-Fe_2O_3 (through the γ-phase). In these transformations, the anions are in cubic or hexagonal close packing, and the metastable intermediate phases occur in the process of cation migration.

KNO_3 transforms from an orthorhombic (aragonite-type) structure II to a rhombohedral (calcite-type) structure I around 403 K. In the structure II, there is approximately hexagonal close packing (as in NiAs), and in I, there is rhombohedral distortion of NaCl with cubic close packing (see Fig. 3-6). I transforms back to II through a rhombohedral ferroelectric intermediate phase III on cooling.[51,52] In both I and II, planes of NO_3^- are parallel to basal planes. The orthorhombic cell of II corresponds to the conventional orthorhombic cell of hexagonal lattices. The orthorhombic a-axis (a_{II}) coincides with the a-axis of the pseudohexagonal cell in which the angle is 61.14°. In $CaCO_3$, there is a greater decrease from hexagonal symmetry, the pseudohexagonal angle being 63° 48′. In both KNO_3 I and II, the c-axis is normal to the basal planes, and the a-axis is a close-packed direction in the plane. When hcp structures are converted to ccp structures by shift (shear) of basal layers into neighboring sites (as in ZnS), the orientation relation with respect to hexagonal cells is $c_I \parallel c_{II}$, $a_I \parallel a_{II}$. That is, the close-packed planes and directions are parallel respectively. In $CaCO_3$, the basal planes remain parallel through the aragonite–calcite transition, indicating change of stacking sequence by translation. Only the orientation relation having $c_I \parallel c_{II}$ might correspond to transformation by shear on basal planes. Even in this,

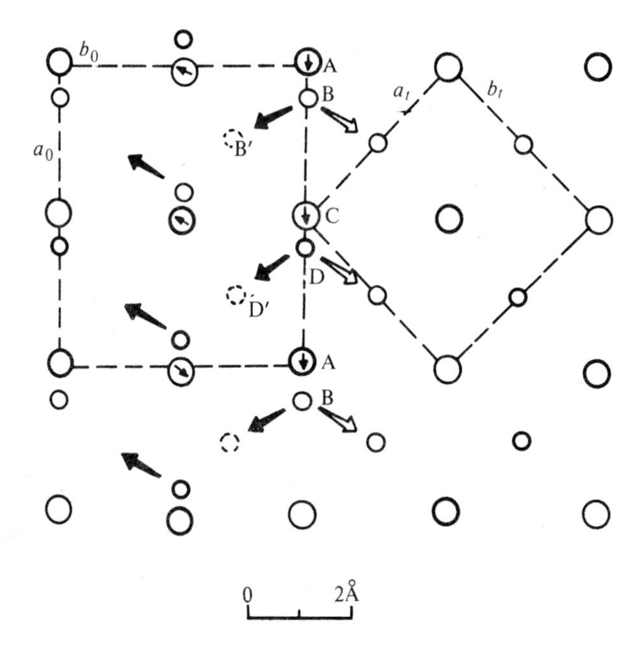

Figure 3-5 Projection along [001] of the structure of a hybrid crystal of PbO composed of orthorhombic (left) and tetragonal (right) forms. (*After Söderquist and Dickens.*[50])

however, appropriate close-packed directions within the plane are not parallel. In KNO_3, the (110) plane of I parallels the (010) plane of the parent II; the c-axes of the two structures are not parallel but differ by 26°, both lying in the plane common to the two structures. Kennedy and coworkers[52,53] find that the II–I transition of KNO_3 produces a variety of orientation relations. They find the relations $(0001)_I \parallel (001)_{II}$, $[a]_I \parallel [b]_{II}$ with the $(001)_{II}$ traces also present, indicating that the transformation does not proceed by shear on the basal planes. Interfaces are produced parallel to the pseudohexagonal basal plane of II, but the basal planes of the two phases do not necessarily form the interface. The II → I transition is also accompanied by kinking of the initially straight needles and by marked surface effects.[50,53]

$RbNO_3$ IV, which is trigonal ($P31m$) at ordinary temperatures, reversibly transforms to a CsCl-type structure III around 437 K, which then reversibly transforms to a rhombohedral NaCl type structure II around 492 K; II reversibly transforms to cubic NaCl structure I at 564 K, where there is incomplete randomization of the orientations of nitrate ions, just as in the melt.[51,54–57] Structures IV, III, and II are related to one another. Thus, in the III–IV transition, any one of the four equivalent cube diagonals can give rise to the trigonal axis. In the sequence I → II → III, the orientation relation is $[100]_I \parallel [100]_{III}$,

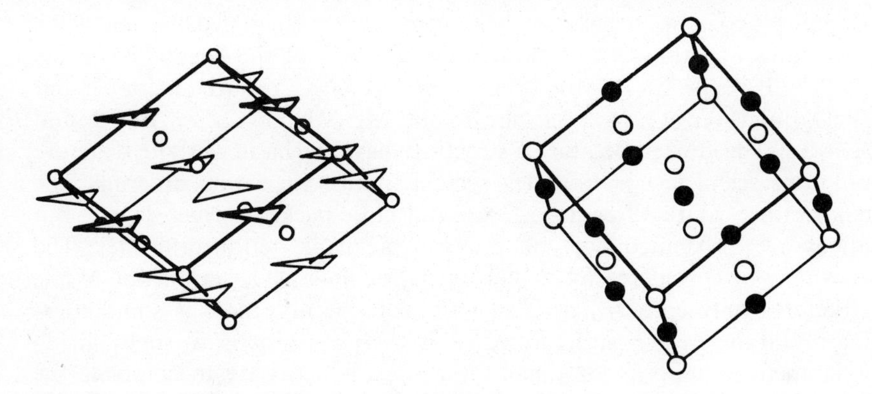

Figure 3-6 Calcite and rock salt structures similarly oriented. (*After Wells.*[1])

$(010)_I \parallel (110)_{III}$. The crystals undergo a regular shape change in II → I → II transformation, implying a coordinated structural rearrangement related by a lattice deformation.

$TlNO_3$ III, which is ordinarily orthorhombic (*Pnma*), has a CsCl-related arrangement of anions, reversibly transforms around 350 K to a rhombohedral structure II. There is no major reorientation of planes of anions in the III → II transformation, and a shear-type mechanism has been suggested. Around 416 K, II reversibly transforms to a cubic structure I; III can also transform directly to I in a continuous manner. It appears that structures of II and I are both based on the arrangement in III.[51,58,59]

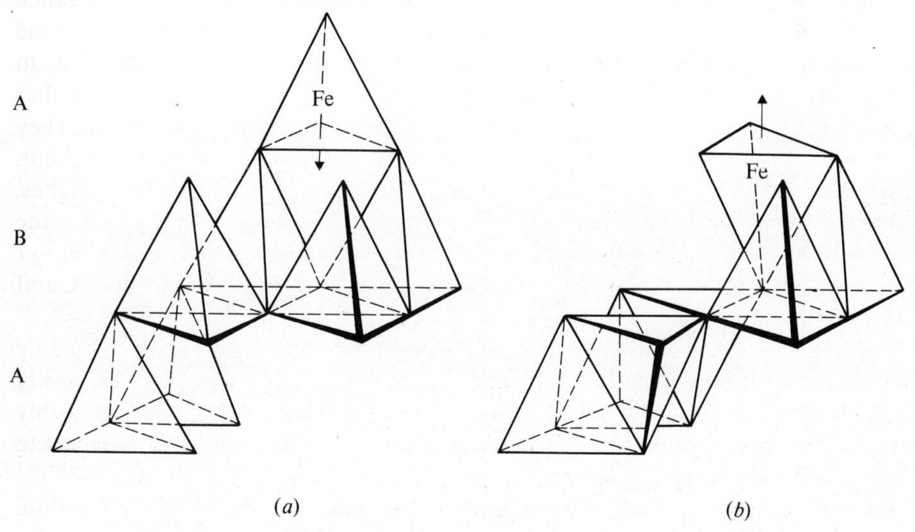

Figure 3-7 Schematic structural relationship between (*a*) β-$NaFeO_2$ and (*b*) γ-$NaFeO_2$. A, B refer to hexagonal close-packing sequence. (*After West.*[62])

A simple topotactic mechanism has been recently suggested for the $\beta \rightleftharpoons \gamma$ transformations of tetrahedrally coordinated oxides[60] of the general formulae Li_3XO_4 (X = P, As, V, Cr, or Mn), AYO_2 (A = Li or Na; Y = Al, Ga, or Fe, but not $LiFeO_2$), and A_2BCO_4 (A = Li, Na; B = Be, Mg, Mn, Fe, Co, Zn, or Cd; and C = Si or Ge). The low-temperature β structures have the basic wurtzite structure with only one set of tetrahedral sites occupied, but with cation ordering. The high-temperature γ structures have hexagonal close-packed oxygen layers, but the cations are distributed over both sets of available tetrahedral sites. The structures may be considered to be built of space-filling MO_4 tetrahedra. While in β structures only corner-sharing of tetrahedra occurs, there is some edge-shearing of tetrahedra in γ structures. In the $\beta \rightleftharpoons \gamma$ transitions, a single, filled–empty tetrahedron jump for only half the cations is necessary to complete the transformation in either direction[60] (see Fig. 3-7).

Structural relations in ferroelectric phase transitions have been reported in several materials.[61] For example, $BaTiO_3$, which has the ideal perovskite (cubic) structure above the Curie point (493 K), transforms to a tetragonal structure (ferroelectric) below the Curie point. In the tetragonal phase, the atoms are displaced from their original symmetric positions along one of the $\langle 001 \rangle$ axes, giving rise to a distortion of the TiO_6 octahedra. The tetragonal phase transforms around 270 K to an orthorhombic ferroelectric phase in which the *a* and *b*-axes are parallel to the pseudocubic face diagonal and the *c*-axis is parallel to the pseudocubic edge; the unit cell thus becomes nearly twice as large as the simple cubic cell. In both the tetragonal and the orthorhombic phases, the distortion of the TiO_6 octahedra is only slight, the distortion resulting from the displacements of Ti and Ba along the polar axis. The antiferroelectric phase of $PbZrO_3$ which has the orthorhombic structure, transforms to the cubic perovskite structure around 500 K. A rather simplified picture of the transformation may be given as follows. In the orthorhombic phase, the *a* and *b* axes are oriented along the pseudocubic $\langle 110 \rangle$ directions. The orthorhombic structure is derived from the

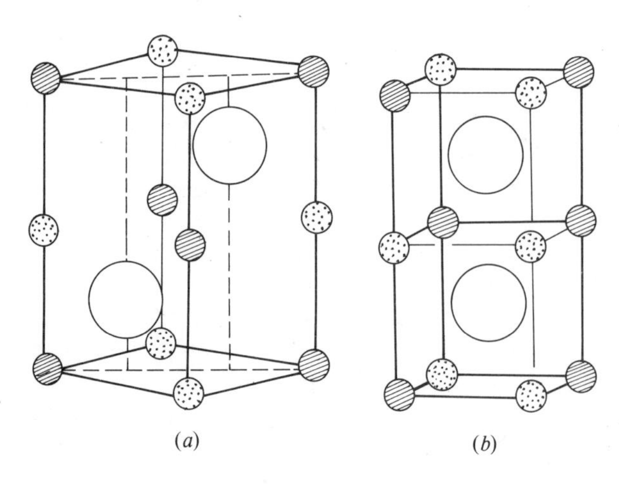

Figure 3-8 When prism (*a*) is converted by strain to the two-cube (*b*), the unit denoted by the open circles is displaced to the centre of the cube. In (*a*) atoms shown by the large open circles are arranged as in hcp. When all the small circles represent cation sites, the deformation represents NiAs → CsCl. When the dot-shaded circles are empty sites, the deformation is rutile → fluorite. When all small circles denote anion sites, the deformation is aragonite → $CsNO_3$. (*After Kennedy.*[63])

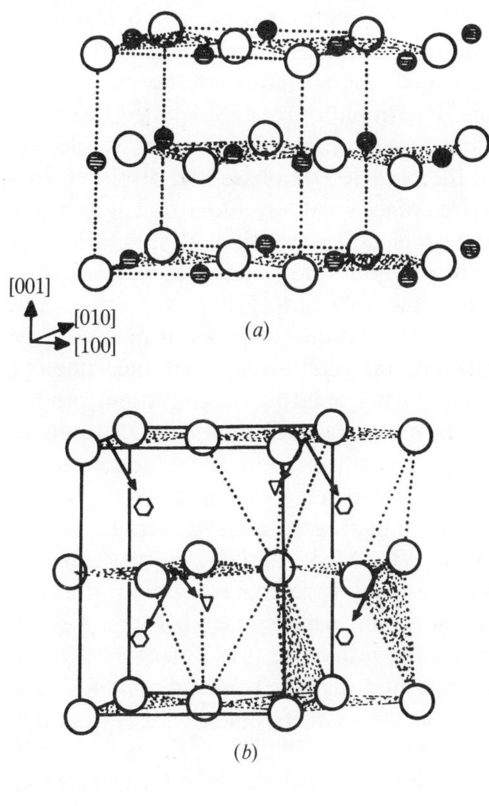

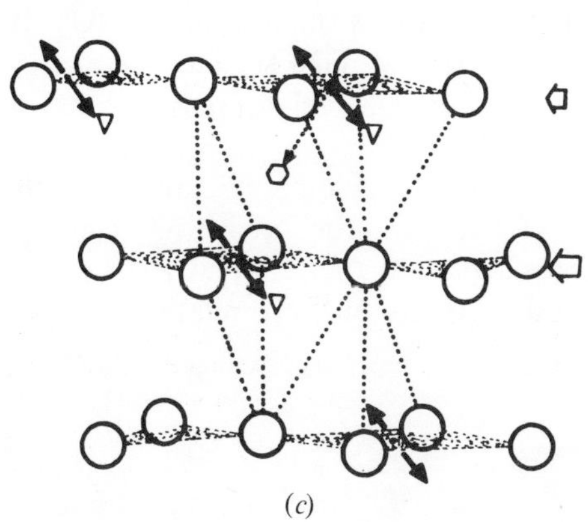

Figure 3-9 Contraction along the [010] direction of the NaCl structure (*a*), besides requiring minor adjustments of [001] stacking (*b*, *c*), displaces the ions shown by shaded circles. In (*b*) they can fall into new octahedral sites (hexagons), giving the NiAs structure, or new tetrahedral sites (triangles), giving the wurtzite structure. In (*c*), if they fall into half the tetrahedral sites (thin arrows), the zinc blende structure results. The (*a*) → (*c*) deformation can represent a rutile–fluorite relationship if the [001] axis is shortened and the shaded circles mark the middle of a line joining two anions. These become displaced into all the tetrahedral sites (shown by full thin and thick arrows). (*After Kennedy.*[63])

cubic structure through antiparallel displacements of Pb ions along ⟨110⟩; oxygen atoms are also displaced antiparallel to one another in the (001) plane. The phase transitions of antiferroelectric $NaNbO_3$ can be understood nicely in terms of such structural relations. In the ferroelectric phase of $NaNO_2$, the mirror symmetry perpendicular to [010] present in the paraelectric high temperature phase (> 478 K) disappears.

The above examples indicate the kind of structural correspondence found in polar and nonpolar phases of ferroelectric crystals. Structural analysis of ferroelectric crystals generally involves analysis of the structure of the paraelectric phase (reference phase) followed by the determination of the detailed structure (atomic positions) of the ferroelectric phase.[60] Atomic positions in the ferroelectric phase differ only slightly from those in the paraelectric phase, the displacements being rather small. A knowledge of the reference structure often makes possible the prediction of the mechanism of the ferroelectric transition, although the real validity of a model can only be established by a study of the structure of the ferroelectric phase, as in the case of Slater's theory[62] of KH_2PO_4.

Before closing this section on structural relations in phase transitions, we shall make a brief reference to deformational relationships among different structures. Such relationships imply that during a lattice deformation, atomic displacements do not require any activation energy. Deformational relations in cubic AB compounds were mentioned earlier in this section. Some new relationships recently pointed out by Kennedy[63] are shown in Figs. 3-8 and 3-9. Figure 3-8 shows relations in NiAs–CsCl, rutile–fluorite, and aragonite–$CsNO_3$ transitions. A similar representation would also relate WC, MnP, and NiAs structures. If alternate pairs of cation sites are vacant, Fig. 3-8*a* represents rutile, with the base of the prism corresponding to (010). If the small black circles in Fig. 3-8 stand for CO_3^{2-} or NO_3^-, then (*a*) would represent aragonite ($CaCO_3$ or KNO_3 II) structure, and (*b*) would represent the cubic and distorted pseudocubic $CsNO_3$, $TlNO_3$, or low $RbNO_3$ structures. Except in the case of aragonite, it is desirable to let the small circles represent cations; the anion tilts within the cation cage. Extension along the cube body diagonal in Fig. 3-8*b* yields calcite-type structures (as in $RbNO_3$ III → II). According to Fig. 3-8, the structure of $AgNO_3$ II corresponds to a deformation between KNO_3 II and $TlNO_3$. Tilts of anions without changing the deformation relationship should relate polymorphs of carbonates, nitrates, borates, and nitrites.

The deformational relations between NaCl, NiAs, zinc blende, and wurtzite structures are depicted in Fig. 3-9. In these relations, the square (001) net of NaCl type becomes hexagonal. Facile transformation of ZnS–NaCl structures (e.g., NH_4F, CdS, MnS) can be understood in terms of these relations. Rutile

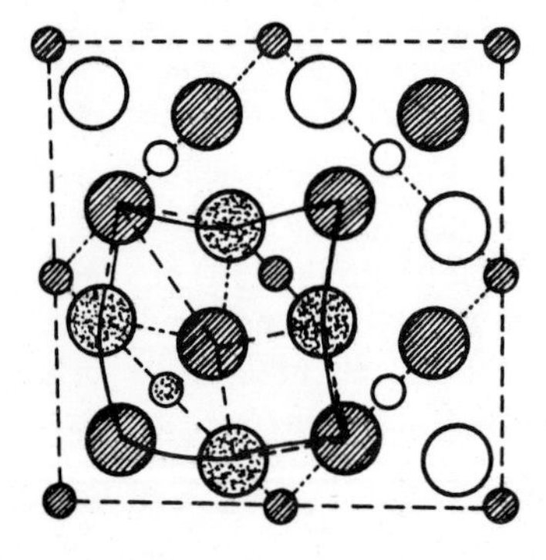

Figure 3-10 Four cells of rutile structure projected down the *c*-axis. A pseudo-fc tetragonal array of anions is outlined by curved lines and a corresponding primitive cell by broken lines. Large circles denote anions, small circles cations, and line shading denotes atoms at height 0 and 1. (*After Kennedy.*[63])

and fluorite structures can also be related by a mechanism other than that shown in Fig. 3-9. In a pseudo-fc tetragonal array of anions (Fig. 3-10), only minor displacements are required to make the curved lines straight. The primitive cell of this array can be transformed to a primitive cubic subcell of fluorite by a deformation where one of the components is a contraction along [111]. Undoubtedly, many structures are related by such deformation relations which enable transformations to occur without appreciable barriers. Examination of orientation relations and twinning will provide exact mechanisms of such transitions.

3-5 POLYTYPISM

Polytypism may be considered to be one-dimensional polymorphism wherein different polytypes of a material differ in the unit cell dimension in one of the three directions. Polytypism is generally exhibited by close-packed and layer structures where the first coordination of an atom is satisfied in more than one way, as in cubic versus hexagonal close packing. Since first-neighbor interactions are the same in different polytypes, and only the second or higher coordinations differ, potential energies of polytypes do not vary significantly. Polytypes of most materials are formed under similar thermodynamic conditions and frequently exist in coalescence. Long-period polytypes are nicely ordered despite the giant unit cell dimensions, although some random disorder of layers (faulted sequences) is almost always present. Formation of such ordered structures with large periodicities is indeed amazing. Undoubtedly, polytypism involves a fine interplay of long-range order versus short-range order forces. Several theories of polytypism have been proposed in the literature. The basic problem lies in finding the clue to long-range ordering over distances so long that they cannot readily be accounted for on the basis of the present understanding of atomic forces.

Although polytypism was first discovered in the case of SiC, it is now known to occur in variety of layered materials like ZnS, CdI_2, TaS_2, layered silicates, and perovskites. The largest c-axis dimension (direction perpendicular to the layers) observed so far appears to be in a SiC polytype with $c = 12{,}000$ Å. Various types of notation have been suggested to specify atomic arrangements in polytypes.[64-66] One of the ways is in terms of the packing scheme of layers employing the ABC notation; this notation becomes unwieldy for higher polytypes. A convenient and concise scheme is that due to Zhdanov, where the successive number of cyclic and anticyclic changes ($A \rightarrow B \rightarrow C$ and $A \rightarrow C \rightarrow B$ respectively) are summed up and given numerically. Another simple notation scheme, due to Ramsdell and Kohn, is to write down the number of layers of one kind of atom in the unit cell followed by an appropriate letter symbol, to signify the crystal symmetry. The six-layered hexagonal and fifteen-layered rhombohedral polytypes of SiC with the sequences ABCACB and ABCBACABACBCACB respectively are represented as (33) and $(32)_3$ in Zhdanov notation, while in the Ramsdell–Kohn notation they are 6H and 15R (Fig. 3-11). Polytypes which have the same

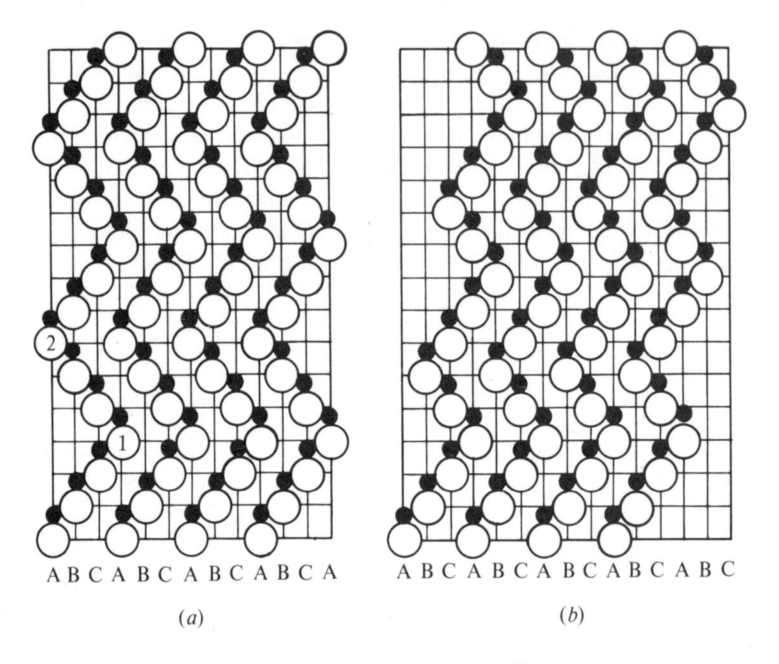

Figure 3-11 Sequence of Si and C atoms in the $11\bar{2}0$ sections of (*a*) 6H and (*b*) 15R polytypes of SiC.

cell size, but different ABC sequences, are often represented by attaching subscripts to the letter symbols (e.g., nH_1, nH_2 etc.). The subject of polytypism has been reviewed by Verma and Krishna,[64] Trigunayat and Chadha,[65] as well as Verma and Trigunayat.[66]

Polytypic Materials

Polytypism has been found in a variety of inorganic substances. Silicon carbide occurs in the cubic (β) and hexagonal (α) crystalline forms, and the α form exhibits a large number (130 or more) of polytypes, including both hexagonal and rhombohedral varieties. The *c*-dimension is ~ 5 Å in 2H, ~ 15 Å in the most common 6H, and 12,000 Å in 4680R. SiC crystals are generally grown at high temperatures (1300–3000 K), and different polytypes often coexist. The Si (or C) layers in the polytypes are separated by 2.52 Å. The β form of SiC transforms irreversibly to the α form at high temperatures, the β form being metastable at all temperatures. The 2H modification is only stable at relatively low temperatures (up to 1800 K). The zigzag sequences of Si and C atoms in two polytypes of SiC are shown in Fig. 3-11.

CdI_2 crystals which are generally grown from solution, vapor, melt, or gel show evidence for a large variety of polytypes (more than 210). The structures consist of different numbers of extended I–Cd–I molecular sheets piled on top of one another. Each minimal sandwich (molecular sheet) consists of a layer of Cd ions nested between two close-packed layers of I atoms, the thickness of the sandwich being 6.84 Å. The cell heights vary from ~7 Å in 2H to ~410 Å in 120R, the most common polytype being 4H. A cubic form of CdI_2 is not known. About forty PbI_2 polytypes have been prepared, and these are isostructural with CdI_2. The thickness of the I–Pb–I sandwich is 6.98 Å. Although $CdBr_2$ is isostructural with CdI_2, polytypism is not as common in this substance.

ZnS crystals are grown around 1300 K. ZnS can exist in the cubic sphalerite (β) form or the hexagonal wurtzite (α) form; the $\beta \rightarrow \alpha$ transformation is reversible and occurs around 1300 K. The variable dimension is along the *c*-axis, just as in SiC. One-dimensional disorder similar to SiC is commonly found in ZnS. The separation between successive layers of Zn (or S) atoms is 3.12 Å. Around 160 polytypes of ZnS are reported, and the common one is 2H. ZnSe, CdSe, CdS, ZnTe, and CdTe are also polytypic.

Group VB chalcogenides such as TaS_2, $TaSe_2$, and NbS_2, which have structures similar to CdI_2 or MoS_2, exhibit polytypism. The top and bottom sheets of the sandwich are of hexagonally packed chalcogen atoms, while the middle sheet is of metal atoms. The X–M–X sandwiches can show either octahedral or trigonal prismatic coordination of metal atoms. The sandwiches stack in different ways giving either pure octahedral (1T), pure trigonal prismatic (2H, 3R, 4H*c*), or mixed-coordination (4H*b*, 6R) polytypes, as shown in Fig. 3-12. The octahedral form (related to CdI_2 structure) is the stable high-temperature form of TaS_2 and $TaSe_2$. In order to obtain the 1T form, these substances must be quenched from above 1100 K in an atmosphere of the chalcogen. In pure state, the 1T form is metastable if it is not reheated beyond 550 K. The trigonal prismatic 2H form is the stable room-temperature phase, and the structure is similar to that of MoS_2. The mixed-coordination (4H*b* and 6R) polytypes are obtained by quenching from about 950 K.

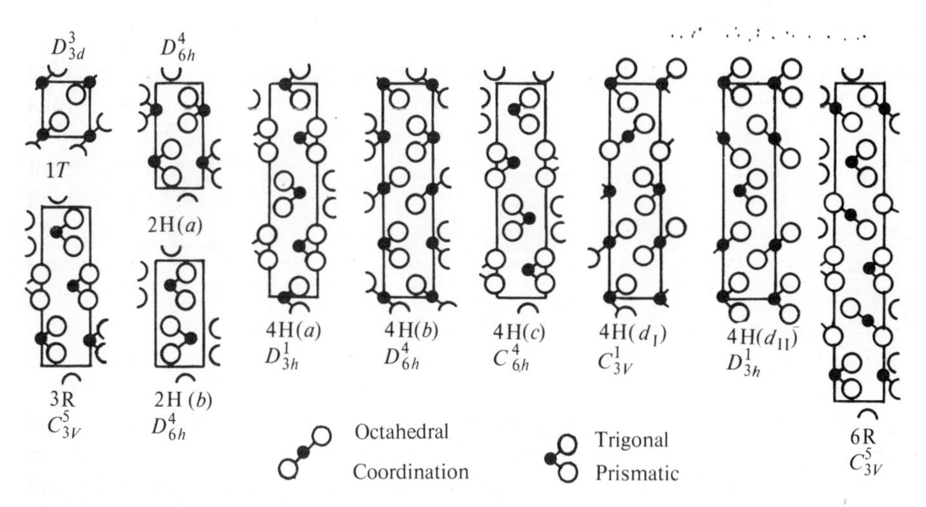

Figure 3-12 $11\bar{2}0$ sections of polytypes of transition metal dichalcogenides.

Mica has been found to show polytypes in crystals of hexagonal, rhombohedral, orthorhombic, monoclinic, and triclinic systems. Several other layered silicates like chlorite, kaolinite, croustedtite, and zussmanite also show polytypism. One-dimensional disorder is commonly observed in layered silicates. Some of the other polytypic substances are ABO_3 perovskites, opal, $K_3Co(CN)_6$, MoS_2, and graphite.

The ABO_3 hexagonal-perovskite polytypes[8] are characterized by a variable stacking of close-packed, ordered AO_3 layers, the B cations occupying all the interlayer oxygen octahedra. The stacking of any AO_3 layer may be cubic or hexagonal with respect to its two neighboring layers, depending on whether it is in the middle of an ABC or of an ABA sequence. If the stacking is entirely cubic, the B-filled octahedra share only corners in three dimensions to form the cubic perovskite structure (3C). If all the stacking is hexagonal, the B-filled octahedra form isolated *c*-axis chains of face-sheared octahedra (Fig. 3-13) as in the case of $CsNiCl_3$ (2H). The 3C structure can only accommodate A-cations within a size range determined by the tolerance factor, *t*. For the ideal cubic structure, $t = 1$, and the structure is stable at atmospheric pressure within the range $0.75 < t < t_c$, where t_c is determined by the effective charge on the B cations. For $t > t_c$, hexagonal stacking of AO_3 layers is stabilized. Formation of hexagonal

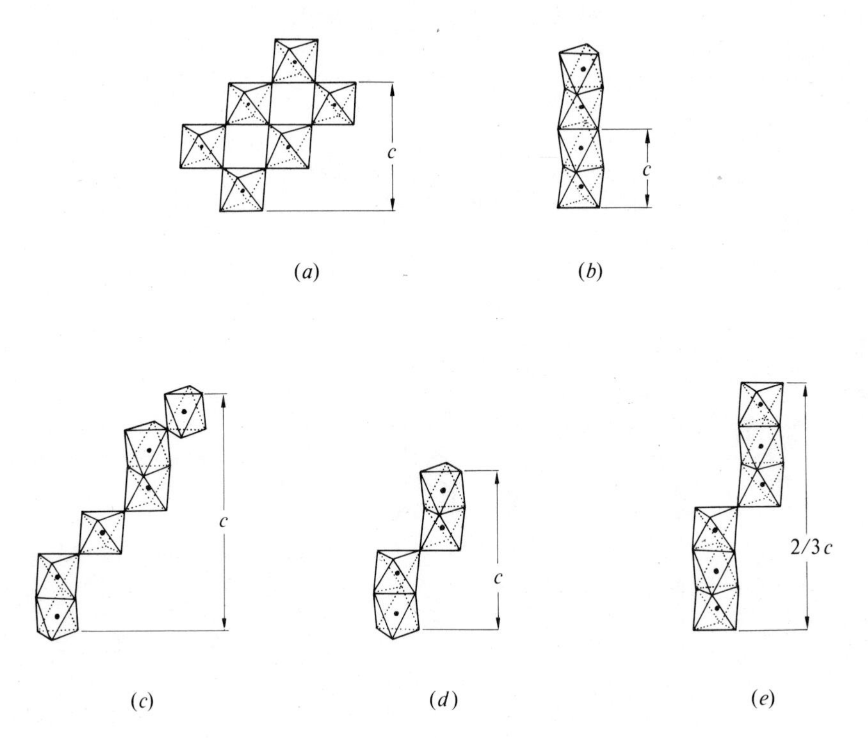

Figure 3-13 Representation of occupied octahedral sites (BO_6) in the polytypes of ABO_3 perovskites: (*a*) 3C, (*b*) 2H, (*c*) 6H, (*d*) 4H, and (*e*) 9R.

stacking occurs at the expense of Madelung energy, and the loss of Madelung energy can be reduced by limiting the length of any face-shared chain to two or three units. Figure 3-13 illustrates the three most probable stacking sequences for achieving this limitation.

The 6H hexagonal structure of perovskites would contain two-to-one cubic to hexagonal stacking in sequence cch cch, while the 4H hexagonal structure would contain a one-to-one sequence ch ch. The 9R rhombohedral structure would contain the sequence chh chh. The energy required to alternate the stacking sequence is 3/2 as large for the 4H structure as for the 6H or 9R structure, and the 4H phase is therefore stable over a limited range. In these polytypes, the dimensions of the unit cell remain the same in two dimensions, while the third dimension varies in length as expected. Typical system showing polytypism are $BaCrO_3$, $BaMnO_3$, $BaFeO_3$, and $BaRuO_3$.

It has been shown recently that direct lattice imaging by high-resolution electron microscopy[67] can be effectively employed to study the layer sequence and local structure of perovskite polytypes.[68–70] For crystals thin enough to approximate phase gratings, the image contrast corresponds to the projected charge density of the crystal structure under optimum defocusing conditions, areas of high projected charge density being indicated by dark contrast. In the lattice images of $BaBO_3$ perovskite polytypes, the Ba^{2+} ions give projected charge densities which may be correlated directly with the stacking of the BaO_3 layers. The images shows chevrons corresponding to columns of Ba cations and BO_6 octahedra which alternate in direction wherever there is a hexagonally close-packed layer (see Fig. 3-13). Thus, in the lattice image of a 4H polytype (chch stacking), the chevrons show reversal of slope every alternate layer (Fig. 3-14). Lattice image studies have shown that stacking faults are present in many of the polytypes.[69,70] Thus, 4H sequences are found in 9H $BaIrO_3$ and six-layer sequences in 9R $BaRuO_3$. Recently, lattice imaging of 6H SiC has been reported.[71] There appears little doubt that the lattice imaging technique is a powerful tool for the study of polytypes and other layered structures.

Polytypic Transitions

Transitions among different polytypes or within the same polytype of a substance are of importance in understanding the relative stabilities of structures. Polytypism has been considered by some workers[64,72] to be a cooperative phenomenon, as in second-order transitions or order–disorder transitions in alloys (see Chaps. 4 and 5 for details of order–disorder transitions). Available information on polytypic transitions, although limited, does not entirely favor this hypothesis. Thus, in ZnS, only one intermediate (3R) polytype appears to have been identified in the transformation of the cubic form to the hexagonal form, in spite of the fact that different ZnS polytypes are synthesized below the β–α transition temperature (1297 K). In SiC, the 2H form which is stable around 1700 K is not formed during the β–α transition.[64] The proportions of 15R and 4H SiC are known to increase relative to 6H if the temperature of preparation (in the range 2670–2770 K) is

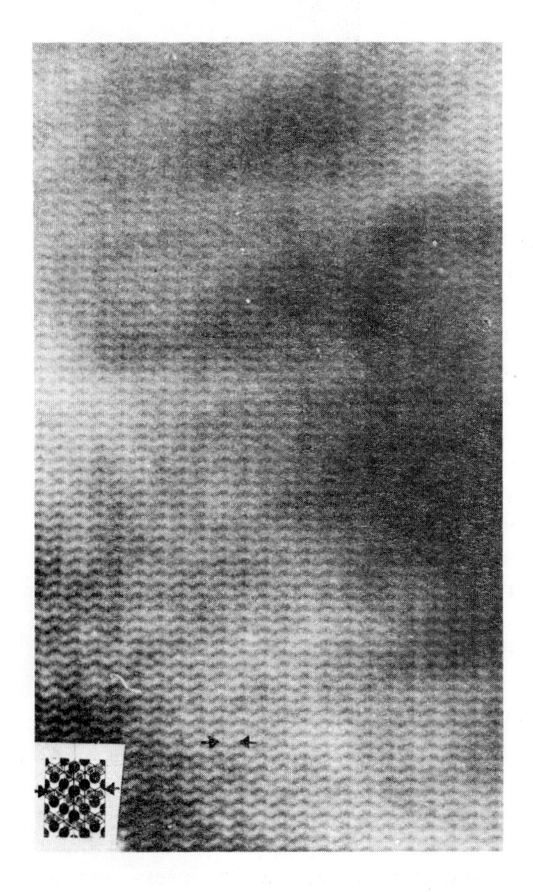

Figure 3-14 Lattice image of 4H $BaCrO_3$. (*After Gai and Rao.*[69]) Idealized projection of chch sequence showing Ba^{2+} (filled circles) and CrO_6 octahedra (shaded parallelograms) is given in inset. The distance between the two arrows is 9.5Å.

lower, suggesting thereby a possible relation between temperature and nature of polytype. The 2H → 3C and 2H → 6H transformations of SiC are believed to proceed through insertion and ordering of stacking faults.[73]

In the perovskite $BaRuO_3$, the transformation of 9R to 4H is noticed around 1500 K at atmospheric pressure.[69] The transition temperature is lowered by substitution of Sr^{2+} for Ba^{2+}. Thus, if x in $Ba_{1-x}Sr_xRuO_3$ is around 0.1, the 9R–4H transition occurs around 1300 K or lower.[74] $BaMnO_3$, which has the two-layer sequence at ordinary temperatures, gives rise to several anion-deficient polytypes with increase in temperature, with the six-layer form itself existing in two different forms.[75] In both $BaRuO_3$ and $BaCrO_3$, different polytypes are formed under different pressures.[76,77]

Interesting intra- and interpolytypic transitions have been observed in transition metal chalcogenides.[78] Thus, $TaSe_2$ undergoes the following interpolytypic transitions: 2H → 6R (~1070 K); 3R → 6R (~1070 K); 4H*b* → 4H*c* (570 K); 1T → 3R (~560 K); 4H*c* → 1T (1150 K); 3R/2H → 1T (1150 K); and so on. The intrapolytypic transitions of $TaSe_2$ are: 2H, 120 K; 1T, 473 K; 4H*b*, 410 K. In 1T–TaS_2, there are first-order transitions at 350 and 150 K, while in 4H*b*–TaS_2, these are at 315 K and 20 K. 2H–TaS_2, on the other hand, shows only a second-order transition at 80 K. There are no marked changes in unit cell parameters in the intrapolytype transitions. Electrical resistivity and other properties show drastic variations at these transitions in the case of 1T and 4Hb polytypes, but there are negligible changes in the case of the 2H polytype. This aspect will be discussed later in Chap. 7 in the light of charge density waves. The ΔH values of the intrapolytypic transitions in these dichalcogenides vary in the range 50–340 kcal mol^{-1}, while the change in unit cell volume is between -0.1 and -0.4 percent. The ΔH values of the intrapolytypic transitions are considerably less than those of interpolytypic transitions which are of the order of 1.5–2 kcal mol^{-1} (e.g., 4H$b \rightarrow$ 4Hc in $TaSe_2$ at 570 K, $\Delta H = -1.5$ kcal mol^{-1} compared to the ΔH of $+0.13$ kcal mol^{-1} for the intrapolytypic transition at 410 K). We see that at least in these dichalcogenide polytypes, most of the interpolytypic phase transitions are of the first order, contrary to popular belief. Transitions among polytypes of the parent compound CdI_2 have, however, been found to occur gradually with increase in temperature eventually giving rise to the stable 4H polytype at the highest temperature.[79] CdI_2 and PbI_2 interpolytypic transformations occur on annealing the crystals at a fixed temperature through rearrangement of stacking faults; long-period polytypes like 12H do not seem to undergo such transformations.[80,81]

3-6 ORIGIN OF LONG PERIODICITIES IN POLYTYPES AND OTHER SYSTEMS

Many explanations have been offered to account for polytypism.[64–66] Frank[82] invoked screw dislocations emanating from surfaces of crystals with different Burgers vectors to explain polytypism. While growth spirals with step heights equal to an integral multiple of the unit cell height have been seen in some polytypes, the phenomenon is not universal. Making use of detailed atomic configurations and layer sequences, attempts have been made to rationalize polytypes of SiC and CdI_2 on the basis of screw dislocations, but the mechanism does not appear to be satisfactory for other systems.[66] Limitations of the screw dislocation mechanism were pointed out by Jagodzinki,[83] who also argued that it would be much easier to produce edge dislocations than screw dislocations since the former require smaller energies.

Jagodzinski[83] proposed an explanation of polytypism based on thermodynamic considerations. He argued that while configurational entropy increases with increasing disorder, vibrational entropy decreases. An interplay of these two factors may account for formation of polytypes with long periods. Vibrational entropy contribution decreases progressively as the periodicity increases, and there is an increase in disorder with larger periodicities as indeed found in many systems. This disorder–order theory has been questioned since it does not fully account for perfectly ordered long-period polytypes or for the temperature–structure relation in polytypes; the assumed model for the variation of vibrational entropy has also been doubted. We must note here that the so-called perfect order may not really be present in polytypes. While x-ray diffraction may show perfection, a detailed study of local structure (in microdomains) may indicate presence of disorder in terms of faulted sequences. This has indeed been found to be true by lattice imaging studies of layered materials.

The cooperative disorder–order (second-order) mechanism of polytype formation (employing a treatment akin to Bragg–Williams–Bethe theory) was referred to earlier in Sec. 3-5. An explanation based on the role of lattice vibrations in creating stacking faults and hence the long periods has also been suggested.[84] Screw-dislocation controlled expansion of stacking faults has been considered to be a plausible mechanism by some workers.[85]

One of the main features of polytypes, particularly those of long periods, that appears to be universal is the presence of stacking faults. Stacking faults manifest themselves in the x-ray diffraction patterns in terms of streaking or arcing. Faults can generate polytypes provided there is a mechanism for their periodic distribution. To put it differently, once a stacking fault is created, the new sequence (with the fault) repeats at regular intervals, giving rise to a new polytypic arrangement (see Fig. 3-15).* The frequency of occurrence and nature of stacking faults will therefore determine the periodicity and symmetry. It has indeed been found in ZnS that increase in one-dimension disorder is accompanied by formation of high periodic polytypes. In perovskite polytypes, stacking faults are present only in the long-period members. Insertion and distribution of stacking faults thus control formation of new phases. Stacking fault formation energies are probably small in layered structures; in fact the difference in energy between the regular superlattice and a disordered state is likely to be an extremely small fraction of the lattice energy. While one could consider a mechanism involving a screw dislocation with a large Burgers vector to be responsible for propagating a wrongly stacked sheet of atoms at regular intervals, one could in principle also explain the phenomenon on the basis of thermodynamic arguments or making use of stacking faults and partial dislocations. The width of a stacking fault ribbon is inversely related to the stacking fault energy, and as such there is no real distinction between linear dislocations and planar stacking faults. In graphite, stacking fault ribbons are bounded by partial dislocations. The ribbons are essentially rhombohedral graphite occurring at different levels in the parent hexagonal crystal.[40] In zussmanite (Fig. 3-15), stacking faults extend right across the layer.[86]

Simple thermodynamic arguments are known to provide the basis for long periodicities in simple systems like CuAu where atoms order on the several sublattices of the unit cell, the ordering pattern switching between alternative sublattices at regular intervals. The operative factor appears to be a lowering of the total electronic energy by decreasing the size of the Brillouin zone;[87] the requisite periodicity for the creation of energy gaps varies with the electron/atom ratio in such intermetallic systems. In ionic compounds, ordering may be caused by the minimization of coulombic energy.

Considerations similar to those in polytypes are also pertinent in under-

* Very recent reports on lattice images of long period SiC and silicate minerals show coexistence of several types of layer sequences.

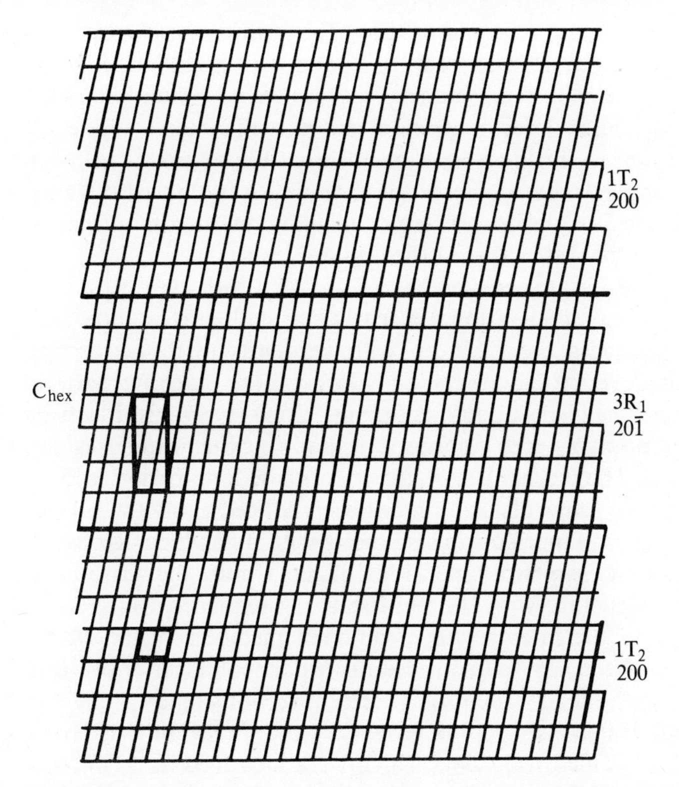

Figure 3-15 Projection of the lattice of zussmanite [$KFe_{13}Si_{17}AlO_{42}(OH)_{14}$] on to the $(1\bar{3}0)$ plane corresponding to the region between (001) planes (in the lattice image) showing structural rearrangement. The hexagonal and triclinic unit meshes are outlined. The (hol) lattice image of zussmanite shows faint traces of (001) planes and the (201) planes traversing them. In the region bounded by the (001) lattice fringes, the (hol) fringes can be interpreted as (200) planes of a single-layer ($1T_2$) structure extending over seven layers, followed by $(20\bar{1})$ planes of a $3R_1$ structure extending over seven layers, then by (200) $1T_2$ planes for another eight layers. (*After Jefferson and Thomas.*[86])

standing long-range ordering in hexagonal barium ferrites and other perovskite layered compounds. In the barium ferrite system, a very large number of crystallographically distinct compounds of the general formula M_pY_q have been reported. They are formed by regular *coherent intergrowth* of $BaFe_{12}O_{19}$ (phase M) with $Ba_2Me_2Fe_{12}O_{22}$ (phase Y with Me = Fe, Ni, etc.) and have *c*-axes from about 100 Å to 1500 Å. In systems where two chemically distinct but related crystal structures have some plane that is identical in dimensions and configuration, that plane constitutes a composition plane across which a crystal can pass, free of strain, although with a change in chemistry, from one structure to another.[88] If such composition planes enclose extended uniform regions, a macroscopic crystal assumes a domain structure, a solid solution of irrational total composition achieving perfect local order in this manner. In a number of systems, the transition from one structure to another recurs at regular intervals. Such *regular recurrent intergrowth* defines a new crystallographic unit. Since an entire range of integral numbers of the two components can be comprised in the repeating unit, coherent intergrowth can generate a homologous series of intergrowth phases with large unit cells.[88] Barium ferrites seem to represent a typical system with such ordering. Attainment of perfect long-range order may be difficult in such systems. Lamellae of wrong structure, varying in thickness, can be coherently intergrown to form crystals with averaged superstructure. Here again, while x-ray diffraction may show streaking of spots because of disorder, lattice imaging microscopy provides detailed information of the local structure at the unit cell level.

Electron microscopy of barium ferrites has shown that although crystallographic repeat units may be extremely long, extensive crystallographic domains of complex stacking sequences are built up with regularity with occasional faults.[88,89] Within a single microscopic crystal, however, the stacking pattern and chemical composition may vary at different points along the *c*-axis. Electron microscopy has revealed domains with compositions and stacking sequences not found by x-ray diffraction. The mechanism of growth of these long-period ferrites is difficult to understand. No screw dislocation has been noticed along the *c*-axis; a simple nucleation and growth mechanism also meets with difficulties. Repeated nucleation would imply that each two-dimensional nucleus must be laid on the template of the growing structure with the right stacking sequence. Since there is no structural obstacle to the intergrowth of different members of the M_pY_q series, a single crystal in the macroscopic sense of a morphological entity can show variation in composition and structure in different sections taken along the common *c*-axis direction. When a single flux grown crystal of barium ferrite was crushed and examined, it yielded fragments which were identified as M_2Y_5 (as polytypes $MYMY_4$ and MY_2MY_3), M_2Y_6 (as $MYMY_5$), and M_2Y_7 (as $MYMY_6$ and MY_3MY_4). In all the crystal fragments which emcompass a change in stacking, there is a sharp and perfect transition from one sequence to the other.

Lattice image studies of ferroelectric bismuth oxides (containing perovskite layers) of the general formula $(Bi_2O_2)^{2+}$ $(A_{n-1}B_nO_{3n+1})^{2-}$ with *c*-axis varying between 15 and 76 Å have shown the presence of ordered structures in most of the crystals, although short random sequences (ordered within each sequence) also occurred.[90] Most of the crystals also showed the presence of edge dislocations.

3-7 ROLE OF DEFECTS AND THE REAL STRUCTURE OF DEFECT SOLIDS

The presence of native point defects in ionic crystals and their role in determining various equilibrium and transport properties are well understood. In substances like alkali or silver halides with small concentrations of Schottky or Frenkel defects, the description of properties in terms of isolated or at best interacting defects (involving primarily coulombic and repulsive interactions) seems to be justified. Presence of native point defects in near-equilibrium concentrations may not have a significant role in phase transitions of ionic solids, as demonstrated recently in the case of CsCl.[18] In systems where deviations in the occupancy of

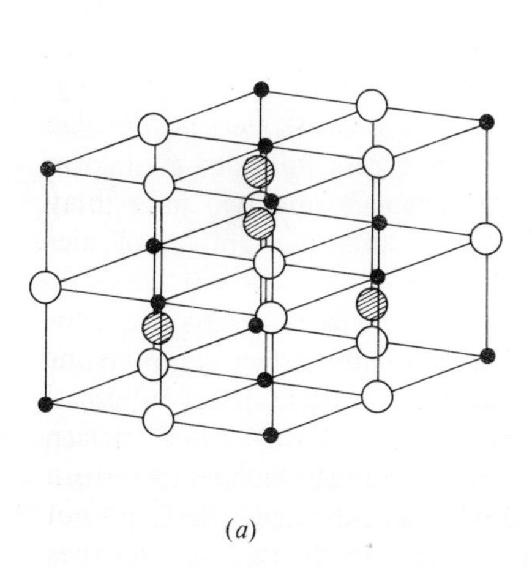

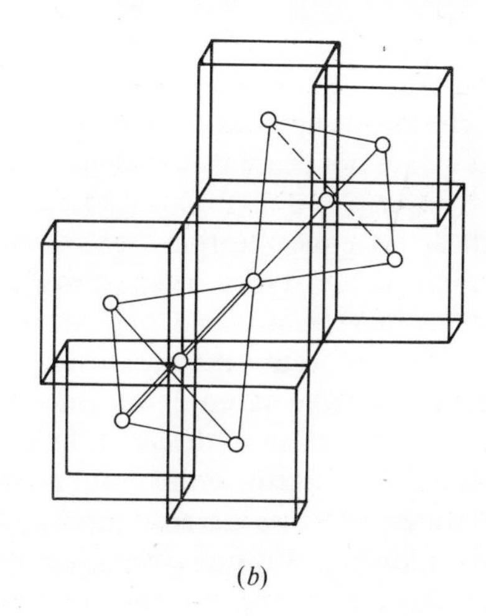

Figure 3-16 (*a*) Koch-Cohen cluster in $Fe_{1-x}O$: full circle, octahedral iron atom; shaded circle, tetrahedral iron atom; open circle, octahedral iron vacancy. (*b*) Associated pairs of vacant anion sites in substoichiometric fluorite structures. Central cation is 6-coordinated surrounded by six 7-coordinated cations: open circle, cation; closed circle, empty anion site.

anion and cation sites are large compared to the assigned crystal structure (e.g., 1 to 20 percent sites associated with vacancies or interstitials), the point-defect model would not be applicable. Recent experimental evidence shows that the real structures of such solids involve complexation or ordering of defects, often giving rise to new structural ramifications. It is therefore important to understand the "real" structure of defect solids in interpreting their properties and phase transitions. The reader is referred to the excellent articles of Anderson[91,92] for a detailed exposition of the subject.

Monoxides of transition metals which generally possess the NaCl structure serve to show the nature of defect ordering. FeO is a well-known cation-deficient oxide. Recent x-ray and neutron diffraction studies, as well as Mössbauer studies,[93-95] show the formation of a defect complex with four tetrahedral iron atoms surrounded by thirteen vacant sites giving the ratio of octahedral cation vacancies to tetrahedral cations as 3.25 (Fig. 3-16). Obviously, the defect center is much more complex than simple cation vacancies or their aggregates. There is a change in the rock salt matrix, and a new structure (essentially, an element of zinc blende structure) compatible with the NaCl matrix is formed. The empty octahedral vacancies in the complex are not really vacancies, and the complex has to dissociate if point-defect attributes of the vacancies (e.g., diffusion) are to manifest themselves. As such, there is a very low concentration of true cation vacancies in $Fe_{1-x}O$.

A case of defect complex formation is found in anion-deficient oxides of fluorite structure[96] shown in Fig. 3-16. Ordered clusters of this type along $\langle 111 \rangle$ are found in M_7O_{12} (e.g., M = Pr) and other intermediate phases. Another defect fluorite phase, where the empty anion sites in M_2O_3 (of type C defect rare earth oxide structure, e.g., M = Pr, Tb, with vacant sites in nonintersecting strings along four ⟨111⟩ directions) are filled by oxygens, is also known; this phase, which extends up to $MO_{1.67}$, is indeed immiscible with $MO_{1.71}$ (M_7O_{12}), showing that we are not dealing with simple vacancies. Such defect clusters are also formed in Y_2O_3–YOF and ZrO_2–Y_2O_3 systems. In anion excess fluorides containing high defect concentrations, 2:2:2 clusters (two vacancies and two interstitials in each of two types of sites) are found to exist,[97] typical examples of such systems being U_4O_9 and $M_x^{3+}M_{1-x}^{2+}F_{2+x}$. When anion excess is not large, the excess anions occupy the interstitial positions which can be treated as point defects. We thus see that point-defect disorder is transformed into defect complexes at high concentration of defects. The reconstructed units in these defect solids are such as to intergrow coherently in three dimensions. Randomization of defects and wide-range disordered compositions are generally found at high temperatures, and the low-temperature structures are almost always well-defined ordered phases.

The case of large vacancy concentrations in solids with itinerant electrons (like TiO and NbO) is interesting. TiO, which belongs to the rock salt family, has about 15 percent anion and cation vacancies. It has a wide miscibility range on either side of the stoichiometric composition. Electron diffraction studies show vacancies in TiO to be ordered below 1190 K, giving a lower symmetry to the structure.[98] Randomization of vacancies (order–disorder transition) occurs at higher temperatures. VO is similar to TiO, although the structure of ordered VO is not exactly known.[98] The quite different variations of cell dimensions of TiO and VO with composition as well as their low mutual solubility to form solid solutions indicates the defect structures of the two oxides to be different. In NbO, where 25 percent of the cations and anions are missing, the structure is considered to be an ordered-defect rock salt phase. In NbC_{1-x}, the carbon vacancies have a strong third-neighbor site preference required for the Nb_6C_5 superstructure observed below 1300 K.

There are several solids where the irrational anion:cation ratios are accommodated by the formation of planar defects or structural singularities. Two types of processes giving rise to such defects can be visualized.[91] In anion-excess structures, interstitial atoms can aggregate into an interstitial disk lying on a crystallographic orientation, the boundary climbing outwards until the singularity extends across the full cross-section of the crystal. Such defect structures are found in the YF_3–YOF and Nb_2O_5–ZrO_2 systems. In the former system, a set of superstructure phases of the general formula $Y_nO_{n-1}F_{n+2}$ is formed with all the additional anions segregating into every nth layer of the fluorite cell along one of the original cubic directions.[99] The structure can be described as layers of modified YF_3 coherently intergrown with $n - 1$ layers of fluorite YOF structure, slightly distorted but without any interstitial anions. In anion-deficient structures, anion vacancies aggregate into a vacancy disk on an appropriate orientation which undergoes a shear displacement until it extends across the crystal (e.g., Magneli phases). In this arrangement, cation coordination is preserved, and the anion coordination is increased, while cation–cation distances are decreased because of the change from corner-sharing to edge-sharing or from edge-sharing to face-sharing of polyhedra. Such planar singularities eliminate (or absorb) a large number of point defects. If deviations from stoichiometry are large, the concentration of planar singularities becomes high, and singularities occur periodically, giving rise to various ordered phases with finite compositions. Across each planar singularity, slices of the parent structure are in proper register or in an antiphase relation with respect to the cation sublattice, the total composition of crystal depending on the number of unit cells of parent structure enclosed between two planar singularities. We shall discuss planar singularities giving rise to shear structures at greater length later in this section.

The role of stacking faults in the formation of polytypes and other long-period crystals was discussed in the previous section. If a stacking fault does not extend right across the crystal, there is a boundary in the stacking plane between regions of perfect and faulted sequences. Such a boundary constitutes a partial dislocation.[40] Stacking sequences of solids may therefore be modified by the passage of glissile partial dislocations throughout the layers. Thus, when cobalt undergoes a transition from hcp to fcc at 790 K, stacking-fault ribbons constituting hcp lamellae bounded by partial dislocations are seen to contract into undissociated perfect dislocations in the electron micrographs. As mentioned earlier, stacking-fault ribbons (rhombohedral form) in graphite are bounded by partial dislocations. We must note that a stacking-fault boundary may be considered to be an antiphase boundary. If antiphase boundaries or planar stacking faults are ordered, they would give rise to a distinct new structure. Hexagonal–rhombohedral transformations in minerals and hcp–fcc transitions in metals generally involve recurrent ordering of antiphase boundaries which can be attained by systematic movements of dislocations.[40] Antiphase boundaries have been invoked to correlate the features of rutile and α-PbO_2 structures.[100] Thus, the conversion of rutile to its α-PbO_2 phase at high pressure can be interpreted as arising from recurrent cooperative shear on every alternate (011) plane. As a result of the introduction of (011) antiphase boundaries, the α-PbO_2 phase may be considered as a polysynthetically twinned version of rutile. Another example of this kind is NiMn, which transforms from CsCl structure to the tetragonal AuCu structure on cooling, the product phase being heavily twinned. This shear transformation occurs on (111) planes; a superlattice corresponding to twice the width of the twin lamellae has indeed been noticed.

The role of dislocations in determining various chemical and physical properties of inorganic solids has been widely recognized.[40] There are several instances in the literature in which dislocations have been considered to play a role in the mechanism of phase transitions of solids.* Thus, Kennedy and Schultz[101] have suggested that in thermally activated transformations, micro-regions may be transferred to the product phase non-diffusively by a dislocation mechanism. The

* The role of dislocations, twins, and impurities on the B–A or C–B transitions of rare-earth sesquioxides, Ln_2O_3, has recently been discussed by Caro et al. in "Defects and Transport in Oxides," ed. M. S. Seltzer and R. I. Jaffee, Plenum Press, New York, 1974. The role of impurities on phase transitions was discussed earlier in Sec. 2-5.

activated process would be the release of stress and disregistry by diffusive mechanisms including dislocation climb. The wurtzite–sphalerite transformation in ZnS is supposed to occur by translation of the close-packed (basal) planes by means of dislocations.[102] In $NaNO_3$, the λ transition has been found to affect the dislocation content.[103] At temperatures below the onset of the λ-transition, a few dislocations are present, but there is multiplication of dislocations at the transition temperature with helical dislocations and dislocation loops on the $\{110\}$ planes. Twin bands that involve twin gliding on $\{100\}$ planes in the [001] direction remain locked during thermal cycling. The I–III transformation in KNO_3 is expected to introduce dislocations,[104] just like the IV–III transformation in $RbNO_3$. Dislocations are also known to play a part in the transformation of ferroelectric perovskites[61] like $BaTiO_3$.

Apart from a few isolated examples, no systematic studies on the role of dislocations in phase transitions of inorganic solids are reported in the literature. However, the recognition of the unity of linear and planar faults and of the importance of antiphase boundaries (which can be created or destroyed by movement of partial dislocations) will be of great value in understanding solid state phenomena.[40] High-resolution electron microscopy has made possible direct examination of dislocations and planar defects (crystallographic shear planes). Crystallographic shear planes (cs) are similar to the imperfect prismatic (or partial) dislocation loops described by Frank[82] in his general dislocation theory; cs planes along with antiphase boundaries are important in understanding the microstructure of several of the oxide systems.

Shear and Block Structures

The structural principles of oxides of W, Mo, and Re forming homologous series of the formula M_nO_{3n-1} or M_nO_{3n-2} (n = variable integer) were difficult to understand until recently. Such apparently nonstoichiometric oxides known as *Magneli phases*[105] are also found in other transition-metal oxides like Ti, V, and Cr with the formulae M_nO_{2n-1}, M_nO_{2n-2}, M_nO_{2n-3}, and so on. Several mixed oxide systems with compositions varying from extreme low- to high-oxygen deficiency are known to form such phases. Wadsley[106] proposed that the decrease in the oxygen/metal ratio can be accommodated by localized variations in a manner by which coordination octahedra share atoms. The variations are confined to specific low-index planes, and their geometry can be described as involving the removal of an oxygen layer from the stoichiometric crystal and followed by a fusion of two half-crystals with a shear displacement which has a component parallel to the missing layer. Creation of a cs plane is schematically shown in Fig. 3-17. Typical crystallographic shear phases in ReO_3 and TiO_2 structures are shown in Table 3-2. Lattice imaging by high-resolution electron microscopy has been particularly useful in studying shear structures.[40,91,92]

Magneli phases of tungsten, W_nO_{3n-1}, arise from quasi-ordered arrays of (120) cs planes, the separation between the cs planes governing the value of n. Oxides of the formula M_nO_{3n-m} are derived from the ReO_3 structure by omission

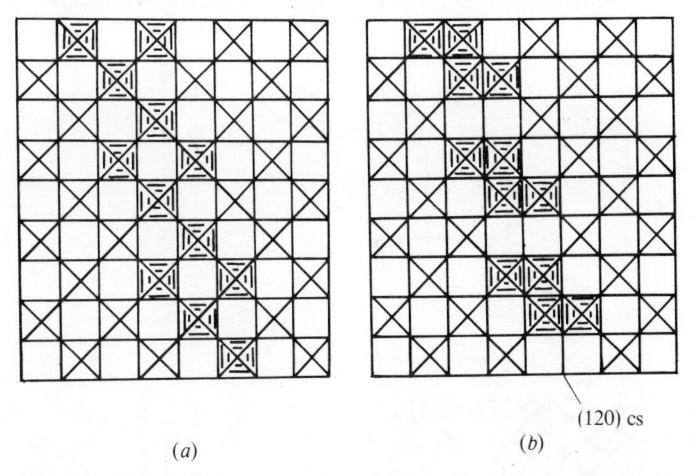

Figure 3-17 Schematic representation of the creation of a crystallographic shear plane in ReO_3-type structure. Corner-shared octahedra rearrange themselves to form edge-shared octahedra separated by oxygen gaps at a (120) cs plane.

of every *n*th (*hk*0) sheet of oxygen sites, where *m* depends on the cs-plane orientation. The spacing between cs planes is related to *n* by $d_{cs} = d_{(hk0)}(n - c)$, where *c* is the fractional collapse. A homologous series is thus represented by a linear plot of composition against the reciprocal superlattice distance ($d^*_{cs} = 1/d_{cs}$) measured from the appropriate electron diffraction pattern. The W_nO_{3n-2} Magneli phases are based on (130) cs planes, the value of *n* (composition) being determined by d_{cs}. Coherent intergrowths of (120) and (130) cs phases are known to occur. In Ti_nO_{2n-1}, the titanium-rich range involves (121) cs planes with face-sharing octahedra, while the oxygen-rich end is based on (132) cs planes (Table 3-1). The (132)-based cs planes are actually composed of (121) cs planes and (011) antiphase boundaries. In the range $n = 9$ to 16, there is swinging of cs planes from (132) to (121) via (253), (374), (495), and so on. It is noteworthy that even in very slightly reduced rutile of the composition $TiO_{1.9986}$, a number of (132) cs planes are found. This shows that even a very small departure from the ideal stoichiometry

Table 3-2 Typical crystallographic shear in ReO_3 and TiO_2 structures

Parent structure	Orientation of cs plane	Formula	*n*	Examples
ReO_3	(100)	M_nO_{3n-1}	2	R–Nb_2O_5
			3	Nb_3O_7F
	(130)	M_nO_{3n-2}	20 etc.	$W_{20}O_{58}$ etc.
	(120)	M_nO_{3n-1}	$8 \le n \le 12$	Mo_8O_{23}
TiO_2	(121)	M_nO_{2n-1}	$4 \le n \le 9$	Ti_4O_7–Ti_9O_{17}
				V_4O_7–V_9O_{17}
	(132)	M_nO_{2n-1}	$16 \le n \le 36$	$Ti_{16}O_{31}$–$Ti_{36}O_{71}$

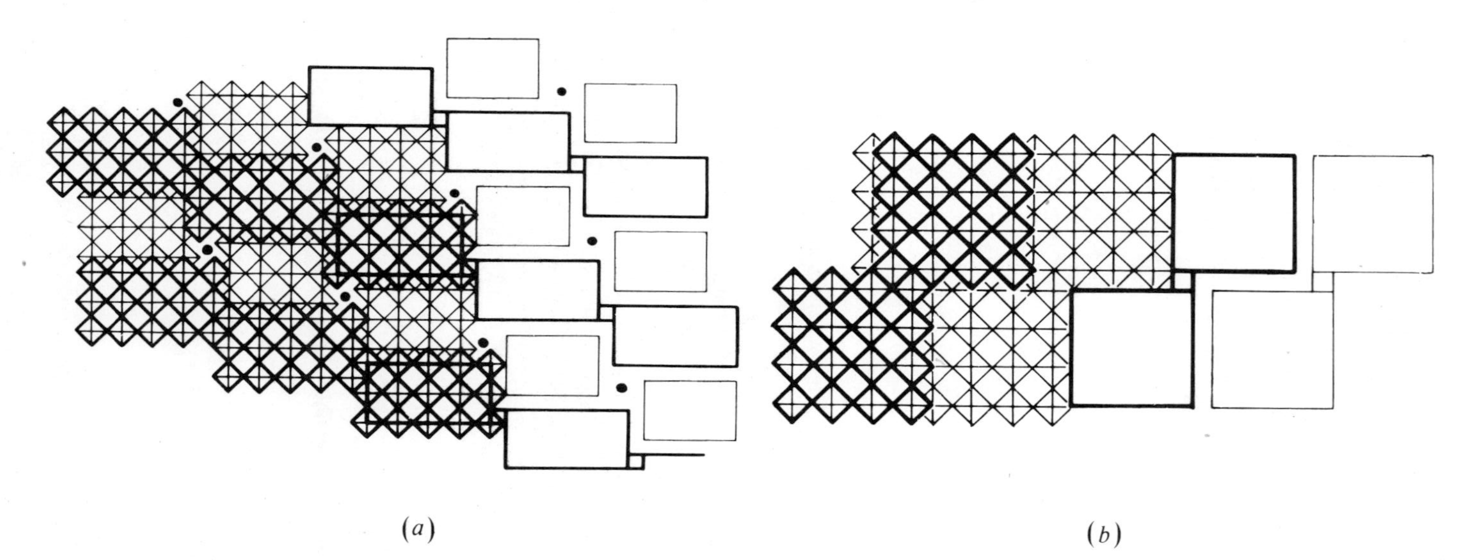

Figure 3-18 (*a*) Structure of H-Nb_2O_5. [010] projection showing columns of octahedra, (5 × 3) in section, at one level (heavy outlines) and (4 × 3) columns at second level. On the right-hand side, a schematic representation outlines the rectangular columns as defined by the niobium atom positions. (*b*) Structure of N-Nb_2O_5. [010] projection showing the columns of (4 × 4) octahedra at both levels.

creates shear structures rather than point defects as one would expect in truly nonstoichiometric compounds. We should therefore not really consider such anion-deficient compositions as nonstoichiometric, but treat them as distinct phases with unique structures.

In some metal oxides, particularly those derived from Nb_2O_5 (including ternary systems like Nb_2O_5–TiO_2, Nb_2O_5–WO_3), intersecting or double cs planes occur, giving rise to the so-called block structures. These structures respond in several ways to changes in metal–oxygen ratios. One cs plane may remain fixed while the other swings, giving rise to different cross-sections of the block. The blocks can get interconnected in different ways by means of edge-sharing or face-sharing octahedra or by making use of tetrahedral sites. Block structures can accommodate a number of distinct compositions, typical ones among niobium oxides being $Nb_{12}O_{29}$, $Nb_{22}O_{54}$, $Nb_{25}O_{62}$, $Nb_{28}O_{70}$, and $Nb_{53}O_{132}$, with general formulae $M_{3n}O_{8n-3}$ and $M_{3n+1}O_{8n-2}$. Many of the polymorphs of Nb_2O_5 are now described in terms of crystallographic shear. Thus, N–Nb_2O_5 and H–Nb_2O_5, which are derived from the ReO_3 structure, differ in the sizes of the blocks and the way blocks are interconnected (Fig. 3-18). There is one polymorph of Nb_2O_5, the B-form, which is based on the PdF_3 structure and contains rutile ribbons of edge-shared octahedra joined by terminal octahedral corners. The structural chemistry of Nb_2O_5 and related derivatives has been nicely reviewed by Wadsley and Andersson.[107] The lattice-imaging technique is ideally suited to the study of the block structures due to the presence of empty channels between corner-shared octahedra.[67,108]

Polymorphic transformations of Nb_2O_5 are known, and all the polymorphs transform to the most stable H-form at high temperatures.[109] H–Nb_2O_5 transforms to B–Nb_2O_5 on application of pressure, the latter being the densest form of all the polymorphs. Raman spectra of the different polymorphs differ significantly, thus providing a diagnostic tool for the study of the transitions.[110]

Faults such as twins, "*Wadsley defects*" (random, isolated, or nonconformist cs planes), special kinds of dislocations, and rotation faults are found in shear and block structures. Recognizing these possibilities, Thomas[40] considers three distinct categories of transformations that these solids may undergo: (i) a non-reconstructive, cooperative, kinetically facile martensitic type of process in which glissile dislocations play an important role; (ii) reconstructive transformations which may depend on large fluctuations for the nucleation of a new configuration or on long-range diffusion for subsequent growth; and (iii) an intermediate situation[92] involving partially reconstructive transformation where there are linked changes of composition and structure.

REFERENCES

1. A. F. Wells, "Structural Inorganic Chemistry," Clarendon Press, Oxford, 1962.
2. R. C. Evans, "Introduction to Crystal Chemistry," Cambridge University Press, 1964.
3. H. Krebs, "Fundamentals of Inorganic Crystal Chemistry," McGraw-Hill, London, 1968.
4. C. N. R. Rao, in "Solid State Chemistry," ed. C. N. R. Rao, Marcel Dekker, New York, 1974.

5. M. J. Buerger, in "Phase Transformations in Solids," eds. R. Smoluchowski, J. E. Mayer, and W. A. Weyl, John Wiley, New York, 1951.
6. M. J. Buerger, *Fortschr. Miner.*, **39,** 9, 1961.
7. C. N. R. Rao and K. J. Rao, "Progress in Solid State Chemistry," ed. H. Reiss, vol. 4, Pergamon Press, Oxford, 1967.
8. J. B. Goodenough and J. M. Longo, *Landolt-Bornstein, New Series, Group III,* vol. 4a, Springer-Verlag, New York, 1970.
9. M. Born and K. Huang, "Dynamical Theory of Crystal Lattices," Oxford University Press, 1956, Chaps. I, III.
10. M. P. Tosi, "Solid State Physics," ed. F. Seitz and D. Turnbull, vol. 16, Academic Press, New York, 1964, pp. 1–113.
11. C. N. R. Rao, "Modern Aspects of Solid State Chemistry," ed. C. N. R. Rao, Plenum Press, New York, London, 1970, chaps. 2, 22.
12. M. L. Huggins and J. E. Mayer, *J. Chem. Phys.*, **1,** 637, 1935.
13. J. E. Jones and A. E. Ingham, *Proc. Roy. Soc.* (*Lond*), **A107,** 636, 1925.
14. B. C. Dick and A. W. Overhauser, *Phys. Rev.*, **112,** 90, 1958.
15. K. J. Rao, G. V. Subba Rao, and C. N. R. Rao, *Trans. Farad. Soc.*, **63,** 1013, 1967.
16. A. May, *Phys. Rev.*, **52,** 339, 1937; **54,** 629, 1938.
17. K. J. Rao and C. N. R. Rao, *Proc. Phys. Soc.* (*Lond*), **91,** 754, 1967.
18. M. Natarajan, K. J. Rao, and C. N. R. Rao, *Trans. Farad. Soc.*, **65,** 2497, 1970.
19. A. K. Shukla, J. C. Ahluwalia, and C. N. R. Rao, *J. Chem. Soc. Faraday I*, **72,** 1288, 1976.
20. F. Hajj, *J. Chem. Phys.*, **44,** 4618, 1966.
21. D. W. Lynch, *J. Phys. Chem. Solids*, **28,** 1941, 1967.
22. K. J. Rao, G. V. Subba Rao, and C. N. R. Rao, *J. Phys. C*, **1,** 1134, 1968.
23. M. L. Huggins, in "Phase Transformations in Solids," ed. R. Smoluchowski, J. E. Mayer, and W. A. Weyl, John Wiley, New York, 1951, p. 238.
24. M. Natarajan and C. N. R. Rao, *J. Chem. Soc.* (*A*), 3087, 1970.
25. M. P. Tosi and F. G. Fumi, *J. Phys. Chem. Solids*, **23,** 359, 1962.
26. P. O. Lowdin, *Phil. Mag. Suppl.*, **5,** 1, 1956.
27. J. F. Colwell, "The Cohesive Energy and Stable Lattice of Cesium Chloride," Ph.D. thesis, Cornell University, 1960.
28. E. Lombardi and L. Jansen, *Phys. Rev.*, **136,** A1011, 1964; **151,** 694, 1966.
29. K. Mansikka, *Ann. Univ. Turku, Ser. AI*, 121, 1968.
30. L. Jansen, in "Modern Quantum Chemistry," ed. O. Sinanoglu, Academic Press, New York, 1965, chap. 3.
31. L. Pauling, "Nature of the Chemical Bond," Cornell University Press, Ithaca, 1962.
32. J. C. Phillips, *Rev. Mod. Phys.*, **42,** 317, 1970.
33. J. C. Phillips, "Bonds and Bands in Semiconductors," Academic Press, New York, 1973.
34. V. Heine and R. O. Jones, *J. Phys.* (*Paris*), **C2,** 719, 1969.
35. D. Penn, *Phys. Rev.*, **128,** 2093, 1962.
36. J. A. Van Vechten, *Phys. Rev.*, **182,** 891, 1969; **187,** 1007, 1969.
37. J. P. Walter and M. L. Cohen, *Phys. Rev. Letts.*, **26,** 17, 1971.
38. T. V. Ramakrishnan, in "Solid State Chemistry," ed. C. N. R. Rao, Marcel Dekker, New York, 1974.
39. J. C. Phillips, and J. A. Van Vechten, *Phys. Rev.*, **B2,** 2147, 1970.
40. J. M. Thomas, *Phil. Trans. Roy. Soc.*, **277,** 251, 1974.
41. H. Manohar, in "Solid State Chemistry," ed. C. N. R. Rao, Marcel Dekker, New York, 1974.
42. J. M. Robertson and A. R. Ubbelohde, *Proc. Roy. Soc.*, **A167,** 36, 1938.
43. A. I. Kitaigorodsky, "Organic Chemical Crystallography," Consultants Bureau, New York, 1973.
44. J. D. Bernal, *Schweizer Arch.*, **26,** 69, 1960.
45. L. S. Dent-Glasser, F. P. Glasser, and H. F. W. Taylor, *Quart. Rev.*, **16,** 343, 1962.
46. G. W. Brindley, *Progress in Ceramic Science*, **3,** 1, 1963.
47. S. Chatterji, A. L. Mackay, and J. W. Jeffery, *J. Appl. Cryst.*, **4,** 175, 1971.
48. W. L. Fraser and S. W. Kennedy, *Acta Cryst.*, **B28,** 3101, 1972; **A30,** 13, 1974.

49. S. W. Kennedy, *J. Appl. Cryst.*, **6,** 293, 1973; *J. Mat. Sci.*, **9,** 1043, 1974.
50. R. Soderquist and B. Dickens, *J. Phys. Chem. Solids*, **28,** 823, 1967.
51. C. N. R. Rao, B. Prakash, and M. Natarajan, "Crystal Structure Transformations in Inorganic Nitrites, Nitrates, and Carbonates," *NSRDS–NBS Monograph* 53, National Bureau of Standards, Washington, D. C., 1975.
52. S. W. Kennedy, A. R. Ubbelohde, and I. Woodward, *Proc. Roy. Soc.*, **A219,** 303, 1953; see also S. W. Kennedy and M. Odlyha, *Australian J. Chem.*, **27,** 1121, 1974.
53. S. W. Kennedy and W. M. Kriven, *J. Mat. Sci.*, **7,** 1092, 1972.
54. S. W. Kennedy, *Phys. stat. solidi* (*a*), **2,** 415, 1970.
55. R. N. Brown and A. C. McLaren, *Acta Cryst.*, **15,** 974, 1962.
56. A. J. Iverson and S. W. Kennedy, *Acta. Cryst.*, **29B,** 1554, 1973.
57. E. W. Courtenay and S. W. Kennedy, *Australian J. Chem.*, **27,** 209, 1974.
58. S. W. Kennedy and J. H. Patterson, *Proc. Roy. Soc.*, **A283,** 498, 1965.
59. W. L. Fraser, S. W. Kennedy, and M. R. Snow, *Acta Cryst.*, **B31,** 365, 1975.
60. A. R. West, *Nature*, **249,** 245, 1974; *Z. Krist.*, **141,** 422, 1975.
61. F. Jona and G. Shirane, "Ferroelectric Crystals," Pergamon Press, New York, 1962.
62. J. C. Slater, *J. Chem. Phys.*, **9,** 16, 1941.
63. S. W. Kennedy, *J. Mat. Sci.*, **9,** 2053, 1974.
64. A. R. Verma and P. Krishna, "Polymorphism and Polytypism," John Wiley, New York, 1966.
65. G. C. Trigunayat and G. K. Chadha, *Phys. stat. solidi.*, **4a,** 9, 1971.
66. A. R. Verma and G. C. Trigunayat, in "Solid State Chemistry," ed. C. N. R. Rao, Marcel Dekker, New York, 1974.
67. J. G. Alpress and J. V. Sanders, *J. Appl. Cryst.*, **6,** 165, 1973.
68. J. L. Hutchison and A. J. Jacobson, *Acta Cryst.*, **B31,** 1442, 1975.
69. P. L. Gai and C. N. R. Rao, *Pramana*, **5,** 274, 1975.
70. P. L. Gai, A. J. Jacobson, and C. N. R. Rao, *Inorg. Chem.*, **15,** 480, 1976.
71. P. L. Gai, J. S. Anderson, and C. N. R. Rao, *J. Phys. D*, **8,** L157, 1975.
72. C. J. Schneer, *Acta Cryst.*, **8,** 279, 1955.
73. P. Krishna and Q. C. Marshall, *J. Cryst. Growth*, **9,** 719, 1971.
74. P. C. Donohue, L. Katz, and R. Ward, *Inorg. Chem.*, **5,** 335, 1966.
75. T. Negas and R. S. Roth, *J. Solid State Chem.*, **3,** 323, 1971.
76. B. L. Chamberland, *Inorg. Chem.*, **8,** 286, 1969.
77. J. M. Longo and J. A. Kafalas, *Mat. Res. Bull.*, **3,** 687, 1968.
78. J. A. Wilson, F. J. Di Salvo, and S. Mahajan, *Adv. Phys.*, **24,** 117, 1975.
79. G. Lal and G. C. Trigunayat, *Acta Cryst.*, **A26,** 430, 1970.
80. R. S. Tiwari and O. N. Srivastava, *J. Appl. Cryst.*, **5,** 347, 1972.
81. R. Prasad and O. N. Srivastava, *Acta Cryst.*, **B30,** 1748, 1974; see also *J. Cryst. Growth*, **19,** 11, 1973.
82. F. C. Frank, *Phil. Mag.*, **42,** 809, 1014, 1951.
83. H. Jagodzinski, *Neues Jahrb. Mineralk.*, **3,** 49, 1954; *Acta Cryst.*, **7,** 300, 1954.
84. H. Piebst, *Z. Phys. Chem.*, **223,** 193, 1963.
85. S. Madrix and I. T. Steinberger, *Israel J. Chem.*, **3,** 243, 1966; see also *Phil. Mag.*, **21,** 1237, 1970.
86. D. A. Jefferson and J. M. Thomas, *J. Chem. Soc.*, *Faraday II*, **70,** 1691, 1974.
87. H. Sato and R. S. Roth, *Phys. Rev.*, **124,** 1833, 1961; **127,** 469, 1962; see also *J. Phys. Chem. Solids*, **28,** 137, 1967.
88. J. S. Anderson and J. L. Hutchison, *Cont. Phys.*, **16,** 443, 1975.
89. J. D. M. McConnell, J. L. Hutchison, and J. S. Anderson, *Proc. Roy. Soc. A.*, **339,** 1, 1974.
90. J. L. Hutchison, J. S. Anderson, and C. N. R. Rao, *Proc. Roy. Soc. A*, **355,** 301, 1977.
91. J. S. Anderson, in "Defects and Transport in Oxides," ed. M. S. Seltzer and R. I. Jaffee, Plenum Press, New York, 1974.
92. J. S. Anderson and R. J. D. Tilley, in "Surface and Defect Properties of Solids," *Chem. Soc. Specialist Periodical Report*, **3,** 1, 1974.
93. F. Koch and J. B. Cohen, *Acta Cryst.*, **B25,** 275, 1969.

94. A. K. Cheetam, B. E. F. Fender, and R. I. Taylor, *J. Phys. C*, **4,** 2160, 1971.
95. N. N. Greenwood and A. T. Howe, *7th International Symposium on Reactivity of Solids*, Chapman & Hall, London, 1972.
96. M. R. Thornber and D. J. M. Bevan, *J. Solid State Chem.*, **1,** 536, 1970.
97. A. K. Cheetam, B. E. F. Fender, D. Steele, R. I. Taylor, and B. J. M. Wollis, *J. Phys. C*, **4,** 3107, 1971; see also *J. Phys. C*, **5,** 2677, 1972.
98. D. Watanabe, O. Terasaki, A. Jostsons, and J. R. Castles, in "Extended Defects in Nonmetallic Solids," North-Holland, Amsterdam (1970); see also C. N. R. Rao, P. L. Gai, and S. Ramasesha, *Phil. Mag.*, **33,** 387, 1976.
99. A. W. Mann and D. J. M. Bevan, *J. Solid State Chem.*, **5,** 410, 1972.
100. I. E. Grey, A. F. Reid, and J. G. Allpress, *J. Solid State Chem.*, **8,** 86, 1973.
101. S. W. Kennedy and P. K. Schultz, *Trans. Faraday Soc.*, **59,** 156, 1963.
102. F. S. d'Aragona, P. Delavignette, and S. Amelinckx, *Phys. stat. solidi,* **14a,** K115, 1966.
103. O. P. Bahl and J. M. Thomas, *J. Mat. Sci.*, **2,** 510, 1967.
104. S. W. Kennedy, *J. Crystal Growth*, **16,** 274, 1972.
105. A. Magneli, *Arkiv Kemi*, **2,** 513, 1950.
106. A. D. Wadsley, in "Non-stoichiometric Compounds," ed. L. Mandelcorn, Academic Press, London 1964, chap. 3; see also L. A. Bursill and B. G. Hyde, *Progress in Solid State Chemistry*, **1,** 178, 1972.
107. A. D. Wadsley and S. Andersson, in "Perspectives in Structural Chemistry," vol. 3, ed. J. D. Dunitz and J. A. Ibers, John Wiley, New York, 1970.
108. J. L. Hutchison and J. S. Anderson, *Phys. stat. solidi*, **9a,** 207, 1972.
109. C. N. R. Rao and G. V. Subba Rao, "Transition Metal Oxides," *NSRDS–NBS Monograph* 49, National Bureau of Standards, Washington, D.C., 1974.
110. A. McConnell, J. S. Anderson, and C. N. R. Rao, *Spectrochim. Acta,* **32a,** 1067, 1976.

CHAPTER

FOUR

VARIOUS KINDS OF PHASE TRANSITIONS

4-1 Nucleation and Growth in Phase Transitions
Critical size of nuclei
Effect of temperature on nucleation rate
Influence of strain on nucleation
Growth of phases during transitions (phase propagation)
Rate equations for phase transitions
Order–disorder approach to kinetics

4-2 Martensitic Transitions
Characteristics of martensitic transitions
Thermodynamics of martensitic transitions
Kinetics of martensitic transitions
Crystallography of martensitic transitions
Typical systems undergoing martensitic transitions

4-3 Order–Disorder Transitions
Kinds of order–disorder transitions
Thermodynamics and kinetics of order–disorder transitions
Experimental methods
Examples of order–disorder transitions
Other types of disorder

4-4 Spinodal Decompositions
The concept of a spinodal
Decomposition inside the spinodal
Examples of spinodal decompositions

4-5 Eutectoid Decompositions

4-6 Transitions in Glasses
Nature of the glass transition
Crystallization of glasses and melts
Switching transitions

4-7 Mesophases
Transitions in mesophases
Thermodynamic aspects

4-8 Transitions in Organic Solids

In this chapter we shall discuss different kinds of transitions which are distinguished by specific phenomena or mechanisms associated with them. Thus, we discuss the kinetics of transformations of a large class of solid state transitions which proceed through the mechanism of nucleation and growth. Similarly, we review martensitic transitions which are accompanied by characteristic crystallographic effects. The subject of disordering transitions, both positional and orientational, is presented concisely without ignoring any relevant aspect. For each kind of transition, a number of illustrative examples are given. We close the chapter with brief presentations of spinoidal and eutectoid decompositions, glass transitions, liquid crystal transitions, and transitions in organic solids.

4-1 NUCLEATION AND GROWTH IN PHASE TRANSITIONS

The study of rates of transformations and factors that influence the rates constitutes the subject of kinetics. Generally, phase transformations are extremely slow at the thermodynamic equilibrium temperatures and take place at measurable rates only after a certain degree of undercooling. A large majority of polymorphic transformations, and transformations involving simple decompositions into two-phase regions, are described by a process known as nucleation and growth, in which the nuclei of a new phase are first formed at a particular rate, followed by the propagation of the new phase at a faster rate. Irriversible transformations of metastable phases to stable phases, as in the case of anatase–rutile and white–gray tin transformations referred to in Sec. 2-5, also generally occur by the nucleation and growth mechanism. We shall now consider the kinetics of phase transitions involving the nucleation and growth mechanism.

For convenience, let us define the temperature at which the free energies of two phases are equal as T_0; T_0 is then the true thermodynamic transition temperature. In the immediate vicinity of this temperature, either while heating (to obtain the high-temperature phase) or while cooling (to obtain the low-temperature phase) and just before the new phase begins to appear, the positions of all the atoms correspond to those of the parent phase (the initial phase undergoing the transformation). The formation of the new phase is caused by fluctuations due to thermal agitations which bring the atoms to new positions corresponding to the product phase. A large number of such fluctuations are unstable, since they are below a certain critical size (volume) and they cause a net increase of free energy.[1-5] Such an unstable minute region of the product phase is known as an "embryo" of the new phase. When the sizes of embryos exceed a minimum critical size, they are capable of continued existence and are called "nuclei" of the product phase. The process of formation of the nuclei is known as nucleation. The "growth" of nuclei requires transfer of atoms from the material in the interface on to these nuclei of the product phase. Most phase changes occur by the growth of a limited number of nuclei. Nucleation is common to all types of solid state transformations.

Critical Size of Nuclei

Depending upon the nature of the material and the phase change involved, two types of nucleation may be distinguished: (*a*) homogeneous, and (*b*) heterogeneous. Homogeneous nucleation takes place when all volume elements of the parent phase are chemically, energetically, and structurally identical. Homogeneous nucleation is therefore an inherently random phenomenon. Since most of the solids contain a variety of defects like vacancies, impurities, dislocations, grain boundaries, and so on, perfectly homogeneous nucleation never occurs;[6] instead, preferred nucleation takes place at defect centers for reasons which will be discussed later. Such preferred nonrandom nucleation is referred to as heterogeneous nucleation. Theoretically, however, heterogeneous nucleation can be treated as an extension of the theory of homogeneous nucleation.[7] The latter was originally developed in the context of vapor condensation in the studies of Volmer and Weber[1] and of Becker and Doring[2] (VWBD). The theory has been modified to include the effect of factors specific to condensed phases,[7] but it is generally referred to as the VWBD theory.

Formation of product-phase nuclei in solids at the transition temperature is caused by the presence of thermal fluctuations. In single-component systems the composition of such nuclei is identical to that of the parent phase, but the sizes and shapes of the nuclei are different. This is a basic assumption of the VWBD theory. During the formation of nuclei, differences in shapes, sizes, and specific volumes create new surfaces, stresses, and strains. Therefore, nuclei will form only if the net free energy change during their formation is negative. Otherwise, the unstable embryo dissolves into the parent phase.

Let us assume that there is no difference between the specific volumes of the parent and the product phases and hence no strain at the interface. Furthermore, we shall assume that the interfacial energy between the two phases is γ and that γ is independent of crystallographic directions. We shall now examine how to calculate the rate of nucleation.

The change in free energy, ΔG, due to the formation of spherical nuclei consists of two terms: (*a*) the bulk free energy decrease per unit volume, ΔG_v, and (*b*) the surface free energy increase per unit area of the surface, γ. If the radius of a spherical embryo is r, then ΔG may be written as equal to

$$\Delta G = -\frac{4\pi}{3} r^3 \Delta G_v + 4\pi r^2 \gamma \tag{4-1}$$

Clearly, for small r, the second term will dominate (it is positive while the first term is negative) and the embryo will therefore be thermodynamically unstable. However, if the embryo attains a critical size of radius r_c, ΔG will begin to decrease and further growth will be thermodynamically favorable. In Fig. 4-1, the variation of ΔG with r is plotted for different temperatures. At T_0, the true transition temperature, ΔG is always positive and no nucleation can occur. That is, a phase transformation can never occur at the true transition temperature. A little supercooling and (theoretically speaking) a little superheating are always necessary for

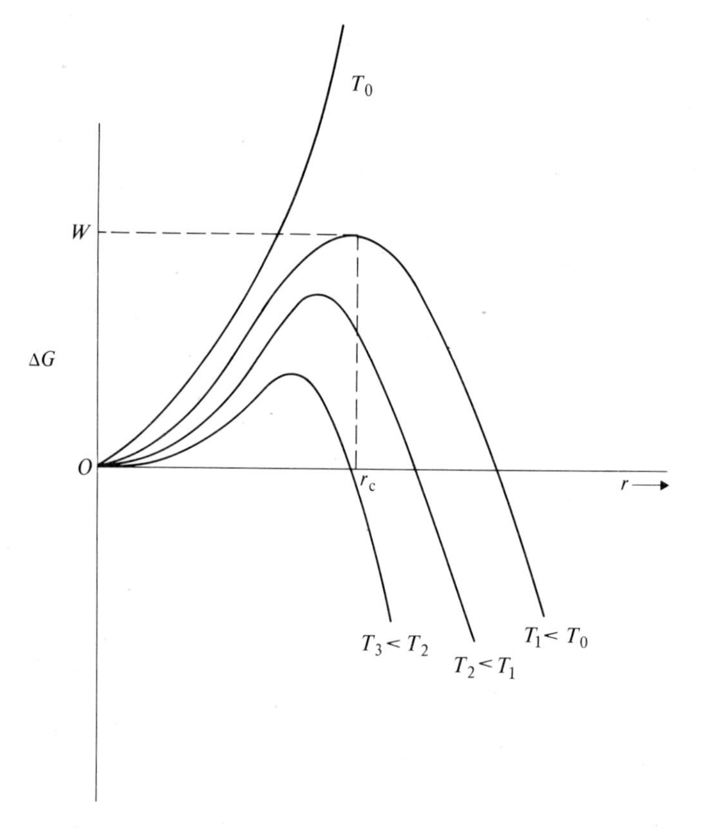

Figure 4-1 Variation of nucleation barrier ΔG as a function of radius for various temperatures (schematic).

the transformations to occur.* Let r_c be the critical radius (known as critical nucleus size) and ΔG_c the critical excess free energy. We can obtain r_c and ΔG_c by letting $(\partial \Delta G/\partial r)$ be equal to zero.

$$r_c = 2\gamma/\Delta G_v \tag{4-2}$$

$$\Delta G_c = \frac{16}{3}\frac{\pi\gamma^3}{\Delta G_v^2} \tag{4-3}$$

Equation (4-3) is a restatement of the fact that no stable nucleus of the product phase can form at T_0 because $\Delta G_c = \infty$.

The rate of nucleation is the number of nuclei that appear per unit volume of the parent per unit time. If there are N sites per unit volume of the parent and

* T_0 lies between T_f and T_r, where T_f and T_r are transformation temperatures in the forward and reverse directions. This accounts for the phenomenon of thermal hysteresis discussed in Chap. 2.

if n_r denotes the embryos of radius r present, the equilibrium constant K is written as

$$K = \frac{n_r}{N} \tag{4-4}$$

K is related to ΔG of Eq. (4-1) by the standard thermodynamic equation[8]

$$K = \frac{n_r}{N} = \exp(-\Delta G/kT)$$

or

$$n_r = N \exp(-\Delta G/kT) \tag{4-5}$$

For embryos of critical size we have the expression

$$n_c = N \exp(-\Delta G_c/kT) \tag{4-6}$$

A critical-sized embryo grows into a nucleus by the jump of a few atoms across the interface. If an activation energy E_a governs such a jump, the rate of interface movement will be proportional to $\exp(-E_a/kT)$. Let there be n_s^* atoms in the interface around the embryo of critical size. If the vibrational frequency of these atoms is ν and the probability that an atom in the interface is vibrating in the direction of the embryo is p, the frequency with which atoms get transferred on to the critical-sized embryo (which is identical to the rate at which the critical sized embryos stabilize into nuclei) is given by

$$n_s^* \nu p \exp(-E_a/kT)$$

The critical-sized embryo may revert to parent-phase structure, and the nuclei themselves may shrink, shedding the atoms away. We can now write the nucleation rate, R, as a product of the numbers of critical-sized embryos and the probability of their conversion to nuclei.

$$\begin{aligned} R &= N \exp(-\Delta G_c/kT) n_s^* \nu p \exp(-E_a/kT) \\ &= A \exp[-(\Delta G_c + E_a)/kT] \end{aligned} \tag{4-7}$$

Heterogeneous nucleation differs from homogeneous nucleation because of preferred sites where the nucleation begins. If impurities or defects are themselves randomly distributed and are in sufficiently large numbers compared to n_c, the only modification will be in γ which will be determined by three terms, the interfaces between defect, parent, and product phases. If γ is replaced by γ_m, then Eq. (4-3) will be valid for the free energy of formation of heterogeneous nuclei.

Effect of Temperature on Nucleation Rate

Let us examine how the nucleation rate is affected by temperature. The temperature dependence[4] of R arises from either A (which contains n^*) or ΔG_c or E_a. Even if n^* should vary, its influence would be very small since it is buried in the pre-exponential term. Since E_a is reasonably constant, it guarantees that R goes to zero at absolute zero of temperature. The behavior of ΔG_c is described by Eq. (4-3) which is itself a function of ΔG_v and γ. To a first approximation, dependence of γ on temperature may be ignored. Dependence of ΔG_v on temperature in the neighborhood of T_0 is fairly linear; that is, $\Delta G_v \propto (T_0 - T)$ (the extent of undercooling). Therefore, ΔG_c is proportional to $(T_0 - T)^{-2}$. Hence, it is guaranteed that at $T = T_0$, R goes to zero in Eq. (4-7). At some temperature, T_m, between T_0 and 0 K, a maximum occurs in the nucleation rate. We can obtain T_m by setting $(\partial \ln R/\partial T)_{T=T_m} = 0$.

$$T_m = (\Delta G_c + E_a)\left[\frac{\partial \Delta G_c}{\partial T}\right]^{-1}_{T=T_m} \tag{4-8}$$

We can obtain $(\partial \Delta G_c/\partial T)$ from a plot of ΔG_c versus temperature. The behavior of R with temperature is shown schematically in Fig. 4-2.

We have assumed hitherto that there is a steady-state concentration of embryos which is instantaneously attained. Normally, in any relatively fast experiment, the distribution of embryos must reestablish a characteristic equilibrium, both in numbers and sizes. This takes a time known as "incubation time" during which no transformation occurs. In many isothermal transformations the presence of incubation times is a common feature. Another important consequence of nucleation theory is the phenomenon of "reversion" or "retrogression."[3,4]

Let us consider a transformation conducted at a temperature $T_2 < T_0$. Let the critical radius for the nuclei be r_{c2}. After a short time, an average nucleus will have grown to a size r (say). If we now reheat the sample fairly fast to a temperature T_1 such that $T_2 < T_1 < T_0$, a new kind of nuclei with critical radius r_{c1} will begin to form. But we know from Fig. 4-1 that $r_{c1} > r_{c2}$. If r is greater

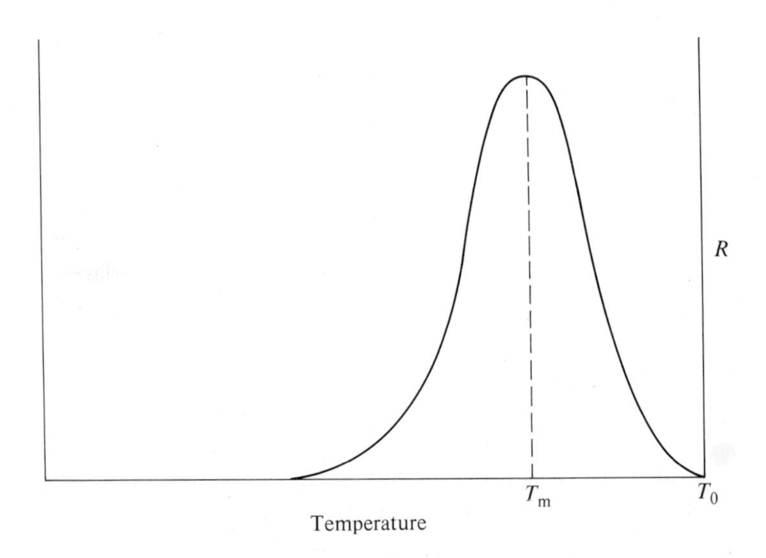

Figure 4-2 Variation of the rate of nucleation as a function of temperature (schematic).

than r_{c2}, then the previously formed nuclei will continue to grow. If $r < r_{c2}$, such a nucleus is unstable at T_1 and so it dissolves and a new equilibrium will have to be established. This is the process of redissolution or reversion.

Influence of Strain on Nucleation

We have so far assumed that the specific volumes of the parent and the product phases are the same and therefore that no strains are developed as a result of mismatch, incoherence, or disregistry. But most transitions in the solid state are associated with volume changes, and hence lattice strains develop because of disregistry across coherent and semicoherent interfaces. It would therefore be incorrect to assume a spherical embryo formation with identical specific volume. An improvement in theory is possible if we assume that n atoms form an embryo with σ as strain energy per unit volume. If υ is the atomic volume in an embryo, Eq. (4-1) then becomes

$$\Delta G = n\upsilon(\Delta G_v + \sigma) + \alpha n^{2/3}\gamma \tag{4-9}$$

where α is a shape factor. If n_c is assumed to be the critical size of the nucleus, n_c and the corresponding ΔG_c can be evaluated by the same procedure as earlier.

In an incoherent interface, as in the case of many of the reconstructive first-order transformations, there is no crystallographic continuity. Since γ is a fairly insensitive term, the strain associated may be considered as simply hydrostatic in nature. If ΔV is the change in volume during the transformation of a volume V of the parent phase, the product phase of volume $(V + \Delta V)$ in the matrix of the parent phase (of volume V) produces the strain. If the parent and product phases are sufficiently soft, then ΔV may be accommodated by a plastic flow. The elastic strain may also be partially annulled by the flow of vacancies toward or away from the point of strain in the stress field that is created by the transformation dilatation. Nabarro[8] has calculated the strain energy per unit volume in cases where the entire strain is accommodated by the parent matrix, assuming different shapes for the product nuclei:

$$\sigma = \tfrac{2}{3}\mu(\Delta)^2 f(c/a) \tag{4-10}$$

where μ is the rigidy modulus of the matrix and Δ is the fractional difference in the volume per atom in the embryo and the matrix and $f(c/a)$ is a function of the spheroidicity, (c/a). In the case of a sphere, $c/a = 1$; $c/a \gg 1$ for a needle, and if $c/a \ll 1$, the product nuclei look like small disks. In Fig. 4-3, a plot of $f(c/a)$ versus c/a is shown. Although the strain energy would be minimum for thin disks, the area per volume for thin disks, being very high, would enhance the surface-energy term in Eq. (4-9). Therefore the optimal shape is one of an oblate spheroid whose volume and surface area are given by

$$\text{Volume} = \tfrac{4}{3}\pi a^2 c \tag{4-11}$$

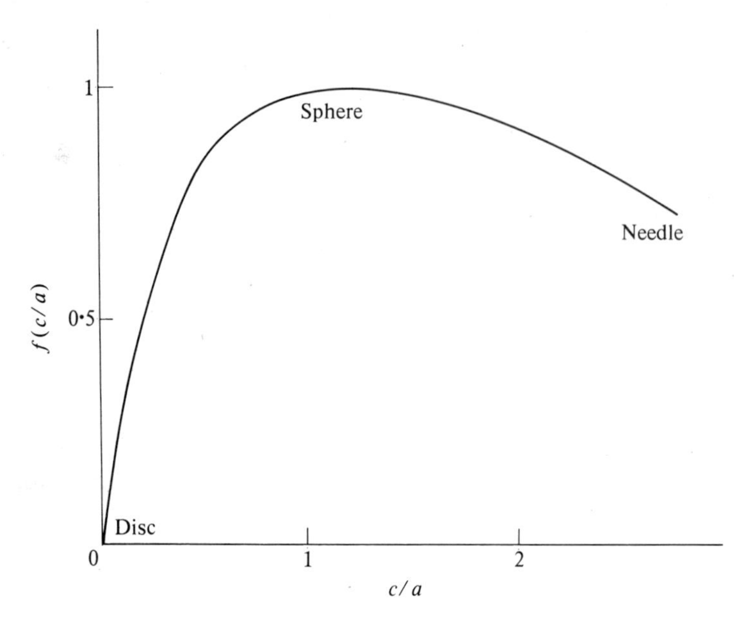

Figure 4-3 Variation of $f(c/a)$. (*After Nabarro.*[8])

$$\text{Area} = \pi a^2 \left[2 + \frac{c^2}{a^2 e} \ln \left(\frac{1+e}{1-e} \right) \right] \tag{4-12}$$

where e is the eccentricity $= (1 - c^2/a^2)^{1/2}$. Using Eqs. (4-9) to (4-12) and setting $(\partial G/\partial X) = 0$, where $X = a$, c, and n, we obtain

$$\Delta G_c = \frac{8\pi}{3} \frac{\pi^3 \mu^2 (\Delta)^4 \gamma^3}{(\Delta G_v)^4} \tag{4-13}$$

This is a powerful function involving both Δ and ΔG_v and hence of undercooling.

Most of the activation energy of a phase transformation is generally utilized in the nucleation process, and hence the nucleation step decides the rate of transformation. Good examples of such behavior may be found in the transitions of calcite[9] and silver sulfate.[10] Factors like dislocations, impurities, etc., markedly affect the nucleation rates. Although several features of solid state transitions like incubation periods, transformation hysteresis, and reversion can be qualitatively understood from the nucleation theory, quantitative agreement is rather poor, the predicted values of ΔG_c differing widely from the experimental values. This is probably due to the assumption that the properties of the embryo are completely describable in terms of the measured bulk properties.

Growth of Phases During Transitions (Phase Propagation)

Phase transformations proceed toward completion by the "growth" or propagation of the critical-sized nuclei of the product phase. In order to achieve this growth, atoms have to be transferred across an interface between the product and parent phases. In a simple situation, we can understand the growth of a phase by assuming that no complications arise because of the lack of coherency at the interface. If we consider the growth to be achieved through an atom-by-atom transfer across the interface[4,11] between two phases I and II, the diffusion barrier seen by the atoms diffusing across the interface may be represented by Fig. 4-4. Here, G_a^{12} and G_a^{21} are the free energies of activation for the atoms to cross the interface from I to II and II to I respectively, and ΔG is the change in free energy of the atom upon transfer. The number of atoms of phase I leaving unit area of interface per unit time may be written as

$$p_1 n_1 A_2 \nu_1 \exp(-G_a^{12}/kT) \tag{4-14}$$

where n_1 is the number of atoms per unit area of I in the interface, ν_1 is the frequency of vibration of the atom, p_1 ($\simeq \frac{1}{6}$) is the probability that a vibration is directed toward the II nucleus, and A_2 is the accommodation coefficient for the II nucleus, i.e., the fraction of the total number of sites on the surface where atoms can be accommodated by the growing lattice. Similarly the number of atoms leaving II per unit area is

$$p_2 n_2 A_1 \nu_2 \exp(-G_a^{21}/kT) \tag{4-15}$$

wherein the symbols have the same meaning but refer to phase II. The net rate of accumulation of atoms on the surface of phase II is obtained by the difference of (4-14) and (4-15):

$$p_1 n_1 A_2 \nu_1 \exp(-G_a^{12}/kT) - p_2 n_2 A_1 \nu_2 \exp(-G_a^{21}/kT) \tag{4-16}$$

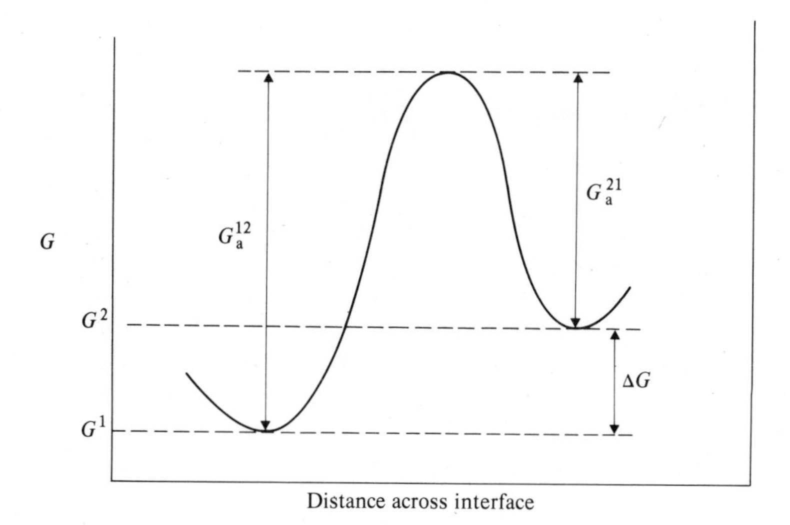

Figure 4-4 Diffusion barriers across the interface for growth of nuclei (schematic).

The rate of advance of the interface, (dR_p/dt), is the product of (4-16) and the volume of one atom in II which we shall designate as λ. We shall make some simplifications: $n_1 \simeq n_2 \simeq n$; $v_1 \simeq v_2 \simeq v$; and $p_1 \simeq p_2 \simeq p$. In polymorphic transformations, the accommodation coefficients may also be set equal. We can thus write

$$\frac{dR_p}{dt} = \lambda pnvA[\exp(-G_a^{12}/kT) - \exp(-G_a^{21}/kT)] \tag{4-17}$$

At the equilibrium temperature T_0, dR_p/dt is zero because $G_a^{12} = G_a^{21}$. At any other temperature, where $G_a^{12} = G_a^{21} - \Delta G$, we have for dR_p/dt,

$$\begin{aligned}\frac{dR_p}{dt} &= \lambda pnvA\left[\exp(-G_a^{12}/kT) - \exp\left(-\frac{G_a^{12} - \Delta G}{kT}\right)\right] \\ &= \lambda pnvA \exp(-G_a^{12}/kT)[1 - \exp(-\Delta G/kT)]\end{aligned} \tag{4-18}$$

For small undercooling, $\Delta G \ll kT$, so that the exponential term may be expanded and the terms higher than the first order neglected:

$$\frac{dR_p}{dt} = \lambda pnvA \exp\left(-\frac{G_a^{12}}{kT}\right)\frac{\Delta G}{kT} \tag{4-19}$$

In order to evaluate ΔG, we note that there is a slight and almost a linear increase in it on undercooling. Since $\Delta G = \Delta H - T\Delta S$, we can assume that ΔH and ΔS are independent of temperature in this region. Furthermore, since $\Delta G = 0$ at the equilibrium temperature T_0, we have $\Delta S = \Delta H/T_0$. Therefore, we can write for ΔG,

$$\Delta G = \Delta H - \frac{\Delta HT}{T_0} = \frac{\Delta H}{T_0}(T_0 - T) \tag{4-20}$$

Equation (4-19) now becomes

$$\frac{dR_p}{dt} = \lambda pnvA \exp\left(-\frac{G_a^{12}}{kT}\right)\frac{\Delta H \Delta T}{kTT_0}$$

or more simply

$$u = \frac{dR_p}{dt} = \lambda pnvA \exp\left(-\frac{G_a^{12}}{kT}\right)\frac{\Delta S \Delta T}{kT} \tag{4-21}$$

An important feature of Eq. (4-21) is that the growth rate should exhibit a maximum at some undercooling because of the dual presence of T. In fact, Hartshorne[13] has derived a similar expression by considering the activation barrier as a simple energy term, and obtained the expression for the linear rate of growth, u,

$$u = \tfrac{1}{2}A_\alpha \exp\left(\frac{-E_a}{kT}\right)\left\{1 - \exp\left[\frac{q}{k}\left(\frac{1}{T_0} - \frac{1}{T}\right)\right]\right\} \tag{4-22}$$

Equation (4-22) simplifies for small values of q, the heat of transformation, and at low values of undercooling ($T \sim T_0$) to

$$u = \tfrac{1}{2}A_\alpha\left(-\frac{\Delta G}{kT}\right)\exp\left(-\frac{E_a}{kT}\right)$$

which is identical to Eq. (4-19) with A_α containing all the constants. The applicability of Eq. (4-22) has been checked recently in the case of transitions of sulfur.[14] The linear growth-rate law has been found to hold good in the case of $AgNO_3$ transition[15] (trigonal to orthorhombic) in the low-temperature region (300–370 K), but it fails at higher temperatures. Although expression (4-21) is oversimplified, it gives us an idea of the kinds of parameters that control growth rates in transformations. In a real transformation, this analysis may not hold good for various reasons, the principal one being the presence of a latent heat which will not allow a constant temperature throughout the matrix.

Rate Equations for Phase Transitions

Having considered the rates of nucleation and growth separately, we can obtain the expression for the rate of a phase transition. The total rate of a transition, I → II, is dependent upon both nucleation and growth rates. As the phase II grows inside the matrix of I, the growth continues until such time as phase I impinges on a growth barrier like domains or free surfaces. The total rate may be written as dx/dt, where x is the fraction of I which has transformed into II in time t. If the nucleation and the growth rates are combined with due correction for impingement of transformed domains, we get the rate expression,[7] $x = f(t)$. If the growth rate is time-independent, then the volume V of the II domain after a time τ (after nucleation) may be written as

$$V = gu^3(t - \tau)^3 \tag{4-23}$$

where g is a shape factor and t is the total time taken for transformation. If the effect of impingement of domains is disregarded, the total volume of all the II domains which grow during transformation may be calculated as

$$\chi_{ex} = \int_0^t VR\,d\tau = gu^3\int_0^t (t - \tau)^3 R\,d\tau \tag{4-24}$$

χ_{ex} is known as the "extended" volume which includes the volume contributed by the "phantom" domains which would nucleate in domains already transformed. The real transformed volume fraction χ is related to χ_{ex} by the relation

$$\chi = 1 - \exp(-\chi_{ex}) \tag{4-25}$$

This relation was obtained by Avrami.[16] Substituting for χ_{ex} and carrying out the integration assuming R also to be time-independent, one gets

$$\chi = 1 - \exp\left[-gu^3 \int_0^t R(t-\tau)^3\, d\tau\right]$$
$$= 1 - \exp\left(-\frac{gu^3Rt^4}{4}\right) \qquad (4\text{-}26)$$

Generally, R is not time-independent, and

$$\chi = 1 - \exp(-kt^n) \qquad (4\text{-}27)$$

can adequately describe the kinetics with $3 \le n \le 4$ for R decreasing with t, and $n > 4$ for R increasing with t. The above expression has been used in the study of isothermal transformation kinetics of a number of materials. Equation (4-27) is frequently referred to as the Avrami equation or Johnson and Mehl equation;[17] a similar relation was also obtained by Erofeev.[18,19]

Equation (4-27) is also obtained by the integration of the empirical rate expression,[4]

$$\frac{dx}{dt} = kt^{n-1}(1-x)n$$

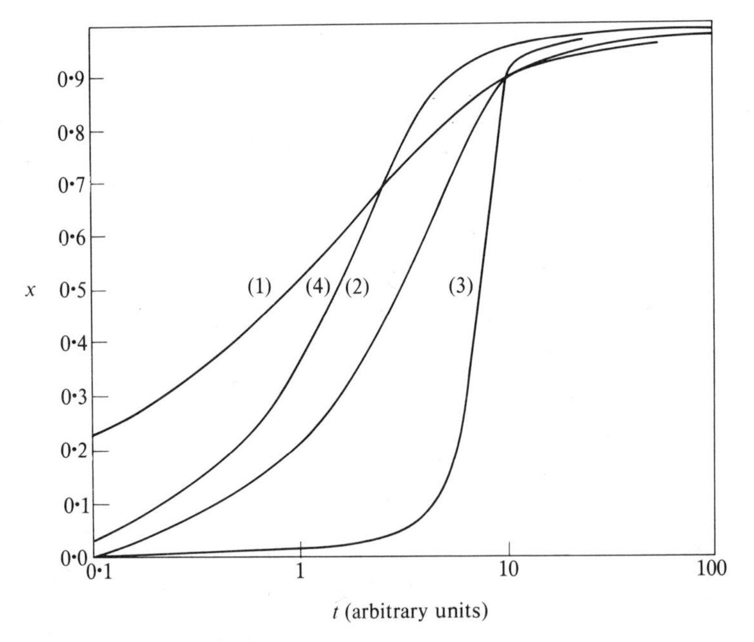

Figure 4-5 Transformation kinetics from Avrami expression. Curves (1), (2), and (3) have same value of k and $n = \frac{1}{2}$, $n = 1$, and $n = 4$ respectively. Curve (4) has $n = 1$ and k half the value of the other curves. (*After Burke.*[4])

Table 4-1 Values of exponent n for the Avrami equation in various cases

	n
Polymorphic or diffusionless or cellular transformations:	
(*a*) Nucleation only at the start of transformation	3
(*b*) Nucleation at constant rate	4
(*c*) Nucleation at increasing rate	4
(*d*) Nucleation at start plus continuing nucleation at grain edges	2
(*e*) Nucleation at start plus continuing nucleation at grain boundaries	1
Diffusion-controlled transformations:	
(*a*) Initial growth of particles nucleated only at the start of transformation	1.5
(*b*) Initial growth of particles nucleated at constant rate	2.5
(*c*) Growth of isolated plates or needles of finite size	1
(*d*) Thickening of plates after their edges have impinged	$\frac{1}{2}$

where $(1 - x)$ may be regarded as the allowance for the impingement effect; here, k is a rate constant parameter and n the time exponent. Both these are good experimental parameters for kinetic studies, with k taking any positive value. In Fig. 4-5, typical variations of x with t are shown. Values of n and k are obtained from Eq. (4-27) by plotting log log $[1/(1 - x)]$ versus log t:

$$\log \log \left(\frac{1}{1-x}\right) = n \log t + n \log k - \log 2.3 \qquad (4\text{-}28)$$

We see that n is given by the slope and k from the intercept. From Eq. (4-27) we also see that $1/k = t^n$ when $x = 1 - 1/e = 0.6321$, so that k is directly obtained from x versus t plots. When $n = 1$, the Avrami equation represents a situation similar to first-order kinetics. For higher values of n, the x–t curves have a sigmoidal

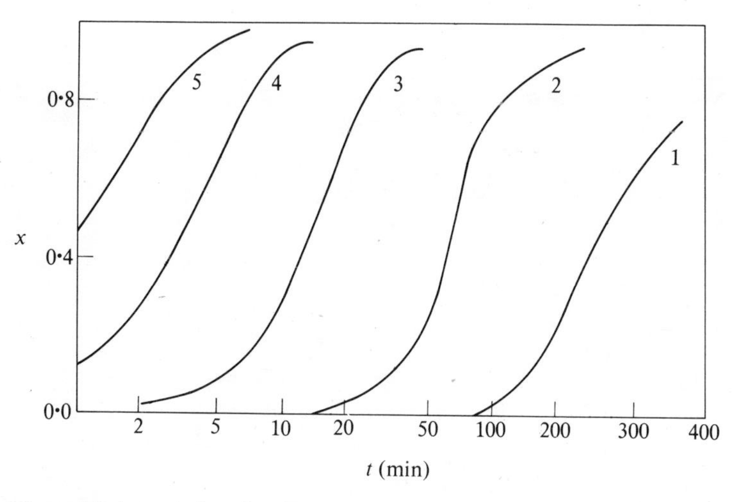

Figure 4-6 Avrami plots for the transformation of gray tin: 1, 298 K; 2, 300.5 K; 3, 303 K; 4, 305.5 K; 5, 308 K. (*After Burgers and Groen.*[20])

shape with a central region where the rate is highest. Two major types of transformations may be treated by the application of the Avrami equation. To one category belong diffusion-controlled transformations such as solid state precipitations, and to the other, diffusionless or cellular transformations typified by polymorphic transitions. In Table 4-1, values of n are listed for a few types of transformation.[3,4]

In the literature, a large number of phase transitions have been investigated by the use of the Avrami equation. Thus, Burgers and Groen[20] investigated the kinetics of white–gray tin transformation employing the Avrami treatment. In Fig. 4-6 the fraction transformed of the gray tin, x, is plotted as a function of time at various temperatures showing the sigmoidal characteristic. The value of n for the white–gray tin transition was 3, while for the gray–white transition it was 1.5–2. The former is consistent with formation of nuclei at the beginning of the

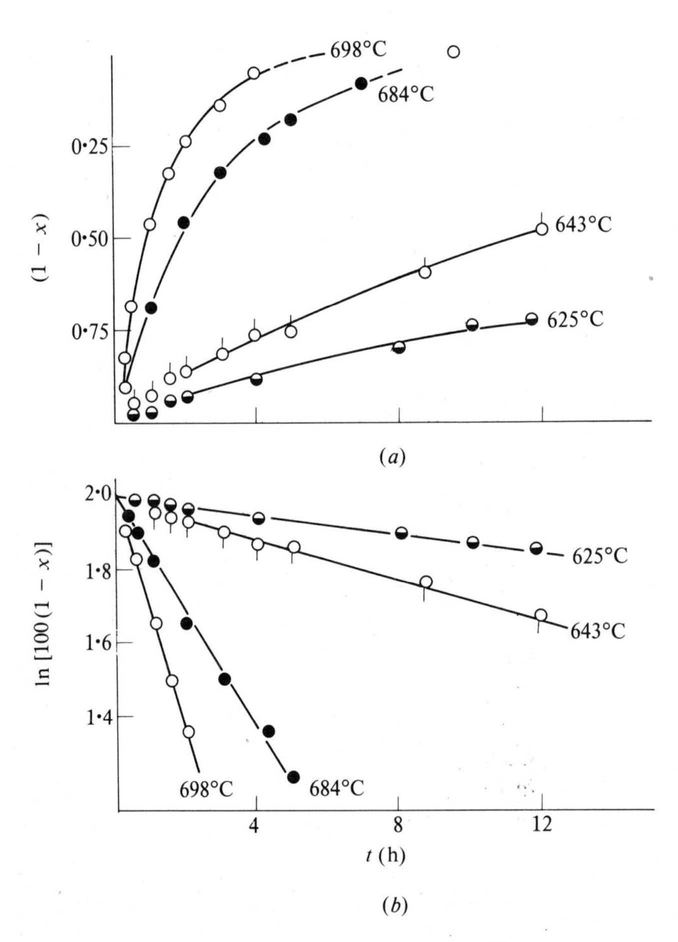

Figure 4-7 First-order rate data on the transformation of spectroscopically pure anatase to rutile. (*After Rao.*[22])

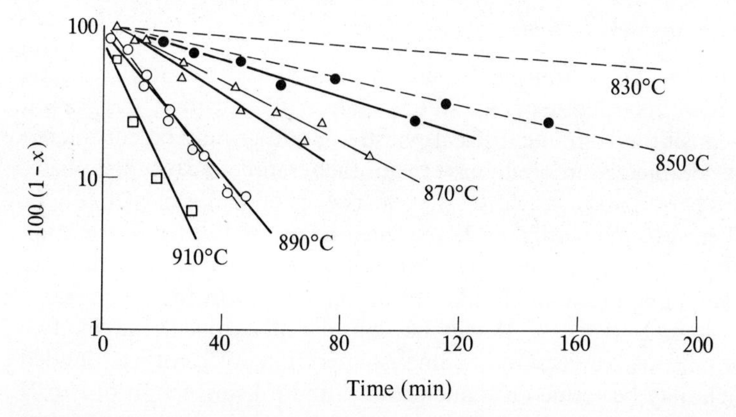

Figure 4-8 First-order plot of the transformation of GeO_2 (catalyst 1 percent Li_2CO_3). Atmosphere: (*a*) dry oxygen (solid line), (*b*) wet oxygen (dotted line). (*After Kotera and Yonemura.*[23])

transformation only. In the reverse transition, the continuing nucleation at the grain edges determine the kinetics. Kinetics of the first-order type are exhibited by anatase–rutile and brookite–rutile transformations[21,22] of TiO_2, as typified by the data in Fig. 4-7. Figure 4-8 gives another example of first-order kinetics seen in the hexagonal to tetragonal transition[23] of GeO_2.* The Avrami plot for the III → IV transition of NH_4NO_3 is given in Fig. 4.9; in this study, the following approximate relation has been used:

$$\frac{dx}{dt} = nkt^{n-1}\, e^{-kt^n} \simeq kx^a(1 - x)^b$$

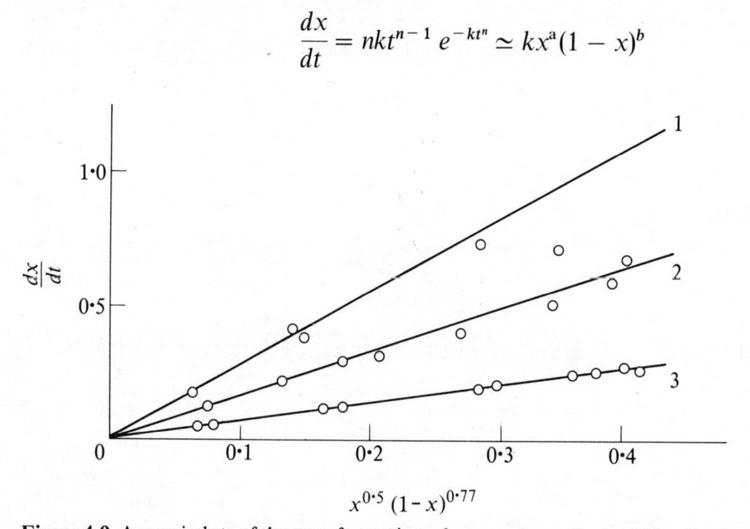

Figure 4-9 Avrami plots of the transformation of ammonium nitrate. (*After Erofeev and Mitskevich.*[19])

* An interesting study of the pressure effect on the kinetics of polymorphic transitions has been carried out by Zeto and Roy[24] on this material. Their results indicate that the nucleation is instantaneous and that there are two kinds of growth processes. One type of growth was enhanced and the other type hindered by pressure. The extrapolated activation energy for transformation was, however, very much different from that of Kotera and Yonemura.[23]

Order–Disorder Approach to Kinetics

Kinetics of diffusionless phase transitions have been analyzed by Honig[25,26] by using notions of order–disorder theory and the formalism of nucleation and growth theory. A phase transition from one distinct phase to another may be considered as going from one completely ordered phase to another completely ordered phase. During the process of transition, however, the coexistence of phases in each other's matrix may be likened to a disordered phase. Thus the process of transformation consists of the growth of one species at the expense of the other passing through a state of what may be approximately likened to maximum disorder. The transformation from phase I to phase II can be considered as occurring by two routes: (*a*) a spontaneous conversion of some isolated units of I not surrounded by II into II, which may be termed as "nucleation," and (*b*) conversion of I to II at I–II interfaces, where activation energy for conversion is likely to be low ("propagation" step). Both nucleation and propagation are characterized by rate constants k_n and k_p.

Let us suppose that at some critical stage of transformation the concentration of isolated I sites is x and that of associated (with II) I sites is y. We shall designate the concentration of isolated II sites by z. The rate of transformation may be written as the rate of decrease of x:

$$-\frac{dx}{dt} = k_n x + k_p y \tag{4-29}$$

Assuming the applicability of lattice statistics, Honig establishes a relation between x and y because in a lattice their concentrations are not independent. x, y, and z are thus related by

$$\frac{xz}{y^2} = C \tag{4-30}$$

It is further assumed that

$$y = \frac{-1 - \sqrt{1 + 4(C - 1)x(1 - x)}}{2(C - 1)} \tag{4-31}$$

in close similarity to order–disorder equilibria. Using the relation (4-31), Eq. (4-29) is written as,

$$-\frac{1}{k_n}\frac{dx}{dt} = x + \frac{Zk_p}{k_n}\,\frac{-1 - \sqrt{1 + 4(C - 1)x(1 - x)}}{2(C - 1)} \tag{4-32}$$

where Z is the lattice coordination number for the I species.

Equation (4-32) is the rate expression from Honig's order–disorder approach. It has been integrated numerically for assumed values of C and k_p/k_n and the variation of x with $k_n t$ examined. Figure 4-10 gives the plot of x versus $k_n t$ for various values of C for a fixed value of k_p/k_n. Some qualitative conclusions may be arrived at by an examination of such plots. (*a*) Increase of k_n leads to decrease

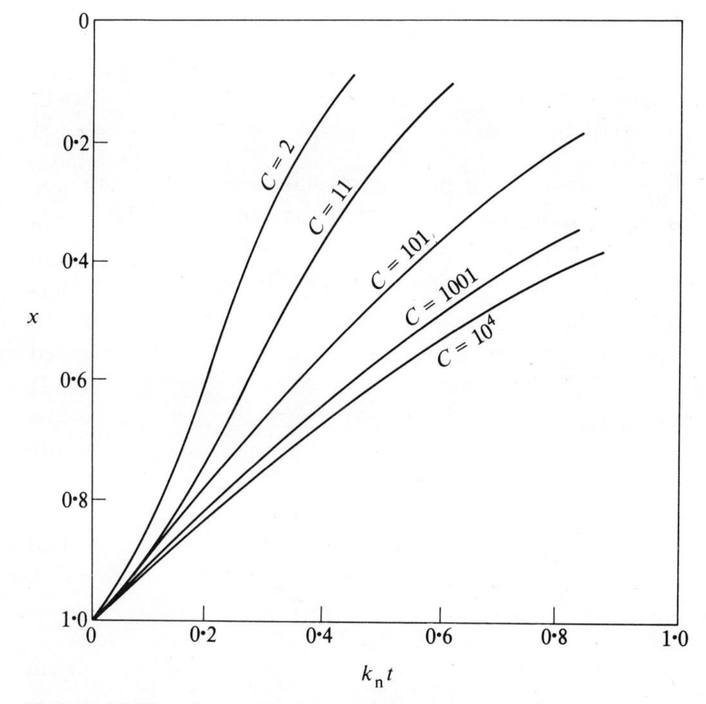

Figure 4-10 Plot of x vs $K_n t$ in order–disorder approach for fixed value of ZK_p/k_n equal to 10. (*After Honig.*[26])

of time, required for the total conversion as it should. (*b*) The shape of the curve is determined by the relative values of C and k_p/k_n. The larger the value of k_p/k_n relative to C, the more sigmoidal the curves become. This is satisfactory because the sigmoidal curves are indicative of autocatalytic behavior and the preponderance of this effect is noticeable only when x and z, and hence C, are small, and k_p (or Zk_p/k_n) is high. (*c*) For fixed values of k_p, the time required for conversion decreases with decreasing C. This is reasonable because, at lower values of x (and z), and hence of C, there is a higher degree of dispersion of the x units, increasing the number of units available for the propagation mechanism.

Equation (4-32) reduces to a linear law when $Zk_p/k_n \ll 1$:

$$-\frac{1}{k_n}\frac{dx}{dt} = x$$

or

$$\ln\frac{1}{x} = k_n t \tag{4-33}$$

Similarly, when $Zk_p/k_n \gg C \gg 1$, one can write Eq. (4-32) as

$$-\frac{1}{k_n}\frac{dx}{dt} = x + \frac{Zk_p}{k_n}\frac{\sqrt{x(1-x)}}{\sqrt{C-1}} \tag{4-34}$$

This equation is valid over all values of x except near zero and unity. Equation (4-34) on integration yields

$$\frac{Zk_p(t - t_0)}{\sqrt{C - 1}} = \cos^{-1}(2x - 1) \tag{4-35}$$

The usefulness of Honig's approach is in providing qualitative explanation for the behavior of diffusionless transitions with minimum reference to the actual mechanism or details of the transition. In fact, x versus $k_n t$ plots from Eq. (4-32) for plausible values of C and Zk_p/k_n are quite comparable to the plots from Avrami equation.[26]

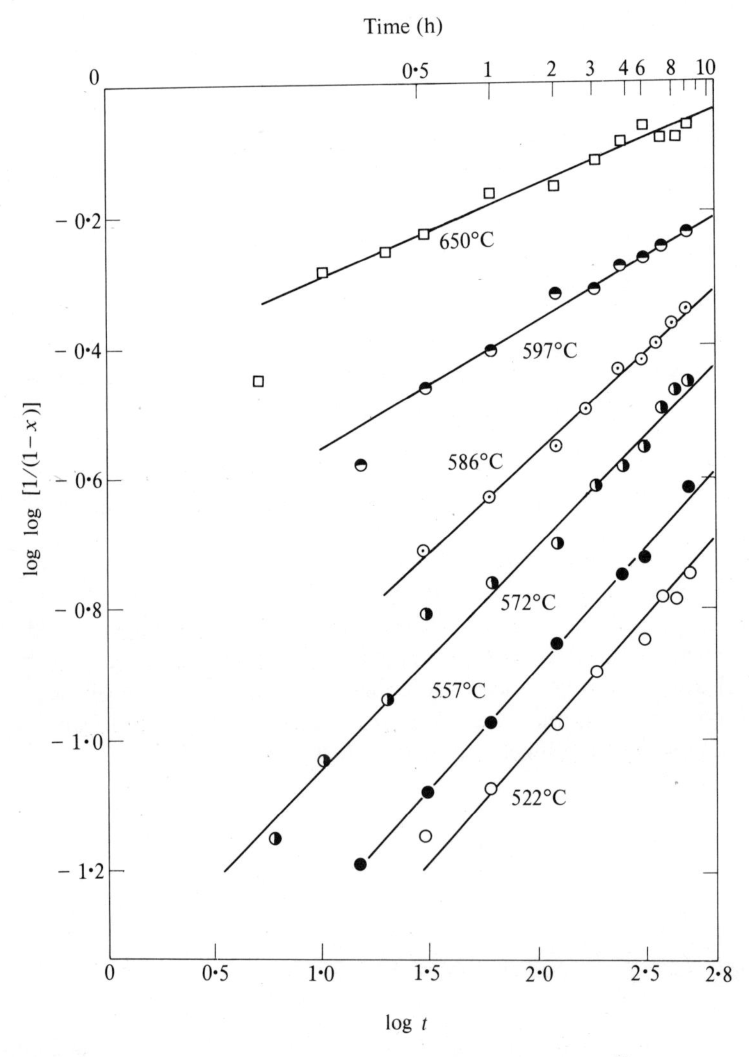

Figure 4-11 Avrami plots for transition of zirconia. (*After Whitney.*[28])

The above equations have been used in the interpretation of kinetic data on many transformations like the transformation in tin[26] and of TiO_2.[21,22,27] An example of the application of the treatments of both Avrami and Honig is found in the investigation of Whitney[28] on the phase-change kinetics of the tetragonal to monoclinic transition of zirconia. In Figs. 4-11 and 4-12, Avrami plots from Eq. (4-28) and Honig plots from Eq. (4-35) for this transition are respectively shown. Both approaches describe the kinetics satisfactorily. Using a further approximation of Honig,[26] namely $C = (1 + k_p/k_n)^2$, the values of Zk_n have been calculated as a function of temperature. In Fig. 4-13 the nucleation rates so obtained are plotted against temperature. Surprisingly, the expression from order–disorder theory also establishes the existence of an expected maximum in the rates of transformation.

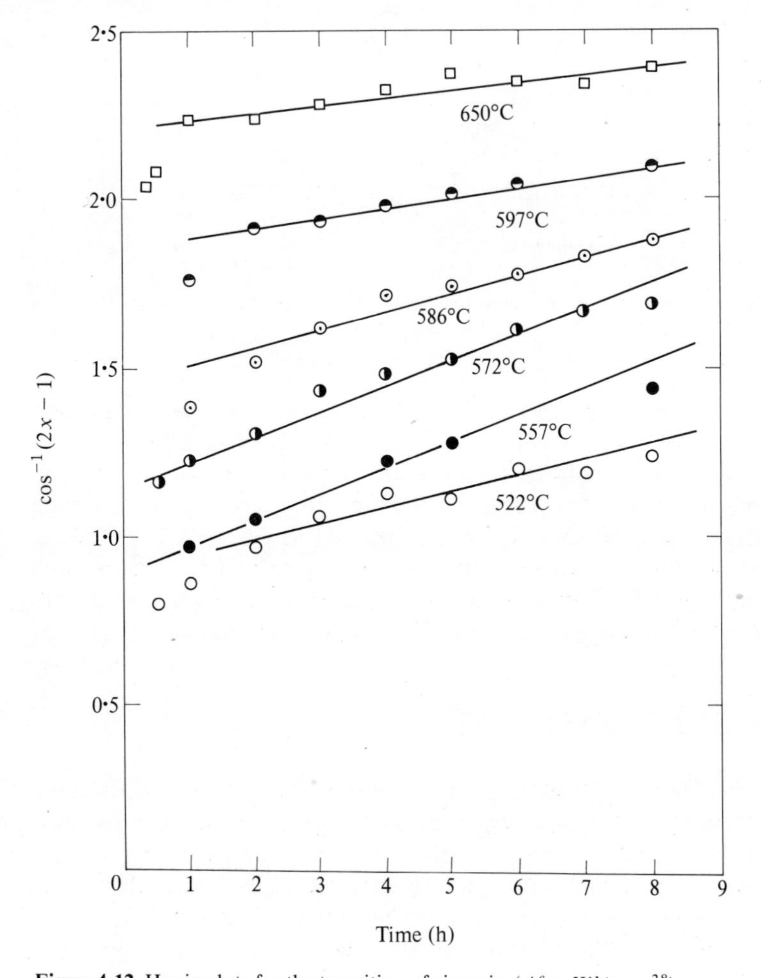

Figure 4-12 Honig plots for the transition of zirconia. (*After Whitney.*[28])

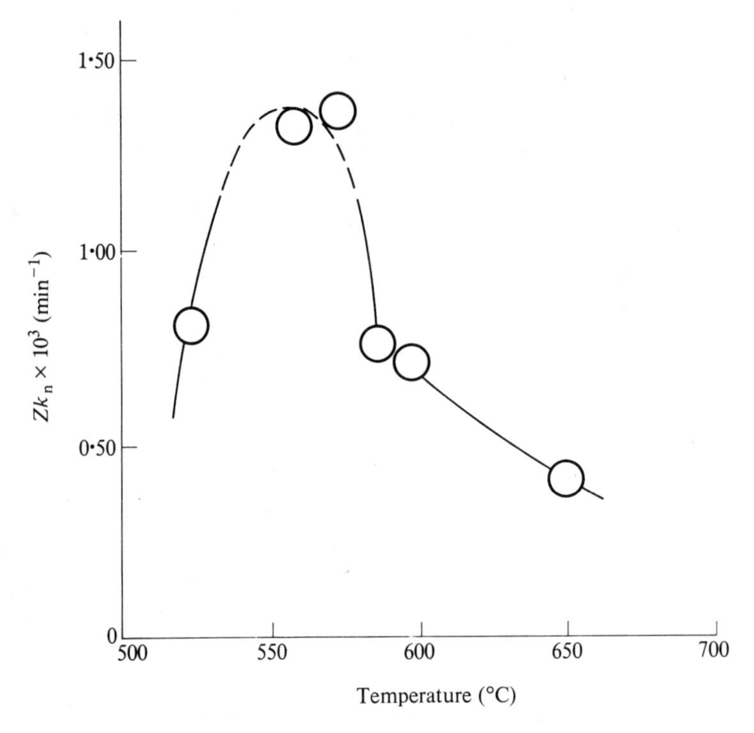

Figure 4-13 Plot of nucleation rates as a function of temperature from order–disorder theory of kinetics. (*After Whitney.*[28])

In the preceding discussions, we have not treated the effect of pressure on the phase transition kinetics, except through Ref. 24. Precious little has been done to investigate pressure effects. Kinetics are generally treated through an equation involving an activation energy, and the pressure effect is sought through the activation barrier ΔG_a which may be decomposed as $\Delta G_a = \Delta E_a + P\Delta V_a - T\Delta S_a$. Interested readers may refer to the work of Eyring and Cagle[29] as well as of Hall[30] and Bundy.[31] Kinetic studies relevant to martensitic and order–disorder transitions are discussed separately in the following sections.

4-2 MARTENSITIC TRANSITIONS

Historically, martensite was the name given to the hard product obtained during the quenching of steels. The name was given in honor of the famous German metallurgist Martens.[32] It was found that the transformation to martensite was associated with certain characteristic structural features. Such features have now been observed in various nonferrous metallic as well as nonmetallic systems. We now regard this class of transformations as martensitic transitions. The study of martensitic transitions is gaining increasing importance in inorganic materials, since the martensitic mechanism provides a general basis for understanding structural changes in many systems (see Sec. 3-4). However, unlike martensitic transitions of metal systems, studies on nonmetallic inorganic systems are rather limited and provide great scope for future investigations. In this section, we shall discuss various features of martensitic transitions along with the thermodynamic, kinetic, and structural aspects in some detail. Although much of the discussion is concerned with the iron system, it would be of value in understanding martensitic transitions in other systems as well.

Characteristics of Martensitic Transitions

As mentioned earlier, martensitic transitions are associated with a number of special features which distinguish them.[32-37] Consider Fig. 4-14, in which a rectangular block of austenite, hereafter referred to as the parent phase, has been partially transformed into a martensite. The section $A_1B_1C_1D_1A_2B_2C_2D_2$ is the transformed martensite plate. The following features are usually and not necessarily[33] associated with this transformation.

(*a*) The transformation occurs through a shearing of discrete volumes of the material. This is evident[34] because the straight-line marking PQRS on the original polished surface is broken into three straight lines PQ, QR′, and R′S′, which nevertheless are (macroscopically) continuous. The continuity also indicates that there is a good match at the interface. The plane surfaces $A_2B_2C_2D_2$ and $A_1'B_1'C_1'D_1'$ remain undistorted and unrotated during the transition. These planes defining the interface between the parent austenite and the transformed martensite are known as the habit planes.[35] These habit planes describe the constant crystallographic orientation relationship between the parent and the martensite phases. Also, the habit plane is usually irrational. The straightness of the edges A_2B_2 and $A_1'B_1'$ indicates the macroscopic homogeneity of the shear in the martensite plate. These rather very

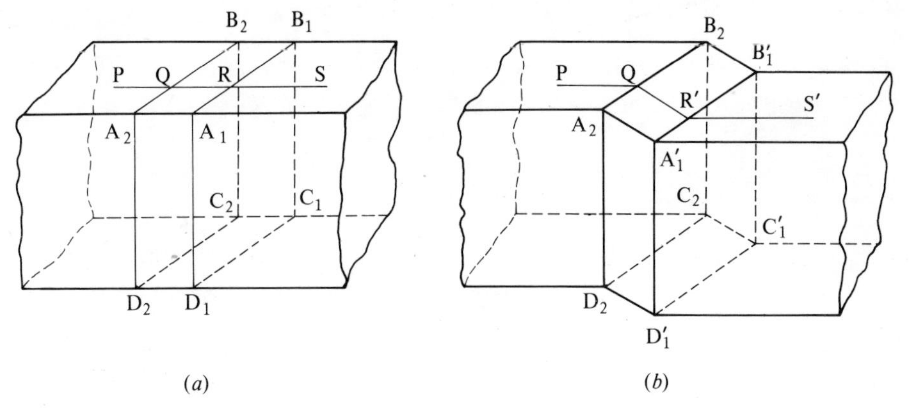

Figure 4-14 Representation of a plate of martensite (*b*), formed from a rectangular block of parent crystal (*a*).

general features of the martensite transitions are utilized in developing the phenomenological crystallographic theories which will be discussed later.

(*b*) These transformations are diffusionless in the sense that no thermally-activated diffusion is required for the growth of the martensite and it is identical to the parent phase in chemical composition. During the transition, the atomic positions in the parent phase change systematically and by distances less than the interatomic distances in the lattice. The systematic aspect of these transitions over macroscopic distances have indeed led to such metaphoric descriptions as "military" transformations.[36]

(*c*) Martensitic transitions often occur with extremely high velocities. The parent martensite interface is glissile. That is, the boundaries can move without any thermal activation.[3] The velocities are sometimes as high as the velocity of sound.[38,39] The transformation kinetics is independent of temperature over wide ranges of temperature, although the total fraction of the parent transformed is a function of the temperature. The transition is either aided or inhibited by applied stresses and strains.[40]

(*d*) A martensite transformation starts on cooling the parent phase at a temperature usually designated[41] as M_s (martensite start). The extent of transformation usually depends on the extent of cooling below M_s. The general behavior of x (the quantity transformed) versus temperature is shown in Fig. 4-15. M_f is the temperature below which no more transformation occurs. Usually the transformation of the entire parent phase will be over by M_f.

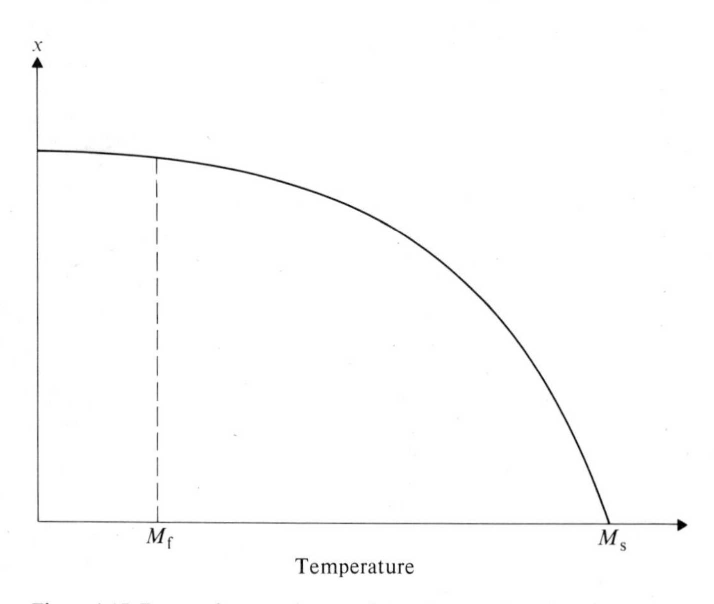

Figure 4-15 Extent of martensite transformation as a function of temperature (schematic).

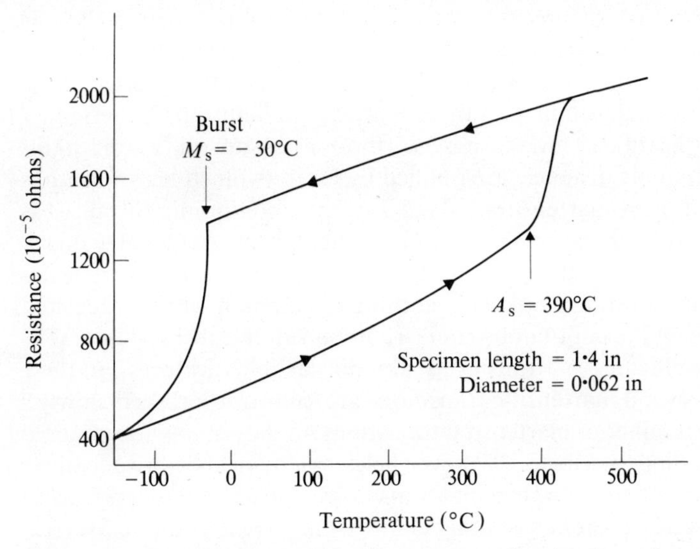

Figure 4-16 Plot of resistivities of Fe–29% Ni alloy as a function of temperature; cooling rate 50°/min. (*After Kauffman and Cohen*;[40] *Shewman.*[42])

(*e*) At any temperature below M_s, plastic deformation increases the quantity of martensite. Deformation of the unstable phase above M_s (but close to M_s) causes transition into the martensite phase. This is true up to a limiting temperature known as M_d which is the highest temperature at which the deformation will give martensite. This effect of deformation is consistent with the shear nature of the transformation.

(*f*) The low-temperature phase that is formed martensitically on cooling reverts to the high-temperature phase on heating well above the M_s temperature. Figure 4-16 is a plot of the resistivities[42] of Fe–29% Ni alloy upon cooling well below M_s (−30°C) and then heating it back. At 390°C, the (bcc) martensite begins to transform back to (fcc) austenite. This temperature is known as A_s (the austenite start temperature). As in the case of martensite, the deformation of austenite helps martensite–austenite transition to start at temperature A_d, which is lower than A_s. Figure 4-16 also shows the behavior of the alloy which is taken through a transition cycle as indicated by the arrows. It appears from the figure that the martensite–austenite transformation can proceed in either direction, given enough heating above or cooling below about 170°C, which means that there is a thermodynamic equilibrium between martensite (bcc α') and austenite (fcc γ) around 170°C.

(*g*) Martensitic transitions are generally polymorphic and are associated with large hysteresis.

None of the above features is, however, unique enough to define a martensitic transition.[33] The occurrence of the habit plane and definite orientation relationship as in (*a*) can be true of precipitations from solid solutions as well. The feature described in (*b*) is also not unique since many martensites in which other features are observed do involve atomic movements greater than the interatomic distances. Indeed, depending on the extent of such diffusion, Lieberman[43] has described a classification of martensites as ortho-martensites (diffusion lengths L less than one interatomic distance, exemplified by fcc to twinned bct transitions in iron-based alloys), para-martensites (where $L \simeq$ one interatomic distance, as in the cubic–twinned ordered orthorhombic structure in AuCu II), quasi-martensites (where $L \gg 1$, as in the β–α transition of brass) and pseudo-martensites (where the mechanisms of transitions have nothing in common with martensites, a typical example being the continuous cubic–rhombohedral transition in GeTe–SnTe alloys). The velocities of transitions are not definite features of these transitions because several martensitic transitions are known to proceed slowly.[3] Also, a considerable number of martensitic transitions are now known to proceed with temperature-dependent kinetics.[40] Nevertheless, many of the above features are usually observed during martensitic transitions. Hence a comprehensive definition of martensitic transitions is rather cumbersome. We may quote Meyrick and Powell,[33] who have recently defined these transitions as follows:

> A martensitic transformation is a structural change generated by atomic displacements and not achieved by diffusion, corresponding to a homogeneous deformation which may be different in small adjacent regions and which gives rise to an invariant plane strain through which the parent and the product are related by a substitutional lattice correspondence, an irrational habit plane and a precise orientation relationship.

Thermodynamics of Martensitic Transitions

Since a martensitic transition is diffusionless, its composition does not vary during the transition. Therefore, the system may be considered as a single component system. In Fig. 4-17 the variation of free energies of α' and γ phases of an alloy like Fe–29% Ni is shown; $G^{\alpha'}$ and G^{γ} intersect at T_0 which is the true transition temperature at which $G^{\alpha'} = G^{\gamma}$ (see Chap. 2). The temperatures marked M_s and A_s are the martensitic and austenitic transition temperatures. At these temperatures the appropriate phases possess enough excess free energy for the transformation to occur. $(A_s - T_0)$ and $(T_0 - M_s)$ are the superheating and the supercooling required to start the transformations to austenite and martensite respectively. Similarly, $(T_0 - M_d)$ is the supercooling necessary for starting martensite transformation under deformation. It should be noted that conversion of austenite (γ phase) to martensite (α' phase) is thermodynamically impossible above T_0. Therefore, M_d cannot be greater than T_0; T_0 is experimentally evaluated[40] as $\frac{1}{2}(M_s + A_s)$. Because of the large hysteresis common to martensitic transitions, it is preferable to narrow down the range by using M_d and A_d data and calculate T_0 as $\frac{1}{2}(M_d + A_d)$. In using this procedure, one makes the assumption that the true T_0 is unaffected by deformations,[40] and this is likely to be incorrect.

The value of T_0 may be calculated theoretically by making some reasonable

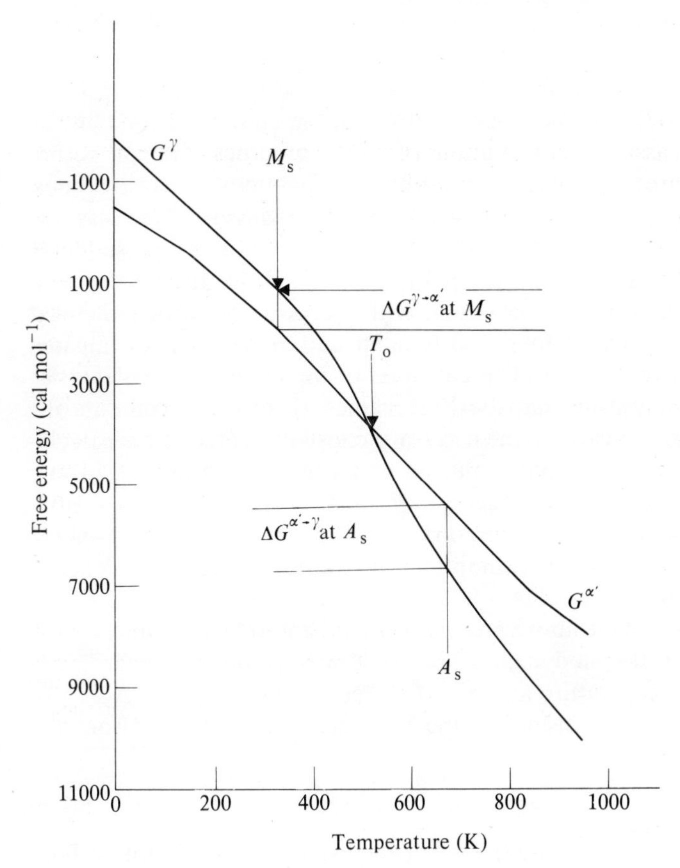

Figure 4-17 Free energy vs temperature for austerite and martensite phases of Fe–29% Ni. (*After Kauffman and Cohen.*[40])

assumptions. In single-component systems (as in pure metals), all that one needs to know are the free energy functions for the two phases. In alloys and other multicomponent systems, calculations of the free energies become difficult unless one assumes ideal mixing.[40] Consider an alloy $A_{1-x}B_x$, where x is the percentage of B in A (usually ~10 percent). Let the transformation be denoted as α' to γ. The free energies for the two phases may be written as

$$G^{\alpha'} = (1 - x)G_A^{\alpha'} + xG_B^{\alpha'} + G_m^{\alpha'}$$
$$G^{\gamma} = (1 - x)G_A^{\gamma} + xG_B^{\gamma} + G_m^{\gamma} \tag{4-36}$$

where G_A and G_B are the free energies per mole of A and B in the respective phases and G_m is the free energy of mixing. For the transition γ–α', the free energy difference $G^{\gamma} - G^{\alpha'} = \Delta G^{\gamma-\alpha'}$ (which should be zero at T_0) is calculated as

$$0 = \Delta G^{\gamma-\alpha'} = (1 - x)\Delta G_A^{\gamma-\alpha'} + x\Delta G_B^{\gamma-\alpha'} + \Delta G_m^{\gamma-\alpha'} \tag{4-37}$$

Equation (4-37) is very general and is readily extended to many-component systems. We should note, however, that it is difficult to calculate G_m.

Various thermodynamic calculations[41] made so far are devoted to the calculation of terms on the right-hand side of Eq. (4-37) from the known thermodynamic properties of the pure A component and from assumed variations of the properties due to the B component. There have been three principal lines of investigations, and we shall consider them briefly. The first was due to Johansson.[44] He assumed that $\Delta G^{\gamma-\alpha'} = 0$ at M_s rather than at T_0, because the martensite forms suddenly without diffusion and is unaffected by rapid quenching. From the known heat capacity of pure iron in α and γ phases and with the assumption that the heat capacities of the two alloy phases are proportional to carbon content, he evaluated the free energies of the two phases. The entropies of mixing were calculated for the two phases separately using statistical mechanics. In order to compute the free energy contributions of carbon, the necessary constants (three in his calculations) were treated as unknowns and evaluated by using three known M_s values. In order to check the validity of the theory, M_s values were calculated at other carbon concentrations. In spite of the good thermodynamic data used in the calculations, the weakness of the assumptions in the theory led to erroneous results. Thus, for pure iron, the values of T_0 and M_s are known to be 910°C and 520°C respectively,[45] while the above analysis shows them to be the same.

A slightly different thermodynamic approach was made by Zener.[46] He considered M_s as the temperature at which the free energy difference $\Delta G^{\gamma-\alpha'}$ of Eq. (4-37) is such as to compensate for the free energy term arising from the strain energy term, ΔG_ε.

$$\Delta G^{\gamma-\alpha'} = -\Delta G_\varepsilon \qquad \text{at } M_s \tag{4-38}$$

Zener then set $(1 - x) \simeq 1$ in Eq. (4-37) (for Fe) and evaluated $\Delta G_B^{\gamma-\alpha'}$ (for carbon) assuming dilute solution behavior* and ignoring $\Delta G_m^{\gamma-\alpha'}$. The values of $\Delta G_B^{\gamma-\alpha'}$ and ΔG_ε are assumed to be independent of temperature. Zener's equation for equilibrium at M_s is given as

$$\Delta G_A^{\gamma-\alpha'} + xG_B^{\gamma-\alpha'} + \Delta G_\varepsilon = 0 \tag{4-39}$$

Noting that $\Delta G_A^{\gamma-\alpha'}$ is the only temperature-dependent term in Eq. (4-39), one can calculate x for each M_s value using appropriate $\Delta G_A^{\gamma-\alpha'}$ term. Taking ΔG_ε to be 290 cal mol^{-1} and $\Delta G_B^{\gamma-\alpha'}$ to be 8100 cal mol^{-1}, Zener obtained good agreement between calculated and experimental M_s values in Fe–C systems.

A novel thermodynamic treatment of martensitic transitions was suggested by Cohen and Paranjpe.[41] In their approach, ΔG_ε is considered to be one of the many nonchemical contributions to the free energy, and the terms $\Delta G_A^{\gamma-\alpha'}$ and $\Delta G_B^{\gamma-\alpha'}$ are decomposed into two parts: $\Delta G_A^{\gamma-\alpha'} = \Delta G_A^{\gamma-\alpha} + \Delta G_A^{\alpha-\alpha'}$ and $\Delta G_B^{\gamma-\alpha'} = \Delta G_B^{\gamma-\alpha} + \Delta G_B^{\alpha-\alpha'}$. In iron–carbon alloys this amounts to assuming the transition to be taking place in two stages, viz., austenite transforming to the bcc lattice

* $RT \ln [(x^\gamma/n^\gamma)/(x^{\alpha'}/n^{\alpha'})]$, where n^γ and $n^{\alpha'}$ are the number of interstitial positions available for carbon in the two alloys (3 and 1 respectively).

which then rearranges to martensite. The basic thermodynamic expression in this treatment[41] is

$$\Delta G^{\gamma-\alpha'} = \Delta G^{\gamma-\alpha} + \Delta G^{\alpha-\alpha'} + \Delta G \text{ (nonchemical terms)} \qquad (4\text{-}40)$$

These authors assume carbon to be in its standard state (graphite) and follow a procedure for the calculation of $\Delta G^{\gamma-\alpha}$ similar to that of Zener; $\Delta G^{\alpha-\alpha'}$ is taken to be the energy needed to elastically deform the bcc iron lattice (with interstitial carbon) into the bct lattice of the martensite of appropriate dimensions. The change in free energy is simply the elastic energy which is equal to $V_m/2$ $(\sum_{i=1}^{3} \sigma_i \varepsilon_i)$, where V_m is the molar volume of the martensite and σ_i and ε_i are the three stresses and strains on the three crystallographic directions. Equation (4-40) with the above substitutions gives the working equation of the Cohen–Paranjpe treatment:[41]

$$\Delta G^{\gamma-\alpha'} = \Delta G_A^{\gamma-\alpha} + xRT \ln (a_B^{\alpha}/a_B^{\gamma}) + RT \ln (a_A^{\alpha}/a_A^{\gamma}) + \frac{V_m}{2} \sum_{i=1}^{3} \sigma_i \varepsilon_i + \Delta G \text{ (nonchemical)} \qquad (4\text{-}41)$$

With ΔG (nonchemical) of approximately the same value as that used by Zener, Eq. (4-41) predicted M_s values for Fe–C systems satisfactorily.

The discussion of thermodynamic treatments presented so far clearly indicates how success has been only fair because of the various assumptions made in the calculations. Furthermore, there has been little effort outside of the conventional martensitic transitions in Fe–C systems. The status of this area of study was reviewed some years ago by Kaufmann and Cohen[40] and by Cohen and Paranjpe,[41] and the interested reader is referred to these articles for further details.

Kinetics of Martensitic Transitions

It was pointed out earlier that martensitic transitions generally take place with extreme rapidity and are often unaffected by quenching. Although there are a few examples of isothermal martensitic transitions,[40] by and large they are athermal transitions. That is, the quantity of martensite formed below M_s is independent of isothermal holding times and is a function only of the temperature. In order to understand the kinetics of martensitic transitions, nucleation and growth theory has been utilized. Classical theory of nucleation was originally applied by Kurdjumov and Maximova,[47] and their ideas were improved by Fisher, Hollomon, and Turnbull.[48] Christian[3] has included the effects of externally applied stresses on the transition. These improved treatments lead to a value of ΔG_c, the critical free energy of nucleation[7] (see Eq. (4-3)), given by

$$\Delta G_c = \frac{KC^2\gamma^3}{(\Delta G_v)^4} \qquad (4\text{-}42)$$

where C is an elastic constant and K is a numerical constant. The nucleation rate, R, is taken to be

$$R = A \exp(-\Delta G_c/kT) \tag{4-43}$$

since E_a for atom transfer across the interface (see Eq. (4-7)) can be assumed to be zero in these fast transitions. Equation (4-43) indicates that R is a sensitive function of temperature.

At M_s, the nucleation rate becomes significant; thus, in this theory, the nucleation is essentially isothermal. It is to be expected that at M_s or at lower temperatures, the transition to martensite becomes complete. However, as the martensite product accumulates, the effective energy of nucleation increases because of the large strains developed in the matrix and leads to a sudden shortage of critical nuclei rendering athermal characteristics to the kinetics. Nevertheless, it is found that the theory of homogeneous nucleation fails to account for the very low M_s temperatures observed in Fe–Ni alloys.[49]*

Heterogeneous nucleation theory has also been invoked to account for the kinetics in these transitions. In one approach it is argued that at high austenite temperature, composition fluctuations lead to carbon-free zones[48] in Fe–C alloys which act as nucleating centres. This leads to embryos with a wide distribution of sizes which become critical at various temperatures lower than M_s. The athermal behavior is now directly evident, because a fixed number of nuclei become critical at any one temperature. This theory, however, suffers from the disadvantage that it should lead to random nucleation or operationally homogeneous kinetics rather than the observed heterogeneous kinetics (taking place at preferred sites) as in β-brass.[50] Furthermore, composition fluctuations which lead to carbon-free zones in concentrated solid solutions (Fe–30% Ni alloys) are unlikely to be present. Cohen et al.[51] have assumed the existence of structural heterogeneities like internal surfaces, local strains, etc., for nucleation purposes. This assumption is valid at least in the case of martensitic transition in cobalt.[52]

Knapp and Dehlinger[53] have approached martensitic kinetics by modifying the condition for nucleation itself. In Eq. (4-1), we assumed that $(\partial \Delta G/\partial r) = 0$ for the attainment of the criticality of the nuclei. Knapp and Delhinger, on the other hand, assume that $\Delta G = 0$ for the rapid, spontaneous growth of nuclei, an assumption which is not altogether valid, as pointed out by Christian.[3]

Experimental studies of the kinetics of martensitic transitions have utilized expressions based on both isothermal and athermal mechanisms. The volume fraction x transformed isothermally has been related to the nucleation rate in isothermal kinetics[54] as

$$x = 1 - [1 + (1 + f)Rt/n_0]^{-f/(1+f)} \tag{4-44}$$

where f is a (constant) fraction of the parent phase transformed by each martensitic plate, n_0 is the total number of martensitic plates formed since the beginning

* M_s temperatures may be evaluated in the above theory as the temperature at which the nucleation rates attain values of 1 nucleus per cc per s, so that $M_s = \Delta G_c/82.9k$.

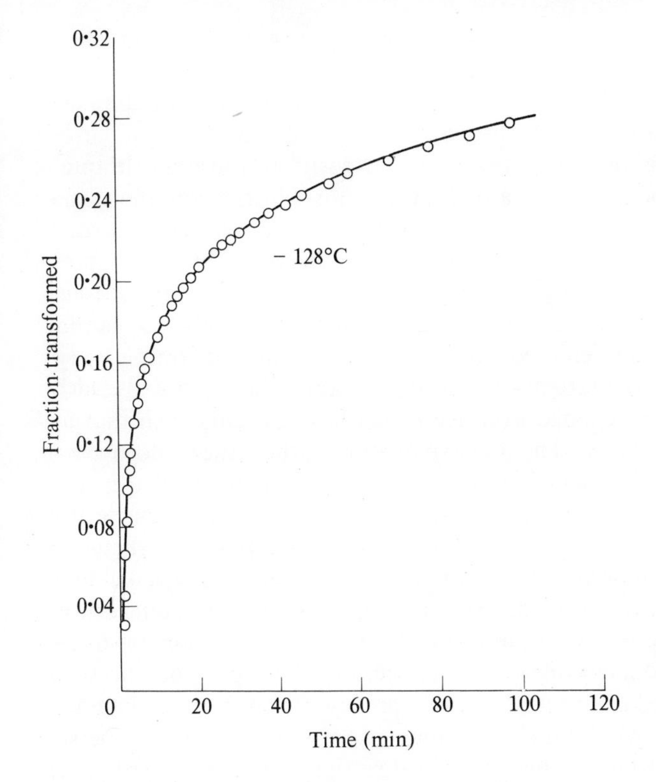

Figure 4-18 Isothermal martensite transformation in an Fe–Ni–Mn alloy. (*After Fisher;*[54] *Cech and Holloman.*[55])

of the transition, and t the time. Fisher[54] analyzed the data of Cech and Holloman[55] treating f and R/n_0 as adjustable parameters and obtained a good fit of the data on an iron–nickel–manganese alloy (Fig. 4-18). The athermal kinetic data of Fe–C alloys have been treated with similar formal kinetic expression by Koistener and Marbuger,[56] who used the expression

$$(1 - x) = \exp\left[-0.011(M_s - T)\right] \tag{4-45}$$

where T is the temperature.

The rapidity with which these transitions occur has from the very beginning led to the assumption that the growth of martensites has a zero barrier. These transitions, which proceed with rates close to that of sound waves,[38,39] have also been looked upon as proceeding by the movement of strain waves.[57] There is, however, little experimental evidence[58] to show the nature and size of these nuclei, and the understanding of the growth mechanisms is at best only well-founded conjecture.

Crystallography of Martensitic Transitions

Probably one of the most important characteristics of martensitic transitions is concerned with surface relief effects. We have seen earlier that straight-line scraches on the parent surface transform into other straight-line scraches after transformation to martensite. We have also seen that, during the transition, there forms an interface between the martensite and the parent phase known as the habit plane which is macroscopically an undeformed and unrotated plane common to the two coexisting phases. These observations have led to the formulation of phenomenological crystallographic theories of martensitic transitions. Although these theories have been developed to a high degree of sophistication, the stages of transition invoked in the theory are purely mathematical constructs and seem to have little or no bearing on the actual mechanism of the transition.[59]

It was pointed out very early by Greninger and Troiano[34] that surface relief effects involve a homogeneous shear in the habit plane. A simple shear cannot transform, for example, a face-centered cubic lattice of an austenite into a body-centered tetragonal lattice of a martensite. A crystallographic theory should clearly indicate how the total shape change from fcc to bct lattice occurs such that an invariant habit plane is preserved. The first explanation of the lattice deformation from fcc to bct was given by Bain[60] and continues to be part of all the later theories. Bain's method of generating a bct unit cell from the fcc parent lattice is shown in Fig. 4-19. The first stage (a) establishes a correspondence between the parent and product phases. The bct cell thus generated is subjected to a homogeneous distortion or a lattice deformation (b) to produce the unit cell of martensite phase of appropriate c/a ratio. While the Bain distortion produces only a cell of appropriate dimensions of the product phase, it does not leave any plane or vector undeformed or unrotated in this process. The rotation which the unit cell has suffered as a whole in the "baining process" can, however, be set right by a rigid body rotation in the opposite direction, but the planes in the final lattice are all distorted. A plane in martensite which has a microscopic if not atomic registry with a plane of the parent phase is obtained by additional operations such as an appropriate slip shear or a twinning shear.

Mathematically, the Bain lattice deformation may be represented by a 3×3 matrix. Referring to Fig. 4-19, the correspondence ${}_{\mathrm{m}}C_{\mathrm{p}}$ and Bain strain $\mathfrak{B}$ are as follows:

$$
{}_{\mathrm{m}}C_{\mathrm{p}} = \begin{bmatrix} 1 & \bar{1} & 0 \\ 1 & 1 & 0 \\ 0 & 0 & 1 \end{bmatrix} \tag{4-46}
$$

and

$$
\mathfrak{B} = \begin{bmatrix} \sqrt{2}a/a_0 & 0 & 0 \\ 0 & \sqrt{2}a/a_0 & 0 \\ 0 & 0 & c/a_0 \end{bmatrix} \simeq \begin{bmatrix} 1.12 & 0 & 0 \\ 0 & 1.12 & 0 \\ 0 & 0 & 0.82 \end{bmatrix}
$$

Or, in general, $\mathfrak{B}$ may be written in the form

$$
\mathfrak{B} = \begin{bmatrix} \eta_1 & 0 & 0 \\ 0 & \eta_2 & 0 \\ 0 & 0 & \eta_3 \end{bmatrix} \tag{4-47}
$$

Thus, Bain strain converts a cube of unit edges into a tetragonal block with edges equal to η_1, η_2, and η_3. Whether or not such deformations lead to any invariant vectors or planes may be seen as follows. The deformation represented by $\mathfrak{B}$ in Eq. (4-47) may be applied on a sphere of unit radius. The resulting ellipsoid is represented in Fig. 4-20. As long as the values of η are such as to

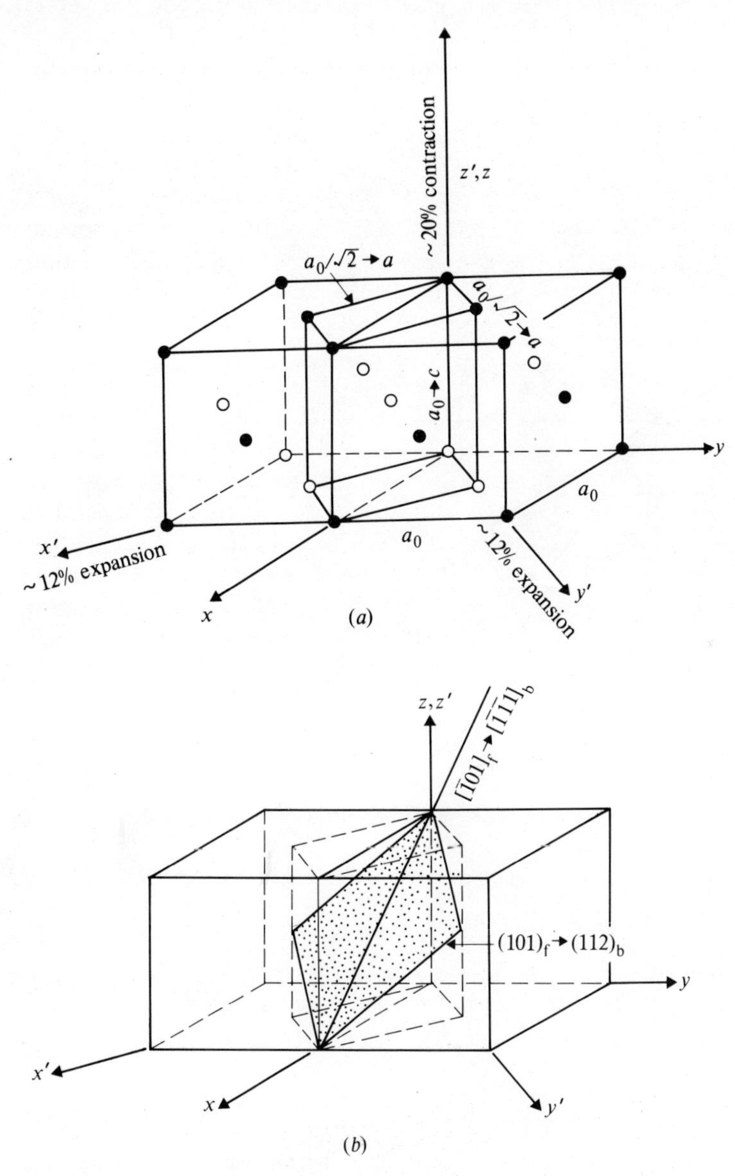

Figure 4-19 The Bain correspondence (*a*) and distortion (*b*) for a fcc → bct transformation, with typical magnitudes of the distortion and correspondences of planes and directions in the lattice before and after the transformation. (*After Wayman.*[59])

enclose unity ($\eta_1 < 1 < \eta_2 < \eta_3$ or $\eta_1 < \eta_2 < 1 < \eta_3$) the ellipsoid and the sphere intersect and two cones (*a*) of "unextended lines" result. The equations of the initial sphere and the distorted ellipsoid are respectively $(x^2 + y^2 + z^2) = 1$ and $(x^2/\eta_1^2 + y^2/\eta_2^2 + z^2/\eta_3^2) = 1$. The cone of intersection is represented by

$$\left(\frac{1}{\eta_1^2} - 1\right)x^2 + \left(\frac{1}{\eta_2^2} - 1\right)y^2 + \left(\frac{1}{\eta_3^2} - 1\right)z^2 = 0 \qquad (4\text{-}48)$$

The vectors drawn from the center to any point on this cone remain undistorted,

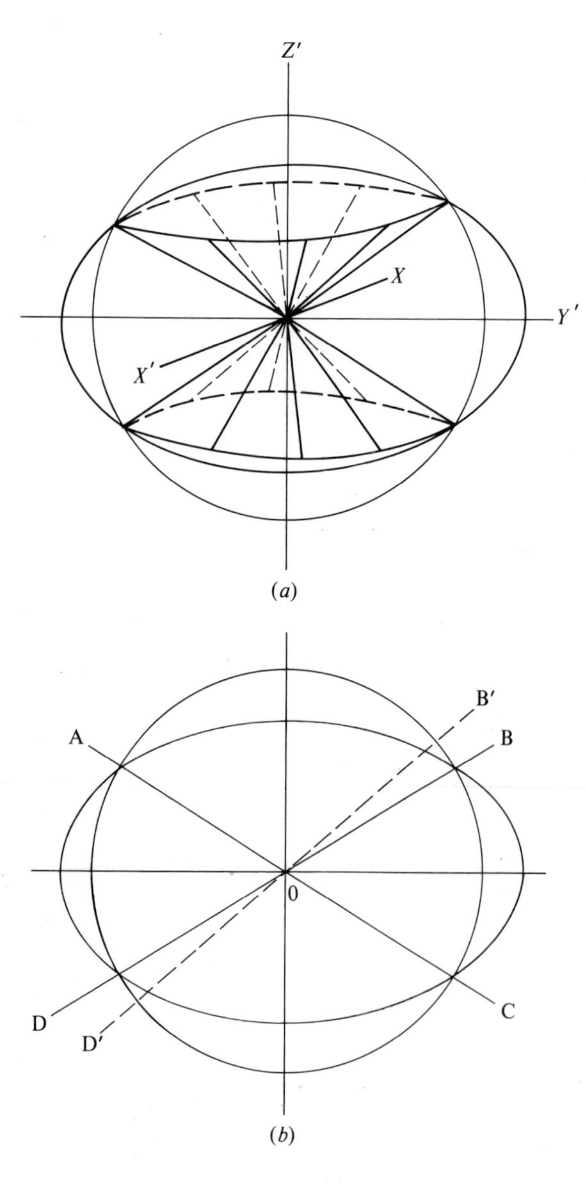

Figure 4-20 Sphere–ellipsoid analog of Bain distortion. Cones of unextended lines (*a*) along with their initial and final positions (*b*) are shown (see text). (*After Wayman.*[59])

but they are rotated with respect to their original positions (*b*) which are described by the equation

$$(\eta_1^2 - 1)x^2 + (\eta_2^2 - 1)y^2 + (\eta_3^2 - 1)z^2 = 0 \tag{4-49}$$

The only possibility that a vector which is undistorted can occur is when one of the ηs is unity. The nature of intersection of the sphere and ellipsoid when η_1 is unity is shown in Fig. 4-21. The intersection takes place along two great circles represented by

$$(\eta_2^2 - 1)y^2 + (\eta_3^2 - 1)z^2 = 0 \tag{4-50}$$

The two planes AOC and BOC are undistorted but, as before, are rotated with respect to their original positions. They represent the analog of the habit plane which is undistorted during the transition.

However, the Bain matrix $\mathfrak{B}$ in real situations would not contain a η which is unity[32,59,61] and, therefore, the theory needs some mechanism by which one of the ηs could be rendered unity. This is achieved by the application of suitable simple shear known as "invariant plane strain." In Fig. 4-22 this shear is represented where the "bained" ellipsoid has been sheared. The ellipsoid is deformed so as to achieve tangency with the original unit sphere along AOC which now represents the undistorted plane. In order to render this plane unrotated, a final operation involving a rigid body rotation in the appropriate direction would be necessary.

This entire process may now be represented as a total shape deformation

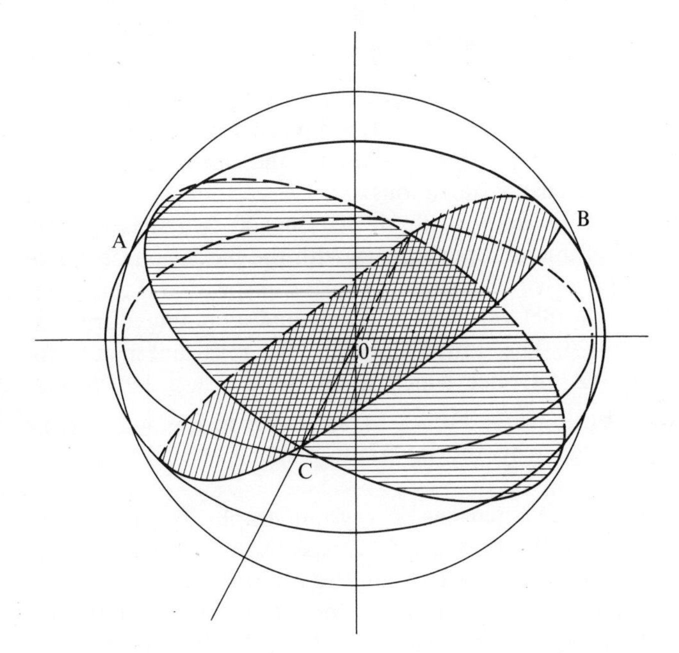

Figure 4-21 The sphere–ellipsoid intersection when one of the principal distortions, η, is unity and the other two are smaller and greater than unity respectively. (*After Wayman.*[59])

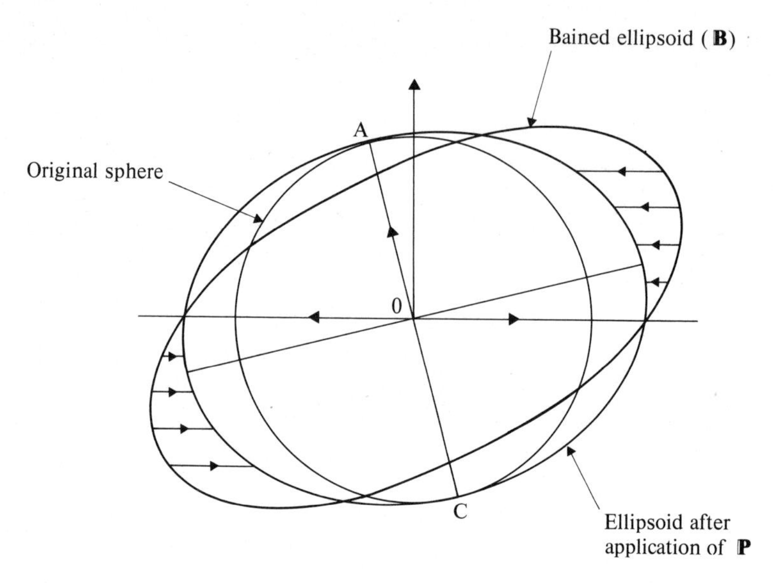

Figure 4-22 Representation of the final shear operation which results in the formation of an undistorted plane. (*After Christian.*[61])

$\mathfrak{P}_1$ which is brought about by three operations: (*a*) a Bain strain $\mathfrak{B}$, (*b*) invariant plane strain $\mathfrak{P}$, and (*c*) a rigid body rotation $\mathfrak{R}$. Mathematically, it may be represented as

$$\mathfrak{P}_1 = \mathfrak{R}\mathfrak{B}\mathfrak{P} \tag{4-51}$$

The order of operations in Eq. (4-51) is immaterial, since they do not represent a physical chronology of events or any of the real steps involved in the mechanism of these transitions.[32] Equation (4-51) represents the sum and substance of all the crystallographic theories of martensitic transitions.

Let us examine what $\mathfrak{P}$ really does in physical terms: $\mathfrak{P}$ is a shear which produces an invariant plane of microscopic registry with the parent phase. Such a shear can be of two types, (*a*) a twinning shear, or (*b*) a slip shear, and these are mathematically equivalent. The net result of slipping and twinning during a transition is shown in Fig. 4-23. The dotted lines are the invariant planes in Figs. 4-23*a* and 4-23*b*. The AZ interface which is on the average undistorted is in reality equal to $(\overrightarrow{AB} + \overrightarrow{BC} + \overrightarrow{CD} + \overrightarrow{DE} + \cdots)$, as shown in Fig. 4-23*c*. It is easy to appreciate at this stage why the invariant plane is a high-index or irrational plane.

The three main approaches to martensitic crystallography differ only in detail in the application of Eq. (4-51). They are due respectively to Bullough and Bilby[62] (BB), Bowles and Mackenzie[63] (BM), and Wechsler, Lieberman and Reed[64] (WLR). The BB theory uses Eq. (4-51) as such, while the BM theory reinterprets it as follows. Multiplying both sides of Eq. (4-51) by $\mathfrak{P}^{-1}$ we get

$$\mathfrak{P}_1\mathfrak{P}^{-1} = \mathfrak{R}\mathfrak{B} \tag{4-52}$$

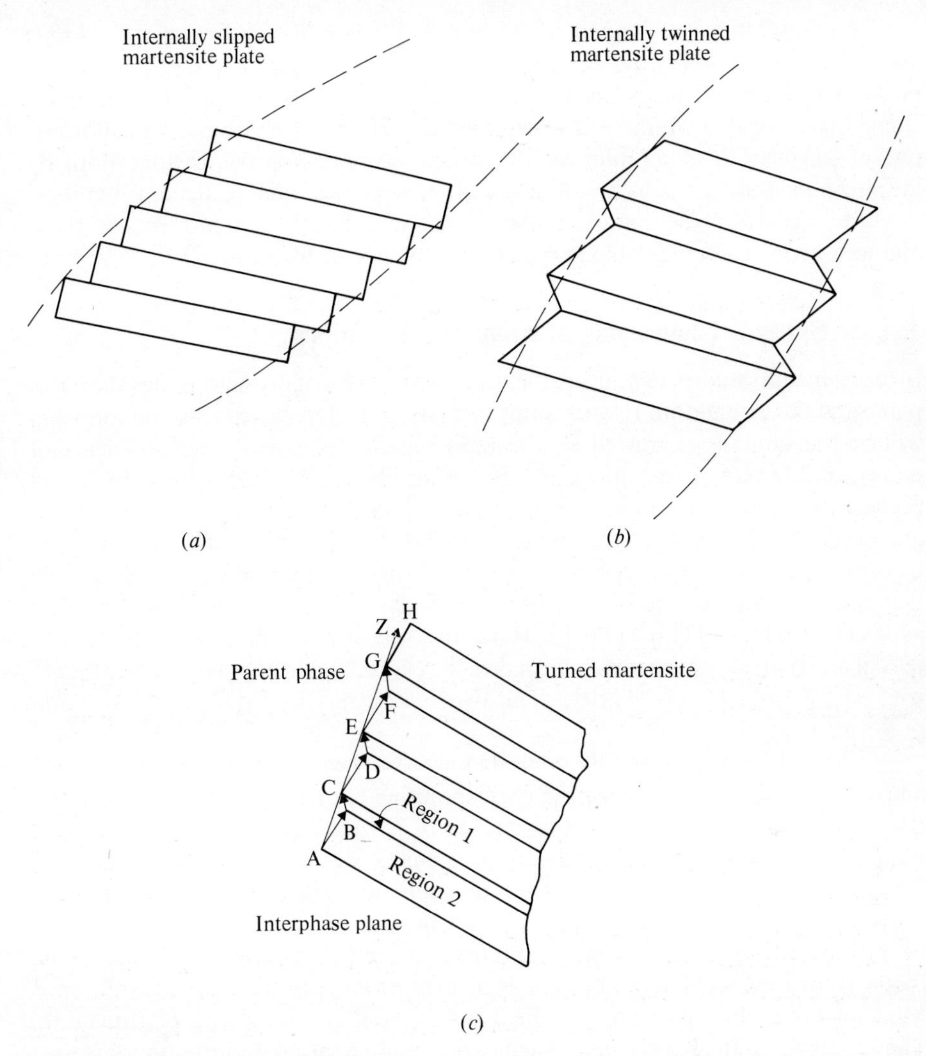

Figure 4-23 Representation of the slipping and twinning mechanisms which result in the martensite habit planes (schematic). (*After Wayman.*[32])

Since both $\mathfrak{P}_1$ and $\mathfrak{P}^{-1}$ represent plane strains, the total operation amounts to formulating an invariant line strain. So investigating an $\mathfrak{R}$ and $\mathfrak{B}$ so as to obtain an invariant line strain solves the problem.* In the WLR approach, the invariant plane strain is applied both before baining and after,[59] and Eq. (4-51) is used essentially in the same form.

* The BM theory allows for a uniform dilatation, δ, of the habit plane up to 2 percent.

The choice of correspondence between product and parent phases (Eq. (4-46)) and hence of the following Bain operation is not unique. Although it can be performed in several ways, the choice is very much dictated by common sense. It is taken to be one which needs minimum displacement of atoms. The choice is one of "inspired"[59] and "informed"[32] guesswork. The analysis is done both by graphical procedures using Wulff nets and by numerical matrix algebra methods, the latter generally yielding more accurate results. Excellent treatments of these methods are already available in special treatments of this subject.[3,32,59,61,65]

Typical Systems Undergoing Martensitic Transitions

In experimental studies of martensitic transitions, one usually determines the habit plane and the orientation relationships (see Sec. 3-4). The orientation relationship will be the same as expressed by the Bain relation in cases where no invariant plane strain needs to be applied.[66] But after the application of the invariant plane strain, there will be very few rational planes and directions in the parent and product phases which have orientation relationships. In the case of martensitic transitions in iron alloys, there are two well-known orientation relationships. The first one is known as the Kurdjumov and Sachs[67] relation, and it is expressed as $(111)_p \parallel (011)_m$; $[\bar{1}11]_p \parallel [\bar{1}1\bar{1}]_m$. Here, the subscripts p and m represent the parent and martensite lattices. A second such relation, established by Nishiyama,[68] is $(111)_p \parallel (110)_m$; $[\bar{2}11]_p \parallel [1\bar{1}0]_m$. The two sets of relations differ by a rotation of $5° 16'$ about $[111]_p$.

Other relevant data usually presented are the shear plane,* shear direction,* amount of shear,* and the rotation corresponding to $\mathfrak{R}$.

In metallic systems where most studies of martensitic transitions have been made, four general types of crystal structure changes have usually been noticed.[61] They are: (*a*) face-centered cubic to body-centered tetragonal (fcc–bct), (*b*) face-centered cubic to face-centered tetragonal (fcc–fct), (*c*) body-centered cubic to hexagonal close-packed (bcc–hcp), and (*d*) body-centered cubic to orthorhombic (bcc–orthorhombic). There are, however, exceptions like the case of uranium.[3] Most of Fe–C, Fe–(low) Ni, and Fe–Cr–C exhibit the first type of transition. They conform to the Kurdjumov–Sachs orientation relation and usually possess a $\{225\}_p$ or $\{259\}_p$ habit plane.† There is still an unconfirmed belief that there is a habit plane jump from $\{225\}_p$ to $\{259\}_p$ as the carbon percentage increases from 1.4 to 1.78 atom percent. That there can be habit planes between $\{225\}_p$ and

* The invariant plane strain $\mathfrak{P}$ referred to earlier may be denoted as

$$\mathfrak{P} = 1 + m\mathfrak{d}\mathfrak{p}'$$

where m is the amount of shear, $\mathfrak{d}$ is the direction of the shear, and $\mathfrak{p}'$ is the unit normal to the invariant plane (which in effect defines the plane). $\mathfrak{d}$ and $\mathfrak{p}'$ are row and column vectors respectively. The description of the shear is usually given as $\{hkl\}[abc]$; e.g., $\{112\}_m[11\bar{1}]_m$, which means shear is applied in the $[11\bar{1}]$ direction on a (112) plane in the martensite phase.

† Habit planes, as pointed out earlier, are irrational planes. The planes are referred to by the indices of the closest poles on the stereogram like $\{225\}_p$ and $\{259\}_p$.

$\{259\}_p$ has been established by the work of Otte and Read[69] on Fe–2.8%Cr, 1.5%C, in which there are habit planes close to the pole $\{124\}_p$. Indium–thallium (~21%Tl) alloy is an example of an fcc–fct transition with $\{110\}_p$ habit plane;[70] bcc–hcp transitions are exemplified by pure metals like lithium[71] and zirconium.[72] In lithium, the habit plane is $\{441\}_p$. Gold–cadmium alloys[73] exhibit a bcc–orthorhombic transition with the habit plane $\{133\}_p$. There are various other types of crystal structures exhibiting martensitic transitions. Pure cobalt[74] exhibits a fcc–hcp transition with the habit plane $\{111\}_p$, while Fe–Ni alloys (with Ni 27–35%) exhibit fcc–bcc transitions[75] with habit plane $\{3, 10, 15\}_p$. Another system which undergoes an essentially perfect martensite transition[76] (fcc–bcc) with $\{3, 10, 15\}_p$ is Fe–24.9% Pt. Martensitic transitions where the habit planes are near poles $\{155\}_p$, $\{2, 11, 12\}_p$ are known in alloy systems of copper and zinc.[77] Nickel–manganese[43] and titanium alloys[78] also undergo martensitic transitions.

Martensitic transitions in nonmetallic inorganic solids are of particular interest. The fast kinetics, analogous crystal structures of the phases connected by the transitions and hysteresis in transformations, etc., all indicate that many inorganic solids may undergo phase transitions indeed through a martensitic mechanism (see Sec. 3-4). A good example of such a study is of $BaTiO_3$ and $KTa_{0.65}Nb_{0.35}O_3$ (KTN) by Di Dominico and Wemple,[79] who used the WLR theory for calculations. The cubic to tetragonal transition is attended by characteristics (see Fig. 4-24) very similar to those found in indium–thallium alloy.[80] The habit plane is irrational and close to $\{110\}_p$. The high-temperature transition in sodium cyanide has been suggested to be martensitic.[41,81] Zirconia (ZrO_2) is an extensively investigated system where the tetragonal–monoclinic transition is martensitic in nature.[82] The large body of literature on this transition has been reviewed by Subbarao et al.[83] Orientation relations for ZrO_2 are $(100)_m \parallel (100)_p$ and $[010]_m \parallel [001]_p$. The observed habit planes are close to $\{100\}_m$ for the plate-shaped products[84] (Fig. 4-25).

Fraser and Kennedy,[85] as well as Kennedy,[86] have studied martensitic or deformational transformations of many inorganic solids using the WLR theory (see Sec. 3-4). The NaCl–CsCl-type transformation in alkali and ammonium halides[85] has been found to agree with the martensitic mechanism. The lattice deformation needed for the NaCl–CsCl transformation by Buerger's dilatation mechanism[87] is approximately 40 percent contraction in the $[111]_p$ direction and about 19 percent expansion in a perpendicular direction. The pure lattice strain leads to the orientation relation $[111]_p \parallel [111]_m$ and $\{\bar{1}10\}_p \parallel \{\bar{1}01\}_m$. The observed orientation relations have been compared with available experimental observations.[88] For example, orientation relations $\{100\}_p \parallel \{110\}_m$, $[010] \parallel [\bar{1}11]_m$ have been shown to be valid for NH_4Br. The habit planes for these transitions have been found to be approximately $\{\bar{1}11\}_p$, $\{210\}_p$, and $\{310\}_p$. The II → I transition in rubidium nitrate has been reported to be martensitic.[86] Martensitic mechanisms are suggested to be operating in several topotactic transformations.[89] The possibility that KNO_3 and $CaCO_3$ may transform through a martensitic mechanism has also been suggested.[90] In view of the orientation relations (Sec. 3-4) between phases, it is possible that the orthorhombic–rhombohedral transition does involve a martensitic mechanism.

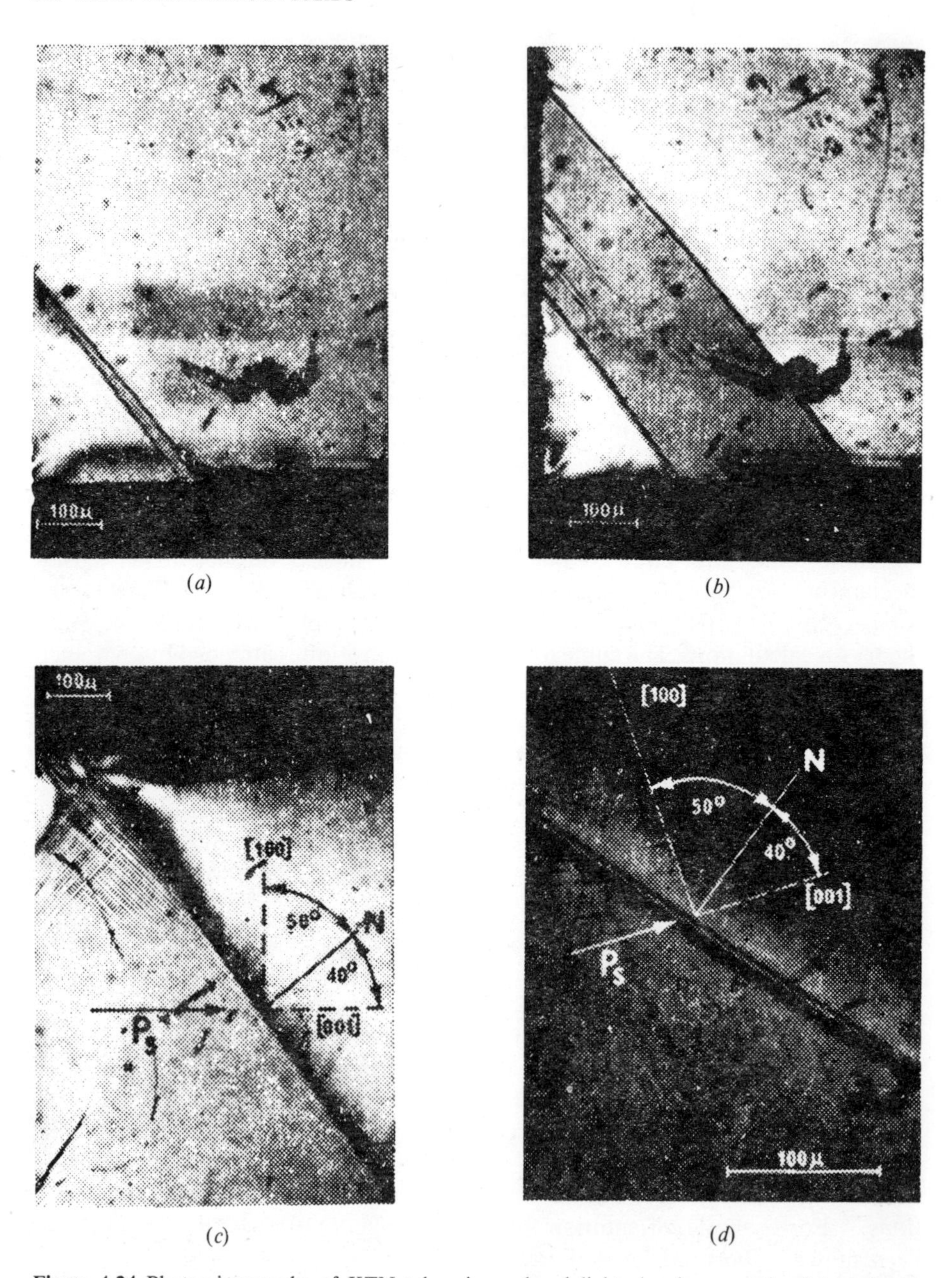

Figure 4-24 Photomicrographs of KTN taken in analyzed light showing growth of ferroelectric spike in (*a*) and (*b*). The strain relief pattern on the paraelectric side of the phase boundary may be seen in (*c*) and (*d*). P_s is the direction of spontaneous polarization. (*After DiDominico and Wemple.*[79])

Figure 4-25 Surface relief in ZrO_2 single crystal following a martensitic transition from tetragonal to monoclinic. Lenticular plates in a scanning electron micrograph. (*After Bansal and Heuer.*[84])

4-3 ORDER–DISORDER TRANSITIONS

The primary characteristic of a crystalline solid is the existence of three-dimensional periodicity in the arrangement of atoms. By virtue of this triply periodic nature, it is required that the position and orientation of every atom (or complex ion) be fixed in the lattice with respect to the position and orientation of every other atom or ion. Such a state of crystalline arrangement corresponds to perfect order. Perfect order is, however, never realized in materials at any temperature other than 0 K. This is because of the thermal agitation in materials at non-zero temperatures which enables atoms and groups to assume such positions and orientations as would diminish the order. It is therefore pertinent to speak of the extent of order or disorder in materials. This is best done in terms of order parameters. The order parameters are defined in such a way that they are equal to unity in the perfectly ordered state and zero in the completely disordered state. We shall defer the mathematical description of order parameters to the next chapter and discuss the nature and variety of order–disorder transitions in materials in this section with suitable examples. By an ordered state we mean that a chosen order parameter is equal to or close to unity. In an order–disorder transition the material goes to a disordered state in which the order parameter essentially goes to zero. The transition may take place discontinuously as a first-order change at a particular temperature and may involve simultaneous change of volume as well. It may also occur in the manner of a lambda transition over a range of temperature during which the order vanishes to zero. We shall not restrict the definition of order–disorder transitions only to the latter case, although they are often inaccurately discussed as synonymous with λ-transitions. In fact, many order–disorder transitions start as λ or cooperative transitions and attain completion as first-order transitions.

Kinds of Order–Disorder Transitions

Three principal kinds of disordering transitions may be distinguished: (*a*) positional disordering, (*b*) orientational disordering, and (*c*) disordering associated with electronic and nuclear spin states. Positional disordering arises either when atoms or ions occupy inappropriate sublattice positions, or when more positions are available for the atoms than are necessary. Consider the example of CuZn.[91] The ordered low-temperature structure corresponds to two interpenetrating simple cubic lattices each of which is occupied exclusively by either copper or zinc atoms. As the temperature increases, copper and zinc atoms begin to exchange positions and appear on both the sublattices (inappropriate lattice positions). When the transition to the disordered state is complete, the probabilities of occupation of a lattice point by copper and zinc atoms become equal. In the case of silver iodide, the transition corresponds to the formation of an enormous number of Frenkel defects. In the disordered state, the Ag^+ ions have an abundance of interstitial sites and are statistically distributed over a very large number of interstitial positions.[92]

Orientational disorder can take place in situations where the ions or the basic units occupying the lattice sites contain more than one atom. In such a situation, more than one distinguishable orientation becomes possible for the ions in the lattice. If these orientations correspond to very small differences in energy, then the disordering can occur into these orientations by thermal agitation. Here again, it is possible that a low-temperature phase may have no disorder while the high-temperature phase which forms after a first-order transition may correspond to very high disorder. A large number of systems exhibiting this type of disordering are known.

Another large class of order–disorder transitions is provided by the disordering of spins. By virtue of the presence of unpaired electrons or spins, atoms or ions behave as tiny magnets and impart magnetism to the lattice when present in a parallelly ordered state. Such spontaneous magnetic polarization in materials is known as ferromagnetism (see Chaps. 5 and 7 for details). As the temperature increases, these elementary magnets on the lattice flip over to other orientations, decreasing the magnetism, and when the disorder is complete, the material becomes paramagnetic. Spins in a paramagnetic material tend to align under the influence of an external magnetic field. The ordered state can also correspond to antiparallel (antiferromagnetic) alignment of spins on two sublattices giving rise to a net magnetic moment of zero. Antiferromagnetic materials also undergo disordering transitions to a paramagnetic state. The magnetic polarization of the lattice may still be finite if alignments of spins on the sublattices are antiparallel but unequal (ferrimagnetism). Here again, a fully disordered state is paramagnetic. Transition metal and rare earth ions, by virtue of the presence of unfilled d and f shells, impart magnetic properties to their compounds in the solid state and provide a host of magnetic order–disorder transitions. Much of our understanding of order–disorder transitions has been through the treatment of magnetic transitions* (Chap. 5). Disordering transitions in which alignment of nuclear spins is involved have been much less studied.

By analogy with ferromagnetic (or antiferromagnetic)–paramagnetic transitions, there are order–disorder transitions involving dipoles. These are the well-known ferroelectric (or antiferroelectric)–paraelectric transitions (see Chap. 7). Metal–insulator transitions in which localized electrons become itinerant can also be discussed as order–disorder transitions (Chap. 7). There are many other ways in which crystalline materials exhibit disorder, such as structural defects, nonstoichiometry, and so on. However, since definitive studies of such order–disorder

* A state between that of a paramagnet and a ferromagnet exists in *spin glasses*. A spin glass may be regarded as a "random solid solution of moment bearing atoms in a non-magnetic host which when cooled to low temperatures has 'frozen' solute moments in local molecular fields, these fields having a distribution of magnitudes and directions such that the net magnetization of any region containing a few tens of solute atoms is zero" (e.g., Au–Fe, Cu–Mn, Mo–Fe). Transitions from a spin glass state to a paramagnetic or ferromagnetic state would be of second order. For more information on spin glasses, the reader is referred to H. O. Hooper and A. M. de Graaf (eds.), "Amorphous Magnetism," Plenum Press, New York, 1973. Also relevant are the following references: S. F. Edwards and P. W. Anderson, *J. Phys., F*, **5,** 965, 1975; D. Sherrington and S. Kirkpatrick, *Phys. Rev. Letts.*, **35,** 1792, 1975; A. B. Harris et al., *Phys. Rev. Letts.*, **36,** 415, 1976.

phenomena as functions of temperature or pressure have not been made on such materials, we shall not discuss these forms of disorder in any detail. We may point out, however, that order–disorder transitions involving vacancies are known to occur in transition metal oxides like TiO and VO (see Sec. 3-7).

Thermodynamics and Kinetics of Order–Disorder Transitions

An order–disorder transition can take place discontinuously as in a first-order transition or continuously as in higher-order cooperative transitions and behave like a λ-transition. An important aspect of such cooperative transitions is that the energy required for disordering is a progressively decreasing function of the disorder itself. Previous disordering events "help" the next disordering event to occur. Ultimately, the energy required for disordering decreases to zero at the end of the transition and the heat capacity rises catastrophically towards the completion of transition. In the case of discontinuous order–disorder transitions, the energy is absorbed discontinuously (Chap. 2). The general thermodynamic considerations of discontinuous and continuous transitions were discussed in Chap. 2. Some order–disorder transitions have features of both cooperative and discontinuous transitions.[93]

The increase in entropy, ΔS, in an order–disorder transition can be related to disorder as follows. The total increase in entropy is made up of electronic, vibrational, rotational, and configurational contributions:

$$\Delta S = \Delta S_{el} + \Delta S_{vib} + \Delta S_{rot} + \Delta S_{conf} \qquad (4\text{-}53)$$

where the subscripts are self-explanatory. The component ΔS_{el} can generally be ignored except in metal–insulator or similar transitions. The vibrational entropy term, ΔS_{vib}, which is determined by the vibrational spectrum of the material in the ordered and disordered phases, is considerable when ΔV, the change in volume at the transition, is very high and when the disordered state has a different crystal symmetry. The rotational entropy term, ΔS_{rot}, becomes important only if free rotation in one, two, or three degrees of freedom occurs in one of the phases (necessarily in the disordered phase). This leaves ΔS_{conf}, the configurational entropy, as the truly dominant term in most order–disorder transitions: $\Delta S \approx \Delta S_{conf}$. If, in the ordered and disordered phases, the total number of configurations (be it positional or orientational in origin) is ω_1 and ω_2 respectively, then

$$\Delta S_c = k \ln (\omega_2/\omega_1) \simeq \Delta S \qquad (4\text{-}54)$$

This simple equation often provides tremendous physical insight into order–disorder transitions, as we shall illustrate later with examples.

In continuous order–disorder transitions, disorder is a function of temperature and there is a finite value of the order parameter at each temperature, the order parameter of relevance here being the long-range order parameter, LRO. In the case of positional disordering, when disorder sets in, correlation between distant neighbors disappears and LRO is reduced to zero, but the preference for unlike neighbors continues to operate because of energy requirements. This leads to the presence of short-range ordering, SRO, and the SRO persists even beyond the transition temperatures in most order–disorder transitions. The equilibrium value of LRO is not attained instantaneously when the material is brought to the appropriate temperature. The rate at which the full value of the disorder or order is attained is generally different in different directions. Any measured property which is dependent on disorder, therefore, attains its proper value with characteristic kinetics. If Q_i is the instantaneous value of a measured property and Q_f is its proper (full) value, in many instances they are related by first-order kinetics[94] as

$$\frac{dQ_i}{dt} = \frac{1}{\tau}(Q_f - Q_i) \tag{4-55}$$

where τ is known as the "relaxation time." Upon integration, Eq. (4-55) becomes

$$Q_i = Q_f - (Q_f - Q_0)\exp(-t/\tau) \tag{4-56}$$

where Q_0 is the initial value of the quantity which is being measured. However, in many instances, application of such empirical kinetics with one relaxation time only is not sufficient. One such example is the isothermal annealing of $AuCu_3$ below its transition temperature, which needs two relaxation times.

Theoretical treatments of the kinetics of order–disorder transitions present many conceptual and mathematical difficulties. Many models of varying rigor are discussed in the literature.[95] They all basically involve the treatment of the time-evolution of correlation functions. These theoretical models have been developed to accommodate two well-known types of transformation mechanisms, namely the nucleation and growth and continuous or homogeneous (or "spinoidal-type") transition mechanism. The critical nuclei required by the nucleation and growth mechanism in the ordering transformations are provided by the small ordered (SRO) regions which exist even above the transition temperature.[94] Other theoretical aspects of the mechanism were discussed earlier in this chapter. Mathematical aspects of the spinodal reactions will be discussed later. It is sufficient to note here that the treatment requires the setting up of diffusion equations for the atomistically inhomogeneous situation that exists in the disordered state.[95,96] Solutions to these equations which are obtained by Fourier transformation techniques reveal that the ordered state occurs spontaneously for certain fluctuations. The time-dependence of the development of these ordered regions can be numerically evaluated.[95]

Kinetic studies have been mostly confined to positional disordering in alloys. A few aspects of ordering (which is not usually the same as disordering) kinetics are worth noting. (*a*) The rates of disordering (when an alloy is upquenched to temperatures above T_c) are usually very much faster than ordering,[97] an ideal example being $AuCu_3$. (*b*) Positional ordering transitions exhibit the phenomenon of "critical slowing down."[94,95] Relaxation times for ordering are very sensitive to temperature and their values decrease as the temperature is raised toward T_c. However, as T_c is approached, the free energy differences between the ordered and disordered states decrease to such low values that the processes of ordering and disordering get very much retarded. This results in a marked increase of relaxation times. Thus, the relaxation time exhibits a minimum in the region close to and below T_c. (*c*) The growth of initial nuclei (SRO region) to small ordered regions below T_c usually takes place fast, and further ordering stops as soon as these ordered regions meet each other. Development of long-range order by merging of these boundaries into larger domains takes place very slowly.[94] Such ordering kinetics are usually described by two relaxation times.

Experimental Methods

A variety of experimental methods have been employed in the investigation of order–disorder transitions. Thermodynamic measurements, such as the determination of heat capacities, have been very useful in the study of λ-transitions. Heat capacity studies also help in understanding how and at what stages the transition entropy is acquired. This is particularly true of magnetic transitions where a large part of the entropy is often gained by the system in the post-transition region. The net entropy gain can usually be given meaningful statistical interpretation.

A variety of scattering techniques have been employed to study these transitions. X-ray diffraction methods have been useful in the study of positional disordering studies in alloys.[94] In the ordered phase, new diffraction lines appear due to the formation of a "superlattice." The intensity of the superlattice lines is related to the order parameter[91] by the equation

$$I = N[X_A(f_A - f_B)\xi]^2 \tag{4-57}$$

where X_A is the fraction of A atoms in the alloy, f_A and f_B are the scattering factors of A and B respectively, and ξ is the long-range order (LRO) parameter. It is often necessary to use appropriate x-ray wavelengths so that $(f_A - f_B)$ may have substantially high values. X-ray diffraction technique is, however, of limited use in studying orientational disorder since it cannot differentiate between free rotation and disorder among a limited number of orientations.[93] Both electron diffraction and neutron diffraction techniques have greater advantages in investigating order–disorder transitions. This is so because even at 100 keV, the wavelength of electrons would be 0.03 Å and can reveal a considerable cross-section of the reciprocal lattice.[94] The scattering cross-sections of elements for neutrons are in general sufficiently well separated and are particularly suited for studying light atom diffraction in the presence of heavy atoms. By virtue of their spin, neutrons interact with magnetic spins in solids. Neutron spectroscopy is thus specially suited in the investigation of magnetic transitions. Raman and infrared spectroscopic techniques are very effective in the study of disorder. In general, the spectra of disordered and hence "averaged" (or more symmetrical) solids consist of less structure than the corresponding ordered states.

If the material under study consists of appropriate nuclei, NMR spectroscopy would be a very useful tool in studying disordering. One normally studies linewidths of the NMR signals which narrow down in disordered states. Other usual parameters are the second moments, and the spin–lattice and spin–spin relaxation times. The variation of the latter quantities helps in the evaluation of orientational or jump barriers during disordering.

Measurements of dielectric constants and magnetic susceptibilities are also useful techniques in the study of these transitions. In principle, any physical property which changes as a consequence of disordering may be measured as a function of temperature and valuable information regarding order–disorder transitions obtained. They include measurements of resistivity, thermoelectric power, Hall coefficient, etc., which are very sensitive to disorder particularly in alloy systems.[94]

Examples of Order–Disorder Transitions

Positional disordering is best exemplified by alloy systems such as Cu–Zn, Au–Cu, Ni–Mn, or Cu–Pd. Many extensive reviews[97,98] and books[94,95,99] are available on the subject of order–disorder transitions of alloys, and the interested reader is referred to them.* It would suffice here to note that several types of measurements have been employed in these investigations. Typical of them are x-ray diffraction,[100] electron diffraction,[101] neutron diffraction,[102] electrical resistivity,[103] Hall coefficient,[104] thermoelectric power,[105] heat capacity,[106] diamagnetic susceptibility,[107] and elastic constants.[108] Among inorganic compounds, many examples may be cited where positional disordering occurs during a transition.

AgI undergoes a phase transition from hexagonal to cubic phase (α AgI) and the latter exhibits very high conductivity. The increase in entropy at this transition is also high ($\sim$4 cal deg^{-1} mol^{-1}). In the high-temperature bcc unit cell, the two Ag^+ ions are statistically distributed over twelve tetrahedral positions in the lattice. Assuming that in the hexagonal lattice the silver ions do not utilize any of the Frenkel defect positions and are perfectly ordered, the transition amounts to an increase of configurational entropy $\simeq k \ln (12/2)^N \simeq R \ln 6 = 3.55$ cal deg^{-1} mol^{-1}. The actual entropy gain is even higher and, with the added possibility that the low-temperature phase also has some disorder, it appears that Ag^+ ions in the cubic phase explore many other sites as well (see Fig. 4-26), although not all the forty-two sites suggested by Strock.[109,110] Cation disorder has similarly been found to occur after the transition[94,110] in Ag_2S, Ag_3SI, Ag_2HgI_4, CuBr, Cu_2S, Na_2MoO_4, Li_2SO_4, KHF_2, Cu_2HgI_4, $RbAg_4I_5$, etc. In all these cases, interstitial sites and unoccupied lattice sites participate along with the cations so that more than the required number of sites are made available for the cations. Cu_2HgI_4 undergoes a transition[111] from ordered tetragonal to a disordered cubic fcc phase. The low-temperature structure is deduced from that of CuI (which also undergoes an order–disorder transition at 408°C) by substituting two Cu^+ ions by one Hg^{2+} and a cation vacancy. Upon transition, the superlattice lines disappear completely and the material

* The reader is referred to the monograph on "Disorder in Crystals" by N. G. Parsonage and L. A. K. Staveley, Oxford University Press, 1977, for a fine discussion of a variety of chemical systems.

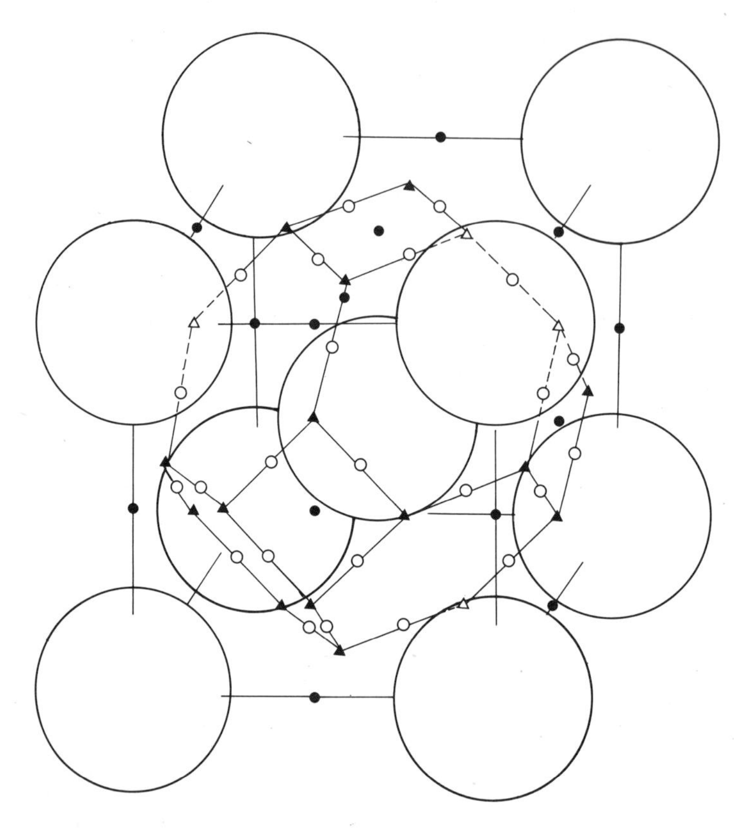

Figure 4-26 Sites (represented by triangles, circles, etc.) available for occupation by Ag^{+} ions in the disordered phase. (*After Strock.*[109])

changes color from red to black. NMR experiments[111] by which quadrupole coupling constants have been evaluated also support randomization of cations (Fig. 4-27). Hg^{2+} ions are found to diffuse randomly, causing high spin–lattice relaxation. Mercuric amidobromide, $HgNH_2Br$, exists in two forms. The stable room-temperature form has an ordered orthorhombic structure, while in the unstable cubic form the Hg atoms are disordered with respect to their positions in a manner equivalent to a type of random walk disorder in the crystal. Calorimetric measurements of ΔS support this model for the disorder.[112]

Order–disorder transitions occur in several spinel structures. Magnetite, Fe_3O_4, has a disordered arrangement of Fe^{2+} and Fe^{3+} at room temperature, and this has been found to undergo a transition[113] (the so-called Verwey transition) to an ordered arrangement of Fe^{2+} and Fe^{3+} on octahedral sites below 120 K. This is also associated with an orthorhombic distortion and increased electrical conductivity. The transition is associated with an entropy change of 2 cal deg^{-1} mol^{-1}. This value of ΔS seems plausible since the total of $(8 + 16)$ tetrahedral and octahedral sites are possibly randomly occupied by the eight Fe^{2+} ions

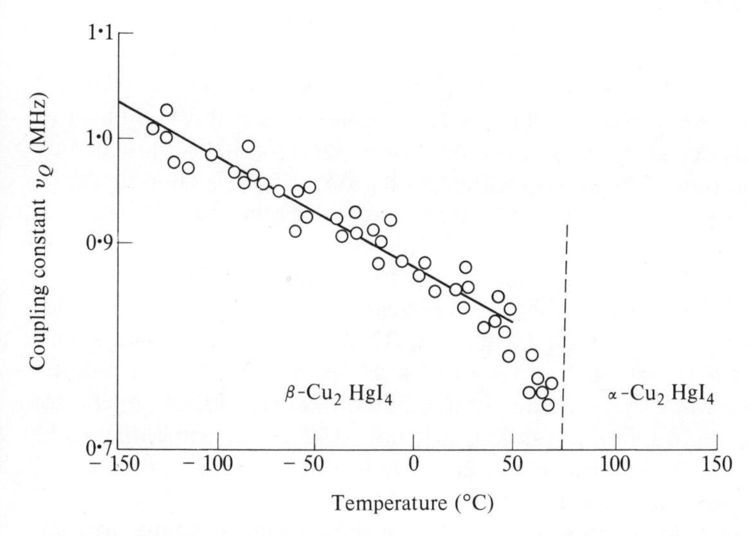

Figure 4-27 Quadrupolar coupling constant of Cu in β-Cu_2HgI_4; V_q becomes zero at the β-α transition. (*After Herzog and Krischner.*[111])

leading to ΔS_c of $k \ln (24/8) = 2.18$ cal deg^{-1} mol^{-1} (see Chap. 7 for further discussion of the Fe_3O_4 transition).

Many order–disorder transitions are known where, instead of ions in the lattice, vacancies arising out of nonstoichiometry undergo disordering. This kind of transition[114] is typified by $TiO_{1.19}$. When it is cooled from 1570 K, the transition occurs at 1260 K with 15 percent of Ti and O vacancies ordered in (110) planes (see Sec. 3-7 for a discussion of the order–disorder transition in stochiometric TiO).

Orientational order–disorder transitions are found in a large number of inorganic solids, and we shall now discuss a few typical examples of this category. In general, any crystalline solid consisting of nonmonatomic ions or molecules in the lattice can exhibit orientational randomization unless its melting point is very low and interaction in the lattice is highly asymmetric. If such ions in the ordered or in the less disordered state have n_1 orientations and in the disordered state have n_2 orientations, the increase in entropy in the order–disorder transition is given by $\Delta S_0 = k \ln (n_2/n_1)^N = R \ln \omega$, where $\omega = n_2/n_1$. This behavior is observed in most orientational disorder transitions.[93,115]

Alkali cyanides provide the simplest examples of salts of linear diatomic ions which exhibit orientational disorder. In KCN, the III → II transition at 83 K is of the λ-type.[116] The gain in entropy is around $R \ln 2$, indicating that CN^- ions gain two possible orientations. A second λ-type transition from orthorhombic (II) to cubic (I) at 168 K is associated with an entropy of approximately $R \ln 4$, indicating that in cubic KCN (I), the CN^- ions now orient in any of the eight $\langle 111 \rangle$ directions (this is more true in NaCN). That this is only an orientational disorder and does not correspond to any free rotation of CN^- ions has been shown by the neutron spectroscopic studies by Atoji[117] and supported by the magnetic resonance work of Fukushima[118] and O'Reilly et al.[119] NaCN exhibits two phase transitions. The high-temperature cubic form transforms to an orthorhombic form at 298 K which further transforms at 172 K to another form (probably monoclinic). The low-temperature transition is associated with a ΔS of $R \ln 2$, while the high-temperature transition is associated with a ΔS of $R \ln 4$. Extensive NMR studies (^{23}Na, ^{14}N, and ^{13}C) carried out on NaCN, along with neutron spectroscopic data, rule out free rotation of CN^- and favor jump reorientation.[118,119]

Elegant neutron scattering studies have been carried out on the order–disorder transitions in alkali hydrogen sulfides (NaHS, RbHS, and CsHS) by Rush and coworkers.[120] In the rhombohedral phase of NaSH, the SH^- ions are disordered in two orientations while they execute librational motion in the high-temperature cubic phase, attaining rapid and random orientation along the cube diagonals. From an analysis of the spectra (Fig. 4-28) in both the phases it is found that SH^- ions do not undergo free rotation.

Potassium thiocyanate,[121] KNCS, has an orthorhombic structure with an ordered antiferroelectric arrangement of NCS^- anions in (100) planes. It undergoes a λ-transition with a T_c of 413 K and an overall entropy change[122] of $\sim R \ln 2$ to a disordered tetragonal structure. The triatomic linear NCS^- ions are randomly oriented in two directions in (100) planes, as confirmed by infrared[123] and Raman[124] spectra.

A nonlinear triatomic ion is exemplified by the nitrite ion. At laboratory temperatures $NaNO_2$ is ferroelectric with an orthorhombic structure.[125] It transforms to an antiferroelectric structure which has a very narrow stability range of one degree (437–438 K).[126,127] It then transforms to the paraelectric phase which also possesses an orthorhombic structure. The transitions have been investigated both by x-ray[127] and spectroscopic[128] techniques. The sum of entropy changes[129] at the two transitions is approximately $R \ln 2$, indicating that the two orientations become available for the NO_2^- ions upon transition. KNO_2 exhibits polymorphic transitions[130] at 260 K and 312 K, from the low-temperature monoclinic structure through rhombohedral to the high-temperature face-centered cubic structure. From elaborate x-ray studies Solbakk and Strømme[130] have concluded that in the rhombohedral phase each NO_2^- has six possible orientations. Similarly, it has been shown that the cubic phase has sixteen equivalent positions, each of which gives two nonequivalent orientations for the NO_2^- ion. However, the entropy increase at the first transition[131] is slightly greater than the expected $R \ln 6$ ($2.3R$), and at the second transition[132] ($\sim 0.19R$) is less than the expected $R \ln (32/6)$ value. It is concluded that the NO_2^- ions do not use all the configurations available to them in the cubic phase.

Nitrate, carbonate, and borate ions are simple tetratomic planar ions which impart many orientational disorder possibilities.[115,126] Sodium and potassium nitrates have high-temperature disordered rhombohedral phases. These transitions may be looked upon as calcite–aragonite transitions with a change in coordination from 6:6 to 9:9. In the calcite structure the nitrogen of NO_3^- is at the center of a distorted octahedron. In the aragonite structure, NO_3^- is displaced from the midpoint along the *c*-axis so that two positions are possible for the NO_3^- groups. $NaNO_3$ undergoes a typical λ-type gradual transition with a T_c of around 548 K. It was first thought from x-ray studies[115,133] (weakening of oxygen

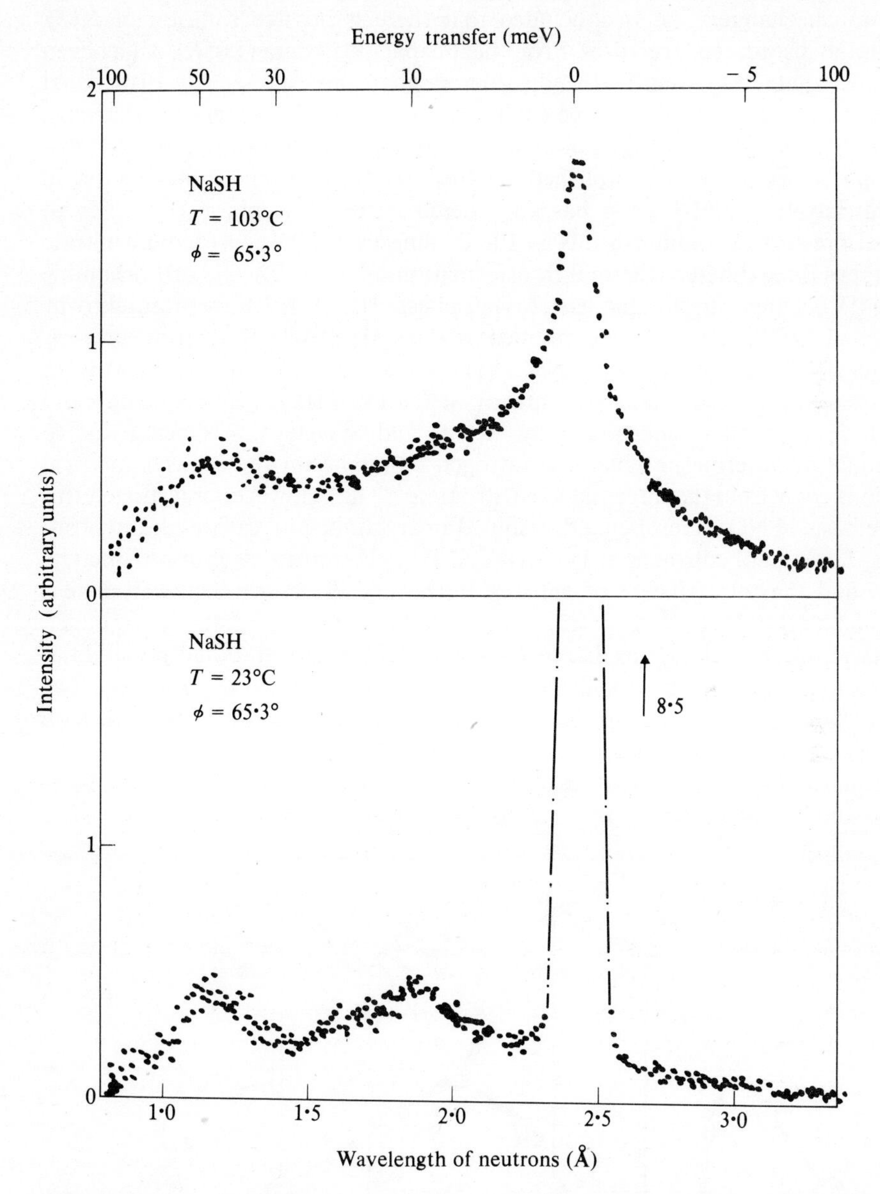

Figure 4-28 Time-of-flight neutron spectra for NaSH. Intensity is corrected for background, chopper transmission, and detector efficiency. Note the broadening of the elastic peak in the cubic phase (*a*) and the presence of smeared broad inelastic peak around 50 meV. (*b*) is the spectrum of NaSH in rhombohedral phase. (*After Rush et al.*[120])

reflections) that the transition corresponds to the onset of free rotation, and the idea was supported by the spectroscopic evidence[134] which indicated a low librational frequency as well as a low rotational barrier. However, since the entropy gain at the transition is very small and the vibration–libration spectra do not show much change,[135] it is concluded that there is no free rotation of NO_3^- ions in the disordered structures. From heat capacity[136] data ($1.05R$), it has been suggested that NO_3^- ions in the disordered phase are statistically distributed between calcite and aragonite-type environments (45 and 55 percent respectively).

KNO_3, as also $AgNO_3$, exhibits a calcite–aragonite transition, and the disordering seems to be accomplished by the two types of environments, as in sodium nitrate.[136] KNO_3 too has an ordered ferroelectric phase III, which at normal pressures is obtained only in the cooling cycle.[126,137] Rubidium nitrate undergoes three different thermal transformations.[126,137–139] The orthorhombic phase (IV) changes to a cubic (CsCl-type) phase, III, at 437 K with an entropy change of $1.07R$, then to a rhombohedral type (II) at 493 K with an entropy change of $0.78R$, and finally to NaCl type cubic phase (I) at 564 K with an entropy of $0.21R$. The change in entropy at the IV → III transition being close to $R \ln 3$, it was first interpreted by Newns and Staveley[115] as being due to positional disordering in which the nitrogen atoms lie on three unsymmetrical positions away from the threefold axis. Strømme[136] has, however, interpreted this on the basis of NO_3^- ions' being distributed in aragonite and calcite-like environments. The sum of entropies at IV → III and III → II transitions is approximately $R \ln 6$ and the total change of entropy (including all the three transitions) is approximately $R \ln 8$. These entropy increases have been consistently explained by Newns and Staveley[115] as due to imposition of two orientational possibilities in the rhombohedral phase and further twofold orientational disorder of NO_3^- ions in planes at right angles to each of the four threefold axes which pass through the N atom in the NaCl phase.

Ammonium chloride provides an important example of order–disorder transitions and has been extensively investigated. The III–II transition (243 K) where

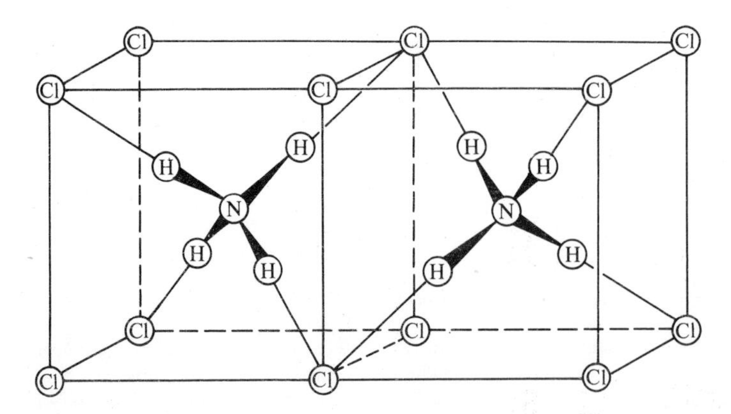

Figure 4-29 Two possible orientations for NH_4^+ ions in phase II of ammonium chloride.

both phases have CsCl-type structure is a λ-type transition. It was initially thought of as due to the onset of free rotation of NH_4^+ ions. From thermodynamic[139] ($\Delta S \simeq 0.7R$), neutron spectroscopic,[140] and NMR[141] studies it is now known that NH_4^+ ions execute only librations and that in the disordered phase II, NH_4^+ ions utilize two possible orientations, as shown in Fig. 4-29. In Fig. 4-30 we show some results of Raman studies[142] consistent with this mechanism. Many other studies on this transition and of other ammonium halides have been excellently

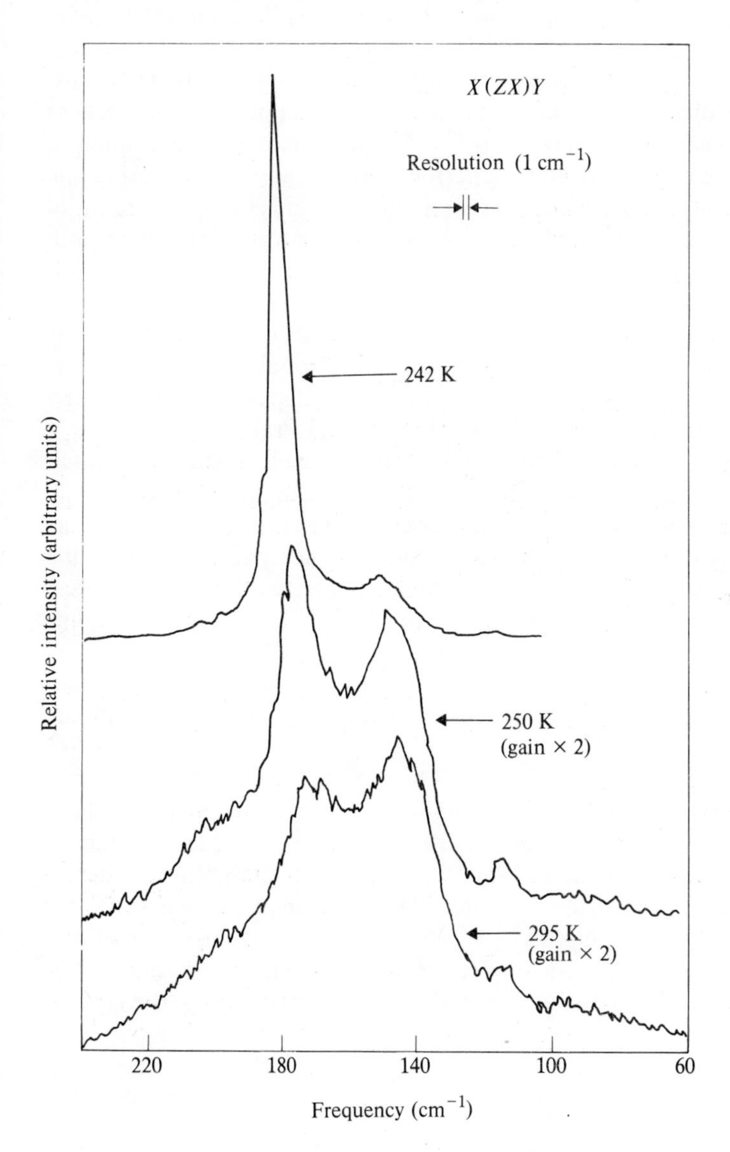

Figure 4-30 Raman spectra of NH_4Cl oriented single crystal in 60–240 cm^{-1} region at various temperatures. Note the vanishing of 144 cm^{-1} band above the transition. (*After Wang and Wright.*[142])

reviewed by Newns and Staveley[115] as well as Rao and Natarajan.[143] The II–I transition of NH_4Cl from CsCl to NaCl-type structure at 456 K is associated with a further disordering entropy of 1.17 cal deg^{-1} mol^{-1}.[139] It is now believed that there is no free rotation of the ammonium ions in the NaCl phase of ammonium halides as well and that NH_4^+ ions execute very complex librational motions.[115,140]

Interpretation of order–disorder transitions becomes complicated when both anions and cations can lead to orientational disorder. NH_4NO_3 and $(NH_4)_2SO_4$ are examples of this kind. The NO_3^- ions in phases II and I (tetragonal and cubic respectively[126,144]) are now definitely known to be orientationally disordered.[145,146] The ions do not seem to be able to exploit all orientations because of some mutually restrictive interactions.[93,115] Ammonium sulfate exhibits a transition[147,148] from one orthorhombic (ferroelectric) to another orthorhombic phase (paraelectric) at 223 K. This is accompanied by an entropy increase of nearly $2R$ and has been interpreted as an order–disorder transition where both SO_4^{2-} and NH_4^+ ions have two orientations each.[149] Since there are two NH_4^+ ions which are in different coordinations[150,151] (one with five nearest neighbors and the other with six), one can expect an entropy increase of $R \ln 8 \simeq 2R$. Many salts with anions like BH_4^-, SO_4^{2-}, ClO_4^-, and BeF_4^{2-} are all known to exhibit complex order–disorder transitions.[115] Transitions in sulfates, phosphates, perchlorates, and chromates have been reviewed by Rao and Prakash.[148]

Many inorganic salts undergo what are known as plastic crystal transformations. This descriptive term only means that the material becomes plastically deformable.[93] A characteristic of these plastic crystalline transitions is that the material gains a very high entropy at the transition as compared to its melting entropy. As a consequence, in the plastic crystalline phase, it is highly disordered. Tungsten hexafluoride (WF_6) is an example of this kind.[93] It is plastic crystalline in the range 265 K to 275 K. The entropies of transition are 7.8 and 3.56 cal deg^{-1} mol^{-1} respectively. In addition to orientational freedom, since it also contains substantial concentration of Schottky defects, it is likely to possess some positional disordering as well.

Other types of disorder Crystalline compounds of transition metal ions exhibit spin disorder. As we have already noted, the three kinds of ordering, namely ferro, antiferro, and ferrimagnetic ordering in magnetic crystals, all disorder to paramagnetic state at transition temperatures. If the net spin of an ion is s then the spin multiplicity of the ion being $(2s + 1) = S$ leads to S possible orientations. At the transition the maximum entropy change due to spin disordering will be $R \ln S$. In cases like $CuCl_2$, however, due to the existence of chains of the type

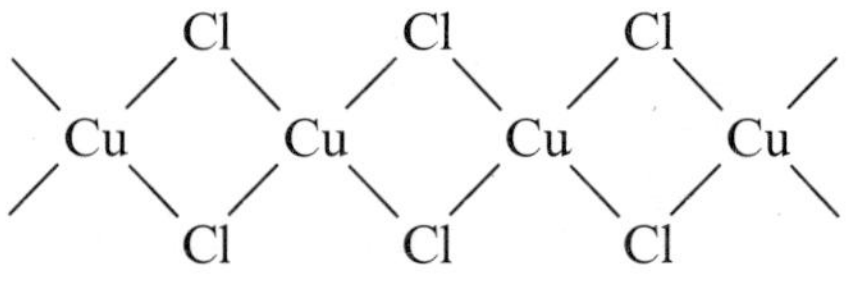

```
        Cl        Cl        Cl
  \    /  \     /  \     /  \    /
    Cu      Cu      Cu      Cu
  /    \  /     \  /     \  /    \
        Cl        Cl        Cl
```

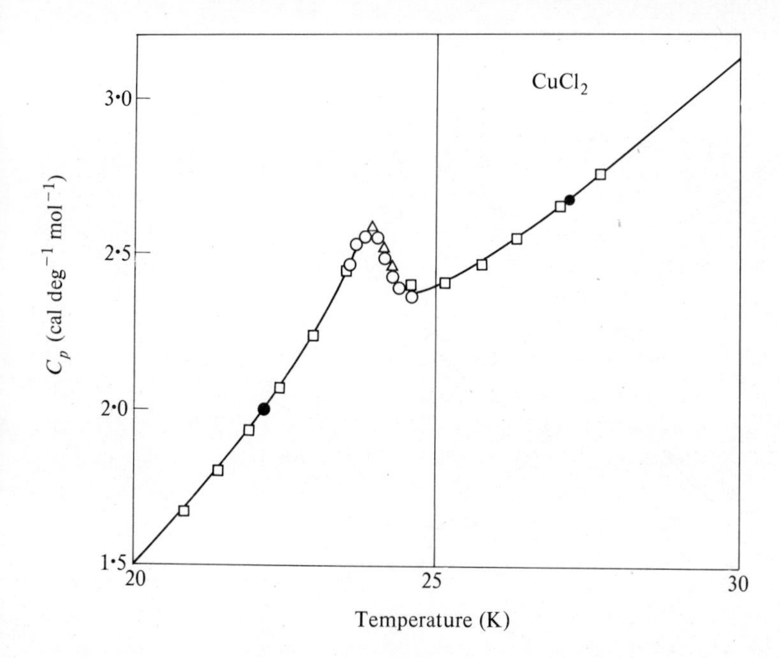

Figure 4-31 Heat capacity of $CuCl_2$ which undergoes a magnetic transition at 24 K. Note the continued increase of heat capacity beyond the transition temperature. (*After Stout and Chisholm.*[152])

the disordering of spins along the chains takes place only at much higher temperatures.[152] Thus, at the transition at 24 K, the increase in entropy of $CuCl_2$ is only 27 percent of the total value of $R \ln 2$. The magnetic contribution to heat capacity continues beyond 24 K (Fig. 4-31). If the individual ions consist of more than one spin-carrying atom, then because of strong coupling the total spin degeneracy also gets reduced.[153]

We have considered so far a number of examples of order–disorder transitions. There are, however, quite a number of disordered materials which do not undergo ordering on cooling. Thus, their entropies will be positive at 0 K. This is in apparent contradiction of the third law of thermodynamics. A good example of such a material would be H_2O which has a residual entropy of $R \ln (3/2)$ (accurate to within 1 percent).[93,154] Hydrates like $ZnF_2 . 4H_2O$ also have large residual entropies at 0 K.[155] This does not mean that the disordered state has lower energy. It so happens because, at very low temperatures, the particles do not possess sufficient energy to rearrange to the lowest energy configuration and just remain in a nonequilibrium state.

4-4 SPINODAL DECOMPOSITIONS

We have been so far discussing transformations which occur without change in composition; that is, the number of phases was constant during a transformation.

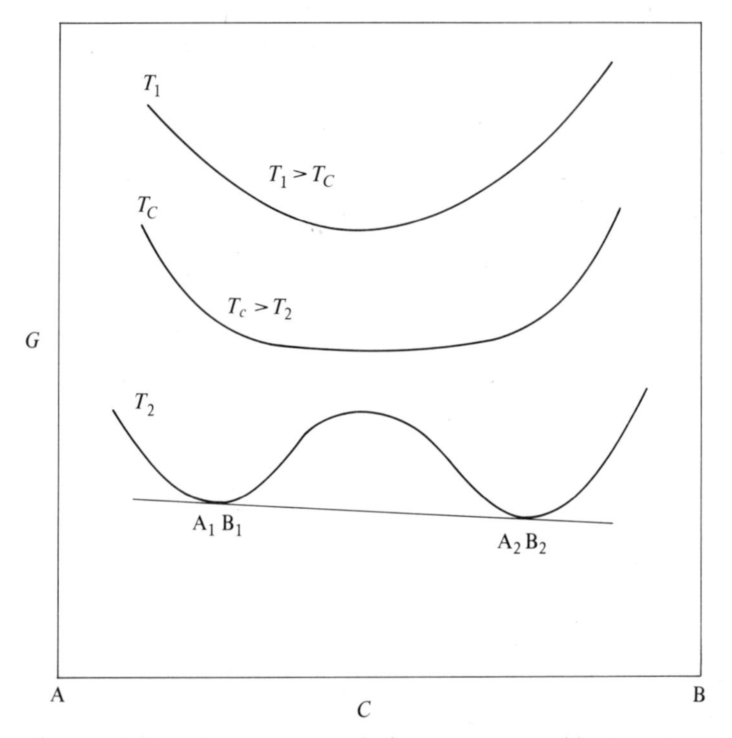

Figure 4-32 Effect of temperature on the free energy–composition behavior (schematic); $T_1 < T_c < T_2$.

A special kind of transformation known as spinodal decomposition, often observed in binary solid solutions of metals and in glasses, arises from thermodynamic instabilities caused by composition.[156] A special feature of this solid state transformation is the absence of any nucleation barrier. The theory of spinodal decompositions is well developed, although there is still some controversy[157] with regard to details. We shall discuss spinodal decompositions following the approach of Shewman[158] along with a few examples of inorganic systems which undergo such transformations.

The Concept of a Spinodal

Let us consider a binary system AB. In Fig. 4-32 we represent the variation of free energy $G(C)$ with composition for different temperatures. At temperature T_1, there is only one phase through the composition range and the free energy is concave upwards. At temperature T_c (critical consolute temperature), the central region of the free energy curve exhibits the typically flat behavior. At any temperature T_2 below T_c, the central region of the free energy curve rises, indicating the occurrence of immiscibility of the two components in the region of the common tangent, A_1B_1–A_2B_2. The material in this region ultimately decomposes to A_1B_1 and A_2B_2 in appropriate proportions.

Let us consider what happens to the free energy of a homogeneous system (quenched to temperature T_2) during fluctuations of composition. For a small fluctuation ΔC around C_0, ΔG may be written as

$$\Delta G = G(C_0 + \Delta C) + G(C_0 - \Delta C) - 2G(C_0) \tag{4-58}$$

The quantities can be expanded in Taylor's series, whereby

$$G(C_0 + \Delta C) = G(C_0) + \Delta C \cdot G'(C_0) + \frac{\Delta C^2}{2} \cdot G''(C_0) + \cdots$$

and

$$G(C_0 - \Delta C) = G(C_0) - \Delta C \cdot G'(C_0) + \frac{\Delta C^2}{2} \cdot G''(C_0) + \cdots \tag{4-59}$$

Combining Eqs. (4-58) and (4-59) we get the expression for the change in free energy as a result of the composition fluctuation:

$$\Delta G = G''(C_0) \cdot \Delta C^2 \tag{4-60}$$

In Fig. 4-33 the free energy corresponding to temperature T_2 of Fig. 4-32 is shown separately. In the regions marked $\Delta G'' > 0$, therefore, a small fluctuation will increase the free energy. Around the stable alloy compositions A_1B_1 and A_2B_2, only a large fluctuation can reduce the free energy. That is, conventional nucleation barriers which are fairly high are present and fluctuations needed are also large. The region covered by $G'' < 0$, that is the region where $G(C)$ curve is concave downward, any fluctuation (small or big) lowers the free energy. The boundary

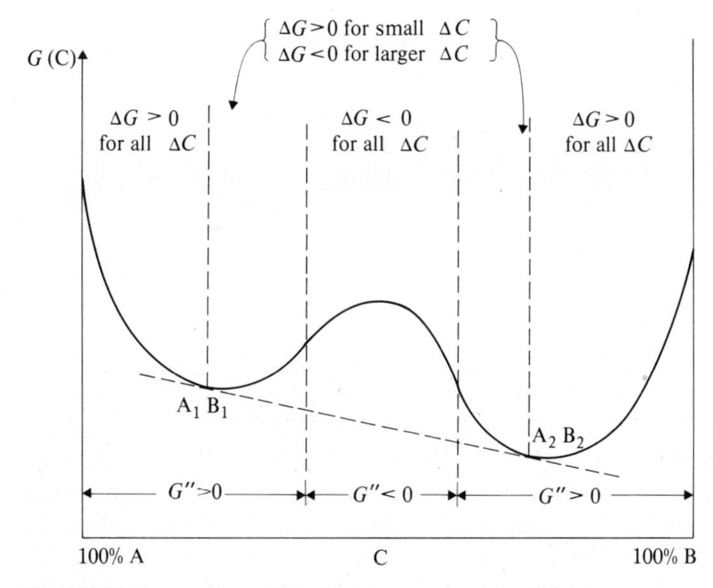

Figure 4-33 Free energy plot indicating the behavior of ΔG for various fluctuations ΔC. (*After Shewman.*[158])

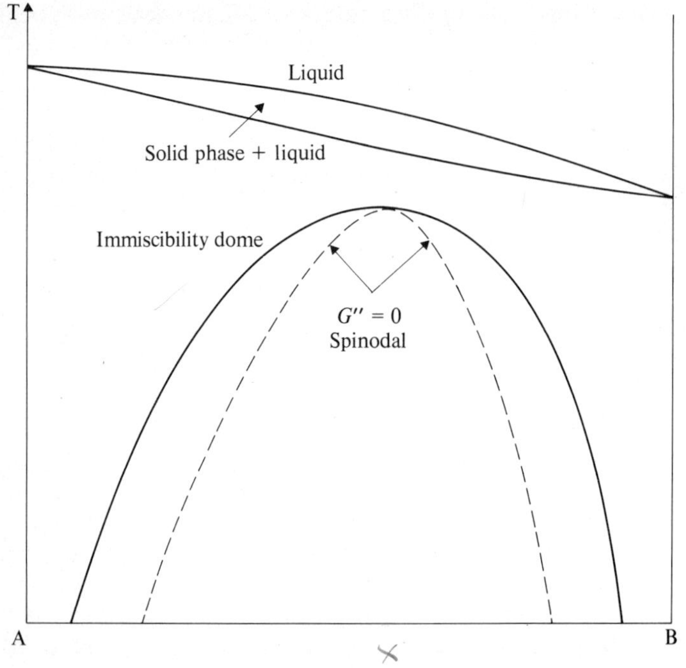

Figure 4-34 Phase diagram showing the immiscibility dome and the spinodal (schematic).

corresponding to $\Delta G'' = 0$ in temperature–composition space is known as a spinodal.

In Fig. 4-34 the phase diagram of the system exhibiting a spinodal region is shown. If a binary compound of an arbitrary composition is quenched and if it is within the region bounded by A_1B_1 and A_2B_2, large fluctuations would be needed to create critical-sized nuclei in the two-phase region between the spinodal and the immiscibility dome while within the spinodal any small fluctuation in composition is already supercritical.

Decomposition Inside the Spinodal

Inside the spinodal, therefore, the decomposition is spontaneous and the value of ΔG increases negatively (in view of Eq. (4-60)) with fluctuations of composition, ΔC. Fluctuation in composition is achieved by diffusion and in this instance, diffusion is against the concentration gradient and hence called "uphill" diffusion.[159] (The diffusion coefficient is formally negative.) Uphill diffusion takes place in order to facilitate the composition fluctuation which accomplishes a considerable decrease in the free energy. The interdiffusion of A and B in the undecomposed matrix is represented by the diffusion equation which may be written for the one-dimensional (moving interface[160]) case as

$$J = -D \cdot \frac{dC}{dx} = -MC \cdot \frac{d\mu}{dx} \tag{4-61}$$

Therefore
$$D = MC \cdot \frac{d\mu}{dC} \tag{4-62}$$

where D is the diffusion coefficient, M is the mobility, and μ is the chemical potential of the given component. C is the concentration and x is the distance from a reference point. It can be shown that $d\mu/dC = (1 - C)G''$ which on substitution into Eq. (4-62) gives

$$D = MC(1 - C)G'' \tag{4-63}$$

By definition, D is independent of concentration and hence of x. We can now write the diffusion equation as

$$\left(\frac{\partial C}{\partial t}\right)_x = -\left(\frac{\partial J}{\partial x}\right)_t = -D\left(\frac{\partial^2 C}{\partial x^2}\right) \tag{4-64}$$

The general solution of Eq. (4-64) has the form[161]

$$C = A(\lambda, t) \exp(2\pi i x/\lambda) \tag{4-65}$$

The time evolution of $A(\lambda, t)$, which relates D with the rate of increase of the amplitude of fluctuation, is given by

$$A(\lambda, t) = A(\lambda, 0) \exp(-4\pi^2 Dt/\lambda^2) \tag{4-66}$$

The quantity $(4\pi^2 D/\lambda^2)$ which is a function of λ is also known as the amplification factor $R(\lambda)$. The variation of the amplitude of a sinusoidal composition fluctuation of wavelength λ is shown in Fig. (4-35). With time, the amplitude increases, and

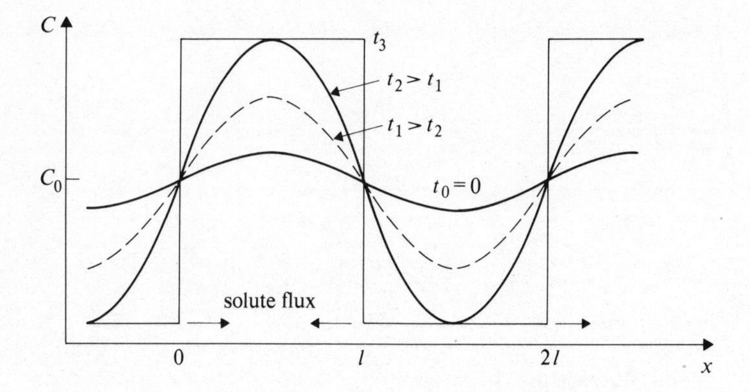

Figure 4-35 Growth of the amplitude of fluctuations as a function of time for decomposition inside the spinodal. The uphill diffusion may be noted. (*After Shewman.*[158])

ultimately when the material inside the spinodal is completely transformed into A_1B_1 and A_2B_2, the amplitude becomes formally infinite. The results are qualitatively the same for the three dimensions.[158]

In the above analysis, the amplification factor becomes very high for shorter wavelengths ($R \propto 1/\lambda^2$) and hence such fluctuations grow faster, the limit of low λ being the interatomic separation in that direction.[161] This is obviously contrary to experience, since much higher wavelengths alone seem to grow[162] and dominate the decomposition process. This drawback of the simple classical diffusion approach was removed by Cahn[163,164] by a consideration of two terms neglected in the above analysis. The terms arise from (*a*) the existence of "diffuse" interfaces (gradient energy terms), and (*b*) interphase elastic strains because the separated phases are not fully coherent.

During diffusion, there is usually cluster formation. Clusters form because the energy of interaction between unlike atoms is greater than between like atoms. Cluster formation sets up a concentration gradient. The increased energy term corresponds to the energy of the diffuse interface between the embryonic cluster and the surrounding matrix. This interface (per unit volume) is proportional to λ^{-1} and its gradient is $\Delta C/\lambda$. It is assumed that the interfacial energy term is equal to $\alpha(\Delta C/\lambda)^2$, where $\alpha > 0$ is a constant.[158] The net gain in free energy due

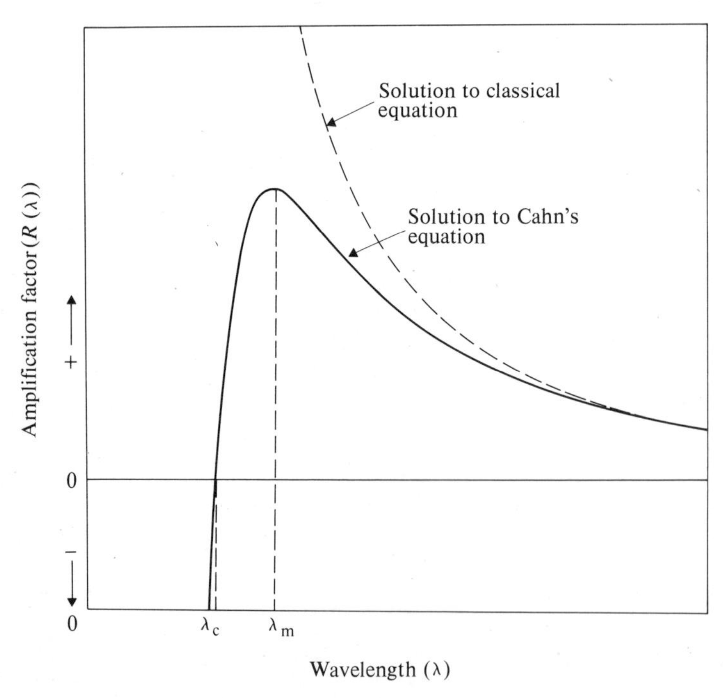

Figure 4-36 Amplification factors for different wavelengths obtained from classical and Cahn diffusion expressions. (*After Hilliard,*[161] *with permission, from "Phase Transformations," copyright by American Society for Metals, 1970.*)

to fluctuation is modified as

$$\Delta G = \Delta C^2 G'' + \alpha(\Delta C/\lambda)^2 = \Delta C^2(G'' + \alpha/\lambda^2) \tag{4-67}$$

In view of Eq. (4-67) we see that not all fluctuations can lead to lowering of free energy, and a lower limit to the fluctuation wavelength, λ, should therefore exist; this is equal to $(\alpha/G'')^{1/2}$, which is always greater than one interatomic distance.

We have assumed that the phases formed during spinodal decomposition are coherent and that there is no strain between the phases and the matrix. However, in cases where the lattice parameters of A_1B_1 and A_2B_2 are different, an interfacial strain is generated and this energy term compensates the free energy $(G''\Delta C^2)$ to some extent. If the lattice strain developed due to concentration variations during phase separation is written as da_0/dC equal to η, then $\eta\Delta C$ will be proportional to the total strain.[158] If E is the Young's modulus and ν the Poisson's ratio, this free energy contribution may be written as equal to $\eta^2(\Delta C)^2E/[2(1-\nu)]$. If this term is included in Eq. (4-67), the net variation in energy due to fluctuation of composition, ΔC, becomes

$$\Delta G = \Delta C^2\left[G'' + \frac{\alpha}{\lambda^2} + \frac{\eta^2 E}{2(1-\nu)}\right] \tag{4-68}$$

This modified free energy term may now be compared with ΔG of Eq. (4-60). This

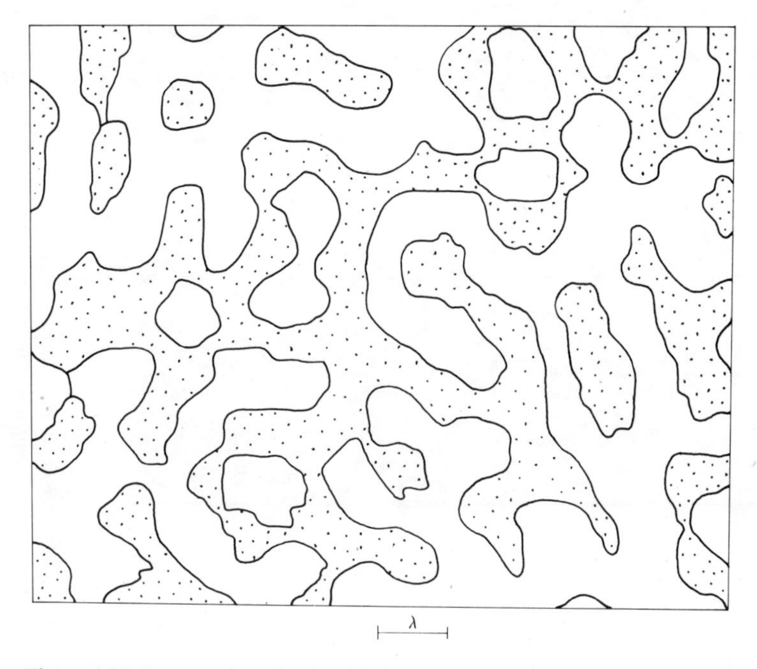

Figure 4-37 Cross-section of spinodal decomposition obtained from computer experiment. (*After Cahn.*[165])

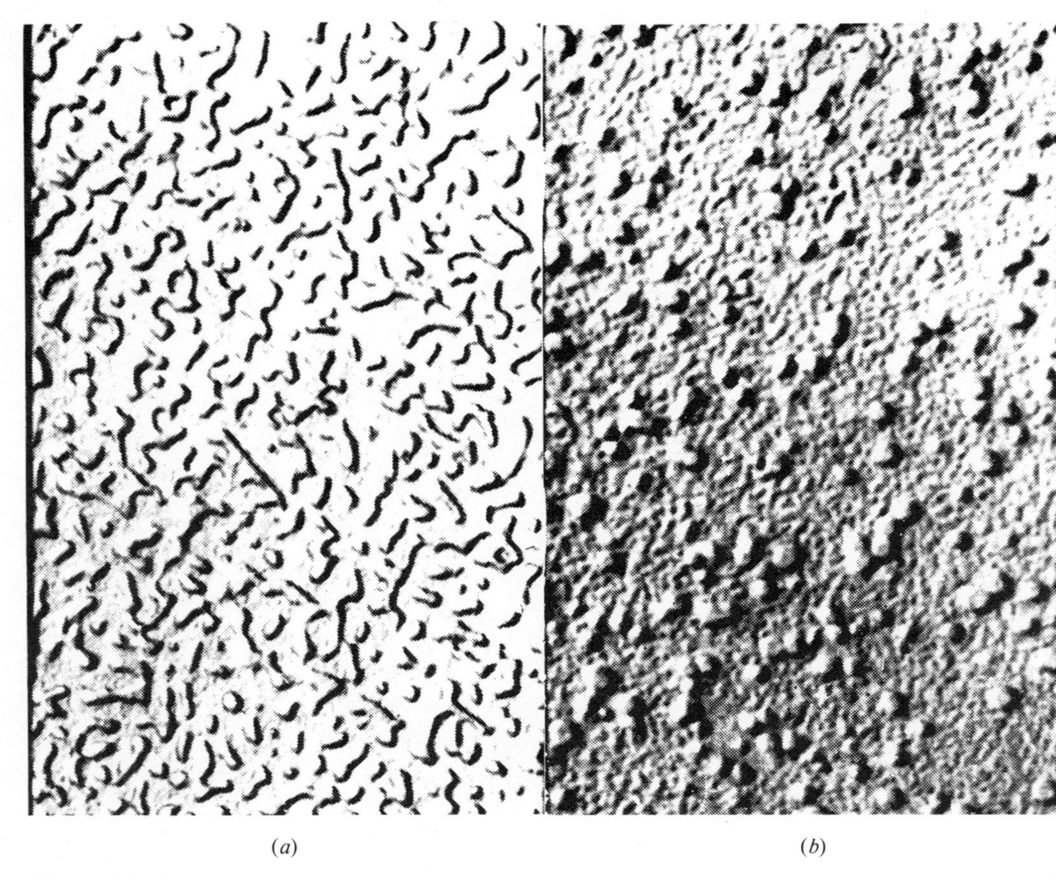

Figure 4-38 (*a*) Spinodal decomposition, and (*b*) nucleation and growth in silica glasses. (*After Ernsberger,*[169] *with permission, from "Properties of Glass Surfaces," Annual Reviews of Materials Science, Vol. 2, copyright 1972 by Annual Reviews Inc.*)

has also the effect of appropriately modifying the diffusion equation and the amplification factor.[161] The behavior of the amplification factor in the classical and Cahn (modified) diffusion equations is represented in Fig. 4-36. There is a maximum, $R(\lambda)$, corresponding to the dominant fluctuation wavelength, λ_m; fluctuations less than λ_c automatically decay.

Cahn[165] has performed computer calculations to show the nature of spinodal decomposition expected from theory. Composition fluctuations were achieved by superposition of sine waves of a fixed wavelength but of random orientation, phase, and amplitude. By superposition of 100 sine waves he obtained a pattern of spinodal decomposition shown in Fig. 4-37. The dotted portions correspond to $C > C_0$, where C_0 is the average composition. When we compare Fig. 4-37 with Fig. 4-38*a* where a photograph of a glass which has undergone spinodal decomposition is shown, the resemblance is remarkable. The point to be noted is the high degree of connectivity although there is no regular periodicity.

The decomposition to equilibrium phases in the region between the immiscibility dome and the spinodal is achieved by the mechanism of homogeneous nucleation and growth (Fig. 4-38*b*), because a critical-sized fluctuation is necessary before the free energy change becomes favorable. This mechanism was discussed earlier in Sec. 4-1. Furthermore, this region of immiscibility is metastable while the spinodal region is unstable. In Table 4-2, some of the essential differences between the two types of decomposition mechanisms in the immiscibility region have been listed.[166,167] Spinodal decompositions are associated with considerable connectivity (Fig. 4-38*a*). This feature has been the subject of detailed investigations, and it has been argued that it is not essential for spinodal decompositions to exhibit interconnectivity.[168–170] The effect of various external constraints such as pressure,[171] magnetic field,[172] and electric field[173] on spinodal decomposition have also been investigated.

Table 4-2 Important differences between nucleation-and-growth and spinodal mechanisms

Nucleation and growth	Spinodal decomposition
1. The composition of the second phase remains unaltered with time (equilibrium phase)	A continuous change of composition occurs until the equilibrium values are attained
2. The interfaces between the nucleating phase and the matrix are discernibly sharp	The interface is initially very diffuse but eventually sharpens
3. There is a marked tendency for random distribution of both sizes and positions of the equilibrium phases	A regularity—though not simple—exists both in sizes and distribution of the phases
4. Particles of separated phases tend to be spherical with low connectivity	The separated phases are generally nonspherical and possess a high degree of connectivity

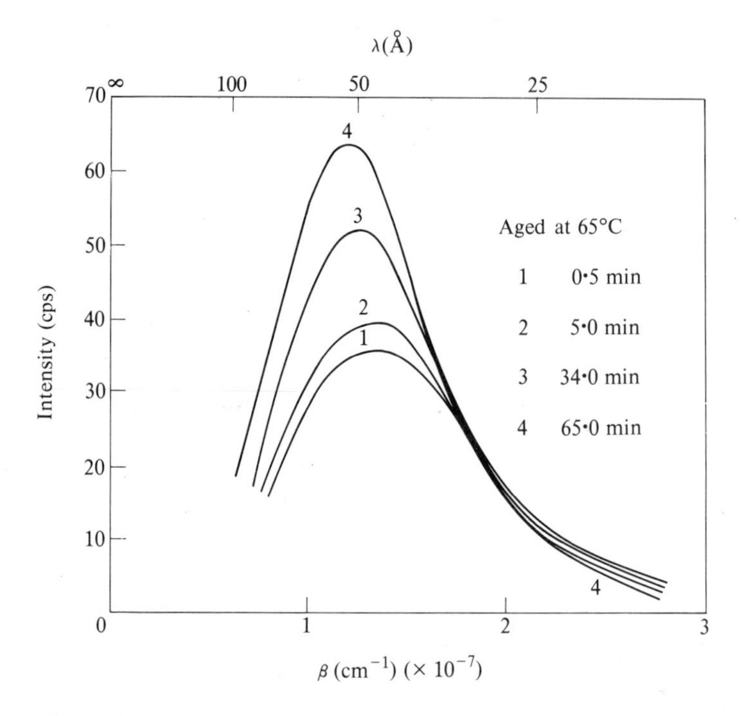

Figure 4-39 Small angle x-ray spectra of Al–22 at % Zn alloy quenched from 425°C and annealed at 65°C for various times. β is $2\pi/\lambda$. (*After Rundman and Hilliard.*[174])

Examples of Spinodal Decompositions

Many intermetallic systems have been found to exhibit spinodal decompositions. Thus, the Al–Zn system with 40 at. % zinc has been examined by Rundmann and Hilliard,[174] and the λ_m in this system is approximately 35 Å. In Fig. 4-39, low-angle x-ray scattering data on this system have been given. Low-angle x-ray scattering is still the best method to obtain the characteristic modulation distances because these modulations produce satellites about the Bragg peaks and the lattice spacing modulations do not contribute to the intensity of satellites in the low-angle scattering regions.[161] Al–20 at % Ag alloy[175] is another system which undergoes spinodal decomposition, as also $SmCo_{5-x}Cu_x$, which is a magnetic alloy.[176]

Inorganic (nonmetallic) systems which have been extensively investigated for spinodal decompositions are the glasses. A special feature of spinodal decomposition in glasses is the absence of strain-energy terms. Particularly well investigated are the soda–silica (Na_2O–SiO_2) glasses.[177,178] These glasses have been annealed at various temperatures below the temperature of complete miscibility and investigated by the low-angle x-ray scattering technique. In Fig. 4-40, the variation of λ_m with temperature has been given for the case of (SiO_2–12.6 mole % Na_2O) glass. Zarzycki and Naudin[179] have examined the spinodal decomposition in B_2O_3–PbO glasses. The diffusion coefficients in these glasses (which also contain small percentages of Al_2O_3) are extremely high when compared to SiO_2–Na_2O systems though the activation barriers are the same. V_2O_5–12.5%P_2O_5 glass also undergoes spinodal decomposition.[180] As examined by electron microscopy, this system has been found to decompose into a pattern similar to that predicted by Cahn[165] by computer simulation. A purely crystalline inorganic solid in which a spinodal decomposition is reported[181] to have occurred is the SnO_2–TiO_2 system containing 50–60 mole % of SnO_2; the periodicity here was about 100 Å.

Spinodal decomposition is indeed an interesting transformation mechanism. Mechanical properties of solids are very much influenced by the nature of the second phase, which is present as a dispersoid. The so-called GP zones (Guinier–Preston zones) are considered as the finest particulate heterophases that can be formed in dispersion. In fact, the formation of GP zones has been explained[158,182] by the mechanism of spinodal decomposition.

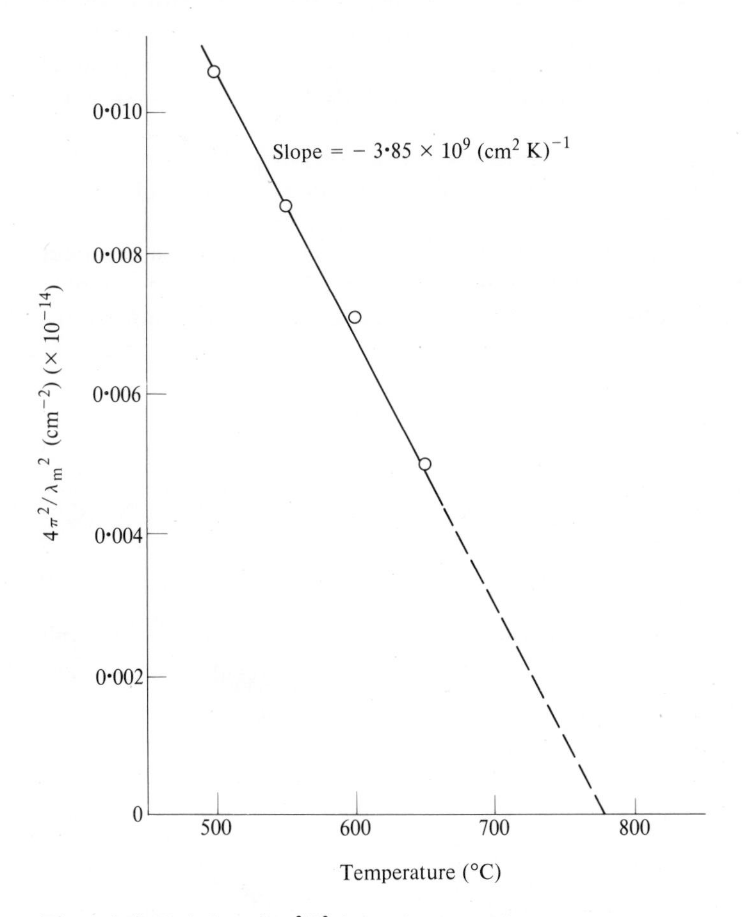

Figure 4-40 Variation of $4\pi^2/\lambda_m^2$ for various annealing temperatures in SiO_2–12.16 mole % Na_2O glass. (*After Neilson.*[178])

4-5 EUTECTOID DECOMPOSITIONS

We have already noted that certain compositions in a phase diagram become unstable at lower temperatures and decompose to stable phases. Such decompositions are often achieved through a spinodal mechanism. For a composition around a eutectic, decomposition to stable phases often occurs by a nucleation and growth mechanism and is termed as a eutectoid reaction or eutectoid decomposition.[42] We shall indicate the nature of this transformation briefly in this section.

A simple form of eutectoid decomposition in a binary phase diagram corresponds to $AB \rightarrow A_1B_1 + A_2B_2$. In the case of steels this decomposition is exemplified by the austenite phase which decomposes into ferrite and Fe_3C. The morphology of this product shows lamellar growth known as pearlite. This eutectoid decomposition is also known as the pearlite reaction. In the pearlite reaction, carbon has out of necessity to be redistributed into the carbon-rich Fe_3C and the carbon-poor ferrite. It occurs through a cooperative growth of the two phases, often with a lamellar morphology. The nucleation of the new phases occur almost always at the grain boundaries. The parent austenite and the product ferrite also bear out orientation relationships (the Kurdjumov–Sachs orientation relations between fcc and bcc phases; see Secs. 3-4 and 4-2).

Eutectic decompositions in nonmetallic systems have attracted much less attention in the literature. However, all such decompositions are likely to proceed by nucleation and growth processes involving cooperative readjustments of solute concentrations in the product phases. The characteristic lengths of the product phases which grow into each other are functions of undercooling, roughly decreasing in proportion to the undercooling. Kinetics of these decompositions are in general described by the Avrami equation with $n = 3$, indicating that nucleation occurs at the beginning of the reaction at the grain boundaries.

When the concentration of the solute is on the low side of the eutectic, the reaction is known as proeutectoid decomposition and when on the high side of eutectic, it is known as hypereutectoid decomposition. In the case of steels, therefore, the kinetics of growth of the ferrite phase in proeutectoid decompositions will be limited by the rate of diffusion of the carbon out of the growing ferrite phase. Here again it leads to interesting morphologies (such as Wiedeman–Stratten plates) due to the intergrowth of phases with the nucleation taking place at grain boundaries. Initially, the nucleated ferrite grows as a grain boundary allotriomorph (that which adapts its shape to the environment) and then grows rapidly to produce a boundary network.

4-6 TRANSITIONS IN GLASSES

The definition of a glass has undergone many refinements during the last five decades.[183–186] The most acceptable definition, due to Secrist and Mackenzie,[186] states that "a glass is a non-crystalline solid." All solids may be classified as either crystalline or amorphous.[187] Glass-forming ability is almost a universal

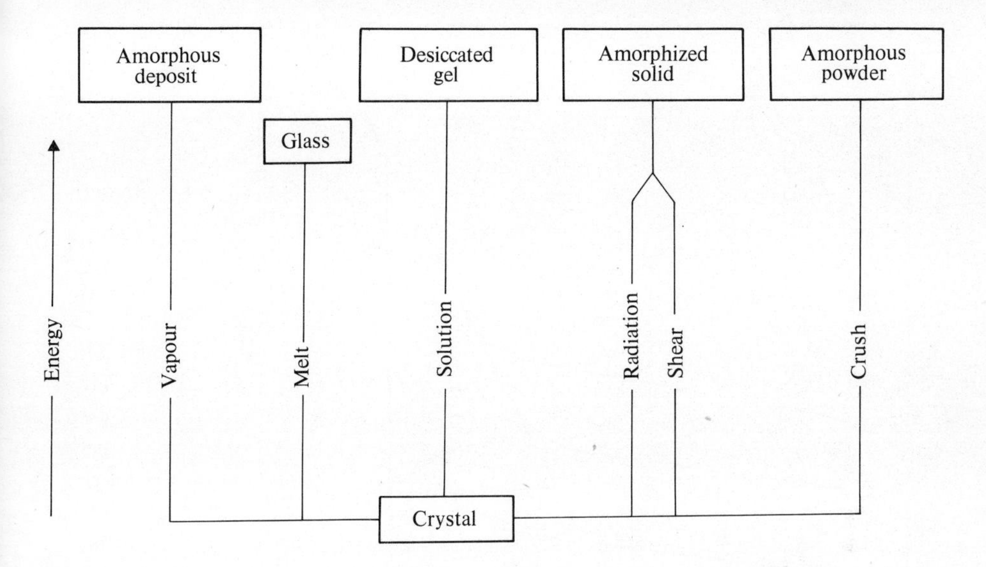

Figure 4-41 Different routes for the formation of amorphous materials. (*After Scholze;*[190] *condensed from Roy.*[189])

property of liquids,[188] both inorganic and organic. With techniques like vacuum evaporation, practically any material can be obtained in the form of thin amorphous films. There are many other routes by which materials can be obtained in the amorphous form,[189,190] as shown in Fig. 4-41. In many instances, the same material can be obtained in the amorphous state by more than one procedure. Amorphous materials obtained from different routes exhibit substantially different physical properties.[191] By the application of pressure during the formation of glass and by varying the rates of quenching, glasses with different physical properties are obtained.[192] The question then arises whether all these forms may be treated as identical except in the chemical sense. Are they the analogs of polymorphic modifications in the crystalline state? In this section, we shall discuss those aspects of glasses and amorphous materials which have a bearing on the kinds of transformations they undergo.

Nature of the Glass Transition

The conventional method of obtaining glasses is by the so-called melt route. When a suitable glass-forming material like B_2O_3 or SiO_2 is heated to a high enough temperature, it melts, and when cooled sufficiently rapidly it becomes a glass. The nature of volume–temperature changes is shown in Fig. 4-42. When the volume decreases to values close to that of the crystal, the rate at which volume decreases also falls, and the behavior of volume changes almost parallels that of the crystalline phase. The departure of the melt-like behavior in the supercooled region (the region below T_m) depends markedly on the rate of cooling. The slower the cooling, the lower is the volume of the glass. The temperature corresponding

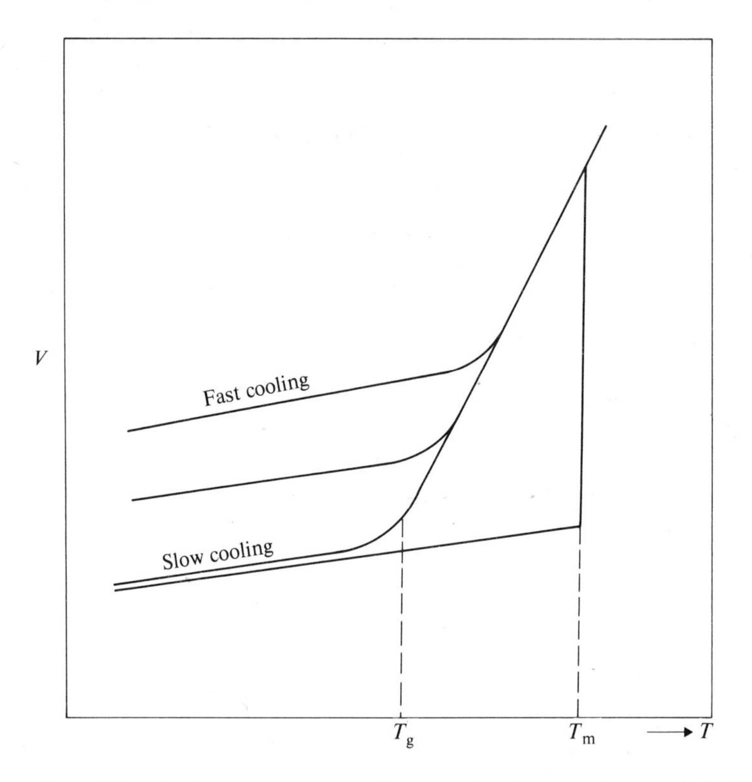

Figure 4-42 Volume–temperature plot for a glass-forming material (schematic).

to this departure is described as the glass transition temperature. Concurrent with the volume change is the enormous increase in the viscosity of the melt. At the glass transition, the shear viscosity of the melt reaches a value of 10^{13} poises.[193] For reasonable values of the shear modulus, G, this value of viscosity corresponds to a relaxation time (η/G) varying anywhere between a few minutes to many hours. Viscosities of glass-forming liquids (except perhaps GeO_2 and SiO_2) may be described by the empirical equation[194-196]

$$\eta = \eta_0 \exp\left[A/(T - T_0)\right] \tag{4-69}$$

where η_0 and T_0 are empirical constants in units of viscosity and temperature respectively.

The variation of heat capacities and entropies corresponding to Fig. 4-42 is shown in Fig. 4-43. The variation of heat capacity, which is more or less sudden in the region of the glass transition, has led to the belief that glass transitions are second-order transitions (in Ehrenfest's classification). However, the glass transition temperature can have only an operational significance since it varies with the cooling rate. The influence of cooling rate[190] on T_g is shown in Fig. 4-44. The dependence of T_g on the cooling rate, q, seems to obey an exponential law[194]

$$q = q_0 \exp\left[-E_a/RT_g\right] \tag{4-70}$$

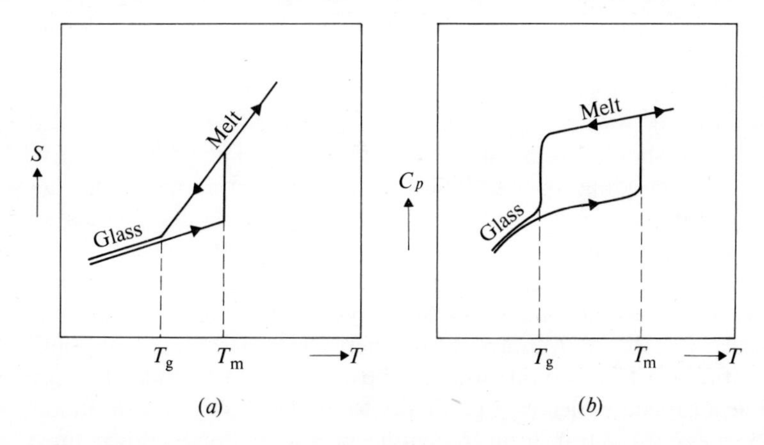

Figure 4-43 (*a*) Variation of entropies and (*b*) heat capacities with temperature for a glass-forming material (schematic).

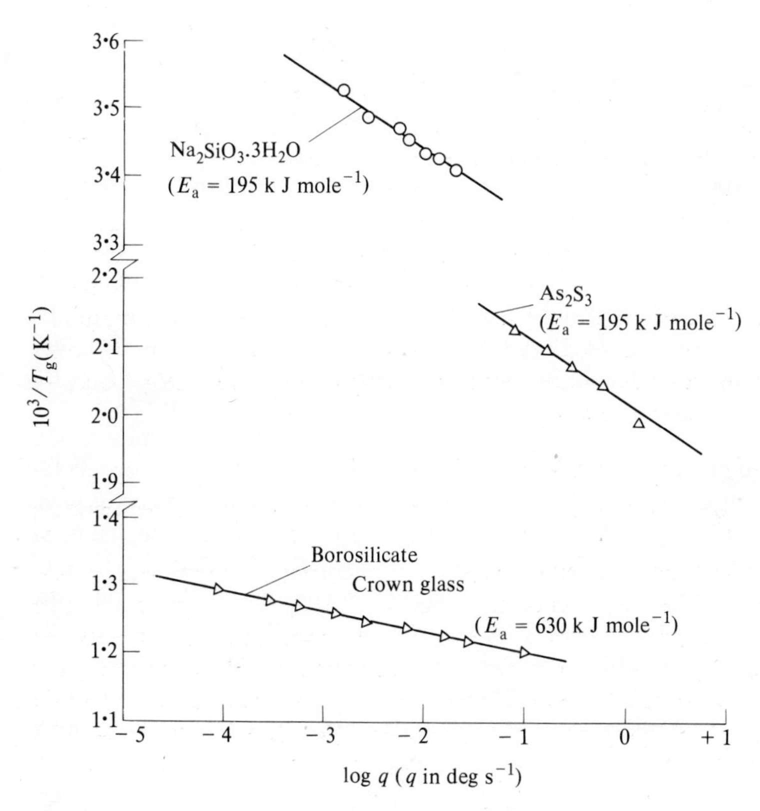

Figure 4-44 The influence of cooling rate on the glass transition temperature. (*After Scholze.*[190])

This naturally raises a question of the lower limit to the value of T_g. From Eq. (4-69) it cannot be lower than T_0. That there should exist a lower limit to T_g under normal circumstances was pointed out by Kauzman.[198]

An inspection of Fig. 4-43 indicates that even if the melt were to be cooled as slowly as needed, T_g should reach a limit when the extrapolated entropy curve touches the one corresponding to crystalline entropy. Any extrapolation further down would result in the paradox that a disordered glass should possess an entropy lower than the corresponding ordered crystal, a result contrary to the fundamental notions of thermodynamics. Thus, at T_0 the properties of supercooled melt must of necessity become similar to their crystalline form, and that state corresponds to a glass. Hence T_0 may be considered the thermodynamic limit to the glass transition.[199] There could, however, be an as yet unreported situation in which liquid heat capacities decrease gradually to solid-like values without any detectable suddenness in the transition. A significant observation in this context is that there are no known glasses where $T_g < T_0$. Angell and coworkers[200-203] have observed through an investigation of transport properties like diffusion coefficient, fluidity, and conductivity that many supercooled liquids obey the equation

$$\begin{aligned} D &= D_0 T^{1/2} \exp\left[-A_D/(T - T_0)\right] \\ \phi &= \phi_0 T^{-1/2} \exp\left[-A_\phi/(T - T_0)\right] \\ \Lambda &= \Lambda_0 T^{1/2} \exp\left[-A_\Lambda/(T - T_0)\right] \end{aligned} \tag{4-71}$$

where D, ϕ, and Λ are the diffusion coefficient, fluidity, and conductance respectively. The pre-exponential and exponential constants are self-evident. The temperature T_0 obtained by transport property measurements and T_0 calculated from calorimetric data (Kauzman limit) have been found to be equal within a narrow limit, in addition to the fact that T_0s obtained from various transport measurements are consistent among themselves (Table 4-3). This again means that at T_0, the liquid-like behavior of the supercooled liquids should cease and therefore T_0 is a limit to T_g.

While T_0 is a thermodynamic parameter, T_g is a kinetic quantity. As a melt is cooled, it gives up heat and the constitutive atoms, ions, or molecules in the melt rearrange to new equilibrium configurations.* This rearrangement or relaxation brings in a time dependence. The relaxation time, as we have already seen, is related to the viscosity and becomes very large in the region close to the glass transition. Thus, the cooling rates will determine when the liquid falls out of equilibrium and hence the value of T_g. The thermodynamic limit of the liquid state, T_0, as estimated from calorimetric data, is lower than T_g, and the excess entropy which the supercooled liquid possesses over that of the crystalline form at T_g is not zero. This entropy is almost entirely configurational and is acquired at melting[199] (the vibrational heat capacities of glass and crystal are not significantly

* It would be more appropriate to call this metastable equilibrium, since the true stable configuration of the material in the supercooled region is crystalline.[198]

Table 4-3 Comparison of T_0 values derived from different transport properties (Angell and Moynihan[200])

Liquid	Property	T_0 (K)	T_g (K)
Isobutyl bromide	fluidity	86.5	95
	dielectric relaxation time	86.5	
n-propanol	fluidity	73.5	98
	dielectric relaxation time	73.5	
glycerol	fluidity	132.0	186
	dielectric relaxation time	132.0	
$Ca(NO_3)_2 . 4H_2O$	conductance	201.0	220
	fluidity	205.0	
	chronopotentiometric diffusion coefficient of Cd^{2+}	203.0	
	chronopotentiometric diffusion coefficient of Tl^{+}	203.0	
$Na_2S_2O_3 . 5H_2O$	conductance	204.0	231
	fluidity	203.0	
0.40 $Ca(NO_3)_2$–0.60 KNO_3	conductance	320.0	338
	fluidity	318–320	

different). The excess entropy therefore gets frozen into glass at T_g. The "frozen" entropy is a measure of the departure from ideality of the glass.

While the influence of cooling rates is profound in the very high viscosity regions close to T_g, its influence is more so just below the normal melting point of the material. Many melts crystallize rapidly when supercooled in a region close to the melting point, and unless avoided by fast cooling or quenching in that region, glasses cannot be obtained. We shall discuss the nature of crystallization later.

Although T_g is not a thermodynamic parameter, it is surprising that it scales with the melting point. The variation of glass transition temperature with melting point[204] is shown in Fig. 4-45. In addition to T_g/T_m being approximately $\frac{2}{3}$, $\Delta S_g/\Delta S_m$ is approximately equal to $\frac{1}{3}$; ΔS_g and ΔS_m are the changes in the entropies at glass transition temperature and melting point respectively.[205]

From our discussions so far it is clear to us that as a melt is supercooled, the heat capacity of the melt (which remains nearly constant in the liquid range) suddenly decreases over a very narrow range of temperature. It is not a sharp discontinuity. It corresponds to the temperature at which the supercooled melt falls out of equilibrium, being unable to relax fast enough with decreasing temperature. The structure of glass naturally corresponds to that of the supercooled melt itself. The relaxational character of the transition is therefore evident.[206] Theories of glass transitions appear as byproducts of the theories of viscosity;[207] we shall briefly discuss two such theories in the literature.

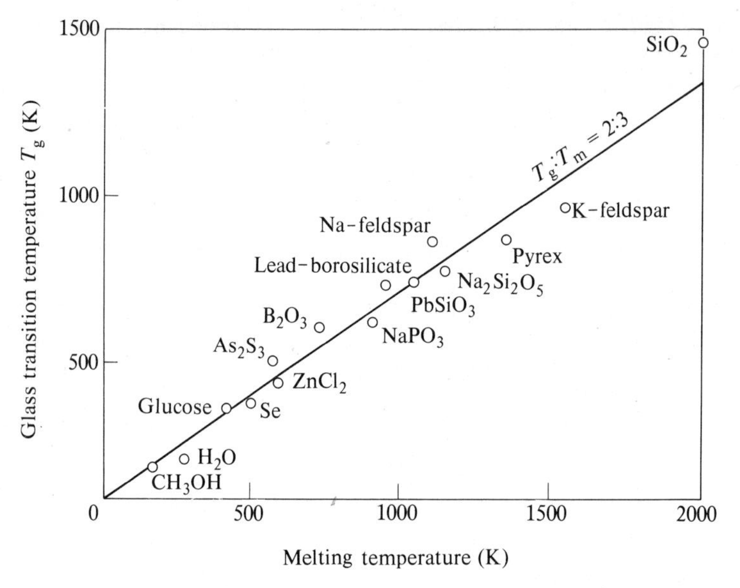

Figure 4-45 Variation of T_g with T_m. (*After Sakka and Mackenzie.*[204])

The free-volume theory for explaining glass transition in liquids was developed largely by Beuche[208] and by Turnbull and Cohen[209] from the broad framework of the free volume concept of transport in liquids.[210,211] The diffusive motion in liquids arise principally from the jumping of molecules into voids which are formed out of the excess volume present in liquids. This occurs only when the voids have volumes greater than a critical value v^* formed by the redistribution of the free volume. The free volume is defined as that part of the excess volume of the liquid which can be redistributed without expense of energy. In liquids there will be random distribution of different-sized voids, and those of greater volume than v^* contribute to transport. Turnbull and Cohen derived an expression for the probability distribution of the free volume in various-sized voids:

$$p(v) = \frac{\gamma}{v_f} \exp\left(-\frac{\gamma v}{v_f}\right) \tag{4-72}$$

where $p(v)$ expresses the probability of a void of volume between v and $v + \delta v$. γ is an overlap factor with a numerical value between $\frac{1}{2}$ and 1, and v_f is the total free volume. Since in general the diffusion coefficient D may be written as

$$D = gu' \int_{v^*}^{\infty} a(v)p(v)\,dv \tag{4-73}$$

where g is a geometric factor and u' is gas kinetic velocity and $a(v)$ is a characteristic jump distance, making use of Eq. (4-72) in Eq. (4-73) we get

$$D = ga^*u' \exp\left(-\frac{\gamma v^*}{v_f}\right) \tag{4-74}$$

Since fluidity, ϕ, and self-diffusion coefficient D are related to one another by the expression $D = (k/3\pi a_0)T\phi$, where a_0 is the molecular diameter and ϕ and η are simply related as $\phi = 1/\eta$, expressions for fluidity and viscosity may be readily derived. The free volume keeps on shrinking with falling temperature. As a consequence, D and ϕ are reduced to extremely low values, causing the transition to a glass.

Viewed from the low-temperature side, the glass expands in the same manner as a crystal, but beyond a certain expansion the additional volume can be redistributed without expense of energy. Once the redistribution occurs, fluid-like properties will emerge and hence the transition. The free volume may now be defined as that volume added after the glass transition (or strictly speaking at a somewhat lower temperature than T_g, namely T_0, where D is infinitely high):

$$V_e = V_l - V_g \cong V_g \Delta\alpha(T - T_0) \tag{4-75}$$

where V_l and V_g are the molar volumes of the liquid and the glass respectively, and $\Delta\alpha = \alpha_l - \alpha_g$ is the difference in the coefficients of thermal expansivity. Thus, we find that from the free-volume theory, if only crystallization of the melt can be avoided, that there should exist a $T_g > 0$ for any liquid, and T_g corresponds to the emergence of a free volume which admits a minimum concentration of voids whose sizes exceed v^*.

Gibbs and coworkers[212-214] took a different approach to the problem of transport in liquids. In their approach, diffusion and viscosity arise because of the cooperative rearrangements in the melt. At a given temperature, therefore, a certain minimum size is associated with the cooperatively rearranging region. This region rearranges to different configurations upon an energy (or an enthalpy) fluctuation. For a region containing z molecules which permit rearrangement, the transition probability may be obtained from simple statistical-mechanical considerations:

$$W(T) = A \exp(-z\Delta\mu/kT) \tag{4-76}$$

Here, $\Delta\mu$ is largely the potential energy hindering the rearrangement. In order that at least one configurational change might occur, there should exist a minimum size z^*, and hence only those clusters or combinations containing over and above z^* molecules can yield nonzero transition probabilities. It has been shown by Adam and Gibbs[213] that the average transition probability is simply equal to

$$\overline{W}(T) = \overline{A} \exp(-z^*\Delta\mu/kT) \tag{4-77}$$

The critical size z^* may be related to the molar configurational entropy S_c by the relation $z^* = Ns_c^*/S_c$, where N is the Avogadro number and s_c^* is the critical configurational entropy (which cannot be lower than $k \ln 2$ since at least two configurations should be possible for z^*). Since $W(T)$ is inversely proportional to $1/\tau$, where τ is the relaxation time (and since τ is related to η as $G\tau$ where G is the shear modulus), the expression for η in Gibbs–Adams theory becomes

$$\eta = A' \exp[(N\Delta\mu s_c^*)/(RTS_c)] \tag{4-78}$$

or more simply

$$\eta = A' \exp\left[B/TS_c\right] \tag{4-79}$$

Therefore, as the melt cools down, S_c, the configurational entropy (which is the excess entropy of the liquid over that of the crystalline value), tends to zero and η reaches values in excess of 10^{13} poises, resulting in a glass transition. The glass transition in this excess-entropy model corresponds to the vanishing of available configurations. Thus the theory predicts the existence of a "configurational ground state" for noncrystalline arrangement of atoms or molecules. Eq. (4-79) may be shown to be equivalent[200] to Eq. (4-69) in the glass transition region by substituting $S_c = \Delta C_p \ln T/T_0$.

Although both the free-volume and the entropy theories have been applied with success in the study of the glass-forming liquids, both have limitations.[200,215,218] The merits of these two theories in the context of glass transition phenomena have been investigated by Goldstein.[219,220] In essence, the free-volume theory assumes that a glass transition occurs when the free volume falls to a minimum (ideally to zero) whereas entropy theory associates a minimum excess entropy for the system at T_g. If we designate excess free volume and excess entropy as V_e and S_e respectively, the variation of these excess quantities may be expressed as

$$dV_e = \left(\frac{\partial V_e}{\partial T}\right)_P dT + \left(\frac{\partial V_e}{\partial P}\right)_T dP \tag{4-80}$$

$$dS_e = \left(\frac{\partial S_e}{\partial T}\right)_P dT + \left(\frac{\partial S_e}{\partial P}\right)_T dP \tag{4-81}$$

At T_g, dV_e and dS_e are independently zero in the two models. Remembering that $V_e = (V_m - V_g)$ and $S_e = (S_m - S_g)$, where the subscripts m and g stand for melt and glass respectively, the above equations may be rewritten as

$$0 = V_g \Delta\alpha \, dT_g - V_g \Delta\beta \, dP$$

$$0 = \frac{\Delta C_p}{T} dT_g - V_g \Delta\alpha \, dP$$

We thus find that if the excess free volume leads to the true description of T_g,

$$\left(\frac{dT_g}{dP}\right) = \frac{\Delta\beta}{\Delta\alpha} \tag{4-82}$$

If the excess entropy leads to the correct description of T_g,

$$\left(\frac{dT_g}{dP}\right) = \frac{T_g V_g \Delta\alpha}{\Delta C_p} \tag{4-83}$$

In the ideal situation, S_e and V_e are equivalent descriptions and we would have

$$\frac{\Delta\beta}{\Delta\alpha} = \frac{T_g V_g \Delta\alpha}{\Delta C_P} \tag{4-84}$$

It had indeed been established much earlier that Eq. (4-84) should hold if the liquid is describable by a single ordering parameter.[221] If there is more than one ordering parameter, Eq. (4-84) becomes an inequality:

$$\frac{\Delta\beta}{\Delta\alpha} > \frac{T_g V_g \Delta\alpha}{\Delta C_P} \tag{4-85}$$

In a large number of cases, experimentally measured (dT_g/dP) values are in agreement with Eq. (4-83) whereas the values from Eq. (4-82) are about twice the experimental values.[219,222]

The problem of liquid–glass transition has been treated by a bond–lattice model by Angell and Rao.[223] The basic feature of their approach is that a lattice of bonds can be abstracted from glass structure. These bonds are "broken" or excited when the temperature is increased. A bond is either "on" or "off" depending on whether it is excited or not. This close similarity to an Ising spin situation makes possible the application of simple statistical mechanics to retrieve thermodynamic quantities. However, when these bonds are excited, (*a*) there can be many stages of excitation, and (*b*) excitations could be cooperative either to a restricted or to an unrestricted extent. If the cooperativity of excitation is unrestricted it would amount to the excitation energy becoming ultimately zero, and the model would degenerate to the Bragg–Williams case of order–disorder transitions (see Chap. 5). However, treating cooperativity of excitations as restricted, and with an assumed functional form for it, Angell and Rao have calculated the excess heat capacities in qualitative agreement with observed glass transitions. Postulating that the probability of a mass transporting event is exponentially related to the inverse concentration of broken bonds, the transport properties in $ZnCl_2$ and water[224] have been shown to be adequately explicable. Another interesting feature of this theory is that the existence of Arrhenius and non-Arrhenius regions in temperature–transport data seems to be a natural consequence of the behavior of the concentration of broken bonds. The advantageous features of the theory are that (*a*) it does not set out to be a theory of transport from which the existence of glass transitions is inferred, and (*b*) the theory has a thermodynamical basis, though admittedly naive. Refinements in this direction might help evolve a suitable theory of glass transition. According to the present status of the theory, an equivalent of a T_0 does not exist and hence there is no true transition at all in glasses!

The theory of configurational states has been found to be applicable in the case of B_2O_3 transitions,[225] but Goldstein[226] has seriously questioned the existence of cooperativity among configurational excitations prior to transformation.

Crystallization of Glasses and Melts

It was mentioned earlier that any liquid may be supercooled into a glass if crystallization can be bypassed. Crystallization is another kind of phase transition which occurs in glasses and supercooled liquids. If we were to consider the nucleation and growth mechanism for crystallization, we see that the nucleation

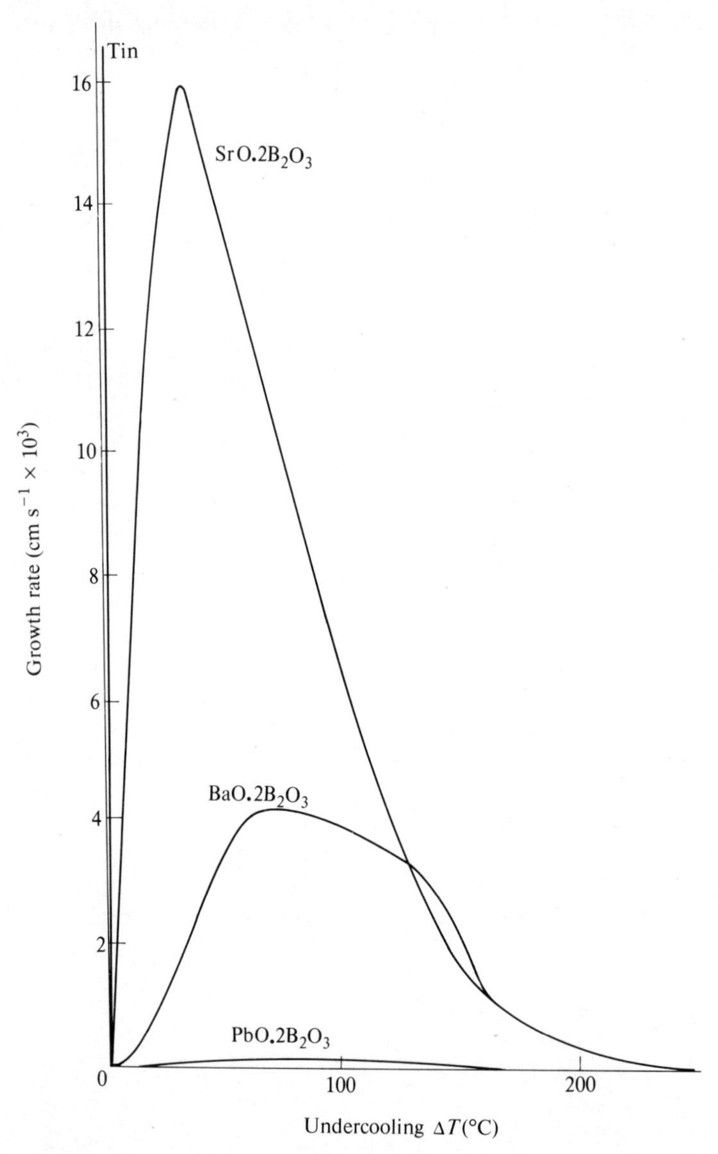

Figure 4-46 Variation of crystallization rates as a function of undercooling. (*After Bergeron.*[227])

rates increase with undercooling and exhibit a maximum (Eq. (4-8)); growth rate also exhibits a similar maximum with undercooling (Eq. (4-21)). An obvious conclusion would be that if a melt is to be converted into a glass it is essential to suppress nucleation completely. The implications of this approach have been discussed by Turnbull.[188]

When crystallization takes place, the interface temperature becomes an important factor.[227] This increases with the increasing enthalpy of fusion. In the

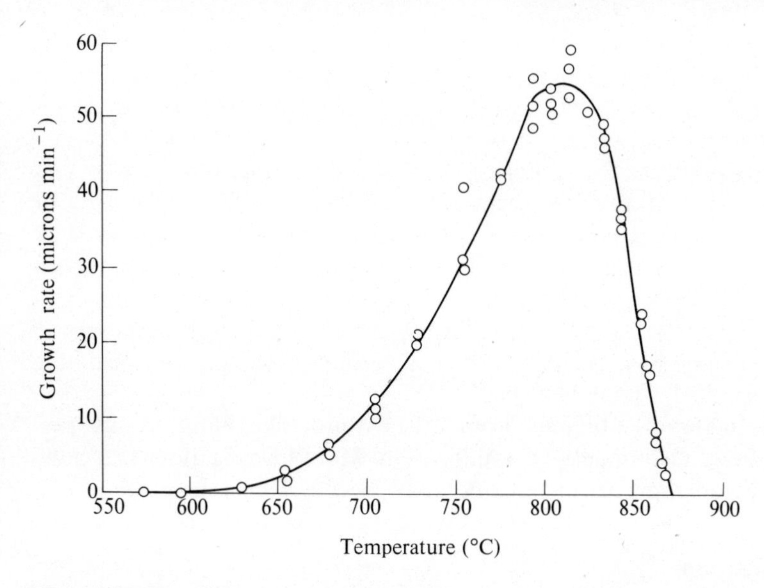

Figure 4-47 Rate of crystallization in sodium silicate melts. (*After Meiling and Uhlmann.*[228])

case of crystallization of sodium disilicate from its melt, it has been found to be less than a degree K ($\Delta H_m \simeq 8$ kcal mol^{-1}) whereas it is as high as 22 K for $PbO.B_2O_3$ crystallization ($\Delta H_m \simeq 32$ kcal mol^{-1}). In Fig. 4-46 the rate of crystallization is shown as a function of undercooling. Meiling and Uhlmann[228] have investigated crystal growth rates in sodium disilicate ($Na_2Si_2O_5$) melts using the following rate expression:*

$$R = \frac{C}{\eta}\left[1 - \exp\left(\frac{\Delta H_m \Delta T}{RTT_m}\right)\right] \tag{4-86}$$

Here, C is related to the fraction of interface sites available for growth and the molecular diameter, η is the viscosity of the melt, and ΔH_m is the molar heat of melting (see Fig. 4-47). Kumm and Scholze[229] have derived, on the basis of the above expression, a useful approximate relation for viscosities of melts at the melting point T_m and at the temperature of maximum crystallization T_{max}:

$$\ln \eta_{T_{max}} - \ln \eta_{T_m} \cong 1 \tag{4-87}$$

Controlled crystallization which has been technically exploited is achieved by nucleating with heterogeneous impurities (TiO_2 is commonly employed). Crystallization is invariably preceded by liquid–liquid phase separation.[230,231] If crystallization into one or more crystalline (stable) phases occurs in the presence of a few nuclei and hence uncontrollably, the process is often referred to as "devitrification." On the other hand, if crystallization is controlled by use of nucleating

* Compare Eq. (4-86) with Eq. (4-22).

agents, a fine-grained product is obtained with special ceramic qualities. The products are known as *vitrocerams or sitalls*. In order that controlled ceramization may be achieved it is necessary to have nucleation and crystallization rate curves fairly well separated.[231]

Many factors influence the tendency for phase separation. One view is that when the bond energy M–O of the second oxide (other than SiO_2) like CaO or BaO is high, it sets up a competition for sharing available oxygens in their own coordination polyhedra. As a result, cations with higher Ze/r (charge-to-radius ratio) should perform well in creating immiscibility regions, as has been found by Warren and Pincus.[232] Various approaches centered on the notion of ionic field strength Ze/r have been made by many groups of workers in elucidating limiting compositions for homogeneity.[233,234]

Amorphous materials obtained from other routes like films, freshly precipitated oxides, etc., also undergo crystallization. More investigations are, however, necessary before a proper understanding of these systems is gained.

Switching Transitions

An important class of transformations is emerging in recent years from the study of inorganic glasses. This is the phenomenon of switching. Literature in this area has been growing rapidly[235–237] since the first report of its device potential by Ovshinsky.[238] Switching devices made by using this phenomenon are often referred to as ovonic devices. Glasses may be obtained normally from sulfides, selenides, and tellurides of Ge, As, Si, etc., in ternary or quaternary compositions. A sputtered thin film or a thin wafer of these glasses is sandwiched between electrodes to obtain a device configuration. The variation of current as a function of applied voltage is shown schematically in Fig. 4-48. In threshold switching (Fig. 4.48*a*) the glass returns to the "off" state below a minimum holding current,

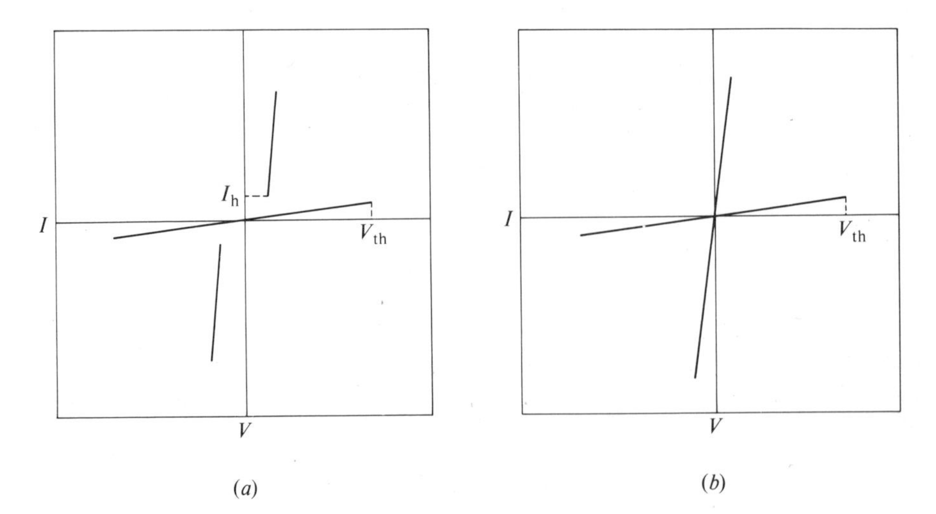

Figure 4-48 I–V characteristics in (*a*) threshold switching and (*b*) memory switching (schematic).

while in memory switching (Fig. 4-48*b*), the "on" state reverts to "off" only on application of a high current pulse. These have very high switching speeds (less than a microsecond) and the switching phenomena do not appear to be associated with any mass transport. However, memory materials have been shown to develop a crystallized conducting filament between the electrodes during switching. Threshold switching is at present considered to be an essentially electronic phenomenon related to the high field behavior of amorphous semiconductors. Switching mechanisms are far from being completely understood[239,240] and continue to be an area of active interest.

In this section we have restricted ourselves to transitions in glasses. Processes such as temperature-dependent preferential occupation of modifier ions in the glass network (which has been termed as an order–disorder transition by Weyl[241]) and large irreversible effects of stress on glasses[242] have not been treated. The interested reader would do well to refer to the original literature on these topics.

4-7 MESOPHASES

The term "mesophase" or "mesomorphic" phase means[243,244] an "intermediate form," and such a description of phases is most appropriate for "liquid crystals."[245] Mesomorphic phases possess properties somewhere between those of crystals and liquids. Crystals exhibit characteristic x-ray diffraction patterns with sharp Bragg reflections arising from the regular stacking of atoms or molecules in the three directions. An important feature of liquids is the flow or, more fundamentally, their inability to withstand shearing forces. Mesomorphic phases share qualities of both crystals and liquids; there is an order in the stacking of constituent atoms or molecules in one or two directions, and there is also the property of flow.[246]

Over 3000 organic compounds are known to exhibit mesomorphism.[247] When heated, these organic solids transform to turbid liquids which have considerable viscosity. These liquids further transform to clear isotropic liquids at a temperature known as the clearing point. Between the temperatures of solid–mesophase and mesophase–liquid transitions, there can be several mesophase–mesophase transitions. A general feature of mesophase-forming compounds is that they are long organic molecules and usually possess polar groups. Three distinct types of mesophases may be identified. They are (*a*) the nematic, (*b*) the cholesteric, and (*c*) the smectic phases shown in Fig. 4-49. In the nematic phases, organic molecules are arranged parallel or almost parallel to one another in the direction of the long axis (Fig. 4-49*a*). Since the parallel and antiparallel arrangements are equally probable, these phases are not ferroelectric even though molecules have permanent dipole moments.[246] The centers of gravity of these aligned molecules do not show any long-range order, but there is long-range order with respect to the alignment itself.* Indeed, the order parameter (see Sec. 4-3 and also Chap. 5) in nematic fluids is conveniently described as

$$\xi = \tfrac{1}{2}\langle 3\cos^2\theta - 1\rangle \qquad \text{(4-88)}$$

* Because of thermal motion, the parallel alignment is lost to some extent.

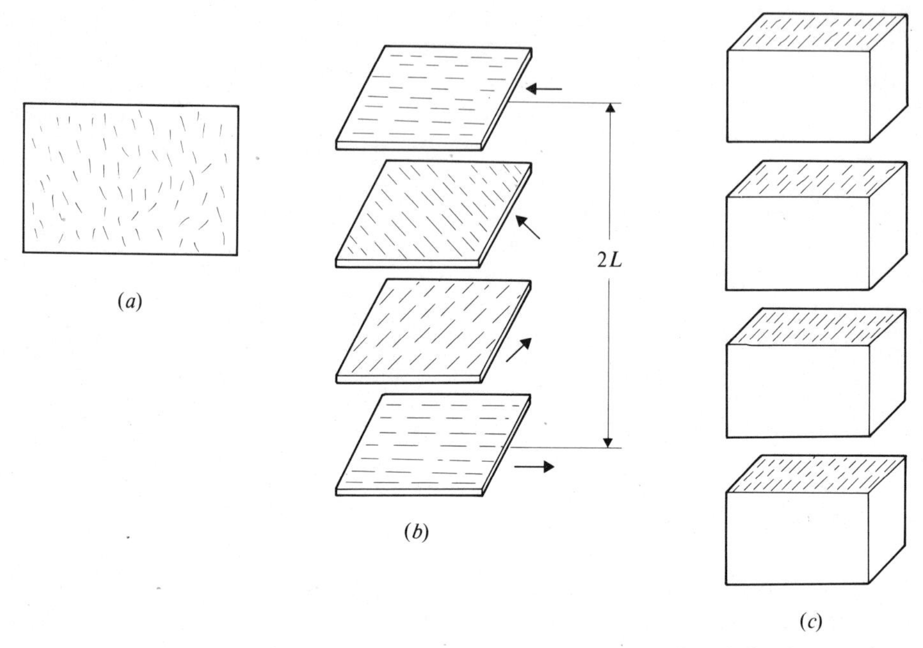

Figure 4-49 (*a*) Nematic ordering, (*b*) cholesteric ordering, and (*c*) smectic ordering in mesophases (schematic).

where θ is the angle between the long axis of the molecule and the preferred direction (the unit vector in this direction is called the "director").[248] For the perfectly ordered state, the average value of $\cos^2 \theta$ is unity, and hence ξ is unity; ξ goes to zero for random orientation. The highest value of ξ measured in nematic liquids is around 0.8, while the lowest around the transition to the isotropic liquid phase varies between 0.3 and 0.5. Examined under a microscope between crossed polars, nematic liquids show typical threadlike textures (*nema* in Greek means thread).

Cholesteric phases may be considered as distorted nematic phases. A large number of cholesterol derivatives exhibit this characteristic. Each of the layers in cholesteric phases has a director and, for each successive layer, the director is twisted by an angle, ϕ (say $2\pi/n$) (see Fig. 4-49*b*). The $(n + 1)$th director will therefore have the same alignment as the first. The distance $2L$ between n layers is known as the pitch of the helical distortion, the value of the pitch being typically around 3000–4000 Å and leading to special optical effects. The pitch is also very sensitive to temperature as well as electrical and magnetic fields. No long-range order is present among the centers of gravity of molecules in each layer in cholesteric phases.

Smectic mesophases are more ordered than either nematic or cholesteric phases (Fig. 4-49*c*). It contains parallel and equidistant layers with constant directors. Thus, a translational order results in one of the directions. Within each layer, positional randomness of centers of gravity continues to exist. Many textures have been found to exist among smectic phases. The same compound may also exhibit several smectic structures. The highest-temperature smectic phase is described as smectic A which, on cooling, leads to smectic C and B textures in that order of stability. The lowest-temperature smectic phase known at present[249] is smectic E. In smectic A phases, the orientation directions of the long axis of the molecules and the plane of the molecules are perpendicular to each other. In smectic C, the long axis makes an angle with the plane of the molecules and allows for a shortening of the interlayer distance. Smectic B corresponds to ordered layers with hexagonal close packing of the molecules,[250] and represents the most ordered of the mesophases analyzed.[246] In addition to the A, B, and C forms of the smectic phases, many other forms (D, E, F, G, and H) have been described in the literature.[251] The classification scheme is generally based on miscibility and optical behavior.[252] De Vries has recently published an extensive classification system.[251]

Transitions in Mesophases

From the general discussion above it is clear that a completely ordered crystal transforms to a completely disordered isotropic liquid through several stages of mesophases. In this process, molecules begin to gain rotational and translational degrees of freedom, and the nature of the transitions is therefore dependent upon the geometry of the molecules. If the component organic molecules are long, they cannot attain rotational degrees of freedom in the crystalline phase, but if the molecules are spherical or nearly so, they would have rotational degrees of freedom in three dimensions, leading to the formation of plastic crystalline phases[253] (see Sec. 4-3). Plastic crystalline phases may also be considered as mesophases. Confining our attention to liquid crystal-forming materials, we find, however, that the following phases are of relevance to the transitions:

(*a*) Crystal: Centers of gravities of the molecules are fixed, and there is no rotational freedom.
(*b*) Smectic phase: Centers of gravity can change in two directions, and molecules can rotate about the long axis.
(*c*) Nematic or cholesteric liquids: Translational degree of freedom is gained in three directions, and rotation is possible only in one direction.
(*d*) Isotropic liquid: Molecules have all the translational and rotational degrees of freedom.

If we denote the different states as C, crystalline solid; S, smectic; N, nematic; Ch, chlolesteric; and L, isotropic liquid, the various stages of transitions with increasing temperature may be represented as follows:[249]

$$\begin{array}{c}\text{Crystalline}\\ \text{solid}\end{array} \xrightarrow{\text{C-S}} \text{smectic mesophases} \xrightarrow[\text{S-Ch}]{\text{S-N}} \begin{array}{c}\text{nematic or}\\ \text{cholesteric}\end{array} \xrightarrow[\text{Ch-L}]{\text{N-L}} \text{liquid}$$

It is interesting that no nematic-to-cholesteric transition has yet been observed. On the basis of this fact, and also the observation that cholesteric and nematic

Table 4-4 Transformations in representative mesophases

Compound	Nature of transition*	Transition temperature (K)	Heat of transition, ΔH (kcal mol^{-1})
4-azoxy anisole	C–N	391	7.06
	N–L	408	0.137
Cholesteryl propionate	C–Ch	372.6	5.21
	Ch–L	387.1	0.16
4,4′-didodecyloxy azoxybenzene	C–S_C	355	10.04
	S_C–L	396	2.86
4,4′-diheptyloxy azoxybenzene	C–S_C	347	9.77
	S_C–N	368	0.380
	N–L	397	0.243
Di-*n*-dodecyl 4,4′-azoxy-α-methyl cinnamate	C–S_C	352	17.45
	S_C–S_A	355	0.024
	S_A–L	361	2.10
Cholesteryl myristate	C–S	344	11.35
	S–Ch	353.1	0.425
	Ch–L	358.6	0.361
Ethyl 4-ethoxy benzylidene-4-amino cinnamate	C–S_C	354	6.52
	S_C–S_A	391	0.501
	S_A–N	429	1.22
	N–L	432	0.12
n-amyl,4-*n*-dodecyloxy benzylidene-4-amino cinnamate	C–S_B	347.7	6.692
	S_B–S_C	369.4	1.309
	S_C–S_A	380.4	0.411
	S_A–L	406.2	2.017
bis N-(4-*n*-hexyloxy benzilidene)-4′-amino phenyl mercury	C–S_B	424	—
	S_B–S_C	466	—
	S_C–S_A	470	—
	S_A–N	563	—
	N–L	606	—

* The subscripts A, B, and C designate the textures of smectic mesophases.

phases are entirely miscible, Friedel[254] considered a cholesteric as a distorted nematic. In Table 4-4 several representative mesophase transitions are listed.[248,255] While transforming through a smectic phase, no compound is known to pass through all the smectic structures.

Thermodynamic Aspects

Most of the transitions involving mesophases seem to be thermodynamically of the first order. The transformations in *n*-amyl, 4-*n*-dodecyloxy benzilidene-4-amino cinnamate as studied by calorimetric methods[256] are shown in Fig. 4-50. Inter-smectic transitions like S_A–S_C (and possibly even smectic–liquid transitions on the basis of symmetry considerations)* are likely to be cooperative transitions of the second order.[246] The major heat of transition always corresponds to the

* The ΔH of smectic-liquid transitions are, however, too large to be classified as second-order transitions.

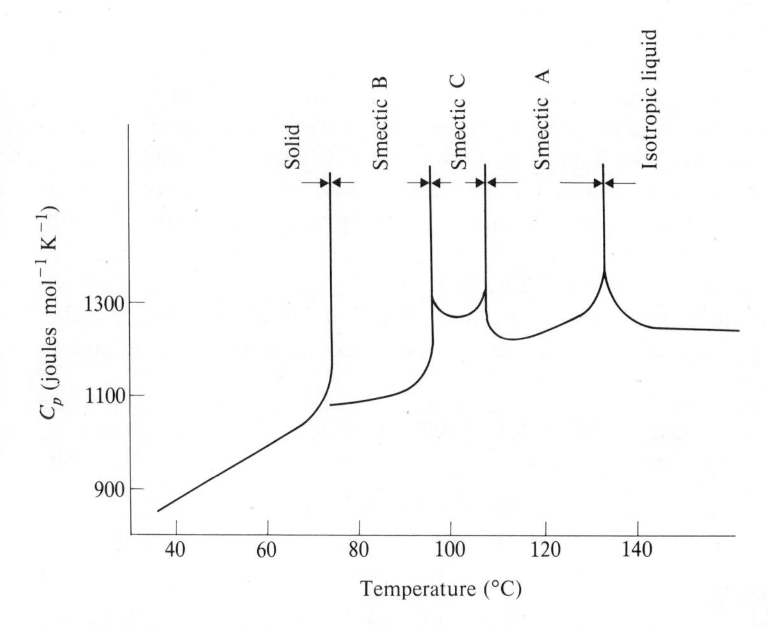

Figure 4-50 Heat capacities during several mesophase transitions in *n*-amyl, 4-*n*-dodecyloxy benzilidene-4-amino cinnomate. (*After Arnold.*[256])

crystal–mesophase transition.[247] As may be seen from Table 4-4, the heat of transition for the change from the mesophase to the liquid phase is a fraction of the heat of the crystal-to-mesophase transition; the ΔH of transitions from nematic or cholesteric to liquid phases are very small fractions of the ΔH for crystal-to-mesophase transitions, and are almost always 2 percent of the latter. This indicates that the major disordering event corresponds to the crystal–mesophase transition. Indeed, C-to-mesophase and mesophase-to-L transitions are considered as major and minor calorimetric events respectively. No simple and systematic relations between entropies of transitions and the nature of disordering events have yet been established. In general, among the mesophase–L transitions, the entropy change for smectic-to-liquid transition is understandably very much greater than the entropy change for nematic or cholesteric–liquid transitions, because the order is higher in a smectic phase than in either a nematic or a cholesteric phase. This is easily seen from the data in Table 4-4. This fact also helps in ascertaining the nature of the mesophase while transforming from the liquid[247] (ΔS being very much higher for L–S than for L–Ch or L–N). Nematic and cholesteric phases are, however, indistinguishable by this criterion. Calorimetric data on a large number of transitions as summarized by Marzatko and Demus[249] are shown in Fig. 4-51.

The effect of pressure on mesomorphism has been studied by Chandrasekhar et al.[257] They have shown that nematic and smectic phases are produced in methoxy- and ethoxy-benzoic acids under pressure. They have also verified that the nematic–isotropic transition obeys the Clausius–Clapeyron equation.

The statistical theory of nematic-to-isotropic transitions was worked out by Maier and Saupe.[258] It was based on the assumption of an average internal field of the Weiss type. The alignment of the long molecules in the nematic phase was shown to be caused primarily by dipole–dipole dispersion forces (of the van der Waals type). These forces have very high angular dependence because of the highly anisotropic optical transition moments. Attractive forces due to permanent dipoles were neglected since there is no observed ferroelectric order in liquid crystals and there are liquid crystals without permanent dipoles. A molecule in the mesophase is assigned a potential energy E, which may be written as $E = E(\xi, V, \theta)$, where ξ is the order parameter, V the molar volume, and θ is the angular position of its long axis; ξ may be obtained from simple Boltzmann statistics.[248]

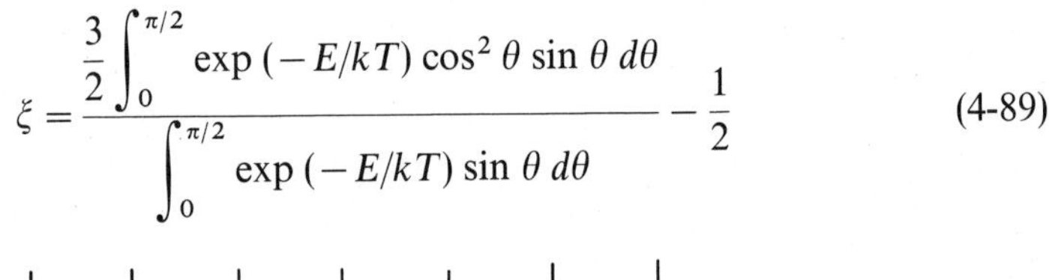

$$\xi = \frac{\dfrac{3}{2}\displaystyle\int_0^{\pi/2} \exp(-E/kT)\cos^2\theta \sin\theta \, d\theta}{\displaystyle\int_0^{\pi/2} \exp(-E/kT)\sin\theta \, d\theta} - \frac{1}{2} \tag{4-89}$$

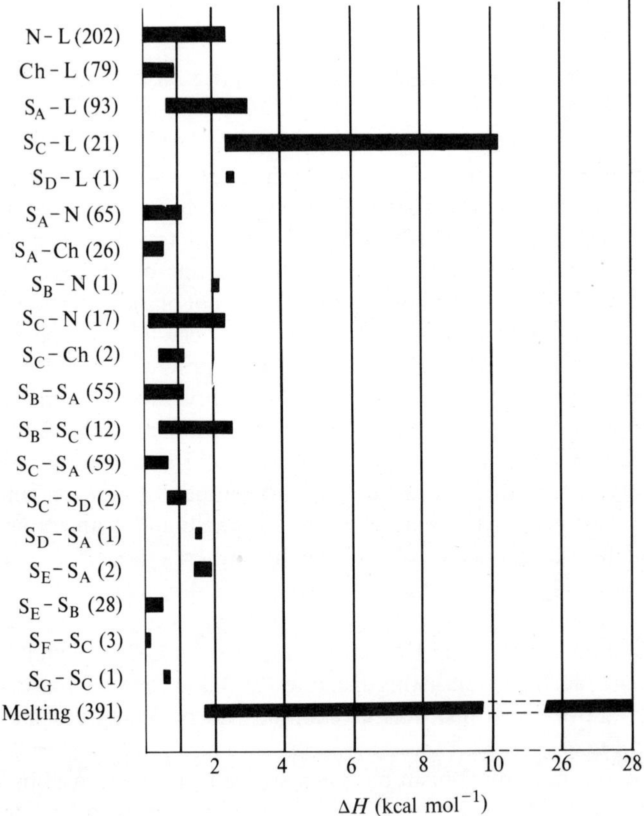

Figure 4-51 Enthalpies of transition for various mesophase-forming materials. (*After Marzotko and Demus.*[249])

In writing this equation, use has been made of Eq. (4-88). The variation of E as a function of ξ is represented as

$$E = -\frac{1}{2}\frac{A\xi}{V^2}(3\cos^2\theta - 1) \tag{4-90}$$

A is a constant which is dependent on the system and can be determined from experimental quantities like clear-point (N–L transition) temperature, and V_N, the molar volume of the nematic phase.[248]

$$\frac{A}{kT_N V_N^2} = 4.55 \tag{4-91}$$

Equations (4-89) and (4-90) may be solved for ξ by graphical or numerical methods. For values of T less than T_N, it is found that ξ has two solutions: $\xi = 0$ (corresponding to the isotropic phase), and $\xi \leq 0.44$. That the true order parameter corresponds to the latter quantity is decided by the behavior of the free energy of the system. Such a state corresponds to a nematic phase. At T_N (or T_c), the order parameter has a value of 0.44 (for all N–L transitions, and this is a limitation of the theory) which suddenly goes to zero in the liquid phase, indicating a first-order transition.

Chandrasekhar and coworkers[259] have worked out a lattice statistical model of the nematic isotropic transitions both in zeroth and first-order approximations, and obtained some interesting results. These workers have modified the original model due to Pople and Karasz[260] for transitions in molecular crystals. In this modification, the orientational barrier is assumed to be proportional to $(1/V^3)$ rather than $(1/V^4)$ while repulsive energies between neighbors are assumed to be proportional to $(1/V^4)$. Disordering is considered for both the position (ξ_p) and the orientation (ξ_o). If the ratio of the barrier for orientation to that of migration (positional disordering) is $\nu = Z_o E_o / Z_p E_p$, where Z and E are the respective coordination numbers and energy barriers, then the nature of transitions exhibited by the system is strongly dependent on the numerical value of ν. For low values of ν, a solid state orientational transition precedes melting (ξ_o reaches low values much before ξ_p), and for very high values of ν, positional melting occurs before orientational disordering (ξ_p becomes very low before ξ_o). The latter corresponds to the formation of a nematic phase. The results of zeroth and first-order cases (considering nearest-neighbor pairs for the orientational order only) are found to be quite similar.

Present theoretical knowledge about mesophase transitions is rather qualitative, partly because of inadequate knowledge of interparticle interaction potentials in mesophases.

4-8 TRANSITIONS IN ORGANIC SOLIDS

Several kinds of phase transformations discussed in the earlier sections also occur in organic solids; transitions can be of the first, second, or higher orders.[261] In this section, we shall make a few brief comments pertinent to organic systems and cite a few interesting examples of phase transitions in organic solids. Cohesion in organic solids is due primarily to dispersion forces.[262] If the constituent organic molecules have permanent dipole moments, a further contribution to cohesive energy is made by dipolar interactions. Since these kinds of bonding are weak in nature, melting points of organic compounds are generally low. Hydrogen bonding often occurs in organic compounds (containing hydrogen atoms bonded to electronegative atoms like fluorine, oxygen, or nitrogen) and contributes to the cohesive energy. An *a priori* prediction of phase transitions in organic solids is difficult. The only general observation that we can make is that whenever the melting point of an organic compound is unusually high and melting entropy unusually low, a solid–solid phase transition is likely.[263]

Organic molecules exhibit rotational transitions according to their shape. If they are highly asymmetric, rotational transitions within the solid state become difficult, and positional melting occurs before the rotational transitions, leading to a variety of mesophase transitions (Sec. 4-7). When the molecules are highly symmetrical, as for example carbon tetrachloride, adamantane, neopentane, pentaerythritol, and camphor, various rotational degrees of freedom may be excited within the solid state, leading to formation of plastic crystals (rotational crystalline state).[115,261,262] The entropy increase in plastic crystal transitions is very high compared to the entropy increase during melting of the same compounds. For example, the first-order (tetragonal–cubic) transition of pentaerythritol at 457 K is accompanied by the formation of a plastic crystalline state with ΔS of 22.8 cal $deg^{-1}\ mol^{-1}$, compared to the melting entropy of 3.16 cal $deg^{-1}\ mol^{-1}$ at 539 K. Such organic molecules usually possess a spherical repulsion envelope and a very low or zero dipole moment. In the case of organic solids where the asymmetry of the molecules is not too high, order–disorder transitions can be expected.[261] A good example is provided by benzothiophene, which undergoes a λ-transition with an entropy gain of 2.75 cal $deg^{-1}\ mol^{-1}$. This is almost exactly $R \ln 4$, indicating that benzothiophene uses the four possible configurations in the disordered state. However, in several organic compounds the disordered state gets frozen during crystallization and no transitions to ordered states occur. Such a situation is exemplified by azulene and various hexasubstituted benzene derivatives.[262]

Many organic solids formed by simple molecules exhibit phase transformations.[37,261] Thus, solid methane and deuterated methanes undergo gradual solid–solid transformations. In the case of solid methane, application of pressure gives rise to doubling of λ-peaks. The fcc structure of methane does not undergo any change during the transition. Cyclohexane undergoes phase transitions in which phase I is stable between the melting point (279.8 K) and 186.1 K, and phase II below 186.1 K. A third phase (III) is obtained by quenching the gas, liquid, or I at 77 K. Annealing III between 120 and 186 K gives phase II. Phase II, showing characteristic far-infrared bands, seems to be orthorhombic, while the high-temperature phase corresponds to a randomized cubic phase.[264] One of the interesting molecular crystals undergoing several phase transformations is thiourea. By virtue of the permanent dipole moment of the thiourea molecule, it exhibits ferroelectricity in the solid state.[265] All the five phases of thiourea have been well studied. While phases I and III are ferroelectric, phases II, IV, and V have been found to be nonpolar (the phases have been numbered from I to V with increasing temperature regions of stability). The explosive HMX (cyclotetramethylenetetranitramine) is known to exist in four polymorphic forms;[266] the reactivity of HMX varies with the polymorphic form.

Paraterphenyl undergoes a phase transition at 110 K when the unit cell dimensions (a and b) double and the space group changes from $P2_1/a$ to $P\bar{1}$. The transition appears to involve rotational disorder in which the paraterphenyl molecules become nonplanar. Ramdas and Thomas[267] have elucidated the nature of the transition by evaluating pairwise interactions between nonbonded atoms, and have predicted the existence of other rotationally ordered phases. Jones et al.[268] have shown that the low-temperature phase with nonplanar paraterphenyl molecules gets transformed to the room-temperature phase under electron irradiation (100 keV) in a microscope. A new form of anthracene ($P\bar{1}a$) produced by application of stress has recently been identified by Thomas and coworkers (personal communication); this new form is topotactically related to the parent form and provides a basis to explain photodimerization of anthracene.

The monoclinic form of *p*-dichlorobenzene transforms to a triclinic structure, and the transformation apparently involves only reorientation of molecules. There is some evidence to show that this transformation begins at one or more nucleation sites and does not occur uniformly through the crystal.[269] The thermal transformation of the metastable β-phase of *p*-nitrophenol to the stable α-phase has been found to occur with the phase boundary moving perpendicular to the [001] axis of the needle-shaped crystal.[270] The structural change in this transformation involves a twist of rings in adjacent links in the chains of molecules.

Geometrical or orientation relationships between parent and transformed phases are well understood in many metal and inorganic systems (see Chaps. 3 and 4). It has not been clear whether such orientation relationships exist in transformations of organic crystals. Mnyukh and coworkers,[271] on the basis of their studies of a large variety of molecular solids, suggest that no such structural relation is possible. Robertson and Ubbelohde[272] had, however, shown long ago that there was some preferred orientation in the transformation of a single crystal of β-resorcinol to the α-form. Recently Jones et al.,[273] on the basis of their microscopic studies of the stress-induced single-crystal phase transformation of 1,8-dichloro-10-methylanthracene, have established that the transition does indeed proceed by a diffusionless displacive transformation (somewhat akin to a martensitic transition) with definite orientation relationships. The transition occurs at an invariant plane with indices (2.88, 0, 1) and the crystallographically equivalent ($\overline{2.88}$, 0, 1). The irrational habit plane seems to be composed of stepped, close-packed planes which give information on the nature of the interface between the structures. The properties of the interface could be formulated in terms of slip dislocations. The mechanism proposed by Jones et al. is similar to that proposed for the stress-induced orthorhombic–monoclinic transition of polyethylene, which is martensitic.[274]

An interesting example of a single-crystal phase transformation is that of 5-methyl-1-thia-5-azoniacyclo-octane-1-oxide perchlorate, which undergoes a reversible topotactic change between 276 and 298 K. Thermodynamic data on the transition are not known, but the structures of the α (276 K) and β (298 K) phases are reported. In the transition, the a parameter of the unit cell doubles while the c parameter halves. It was first thought that the mechanism involved a cooperative process of inversion and rotation of half of the molecular cations.[275] Recently, Parkinson et al.[276] have shown that the transition occurs on recurrent (102)-type planes; the recurrent passage of glissile partial dislocations on alternate (102) planes of the α-form yields the β-form. This mechanism has some features of martensitic transitions and also bears some resemblance to the mechanism of rutile-α-PbO_2 transition of TiO_2 (see Chap. 3). Recently, the transformation of the yellow form of 2-(4′-methoxyphenyl)-1,4-benzoquinone to the red form (both orthorhombic, *Pbca*) has been found to involve nucleation and migration of well-defined fronts; molecules in the two phases are related to each other as diastereo isomers.[276a]

A variety of organic compounds can be obtained in the form of glasses, and transitions of organic glasses have been reported in the literature.[230,261] A glassy state is common among organic polymers, and glass transitions in high polymers have been discussed by many authors.[214,277,278] Organic polymers also show other phase transitions, particularly under pressure, as mentioned earlier in the case of polyethylene. Phase transitions in organic systems, particularly polymers, can be studied effectively employing vibrational spectroscopy. Such studies provide information on the symmetry of the crystal and structure of the molecules concerned. Thus, a study of the pressure-induced II–III transition of teflon employing Raman spectroscopy[279] has provided information on the nature of phase III (phases I, II, and IV are low-pressure phases with helical conformation). An infrared study of cyclohexane was referred to earlier in this section.[264] Thiourea, glycine derivatives, and other organic ferroelectric materials have similarly been investigated by infrared and Raman spectroscopy. Optical microscopy employing a diamond anvil cell along with x-ray diffraction has been most useful in detecting and characterizing high-pressure phases of organic solids. Thus, high-pressure phases of polyethylene and CCl_4 have been studied in this manner.[280] Proton magnetic resonance (second moment) studies of organic crystals have been most effective in providing information on the rotation or reorientation of molecules accompanying phase transitions.[261] Transitions in methanol and methyl mercaptan have been investigated by positron annihilation.[281] Such studies have been useful in understanding the mechanism of annihilation.* Before closing this section, it should be pointed out that phase transitions of organic crystals continue to provide good scope for investigation, and many of the mechanisms that we are used to in inorganic systems have yet to be properly characterized in organic systems.

* A study of the *Pm3m*–*Fm3m* transition of NH_4Cl by positron annihilation[282] seems to support the free-volume model.

REFERENCES

1. M. Volmer and A. Weber, *Z. Phys. Chem.*, **119**, 277, 1925.
2. R. Becker and W. Doring, *Ann. Phys.*, **24**, 719, 1935.
3. J. W. Christian, "The Theory of Transformations in Metals and Alloys," Pergamon Press, Oxford, 1965 (second edition, part I, 1975).
4. J. Burke, "The Kinetics of Phase Transformations in Metals," Pergamon Press, Oxford, 1965.
5. R. Smoluchowski, in "Phase Transformations in Solids," ed. R. Smoluchowski, J. E. Mayer, and W. A. Weyl, John Wiley, New York, 1951.
6. R. A. Swalin, in "Kinetics of High Temperature Processes," ed. W. D. Kingery, John Wiley, New York, 1959.
7. D. Turnbull, in "Solid State Physics," ed. F. Seitz and D. Turnbull, vol. 3, Academic Press, New York, 1956.
8. F. R. N. Nabarro, *Proc. Roy. Soc.*, **A175**, 519, 1940; *Proc. Roy. Soc.* (*London*), **52**, 90, 1940.
9. M. Chaudron and Pruna, *Proc. Internatl. Symp. Reactivity of Solids* (1952).
10. G. Johansson, *Arkiv Kemi*, **8**, 33, 1954.
11. R. Smoluchowski, in "Handbook of Physics," ed. E. U. Condon and H. Odishaw, McGraw-Hill, New York, 1958.
12. J. H. de Boer, *Discussions of Faraday Soc.*, **23**, 171, 1957.
13. Cited by de Boer in Ref. 12.
14. C. Briske and N. H. Hartshorne, *Trans. Faraday Soc.*, **63**, 1546, 1967.
15. S. W. Kennedy and P. K. Shultz, *Trans. Faraday Soc.*, **59**, 156, 1963.
16. M. Avrami, *J. Chem. Phys.*, **7**, 1103, 1939; **8**, 212, 1940; **9**, 177, 1941.
17. W. A. Johnson and R. F. Mehl, *Trans. AIME*, **135**, 416, 1939.
18. B. V. Erofeev, *DAN, USSR*, **52**, 515, 1946.
19. P. P. Budnikov and A. M. Ginstling, in "Principles of Solid State Chemistry," trans. and ed. K. Shaw, Maclaren, London, 1968.
20. W. G. Burgers and L. J. Groen, *Discussions of Faraday Soc.*, **23**, 183, 1957.
21. C. N. R. Rao, S. R. Yoganarasimhan, and P. A. Faeth, *Trans. Faraday Soc.*, **57**, 504, 1961.
22. C. N. R. Rao, *Canad. J. Chem.*, **39**, 498, 1961.
23. Y. Kotera and M. Yonemura, *Trans. Faraday Soc.*, **59**, 147, 1963.
24. R. J. Zeto and R. Roy, in "Reactivity of Solids," ed. J. W. Michell et al., Wiley-Interscience, New York, 1969.
25. J. M. Honig, *J. Chem. Phys.*, **28**, 723, 1958.
26. J. M. Honig, in "Kinetics of High Temperature Processes," ed. W. D. Kingery, John Wiley, New York, 1959.
27. S. R. Yoganarasimhan and C. N. R. Rao, *Trans. Faraday Soc.*, **58**, 1579, 1962.
28. E. D. Whitney, *Trans. Faraday Soc.*, **61**, 1991, 1965.
29. H. Eyring and F. W. Cagle, Jr., *Z. Electrochem.*, **56**, 480, 1952.
30. H. T. Hall, *Proc. Symp. High Temp.* (*Stanford Res. Inst.*), 161, 1956.
31. F. P. Bundy, in "Reactivity of Solids," ed. J. W. Michell et al., Wiley-Interscience, New York, 1969, p. 817.
32. C. M. Wayman, "Introduction to the Crystallography of Martensitic Transformation," Macmillan, New York, 1964.
33. G. Meyrick and G. W. Powell, *Ann. Rev. Materials Sci.*, ed. R. A. Huggins, R. W. Bube, and R. W. Roberts, **3**, 327, 1973.
34. A. B. Greninger and A. R. Troiano, *Trans. AIME*, **140**, 307, 1940.
35. J. A. Klostermann, in "Topics in Physical Metallurgy," ed. A. Q. Khan and M. J. Brabers, Elsevier, Amsterdam, 1972.
36. J. W. Christian, "Physical Properties of Martensite and Bainite," *Iron and Steel Institute Special Rep. No.* 93, 1965.
37. C. N. R. Rao and K. J. Rao, in "Progress in Solid State Chemistry," ed. H. Reiss, vol. 4, Pergamon, Oxford, 1967.

38. R. F. Bunshah and R. F. Mehl, *J. Metals*, **5,** 1251, 1953.
39. E. S. Machlin and M. Cohen, *J. Metals*, **3,** 746, 1951.
40. L. Kaufmann and M. Cohen, *Prog. Metal Phys.*, ed. B. Chalmers and R. King, **7,** 165, 1958.
41. M. Cohen, in "Phase Transformations in Solids," ed. R. Smoluchowski, J. E. Meyer, and W. A. Weyl, John Wiley, New York, 1951.
42. P. G. Shewman, "Transformations in Metals," McGraw-Hill, New York, 1969.
43. D. S. Lieberman, "Mechanism of Phase Transformations in Crystalline Solids," *Institute of Metals Monograph No.* 33, 1969.
44. C. H. Johansson, *Arch. Eisenhuttener*, **11,** 241, 1937.
45. F. Wever and N. Engel, cited in Ref. 41.
46. C. Zener, *Trans. AIME*, **167,** 550, 1946.
47. G. V. Kurdjumov and O. P. Maximova, *Dokl. Akad. Nauk SSSR*, **61,** 83, 1948.
48. J. C. Fisher, J. H. Hollomon, and D. Turnbull, *Trans. AIME*, **185,** 691, 1949.
49. L. Kaufman and M. Cohen, in "Mechanism of Phase Transformations in Metals," Institute of Metals Monograph and Report Series, **18,** 187, 1955.
50. A. B. Greninger and V. C. Mooradian, *Trans. AIME*, **128,** 337, 1938.
51. M. Cohen, E. S. Machlin, and V. G. Paranjpe, "Thermodynamics in Physical Metallurgy," American Society of Metals, 1949, p. 242.
52. J. W. Christian, *Proc. Roy. Soc.* (*London*), **A206,** 51, 1951; *Acta Metall.*, **6,** 377, 1958; **7,** 218, 1959.
53. H. Knapp and U. Dehlinger, *Acta Metall.*, **4,** 289, 1956.
54. J. C. Fisher, *Acta Metall.*, **1,** 32, 1953.
55. R. E. Cech and J. H. Holloman, *Trans. AIME*, **197,** 685, 1953.
56. D. P. Koistener and R. E. Marbuger, *Acta Metall.*, **7,** 59, 1959.
57. E. S. Machlin and M. Cohen, *J. Metals*, **3,** 1019, 1951.
58. M. H. Richman, M. Cohen and H. G. F. Wilsdorf, *Acta Metall.*, **7,** 819, 1959.
59. C. M. Wayman, *Advances in Materials Research*, ed. H. Hermann, **3,** 147, 1968.
60. E. C. Bain, *Trans. AIME*, **70,** 25, 1924.
61. J. W. Christian, *J. Inst. Metals*, **84,** 386, 1955–1956.
62. R. Bullough and B. A. Bilby, *Proc. Phys. Soc.*, **69B,** 1276, 1956.
63. J. S. Bowles and J. K. Mackenzie, *Acta Metall.*, **2,** 129, 1954; **2,** 138, 1954; **2,** 224, 1954; **10,** 625, 1962.
64. M. S. Wechsler, D. S. Lieberman, and T. A. Read, *Trans. AIME*, **197**, 1503, 1953.
65. D. S. Lieberman, *Acta Metall.*, **6,** 680, 1958.
66. W. S. Owen and F. J. Schoen, in "Structural Characteristics of Materials," ed. H. M. Finniston, Elsevier, Amsterdam, 1971.
67. G. Kurdjumov and G. Sachs, *Z. Physik*, **64,** 325, 1930.
68. Z. Nishiyama, *Sci. Rep. Tohoku Univ.*, **23,** 638, 1934.
69. H. M. Otte and T. A. Read, *Trans. AIME*, **209,** 412, 1957.
70. J. S. Bowles, C. S. Barrett, and L. Guttman, *Trans. AIME*, **188,** 1478, 1950.
71. C. S. Barrett and O. R. Trautz, *Trans. AIME*, **175,** 599, 1948.
72. W. G. Burgers, *Physica*, **1,** 561, 1934.
73. L. C. Chang and T. A. Read, *Trans. AIME*, **189,** 47, 1951.
74. J. S. Bowles and C. S. Barrett, *Progr. Metal Physics*, ed. B. Chalmers, **3,** 1, 1952.
75. R. P. Reed, *U.S. Department of Commerce, NBS Rep. No.* 9256, 1966.
76. E. J. Efsik and C. M. Wayman, *Trans. AIME*, **233,** 919, 1965.
77. H. Warlimont and L. Delaey, "Progress in Materials Science," eds. B. Chalmers, J. W. Christian and T. B. Massalski, Vol. 18, Pergamon Press, Oxford, 1974.
78. J. W. Christian, in "Topics in Physical Metallurgy," ed. A. Q. Khan and M. J. Brabers, Elsevier, Amsterdam, 1972.
79. M. Di Dominico and S. H. Wemple, *Phys. Rev.*, **155,** 539, 1967.
80. M. W. Burchardt and T. A. Read, *Trans. AIME*, **197,** 1516, 1953.
81. L. A. Seigel, *J. Chem. Phys.*, **17,** 1146, 1949.
82. G. M. Wolten, *J. Am. Ceram. Soc.*, **46,** 418, 1963.

83. E. C. Subbarao, H. S. Maiti, and K. K. Srivastava, *Phys. Stat. Solidi*, **21** *a*, 9, 1974.
84. G. K. Bansal and A. H. Heuer, *Acta Met.*, **20,** 1281, 1972.
85. W. L. Frazer and S. W. Kennedy, *Acta. Cryst.*, **A30,** 13, 1974.
86. S. W. Kennedy, *J. Materials Sci.*, **9,** 1392, 1974.
87. M. J. Buerger, in "Phase Transformations in Solids," ed. R. Smoluchowski, J. E. Mayer, and W. A. Weyl, John Wiley, London, 1951.
88. W. L. Frazer and S. W. Kennedy, *Acta Cryst.*, **B28,** 3101, 1972.
89. S. W. Kennedy, *J. Materials Sci.*, **9,** 1557, 1974.
90. S. Swaminathan and S. Srinivasan, *Acta. Cryst.*, **A31,** 628, 1975.
91. H. Sato, in "Physical Chemistry: An Advanced Treatise," ed. H. Eyring, D. Henderson, and W. Jost, vol. 10, Academic Press, New York, 1970.
92. W. Van Gool, in "Fast Ion Transport in Solids," ed. W. Van Gool, North-Holland, Amsterdam, 1973.
93. L. A. K. Staveley, "Technica," *Revista de Engenharia, Separata* 1o, no. 414, p. 173, Lisbon, 1972.
94. M. A. Krivoglaz and A. Smirnov, "The Theory of Order–Disorder in Alloys," Macdonald, London, 1964.
95. H. Yamouchi and D. de Fontaine, in "Order–Disorder Transformation in Alloys," ed. H. Warlimont, Springer-Verlag, Berlin, 1974, p. 148.
96. L. E. Tanner and H. J. Leamy, in Ref. 95, p. 180.
97. J. M. Cowley, *J. Appl. Phys.*, **21,** 24, 1950.
98. H. Lipson, "Progress in Metal Physics," ed. B. Chalmers, vol. 2, Pergamon Press, New York, 1957; see also L. Guttman, in "Solid State Physics," ed. F. Seitz and D. Turnbull, vol. 3, Academic Press, New York, 1956.
99. B. H. Kear, T. Sims, N. S. Stoloff, and J. H. Westbrook (eds.), "Ordered Alloys, Structural Applications and Physical Metallurgy," Claitors Publishing Division, Baton Rouge, 1970.
100. F. W. Jones and C. Sykes, *Proc. Roy. Soc.* (*London*), **A161,** 440, 1947.
101. L. H. Germer, F. E. Haworth, and J. J. Lander, *Phys. Rev.*, **61,** 614, 1942.
102. C. G. Shull and M. K. Wilkinson, *Phys. Rev.*, **97,** 304, 1955.
103. R. McGeary and S. Siegel, *Phys. Rev.*, **65,** 347, 1944.
104. A. P. Komar, doctoral dissertation, Urals Branch of the Academy of Sciences of the USSR, 1942.
105. V. E. Pamin and V. P. Fadin, in "Order–Disorder Transition in Alloys," ed. H. Warlimont, Springer-Verlag, Berlin, 1974, p. 28.
106. A. Moser, *Physik Z.*, **37,** 737, 1936.
107. H. Sato, *Nippon Kinzo ku Gakkaishi*, **6,** 435, 1942.
108. R. Artman, *J. Appl. Phys.*, **23,** 475, 1952.
109. L. W. Strock, *Z. Physik Chem.*, **B25,** 441, 1934; **B31,** 132, 1936.
110. S. Geller, *Science*, **157,** 310, 1967; see also H. Wiedersich and S. Geller, in "The Chemistry of Extended Defects in Non-Metallic Solids," ed. L. Eyring and M. O'Keefe, North-Holland, Amsterdam, 1970, p. 629.
111. G. W. Herzog and H. Krischner, in "Reactivity of Solids," ed. J. S. Anderson, M. W. Roberts and F. S. Stone, Chapman and Hall, London, 1972, p. 140; see also K. D. Becker, G. W. Herzog, D. Kanne, H. Richtering, and E. Stadler, *Ber. Bunsenges, Phys. Chem.*, **74,** 527, 1970.
112. R. D. Worswick, D. F. Mayers, and L. A. K. Staveley, *J. Chem. Soc. Faraday II*, **68,** 539, 1972.
113. K. Kamigaki, M. Ohashi, and T. Kaneko, in "Ferrites," ed. Y. Hoshino, S. Iida, and M. Sugimoto, University Park Press, Baltimore, 1971, p. 598.
114. J. R. Castles, J. M. Cowley, and A. E. C. Sparago, *Acta Cryst.*, **A27,** 376, 1971.
115. D. M. Newns and L. A. K. Staveley, *Chem. Rev.*, **66,** 267, 1966; see also N. G. Parsonage and L. A. K. Staveley, "Disorder in Crystals," Oxford University Press, 1977.
116. H. Suga, T. Matsno, and S. Seki, *Bull. Chem. Soc. Japan*, **38,** 1115, 1965.
117. M. Atoji, *J. Chem. Phys.*, **54,** 3514, 1971.
118. E. Fukishima, *J. Chem. Phys.*, **49,** 4721, 1968.
119. D. E. O'Reilly, E. M. Peterson, C. E. Scheie, and P. K. Kadaba, *J. Chem. Phys.*, **58,** 3018, 1973.
120. J. J. Rush, L. A. de Graaf, and R. C. Livingston, *J. Chem. Phys.*, **58,** 3439, 1973.
121. C. Akers, S. W. Peterson, and R. D. Willett, *Acta Cryst.*, **B24,** 1125, 1968.

122. M. Sakiyama, H. Suga, and S. Seki, *Bull. Chem. Soc. Japan*, **36,** 1025, 1963.
123. R. Savoie and M. Pezolet, *Can. J. Chem.*, **45,** 1677, 1967.
124. Z. Iqbal, L. H. Sarma, and K. D. Moller, *J. Chem. Phys.*, **57,** 4728, 1972.
125. S. Sawada, S. Nomura, S. Fujii, and I. Yashida, *Phys. Rev. Letters*, **1,** 320, 1958.
126. C. N. R. Rao, B. Prakash, and M. Natarajan, "Crystal Structure Transformations in Inorganic Nitrites, Nitrates and Carbonates," *NSRDS–NBS Monograph* 53, National Bureau of Standards, Washington, D.C., 1975.
127. Y. Yamada, I. Shibuya, and S. Hoshino, *J. Phys. Soc. Japan*, **18,** 1594, 1963.
128. E. V. Chisler and M. S. Shur, *Phys. Stat. Solidi*, **17,** 163, 173, 1966.
129. M. Sakiyama, A. Kimoto, and S. Seki, *J. Phys. Soc. Japan*, **20,** 2180, 1965.
130. J. F. Solbakk and K. O. Strømme, *Acta Chem. Scand.*, **23,** 300, 1969; K. O. Strømme, *Z. Anorg. Allg. Chem.*, **389,** 315, 1972.
131. J. D. Ray and R. A. Ogg, *J. Phys. Chem.*, **60,** 1599, 1956.
132. K. J. Rao and C. N. R. Rao, *Brit. J. Appl. Phys.*, **17,** 1653, 1966.
133. F. C. Kracek, *J. Amer. Chem. Soc.*, **53,** 2609, 1931.
134. R. A. Schroeder, C. E. Weir, and E. R. Lippincott, *J. Res. Natl. Bur. Standards*, **66A,** 407, 1962.
135. R. M. Hexter, *Spectrochim. Acta*, **10,** 291, 1958.
136. K. O. Strømme, *Acta Chem. Scan.*, **23,** 1616, 1969; **24,** 1477, 1970; **25,** 211, 1971.
137. C. N. R. Rao, in "Modern Aspects of Solid State Chemistry," ed. C. N. R. Rao, Plenum Press, New York, 1970, p. 589.
138. P. P. Salhotra, E. C. Subbarao, and P. Venkateswarlu, *Phys. Stat. Sol.*, **29,** 859, 1968.
139. A. Arell, *Ann. Acad. Sci. Fenn. Ser. A*, **6,** no. 57, 204, 1966; P. Schwartz, *Phys. Rev.*, **B4,** 920, 1971.
140. H. A. Levy and S. W. Peterson, *Phys. Rev.*, **86,** 766, 1952; *J. Chem. Phys.*, **21,** 366, 1953.
141. R. Bersohn and H. S. Gutowsky, *J. Chem. Phys.*, **22,** 651, 1954.
142. C. H. Wang and R. B. Wright, *J. Chem. Phys.*, **58,** 1411, 1973.
143. C. N. R. Rao and M. Natarajan, "Crystal Structure Transformations in Binary Halides," *NSRDS–NBS Monograph* 41, National Bureau of Standards, Washington, D.C., 1972.
144. R. N. Brown and A. C. McClaren, *Proc. Roy. Soc.* (*London*), **266,** 329, 1962.
145. Y. Shinnaka, *J. Phys. Soc. Japan*, **14,** 1073, 1959.
146. M. Nagitani, T. Seiyama, M. Sariyama, H. Suga, and S. Seki, *Bull. Chem. Soc. Japan*, **40,** 1833, 1967.
147. B. T. Matthias and J. P. Rameika, *Phys. Rev.*, **103,** 262, 1956.
148. C. N. R. Rao and B. Prakash, "Crystal Structure Transformations in Inorganic Sulfates, Phosphates, Perchlorates and Chromates," *NSRDS–NBS Monograph* 56, National Bureau of Standards, Washington, D.C., 1976.
149. D. E. O'Reilly and T. Tsang, *J. Chem. Phys.*, **46,** 1291, 1967.
150. V. V. Udalova and Z. G. Pinsker, *Kristallografia*, **8,** 538, 1963.
151. E. O. Schlemper and W. C. Hamilton, *J. Chem. Phys.*, **44,** 4498, 1969.
152. J. W. Stout and R. C. Chisholm, *J. Chem. Phys.*, **36,** 979, 1962.
153. R. M. Clay, C. E. Dyball, and L. A. K. Staveley, *Proc. First Internatl. Conf. Calorimetry and Thermodynamics*, 1969.
154. L. Pauling, "Nature of the Chemical Bond," Cornell University Press, Ithaca, 1960.
155. R. O. Cook, A. Davies, and L. A. K. Staveley, *J. Chem. Soc. Faraday I*, **68,** 1384, 1972.
156. J. Cahn, *Trans. AIME*, **242,** 168, 1968.
157. H. J. Stevens, in "Introduction to Glass Science," ed. L. D. Pye, H. J. Stevens, and W. C. LaCource, Plenum Press, New York, 1972, p. 197.
158. P. G. Shewman, Ref. 42, pp. 291–297.
159. J. W. Christian, Ref. 3, p. 182.
160. D. Lazarus, in "Solid State Physics," ed. F. Seitz and D. Turnbull, vol. 10, Academic Press, New York, 1960.
161. J. E. Hilliard, in "Phase Transformations," American Society for Metals, Metals Park, Ohio, 1970, p. 497.
162. V. Daniel and H. Lipson, *Proc. Roy. Soc.* (*Lond*), **A181,** 368, 1943; **A182,** 378, 1944.
163. J. W. Cahn, *Acta Metall.*, **9,** 795, 1961.

164. J. W. Cahn, *Acta Metall.*, **10,** 179, 1962.
165. J. W. Cahn, *J. Chem. Phys.*, **42,** 93, 1965.
166. J. W. Cahn and R. J. Charles, *Phys. Chem. Glasses*, **6,** 181, 1965.
167. H. Rawson, "Inorganic Glass Forming Systems," Academic Press, New York, 1967.
168. W. Haller and P. B. Macedo, *Phys. Chem. Glasses*, **9,** 153, 1968.
169. E. M. Ernsberger, *Ann. Rev. Materials Sci.*, **2,** 529, 1972.
170. T. P. Seward, D. R. Uhlmann, and D. Turnbull, *J. Am. Ceram. Soc.*, **51,** 634, 1968.
171. J. W. Cahn, *General Electric Research Laboratory Report*, RL3561M, 1964.
172. J. W. Cahn, *J. Appl. Phys.*, **34,** 3581, 1963.
173. R. W. Hooper and D. R. Uhlmann, *Phys. Chem. Glasses*, **14,** 37, 1973.
174. K. B. Rundmann and J. E. Hilliard, *Acta. Met.*, **15,** 1025, 1967.
175. K. Kallstrom and J. E. Hilliard, *J. Metals*, **20,** 69, 1968.
176. F. Hofer, *IEEE Trans. Magn. Mag.*, **6,** 221, 1970.
177. M. Tomazowa, H. Herman, and R. K. MacCrone, "The Mechanism of Phase Transformations in Crystalline Solids," *Monograph and Report Series* No. 33, Institute of Metals, London, 1969, p. 6.
178. G. F. Neilson, *Phys. Chem. Classes*, **10,** 54, 1969.
179. J. Zarzycki and F. Naudin, *Compt. Rend.*, **265,** 1456, 1967.
180. G. W. Anderson and F. U. Luehrs, *J. Appl. Phys.*, **39,** 1634, 1968.
181. U. S. Stubican and A. H. Shultz, *J. Am. Ceram. Soc.*, **51,** 290, 1968.
182. J. W. Cahn, Ref. 177, p. 31.
183. W. H. Zakariasen, *J. Am. Chem. Soc.*, **54,** 3841, 1932.
184. G. W. Morey, "The Properties of Glass," Reinhold Publishing Corp., New York, 1938.
185. J. E. Stanworth, "Physical Properties of Glass," Clarendon Press, Oxford, 1950.
186. D. R. Secrist and J. D. Mackenzie, in "Modern Aspects of Vitreous State," ed. J. D. Mackenzie, Vol. 3, Butterworths, London, 1960.
187. N. F. Mott, *Scientific American*, **217,** 80, 1967.
188. D. Turnbull, *Contemporary Physics*, **10,** 473, 1969.
189. R. Roy, *J. Non Cryst. Solids*, **3,** 33, 1970.
190. H. Scholze, in "Reactivity of Solids," ed. J. S. Anderson, M. W. Roberts, and F. S. Stone, Chapman and Hall, London, 1972, p. 160.
191. D. R. Secrist and J. D. Mackenzie, *J. Am. Ceram. Soc.*, **48,** 487, 1965.
192. H. M. Cohen and R. Roy, *J. Am. Ceram. Soc.*, **44,** 523, 1961.
193. G. Tamman, "Der Glazustand," Voss, Leipzig, 1933, p. 18.
194. H. Vogel, *Physik. Z.*, **22,** 645, 1921.
195. G. S. Fulcher, *J. Am. Ceram. Soc.*, **77,** 3701, 1925.
196. G. Tamman and W. Hesse, *Z. Anorg. Allgem. Chem.*, **156,** 245, 1926.
197. G. M. Bartenev, "The Structure and Mechanical Properties of Inorganic Glasses," Wolters-Noordhoff Publ., Groningen, 1970.
198. W. Kauzman, *Chem. Rev.*, **48,** 219, 1948.
199. C. A. Angell, *J. Am. Ceram. Soc.*, **51,** 117, 1968.
200. C. A. Angell and C. T. Moynihan, in "Molten Salts," ed. G. Mamantov, Marcel Dekker, New York, 1969.
201. A. J. Easteal and C. A. Angell, *J. Chem. Phys.*, **56,** 4231, 1972.
202. C. A. Angell and D. B. Helphrey, *J. Phys. Chem.*, **75,** 2306, 1971.
203. A. J. Easteal and C. A. Angell, *J. Phys. Chem.*, **74,** 3987, 1970.
204. S. Sakka and J. D. Mackenzie, *J. Non Cryst. Solids*, **6,** 145, 1971.
205. I. Gutzov, in "Amorphous Materials," ed. R. W. Douglas and B. Ellis, Wiley Interscience, London, 1972, p. 159.
206. A. Q. Tool, *J. Am. Ceram. Soc.*, **29,** 240, 1946.
207. M. Goldstein, *J. Chem. Phys.*, **51,** 3728, 1969.
208. F. Beuche, *J. Chem. Phys.*, **21,** 1850, 1953; **24,** 418, 1956; **30,** 748, 1959.
209. M. H. Cohen and D. Turnbull, *J. Chem. Phys.*, **31,** 1164, 1959; D. Turnbull and M. H. Cohen, *J. Chem. Phys.*, **34,** 120, 1961.

210. A. K. Doolittle, *J. Appl. Phys.*, **22,** 1471, 1951.
211. M. F. Williams, R. F. Landel, and J. D. Ferry, *J. Am. Chem. Soc.*, **77,** 3701, 1955.
212. J. H. Gibbs and E. A. DiMarzio, *J. Chem. Phys.*, **28,** 373, 1958.
213. G. Adam and J. H. Gibbs, *J. Chem. Phys.*, **43,** 139, 1965.
214. J. H. Gibbs, in "Modern Aspects of the Vitreous State," ed. J. D. Mackenzie, vol. 1, Butterworths, London, 1960.
215. R. J. Greet, *J. Chem. Phys.*, **45,** 2479, 1966.
216. A. A. Miller, *J. Phys. Chem.*, **69,** 3190, 1965.
217. D. R. Uhlmann, in "Amorphous Materials," ed. R. W. Douglas and B. Ellis, Wiley-Interscience, New York, 1972.
218. P. B. Macedo and T. A. Litowitz, *J. Chem. Phys.*, **42,** 245, 1965.
219. M. Goldstein, *J. Chem. Phys.*, **39,** 3369, 1963.
220. M. Goldstein, in "Modern Aspects of the Vitreous State," ed. J. D. Mackenzie, vol. 3, Butterworths, London, 1964.
221. R. O. Davies and G. O. Jones, *Adv. Phys.*, **2,** 370, 1953.
222. J. M. O'Reilly, *J. Polymer Sci.*, **57,** 429, 1962.
223. C. A. Angell and K. J. Rao, *J. Chem. Phys.*, **57,** 470, 1972; see also K. J. Rao and C. A. Angell, in "Amorphous Materials," ed. R. W. Douglas and B. Ellis, Wiley-Interscience, New York, 1972.
224. C. A. Angell, *J. Phys. Chem.*, **75,** 3698, 1971.
225. R. D. Corsaro and J. Jarzynski, *J. Chem. Phys.*, **60,** 5128, 1974.
226. M. Goldstein, in "Phase Transitions," ed. H. K. Henisch, R. Roy, and L. E. Cross, Pergamon Press, Oxford, 1973.
227. C. G. Bergeron, in "Introduction to Glass Science," ed. L. D. Pye, H. J. Stevens, and W. C. La Course, Plenum Press, New York, 1972.
228. G. S. Meiling and D. R. Uhlmann, *Phys. Chem. Glasses*, **8,** 62, 1967.
229. K. A. Kumm and H. Scholze, *Torid. Ztg.*, **93,** 332, 360, 1969.
230. R. H. Doremus, "Glass Science," John Wiley, New York, 1973.
231. D. R. Stewart, in "Introduction to Glass Science," ed. L. D. Pye, H. J. Stevens, and W. C. La Course, Plenum Press, New York, 1972.
232. B. E. Warren and A. G. Pincus, *J. Am. Ceram. Soc.*, **23,** 301, 1940.
233. E. M. Levin and S. Block, *J. Am. Ceram. Soc.*, **41,** 49, 1958.
234. F. P. Glasser, I. Warshaw, and R. Roy, *Phys. Chem. Glasses*, **1,** 39, 1960.
235. H. Fritzsche, in "Electronic and Structural Properties of Amorphous Semiconductors," ed. P. G. Le Comber and J. Mart, Academic Press, New York, 1973.
236. A. C. Warren, *IEEE Trans. Electronic Devices*, **ED-20,** 123, 1973.
237. J. R. Bosnell, *Physics in Technology*, **4,** 113, 1973.
238. S. R. Ovshinsky, *Phys. Rev. Letters*, **21,** 1450, 1968.
239. P. J. Walsh and G. C. Vezzoli, *Appl. Phys. Letters*, **25,** 28, 1974.
240. H. K. Henisch, R. W. Pryor, and G. J. Vendura, Jr., *J. Non-Cryst. Solids*, **8–10,** 415, 1972.
241. W. A. Weyl, in "Phase Transformations in Solids," ed. R. Smoluchowski, J. E. Mayer, and W. A. Weyl, John Wiley, New York, 1951.
242. J. D. Mackenzie, *J. Am. Ceram. Soc.*, **46,** 461, 1963; **47,** 76, 1964.
243. G. Friedel and E. Friedel, *Z. Krist.*, **79,** 1, 1931.
244. G. H. Brown and W. G. Shaw, *Chem. Rev.*, **57,** 1049, 1957.
245. O. Lehmann, *Z. Phys. Chem.*, **4,** 462, 1889.
246. P. G. de Gennes, "The Physics of Liquid Crystals," Oxford University Press, 1974.
247. R. S. Porter, E. M. Barrall II, and J. F. Johnson, *Acc. Chem. Res.*, **2,** 53, 1969.
248. A. Saupe, *Angewandte Chemie* (*internatl. ed.*), **7,** 97, 1968.
249. D. Marzotko and D. Demus, in "Liquid Crystals," ed. S. Chandrasekhar, Indian Academy of Sciences, Bangalore, India, 1975, p. 189.
250. H. Arnold, *Mol. Cryst.*, **2,** 63, 1966.
251. A. de Vries, in "Liquid Crystals," ed. S. Chandrasekhar, Indian Academy of Sciences, Bangalore, India, 1975, p. 93.
252. H. Arnold, D. Demus, and H. Sackmann, *Physik Chem.*, **222,** 127, 1963.

253. A. Ubbelohde, "Melting and Crystal Structure," Oxford University Press, 1965, p. 102.
254. G. Friedel, *Ann. Phys.*, **18,** 273, 1922.
255. G. H. Brown, J. W. Doane, and V. D. Neff, "A Review of the Structure and Physical Properties of Liquid Crystals," Butterworths, London, 1971.
256. H. Arnold, *Z. Physik. Chem.* (*Leipzig*), **240,** 177, 1969.
257. S. Chandrasekhar, S. Ramaseshan, A. S. Reshamwala, B. K. Sadashiva, R. Shashidhar, and V. Surendranath, in "Liquid Crystals," ed. S. Chandrasekhar, Indian Academy of Sciences, Bangalore, India, 1975, p. 117.
258. W. Maier and A. Saupe, *Z. Naturforsch.*, **14A,** 882, 1959; **15A,** 287, 1960.
259. S. Chandrasekhar, R. Shashidhar, and N. Tara, *Mol. Cryst. and Liq. Cryst.*, **10,** 337, 1970; **12,** 245, 1970; S. Chandrasekhar and R. Shashidhar, **16,** 1, 1972.
260. J. A. Pople and F. E. Karasz, *J. Phys. Chem. Solids*, **18,** 28, 1961; F. E. Karasz and J. A. Pople, **20,** 294 (1961).
261. E. F. Westrum, Jr., and J. P. McCullough, in "Physics and Chemistry of the Organic Solid State," ed. D. Fox, M. M. Labes, and A. Weissberger, Vol. 1, Interscience, New York, 1963.
262. A. I. Kitaigorodskii, "Molecular Crystals and Molecules," Academic Press, New York, 1973.
263. A. Bondi, "Physical Properties of Molecular Crystals," John Wiley, New York, 1968.
264. Y. A. Satay and A. Ron, *Chem. Phys. Letts.*, **25,** 384, 1974.
265. F. Jona and G. Shirane, "Ferroelectric Crystals," Pergamon Press, Oxford, 1962.
266. W. C. McCrone, in "Physics and Chemistry of the Organic Solid State," ed. D. Fox, M. M. Labes, and A. Weissberger, vol. 2, Interscience, New York, 1965.
267. S. Ramdas and J. M. Thomas, *J. Chem. Soc., Faraday II*, **72,** 1251, 1976, and the references cited therein.
268. W. Jones, J. M. Thomas, and J. O. Williams, *Mat. Res. Bull.*, **10,** 1031, 1975.
269. Yu. V. Mnyukh, N. N. Petropavlov, and A. I. Kitaigorodskii, *Dokl. Akad Nauk SSSR*, **166,** 80, 1966.
270. P. Coppens and G. M. J. Schmidt, *Acta Cryst.*, **18,** 62, 654, 1965.
271. Yu. V. Mnyukh and N. A. Panfilova, *J. Phys. Chem. Solids*, **34,** 159, 1973; Yu. V. Mnyukh and N. N. Petropavlov, *ibid.*, **33,** 2079, 1973.
272. J. M. Robertson and A. R. Ubbelohde, *Proc. Roy. Soc.*, **A167,** 136, 1938.
273. W. Jones, J. M. Thomas, and J. O. Williams, *Phil. Mag.*, **32,** 1, 1975.
274. P. Allan, E. B. Crellin, and M. Bevis, *Phil. Mag.*, **27,** 127, 1973.
275. I. C. Paul and K. T. Go, *J. Chem. Soc. B*, 33, 1969.
276. G. M. Parkinson, J. M. Thomas, J. O. Williams, M. J. Goringe, and L. W. Hobbs, *J. Chem. Soc., Perkin II*, 836, 1976.
276a. G. R. Desiraju, I. C. Paul and D. Y. Curtin, *J. Am. Chem. Soc.*, **99,** 1594, 1977.
277. F. Beuche, "Physical Properties of Polymers," Interscience, New York, 1962.
278. G. Gee, *Contemp. Phys.*, **11,** 313, 1970.
279. C. K. Wu and M. Nicol, *Chem. Phys. Letts.*, **21,** 153, 1973.
280. G. J. Piermarini and A. B. Braun, *J. Chem. Phys.*, **58,** 1974, 1973; D. C. Bassett, S. Block, and G. J. Piermarini, *J. Appl. Phys.*, **45,** 4146, 1974.
281. S. Y. Chuang and S. J. Tao, in "Phase Transitions," ed. H. K. Henisch, R. Roy, and L. E. Cross, Pergamon Press, New York, 1973, p. 63.
282. K. P. Singh, R. M. Singru, and C. N. R. Rao, *J. Phys. C.*, **5,** 1067, 1972.

CHAPTER

FIVE

STATISTICAL MECHANICS AND PHASE TRANSITIONS

In Chap. 2, thermodynamic theories of phase transitions were examined. In the case of second-order transformations, it was found that the long-range order parameter rapidly decreases to zero as the critical temperature, T_c, is approached. Heat capacities and similar derivative properties increase rapidly and approach infinity near the transition temperature. A large variety of solid state transitions show such behavior, generally referred to as critical phenomena.[1] Typical of these are the order–disorder transitions in alloys and the ferromagnetic–paramagnetic or antiferromagnetic–paramagnetic transitions in inorganic solids. Striking similarities found in the variation of different physical properties near the transition temperature are noteworthy. Thus, the dimensionless quantity, $\varepsilon = (T - T_c)/T_c$ is related to the long-range order parameter (p in order–disorder transitions and magnetization, M, in magnetic transitions) by the equation

$$p, M = A(-\varepsilon)^{\lambda} \tag{5-1}$$

where the exponent λ is approximately $\frac{1}{3}$. A large number of exponents for the variation of corresponding quantities are known.[2] Such similarities in the behavior of diverse systems in the critical region points to the fact that the basic physical processes leading to the transitions are similar. These transitions are cooperative in nature and are produced by the mutual interaction of many particles. The cooperativity renders the process of transition easier (note that these are continuous transitions) as the critical temperature is approached.[3,4] Thus, for example, small changes in temperature produce large-scale fluctuations in the order parameter near T_c because the energy for disordering is directly dependent on the extent of the disorder that has already occurred. In a sense, this corresponds to a feedback mechanism in which a previous event conditions the events to occur. In order to understand the nature of critical phenomena or cooperative transitions, we therefore need to employ a more powerful microscopic theory which takes into account the details of atomic interactions than simple thermodynamic theories. This is provided by statistical mechanics.[5,6]

In all statistical-mechanical problems, the approach is identical. The first step is to write down the hamiltonian or the total energy of the system. In the case of solid state transitions, we need to know only the potential energies of interaction, and these would depend on the choice of a model. The partition function for the system is then written as

$$Z = \sum_{v} g(v) \exp\left[-E(v)/kT\right] \tag{5-2}$$

where v is a configuration of the system, $g(v)$ the degeneracy of the configuration, and $E(v)$ the corresponding energy. The next part of the problem involves the difficult task of finding $g(v)$, which is dependent on the model chosen. From Eq. (5-2), all the thermodynamic quantities can be readily obtained by making use of standard relations. What we are interested in is to find out whether thermodynamic quantities like heat capacity derived by using Eq. (5-2) show singularities as a function of temperature and, if so, how these quantities vary in the critical region. Answers to these are then checked against the chosen models.

The subject of critical behavior is a vast one, and to discuss all facets of this highly specialized topic would be clearly beyond the scope of this book. We shall therefore only highlight the important results obtained in this area. We shall first consider the Ising model and show how it can be used to understand magnetic as well as order–disorder transitions.

5-1 ISING MODEL

The Ising model[8] or, more appropriately, the Lenz–Ising model,[9] was originally proposed to discuss transitions in magnetic systems and is easily understood in the case of a ferromagnetic system. The hamiltonian of a spin system in a magnetic field where only pairwise interactions among nearest neighbors are considered may be written as

$$\mathscr{H} = -\tfrac{1}{2}\sum_{i,j} J_{ij}\boldsymbol{\sigma}_i \cdot \boldsymbol{\sigma}_j - \mu \sum_{i} \boldsymbol{\sigma}_i \cdot \mathbf{H} \tag{5-3}$$

where $\boldsymbol{\sigma}_i$ and $\boldsymbol{\sigma}_j$ are any two spins. The first term of Eq. (5-3) is the exchange energy, where J_{ij} is the exchange parameter. The second term gives the interaction of the individual spins with the external field $\mathbf{H}$, and μ is the magnetic moment of the spin. Equation (5-3) is known as the Heisenberg hamiltonian. We shall not discuss the statistical mechanics of a Heisenberg model,[10] but limit ourselves to the Ising model which is a simplified case of the Heisenberg model. In the Ising model we assume that the spins are aligned only along one axis (say z) and obtain the truncated Heisenberg hamiltonian as

$$\mathscr{H}_{\mathrm{I}} = -\tfrac{1}{2}\sum_{i,j} J_{ij}\sigma_i^z\sigma_j^z - \mu H \sum_i \sigma_i^z \tag{5-4}$$

where the sum is carried over all the nearest-neighbor pairs.

Equation (5-4) assumes in effect that the spins are quantized in the z-direction only (an arbitrary easy axis of magnetization), σ_i^z and σ_j^z being the spins along the z-axis. The Ising model therefore represents the case of a highly uniaxial anisotropy. Since σ_i or σ_j can only take two identical values with opposite signs, Eq. (5-4) can be rewritten as

$$\mathscr{H}_{\mathrm{I}} = -\tfrac{1}{2}J\sum_{i,j} \tau_i\tau_j - \mu H \sum_i \tau_i \tag{5-5}$$

where the summation is over all values of τ (equal to ± 1). The generality of the Ising model is now at once clear. The hamiltonian $\mathscr{H}_{\mathrm{I}}$ or, more generally, the interaction energy E_{I} for any lattice of particles where only nearest-neighbor interactions are considered and the state of the particle can be described by a variable $\tau_i = \pm 1$ is represented by Eq. (5-5) with the appropriate values of J and μH. As an example, consider the case of the order–disorder transitions in binary alloys. The transition corresponds to the randomization of the occupation of atoms on the "right" (appropriate sublattice) and the "wrong" (inappropriate sublattice) sites. The right/wrong occupation may be indicated as $\tau_i = \pm 1$ along with the appropriate pair interaction energy J. While $\mu H \Sigma \tau_i$ corresponds to the interaction energy in the field in the magnetic case, it corresponds to a chemical potential term in an alloy of variable composition which becomes zero in an alloy of fixed composition. Spin disordering and alloy disordering problems will thus have a similar hamiltonian, rendering the Ising model of a ferromagnet (in the absence of external field) formally identical to that of an ordered alloy.

The partition function for the Ising model may now be written as

$$Z = \sum_{i=1}^{N} \sum_{\tau_i,\tau_j=\pm 1} \exp\left\{-\frac{J}{2kT}\sum_{i,j}\tau_i\tau_j - \frac{\mu H}{kT}\sum_i \tau_i\right\} \tag{5-6}$$

The thermodynamic properties of the system are derived from Eq. (5-6). The free energy, F, is given by

$$F = -kT \ln Z \tag{5-7}$$

and the other thermodynamic quantities are easily obtained from Eq. (5-7).

The problem involved in evaluating Z may be easily visualized. For a large system of N particles, even an oversimplified expression like Eq. (5-6) contains

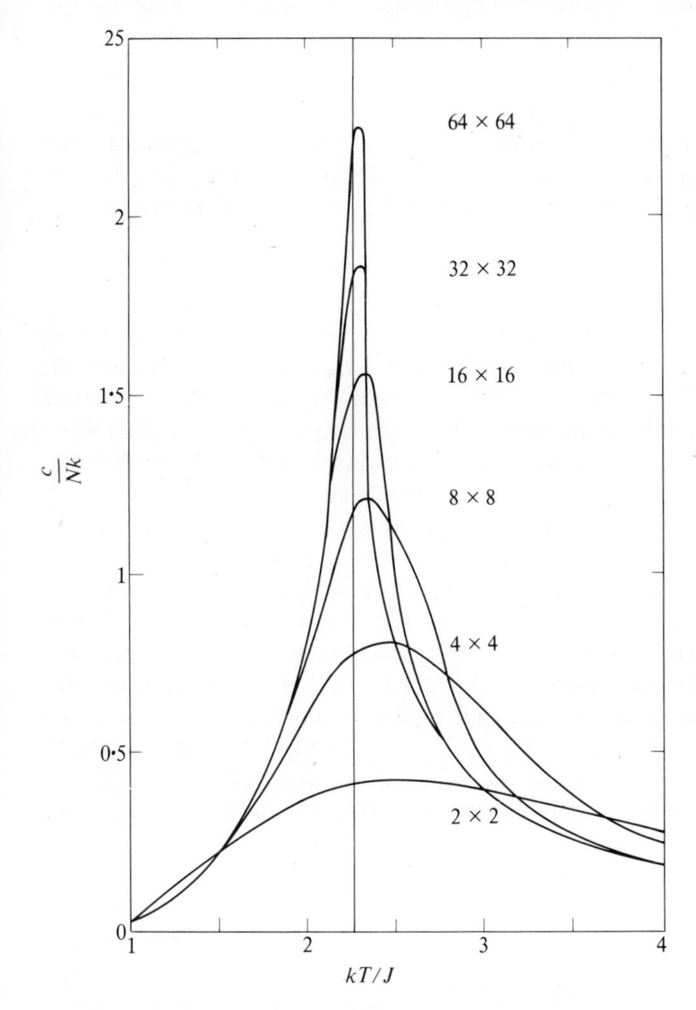

Figure 5-1 Heat capacities of square Ising nets with increasing size. (*After Firdinand and Fisher.*[11])

2^N terms. With such an expression it is our interest to find out whether the system exhibits a phase transition at all. At first sight, Eq. (5-6), being a sum of exponentials (and the exponentials in turn being "entire" analytical functions), gives the impression that there cannot be any singularities resulting from such an expression and, hence, any phase transitions. While this is indeed so, irrespective of the size N, for the Ising model in one dimension (an Ising chain), the situation is different in the two-dimensional case with sufficiently large N. Firdinand and Fisher[11] have calculated the heat capacities for an Ising net increasing the size gradually. Even with a net size as small as 32×32 (note that in real systems $N \approx 10^{20}$), there was a remarkable sharpness in the increase of specific heat (Fig. 5-1).

Order Parameters

Before we proceed further with our discussion of the Ising model, it would be in order to define what are known as order parameters. Let us consider the case of β-brass which is an alloy of the formula CuZn (Fig. 5-2). It has a body-centered cubic structure with an atom of one kind (either Zn or Cu) at the body center and of the other kind (Cu or Zn atom respectively) at the corners. The lattice can be subdivided into two equivalent interpenetrating sublattices, each of which is simple cubic, and each sublattice is completely occupied by a particular kind of atoms. This arrangement corresponds to a completely ordered state of the alloy which, in reality, exists only at very low temperatures. As the temperature is increased, exchange of atoms on the two sublattices occurs, giving rise to disorder. The maximum disorder corresponds to 50 percent of Cu atoms being exchanged with 50 percent Zn atoms at random, which renders the two sublattices indistinguishable. At the lowest temperature, namely absolute zero, the probability of Cu or Zn atoms being on the corresponding "right" lattice site is unity. At a high enough temperature, when the lattice occupation is completely random, this probability decreases to 0.5.

In a general alloy system AB, if A belongs to a sublattice of A, and B to a sublattice of B, as the temperature increases some atoms of A will wrongly occupy sublattice positions corresponding to B; a corresponding number of B atoms will similarly be occupying wrong positions belonging to the A sublattice. If R denotes the number of right atoms and W the number of wrong atoms, $R + W$ gives the total number of atoms of a particular kind. The highest order corresponds to $W = 0$ and we shall assign unity as the value of the order parameter for this state. In the completely disordered state, $R = W$ and the order parameter

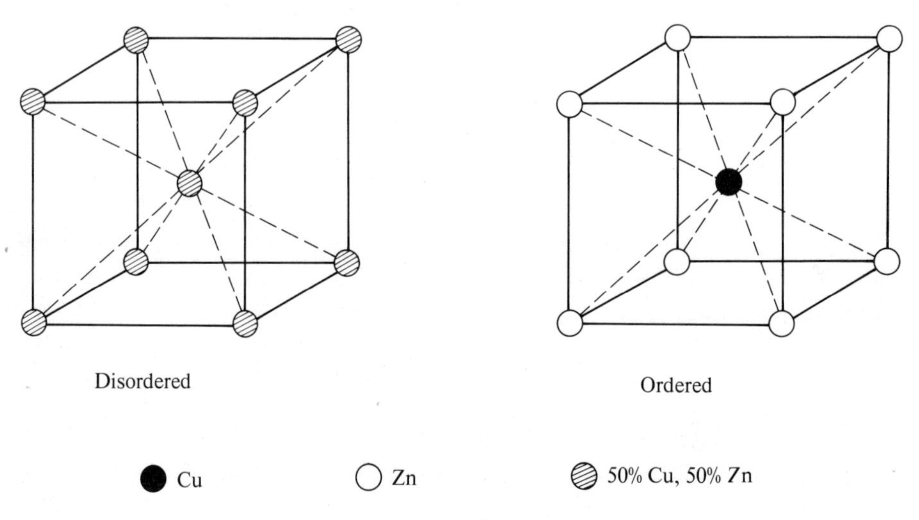

Figure 5-2 Ordered and disordered structures of CuZn.

corresponding to this state may be defined as zero. The expression for the order parameter, ξ, can be written as

$$\xi = \frac{R - W}{R + W} \tag{5-8}$$

Since ξ is determined from the averaged occupation probabilities over the entire lattice without any reference to the distances between right or wrong atoms, it is known as the *long-range order parameter*. This is the same ξ that was discussed in Chap. 2. One can see that if the lattices are so defined that R and W are interchanged, ξ becomes -1 for complete order and zero for disorder.

A *short-range order parameter* may be defined similarly. In the kind of lattice considered above, all the nearest neighbors of A atoms are atoms of B in the perfectly ordered state, and vice versa. If R_1 and W_1 represent the number of right and wrong nearest neighbors, then we can define an order parameter, ξ_1, with respect to nearest neighbors:

$$\xi_1 = \frac{R_1 - W_1}{R_1 + W_1} \tag{5-9}$$

Here, $R_1 + W_1 = zN$, where z is the number of nearest neighbors and ξ_1 corresponds to the pair correlation coefficient at the nearest-neighbor distance. We can similarly define $\xi_2, \xi_3, \ldots,$ etc., as the order parameters with respect to the second, third, ..., etc., neighbors. Since there is always a tendency for the atoms to have the "right" neighbors, we have $\xi_1 > \xi_2 > \ldots$, and in general $\xi_i \geq \xi_{i+k}$. As i gets larger, ξ_i approaches a limiting value defined by the long-range order parameter ξ as follows:

$$\frac{R_\infty}{R_\infty + W_\infty} = \left(\frac{R}{R+W}\right)^2 + \left(\frac{W}{R+W}\right)^2$$

$$= \frac{(1+\xi)^2}{2} + \frac{(1-\xi)^2}{2} = \tfrac{1}{2}(1+\xi^2)$$

$$\frac{W_\infty}{R_\infty + W_\infty} = 1 - \frac{R_\infty}{R_\infty + W_\infty} = 1 - \frac{(1+\xi^2)}{2} = \tfrac{1}{2}(1-\xi^2)$$

$$\therefore \xi_\infty = \frac{R_\infty - W_\infty}{R_\infty + W_\infty} = \xi^2 \tag{5-10}$$

With these definitions of order parameters, we shall proceed with the discussion of the statistical mechanics of an Ising chain.

One-dimensional Ising Model

Interest in the one-dimensional Ising model is both historical and demonstrative. It is historical[9] because Ising solved it in the case of a spin system and failed to notice any transition. It is demonstrative because it is the simplest of the Ising problems. It was nearly two decades after Ising's work that a rigorous solution of a two-dimensional Ising model was obtained by Onsager.[12] The two-dimensional problem itself is rather complex[13] and will be briefly considered later in the section.

Let us consider an Ising chain containing a total of N spins. Let the chain be closed into a loop so that end effects are eliminated (Fig. 5-3). Let us further denote by p and n the number of positive (up) and negative (down) spins ($p + n = N$). The Ising model energy (the hamiltonian) may be written as

$$\mathscr{H}_{\mathrm{I}} = E = 2hJ - \mu H(p - n) \tag{5-11}$$

where we imagine that there are $2h$ pairs of antiparallel spins in the arrangement with an interaction energy of J per pair (the parallel-pair interaction energy is taken as zero) and H is the field acting in the direction of positive spins. The combinational factor leading to $2h$ pairs of antiparallel spins is obtained as follows. Divide the entire ring into two (imaginary) subrings of only p and n spins. Insert h cuts in each of the rings. The number of ways of doing this would be equal to $\binom{p}{h}$ and $\binom{n}{h}$ respectively for the two rings. After effecting the cuts, we can insert the h cuts of the p subring into the h cuts of the n subring so that $2h$ antiparallel pairs are generated. The total number of ways of obtaining $2h$ pairs of antiparallel spins therefore becomes equal to

$$g(p, h) = \binom{p}{h}\binom{n}{h} \equiv \binom{p}{h}\binom{N - p}{h} \tag{5-12}$$

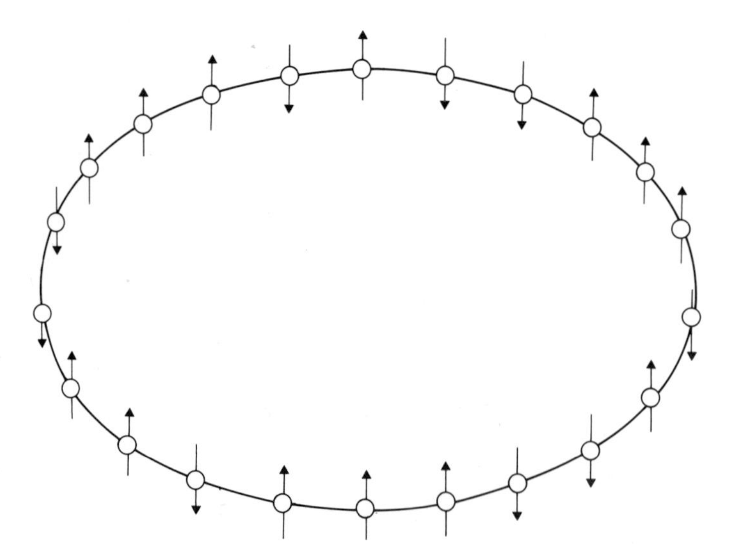

Figure 5-3 Ising chain whose ends are joined to avoid end effects.

Noting that $p - n = 2p - N$, the partition function can be written as

$$Z(p, h) = \sum_{p=-N}^{N} g(p, h) \exp\left[-\{2hJ - \mu H(2p - N)\}/kT\right] \tag{5-13}$$

We also note that $Z(p, h) = Z(\xi, \xi_1)$, since

$$\xi = \frac{p - n}{N} \tag{5-14}$$

and

$$\xi_1 = \frac{N - 2h}{N} \tag{5-15}$$

By applying the minimum free energy condition in the form

$$\left(\frac{\partial \ln Z}{\partial p}\right) = 0 \quad \text{and} \quad \left(\frac{\partial \ln Z}{\partial h}\right) = 0 \tag{5-16}$$

and using Stirling's approximation,[7] we obtain the two relations:

$$\frac{(p - h)(n - h)}{h^2} = \exp(2J/kT) \tag{5-17}$$

and

$$\left(\frac{n - h}{p - h}\right)\left(\frac{p}{n}\right) = \exp(-2\mu H/kT) \tag{5-18}$$

Eliminating h between Eqs. (5-17) and (5-18), we obtain

$$\frac{(p - n)^2}{pn} = [\exp(2J/kT)][\exp(\mu H/kT) - \exp(-\mu H/kT)]^2 \tag{5-19}$$

Since the magnetization M (corresponding to an order parameter ξ) and M_∞ (at absolute zero) are related to p and n as

$$\frac{M}{M_\infty} = \frac{\mu(p - n)}{\mu N} = \frac{(p - n)}{N} = \xi \tag{5-20}$$

we can transform Eq. (5-19) to

$$\frac{M/M_\infty}{[1 - (M/M_\infty)^2]^{1/2}} = \exp(J/kT) \sinh(\mu H/kT) \tag{5-21}$$

$$\frac{M}{M_\infty} = \frac{\sinh(\mu H/kT)}{[\sinh^2(\mu H/kT) + \exp(-2J/kT)]^{1/2}} \tag{5-22}$$

Equation (5-22) contains the important information that when H becomes zero or the external magnetic field is removed, the value of M/M_∞ becomes zero or the long-range order parameter goes to zero. Therefore at no temperature other than absolute zero can there be any ordering in the absence of an external field. This means that there is no phase transition for a one-dimensional Ising model.

The reason for the lack of phase transition in one dimension may be understood from fundamental thermodynamic considerations[5,14] as well. Let us suppose that in a long chain of N ordered spins a particular spin is flipped. If this flipping is spontaneous at all temperatures (other than absolute zero), there can be no ordering and hence no phase transition. This question is answered by finding out the change in free energy ΔF which is equal to $\Delta E - T\Delta S$ (ΔE is the change in the internal energy and ΔS is the change in entropy). Let the energy for spin flipping be W. The value of ΔS will be $k \ln N$, since any of the N different spins may be flipped to produce disorder. Therefore

$$\Delta F = W - kT \ln N \tag{5-23}$$

which is always negative for any reasonable value of N and T. This implies that disordering can occur spontaneously. Even when the temperature is very low, the system moves to order gradually, since the probability of the system in the disordered condition decreases as $\exp(-W/kT)/[1 + \exp(-W/kT)]$ and there can be no phase transition in a one-dimensional Ising system.

Two-dimensional Ising Model

Let us first examine from physical reasoning whether a two-dimensional Ising system can exhibit a phase transition at all. Following Fisher,[14] we shall consider a completely ordered square lattice (Fig. 5-4) in which we want to break the order by flipping the spins in some region as indicated. The line which indicates the boundary may be described as a domain wall. The question, as before, would be whether the formation of such a domain can be spontaneous at all temperatures. Let the sides of the square lattice in Fig. 5-4 be equal to L and the energy required to create a unit of the domain wall be W. Let us suppose that we begin to form a wall from one edge. In principle, the building-up of the wall can proceed by travelling in three directions, viz., left, right, or forward (it is possible even to travel backwards, after building the wall to a certain extent). Suppose we build a wall of length S equal to fL, where f is greater than unity. The energy required to create such a wall is equal to $fLW = \Delta E$. In order to estimate the entropy, we note that we can start building the wall lengthwise or breadthwise. Also, since we can proceed in any of the three directions left, right, or forward while building the wall, a lower limit of the number of configurations would be equal to $2L \times (3)^{fL}$. We therefore obtain

$$\begin{aligned} \Delta S &\leq k \ln [2L(3)^{fL}] \\ &\leq fLk \ln 3 + k \ln 2L \end{aligned} \tag{5-24}$$

The free energy needed for the creation of a wall may be written as

$$\Delta F \geq fLN - T[fLk \ln 3 + k \ln 2L] \tag{5-25}$$

Since the number of lattice points, N, is equal to L^2, we can rewrite Eq. (5-25) as

$$\Delta F \geq fN^{1/2}(W - kT \ln 3) - \tfrac{1}{2}kT \ln 2N \tag{5-26}$$

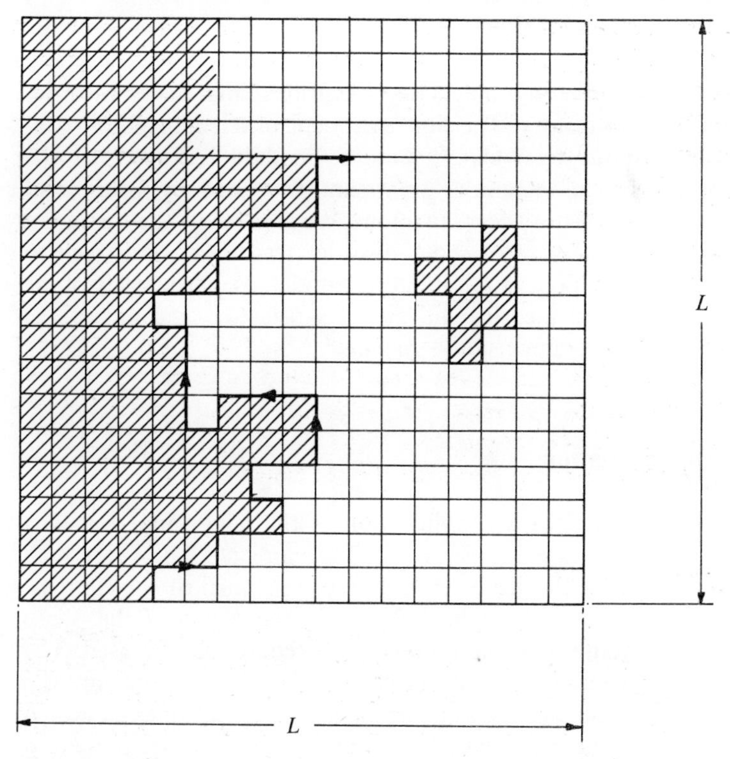

Figure 5-4 Illustration of stepwise construction of domain wall across a two-dimensional square lattice. (*After Fisher.*[14])

For a large system the second term is negligible. For temperatures less than T_c (where T_c is equal to $W/k \ln 3$), the free energy change would be positive for putting a domain wall. Therefore, below T_c, the system would be spontaneously ordered, and hence a phase transition must occur in a two-dimensional system.

The rigorous solution of the two-dimensional Ising model was first obtained by Onsager,[12,15] and several books and reviews have treated the two-dimensional Ising model extensively.[1,5,13,16,17] The principal results of Onsager's treatment are: (i) a phase transition can occur in a two-dimensional Ising model, and (ii) the heat capacity of a square Ising system increases logarithmically and symmetrically to infinity as the critical temperature is approached. We will compare the critical exponents obtained by this rigorous method with those from other treatments at a later stage. The problem of the three-dimensional Ising model has not yet been rigorously solved. However, several reliable approximate methods[2,18,19] have been developed and even these methods require fairly sophisticated mathematical techniques. We shall be comparing the exponents obtained from such methods at a later stage.

5-2 APPROXIMATE METHODS

Approximate methods for treating magnetic transitions and order–disorder problems have a fairly long history. The first treatment of ferromagnetic–paramagnetic transitions was due to Weiss,[20] and the method is known as the molecular field approximation. A similar treatment was used by Bragg and Williams[21] in the case of order–disorder transitions. We give below the treatment of Bragg and Williams for the case of order–disorder transitions. It is well to remember in this context that if one is not interested in details, particularly of the critical behavior, effective field theories will give a satisfactory account of the overall behavior found in three-dimensional systems.[22]

Bragg-Williams Approximation

This model may be considered as a simplification of the Ising model[4] and is based on the assumption $\xi_1 = \xi_2 = \xi_3 = \ldots = \xi_\infty$. Therefore, $g(\xi, \xi_1) = g(\xi)$. As a result of this assumption, which neglects all variations in statistical correlations, the ability of the model to account for finer details in the region of the phase transitions is lost. To compute $g(\xi)$, the following procedure may be used. The expression for long-range order is given by Eq. (5-8). The "right" atoms are the A and B atoms on their own sublattices, while wrong atoms are the ones for which sublattice positions are interchanged. Since $N/2$ A and $N/2$ B atoms are present in the system, we have

$$\text{Number of A atoms in right sites} = R = \frac{N}{2}\left(\frac{1+\xi}{2}\right) = X \qquad \text{(say)}$$

$$\text{Number of A atoms in wrong sites} = W = \frac{N}{2}\left(\frac{1-\xi}{2}\right) = Y \qquad \text{(say)}$$

$$\text{Number of B atoms on right sites} = R = \frac{N}{2}\left(\frac{1+\xi}{2}\right) = X$$

$$\text{Number of B atoms on wrong sites} = W = \frac{N}{2}\left(\frac{1-\xi}{2}\right) = Y$$

Since $g(\xi)$ is the number of ways a distribution of the above kind can be effected, it is enough to compute the number of ways right and wrong sites can be chosen for either kind of atoms (A or B). This is simply given by the combinatorial factor,

$$g(\xi) = \frac{(N/2)!}{(N/2 - X)!\,X!} \times \frac{(N/2)!}{(N/2 - Y)!\,Y!}$$

$$= \frac{(N/2)!}{\left[(N/2)\left(1 - \frac{1+\xi}{2}\right)\right]!\left[(N/2)\left(\frac{1+\xi}{2}\right)\right]!}$$

$$\times \frac{(N/2)!}{\left[(N/2)\left(1 - \frac{1-\xi}{2}\right)\right]!\left[(N/2)\left(\frac{1-\xi}{2}\right)\right]!}$$

$$= \left\{\frac{(N/2)!}{\left[(N/2)\left(\frac{1-\xi}{2}\right)\right]!\left[(N/2)\left(\frac{1+\xi}{2}\right)\right]!}\right\}^2 \tag{5-27}$$

The energy of the configuration, $E(\xi)$, is evaluated as follows. There are AA, AB, and BB pairs present in the configuration. Since all the first neighbors of an atom on the A sublattice are always present in the B sublattice, and since the number of nearest neighbors is z, the number of AA pairs would be the product of four terms: (*a*) the total number of A sites, (*b*) the probability of occupation of A by A (i.e., the right occupation), (*c*) the number of nearest-neighbor lattice positions z, and (*d*) the probability of occupation of B sites by A (i.e., wrong occupation). The appropriate number of pairs is evaluated as follows:

$$\text{Number of A–A pairs} = \frac{N}{2}\left(\frac{1+\xi}{2}\right)z\left(\frac{1-\xi}{2}\right) = \frac{Nz}{8}(1 - \xi^2)$$

$$\text{Number of A–B pairs} = \frac{N}{2}\left(\frac{1+\xi}{2}\right)z\left(\frac{1+\xi}{2}\right) + \frac{N}{2}\left(\frac{1-\xi}{2}\right)z\left(\frac{1-\xi}{2}\right)$$

$$= \frac{Nz}{8}(1 + \xi)^2 + \frac{Nz}{8}(1 - \xi)^2$$

$$= \frac{Nz}{4}(1 + \xi^2)$$

(the second term arises through both A and B being on wrong sites).

$$\text{Number of BB pairs} = \frac{N}{2}\left(\frac{1+\xi}{2}\right)z\left(\frac{1-\xi}{2}\right) = \frac{Nz}{8}(1 - \xi^2)$$

If the energies of interaction for AA, BB, and AB pairs are V_{AA}, V_{BB}, and V_{AB} respectively, the total configurational energy is given by

$$E(\xi) = \frac{Nz}{8}(1 - \xi^2)[V_{AA} + V_{BB}] + \frac{Nz}{4}(1 + \xi^2)V_{AB}$$

$$= \frac{Nz}{8}[(V_{AA} + V_{BB} + 2V_{AB}) - \xi^2(V_{AA} + V_{BB} - 2V_{AB})]$$

$$= E(0) - \frac{NzV\xi^2}{4} \tag{5-28}$$

where $E(0)$ corresponds to energy for the completely disordered state ($\xi = 0$). and $V = \frac{1}{2}(V_{AA} + V_{BB}) - V_{AB}$.

Since we know both $g(\xi)$ and $E(\xi)$, we can write the partition function

$$Z = g(\xi) \exp[-E(\xi)/kT] \tag{5-29}$$

The free energy of the system would correspond to $-kT \ln Z(\xi)$. For equilibrium, it is necessary that $(\partial/\partial\xi)[-kT \ln Z(\xi)]$ be zero. So, the equilibrium value of ξ is determined from the equation

$$\frac{\partial \ln Z(\xi)}{\partial \xi} = 0 \tag{5-30}$$

From equations (5-27), (5-28), and (5-29),

$$\ln Z(\xi) = \ln g(\xi) - \frac{E(\xi)}{kT}$$

$$= 2\left\{\ln\left(\frac{N}{2}\right)! - \ln\left[\frac{N}{2}\left(\frac{1-\xi}{2}\right)\right]! - \ln\left[\frac{N}{2}\left(\frac{1+\xi}{2}\right)\right]!\right\}$$

$$- \frac{E(0)}{kT} + \frac{NzV\xi^2}{4kT} \tag{5-31}$$

Using Stirling's approximation and cancelling appropriate terms, we have

$$\ln Z(\xi) = \frac{N}{2}[(1 - \xi)\ln(1 - \xi) + (1 + \xi)\ln(1 + \xi)]$$

$$+ N \ln 2 - \frac{E(0)}{kT} + \frac{NzV\xi^2}{4kT} \tag{5-32}$$

Therefore, $$\frac{\partial \ln Z(\xi)}{\partial \xi} = 0 = \frac{N}{2}\left[\ln\frac{(1+\xi)}{(1-\xi)}\right] + \frac{NzV\xi}{2kT}$$

and $$\left(\frac{1-\xi}{1+\xi}\right) = \exp(zV\xi/kT) \tag{5-33}$$

Or $$\xi = \tanh(zV\xi/2kT) \tag{5-34}$$

Equation (5-34) may also be written as

$$\frac{1}{\xi} \ln \left(\frac{1-\xi}{1+\xi} \right) = \frac{zV}{2kT} \tag{5-35}$$

The configurational free energy of the system can be written as $F(\xi) = -kT \ln Z(\xi)$, as mentioned earlier. From Eq. (5-32) one can see that $F(0) = E(0)$. In Fig. 5-5, $[F(\xi) - F(0)]/2kT$ is plotted for values of ξ between -1 and $+1$ and for assumed values of $zV/2kT$. It is seen that for $zV/2kT > 1$, two free energy minima always exist for finite values of $\pm\xi$. As the ratio $zV/2kT$ approaches unity, the minima tend to merge at $\xi = 0$, and for all values of $zV/2kT < 1$, there is only one minimum corresponding to $\xi = 0$; that is, only the completely disordered state is stable. The critical point corresponds to $zV/2kT = 1$, or

$$T_c = \frac{zV}{2k} \tag{5-36}$$

The above result can be obtained by setting $\partial F/\partial \xi = 0$ and $\partial^2 F/\partial \xi^2 = 0$, the conditions for a critical point. Utilizing the above definition of T_c, Eq. (5-34) may be rewritten as

$$\xi = \tanh (2T_c \xi/T) \tag{5-37}$$

This represents a universal function, and the behavior of ξ with respect to T/T_c is represented in Fig. 5-6. Value of ξ can also be obtained graphically using Eq. (5-33). Values of $\ln [(1-\xi)/(1+\xi)]$ are plotted against ξ in Fig. 5-7, and in the same graph a plot of $zV\xi/2kT$ against ξ is shown (straight line). There are three intersections, one at $\xi = 0$ and two others for positive and negative values of ξ. As T is increased, the two values of ξ will tend to merge at $\xi = 0$ so that at $T = T_c$ there will be just two overlapping straight lines.

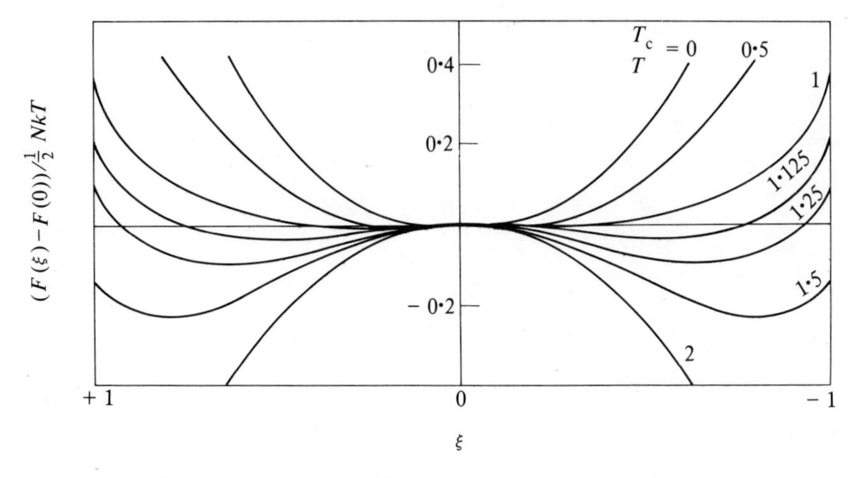

Figure 5-5 Variation of configurational free energy as a function of order parameter, ξ.

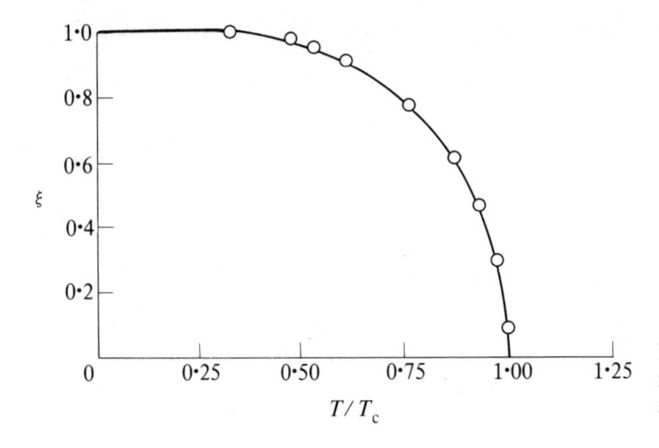

Figure 5-6 Variation of ξ as a function of T/T_c in zeroth-order approximation.

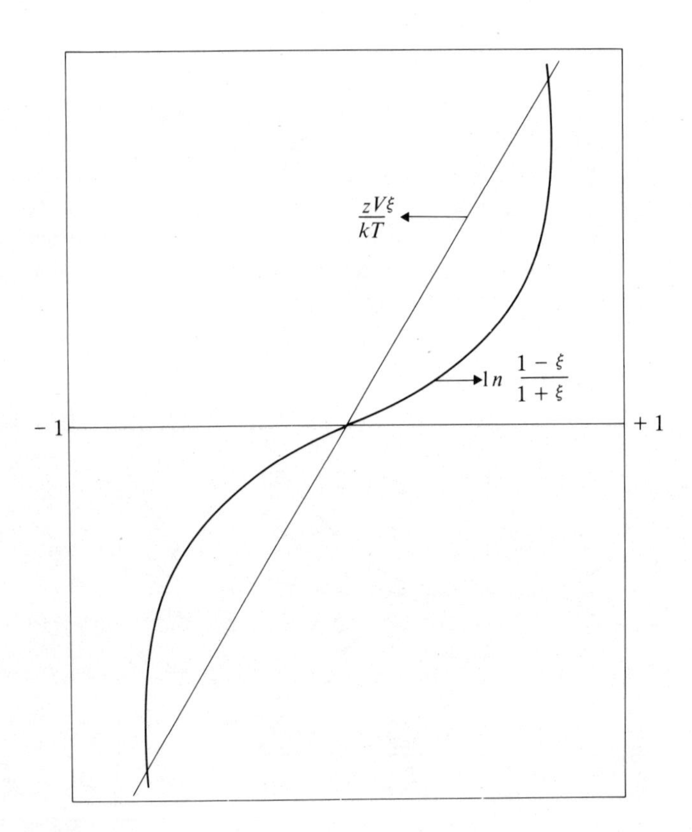

Figure 5-7 Graphical evaluation of ξ.

Configurational heat capacity in the Bragg–Williams model may be calculated from Eq. (5-28) and the thermodynamic relation

$$C_v = \left(\frac{\partial E}{\partial T}\right)_v \tag{5-38}$$

The $(\partial\xi/\partial T)$ that is needed for the evaluation of heat capacity is obtained from relation (5-33):

$$\frac{\partial \xi}{\partial T} = \left[\frac{zV(\xi^2 - 1)\xi}{T\{zV(\xi^2 - 1) - 4kT\}}\right] \tag{5-39}$$

The variation of heat capacity evaluated by this model is shown in Fig. 5-8.

The equivalence of the Bragg–Williams and the molecular field approaches can be visualized as follows. The potential energy for the order–disorder transition in a binary alloy of constant composition is obtained from Eq. (5-5) as

$$E = -\tfrac{1}{2}\sum u\tau_i\tau_j \tag{5-40}$$

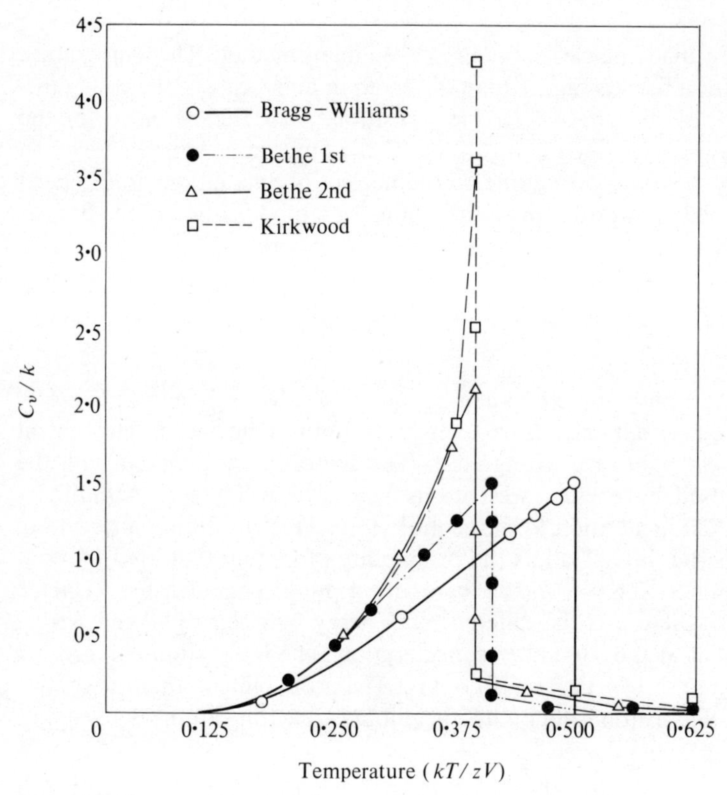

Figure 5-8 Heat capacities in various approximation procedures for a cooperative transition. (*After Sato.*[4])

where u is the appropriate interaction energy. Equation (5-40) works out as if the atom τ_j is under the influence of a fluctuating field $\Sigma u\tau_i$, with the summation carried over nearest neighbors. Instead of the fluctuating field, one can substitute an average field obtained from Eq. (5-28):

$$H_0 = \frac{zV\xi}{2} \tag{5-41}$$

From the Boltzmann principle, R/W can be written as

$$\begin{aligned} \frac{R}{W} &= \exp\left(\frac{2H_0}{kT}\right) = \frac{1+\xi}{1-\xi} \\ &= \exp\left(\frac{zV\xi}{kT}\right) \end{aligned} \tag{5-42}$$

From the above relation, we readily obtain Eq. (5-34):

$$\xi = \tanh\left(\frac{zV\xi}{2kT}\right)$$

The mean field expressed by Eq. (5-41) gives it the name "*mean-field*" or "*Weiss field*" approximation.

There are many inadequacies in the Bragg–Williams method. The temperature of the transformation itself is higher than observed in many cases. The configurational heat capacities go to zero after the transition. Also, the exponent for the heat capacity rise is zero, which is incorrect. These limitations can be traced to the assumption $\xi_1 = \xi_2 = \ldots = \xi_\infty$ and to the neglect of fluctuations in the local order. Bethe[6,23] tried to improve this shortcoming by a modification of the Bragg–Williams model.

Bethe's Model

The improvement in Bethe's method can be understood with the aid of Fig. 5-9. A is the central atom, and it has z nearest neighbors (four in the figure). The central atom itself may be a right or a wrong atom. The central atom interacts with the atoms nearest to itself, but these nearest atoms themselves will interact with others outside the first shell in addition to the central atom. This additional interaction, neglected in the earlier model, alters the probability of finding that kind of atom as the first neighbor. This is taken care of in Bethe's model by a factor $\theta = \exp(-u/kT)$, where u is the difference in energy between right and wrong atoms when present at the site under consideration. The interaction energies, as before, are defined by $V = \frac{1}{2}(V_{AA} + V_{BB}) - V_{AB}$. The probability r_n that the central atom is right and that n atoms out of the z neighbors are wrong atoms is given by

$$r_n = \binom{z}{n} \cdot \theta^n \cdot x^n \tag{5-43}$$

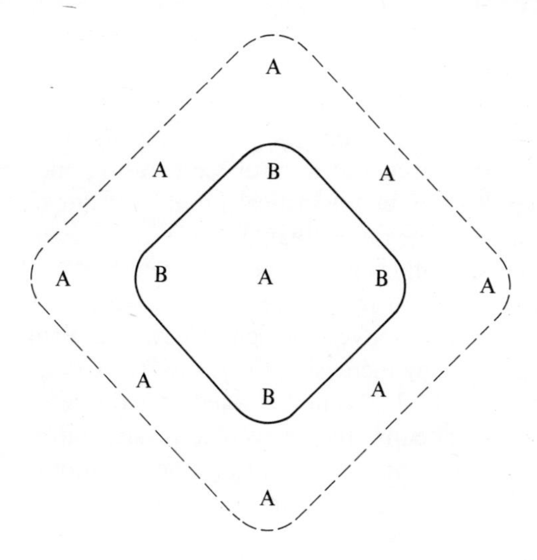

Figure 5-9 Bethe's first (the inner square) and second (the outer square) approximations.

where $x = \exp(-V/kT)$. Similarly, the probability W_n for the same group but with the central atom being wrong is

$$W_n = \binom{z}{n} x^{(z-n)} \cdot \theta^n \tag{5-44}$$

The total relative probabilities that the central atoms are "right" or "wrong" is therefore given by

$$r = \sum_{n=0}^{z} r_n = (1 + \theta x)^z \tag{5-45}$$

$$W = \sum_{n=0}^{z} W_n = (\theta + x)^z \tag{5-46}$$

Since the sum of Eqs. (5-43) and (5-44) gives the probability of finding n atoms wrong in the shell with either kind of atoms at the center, the probability that one atom is wrong in the shell is given by $(n/z)(r_n + W_n)$. The general relative probability that one atom in the shell is wrong is then given by

$$W = \sum_{n=0}^{z} \frac{n}{z}(r_n + W_n) = \frac{\theta x r}{1 + \theta x} + \frac{\theta - W}{\theta + x} \tag{5-47}$$

For a case like β-brass, we have the consistency relation in which the probabilities of either the central site (W) or the neighboring site (W') being occupied wrongly are identical. Since $W = W'$, we obtain from Eqs. (5-46) and (5-47),

$$\theta = \left(\frac{\theta x}{1 + \theta x}\right)^{z-1} \tag{5-48}$$

This expresses θ as a function of x. From the definition of the long-range order parameter, $\xi = (r - W)/(r + W)$, the behavior of ξ as a function of temperature is obtained.

A considerable improvement over the Bragg–Williams method results from this procedure (Fig. 5-8). The transformation occurs at a lower temperature and, more importantly, short-range order persists after the critical point. A point of interest in Bethe's method is that a pair of atoms rather than a single atom (as in Bragg–Williams) is being treated in an essentially similar molecular field.[4]

Calculations become more complicated with face-centered cubic lattices. A general improvement over the method outlined above has been achieved in what is known as Bethe's second approximation,[24] by increasing the size of the cluster of atoms under explicit consideration (Fig. 5-8). It should be noted that the same results were obtained by Fowler and Guggenheim[25] by means of a quasichemical approximation. In this method, the equilibrium number of various pairs of atoms like AA, BB, and AB are obtained by assuming simple chemical kinetics.

Mention may now be made of various other improved approximations without going into details. Kirkwood[26] employed an expansion technique in which moments of probability spreads were used to compute the energy of the system as a function of disorder. Another general method of evaluating the partition function is known as the cluster variation method.[27] This method is an extension of the quasichemical approximation to larger clusters of Bethe's model (keeping in view certain consistency relations). Larger cluster sizes give better descriptions of $g(\xi, \xi_1)$. In this approach, the Bragg–Williams approximation will have single atom clusters, and hence its description is known as a zeroth-order approximation. A comparison of the behavior of heat capacities obtained by the various approximations is given in Fig. 5-8. In Table 5-1, the critical parameters that are usually compared for these approximate models are listed.[28]

As mentioned earlier, a rigorous solution of the three-dimensional Ising

Table 5-1 Critical parameters of Ising models in various approximations

	Square $Z = 4$		Triangular $Z = 6$		Simple cubic $Z = 6$		Body-centered cubic $Z = 8$		Face-centered cubic $Z = 12$	
Approximation	β_c	$\frac{RT_c}{E_c}$	β_c	$\frac{RT_c}{E_c}$	β_c	$\frac{RT_c}{E_c}$	β_c	$\frac{RT_c}{E_c}$	β_c	$\frac{RT_c}{E_c}$
Zeroth (Bragg–Williams	0.607	2.00	0.717	2.00	0.717	2.00	0.779	2.00	0.846	2.00
Bethe (first)	0.500	1.44	0.667	1.65	0.667	1.65	0.750	1.74	0.828	1.77
Bethe (second)	—	—	—	—	0.656	1.58	—	—	—	—
Kikuchi	0.439	1.21	0.600	1.30	0.646	1.53	—	—	—	—
Exact	0.414	1.135	0.578	1.214	—	—	—	—	—	—

$\beta_c = \exp(-V/kT_c)$.
E_c = total change in configurational energy = $NzV/4$.

problem has not been achieved. However, several powerful approximate procedures have been developed.[2,18,19] Particularly notable are the series expansion procedures. These procedures have been used with success to compute critical exponents.

5-3 CRITICAL EXPONENTS AND SCALING LAWS

The behavior of physical quantities near the critical point was described by Eq. (5-1), where λ is known as a critical exponent. It follows from Eq. (5-1) that, in general, the variation of any measurable physical quantity, ϕ, and ε are related through λ:

$$\lambda = \lim_{\varepsilon \to 0} \left| \frac{\ln \phi}{\ln |\varepsilon|} \right| \tag{5-49}$$

Although we usually learn only about the variation of order parameters and heat capacities near the critical points for order–disorder transitions, many more quantities are actually studied in magnetic transitions.[1,2] A few such important quantities and the corresponding exponents are listed in Table 5-2. The values of these exponents may be predicted by the models discussed earlier, such as mean-field theories or the two- and three-dimensional Ising models. The predicted values are given in Table 5-3 along with the experimental values of exponents for ferromagnetic substances.

The exponents are not all independent of one another. Several relations have been established among these quantities:

$$\begin{aligned} \alpha + 2\beta + \gamma' &= 0 && \text{Essam and Fisher}^{29} \\ \alpha' + 2\beta + \gamma' &\geq 0 && \text{Rushbrooke}^{30} \\ \alpha' + \beta(\delta - 1) &\geq 2 && \text{Griffiths}^{31} \\ \gamma' &\geq \beta(\delta - 1) && \text{Griffiths}^{31} \\ \gamma(\delta + 1) &\geq (2 - \alpha)(\delta - 1) && \text{Griffiths}^{31} \end{aligned} \tag{5-50}$$

Table 5-2 Critical exponents: definition in ferromagnets

Critical exponent	Definition	Quantity
α	$C_{H=0} \sim \varepsilon^{-\alpha}, \varepsilon > 0$	Specific heat at $H = 0$
α'	$C_{H=0} \sim (-\varepsilon)^{-\alpha'}, \varepsilon < 0$	which is also C_M
β	$M_0 \sim (-\varepsilon)^{\beta}$	Zero field magnetization
γ	$\chi_T \sim \varepsilon^{-\gamma}, \varepsilon > 0$	Zero field isothermal susceptibility
γ'	$\chi_T \sim (-\varepsilon)^{\gamma'}, \varepsilon < 0$	
δ	$H \sim \|M\|^{\delta}$	Critical isotherm

Table 5-3 Theoretical and experimental values of critical exponents

Exponent	α'	β	γ'	δ	α	γ
Classical	0	$\frac{1}{2}$	1	3	0	1
Experimental*	<0.16	0.33 ± 0.03	—	0.41 ± 0.1	<0.16	1.33 ± 0.03
2-dimensional Ising model	0	$\frac{1}{8}$	$\frac{7}{4}$	15	0	$\frac{7}{4}$
3-dimensional Ising model lattice gas	$\sim\frac{1}{8}$	$\sim\frac{5}{16}$	$\sim\frac{5}{4}$	~ 5	$\sim\frac{1}{8}$	$\sim\frac{5}{4}$

* For ferromagnetic substances.

Many other such relations are reported in the literature.[1,2] Such relations reduce the minimum number of exponents required in order to estimate others. The efforts made to establish the minimum number of quantities essential to estimate all the exponents have led to what is known as the *scaling hypothesis.*[32]

Two independent approaches[33–35] have been made to arrive at the minimum number of exponents, both of which rest on the assumption (the scaling hypothesis) that the thermodynamic potential of interest has the form of a homogeneous function.[1] It is established by these approaches that all of the critical exponents may be expressed as functions of just two parameters. However, these parameters are not themselves predicted in such analyses; they merely establish that the measurement of just any two exponents is sufficient to predict the exponents for all other quantities. The exponent relations (5-50) can also be proved by use of the scaling hypothesis.

The scaling hypothesis states that the correlation length, ζ, should be the longest and the only relevant length in explaining critical phenomena. The correlation length itself is considered as a measure of the average distance over which the fluctuations (of magnetization) are correlated. The scaling hypothesis also states that ζ, diverging like $|T - T_c|^{-\nu}, \nu > 0$, counts for the dominating temperature dependence of all quatities near T_c; physical quantities depend on $|T - T_c|$ only through their dependence on ζ. Thus, if we increase the unit of length by a factor s, then in the new unit, the system appears shrunk by the factor s and the new correlation length becomes ζ/s. Since this correlation length is proportional to $|T - T_c|^{-\nu}$, a decrease in correlation length gives rise to an increase in $|T - T_c|$. The temperature dependence of a physical quantity near T_c can be understood from the way it behaves under a change of scale.

A simple example for illustrating the scaling hypothesis is the following. The free energy per unit volume $F(\zeta)$ becomes $s^d F(\zeta)$ when the volume of the system is shrunk. Here, d is the dimension. We therefore have $F(\zeta/s) = s^d F(\zeta)$. Since s is arbitrary, we shall set $s = \zeta$. We then get

$$F(\zeta) = s^{-d} F(\zeta/s) = \zeta^{-d} F(1) \propto |T - T_c|^{\nu d} \tag{5-51}$$

This is because $\zeta \propto |T - T_c|^{-\nu}$. Another result is that in the limit $T = T_c$, ζ becomes infinite and there is no length parameter, and hence the systems would look the same if a change in length scale is made. It is obvious that the scaling hypothesis is a powerful technique. A proper understanding of this hypothesis becomes possible by the renormalization group formulation discussed later in this chapter.

5-4 TYPICAL SYSTEMS EXHIBITING CRITICAL PHENOMENA

In Table 5-4, a number of order–disorder transitions are listed.[28,36,37] Unfortunately, exponent measurements on alloy systems reported in the literature are not detailed enough. In magnetic systems, however, studies have been more extensive and detailed. From the large variety of magnetic materials that chemistry

Table 5-4 Order–disorder transformations in binary metal systems*

Alloy	Trans. temp. (°C)	Lattice type disorder–order
1. Ag_3Pt	~800	FCC–fcc
AgPt	500	FCC–complex
$AgPt_3$	625	FCC–fcc
2. Au_3Cu	240	FCC–fcc
AuCu	408	FCC-(orth)–tet.
$AuCu_3$	391	FCC–fcc
3. Cd_3Mg	85	Hex.–hex.
CdMg	253	Hex.–hex.
$CdMg_3$	153	Hex.–hex.
4. $CoPt_3$	700–800	FCC–fcc
CoPt	825	FCC–tet.
5. Cu_4Pd	478	FCC–tet.
Cu_3Pd_2	~600	FCC–bcc
CuPd	600	FCC–bcc
6. $AlFe_3$	575	BCC–bcc
$AlNi_3$	>1125	FCC–fcc
7. Fe_3Pd	780	FCC–fcc
FePd	~750	FCC–tet.
$FePd_3$	760	FCC–fcc
8. MnNi	~650	FCC–tet.
$MnNi_3$	510	FCC–fcc
9. FeV	1234	BCC–complex
FePt	~700	FCC–fcc
10. Au_3Zn	270, 425	Complex?
$AuZn_3$	225, 515	Complex?

* From Ref. 28; data in the table are based on the information collected by G. J. Diener, C. E. Dixon, F. E. Jaumot, Jr., J. B. Newkirk, R. A. Oliani, and F. N. Rhiner.

has afforded, nearly all possible types of systems have been identified and studied.[22] Although in this book we have confined ourselves to Ising systems, we must note that, in reality, the dimensionality of spin itself can be three. This along with the lattice dimensionality of three gives the possibility of nine different types of magnetic systems. This is further doubled by the fact that J, the coupling parameter, can have either positive (ferromagnetic) or negative (antiferromagnetic) signs. In all, therefore, eighteen different types of magnetic systems are possible. In the words of de Jongh and Miedema,[22] experimentalists have been successful to such an extent "that one sometimes wonders how artificial and unphysical such a model has to be, in order to prevent the discovery of an approximation in the laboratory." In Table 5-5 several examples which approximate to Ising spin systems in one, two, and three dimensions are listed.

Table 5-5 Model systems in magnetic transitions*

Model	Example	T_c (K)	Remarks
One-dimensional Ising	$CoCl_2 \cdot 2NC_5H_5$	—	A critical temperature due to 3-D Ferromagnetic ordering occurs at very low temperatures
	$Dy(C_2H_5SO_4)_2 \cdot 9H_2O$	—	A critical temperature due to 3-D Ferromagnetic ordering occurs at very low temperatures
	$K_3Fe(CN)_6$	—	Antiferromagnetic ordering occurs at very low temperatures
Two-dimensional Ising	Rb_2CoF_4	101	Antiferromagnetic ordering
	K_2CoF_4	107	Antiferromagnetic ordering
	$FeCl_2$	23.55	Ferromagnetic ordering
Three-dimensional Ising	$DyPO_4$	3.39	Antiferromagnetic ordering
	$Dy_3Al_5O_{12}$	2.54	Antiferromagnetic ordering
	$DyAlO_3$	3.52	Antiferromagnetic ordering
	$CoRb_3Cl_5$	1.14	Antiferromagnetic ordering

* Original references to the literature may be found in Ref. 22.

5-5 UNIVERSALITY OF CRITICAL EXPONENTS AND THEIR DEPENDENCE ON DIMENSIONALITY

The discussion so far has led us to two principal conclusions. They are: (*a*) cooperative transitions are a statistical problem, and (*b*) Ising models in more

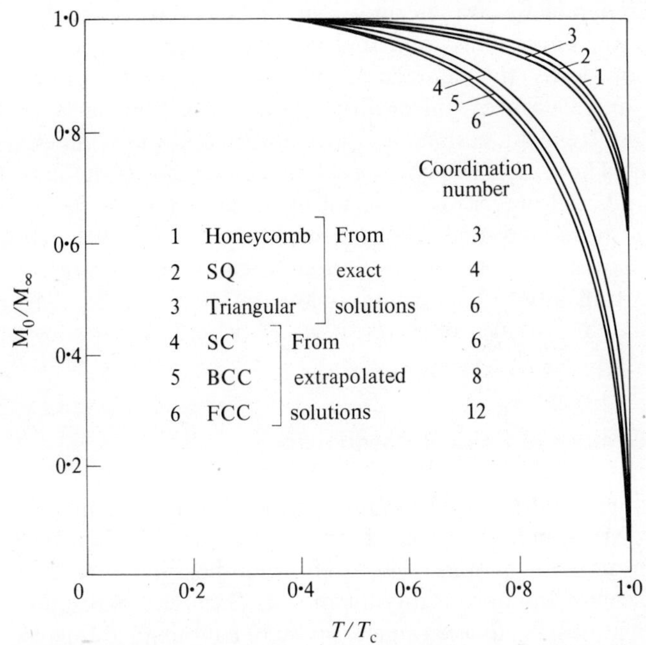

Figure 5-10 Effect of lattice dimensionality and structure on the critical phenomena in Ising models. (*After Fisher*[14] *and Domb.*[18])

than one dimension lead to phase transitions.* Two important observations regarding critical phenomena are to be noted. The first concerns the coordinations of spins in a given dimensionality of an Ising system.[18] This is demonstrated in Fig. 5-10. Curves (3) and (4) in the figure refer to two-dimensional triangular and three-dimensional simple cubic structures with the same coordination number of six, but the behavior of order parameters is very different, and so are the critical exponents. We see that β is 0.125 for two dimensions and 0.313 for three dimensions. This shows the clear dominant dependence of critical behavior on dimensionality.

The second observation is connected with the nature of the potentials employed in describing critical behavior. The fact that critical exponents in diverse systems like magnets and alloys are the same indicates that critical behavior is insensitive to the detailed nature of interparticle interactions.[1,14] This is further demonstrated in the ESR studies of Muller and Berlinger[43] on $SrTiO_3$ and $LaAlO_3$. In the region of $0.1T_c$ to T_c, the order parameter changed from $\frac{1}{2}$ to $\frac{1}{3}$, characteristic of critical behavior. This is plausible since, in the critical region,

* We have not so far discussed Heisenberg models. If in Eq. (5-3) we use $\sigma_i^x\sigma_j^x + \sigma_i^y\sigma_j^y$, it is known as the planar Heisenberg model,[38] and if we use Eq. (5-3) as such, untruncated, it is known as the three-dimensional Heisenberg model.[39-41] Yet another possibility is to allow spins to have unrestricted orientations, and this leads to a "spherical" model.[42] It would be useful to remember that a Heisenberg model makes transitions even more difficult;[14] one- and two-dimensional Heisenberg models do not exhibit any transitions.

fluctuations in the order parameter are enormous and the system senses only changes occurring over large dimensions compared to interatomic distances.[1,44] This line of investigation leads to the idea of the universality of critical phenomena.[1,32,44] The implication of universality is that transitions may be classified simply according to the dimensionality of the lattice and the symmetry of the ordering parameter. The critical behavior of systems belonging to the same class is expected to be similar. However, the behavior of systems in the transition region as predicted by mean-field and Ising theories indicates clearly the importance of long and short-range interactions. Indeed, even an Ising chain has been shown to exhibit a transition[45] if interactions are considered to be long-range and if the interatomic potential is of the form $1/r^{1+\delta}$, where δ ranges from 0 to 1.

The Renormalization Group and Critical Phenomena

Although the idea of the renormalization group first appeared in relativistic field theories, its most successful application has been to the theory of critical phenomena. The pioneering work of Wilson[46–49] has made possible an understanding of the origin of scaling and universality hypotheses. The renormalization group is a set of transformations, R_s, in a parameter space of coupling parameters which are nonsingular. Each point in the parameter space represents a possible probability distribution describing the statistical mechanical system. The concept of scaling appears in the scale change, which is a part of R_s. Universality shows itself in terms of critical exponents, which are properties of R_s near a fixed point and are to a great extent independent of the details of the microscopic hamiltonian. The renormalization group method provides a powerful averaging technique which can handle small and big fluctuations in the critical region. Furthermore, the renormalization group operator leaves the partition function unchanged. The subject of the renormalization group has been discussed in several recent articles and reviews.[48–52] We shall briefly examine the formalism of the renormalization group within the framework of statistical mechanics of an n-component classical field in a d-dimensional space. If $n = 3$, $d = 3$, the classical field would describe the fluctuation of magnetization in a ferromagnet.

Let us consider a large class of probability distributions for a set of random variables ϕ_{ik}, and label k to range over discrete points in a sphere of radius Λ in k-space. The density of points is $L^d(2\pi)^{-d}$, where L^d is the volume of a d-dimensional lattice. Any probability distribution for the random variables can be specified by a set of parameters. Let each set of parameters be a point in a parameter space, so that a probability distribution P is represented by a point μ in this space. Such a parameter space is constructed as follows:

$$P \propto \exp(-\mathscr{H}) \tag{5-52}$$

$$\mathscr{H} = \sum_{m=1}^{\infty} L^{-(m-1)d} \sum_{k_1,k_2\cdots k_{2m-1}} \sum_{i_1,i_2\cdots i_{2m}} \phi_{i_1k_1}\phi_{i_2k_2}\cdots\phi_{i_{2m}k_{2m}u_{2m}} + \text{constant} \tag{5-53}$$

Here, $k_{2m} = -(k_1 + k_2 + \ldots + k_{2m-1})$, and u_{2m} is a function of $k_1, k_2 \ldots k_{2m-1}$. We define the parameter space as the space of all possible μ:

$$\mu \equiv (u_2, u_4, u_6 \ldots) \tag{5-54}$$

We consider u_{2m} as coupling parameters. We should note that Λ, the cutoff in k, is fixed for all probability distributions, and $\mathscr{H}$ is just the logarithm of the probability distribution (and not energy divided by temperature). Concepts of temperature and energy are irrelevant to the parameter space. They only come in as inputs in determining a particular probability distribution corresponding to a particular point in the parameter space.

Let us consider a transformation involving a change of a probability distribution from P to P'. This transformation may be represented as

$$\mu' = R_s \mu \tag{5-55}$$

where point μ is transformed to μ' in the parameter space (note μ and μ' represent P and P' respectively). Such a transformation is defined by

$$P' \propto \exp(-\mathscr{H}') = \left[\prod_{i, \Lambda/s < k' < \Lambda} \int d\phi_{ik'} \exp(-\mathscr{H}) \right]_{\phi_k \to \alpha_s \phi_{sk}} \tag{5-56}$$

The definition of μ is given by Eq. (5-53) and μ' is similarly defined from $\mathscr{H}'$ by writing it in the same form as Eq. (5-53). In Eq. (5-56), we integrate $\phi_{ik'}$ with k' between Λ/s and Λ, relabel random variables by enlarging the wave vectors by a factor s, and multiply the variables by a constant factor α_s. P' is equivalent to P as far as random variables ϕ_k with $k < \Lambda/s$ are concerned, provided that proper relabeling and multiplication by α_s are carried out while computing averages. Thus,

$$\langle | \phi_{ik} | \rangle_P^2 = \alpha_s^2 \langle | \phi_{isk} |^2 \rangle_{P'}$$

If we define $G(k, \mu) = \langle | \phi_{ik} |^2 \rangle_P$, then

$$G(k, \mu) = \alpha_s^2 G(sk, R_s \mu) \tag{5-57}$$

The number of random variables in P' is smaller by a factor s^{-d} than in P; change of scale $k \to sk$ renders the density of points in k-space smaller by the same factor. That is, the volume of the system described by P' has shrunk by a factor $s^{-d}(L'^d = s^{-d} L^d)$, and the density of points is $L'^d(2\pi)^{-d}$. L or L' has no role to play in calculating quantities of interest, and is therefore not included as a parameter. The set of R_s, $1 \le s < \infty$, will be the renormalization group.

From Eq. (5-56) we see that having two transformations R_s and $R_{s'}$ is equivalent to a single transformation $R_{ss'}$:

$$R_s R_{s'} \mu = R_{ss'} \mu \tag{5-58}$$

In order for Eq. (5-58) to hold, $\alpha_s \alpha_{s'} = \alpha_{ss'}$, and hence there will be the severe restriction on α_s

$$\alpha_s = s^y \tag{5-59}$$

where y is a constant. If $\phi_k \to s^y \phi_{sk}$ in Eq. (5-56) is regarded as a scale change,

y may be interpreted as the dimension of ϕ_k in units of length. Such a definition is not useful, and we shall determine y with respect to a fixed point. A fixed point is that satisfying

$$R_s\mu^* = \mu^* \tag{5-60}$$

Equation (5-60) may be viewed as an equation to be solved for μ^*, and the equation will not have a solution unless y in Eq. (5-59) is properly chosen. Equation (5-60) is in a way an eigenvalue equation for the eigenvalue y and eigenvector μ^*. Let us assume that there is a solution to this equation with a definite y and define a quantity η for this y as

$$y = 1 - \eta/2 \tag{5-61}$$

Therefore,

$$\alpha_s = s^{1-\eta/2} \tag{5-62}$$

We shall later show that η is a critical exponent. Equation (5-57) now becomes

$$G(k, \mu) = s^{2-\eta}G(sk, R_s\mu) \tag{5-63}$$

We should note here that R_s is a refined scale transformation keeping the cutoff fixed. R_s tells us how coupling parameters change when the system is shrunk by a factor s. At the same time, the multiple integral in Eq. (5-56) and determination of α_s by a fixed point equation render R_s more than a mere change of scale. Equation (5-56) ensures that Λ changes Λ/s and lets the scale change bring Λ/s back to Λ.

Let us now examine R_s near a fixed point μ^* as defined by Eq. (5-60). Characteristics of critical phenomena are related to those of R_s operating near μ^*. If μ is near μ^*, $\mu = \mu^* + \delta\mu$ where $\delta\mu$ is small. We can then write

$$\delta\mu' = R_s^L\delta\mu \tag{5-64}$$

since $\mu' = \mu^* + \delta\mu'$ and $R_s\mu^* = \mu^*$. If $0\left((\delta\mu)^2\right)$ terms are ignored in calculating $\delta\mu'$ from Eq. (5-64), R_s^L becomes a linear operator. We can in principle construct a matrix to represent R_s^L and determine the eigenvalues and eigenvectors of the matrix. Noting that the eigenvalues $\lambda_j(s) = s^{y_j}$, we can show that

$$\delta\mu' = \sum_j t_j s^{y_j} e_j \tag{5-65}$$

where e_j stands for eigenvector. If $y_1 > 0$ (and all other y_js are negative) and s is very large,

$$\delta\mu' = R_s^L\delta\mu = t_1 s^{y_1} e_1 + 0(s^{y_2}) \tag{5-66}$$

If $t_1 = 0$, $R_s^L\delta\mu \rightarrow 0$ as s increases, and μ is moved toward the fixed point by R_s. The subspace defined by $t_1 = 0$ is considered to be the critical surface, and points on the critical surface are pushed to the fixed point by R_s.

Let us examine the effect of R_s on the probability distribution (5-53). This particular probability distribution, represented by a point $\mu(T)$ in the parameter space, corresponds to a set of coupling parameters which are smooth functions of T. The trajectory $\mu(T)$ should be smooth and hit the critical surface at a temperature T_c. At a temperature T very close to T_c, the distance from $\mu(T)$ to the critical surface, t_1, is proportional to $(T - T_c)$. Assuming $\mu(T) = \mu^* + \delta\mu(T)$,

$$R_s^L \delta\mu(T) = A(T - T_c)s^{1/v}e_1 + 0\,(s^{y_2}) \tag{5-67}$$

where $1/v = y_1$ and A is a constant. Making use of Eqs. (5-63) and (5-67), we can write for large s,

$$G(k, \mu(T)) = s^{2-\eta}[G(sk, \mu^*) + A(T - T_c)s^{1/v}e_1 + 0(s^{y_2})] \tag{5-68}$$

In the case of $T = T_c$, if we take $s = \Lambda/2k$, in the limit of small k we get

$$G(k, \mu(T_c)) \propto k^{-2+\eta} \tag{5-69}$$

which defines the critical exponent η which is related to the fixed point of Eq. (5-59). The power law (5-69) results from the fact that $R_s\mu(T_c)$ approaches μ^* for large s. In the case of $T - T_c > 0$, $k = 0$, taking $s = t_1^{-v}$ we can show that

$$G(0, \mu(T)) \propto (T - T_c)^{\gamma} \tag{5-70}$$

where $\gamma = v(2 - \eta)$.

The assumption that μ must be near μ^* may be relaxed. The critical surface can be taken as a curved surface extending away from μ^*, and for large s, $R_s\mu$ will approach μ^* and the linear approximation becomes applicable.

We can define the correlation length, ζ (see Sec. 5-3) as $\zeta = |t_1|^{-v}$. Equation (5-67) then becomes

$$R_s^L \delta\mu = (s/\beta)^{1/v}e_1 + 0(s^{y_2}) \tag{5-71}$$

The effect of R_s would thus be to reduce the correlation length by a factor s. If we ignore the second term in Eq. (5-71), we get the scaling hypothesis discussed earlier in Sec. 5-3. The scaling hypothesis becomes valid if R_s (near μ^*) is dominantly determined by one eigenvalue for large s.

Hitherto, we have outlined the features of renormalization group without going to rigorous proofs and calculations. Wilson and Fisher[47] gave the first simple analytical illustration of the renormalization group for small $\varepsilon = 4 - d$, in which case there were no mathematical complications. Studies have recently been reported in the literature for the large n limit; critical exponents have been computed as power series in $1/n$. The reader is referred to some of the reviews[48–52] in the literature for a detailed understanding of this important topic.

5-6 HIGHER CRITICAL POINTS

Another important topic of current interest relates to the phenomenon of higher critical points. The existence of a tricritical point was first recognized by Griffiths[53] in the transitions of He^3–He^4 mixtures. It is now known to occur in many other transitions such as those of ND_4Cl and in metamagnetic (a term which describes the behavior of antiferromagnetic materials in which the layers are weakly coupled) antiferromagnetic transitions[54] in dysprosium–aluminum garnet, $FeCl_2$, $Ni(NO_3)_2 \cdot 2H_2O$, etc. The phenomenon may be briefly described with reference to Eq. (5-4). Let us consider the hamiltonian[55] which represents a system of unit spin-ions at lattice sites so that $\sigma_i = \pm 1$ or 0. The system allows a further term representing interaction with the crystal field so that Eq. (5-4) is modified as

$$\mathscr{H} = -\tfrac{1}{2}\sum_{i,j} J_{ij}\sigma_i^z\sigma_j^z - \mu H \sum_i \sigma_i^z + \Delta \sum_i (\sigma_i^z)^2 \tag{5-72}$$

In Eq. (5-72), Δ represents the energy difference between the singlet and triplet states. When Δ is zero, the problem reduces to an Ising lattice. The behavior of the system described by Eq. (5-72) has been theoretically investigated. It has been found that, for small values of Δ, the ferromagnetic–paramagnetic transitions are second-order while, beyond a critical value of Δ, they become first-order. By the application of an external magnetic field, however, the second-order transition branches off in two directions (depending on the direction of the external field). Thus, at this critical point, the point at which the critical Δ-value changes the character of the transition is actually the confluence of three second-order transition lines: hence the name "tricritical point."

It is to be recognized that the hamiltonian in Eq. (5-72) leads to two order parameters: one is the normal $\Sigma_i \sigma_i^z$, and the other, $\Sigma_i (\sigma_i^z)^2$, the value of the latter being dependent on its conjugate field Δ. In metamagnets, Δ corresponds to the physically inaccessible staggered field. In situations where two ordering parameters (which are related to each other) are present, the existence of a tricritical point may normally be expected. Experimental studies of the tricritical point in ND_4Cl have been reported recently by Yelon.[54]

Theoretical studies of critical behavior using renormalization group analysis near tricritical points have been reported by many workers.[56,58] Fisher and Nelson[56] have reported that the transitions in MnF_2, which is a weakly anisotropic antiferromagnet, may be regarded as a bicritical point. The existence of other multicritical points such as tetracritical points[54] have also been suggested.

REFERENCES

1. D. Sette, in "Essays in Physics," vol. 5, ed. G. K. T. Conn and G. N. Fowler, Academic Press, London, 1973.
2. H. E. Stanley, "Introduction to Phase Transitions and Critical Phenomena," Clarendon Press, Oxford, 1971.
3. H. N. V. Temperley, "Changes of State," Cleaver-Hume Press, London, 1956.
4. H. Sato, in "Physical Chemistry—An Advanced Treatise," vol. 10, ed. H. Eyring, D. Henderson, and W. Jost, Academic Press, New York, 1970.
5. G. H. Wannier, "Statistical Physics," John Wiley, New York, 1966.
6. E. A. Guggenheim, "Mixtures," Oxford University Press, 1952.
7. H. Eyring, D. Henderson, B. J. Stover, and E. M. Eyring, "Statistical Mechanics and Dynamics," John Wiley, New York, 1964.
8. E. Ising, *Z. Phys.*, **31,** 253, 1925.
9. S. G. Brush, *Rev. Mod. Phys.*, **39,** 883, 1967.
10. See for example "Critical Phenomena," ed. M. S. Green, Academic Press, New York, 1971; "Phase Transitions and Critical Phenomena" (first four vols.), ed. C. Domb and M. S. Green, Academic Press, London, New York, 1972.

11. A. E. Firdinand and M. E. Fisher, *Phys. Rev.*, **185,** 832, 1969.
12. L. Onsager, *Phys. Rev.*, **65,** 117, 1944.
13. G. F. Newell and E. W. Montroll, *Rev. Mod. Phys.*, **25,** 353, 1953.
14. M. E. Fisher, "Essays in Physics," vol. 4, Academic Press, London, 1972.
15. L. Onsager and B. Kaufmann, *Phys. Rev.*, **76,** 1232, 1244, 1949.
16. M. S. Green and C. A. Hurst, "Order–Disorder Phenomena," John Wiley, New York, 1964.
17. L. Shultz, D. Mattis, and E. Lieb, *Rev. Mod. Phys.*, **36,** 856, 1964.
18. C. Domb, *Adv. Phys.*, **9,** 149, 1960.
19. M. E. Fisher, *Rep. Prog. Phys.*, **30,** 310, 1967.
20. P. Weiss, *J. Phys. Paris*, **6,** 661, 1907.
21. W. L. Bragg and E. J. Williams, *Proc. Roy. Soc.* (*London*), **A145,** 699, 1934.
22. L. J. de Jongh and A. R. Miedema, *Adv. Phys.*, **23,** 1, 1974.
23. H. A. Bethe, *Proc. Roy. Soc.* (*London*), **A150,** 552, 1935.
24. T. S. Chang, *Proc. Roy. Soc.* (*London*), **A161**, 546, 1937; *Proc. Cambridge Phil. Soc.*, **34,** 224; **35,** 81, 1938.
25. R. H. Fowler and E. A. Guggenheim, *Proc. Roy. Soc.* (*London*), **A174,** 189, 1940.
26. J. G. Kirkwood, *J. Chem. Phys.*, **6,** 70, 1938.
27. R. Kikuchi and S. G. Brush, *J. Chem. Phys.*, **47,** 195, 1967.
28. R. Smoluchowski, in "Hand Book of Physics," ed. E. U. Condon and Hugh-Odishaw, McGraw-Hill, New York, 1958.
29. J. W. Essam and M. E. Fisher, *J. Chem. Phys.*, **38,** 802, 1963.
30. G. S. Rushbrooke, *J. Chem. Phys.*, **39,** 842, 1963.
31. R. B. Griffiths, *J. Chem. Phys.*, **43,** 1958, 1965.
32. L. P. Kadanoff, W. Godze, D. Hamblen, R. Hecht, E. Lewis, V. V. Palciauskas, M. Rayl, J. Swift, D. Arpnes, and J. Kane, *Rev. Mod. Phys.*, **39,** 395, 1967.
33. B. Widom, *J. Chem. Phys.*, **43,** 3892, 3898, 1965.
34. C. Domb and D. L. Hunter, *Proc. Phys. Soc.*, **86,** 1147, 1965.
35. L. P. Kadanoff, *Physics*, **2,** 263, 1966.
36. L. Guttman, in "Solid State Physics," ed. F. Seitz and D. Turnbull, vol. 3, Academic Press, New York, London, 1956.
37. M. A. Krivoglaz and A. S. Smirnov, "The Theory of Order–Disorder in Alloys," Macdonald, London, 1964.
38. V. G. Vaks and A. I. Larkin, *Sov. Phys. JETP*, **22,** 678, 1966.
39. G. Heller and H. A. Kramers, *Proc. Sect. Sci. K. ned Acad. Wet.*, **37,** 378, 1934.
40. H. E. Stanley and T. A. Kaplan, *Phys. Rev. Lett.*, **16,** 981, 1966; **17,** 913, 1966.
41. P. J. Wood and G. S. Rushbrooke, *Phys. Rev. Lett.*, **17,** 307, 1966.
42. T. H. Berlin and M. Kac, *Phys. Rev.*, **86,** 821, 1952.
43. K. A. Muller and N. Berlinger, *Phys. Rev. Lett.*, **26,** 13, 1971.
44. L. P. Kadanoff, in "Critical Phenomena," ed. M. S. Green, Academic Press, New York, 1971.
45. Results of F. J. Dyson, C. J. Thompson, and P. W. Anderson, quoted in Ref. 14.
46. K. G. Wilson, *Phys. Rev. Lett.*, **28,** 584, 1972.
47. K. G. Wilson and M. E. Fisher, *Phys. Rev. Lett.*, **28,** 240, 1972.
48. K. G. Wilson, *Physica*, **73,** 119, 1974.
49. K. G. Wilson and J. Kogut, *Phys. Repts.*, **12C,** 77, 1974.
50. M. E. Fisher, *Rev. Mod. Phys.*, **46,** 587, 1974.
51. S. Ma, *Rev. Mod. Phys.*, **45,** 589, 1973.
52. S. Ma, *J. Math. Phys.*, **15,** 1866, 1974.
53. R. B. Griffiths, *Phys. Rev. Lett.*, **24,** 715, 1970; see also M. Blume, V. J. Emery, and R. B. Griffiths, *Phys. Rev.*, **A4,** 1071, 1971.
54. W. B. Yelon, in "Anharmonic Lattices, Structural Transitions and Melting," ed. T. Riste, Noordhoff, Leiden, 1974.
55. M. Blume, in "Anharmonic Lattices, Structural Transitions and Melting," ed. T. Riste, Noordhoff, Leiden, 1974.
56. M. E. Fisher and D. R. Nelson, *Phys. Rev. Lett.*, **32,** 1350, 1974.
57. E. K. Reidel and F. J. Wegner, *Phys. Rev. Lett.*, **29,** 349, 1972.
58. D. R. Nelson, J. M. Kosterlitz, and M. E. Fisher, *Phys. Rev. Lett.*, **33,** 813, 1974.

CHAPTER

SIX

SOFT MODES AND PHASE TRANSITIONS

In earlier chapters we examined phase transitions in solids, particularly critical behavior, in terms of order parameters and learnt how the statistical-mechanical approach provides a basis for understanding the general features of phase transitions. Another unifying concept which makes possible a microscopic understanding of structural phase transitions in solids is that of the soft mode. In simple terms, a soft mode is a vibrational mode, the square of whose frequency goes toward zero as the temperature approaches the phase transition temperature. Structural phase transitions are generally accompanied by crystal distortions or displacements of ions, the mean value of such displacements corresponding to an order parameter; vibrational soft modes are expected to be associated with all such transitions.

If we define a phase transition as the appearance of long-range order in some degree of freedom, the order being absent before the occurrence of the transition, the transition can be described by the order parameter. For long-range order to exist, the order parameter must be nonzero below the phase transition temperature, and it becomes zero above the transition temperature. In second-order structural transitions, the order parameter measures the magnitude of change in atomic configuration from the old structure, and the atomic displacements generally parallel the variation of a particular normal mode of lattice vibration. The normal mode would then describe thermal fluctuations in the order parameter. The normal mode frequency decreases as the temperature approaches the transition temperature (or the mode softens) in anticipation of the new structure resulting from the imposition of the soft mode eigenvector into the old structure.

Historically, Raman and Nedungadi[1] were the first to observe a soft mode in a structural phase transition by Raman scattering. As early as 1940, they reported that the α–β transition of quartz was accompanied by a decrease in the frequency of a totally symmetric optical phonon as the temperature approaches the phase transition temperature. On the basis of the Lyddane–Sachs–Teller (LST) relation,[2] Frohlich[3] in 1949 predicted that the static dielectric constant of ferroelectric perovskites like $BaTiO_3$ would go to infinity when the frequency of the lowest transverse optical mode goes to zero. The behavior of the static dielectric constant, ε_0, of a ferroelectric material above the transition temperature is given by

$$\varepsilon_0 = \frac{4\pi C}{T - T_c} \tag{6-1}$$

where T_c is the critical temperature (the use of the term "critical" may not exactly imply the critical behavior discussed in Chap. 5). From Eq. (6-1) we see that as $T \to T_c$, $\varepsilon_0 \to \infty$. The LST relation[2] may be written as

$$\frac{\varepsilon_0}{\varepsilon_\infty} = \frac{\omega_{\text{l.o}}^2}{\omega_{\text{t.o}}^2} \tag{6-2}$$

Since ε_0 tends to infinity during a ferroelectric transition, the transverse optical mode, $\omega_{\text{t.o}}$ tends to zero (unless the longitudinal mode $\omega_{\text{l.o}}$ tends to infinity, which is unphysical). This amounts to stating

$$\varepsilon_0 = \frac{4\pi C}{T - T_c} = \frac{\varepsilon_\infty \omega_{\text{l.o}}^2}{\omega_{\text{t.o}}^2}$$

or

$$\omega_{\text{t.o}}^2 = \frac{\varepsilon_\infty \omega_{\text{l.o}}^2}{4\pi C}(T - T_c) = \gamma(T - T_c) \tag{6-3}$$

Such behavior of $\omega_{\text{t.o}}$ was indeed predicted by Frohlich.[3] If $\omega_{\text{t.o}}^2$ is plotted against T, it goes to zero approximately linearly as T_c is approached. This is what is in fact implied by the phrase that the mode softens. We may note that in Eq. (6-3), we have assumed that $\omega_{\text{l.o}}$ is temperature-independent.

The concept of the soft mode was, however, properly understood only after Anderson[4] and Cochran[5] independently proposed in 1959 their soft-mode theory of ferroelectrics. According to this lattice dynamical theory, most transitions accompanied by crystal distortions are characterized by soft optical phonons whose frequency decreases as the transition temperature is approached from above or below. Soft-mode theory has been reviewed extensively in the literature.[6,7] Before discussing the lattice dynamical theory, we shall briefly examine the relation of the soft mode to order parameter and symmetry.

6-1 LANDAU'S THEORY AND SOFT MODES

The fact that there should be softening of a mode during the transformation of any solid in which long-range forces are operative (such as ionic solids in which Coulomb forces operate) can be inferred from Landau's theory (Chap. 2). In order to apply Landau's theory, we need to identify an order parameter which varies between zero and unity. In phase transformations like the cubic-to-tetragonal transitions in perovskites, the ionic displacements may themselves be considered to represent an order parameter. If η is the ionic displacement, then the free energy $\phi(P, T, \eta)$ is given by

$$\phi(P, T, \eta) = \phi_0(P, T) + a\eta + b\eta^2 + c\eta^3 + d\eta^4 + \dots$$
$$= \phi_0(P, T) + b\eta^2 + d\eta^4 + \dots \tag{6-4}$$

Equation (6-4) is identical to Eq. (2-15) with η replacing ξ. By the same arguments outlined earlier, we obtain,

$$b(P, T) = B(T - T_c) \tag{6-5}$$

and therefore

$$\eta^2 = -\frac{b}{2d} = \frac{B(T - T_c)}{2d}$$

or

$$\eta = \eta_0(T - T_c)^{1/2} \tag{6-6}$$

The exponent $\frac{1}{2}$ is characteristic of mean-field theories. Landau's theory is a mean-field theory and assumes the existence of long-range forces which play a dominant role. In order to see how Eq. (6-6) is connected with a soft mode, let us assume the simple one-dimensional harmonic oscillator model. In such a case, ϕ would be given by

$$\phi = \tfrac{1}{2}\omega^2 Q^2 + \text{other noncritical terms} \tag{6-7}$$

where ω is the vibration frequency and Q the mean value of the normal coordinate. Comparing Eq. (6-4) and (6-7) we get

$$\eta = Q \qquad \text{and} \qquad b = \omega^2$$

Making use of Eq. (6-5), we have

$$\omega^2 = B(T - T_c) \tag{6-8}$$

Thus, wherever the assumption of the existence of long-range forces is reasonable, we would expect the existence of a vibrational mode frequency whose variation with temperature is approximately represented by Eq. (6-8) which represents a soft mode.

6-2 BROKEN SYMMETRY AND SOFT MODES

One of the important features of phase transitions is that the appearance of a nonzero order parameter in the low-temperature ordered phase (e.g., the ferroelectric phase) breaks the inherent symmetry of the problem. In other words, some symmetry elements of the high-temperature disordered phase are lost on cooling below T_c. Two distinct cases of broken symmetry can be considered:[7] (*a*) broken symmetry corresponds to a group of continuous transformations, and (*b*) symmetry that is broken involves a discrete group. In case (*a*), there is always a zero-frequency normal mode at $T < T_c$ which restores the lost symmetry (Goldstone mode), an example of such a case being the isotropic Heisenberg ferromagnet. In the low-symmetry phase the free energy has an infinite number of minima in configuration space connected with the symmetry operation broken down at T_c. A continuous group of symmetry operations sends the system from one minimum into another. In ferroelectrics, a discrete symmetry is broken (case (*b*)) and the free energy in the low symmetry phase has a finite number of minima connected with the symmetry operation broken at T_c. The frequency of the symmetry mode will be nonzero at all temperatures below T_c. As $T \to T_c$, the free energy minima merge into a minimum corresponding to the high-temperature phase (with zero order parameter); at $T = T_c$ the frequency of the soft mode will be zero.

At $T = T_c$ both cases (*a*) and (*b*) will show similar behavior in the case of second-order transitions (i.e., $\omega = 0$). However, when $T < T_c$, case (*a*) will continue to have $\omega = 0$, while in case (*b*), the optical soft mode is nonzero. Thus, the existence of a soft mode $\omega \neq 0$ at $T < T_c$ which goes to zero as $T \to T_c$ is a consequence of breaking a discrete symmetry. The symmetry-breaking mode of the high-temperature phase becomes the symmetry-restoring mode of the low-temperature phase.

6-3 LATTICE DYNAMICS AND SOFT MODES

We shall examine here a particularly simplified form of the lattice dynamical theory. Following Barker,[8] consider Fig. 6-1, in which a positively charged ion of mass m, charge z, and polarizability α is connected to a rigid point by a spring of force constant f. The equation of motion is given by

$$m(\partial^2\mathbf{x}/\partial t^2) = -f\mathbf{x} + z\mathbf{E}_{\text{loc}} \tag{6-9}$$

The polarization $\mathbf{P}$ produced by the displacement of the ion is given by

$$\mathbf{P} = z\mathbf{x}/v + \alpha\mathbf{E}_{\text{loc}}/v \tag{6-10}$$

$\mathbf{x}$ and v are the displacement and volume of the ion respectively, while $\mathbf{E}_{\text{loc}}$ is the local field at the ion site. Let us first of all evaluate $\mathbf{E}_{\text{loc}}$. Consider the ions situated at the cubic environment of Fig. 6-1. We may assume the usual simple exponential time-dependence for the fields and displacements. We may further assume that $\mathbf{k}$ (the wave vector) is approximately zero and use the form $\exp(-i\omega t)$ for the time-dependence of the fields (t is the time and ω is the frequency). Let us choose the vibration direction to be $\mathbf{x}$. We then have two simple choices for the wave vector. If $\mathbf{k}$ is parallel to $\mathbf{x}$, the vibration is known as a longitudinal phonon. If $\mathbf{k}$ is perpendicular to $\mathbf{x}$ (along $\mathbf{y}$ or $\mathbf{z}$), then it is known as a transverse phonon.

The local field, $\mathbf{E}_{\text{loc}}$, for the transverse phonon contains in addition to the macroscopic field $\mathbf{E}$, a Lorentz field $4\pi\mathbf{P}/3$. Therefore, for transverse waves,

$$\mathbf{E}_{\text{loc}}(t) = \mathbf{E} + 4\pi\mathbf{P}/3 \tag{6-11}$$

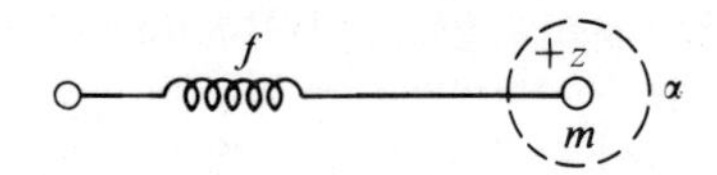

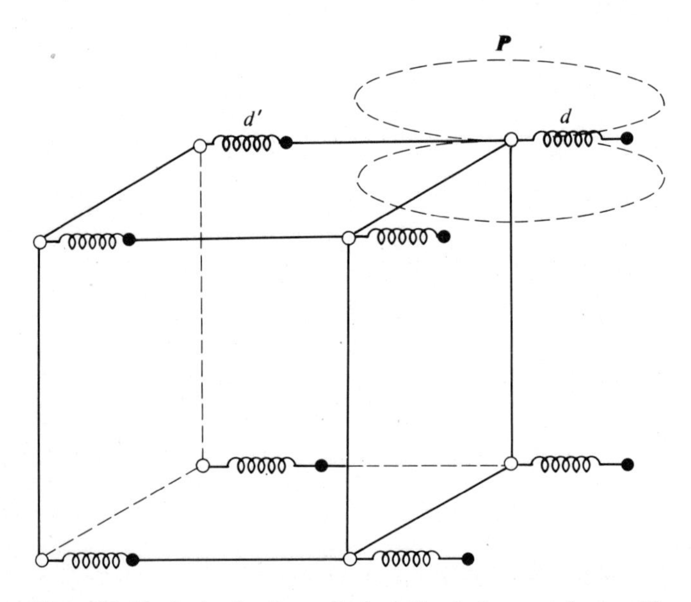

Figure 6-1 The basic vibrating unit of a lattice is shown at the top. The arrangement of these units in a cubic cell is shown in the bottom figure. d and d' are two different ions. The other quantities are explained in the text.

For longitudinal vibrations,[8] $\mathbf{E}_{\text{loc}}$ consists of yet another term due to the depolarization field, $-4\pi\mathbf{P}$. Therefore,

$$\mathbf{E}_{\text{loc}}(l) = \mathbf{E} + 4\pi\mathbf{P}/3 - 4\pi\mathbf{P} = \mathbf{E} - 8\pi\mathbf{P}/3 \tag{6-12}$$

Combining the different equations, we obtain

$$\mathbf{E}_{\text{loc}}(t) = \frac{\mathbf{E} + (4\pi z\mathbf{x}/3v)}{1 - (4\pi\alpha/3v)} \tag{6-13}$$

$$\mathbf{E}_{\text{loc}}(l) = \frac{\mathbf{E} - (8\pi z\mathbf{x}/3v)}{1 + (8\pi\alpha/3v)} \tag{6-14}$$

Now we can eliminate $\mathbf{E}_{\text{loc}}$ in Eq. (6-9) by using Eq. (6-13) and obtain the equation of motion for the transverse waves as

$$m\left(\frac{\partial^2\mathbf{x}}{\partial t^2}\right) = -f\mathbf{x} + z\left[\frac{\mathbf{E} + (4\pi z\mathbf{x}/3v)}{1 - (4\pi\alpha/3v)}\right]$$

or

$$\left(\frac{\partial^2\mathbf{x}}{\partial t^2}\right) = \left[-\frac{f}{m} + \frac{4\pi z^2/3vm}{1 - (4\pi\alpha/3v)}\right]\mathbf{x} + \left[\frac{z/m}{1 - (4\pi\alpha/3v)}\right]\mathbf{E} \tag{6-15}$$

As already stated, if we assume the displacements to be of the form $\mathbf{x} = \mathbf{x}_0 \exp(i\omega t)$, Eq. (6-15) becomes

$$-\omega^2\mathbf{x} = \left[-\frac{f}{m} + \frac{4\pi z^2/3vm}{1 - (4\pi\alpha/3v)}\right]\mathbf{x} + \left[\frac{z/m}{1 - (4\pi\alpha/3v)}\right]\mathbf{E} \tag{6-16}$$

For the longitudinal waves, the same procedure yields

$$-\omega^2\mathbf{x} = \left[-\frac{f}{m} - \frac{8\pi z^2/3vm}{1 + (8\pi\alpha/3v)}\right]\mathbf{x} + \left[\frac{z/m}{1 + (8\pi\alpha/3v)}\right]\mathbf{E} \tag{6-17}$$

Equations (6-16) and (6-17) bring out the essential features of lattice vibrations. When the external macroscopic field is set to zero, the above equations give the natural mode frequencies for the long-wavelength limit. Therefore, the transverse and longitudinal mode frequencies would now be equal to

$$-\omega^2 \text{ (transverse)} = \left[-\frac{f}{m} + \frac{4\pi z^2/3vm}{1 - (4\pi\alpha/3v)}\right] \tag{6-18}$$

$$-\omega^2 \text{ (longitudinal)} = \left[-\frac{f}{m} + \frac{8\pi z^2/3vm}{1 + (8\pi\alpha/3v)}\right] \tag{6-19}$$

The two terms in Eq. (6-18) have opposite signs, and the term $1 - (4\pi\alpha/3v)$ decreases the transverse vibrational frequency. Further the frequency goes to zero whenever α/v is large enough to bring about the equality

$$\frac{f}{m} = \frac{4\pi z^2/3vm}{1 - (4\pi\alpha/3v)} \tag{6-20}$$

The factor $1 - (4\pi\alpha/3v)$ which reduces the effective restoring force is a result of higher polarization. Increasing the polarization factor alters the longitudinal frequency in an opposite manner, as evidenced by Eq. (6-19). Even from such an oversimplified model we see that a transverse phonon frequency can be low and that the frequency can go to zero on cooling since v accordingly varies with temperature (assuming a positive coefficient of thermal expansion).

The model presented above is rather oversimplified. The cubic lattice considered above consisted of one particle of charge z. Therefore it did not possess any acoustic modes. A more realistic two-particle model can be solved very similarly. The expression for the transverse optical mode in a model of that kind[9] will be the same as that in Eq. (6-18), but with m replaced by the reduced mass, μ, and α by the sum of the polarizabilities of the two kinds of ions $(\alpha_+ + \alpha_-)$. Thus, for a diatomic cubic lattice of the NaCl type, the frequency for the transverse optical phonon mode (for $\mathbf{k} \simeq 0$ limit) may be written as

$$-\omega_{\text{t.o}}^2 = \left[-\frac{f}{\mu} + \frac{4\pi z^2/3v\mu}{1 - [4\pi(\alpha_+ + \alpha_-)/3v]}\right] \tag{6-21}$$

The bracketed quantity in Eq. (6-21) is the effective force constant, f_{eff}. The transverse optical mode becoming zero leads to the instability for the following reasons. Combining Eq. (6-21) and (6-9) we have

$$\left(\frac{m_1 m_2}{m_1 + m_2}\right)\left(\frac{\partial^2 \mathbf{x}}{\partial t^2}\right) = -f_{\text{eff}}\mathbf{x} \tag{6-22}$$

since f_{eff} is zero at the transition. This has the solution of the type $\mathbf{x} = at + b$. Therefore, with time, the displacement should build up, breaking the crystalline arrangement. However, the crystal distorts and undergoes a transformation before this happens, because the repulsive forces will begin to operate. In order to appreciate how this transition proceeds, we can include short-range forces in the original expression (6-9) itself and rewrite Eq. (6-22) as

$$\left(\frac{m_1 m_2}{m_1 + m_2}\right)\left(\frac{\partial^2 \mathbf{x}}{\partial t^2}\right) = -f_{\text{eff}}\mathbf{x} + \beta\mathbf{x}^3 + \gamma\mathbf{x}^5 + z\mathbf{E} \tag{6-23}$$

where f_{eff} is from Eq. (6-21). The right-hand side of Eq. (6-23) represents the total restoring force. This is equal to $(dV/d\mathbf{x})$, where V is the net potential. In the absence of the macroscopic field, $\mathbf{E}$, we can write

$$(d^2V/d\mathbf{x}^2) = -f_{\text{eff}} + (2\beta)\mathbf{x}^2 + (5\gamma)\mathbf{x}^4 \tag{6-24}$$

From Eq. (6-24), we obtain V after appropriate integration. A plot of such a potential as a function of $\mathbf{x}$ is given in Fig. 6-2*a* for various values of f_{eff}. The values of β and γ are chosen to fit the behavior of $BaTiO_3$. As the temperature is lowered, the frequency $\omega_{\text{t.o}}$ (the transverse optical mode) decreases in value and the potential well dips on the sides. At the transition temperature, the particle begins to vibrate in a side well following a first-order transition and a tetragonal distortion. The new equilibrium position being $\mathbf{x}_s$ apart, it leads to a spontaneous polarization, $\mathbf{P} = z\mathbf{x}_s/v$. In Fig. 6-2*b*, the variation of ω^2 with temperature for the same is given. At T_t, slightly before ω^2 becomes zero, a first-order transformation occurs. T_c is the extrapolated Curie temperature. In Figs. 6-2*c* and 6-2*d*, the behavior of a system for which $\gamma = 0$ in Eq. (6-23) is shown schematically. This represents a second-order transition in the sense that $\omega_{\text{t.o}}$ gradually goes to zero before crystal distortion occurs.

We thus arrive at a simple picture of the soft mode. It is a vibrational mode, the square of whose frequency, when plotted as a function of temperature, decreases to zero toward the transition temperature. In our discussion we have chosen the cubic structure which approximates the high-temperature forms of perovskites like $BaTiO_3$ and $SrTiO_3$. One of the low-energy normal modes in these cubic structures whose temperature dependence is anomalous (because it is the opposite of the normal behavior of vibrational modes), softens as the temperature is lowered and the consequent instability distorts the crystal to one of lower symmetry. This soft mode is often referred to as the "Cochran mode" or the "ferroelectric mode."[10,11] We may note here that the mode in the (paraelectric) cubic phase is only Raman-active, while after distortion the new modes in the (noncentrosymmetric, ferroelectric) distorted phase are both Raman and infrared-active.

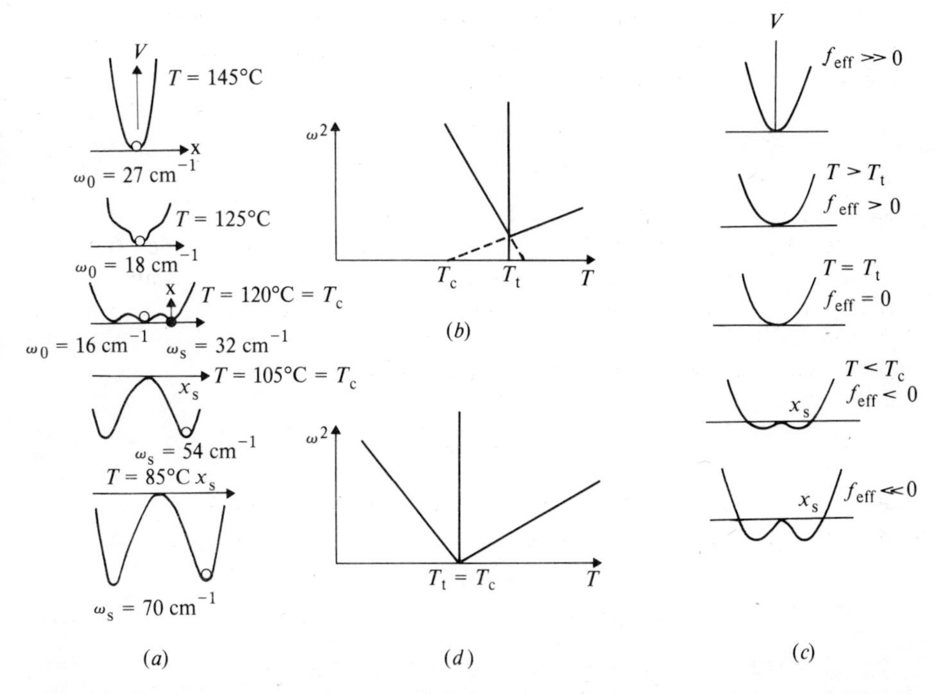

Figure 6-2 (*a*) Schematic representation of the variation of potential V for the case of $BaTiO_3$ (first-order transition). ω_0 values correspond to vibration at the centre of the well such that $\omega_0^2 = f_{eff}/\mu$. ω_s is the frequency of the vibration in a side well such that $\omega_s^2 = (f_{eff} - \beta x_s^2 - \gamma x_s^4)/\mu$. (*b*) Corresponding variation of ω^2 with temperature. T_t and T_c are the first-order transition temperature and the extrapolated critical temperature respectively. (*c*) Similar variation of potential when γ is zero and β is positive (second-order transition). (*d*) Variation of ω^2 with temperature for the case (*c*). Note that $T_t = T_c$. (*After Barker.*[8])

We have chosen the $\mathbf{k} \sim 0$ transverse modes in our discussion simply because these are the modes which respond to electromagnetic radiation and are readily accessible for conventional spectroscopy. This does not mean that phonons at the zone boundary are unimportant. Indeed, as we shall be discussing later, the 110 K transition in $SrTiO_3$ is due to the softening of the zone boundary phonons. To study these phonons, neutron scattering is the only method available. A soft mode is not necessarily an anomalous mode of the high-temperature phase. It can also be a mode of the low-temperature phase, as in the cases of GeTe, α-quartz, and so on. Soft modes are not confined only to displacive transitions; furthermore, neither of the phases in a transition need be noncentrosymmetric. In fact, in transitions of ammonium halides where both phases are cubic, a tunnelling mode coupled to the zone boundary phonon is involved in the transition. These transitions are of the order–disorder type. We may therefore conclude that structural transitions of both displacive and order–disorder types involve soft modes. Another aspect worth noting is that a soft mode need not be an optical mode; it could be an acoustic mode, as in the case of Nb_3Sn. In Fig. 6-3, the known types of soft modes are schematically represented.

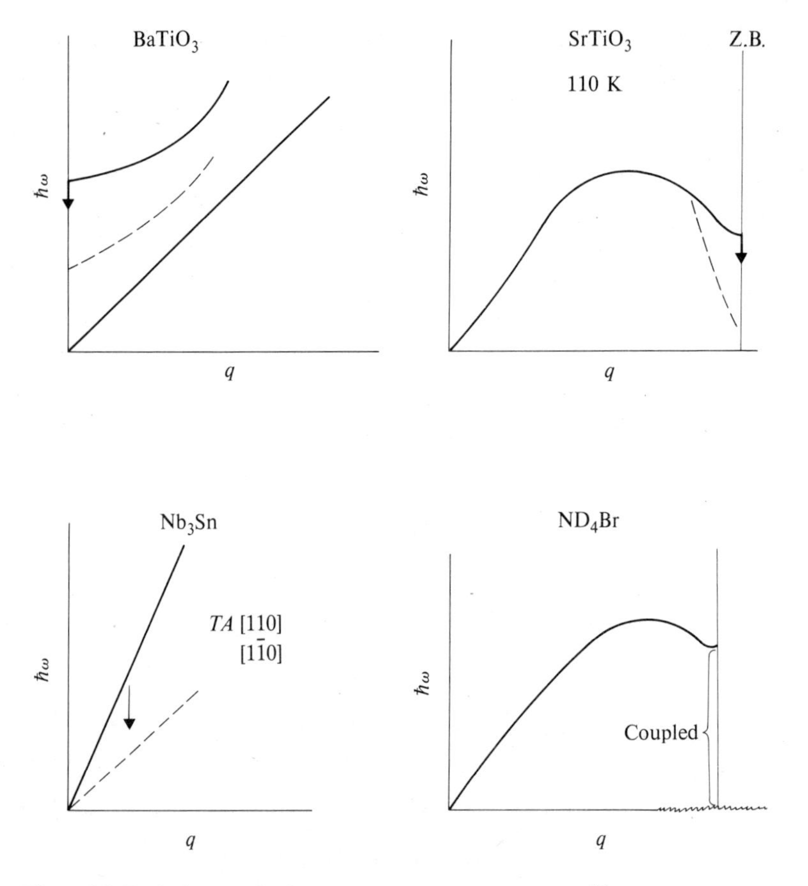

Figure 6-3 Typical types of soft-mode transitions. (*After Shirane.*[30])

A few words about soft modes in displacive and order–disorder transitions of ferroelectrics (or antiferroelectrics) would be in order.[7] In displacive systems, we essentially have a single minimum potential with only a slight anharmonicity. Further, the real as well as the imaginary parts of the complex soft-mode frequency will be generally different from zero if $T \neq T_c$, and the soft mode will be of a resonant type. The transition of $BaTiO_3$ is a typical displacive transition. In order–disorder systems, anharmonicity is large and the potential has two minima of equal depth. In such systems, the imaginary part of the soft-mode frequency will be nonzero if $T \neq T_c$, while the real part will be nonzero only if the tunnelling splitting of the ground state is significant. If tunnelling splitting is not significant, the real part will be zero (at $T \neq T_c$) as in $NaNO_2$ or triglycine sulphate. Tunnelling is important in KH_2PO_4, and a resonant-type response is found. Recently it has been found, on the basis of the analysis of data on a large number of compounds exhibiting displacive phase transitions, that the transition temperature decreases with hydrostatic pressure if the transitions are associated with soft-zone center optic phonons.[12] The transition temperature increases in the case of soft-zone boundary phonons. This difference in behavior is explained in terms of the roles of short-range and long-range forces in the lattice dynamics of these systems.

Schneider, Stoll, and Beck[13] have studied three exactly soluble models for systems undergoing structural phase transitions. Two of the models are described by a lattice dynamic hamiltonian, the transition being driven by a spherical constraint in one and by a long-range anharmonic interaction in the other. The third model is a continuous model based on an effective free energy of the long-wavelength fluctuations of the order parameter field. All the models show a strongly temperature-dependent vibrational mode at $T > T_c$. In the first two models, it is an undamped soft mode with $\omega \rightarrow 0$ as $T \rightarrow T_c$. In the third model, the mode gets overdamped and the linewidth goes to zero at $T \rightarrow T_c$. The equation of motion for dynamical quantities like the displacement or the order parameter contain similar anharmonic terms in all the three cases. All the models show identical critical behavior and obey dynamic scaling, although the dynamic critical properties are different.

Damping and Central Modes

Investigation of the soft mode is becoming an increasingly important aspect of phase transitions. One of the aspects of interest in this field relates[14] to the damping of soft modes due to anharmonic interactions and the development of the central mode close to $\omega = 0$. Experimentally, a central mode was observed in $SrTiO_3$ by Riste et al.[15] in their neutron inelastic scattering work and was earlier predicted theoretically by Cowley.[16] The damped harmonic oscillator expression for the soft mode may be obtained by a suitable phenomenological[7] modification of Eq. (6-9):

$$m\ddot{x} = -\bar{\omega}^2 x + F \exp(i\omega t) - \int_0^t M(t - t')\dot{x}(t')\, dt' \qquad (6\text{-}25)$$

where $\dot{x}(t') = \partial x/\partial t$ and the soft-mode frequency is $\bar{\omega}$ which is given by $\omega_0(T - T_c)^{1/2}$. While the first term on the right-hand side of Eq. (6-25) represents the restoring force of the soft mode, the second describes the effect of an external oscillating force F, of frequency ω, and the last term represents the damping effect due to phonon–phonon interactions. M in Eq. (6-25) represents a memory function which indicates the dependence of the response of the system upon its previous history. The integro-differential equation has been solved by Blinc and Zeks[7] using a Laplace transform and will not be dealt with here. The important conclusions from this study are: (*a*) the renormalized soft-mode frequency, ω_∞, turns out to be

$$\omega_\infty^2 = \bar{\omega}^2 + \frac{\omega^2 \Gamma \tau}{1 + \omega^2 \tau^2} \qquad (6\text{-}26)$$

in which Γ is the damping coefficient. When $\omega\tau \gg 1$, it is obvious that

$$\omega_\infty^2 = \bar{\omega}^2 + \Gamma\tau^{-1} \qquad \text{which is} \propto (T - T_c^*) \tag{6-27}$$

such that $T_c^* < T_c$. (*b*) The intensity function $I(\omega)$ becomes

$$I(\omega) = \text{constant}\left[\frac{\Gamma_{\text{eff}}}{(\omega_\infty^2 - \omega^2)^2 + (\Gamma_{\text{eff}}\omega)^2}\right] \tag{6-28}$$

in which Γ_{eff} is the frequency-dependent damping function,

$$\Gamma_{\text{eff}} = \frac{\Gamma}{1 + \omega^2\tau^2} \tag{6-29}$$

The system behaves differently in the two limits of fast and slow relaxation. When $\omega\tau \ll 1$, Eq. (6-29) represents a damped oscillator with no special behavior. However, when $\omega\tau \gg 1$, the soft mode renormalizes its energy quickly with other phonons leading to further escalation of the effective damping constant. This leads to a strong central peak at $\omega = 0$ in its spectrum. When the two peaks, corresponding to ω_∞ and 0, are well separated, the ratio of the intensities of the "central" and the soft modes may be roughly approximated to

$$\frac{I_c}{I_s} \approx \frac{1}{(\omega_\infty\tau)^2} \tag{6-30}$$

where Γ has been taken as approximately equal to ω_∞. The central peak is thus always weak (not nonexistent!) except close to T_c where (since $\bar{\omega}$ decreases) it begins to "mix" with the soft mode.

Many other theoretical approaches have been made to account for the behavior of the central mode, such as those of Cowley et al.,[17] Shirane and Axe,[18] and Schwabl.[19]

Two important conclusions[6] may be arrived at from the above treatment of central modes. The first one is that anharmonic effects are partly contained in the central mode, and therefore the soft mode need not have to soften all the way to zero value. The second conclusion is that the central mode is not a necessary aspect of critical behavior and can occur in any temperature regime where mean field theory is applicable. However, it has been found from measured integrated intensities of central modes that, in cases like $SrTiO_3$[15,20] and NH_4Cl,[21] they do exhibit criticality. A thorough study of the central mode in KH_2PO_4 has recently been made by Lagakos and Cummins[22] using Raman and high-resolution Brillouin scattering in which they have been able to explain all aspects of spectra using three interacting modes.

6-4 TYPICAL EXAMPLES OF SOFT-MODE STUDIES

Strontium titanate is a cubic perovskite which exhibits a soft mode,[23] and several studies[24–28] have been reported on this compound. Temperature-dependence of

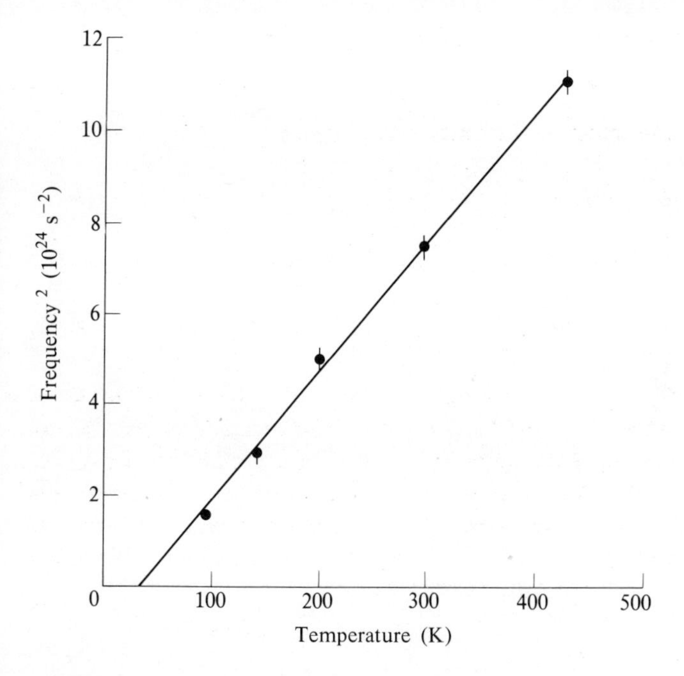

Figure 6-4 Variation of frequency squared of the zone center soft mode in strontium titanate. (*After Cowley.*[15])

the lowest-frequency transverse optical mode in $SrTiO_3$ was studied by neutron scattering, and it was found that the square of the frequency decreases linearly with temperature and extrapolates to a T_c of 32 ± 5 K (Fig. 6-4), in agreement with other dielectric measurements. However, experimentally it is known that when cooled to temperature around 30 K, $SrTiO_3$ deviates from the Curie behavior and does not become ferroelectric until zero Kelvin.[29] $SrTiO_3$ is considered to be a good example of an incipient ferroelectric.[30] It is also a good example to illustrate the softening of a transverse mode in a perovskite.

$SrTiO_3$ has another soft mode connected with the rotation of oxygen octahedra.[26] It exhibits a transition at 110 K, where large changes occur in elastic properties, but no significant change occurs in the dielectric constant.[30] The fact that a real structural transition takes place to a tetragonal structure was first established by the ESR studies of Unoki and Sakudo.[26] It was later shown by neutron spectroscopy that the transition occurs due to the softening of a zone-boundary phonon[28] (Fig. 6-5) associated with the rotation of the oxygen octahedra. The Raman spectrum of the tetragonal phase reveals the presence of two soft phonon modes[31] (Fig. 6-6). The zone-boundary phonon mentioned earlier appears to be the progenitor of these two soft modes.

An interesting example of a nonferroelectric transition where soft-mode studies have been made is that of quartz. As pointed out earlier, the first studies of a soft mode were performed on the low-temperature α-phase of quartz by Raman

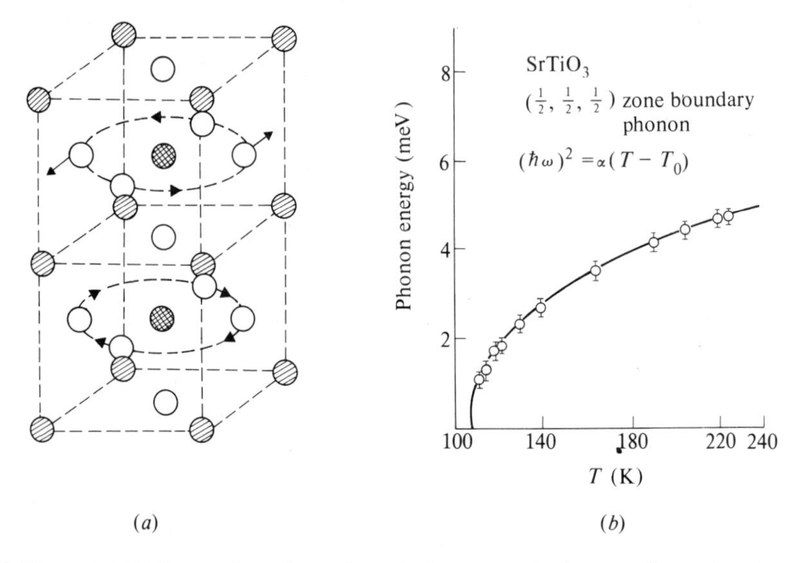

Figure 6-5 (*a*) The zone boundary soft-mode eigenvectors in the case of strontium titanate. (*b*) Variation of soft-mode frequency with temperature. (*After Shirane and Yamada.*[20])

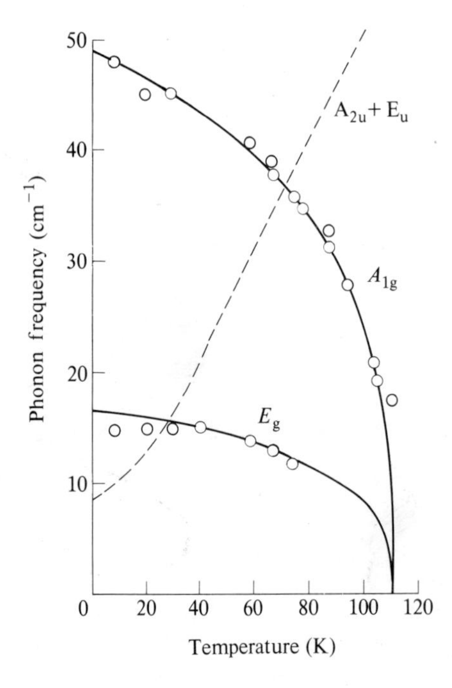

Figure 6-6 Soft-mode frequencies in the low-temperature tetragonal phase of $SrTiO_3$ as studied by Raman spectra. (*After Worlock et al.*[23])

and Nedungadi.[1] Recently, Raman studies of the same soft mode have been made by Scott and Porto[32] and Shapiro et al.[33] Spectra of quartz illustrating the soft mode at various temperatures are shown in Fig. 6-7. Soft-mode studies of the β-phase have been recently accomplished by neutron-scattering studies by Axe and Shirane.[34] In Fig. 6-8, the variation of the square of this soft-mode frequency with temperature is given along with the soft-mode eigenvectors; this soft-mode is of a high symmetry and is neither Raman nor infrared-active.

Recently, it has been found that a soft mode is associated with the transition of sodium azide. NaN_3, which has the rhombohedral structure, reversibly changes to a monoclinic structure around 292 K. In the rhombohedral phase, the linear azide ion lies along the [111] direction of the unit cell, the Na^+ ions lie in planes parallel to the (111) plane, and the lines joining any three Na^+ ions form an equilateral triangle. In the monoclinic phase there is a distortion of the equilateral triangles of Na^+ ions to isosceles triangles, and the azide ion tilts from the [111] direction of the rhomohedral cell. The transition is of the second order. Raman studies show that the frequency of the vibrational mode (corresponding to an oscillation of the tilt angle of the linear azide ion) in the monoclinic phase softens with a $(T_c - T)^{1/2}$ dependence.[35,36] ESR studies[37] of Mn^{2+}-doped NaN_3 show that the zero-field splitting varies as $(T_c - T)^{1/2}$ and that the intensity of the resonance decreases near T_c.

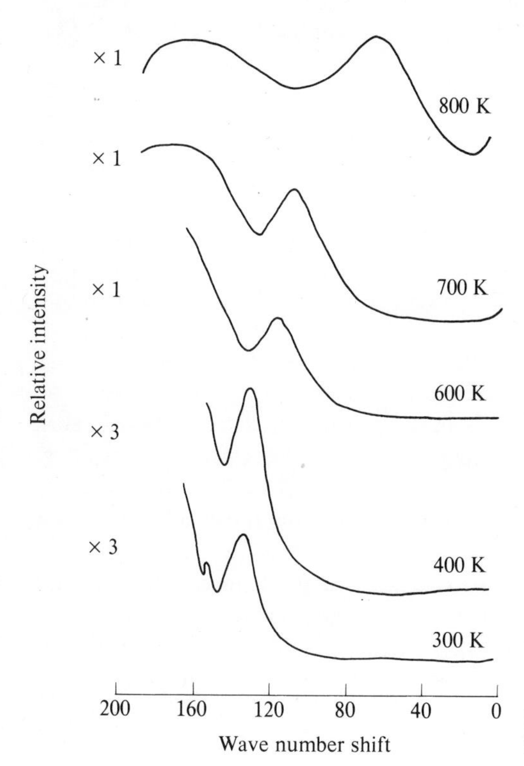

Figure 6-7 Raman spectra of α-quartz revealing the soft mode. (*After Scott and Porto.*[24])

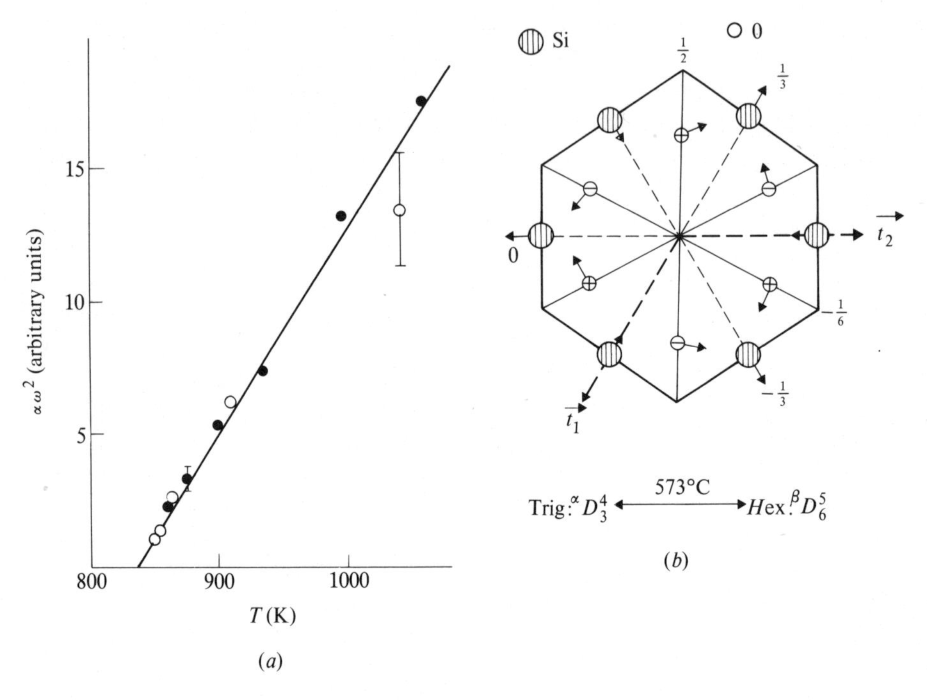

Figure 6-8 (*a*) Variation of soft-mode frequency squared with temperature for β-quartz. (*b*) Corresponding eigenvectors. (*After Axe and Shirane.*[26])

As good examples of transitions where the soft phonons are coupled modes, we may consider KD_2PO_4[30] and ND_4Br.[38] In ND_4Br, ND_4^+ groups have the same orientation in the ordered structure while they are randomized in two possible (antiparallel and parallel) orientations in the disordered structure. This disordering frequency or flipping frequency mode is believed to be coherently coupled to the Br vibrational (zone-boundary) mode. This coupled mode constitutes the soft mode in ND_4Br.

Structural instabilities in Nb_3Sn and V_3Si (see Refs. 30, 39–42) which give rise to relatively high superconducting transition temperatures involve acoustic phonons. Transitions in these compounds may be considered to be Jahn–Teller transitions driven by the conduction electrons, the large electron–phonon interaction being responsible for the high T_C. The lattice-mode behavior in these systems is similar to that found in localized electron systems, although the exact mechanism is quite different.

Soft-mode studies have been extended to investigate semiconductor–metal transitions (see Chap. 7 for details). NbO_2 is a semiconductor at normal temperatures and undergoes a transition around 1070 K to a metallic phase.[43] The high-temperature phase has the rutile structure and the low-temperature phase has a body-centered tetragonal structure of large unit cell[44,45] (32 formula units as compared to 2 of the rutile phase). Neutron-scattering studies by Shapiro et al.[46] show that a zone-boundary phonon softens as the rutile phase is cooled to the phase transition temperature. The metallic band structure of the high-temperature phase becomes unstable with respect to charge density fluctuations, and it is argued that the electron–phonon coupling renormalizes the phonon frequency so as to cause the instability to occur first in the phonon response.[46]

Magnetic transitions such as those of $KCoF_3$ and $RbCoF_3$ are now known to involve soft modes which are simply magnons.[47,48] Figure 6-9 presents the magnon

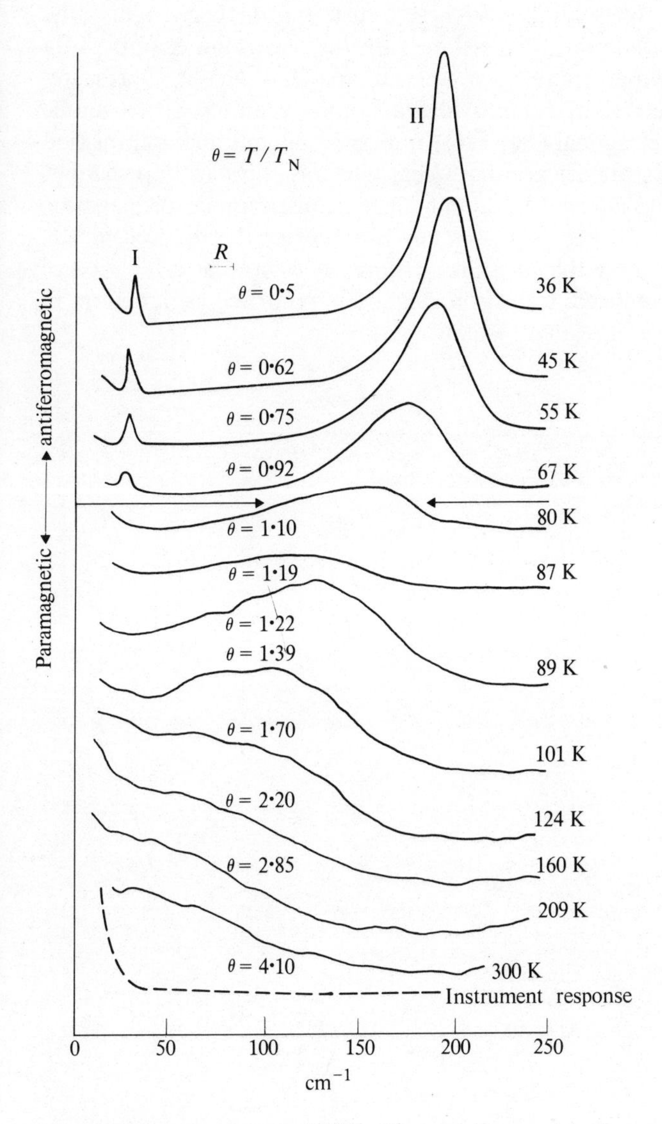

Figure 6-9 Magnon spectra of NiF_2. The one-magnon peak disappears for $T > T_N$ while the two-magnon peak (II) persists. (*After Fleury.*[41])

spectra of NiF_2 at various temperatures. The two-magnon peak (II) of antiferromagnetic NiF_2 softens rapidly toward the transition temperature.[49] The peak, however, persists because of the probable existence of spin waves in the paramagnetic phase.

Another important type of transition in which soft modes occur is the cooperative Jahn–Teller transitions, where the transitions are driven by the interaction between localized orbital electronic states and the crystal lattice.[50] Typical systems exhibiting such transitions are rare-earth zircons (e.g., $TmVO_4$) and perovskites (e.g., $PrAlO_3$). We shall discuss these transitions at some length in the next chapter. We close the present discussion with the interesting example of a transition in TeO_2 involving a pure shear acoustic mode.[51] This is a pressure-induced second-order transition and provides a unique example of soft-mode studies under pressure. Tetragonal (D_4^4) TeO_2 undergoes a continuous transition to the orthorhombic (D_2^2) structure around 9 kbar which is completely reversible. It is strain-induced[52] and is driven by a soft-shear acoustic mode propagating along the [110] direction. In Fig. 6-10 we show the plot of the reduced elastic constant of the soft mode (note that it is proportional to ω^2/ω_0^2) as a function of pressure. Such a strain-induced transition has been reported as function of temperature[53] in $PrAlO_3$ and related systems.

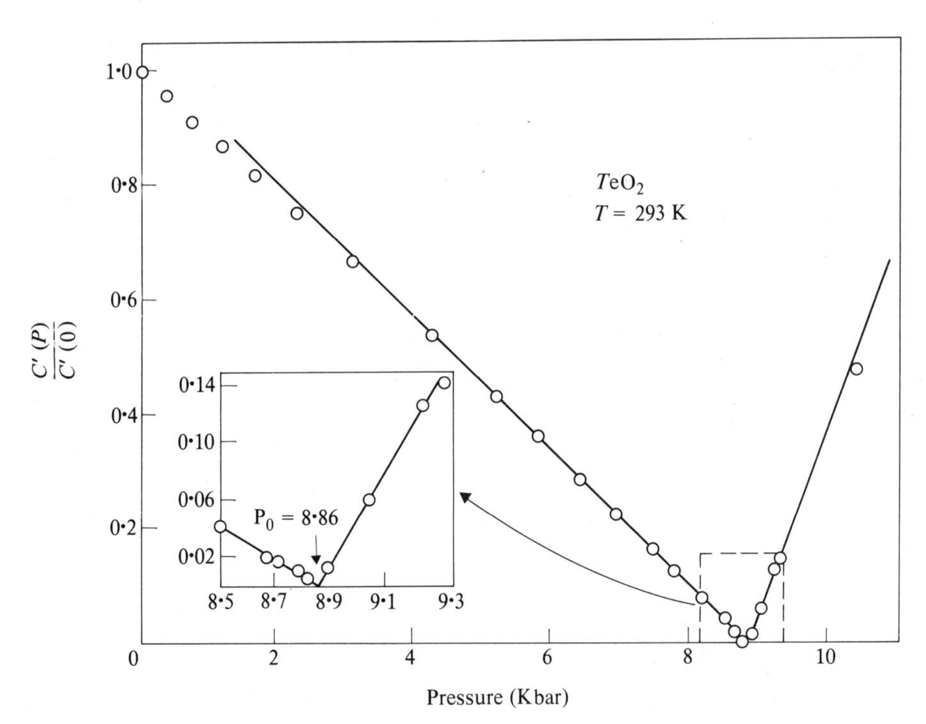

Figure 6-10 Plot of the reduced elastic constant of the soft mode of TeO_2 as a function of temperature. (*After Peercy et al.*[43])

Table 6-1 Some typical soft-mode transitions*

	Method of study	Soft mode	Structural change	Transition temperature
$PbTiO_3$	NS & RS	Zone center T.O phonon	Cubic to tetragonal	763 K
$BaTiO_3$	NS	Zone center T.O phonon	Cubic to tetragonal	403 K
$KTaO_3$	NS & RS	Zone center T.O phonon	Cubic to tetragonal?	~0 K
$KNbO_3$	NS	Zone center T.O phonon	Cubic to tetragonal	693 K
$LaAlO_3$	NS	Zone center T.O phonon	Cubic to rhombohedral	535 K
$SrTiO_3$	NS	Zone center T.O phonon	Cubic to tetragonal	110 K
$KMnF_3$	NS	Zone center T.O phonon	Cubic to tetragonal	186 K
$KMnF_3$	NS	Zone center T.O phonon	Tetragonal to orthorhombic	91 K
$KCoF_3$	RS	Magnon	Cubic to tetragonal	114 K
$RbCoF_3$	RS	Magnon	Cubic to tetragonal	101 K
$Tb(MoO_4)_3$	NS	Zone center T.O phonon	Tetragonal to orthorhombic	433 K
NbO_2	NS	Zone center T.O phonon	Rutile to body-centered tetragonal	1073 K
SiO_2	NS & RS	Zone center T.O phonon	Hexagonal to trigonal	846 K
$AlPO_4$	RS	Zone center T.O phonon	Hexagonal to trigonal	853 K
Na_2WO_3	NQR	Zone center T.O phonon	Cubic to tetragonal	400 K
GeTe	RS	Zone center T.O phonon	Cubic to rhombohedral	670 K
ND_4Br	NS	Zone boundary (coupled to flipping mode)	Cubic (disordered) to cubic (ordered)	215 K
KD_2PO_4	NS	Zone center T.O phonon	Tetragonal (disordered) to tetragonal (ordered)	220 K
KH_2PO_4	RS	Zone center T.O phonon	Tetragonal (disordered) to tetragonal (ordered)	122 K
$TbVO_4$	RS	Acoustic phonon electron coupled mode	Tetragonal to orthorhombic	34 K
Nb_3Sn	NS	Acoustic phonon electron coupled mode	Cubic to tetragonal	46 K

* Detailed references to the original literature may be obtained from two recent reviews of Scott[6] and Shirane.[30] NS = neutron spectroscopy; RS = Raman spectroscopy; NQR = nuclear quadrupole resonance spectroscopy.

Soft-mode behavior has been seen in the martensite (fct → fcc) transition of In–Tl alloys.[54] In this system, the shear elastic constant term $\frac{1}{2}(C_{11} - C_{12})$ obtained from ultrasonic velocity measurements goes to zero at the transition temperature. Undoubtedly there will be increasing efforts to identify soft modes in many such martensite transitions involving deformation of the lattice. As pointed out in Chaps. 3 and 4, transition mechanisms of many systems are likely to involve lattice deformation (or martensitic character), thus providing a number of interesting possibilities.

Soft-mode anomalies form the basis of several device or materials applications. Fleury[55] has discussed the variation of the order parameter, susceptibility, and soft-mode frequency on external variables like temperature, stress, and ordering field in terms of device applications. Typical of the devices are acoustic–optic modulators, tunable IR filters and modulators, tunable optic and IR light sources, and so on.

REFERENCES

1. C. V. Raman and T. M. K. Nedungadi, *Nature*, **145,** 147, 1940.
2. R. H. Lyddane, R. G. Sachs, and E. Teller, *Phys. Rev.*, **59,** 673, 1941.
3. H. Frohlich, "Theory of Dielectrics," Clarendon Press, Oxford, 1949; see also H. Frohlich, in "Ferroelectricity," ed. E. F. Weller, Elsevier, Amsterdam, 1967.
4. P. W. Anderson, "Fizika Dielektrikov," ed. G. I. Skanavi, Akad. Nauk SSSR, Moscow, 1959.
5. W. Cochran, *Phys. Rev. Lett.*, **3,** 412, 1959; *Adv. Phys.*, **9,** 387, 1960; **10,** 401, 1961.
6. J. F. Scott, *Rev. Mod. Phys.*, **46,** 83, 1974.
7. R. Blinc and B. Zeks, "Soft Modes in Ferroelectrics and Antiferroelectrics," North-Holland, Amsterdam, 1974.
8. A. S. Barker, in "Ferroelectricity," ed. E. F. Weller, Elsevier, Amsterdam, 1967; see also A. S. Barker, in "Far Infrared Properties of Solids," ed. S. S. Mitra and S. Nudelman, Plenum Press, New York, 1970.
9. M. Born and K. Huang, "Dynamical Theory of Crystal Lattices," Oxford University Press, London, 1954.
10. E. J. Samuelsen, E. Andersen, and J. Feder (eds.) "Structural Phase Transitions and Soft Modes," Universitets forlaget, Oslo, 1971.
11. J. C. Burfoot, "Ferroelectrics," Von Nostrand, London, 1967.
12. G. A. Samara, T. Sakuda, and K. Yoshimitsu, *Phys. Rev. Lett.*, **35,** 1767, 1975.
13. T. Schneider, E. Stoll, and H. Beck, *Physica*, **79A,** 201, 1975.
14. P. A. Fleury, *Ann. Rev. Materials Sci.*, **6,** 217, 1976.
15. T. Riste, E. J. Samuelsen, K. Otnas, and J. Feder, in "Structural Phase Transitions and Soft Modes," ed. E. J. Samuelsen, E. Andersen, and J. Feder, Universitets forlaget, Oslo, 1971.
16. R. A. Cowley, *J. Phys. Soc. Japan Suppl.*, **28,** 239, 1970.
17. R. A. Cowley, G. J. Coombs, R. S. Katiyar, J. F. Ryan, and J. F. Scott, *J. Phys.*, **C4,** L203, 1971.
18. G. Shirane and J. D. Axe, *Phys. Rev. Lett.*, **27,** 1803, 1971; *Phys. Rev.*, **B4,** 2957, 1971.
19. F. Schwabl, *Phys. Rev. Lett.*, **28,** 500, 1972; *Solid State Comm.*, **13,** 181, 1973.
20. S. M. Shapiro, J. D. Axe, G. Shirane, and T. Riste, *Phys. Rev.*, **B6,** 4332, 1972.
21. P. D. Lazay, J. H. Lunacek, N. A. Clark, and G. B. Benedek, in "Light Scattering in Solids," ed. G. B. Wright, Springer-Verlag, New York, 1969, p. 593.
22. N. Lagakos and H. Z. Cummins, *Phys. Rev.*, **B10,** 1063, 1974.
23. R. A. Cowley, *Phys. Rev. Letters*, **9,** 159, 1962.
24. P. A. Fleury, J. F. Scott, and J. M. Worlock, *Phys. Rev. Letters*, **21,** 16, 1968.

25. K. A. Muller, *Helv. Phys. Acta.*, **31,** 173, 1958.
26. H. Unoki and T. Sakudo, *J. Phys. Soc. Japan*, **23,** 546, 1967.
27. J. Feder and E. Pytte, *Phys. Rev.*, **B1,** 4803, 1970.
28. G. Shirane and Y. Yamada, *Phys. Rev.*, **177,** 858, 1969.
29. A. A. Maradudin, in "Ferroelectricity," ed. E. F. Weller, Elsevier, Amsterdam, 1967.
30. G. Shirane, *Rev. Mod. Phys.*, **46,** 437, 1974.
31. J. M. Worlock, J. F. Scott, and P. A. Fleury, in "Light Scattering Spectra of Solids," ed. G. B. Wright, Springer-Verlag, New York, 1969.
32. J. F. Scott and S. P. S. Porto, *Phys. Rev.*, **161,** 903, 1967.
33. S. M. Shapiro, D. C. O'Shea, and H. Z. Cummins, *Phys. Rev. Lett.*, **19,** 361, 1967.
34. J. D. Axe and G. Shirane, *Phys. Rev.*, **B1,** 342, 1970.
35. Z. Iqbal, *J. Chem. Phys.*, **59,** 1769, 1973.
36. G. J. Simonis and C. E. Hathway, *Phys. Rev.*, **B10,** 4419, 1974.
37. F. J. Owens, *Chem. Phys. Lett.*, **35,** 269, 1975.
38. Y. Yamada, H. Takatera, and D. L. Huber, *J. Phys. Soc. Japan*, **36,** 641, 1974.
39. J. D. Axe and G. Shirane, *Phys. Rev.*, **B8,** 1965, 1973.
40. J. Perel, B. W. Batterman, and E. I. Blount, *Phys. Rev.*, **166,** 616, 1968.
41. S. Barisic, *Phys. Rev.*, **B5,** 932, 941, 1971.
42. J. Labbie and J. Friedel, *J. Phys. Radium*, **27,** 153, 303, 1966.
43. C. N. R. Rao, G. R. Rao, and G. V. Subbarao, *J. Solid State Chem.*, **6,** 340, 1973.
44. T. Sakata, K. Sakata, and I. Nishida, *Phys. Stat. Solidi*, **20A,** K 155, 1967; K. Sakata, *J. Phys. Soc. Japan*, **26,** 582, 1969.
45. A. K. Cheetam and C. N. R. Rao, *Acta Cryst.*, **B32,** 1579, 1976.
46. S. M. Shapiro, J. D. Axe, G. Shirane, and P. M. Raccah, *Solid State Comm.*, **15,** 377, 1974.
47. Y. Allain, J. Denis, A. Herpin, M. Lecompte, P. Mariel, J. Nouet, R. Plique, and A. Zarembovitch, *J. Phys. Paris*, **32,** *Supplement* C1, 611, 1971.
48. J. Nouet, D. Toms, and J. E. Scott, *Phys. Rev.*, **B7,** 4874, 1973.
49. P. A. Fleury, in "Light Scattering Spectra of Solids," ed. G. B. Wright, Springer-Verlag, New York, 1969.
50. G. A. Gehring and K. A. Gehring, *Rep. Prog. Phys.*, **38,** 1, 1975.
51. P. S. Peercy, I. J. Fritz, and G. A. Samara, *J. Phys. Chem. Solids*, **36,** 1105, 1975; see also *Phys. Rev. Lett.*, **32,** 466, 1974.
52. P. W. Anderson and E. I. Blount, *Phys. Rev. Lett.*, **14,** 217, 1965.
53. P. A. Fleury, P. D. Lazay, and L. G. van Uitert, *Phys. Rev. Lett.*, **33,** 492, 1974.
54. D. J. Gunton and G. A. Saunders, *Solid State Comm.*, **14,** 865, 1974.
55. P. A. Fleury, in "Phase Transitions," ed. H. Henisch, R. Roy, and L. E. Cross, Pergamon Press, Oxford, 1973.

CHAPTER

SEVEN

PROPERTIES OF SOLIDS AND PHASE TRANSITIONS

Phase transitions in solids are often accompanied by interesting changes in their properties. Several techniques are employed to investigate phase transitions, depending on the nature of the solid and properties of interest. Such studies are not only of academic value in understanding the structural and mechanistic aspects of phase transitions, but can also be of technological importance. The literature abounds in studies of phase transitions in solids using a wide range of techniques including diffraction, thermal, optical, electrical, magnetic, dielectric, spectroscopic, and other measurements. Case histories and examples of such studies on a wide variety of inorganic solids can be found in some of the literature reviews.[1-7]

It would be difficult here to describe all the techniques and material properties that have been employed to study phase transitions. We shall therefore limit our discussion to three important aspects of solid materials: magnetic, electrical, and dielectric properties. The discussion of magnetic, electrical, and dielectric transitions should clearly illustrate how the study of phase transitions encompasses a wide range of methods and techniques and offers exciting possibilities for investigation. In this context, specific mention must be made of insulator–metal transitions in oxides, sulfides, and other materials where almost all the available techniques have been employed to understand the nature of transitions. Before proceeding with the discussion of the three properties, we shall briefly comment on other techniques commonly employed in the study of phase transitions.

7-1 SOME TECHNIQUES EMPLOYED IN THE STUDY OF PHASE TRANSITIONS

The two important thermodynamic variables in the study of phase transitions are temperature and pressure. Any study of a phase transition would therefore involve measurements of properties as a function of temperature or pressure. X-ray diffraction forms an essential part of any study, quite apart from the other techniques one may employ. Diffraction cameras or diffractometer attachments with variable temperature (or pressure) are commercially available. While most studies in the literature routinely employ powder diffraction methods, often because of the unavailability or instability of single crystals, single-crystal measurements by Laue or Weisenberg methods can provide valuable structural and mechanistic information in situations that retain the single crystals or the crystal axis through the transitions. The formation of hybrid crystals,[8] structural intermediates or superstructures, and the existence of orientational relations between the initial and transformed phases (see Chaps. 3 and 4) can be readily examined by x-ray and electron diffraction. Electron diffraction has certain special advantages, because of the short wavelength of electrons, in studying superstructures and small domains. Neutron diffraction studies are most useful in studying positions of light atoms and magnetic structures. The analysis of powder neutron diffraction profiles[10] yields valuable structural information, and this technique will undoubtedly become more popular in the years to come.

Thermal measurements have been widely used to identify and characterize transitions. Heat capacity measurements provide precise enthalpy changes and indicate the thermodynamic order of transitions. Differential thermal analysis (DTA) has been routinely employed to obtain the same information.[11] Being a dynamic technique (where the substance is heated or cooled at a constant rate), DTA suffers from disadvantages. The ΔH values obtained by DTA are not very reliable, particularly in the case of second-order transitions. However, if suitable standards (e.g., transformations of silica, CsCl, K_2SO_4, and so on, or thermal decomposition of calcium oxalate or $CaCO_3$) are employed, areas of DTA peaks may provide reasonable estimates of enthalpy changes. Information on the activation energies of transformations has also been obtained by fitting the DTA peak to first-order kinetic equations,[11] but it may not be very meaningful. Thermal hysteresis in phase transitions[11] is also conveniently studied by DTA. Differential scanning calorimetry (DSC) has become popular in recent years for obtaining heat capacity data and ΔH of transitions, the ΔH values of DSC being very much more reliable than those of DTA. Comparisons of typical data obtained from different measurements of ΔH are shown in Fig. 7-1. Measurements of thermal expansion of solids have also been employed in the study of phase transitions; dilatometry and x-ray diffraction directly provide this information.

The optical microscope is a valuable tool for studying phase transformations, particularly with respect to the movement of boundaries, growth of nuclei, and

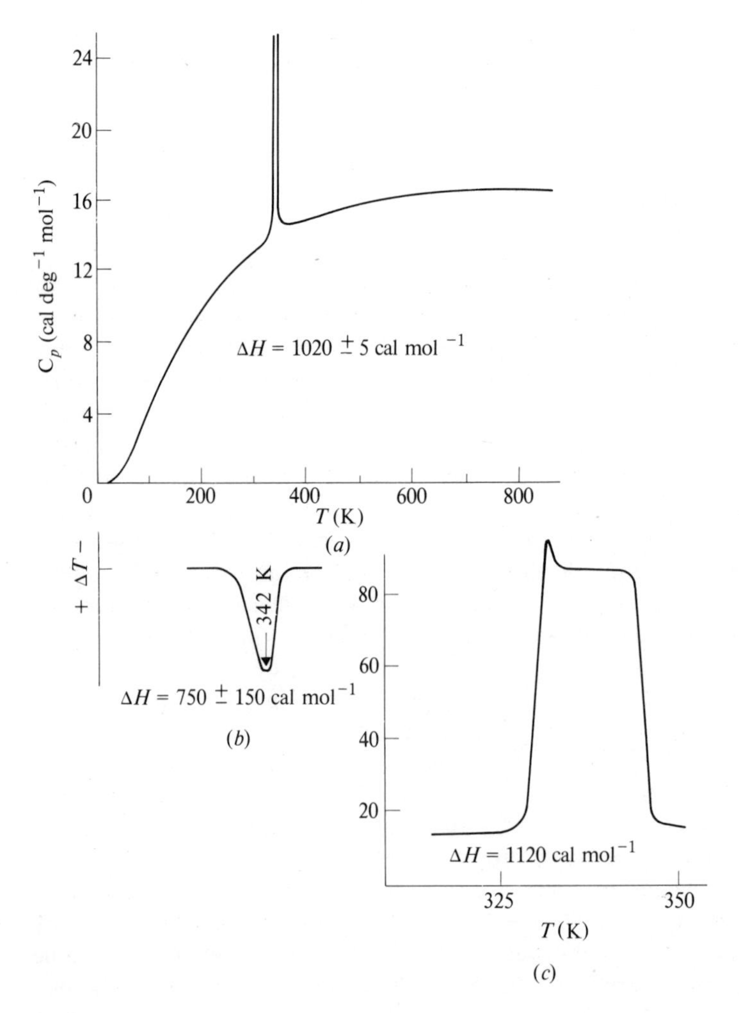

Figure 7-1 Enthalpy change in the VO_2 transition. (a) From heat capacity. (*After Berglund et al.*[12]) (b) From DTA. (*After Rao et al.*[13a]) (c) From DSC. (*After Chandrasekhar et al.*[13b])

changes in grain size. Pressure transitions can also be studied by using an optical microscope and a diamond anvil press. Electron microscopic examination would give useful information on dislocations and structural aspects if the solid can be studied in the transition region. A variable-temperature stage would undoubtedly be of great value in this regard. High-resolution (2–3 Å) lattice imaging[14] of transforming solids (see Chap. 3) is an area of great potential.

Magnetic and electrical properties are used widely in the study of transitions of a variety of inorganic solids. These, along with dielectric properties, are discussed at some length in the subsequent sections. Optical spectroscopy in the infrared, visible, and ultraviolet regions has been used to study solids undergoing transitions. Laser Raman spectroscopy has been particularly exploited in recent years to investigate phase transitions. We shall be describing typical studies employing spectroscopic methods. Neutron scattering and Raman spectroscopy yield direct information on soft modes. X-ray and ultraviolet photoelectron spectra of solids through their phase transitions can provide valuable information on the changes in electronic structure (if any). Positron annihilation is a technique in which phase transition studies enable us to understand the phenomenon of annihilation.

Preparation, purification, and characterization of materials undoubtedly form an important part of phase-transition studies. The purity of the material is particularly crucial, since it has been known that impurities affect characteristics of transitions significantly. It is therefore important that efforts are made to use the purest material possible while studying phase transitions. In this context, all the well-known techniques for the analysis and characterization of materials like mass spectrometry, spectrography, atomic absorption spectrophotometry, and electron microprobe analysis have to be employed. The stoichiometry of the material is itself an important factor in studies of materials like oxides, sulfides, or hydrates. It is possible that under the conditions of the experiment, the stoichiometry of the substance changes appreciably. For example, in the high-temperature transition of ZrO_2 (2550 K) when it becomes cubic,[3] an appreciable loss of oxygen has been noted under the vacuum conditions employed to record the x-ray diffraction patterns. It would be important to carry out precise thermogravimetric studies to ensure the stoichiometry of the sample in many such systems.

7-2 MAGNETIC PROPERTIES

The outer electrons of atoms in solids can be described either by the Heitler–London localized-electron (valence-bond) approach or by the collective-electron (molecular-orbital) approach. One can think of a critical distance between atoms, R_c, above which ($R > R_c$) electrons are best described by the localized-electron approach, the collective-electron approach becoming applicable when $R < R_c$. In the collective-electron approach, we make use of the Fermi–Dirac statistics and our knowledge of the crystal structure. In the case of localized electrons, we solve a multi-electron problem for the outer atomic orbitals, the crystalline (ligand) field and the Pauli exclusion principle determining the coupling between neighboring atomic moments as well as the intra-atomic exchange and multiplet structure. Spontaneous atomic moments occur only when localized electrons are present. There would be interaction between localized and collective electrons when they are simultaneously present as a result of internal exchange fields. In ionic solids, coupling between neighboring atomic moments occurs because of covalency effects induced by the interactions of the overlapping orbitals from neighboring atoms responsible for the magnitude and sign of the ligand fields. In metals, the nature of collective electrons is determined by collective electron correlations.

Magnetic measurements give direct information regarding electron correlations and ligand field potentials. The Weiss molecular-field approach gives the basis for understanding the temperature variation of magnetic susceptibility and magnetization. Measurement of magnetic susceptibility and magnetization as a function of temperature, along with techniques like neutron diffraction, inelastic neutron scattering, and Mössbauer spectroscopy, provides information on magnetic moments, the nature of coupling, and magnetic order in solids. While it would be out of the scope of this book to discuss magnetism in detail, we shall briefly summarize various types of magnetic behavior in solids in order to be able to examine magnetic transitions. An excellent treatment of magnetism and the chemical bond has been presented by Goodenough.[15] The reader is referred to this monograph and other works in the literature[16,17] for a detailed study of magnetism and magnetic materials. Goodenough[15] has tabulated magnetic transition temperatures and associated structural information on a variety of inorganic solids.

Types of Magnetism

When a substance is placed in a magnetic field H, it develops a certain amount of magnetization. The magnetization I (magnetic moment per unit volume) is given by $I = \chi H$, where χ is known as magnetic susceptibility. The magnetic induction B is defined as

$$B = H + 4\pi I = \mu H$$

where μ is the permeability of the material. We see that $\mu = 1 + 4\pi\chi$.

The magnetization of a solid arises from the spin and the orbital motion of the electrons. The orbital motion of an electron about the nucleus gives rise to a magnetic moment μ_L which is related to the orbital angular momentum M_L by the expression

$$\mu_L = -\frac{e}{2mc}(M_L)$$

The spin magnetic moment μ_s is given by

$$\mu_s = -\frac{e}{2mc}(2M_s)$$

The total angular momentum of an atom arises from a combination of the orbital and the spin angular momenta. The magnetic moment μ is related to the total angular momentum M_J by the relationship

$$\mu = -\frac{e}{2mc}(gM_J)$$

where
$$g = 1 + \frac{J(J+1) + S(S+1) - L(L+1)}{2J(J+1)}$$

The factor g is called the Landé g factor, and its value is 1 when $S = 0$ and 2 when $L = 0$. The magnitude of M_J is $\sqrt{J(J+1)}\hbar$, and its possible orientations are such that the components in an arbitrary direction (z-direction) are $m_J\hbar$, where $m_J = J, J-1, \ldots, -J$. The allowed values of the components of the magnetic moment are

$$\mu_z = -\frac{e}{2mc}(gm_J\hbar) = -m_J g\mu_B$$

Atoms or ions having no resultant magnetic moment ($J = 0$) are called diamagnetic, while those having a resultant magnetic moment are called paramagnetic. In paramagnetic solids at any temperature above absolute zero, the different energy states corresponding to the different values of m_J would be populated according to the Boltzmann distribution function. At high temperatures, the magnetic susceptibility, $\chi = I/H$, becomes equal to

$$\frac{Ng^2J(J+1)\mu_B^2}{3kT} = \frac{C}{T}$$

where
$$C = \frac{Ng^2J(J+1)\mu_B^2}{3k}$$

The variation of $1/\chi$ as a function of T is shown in curve a of Fig. 7-2.

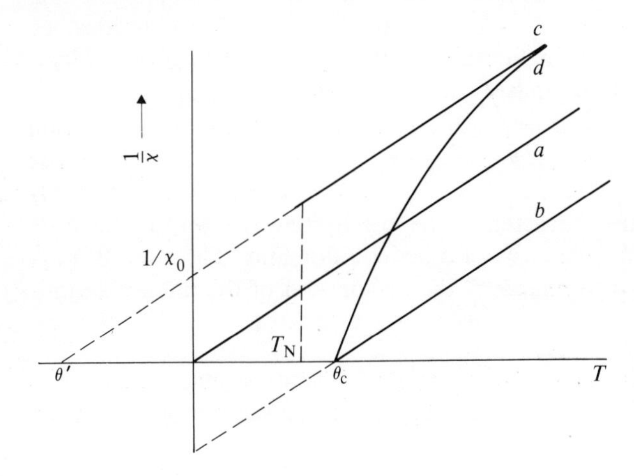

Figure 7-2 Variation of reciprocal susceptibility with temperature: (a) paramagnetic down to O K (no interaction), (b) ferromagnetic below $\theta_c = T_c$ (positive interaction), (c) antiferromagnetic below T (negative interaction), and (d) ferromagnetic below θ_c (negative interaction).

In solids containing paramagnetic ions, there is often an interaction between the spins on adjacent paramagnetic ions. If two atoms i and j carry spins S_i and S_j, the interaction energy is given by

$$W_{\text{ex}} = -2J_{\text{ex}}S_iS_j$$

where J_{ex} is the exchange integral. If J_{ex} is positive, the energy is lowest when S_i and S_j are parallel; if J_{ex} is negative, the exchange energy is lowest when S_i and S_j are antiparallel. As a result of this interaction, the energy of the solid is lowered below a critical temperature if there is an ordered arrangement of spins over the space lattice.

Ordering can be of three types: (1) The atomic moments are aligned parallel (ferromagnetic). (2) The atomic moments form two sublattices. The moment on one is equal in magnitude but aligned antiparallel to that on the other, giving a net moment of zero (antiferromagnetic). (3) In the third case, we have antiparallel arrangement, but the magnetic moments in the two opposite directions are not equal. This may arise because the opposing magnets have different moments, or because the number of atoms having one spin direction is different from that having the opposite spin direction. We would therefore have a net moment despite the antiparallel arrangement (ferrimagnetic). In all these cases, order is destroyed above a critical temperature characteristic of the material and the solid becomes paramagnetic.

Ferromagnetism Several important characteristics of ferromagnetism have been explained by Weiss[18] by assuming an internal field proportional to the magnetization of the sample. The field H_m acting on a dipole is given by

$$H_m = H + \lambda I$$

where λ is the Weiss field constant. In the ferromagnetic region,

$$I_s = NJg\mu_B B_J(x)$$

where I_s is the spontaneous magnetization at $H = 0$. $B_J(x)$ is the Brillouin function, where $x = Jg\mu_B I_s/kT$. At $T = 0$, $I_s = NJg\mu_B$, and $I_s = 0$ at $T = T_c$ (critical or Curie temperature). The paramagnetic susceptibility χ above the transition temperature is given by the relationship (see curve b of Fig. 7-2)

$$\chi = \frac{C}{T - \theta_c}.$$

Ferromagnetic materials are characterized by the hysteresis loop (in the B–H curve) which is explained on the basis of magnetic domains. The overall magnetization of a material is determined by the vector sum of the magnetizations of all domains.

Antiferromagnetism Antiferromagnetic materials become paramagnetic above the transition temperature T_N (Néel temperature), and the susceptibility is given by (see curve c of Fig. 7-2)

$$\chi = \frac{C}{T + \theta'}$$

where θ' is the asymptotic Curie point. Below the transition temperature, the susceptibility depends on whether it is measured parallel or perpendicular to the axis of the spins. At the transition temperature T_N, $\chi_{\parallel} = \chi_{\perp}$. Below T_N, $\chi_{\parallel}$ decreases with decreasing temperature while $\chi_{\perp}$ remains constant.

Some antiferromagnetic substances can be made ferromagnetic by the application of a sufficiently high magnetic field parallel to the spin axis. This phenomenon is known as *metamagnetism*. By rotating the spins slightly away from their usual orientation (spin canting), an antiferromagnetic material can be made weakly ferromagnetic, and this phenomenon is known as parasitic ferromagnetism.

Ferrimagnetism Several materials are known to be ferrimagnetic. These solids possess a net resultant magnetization due to the unequal antiparallel spin moments. Using the Weiss molecular field for a system containing only one type of magnetic ion situated on different lattice sites, Néel[18] developed a theory for ferrimagnetism. Below the Curie temperature, the magnetization on each sublattice follows an I_s versus T curve of the Brillouin form and the net magnetization is given by the resultant. Depending on the relative variations of the two components, the resultant I–T plot can take different shapes. Above the Curie temperature, the paramagnetic susceptibility is given by

$$\frac{1}{\chi} = \frac{T}{C} + \frac{1}{\chi_0} - \frac{\rho}{T - \theta}$$

where χ_0, θ, and ρ are constants, $\theta \neq \theta_c$ (see curve d of Fig. 7-2).

Techniques Employed

Magnetic properties of solids can be studied by a variety of techniques such as susceptibility measurements, neutron diffraction, Mössbauer spectroscopy, and magnetic resonance spectroscopy (including NMR, ESR, and NQR). In Fig. 7-3, magnetic susceptibility measurements on the Ni–S system[19] are shown to typically illustrate the variation of χ with temperature and composition. We shall be examining χ–T behavior of several systems later in this section while examining magnetic transitions. In Fig. 7-4, the neutron diffraction pattern of CoO is shown to illustrate the appearance of magnetic Bragg peaks appearing below the magnetic ordering temperature ($T_N = 293$ K). Above the ordering temperature, only nuclear Bragg peaks will be present. Spin arrangements in magnetic solids can be determined by an analysis of the diffraction pattern. Inelastic neutron scattering provides valuable information on phonons and magnons in crystals. Neutron inelastic scattering of CoO is shown in Fig. 7-4 to illustrate the nature of information obtained by this technique.[20]

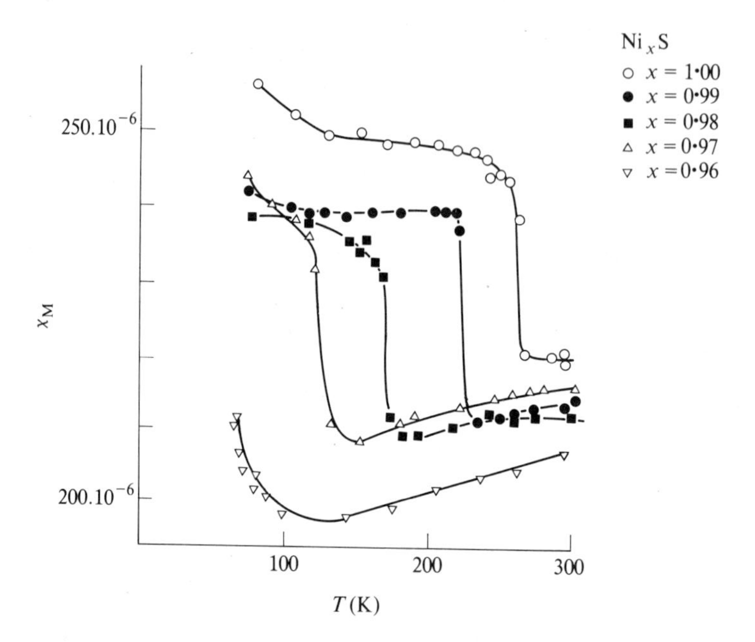

Figure 7-3 Magnetic susceptibilities of Ni_xS system. (*After Berthelemy et al.*[19])

Mössbauer spectroscopy is ideally suited for studying the chemical environment of Mössbauer nuclei like Fe, Sn, I, Eu, Au, etc. (in terms of the isomer shift), electric field gradient at the nuclei (in terms of quadrupole splitting), and magnetic hyperfine fields in magnetically ordered solids. We shall be discussing specific applications of this technique later. Where the parent substance does not contain a Mössbauer nucleus, one can dope it with an appropriate impurity (e.g., Fe^{3+} in V_2O_3) to examine the solid.

NMR spectroscopy has been employed to study phase transitions of solids containing the appropriate nuclei (e.g., V in VO_2 and V_2O_3, or Mn in $MnCr_2O_4$). Phase transitions in NaCN and NaHS have been studied by NMR spectroscopy. Studies of hindered rotation of CH_3 or NH_4^+ groups and phase transitions in hydrogen-bonded ferroelectrics like KH_2PO_4 are other important applications of NMR spectroscopy. ESR spectra of solids undergoing transitions have been reported in the literature; a useful application of ESR spectroscopy is to study a diamagnetic crystal doped with a paramagnetic ion (Mn^{2+} in KNO_3) in the region of the phase transition. NQR spectroscopy has been employed to study phase transitions of halides (e.g., $CsPbCl_3$), nitrates, and nitrites ($NaNO_3$ and $NaNO_2$) containing nuclei like halogens, nitrogen, and others (Nb in $KNbO_3$) with quadrupole moments. Ferromagnetic or antiferromagnetic resonance experiments also provide useful information on magnetically ordered solids.

Optical spectra are sensitive to magnetic ordering in crystals. Thus, formally spin-forbidden ligand field transitions in antiferromagnetic crystals are intensified by coexcitation of magnons.[21] Analogous intensification in ferromagnetic materials takes place by annihilation of thermally created magnons; cold magnon–

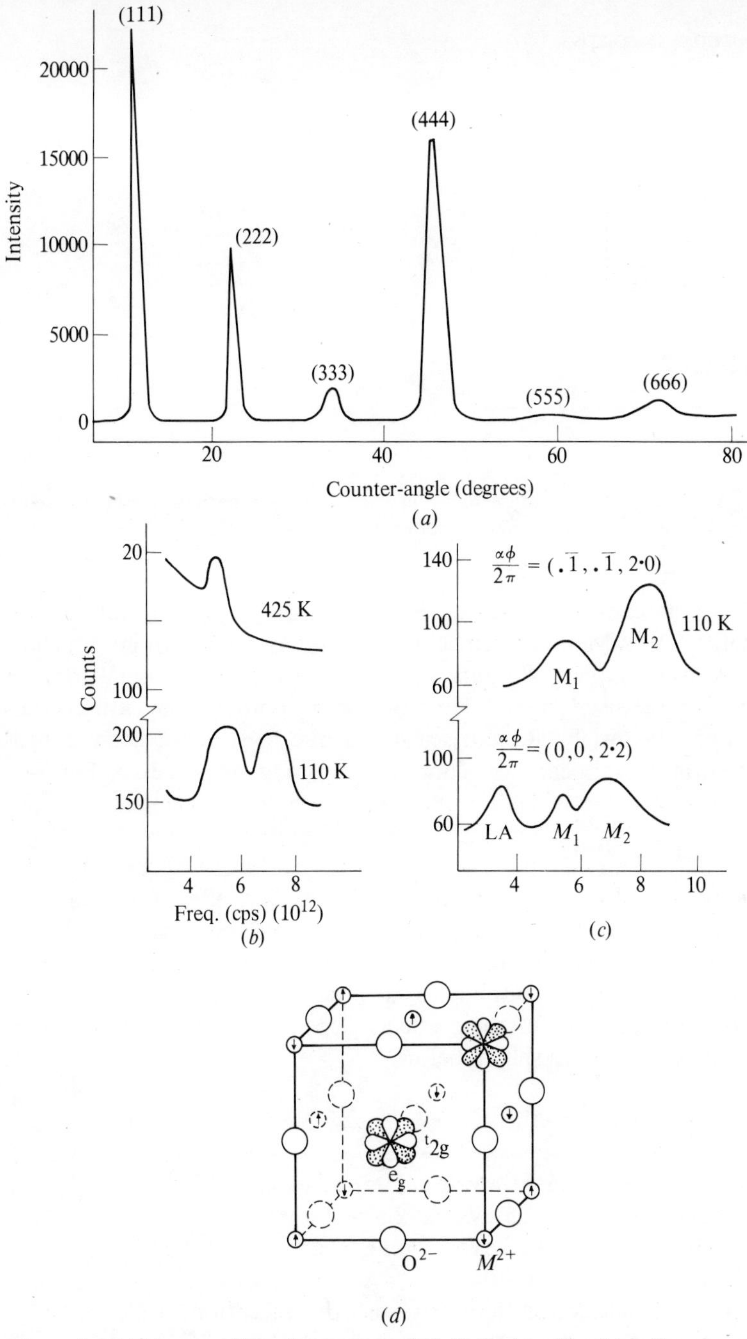

Figure 7-4 (*a*) Neutron diffraction pattern of CoO. Peaks with odd indices are magnetic and with even indices are nuclear. (*b*) Neutron inelastic scattering of CoO. (*After Bugers et al.*[20]) Observed neutron groups for constant Q scans. Peaks are believed to be due to magnetic scattering. Rise in intensity at low frequency at 425 K is associated with paramagnetic scattering. (*c*) Peaks M_1 and M_2 are magnetic excitations and LA from longitudinal acoustic mode in the neutron elastic scattering spectrum of CoO. (*d*) Rock salt structure exhibited by transition metal monoxides (TiO to NbO). Antiferromagnetism in MnO, CoO and NiO is illustrated.

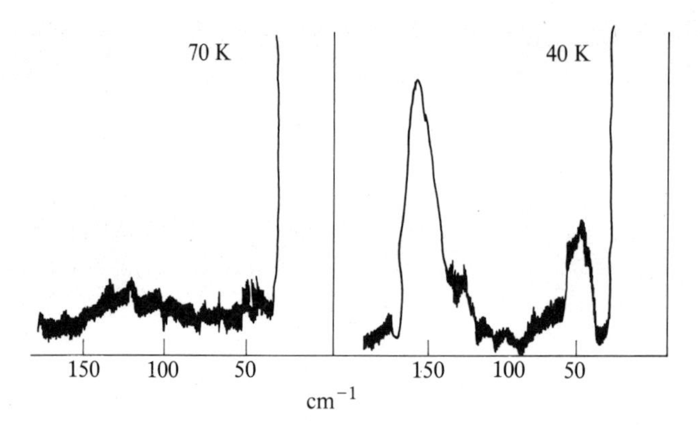

Figure 7-5 Light scattering from one and two-magnon states of FeF_2. The spins orient themselves below T_N (70 K) and spin waves propagate and scatter light. (*After Porto.*[22])

exciton combinations cannot be created in ferromagnetic phases, but only in antiferromagnetic phases. Metamagnetic compounds may occupy an intermediate position. Light scattering (laser Raman) spectroscopy is another useful tool for studying magnons[22] (see also Chap. 6). Thus, on cooling antiferromagnetic crystals like MnF_2 or FeF_2 below T_N, Raman scattering due to spin waves is seen as evidenced by the dramatic appearance of one- and two-magnon processes (Fig. 7-5).

Magnetic Atoms in Crystals

Since the neighboring atoms in a crystal have profound effects on magnetic properties, the hamiltonian is modified to include perturbing potentials due to electrostatic interaction between electrons (Δ_{ex}, intra-atomic exchange), ligand-field effects (Δ_{cf}), and spin–orbit coupling (Δ_{L-S}) besides the Heisenberg exchange term. The relative magnitudes of these effects depend on the position of the element in the periodic table, as shown below.

	Δ_{ex}	Δ_{cf}	Δ_{L-S}
Fe group (3*d*)	1.25–5.0 eV	1.25–2.5 eV	0.01–0.1 eV
Pt group (5*d*)	0.5 –2.5 eV	2.5 –5.0 eV	0.1 –0.6 eV
Rare earth (4*f*)	0.5 –5.0 eV	~0.02 eV	0.1 –0.4 eV

In 3*d* transition-metal oxides and fluorides, with the exception of Co^{3+}, Ni^{3+}, and tetravalent ions, $\Delta_{ex} > \Delta_{cf} > \Delta_{L-S}$ (medium-field case). Consideration of ligand-field splittings in different environments of the metal ion provides information on site preference energies. Thus, for an octahedral 3*d* cation containing n electrons in t_{2g} and m electrons in e_g levels, $t_{2g}^n e_g^m$, the ligand field stabilizes the octahedral site by $(4n - 6m)D_V$, if we ignore covalency effects; for a tetrahedral site, the stabilization is $(6m - 4n)D'_V$. There would be no ligand-field stabilization

for d^0, d^5, or d^{10} ions. Such simple considerations satisfactorily account for the observed cation distribution in spinels. Octahedral site stabilization of the Cr^{3+} (d^3) ion, for example, is responsible for the normal spinel structure of chromites; ferrites with d^5 ions (no stabilization) are inverse spinels.

The orbital contribution to the magnetic moment is quenched in cubic fields in many ions, and the observed moments are close to their spin-only values. Appreciable orbital contributions can, however, be obtained in octahedral d^1, d^2, d^6, and d^7 configurations and in tetrahedral d^3, d^4, d^8, and d^9 configurations. Further splittings can also occur through Jahn–Teller distortions from cubic symmetry, as in the case of octahedral Mn^{3+} (d^4) and Cu^{2+} (d^9) ions, the distortion stabilizing the octahedral site for the ions. Crystals containing such ions undergo tetragonal distortion ($c/a > 1$ or < 1). The $c/a > 1$ distortion is generally found in spinels (e.g., Mn_3O_4, $c/a \approx 1.16$; $CuFe_2O_4$, $c/a \approx 1.06$). Tetrahedral Fe^{2+} ions and Mn^{3+} and Cu^{2+} in perovskites (e.g., $LaMnO_3$) may give rise to orthorhombic distortions. Tetragonal distortions of tetrahedral sites also occur with $c/a > 1$ or < 1. Thus, Ni^{2+} and Cu^{2+} in $NiCr_2O_4$ and $CuCr_2O_4$ spinels have $c/a = 1.04$ and 0.91 respectively. Although Jahn–Teller distortions split t_{2g} orbitals just like the e_g orbitals, the distortions in the former are smaller since they are non-bonding orbitals (see Sec. 7-4 for a discussion of the cooperative Jahn–Teller effect).

Orbital effects are normally quenched by ligand fields. However, when the t_{2g} orbitals in cubic fields are partially filled, the spin-orbit energy due to the unquenched orbital angular momentum can become comparable to the Jahn–Teller stabilization energy. In the presence of long-range order, the orbital states get coupled to the ordered spin arrangement through spin-orbit interaction, giving rise to crystal distortion. While the Jahn–Teller distortion removes the degeneracy completely (quenching the orbital effect), spin-orbit stabilized distortion will have the opposite sign and disappears above the magnetic ordering temperature. Spin-orbit distortions have been observed in FeO and CoO.

Earlier in the discussion, we mentioned transition metal ions where the exchange energy is greater than the ligand-field splitting. In $4d$ and $5d$ ions and also in some of the $3d$ ions, Δ_{cf} can be larger than Δ_{ex} (strong-field case). Thus, low-spin states occur for octahedral d^n ions with $4 < n < 7$ and tetrahedral ions with $3 < n < 6$. Diamagnetic Co^{3+} ($t_{2g}^6 e_g^0$) is found in cobaltite spinels like Co_3O_4. However, in the perovskite $LaCoO_3$, the diamagnetic low-spin state is only 0.05 eV below the paramagnetic high-spin state ($t_{2g}^4 e_g^2$), giving rise to unusual magnetic properties as a function of temperature.[23] Such materials exhibit transitions from low-spin states to high-spin states at a temperature where $\Delta_{cf} = \Delta_{ex}$. $MnAs_{0.94}P_{0.06}$ also seems to undergo this kind of spin-state transition accompanied by a thermal expansion through a critical lattice parameter. All rare-earth cobaltites show low-spin–high-spin transitions, although it is only in $LaCoO_3$ that the transition is followed by a symmetry change from $R\bar{3}c$ to $R\bar{3}$. The transition in $LaCoO_3$ has features of a first-order phase transition, but in other cobaltites the transition is of the second or a higher order. In all these cobaltites, the transition seems to occur when the high-spin and low-spin states are in the ratio

1:1. Co_2O_3 prepared under high pressure has Co^{3+} ions in the low-spin state, and the oxide transforms to high-spin state accompanied by an increase in cell volume.[24] In coordination complexes where high–low-spin transitions have been seen, there appears to be no change in the crystal structure or volume.

The magnetization vector in crystals in the absence of an applied field aligns itself parallel to a preferred direction(s). In cobalt (hexagonal), the preferred direction is the *c*-axis, while the preferred directions are along the cube edge and the diagonal respectively in Fe and Ni. Coupling between electron spins and orbital motion of electrons gives rise to magnetocrystalline anisotropy. Since directional properties of orbitals are oriented with respect to the crystal lattice, the effect of magnetic field on spin moments depends on spin orientation with respect to the lattice. Magnetization also causes elastic changes in the dimensions of magnetic materials, and this effect is called magnetostriction.

Superexchange Interactions

The term superexchange is generally employed with respect to magnetic insulators where magnetic interactions take place between localized electrons on neighboring cations, often through an intermediary anion. The work of Anderson,[25] Goodenough,[15] and Kanamori[26] has been largely responsible for the present-day understanding of this phenomenon. Magnetic interaction between cations can be large despite long intercationic distances, due to the role played by the intervening anion. Thus, in NiO the Ni–O–Ni interaction determines the magnetic ordering temperature ($T_N = 523$ K), although two Ni^{2+} ions are separated by ~ 4 Å (see Fig. 7-4*d*). Consideration of the spatial relations between cation and anion orbitals will show different types of interaction (overlap) that can occur in crystals, giving rise to covalent mixing of anion and cation orbitals. Goodenough and Kanamori have derived the signs and magnitudes of various d^n–anion–d^m superexchange interactions. For example, d^3–anion–d^3 interaction would be antiferromagnetic if the cation–anion–cation angle is 180°. If the cation–anion–cation angle is 90°, the interaction would be ferromagnetic; direct overlap of the half-filled t_{2g} orbitals (cation–cation interaction) would, however, be antiferromagnetic. Since the cation–cation interaction is very sensitive to the intercationic distance, we would expect a small antiferromagnetic contribution at large intercationic distances. Thus, in spinels of the type MCr_2X_4 (M = Zn or Cd, X = O, S, or Se), the paramagnetic Curie temperature becomes more positive (increased ferromagnetic interaction) as the cation–cation separation increases, with $CdCr_2S_4$ and $CdCr_2Se_4$ being ferromagnetic ($r_{Cr-Cr} > 3.6$ Å).

Superexchange effects are far greater in σ-type interactions than in π-type interactions. For cations of the same electronic configuration, the interaction is greatest for the highest-valency cations (e.g., $Fe^{3+} > Mn^{2+}$). Covalency also increases on going to the right of the periodic table (e.g., T_N increases in the order MnO, FeO, CoO, NiO). Increasing covalency effects also vary in the order O^{2-}, S^{2-}, Se^{2-} (T_c increases from 122 K to 173 K from MnO to MnSe).

In compounds containing mixed-valency cations, double exchange can provide energy stabilization. An example for this is the perovskite $La_{1-x}Ca_x$ $Mn^{3+}_{1-x}Mn^{4+}_xO_3$, where the compositions $0.1 < x < 0.5$ are ferromagnetic conductors although the end members are magnetic insulators. In the double exchange process the transformations involved are $Mn^{3+} \rightarrow Mn^{4+}$ and $Mn^{4+} \rightarrow Mn^{3+}$, so that the final and initial states are degenerate; the mobile electron is coupled parallel to the ionic spin and there is spin conservation in the transfer process.

Collective-electron Model

In the localized-electron model, electron transfer involves the expenditure of energy equal to the Coulomb energy and there is a change in the valence of the cation. If we modify the localized model by introducing bands, the electrons gain kinetic energy in moving through the crystal. In wide-band materials, the energy gain is greater than the coulombic effect giving rise to the metallic state. In this state, there is no spontaneous moment and the material exhibits a weak temperature-independent paramagnetism (Pauli paramagnetism). The susceptibility is then given by

$$\chi = \frac{N\mu^2}{3kT_F}$$

where T_F is the Fermi temperature ($\sim 10^4$–10^5 K). The broad-band limit is the opposite extreme from the localized model. When both localized and collective electrons coexist in a solid, there is a collective-electron contribution to the atomic moment, if the bands are narrow.

Solids which exhibit magnetic behavior in the intermediate region between localized and collective limits are indeed interesting. It is most instructive to examine these solids following Goodenough's conceptual phase diagrams in terms of the transfer energy (overlap integral), b. Such a diagram[27] in the case of a single d electron per orbital ($n_l = 1$) is given in Fig. 7-6. More sophisticated diagrams have been given by Goodenough[28,29] in his recent articles. The interaction in a system with $n_l = 1$ (integral number of d electrons for each transition metal ion on equivalent lattice sites) is antiferromagnetic, with the Néel temperature increasing with b (since T_N is proportional to b^2) up to a critical value b_c. When $b > b_c$, the bands continue to broaden, eventually overlapping at a new critical value b_g. On increasing b further, we reach the band limit (b_p in Fig. 7-6). When $b_p > b_g$, there is Pauli paramagnetism and metallic conductivity. The collective-electron regime where there is antiferromagnetism is limited to the region $b_c < b < b_m$, and within this region, T_N decreases with increasing b ($T_N = 0$ when $b = b_m$). The maximum value of T_N is when $b = b_c$ (Fig. 7-6). When $b < b_c$, the paramagnetic susceptibility follows the Curie–Weiss law.

A large overlap integral may be due to strong cation–cation or cation–anion–cation interactions. Since b directly depends on the atomic separation R, the occurrence of a localized–collective-electron transition at $b = b_c$ would imply a critical distance R_c for such a transition. One of the characteristic features

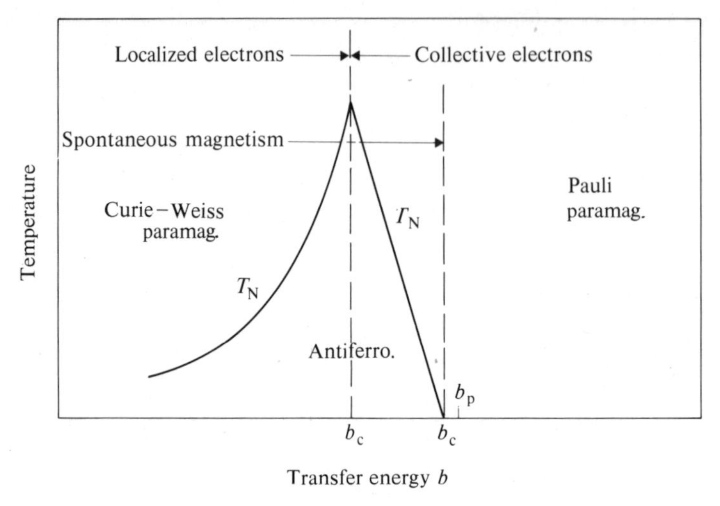

Figure 7-6 Conceptual b–T phase diagram of Goodenough.[27]

associated with a semiconductor⇌metal transition is a marked discontinuity in the magnetic susceptibility. This occurs in addition to the crystallographic changes and specific heat effects accompanying the transition. If localized electrons are simultaneously present, a bonding-band⇌metallic-band transition coincides with (or lies above) a Néel temperature, since intra-atomic exchange between localized and collective *d*-electrons gives rise to an antiferromagnetic order of the localized electrons which reflects antiparallel correlations of the collective electrons. If the collective *d*-bands are more than half filled, there would be ferromagnetic ordering of localized electrons reflecting the parallel-spin correlations of the collective electrons. We shall examine the relevance of these concepts in some of the transition metal oxide systems in this section. Electron transport properties of materials will be discussed in the light of these concepts later in this chapter. We shall now examine magnetic properties of illustrative cases of inorganic solids of different structures.

Case Studies of Magnetic Transitions

(*a*) Rock salt structures Monoxides of 3*d* transition metals have the rock salt structure and exhibit properties shown in Table 7-1. MnO, FeO, CoO, and NiO show typical localized-electron behavior ($b < b_c$, $R > R_c$), with T_N increasing with b. In these oxides, there is 180° cation–anion–cation superexchange interaction. In TiO ($b > b_m$, $R < R_c$), we have the band regime and it is Pauli paramagnetic. In VO also, $R < R_c$, but the difference between the two is much smaller than in TiO. The existence of an energy gap in VO (since it is not truly metallic) indicates that $b < b_g$; since it is not Pauli paramagnetic, $b < b_p$. The absence of magnetic order requires $b > b_m$. Therefore, in VO, $b_m < b < b_g < b_p$. The $\Delta b(= b - b_m)$ is probably small since χ increases with x in VO_x (Fig. 7-7).[30]

Table 7-1 Oxides of rock salt structure*

	R, Å	R_c, Å†	Properties
TiO	2.94	3.02	metallic, Pauli-paramagnetic
VO	2.89	2.92	semimetal, weak temperature-dependence of χ
MnO	3.14	2.66	semiconductor, Curie–Weiss, $T_N = 122$ K
FeO	3.03	2.95	semiconductor, Curie–Weiss, $T_N = 198$ K
CoO	3.01	2.87	semiconductor, Curie–Weiss, $T_N = 293$ K
NiO	2.95	2.77	semiconductor, Curie–Weiss, $T_N = 523$ K

* See Fig. 7-4*d* for rock salt structure of these monoxides. In TiO, cation–cation overlap via t_{2g} orbitals occurs.

† After Goodenough.[15]

Neutron diffraction, neutron inelastic scattering, and related techniques have provided a detailed picture of the magnetic ordering in oxides like MnO, CoO, and NiO (see Figs. 7-4 and 7-5). Thus, in CoO, magnetic excitations exist both above and below T_N. Neutron inelastic scattering[20] gives two peaks in the paramagnetic phase due to transitions between the spin-orbit levels of Co^{2+}. Two bands of excitation seen in the antiferromagnetic phase are due to transitions from ground state of Co^{2+} to its conjugate ($J = \frac{1}{2}$) state and to the lowest state

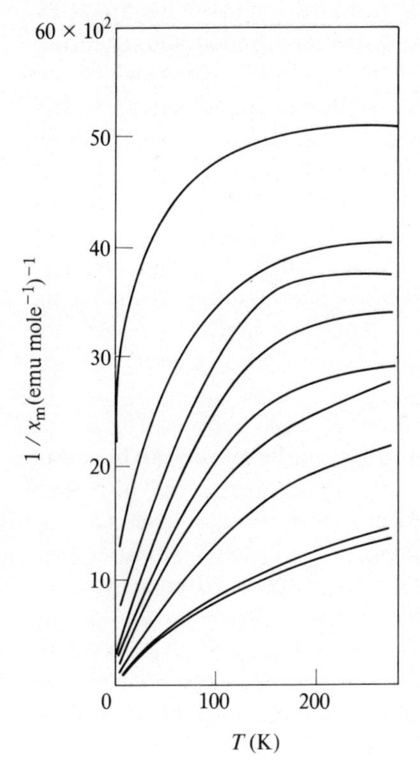

Figure 7-7 Variation of $1/\lambda$ with temperature in VO_x. (*After Banus and Reed.*[30]) Value of x decreases from 1.32 for the curve at the bottom of the figure to 0.79 for the topmost curve. Values of x for curves 5 and 6 from the bottom are 1.02 and 0.99 respectively.

of the next spin-orbit level ($J = \frac{3}{2}$). The spin-wave model for these magnetic excitations leads to a next-nearest-neighbor exchange constant of 0.35 (10^{12} cps). The nearest-neighbor exchange constant and tetragonal distortion are both small in CoO.

$LiVO_2$ and $NaVO_2$ have rock salt structures with Li^+ (or Na^+) and V^{3+} on alternate (111) cation planes introducing a unique [111] axis and rhombohedral ($\alpha < 60°$) symmetry. Both these show the spin-only value of susceptibility at high temperatures. The intercationic distance in $LiVO_2$ is 2.84 Å $< R_c$ (V) = 2.95 Å, and in $NaVO_2$ it is greater than R_c (V). $LiVO_2$ shows a sharp drop in χ at 463 K, while $NaVO_2$ only shows a small change at 330 K.[31] The large drop in $LiVO_2$ is due mainly to molecular orbital formation (bonding) in the basal plane, as evidenced by the large c/a ratio (hexagonal basis) in $LiVO_2$.

MnS occurs in three modifications: the green form, α-MnS, with rock salt structure, and the pink form β-MnS in zinc blende or wurtzite structure. All three forms are antiferromagnetic,[32] with α-MnS having a T_N of 152 K.[33] At higher temperatures, the susceptibility obeys the Curie–Weiss law, with the magnetic moment corresponding to five unpaired electrons. Both forms of β-MnS are also antiferromagnetic. The Néel temperature of the zinc-blende-type MnS is around 100 K, while in the wurtzite type, antiferromagnetism occurs at still lower temperatures, probably because of stacking faults.[34]

Magnetic structures of all the three forms of MnS have been deduced by neutron diffraction.[35] In α-MnS, the moments within the (111) plane are ferromagnetically aligned, and successive (111) planes are antiferromagnetically coupled. In the zinc-blende-type β-MnS, the spins lie in planes which are perpendicular to one of the crystallographic axes. In the wurtzite-type β-MnS, the hexagonal close-packed planes of Mn are arranged as ABAB..., etc., with the sulfur atoms in the tetrahedral holes. The internal arrangement of the spins in each of the close-packed planes is such that $\frac{2}{3}$ of the nearest neighbors are parallel and $\frac{1}{3}$ are antiparallel. In adjacent planes, the spins are reversed. Antiferromagnetism in all these compounds can be explained by the superexchange mechanism involving intermediate anions. In α-MnS, interaction may involve the d_{z^2} and $d_{x^2-y^2}$ orbitals of Mn and the $3p$ orbitals of sulfur, whereas in β-MnS, the superexchange may involve d_{xy}, d_{yz}, d_{xz} orbitals of Mn and an sp hybrid of sulfur orbitals.

Specific heat measurements on α-MnS show that T_N is between 152 K and 155 K. At temperatures below 4 K, a large contribution from nuclear hyperfine interaction to the heat capacity is observed. Specific heat measurements also show that antiferromagnetism in β-MnS occurs at lower temperatures. There is a knee in the electrical conductivity curve of α-MnS near the Néel temperature. EPR studies of α-MnS have shown that the resonance line shape is Lorentzian with a g-value (2.005) quite close to the value of dilute Mn^{2+} in diamagnetic crystals. The intensity of the line decreases as the temperature is decreased and there is no residual absorption below the Néel temperature. The close correspondence of the g value with that of the Mn^{2+} ion suggests that there are no free conduction electrons and the conduction is through a hopping mechanism.

(*b*) Rutile and corundum structures In the rutile structure, there are 135° cation–anion–cation interactions (due to corner sharing of body-centered octahedra and corner octahedra) besides 90° interactions (due to edge-sharing of octahedra along the *c*-axis). The 90° and 135° interactions can be cooperative only if the 90° interactions are ferromagnetic. Compounds like MnF_2, FeF_2, CoF_2, and NiF_2 have body-centered ordering with low Néel points. The 90° interactions in MnF_2 are, however, ferromagnetic. In CrF_2 or $CrCl_2$ (d^4), Jahn–Teller distortion occurs above room temperature. While CrF_2 has body-centered ordering, in $CrCl_2$ there is competition between the 90° and 135° interactions because of the large cation–cation distance. Antiferromagnetic CuF_2 also shows Jahn–Teller distortion similar to that of CrF_2. CrF_2 is metallic and ferromagnetic ($T_c = 394$ K), indicating that cation–cation interactions along the *c*-axis are eliminated; 180°-type cation–anion–cation coupling should be present in this system. If all the interactions in the rutile structure are antiferromagnetic, spiral configurations of the kind found in MnO_2 can result.

TiO_2 and VO_2 are the only rutile-type oxides where the intercationic distance can be less than R_c. Ti^{4+} has no outer *d*-electrons and is an insulator; however, if there are a few anion vacancies in TiO_2, R_{cc} (*c*-axis) $< R_c$. VO_2 has the rutile structure above 340 K. At room temperature, chains of octahedra along the [001] axis are puckered and V^{4+} ions are shifted so as to form metal–metal pairs within the chains. Such bonding traps all *d*-electrons into homopolar bonds and quenches the metallic conductivity along the *c*-axis. VO_2 undergoes a transition at 340 K from monoclinic to rutile structure accompanied by a semiconductor–metal transition and a paramagnetic–diamagnetic transition ($\mu_{eff} \rightarrow 1.73\mu_B$). The Curie–Weiss law is not obeyed at low temperatures, and there is no magnetic ordering as evidenced by neutron diffraction experiments. In Fig. 7-8 the χ–T curves for VO_2–TiO_2 solid solutions[36] are given, and show how the increase in the proportion of TiO_2 eliminates the VO_2 transition. It is to be noted that with increase in the percentage of TiO_2, the solid solution becomes more rutile-like at room temperature. We shall be discussing the VO_2 transition at length in the section on electrical properties.

In the corundum structure, cation–anion–cation (cac) interactions are of 135° and 90°. In Cr_2O_3 ($3d^3$) with no e_g electrons, cac interactions are weak, and in Fe_2O_3 ($3d^5$), with half-filled e_g orbitals, they are strong. Accordingly, T_N in Fe_2O_3 is much higher (953 K) than in Cr_2O_3 (307 K). Along the *c*-axis, however, intercationic distance in Cr_2O_3 is less than R_c ($3d$), causing variations in atomic moment with temperature (see Fig. 7-9). Fe_2O_3 exhibits weak parasitic ferromagnetism in the range $253 < T < 953$ K. In this temperature range, atomic moments are nearly in the basal plane. Antisymmetric spin-coupling[40] is parallel to the *c*-axis and the anisotropic superexchange cants spins in the basal plane to produce a net moment. At $T < 253$ K, the spins are aligned parallel to the *c*-axis and the parasitic ferromagnetism disappears. Such a transition, also referred to as a spin–flip or Morin transition,[41] is seen in iron (II) sulfide. The Morin transition in Fe_2O_3 has been investigated by a variety of techniques including NMR, Mössbauer, and neutron scattering.[4]

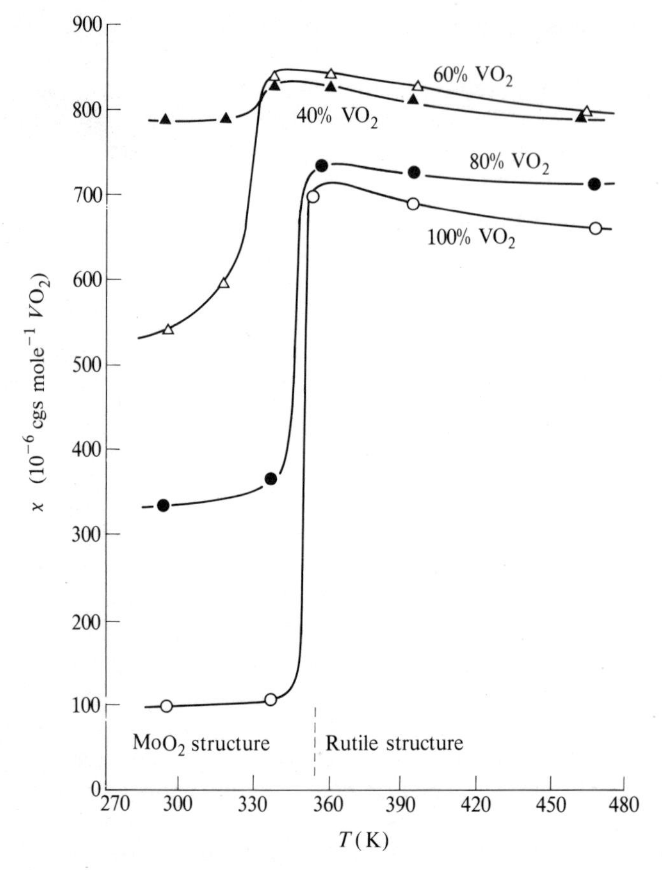

Figure 7-8 Susceptibility data for VO_2–TiO_2 system. (*After Rüdorff et al.*[36])

In transition metal dihalides which crystallize in the $CdCl_2$ structure, 90° interactions within the layer are antiferromagnetic if the 3*d* orbitals are half-filled, but are ferromagnetic if the t_{2g} orbitals are more than half-filled. $FeCl_2$ is metamagnetic. Results from a recent spectroscopic study[42] of the phase transition from antiferromagnetic (metamagnetic) to ferromagnetic state in $FeCl_2$ are shown in Fig. 7-10.

In transition metal trichlorides, one third of the cations are removed from the dichloride layer, but 90° interactions are still present. Such competing interactions in $FeCl_3$ produce the spiral configuration. In ferromagnetic layers of $CrCl_3$, 90° intralayer interactions are ferromagnetic.

Ti_2O_3 and V_2O_3 are both corundum structures in the high-temperature metallic phases (above 410 and 150 K respectively). In the low-temperature phase of Ti_2O_3 there is homopolar bonding of *c*-axis pairs and there is no antiferromagnetic ordering. V_2O_3 shows a cooperative (antiferromagnetic–paramagnetic) transition at 150 K accompanying a monoclinic-corundum structure change and

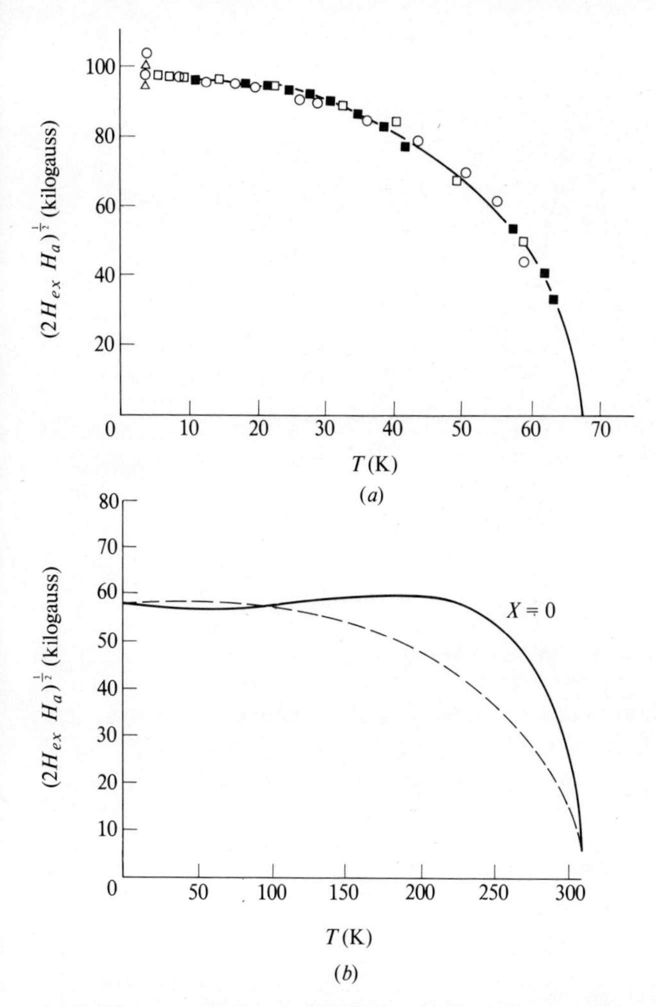

Figure 7-9 Critical field $H_c = (2H_{ex}H_a)^{1/2}$ vs temperature from antiferromagnetic resonance. (a) MnF_2; experimental points from refs. 37 and 38. Solid line is Brillouin function for $S = 5/2$ ($T_N = 67.7$ K). (b) Cr_2O_3; broken curve is the Brillouin function for $S = 3/2$ and the solid curve is experimental. (*After Foner.*[39]) Deviations between the two curves here may arise from the intercationic distance being less than R_c (3d). Further, the c axis in Cr_2O_3 being the easy axis of magnetization may also cause such deviations ($T_N = 307$ K).

also a noncooperative transition around 450 K. The χ–T curve corresponding to the low-temperature transition[43] of V_2O_3 is shown in Fig. 7-11, and the Mössbauer spectra of ^{57}Fe-doped V_2O_3 at two temperatures[44] are shown in Fig. 7-12. We shall be discussing transitions in V_2O_3 and Ti_2O_3 in greater detail in the section on electrical transitions.

Ti_2S_3 (hexagonal) is metallic and Pauli-paramagnetic, while V_2S_3 (monoclinic or hexagonal) is antiferromagnetic. Rhombohedral Cr_2S_3 is ferrimagnetic below

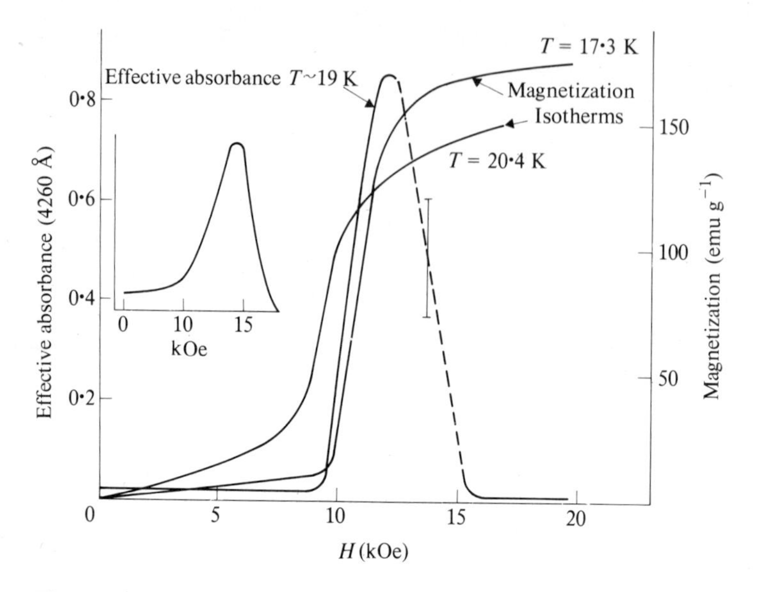

Figure 7-10 Absorbance of $FeCl_2$ at 19 K as a function of magnetic field. Magnetization curves are also shown. In the inset, a plot of the integrated band area of the ligand-field zero-phonon line at 4272 Å is plotted against magnetic field. (*After Robbins and Day.*[42])

120 K with neutron diffraction measurements indicating collinear spin structure with magnetic sublattices. Trigonal Cr_2S_3 has a structure similar to Cr_5S_6 (NiAs–$Cd(OH)_2$-type superstructure) and exhibits different magnetic properties as described later under NiAs structures.

(*c*) Nickel arsenide structure In the NiAs structure (cac angle $\approx 135°$), predominant cac and cc exchange interactions are between basal plane layers, with weaker cc

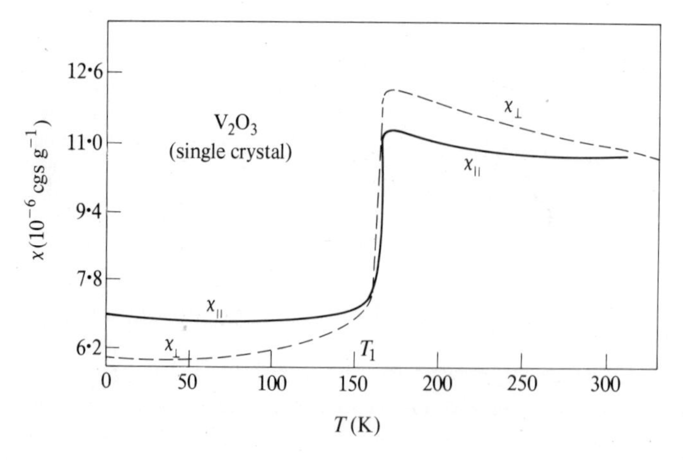

Figure 7-11 Single-crystal magnetic susceptibility of V_2O_3 as a function of temperature. (*After Carr and Foner.*[43])

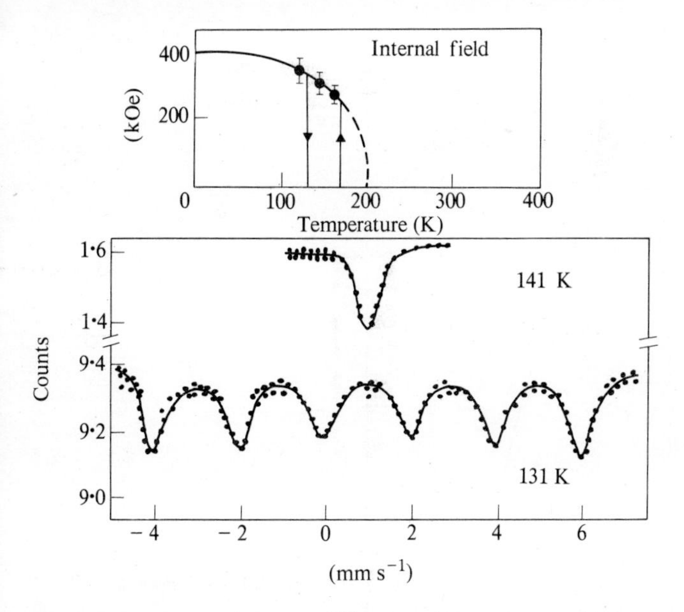

Figure 7-12 Mössbauer spectra of ^{57}Fe-doped V_2O_3 above and below T_N. (*After Shinjo and Kosuge.*[44]) Notice that the internal field sharply drops to zero at T_N.

interactions existing within a plane. Except in the case of $3d^4$ cations, the magnetic order of stoichiometric NiAs compounds consists of ferromagnetic basal planes coupled antiparallel to one another.[15] Interstitial ions generally favor ferromagnetic ordering of the cation sublattice. With the exception of monoclinic CrS, no static Jahn–Teller distortions are associated with $3d^4$ ions in the NiAs structure. NiAs compounds with d^4 ions as in CrTe, MnAs, and MnSb are ferromagnetic. $CrS_{1+\delta}$ is antiferromagnetic (ferrimagnetic, if defects are ordered) and stoichiometric CrS undergoes a monoclinic–hexagonal (semiconductor–metal) transition. MnAs, MnSb, and MnBi show low moments because of the presence of interstitial ions. MnAs and MnBi undergo first-order phase changes at T_c with a discontinuous change in a and c parameters.

Cr_5S_6 has a trigonal superstructure of the NiAs–$Cd(OH)_2$ type with ordered vacancies in every alternate layer. At room temperature, the cell volume is six times that of the NiAs subcell. The three-dimensional order of the vacancies disappears at about 600 K, but up to 900 K the vacancies remain confined to every other metal layer.[32] Cr_5S_6 is a metallic conductor and is antiferromagnetic below 158 K, ferrimagnetic between 158 K and 305 K, and paramagnetic above 305 K[45] (Fig. 7-13). Various mechanisms have been proposed to explain these magnetic transitions. Van Laar,[46] on the basis of a neutron diffraction study, has argued that the spin configuration in Cr_5S_6 is spiral-type below the transition temperature (160 K); above this temperature, the spiral unwinds to give rise to collinear Néel-type ferrimagnetism (Fig. 7-14). According to this mechanism, the transition should be of second order, whereas the thermal hysteresis observed

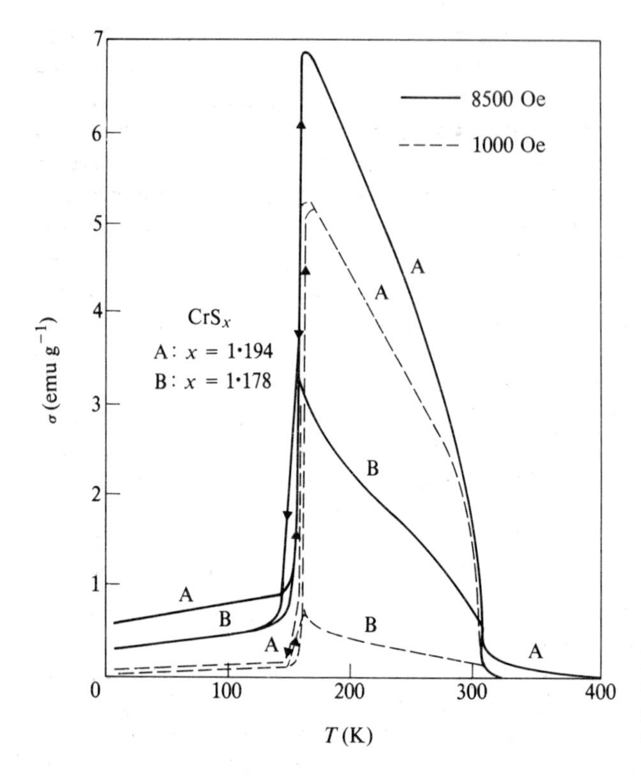

Figure 7-13 Magnetization of Cr_5S_6 at various temperatures for compositions $CrS_{1.194}$ and $CrS_{1.178}$. (*After Dwight et al.*[45])

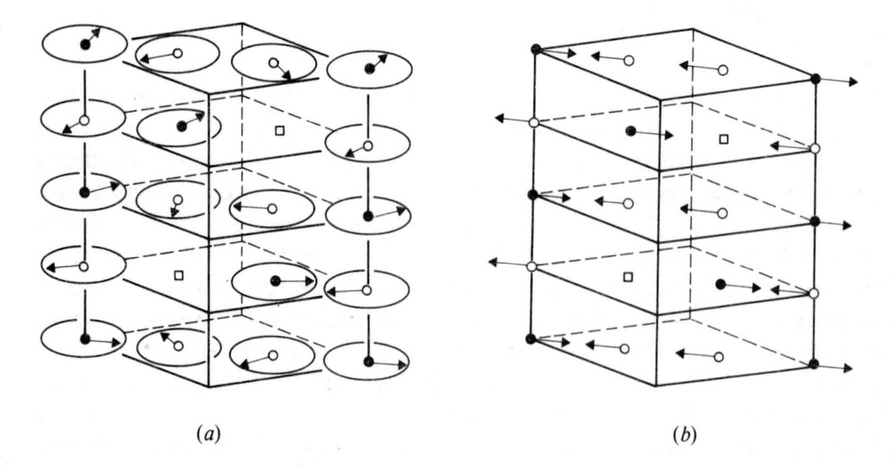

Figure 7-14 (*a*) Antiferromagnetic spin arrangement in Cr_5S_6. (*b*) Ferrimagnetic spin arrangement in Cr_5S_6. (*After Van Laar.*[46])

in the transition indicates a first-order transition. Dwight et al.[47] have investigated this transition as a function of pressure, temperature, and applied field. The values of $(\partial T_c/\partial P)$ and $(\partial T_t/\partial P)$ are 1.83 deg kbar^{-1} and 0.04 deg kbar^{-1} respectively. Their studies show, for the observed ground-state spiral configuration, not only that all the nearest-neighbor interactions should be antiferromagnetic, but also that the antiferromagnetic next-nearest-neighbor interactions should be present. The secondary magnetostrictive forces are responsible for the thermal hysteresis. The pressure dependence of σ_0 indicates that some of the magnetization arises from band electrons. Popma and Haas[48] have carried out ferrimagnetic resonance experiments on Cr_5S_6 to examine magnetic anisotropy. The resonance field was dependent on temperature; at T_c, the resonance field was 12.5 kOe which corresponds to $g = 2$.

Cr_3S_4 has the defect NiAs–Cd(OH)$_2$ monoclinic structure with ordered vacancies in every other metal layer.[32] Cr_3S_4 is metallic and antiferromagnetic with a Néel temperature of 280 K. The magnetic unit cell does not coincide with the crystallographic unit cell. The unit cell is doubled in the a and c-directions with spins in $(10\bar{1})$ planes in "phase." At low temperatures, Cr_7S_8 has a NiAs–Cd(OH)$_2$ type unit cell similar to other chromium sulfides[32] with a superlattice of $a = 2a'$ and $c = 3c'$. Cr_7S_8 is metallic and antiferromagnetic with $T_N = 125$ K.

The crystal structure of trigonal Cr_2S_3 is similar to that of Cr_5S_6 except that both the 3(d) and the 2(a) sites are vacant.[32] This gives rise to an arrangement in which two of each three possible metal sites are vacant. Trigonal Cr_2S_3 is paramagnetic above about 125 K. As the temperature is lowered, magnetization increases with a maximum at 95 K and further on it decreases. Between 15 K and 4.20 K, Cr_2S_3(tr) behaves as an antiferromagnet. At 4.2 K, the magnetization at $H = 0$ has zero value, but at 80 K it has $\sim 10^{-2}$ μ_B/Cr atom. Neutron diffraction measurements on Cr_2S_3(tr) at 4.2, 78, and 300 K show that the maximum in the magnetization cannot be attributed to any change in the spin arrangement. Qualitatively, the magnetic structures of Cr_2S_3(tr) at 4.2 K and 78 K are essentially the same. The spin arrangement can be described as a screw-type spiral structure with a periodicity of exactly twice the crystallography c-parameter.

Nonstoichiometric VS_{1-x} phase ($0.85 \leq S/V \leq 1.05$) has the MnP structure derived through an orthorhombic distortion of the NiAs structure. The transition between NiAs and MnP structures is of second order.[32] The nonstoichiometry is due primarily to randomly distributed sulfur vacancies. The stability of the MnP structure in VS_{1-x} has been interpreted to be associated with a particular range of electron concentration (0.3 electron/Å^3). Knight shift measurements[49] on VS_x with NiAs and MnP structures show a change in the shift at $V/S = 0.94$, indicating a change associated with the conduction band. Band structure calculations show that the NiAs–MnP transition of VS is due to the charge density wave in the conduction band. The nonstoichiometric $V_{1-x}S$ system has been studied recently by Delamaire et al.[50] For $x = 0.16$ to 0.365, $V_{1-x}S$ exists as a single homogeneous nonstoichiometric phase with a gradual change in lattice parameters. Grønvold et al.[51] have investigated the V–S system with various S/V ratios. According to them $VS_{1\pm x}$ phases have the NiAs–orthorhombic structure with the a and b-axes doubled. V_7S_8 and V_7Se_8 have superlattice structures closely related to the NiAs type, with ordering of the vacancies. Besides the hexagonal compound with $a = 2a'$ and $c = 4c'$, a new monoclinic compound with $a = 2a'\sqrt{3}$ and $b = 2a'$ and $c = 4c'$ has been reported (a' and c' refer to the NiAs cell). Magnetic susceptibilities of various $V_{1-x}S$ phases have been studied[52] (see Fig. 7-15), and the results show that vanadium atoms in these phases have both

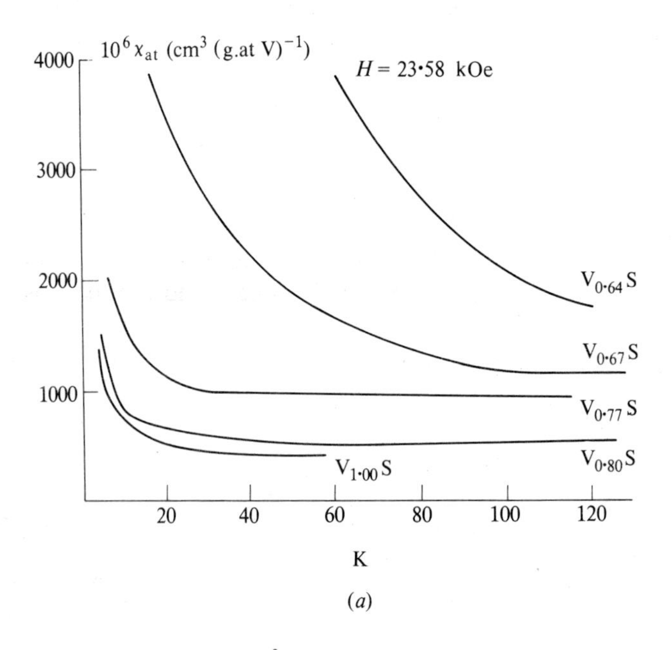

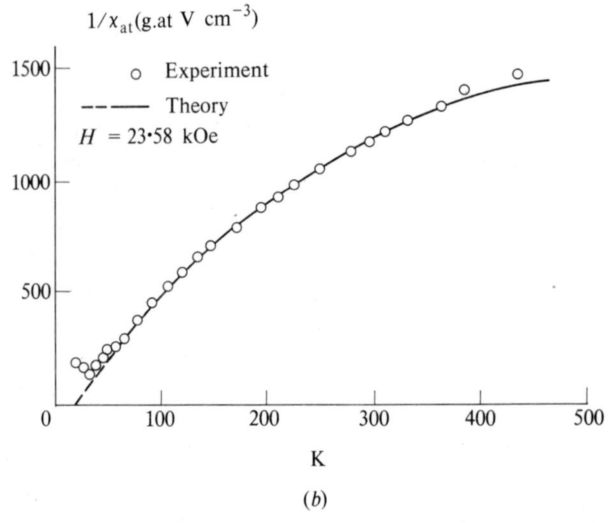

Figure 7-15 (*a*) Magnetic susceptibility of $V_{1-x}S$ phases. (*b*) Reciprocal susceptibility of V_5S_8 as a function of temperature. (*After De Vries and Haas.*[52])

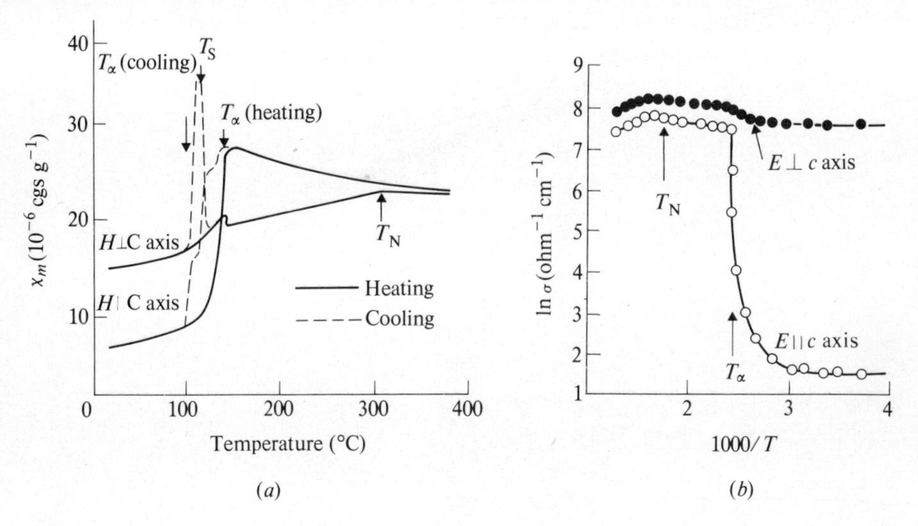

Figure 7-16 Temperature-dependence of (*a*) magnetic susceptibility and (*b*) logarithm of electrical conductivity of nominal FeS. (*After Hirahara and Murakami.*[53])

localized and itinerant *d*-electrons. Susceptibility data on V_5S_8 (monoclinic structure derived from NiAs) give a Néel temperature of 30 K.

Nonstoichiometric phases of FeS exhibit interesting and complex magnetic properties.[15,29,32] All these have structures related to NiAs. $Fe_{1-x}S$ compounds show two magnetic transitions, called α and β, T_α varying with the percentage of S, and T_β corresponding to T_N (598 K). The high T_N implies that the α-spin electrons in the σ-bonding orbitals are localized. Cation clustering at room temperature establishes itinerant character (below T_N) of the sixth *d* electron per iron atom which has its spin antiparallel to the net spin on a cation subarray.[29] The α-transition seems to correspond to the boundary between the 1C and 2C-type NiAs superlattice structures.[32] Fe^{2+} ions move together in groups of three in the (001) plane and S^{2-} suffers a small displacement along the *c*-axis. It has been shown recently that the α-transition is accompanied by a change from a ferroelectric to a paraelectric state. The polar axis in the ferroelectric 2C phase is parallel to the *c*-axis, along which electrical conductivity also changes sharply[53] (Fig. 7-16). Just below T_α, a spin rotation (T_s) is seen from parallel to the *c*-axis to perpendicular to *c*-axis[53] (Fig. 7-16). Both T_α and T_s occur at different temperatures, depending on stoichiometry.[54] The spin-flip (Morin transition) apparently proceeds by two separate steps, denoted T_{MK} and $T_{M\alpha}$ by Van den Berg.[54] Apart from the α and β transitions, a γ-peak has been noticed ($T_\gamma < T_\alpha < T_\beta = T_N$) in the magnetic susceptibility curve, the peak becoming more prominent as x (in $Fe_{1-x}S$) increases. In Fig. 7-17, the "complete" but complex phase diagram of $Fe_{1-x}S$ given by Van den Berg[54] has been reproduced. The shaded part of the phase diagram is connected with the γ-peak. The plot of $T_{M\alpha}$ versus x extrapolates to T_N, indicating that the spins are parallel to the *c*-axis

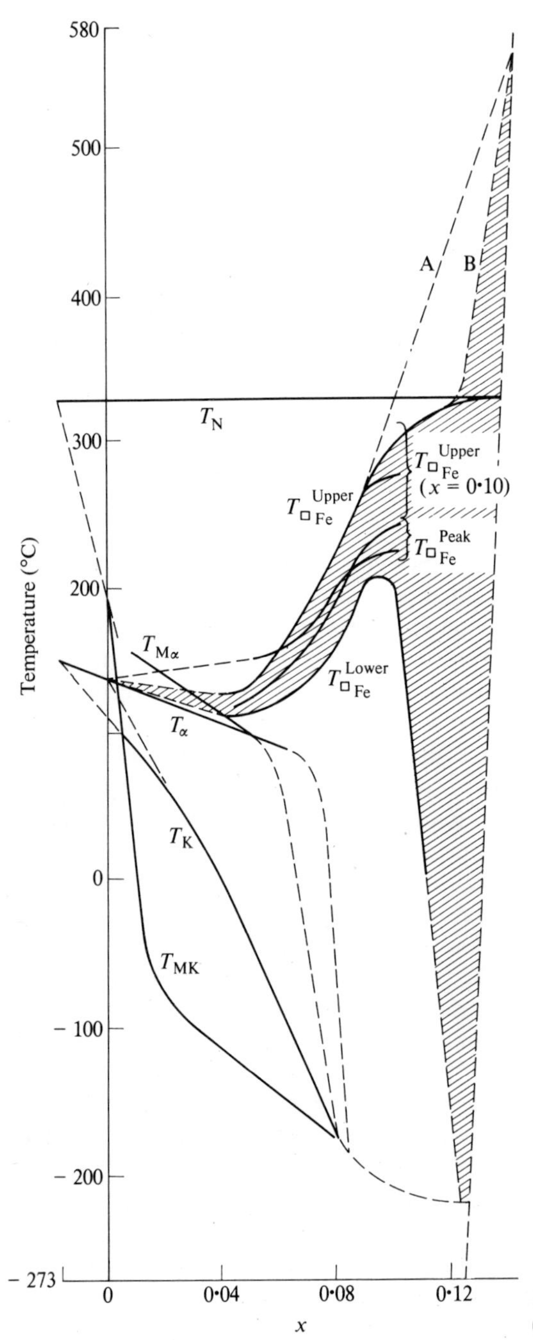

Figure 7-17 Phase diagram of $Fe_{1-x}S$. (*After van den Berg.*[54])

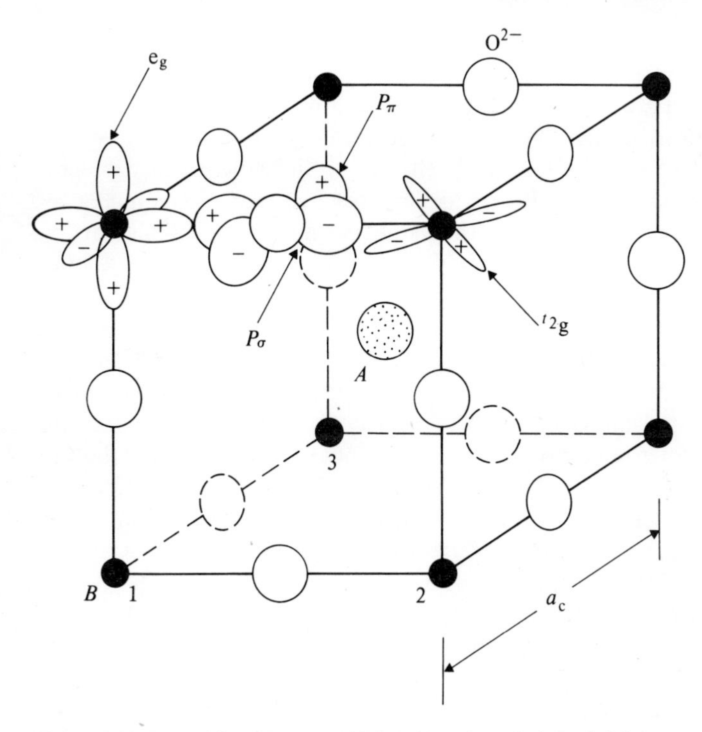

Figure 7-18 Perovskite structure (ABO_3). B cations 1, 2, and 3 have overlap integrals $\Delta^{\pi}_{cac} < \Delta^{\sigma}_{cac}$ (between 1 and 2 or 1 and 3) and an overlap integral Δ_{cc} between 2 and 3.

all the way up to T_N in $Fe_{1.02}S$ (intrinsic ferrous sulfide). We should note here that in Fe_7S_8 ($x = \frac{1}{8}$), the antiferromagnetic superstructure is caused by the ordering of iron vacancies on to every second iron plane.[55] Fe_7S_8 is actually ferrimagnetic, and the slope of the $1/\chi$ versus T plot above 830 K assumes the same value as in FeS.

(*d*) Perovskites The perovskite structure (Fig. 7-18), found in a number of compounds of the formula ABX_3, is ideally suited to the study of 180° cation–anion–cation interactions, since there are no 90° interactions if the A cation is nonmagnetic. The ideal perovskite structure is cubic, but cubic symmetry is rarely encountered. There are usually rhombohedral or orthorhombic distortions, depending on the ionic sizes. The smaller the A cation, the greater is the distortion to orthorhombic symmetry $(a < c/\sqrt{2} < b)$. Such distortions frequently lead to parasitic ferromagnetism superimposed on antiferromagnetism. Spin-orbit effects similar to those in rock salt structure are encountered in perovskites; Jahn–Teller distortions also occur in perovskites.[15] Goodenough and Longo[7] have compiled properties of all known perovskites.

Perovskites like $LaMnO_3$ or $LaCrO_3$ are antiferromagnetic insulators, while those like $SrCrO_3$ are metallic and Pauli-paramagnetic. Metallic conductivity in perovskites is due entirely to the large cation–anion–cation interactions, since the

B cations are separated along the cube face by fairly long distances. Accordingly, ReO_3 (cubic perovskite without the central A ion) is metallic. Several transition metal (B_{ion}) oxides with perovskite structure[29,56] are shown in Fig. 7-19 along with the spins of the B cations. Generally, low-spin states favor collective behavior of *d*-electrons, while high spins favor localized behavior.[57] Since the transfer integral, *b*, would be expected to increase with covalency, we have shown *b* as increasing with valence state of the cation; *b* for the same valence state should vary as $5d > 4d > 3d$. The A cation also affects cation–anion interactions, although indirectly.

Following the arguments of Goodenough,[7,15,29,56] we find that all the perovskites within the dotted line $b_\sigma \approx b_c$ are described by the localized model; compounds with $b_c > b_\pi$ also come under this category. The narrow region $b_m > b_\pi > b_c$ has been established on the basis of electrical, magnetic, and associated properties of the compounds. Thus $LaNiO_3$ ($S = \frac{1}{2}$) is metallic and Pauli-paramagnetic ($b_\pi > b_m$). Similarly, $AMoO_3$ (A = Ba, Sr, Ca) compounds and $SrCrO_3$ in the third column ($S = 1$) are Pauli-paramagnetic and metallic. The other compounds in this column are antiferromagnetic with T_N of 90 K ($CaCrO_3$, $b_m > b_\pi > b_c$), 240 K ($PbCrO_3$); 137 K ($LaVO_3$, $b_c > b_\pi$) and 110 K (YVO_3, $b_c > b_\pi$), the last two corresponding to a localized-electron situation. In $A^{2+}CrO_3$ compounds, a change in the A ion can change the magnetic property from antiferromagnetic to Pauli-paramagnetic. Since A ion interactions are indirect, it would appear that the region $b_m > b_\pi > b_c$ is quite narrow. Because of the narrowness of this region, very few compounds with this behavior are known. Pressure experiments on perovskites are valuable in the study of this region. Thus, $dT_N/dp < 0$ in $CaCrO_3$, while $dT_N/dp > 0$ in $YCrO_3$ and $CaMnO_3$.[57] Since increasing pressure increases b_π (by decreasing lattice dimensions), $dT_N/dp > 0$ for $b_c > b_\pi$ (localized behavior) and $dT_N/dp < 0$ for $b_m > b_\pi > b_c$ (collective behavior). Studies[58] on $Ca_{1-x}Sr_xMnO_3$ show that Sr substitution increases both the lattice parameter and T_N, and the interpretation of the results becomes difficult, unlike the case of the pressure experiments.

In Fig. 7-19, $LaCoO_3$ is shown twice, since the Co^{3+} ion in this compound can have either the low-spin or the high-spin configuration. The compound does indeed show a low-spin–high-spin transition,[23] as discussed earlier. This compound is also unique in the sense that it exhibits localized as well as collective electronic properties depending on the conditions, an aspect that will be discussed later under electrical properties. Substitution of La^{3+} in $LaCoO_3$ by Sr^{2+} gives rise to ferromagnetism and itinerant *d*-electron behavior[59,60] above a critical concentration ($\sim$15 percent) of Sr^{2+} (Co^{4+}–O–Co^{3+} interaction is ferromagnetic while Co^{3+}–O–Co^{3+} interaction is antiferromagnetic). $La_{0.5}Sr_{0.5}CoO_3$ is a metallic ferromagnet with $T_c = 232$ K.

Rare-earth orthoferrites, $LnFeO_3$, which are generally orthorhombic, exhibit parasitic ferromagnetism.[7,15] The important contributions here are: (*a*) Fe^{3+} spins canted in a common direction either by cooperative buckling of oxygen octahedra or by anisotropic superexchange, and (*b*) canting of the antiferromagnetic rare-earth sublattice because of interactions between two sublattices.

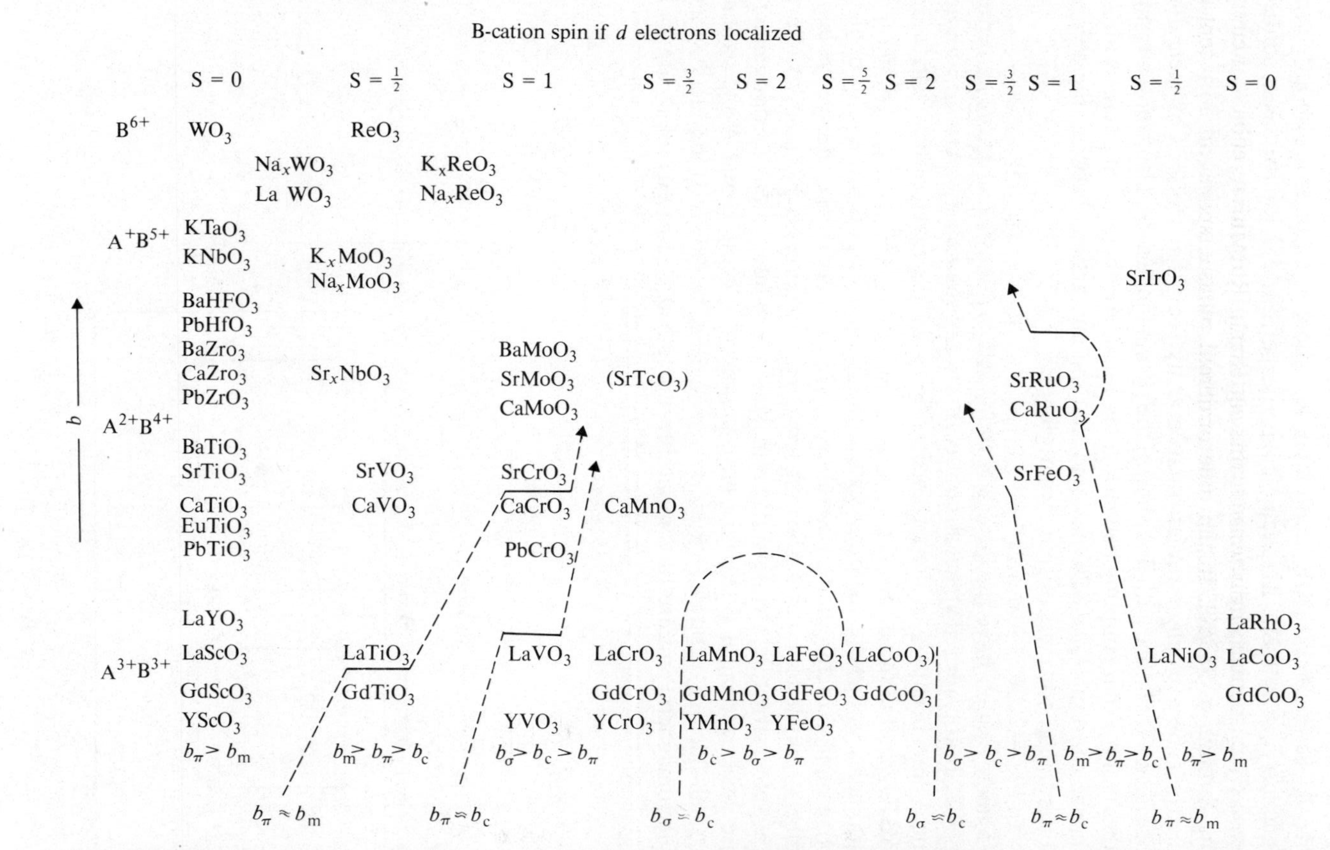

Figure 7-19 Periodic table of perovskite oxides containing transition metal ions in different spin configurations. (*Following Goodenough.*[15])

Fluoride perovskites of the general formula KMF_3 (M = Cr, Mn, Fe, Co, Ni, or Cu) are antiferromagnetic[15,29] with T_N increasing in the series; they are cubic above T_N. Tetragonal K_2NiF_4 containing KF and $KNiF_3$ units is also antiferromagnetic ($T_N = 180$ K). Magnetic properties of $RbMnF_3$ have been studied extensively, particularly by neutron scattering. $RbMnF_3$ retains its cubic symmetry going through T_N (83 K). In the ordered phase, spins on adjacent Mn^{2+} ions along the cube axes align antiferromagnetically such that the ions of each sublattice form a fcc lattice with doubling of the paramagnetic cell. Neutron scattering studies[61] show that coupling between spins was Heisenberg in character with an exchange constant J_1 of 0.29 meV and that the interactions between the second and third-neighbor pairs of spins are negligible.

***(e)* Spinels** Spinels have the general formula AB_2O_4 and the structure shown in Fig. 7-20. In the normal spinel structure, B ions occupy half the octahedral holes while A ions occupy $\frac{1}{4}$ of the tetrahedral holes. In the inverse spinel structure, $B[AB]O_4$, half of the B ions are in tetrahedral holes, and the A ions are in octahedral holes along with the other half of the B ions, the preference of normal or inverse spinel structure being determined by the site preference energies. A large number of magnetic materials showing ferrimagnetism possess the spinel structure. In the spinel structure, strong antiferromagnetic A–B interactions predominate to cause Néel ordering if B-site ions have half-filled e_g orbitals and A-site cations have half-filled t_{2g} orbitals (particularly if A = Fe^{3+}); 90° B–B interactions are antiferromagnetic and are of comparable strength if t_{2g} orbitals (of B) are half-filled or contain one or two electrons. A–A interactions are generally very weak.

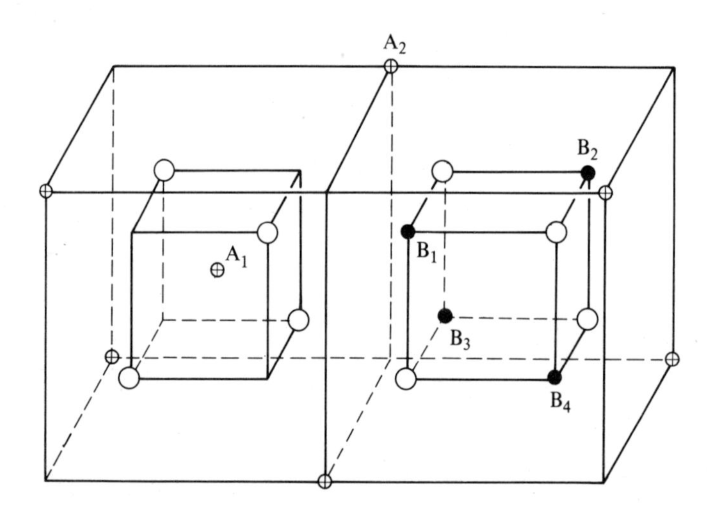

⊕ Tetrahedral sites
● Octahedral sites
○ Anion sites

Figure 7-20 Spinel structure.

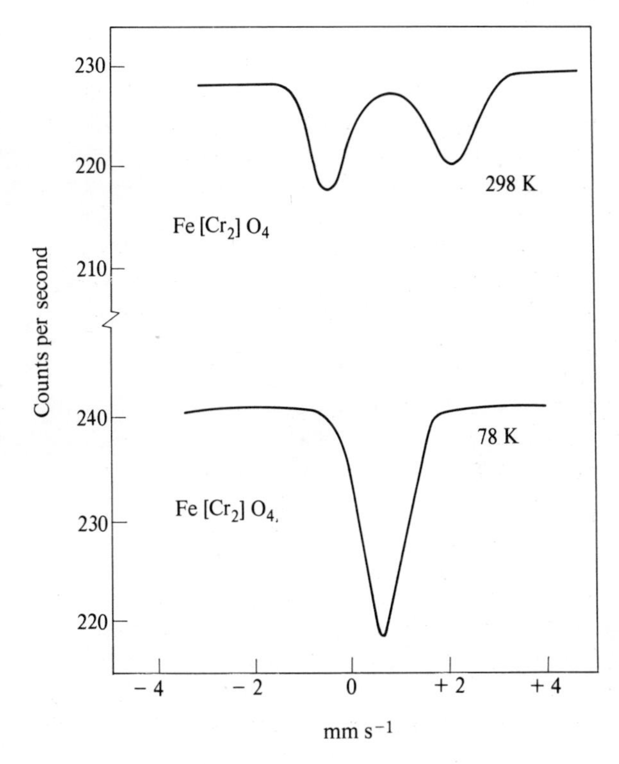

Figure 7-21 ^{57}Fe Mössbauer spectra of $Fe[Cr_2]O_4$ at 298 K and 78 K (experimental points are not shown). Notice the large quadrupole splitting due to tetragonal distortion. (*After Mathur.*[62])

In spinels containing Cu^{2+} or Mn^{3+} ions, Jahn–Teller effect stabilizes a static distortion (to tetragonal, $c/a > 1$), provided that the entropy contribution to the free energy does not stabilize the dynamic Jahn–Teller effect. In spinels like $FeCr_2O_4$, Jahn–Teller distortion with $c/a < 1$ is seen.

In Fig. 7-21, Mössbauer spectra of $FeCr_2O_4$ ($T_c = 90$ K) are shown at temperatures above and below the cubic–tetragonal transformation temperature.[62] The tetragonal distortion increases with decrease in temperature, and the magnitude of quadrupole splitting is determined by the distortion. The Mössbauer spectrum of cubic $Ge[Fe_2]O_4$ shows a large quadrupole splitting due to the presence of a trigonal field at the B site of nominal cubic symmetry;[62] quadrupole splitting in $Zn[Fe_2]O_4$ is, however, much smaller. Thus, the presence of an electric field gradient due to loss of cubic symmetry is nicely seen in the Mössbauer spectra.[62] Other techniques generally employed to study tetragonal distortions are x-ray crystallography and electronic spectroscopy. The tetragonal–cubic transition temperature in $Zn_xGe_{1-x}[Co^{2+}_{2-2x}Mn^{3+}_{2x}]O_4$ is shown as a function of x (Mn^{3+} concentration) in Fig. 7-22.[63] The transition is abrupt. This fact, along with the site preference energies, can be used to determine the oxidation states in the system. Cubic–tetragonal transitions in several spinel systems have been discussed by Goodenough[15] and Mathur.[62]

Magnetic ordering in spinels can be readily studied by Mössbauer spectro-

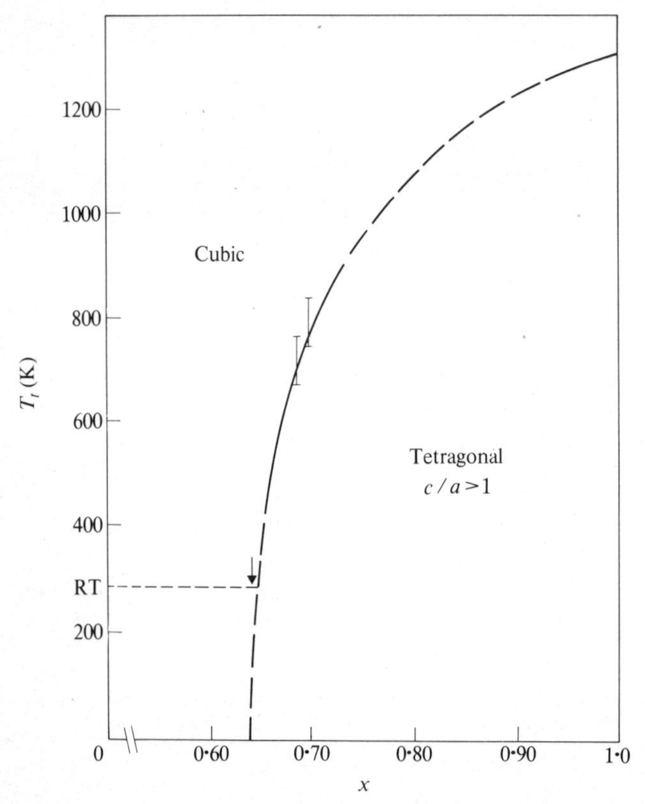

Figure 7-22 Cubic⇌tetragonal transition temperature, T_t, as a function of x in $Zn_xGe_{1-x}[Co_{2-2x}Mn_{2x}]O_4$; $c/a > 1$. (*After Wickham and Croft.*[63])

scopy. In Fig. 7-23, Mössbauer spectra of $Fe[CrNi]O_4$ ($T_c = 598$ K) are given at three temperatures. The paramagnetic spectrum at 688 K shows only a small quadrupole splitting. The low-temperature spectrum shows hyperfine structure characteristic of the ferrimagnetic state. Similar spectra are also shown by $NiFe_2O_4$, $CoFe_2O_4$, $MnFe_2O_4$, and $MgFe_2O_4$. In Fig. 7-24, the count rate is plotted against temperature to illustrate the change at T_c. A plot of the internal field against temperature shows a sharp drop to zero at T_c (just as in Fig. 7-12). In cubic spinels with only nearest-neighbor A–B and B–B interactions, the spiral configuration becomes the ground state.[17] Detailed studies on ferrimagnetic $CoCr_2O_4$ indeed establish the conical spiral configuration to be stable.

Fe_3O_4 (magnetite) is an inverse spinel with the cation distribution $Fe^{3+}[Fe^{2+}Fe^{3+}]O_4$, where the octahedral sites are occupied by both Fe^{2+} and Fe^{3+} ions. It is ferrimagnetic, with $T_c = 860$ K. At 120 K, Fe_3O_4 undergoes a cubic–orthorhombic transition which is accompanied by a sharp change in resistivity[64] (Fig. 7-25) and a specific heat anomaly. Verwey[65] proposed that above 120 K (T_t), there was rapid exchange between Fe^{2+} and Fe^{3+} (at B sites)

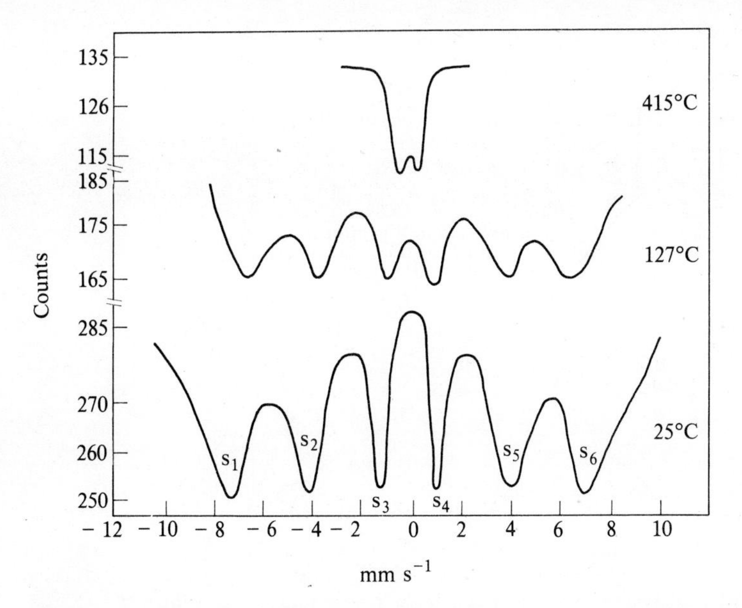

Figure 7-23 ^{57}Fe Mössbauer spectra of $Fe^{3+}Cr^{3+}Ni^{2+}O_4$ at different temperatures (experimental points are not shown). (*After Mathur.*[62])

while below this temperature they were ordered in the orthorhombic phase. This so-called Verwey transition has been investigated by neutron diffraction.[66] Spin waves in Fe_3O_4 have been investigated by neutron inelastic scattering[67] and the magnons disappear at 1.11 T_c. Mössbauer studies have been useful in understanding the nature of the Verwey transition. If the electron exchange between Fe^{2+}

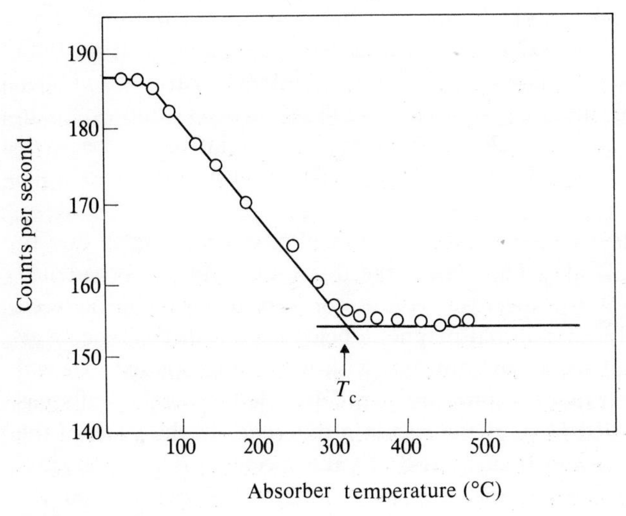

Figure 7-24 Plot of count rate against temperature of $Fe[CrNi]O_4$ absorber. (*After Mathur.*[62]) Notice the break at T_c.

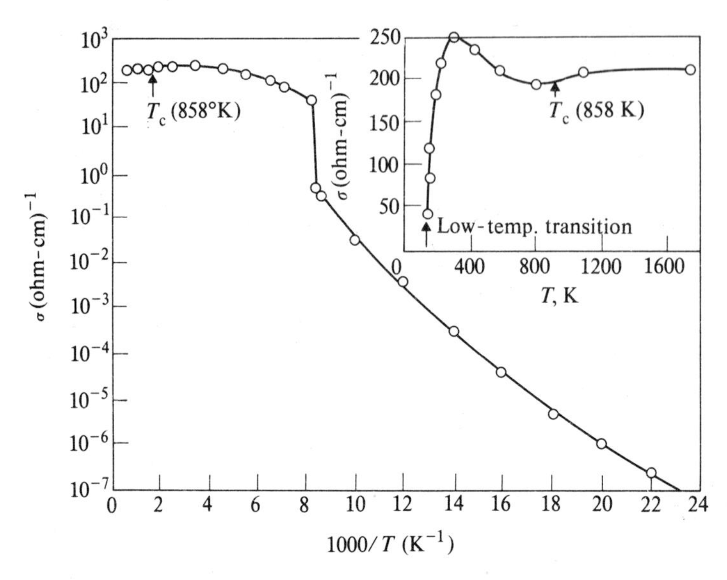

Figure 7-25 Conductivity behavior of Fe_3O_4 as a function of temperature. (*After Miles et al.*[64])

and Fe^{3+} (B sites) is fast above T_t and if the exchange frequency is larger than the Larmor frequency, the Mössbauer spectrum should show an effective magnetic field which is an average of the Fe^{3+} and Fe^{2+} ions besides the hyperfine split spectrum (with a different effective field) due to the Fe^{3+} ions at the A sites. The ratio of the absorption intensities for the two sites should be 2 to 1, corresponding to the actual ratio of the ions on each site. Below the transition temperature, if the Fe^{3+} and Fe^{2+} ions are separately ordered, three sets of effective magnetic fields will be observed (corresponding to Fe^{3+} and Fe^{2+} ions at B sites and Fe^{3+} ions at the A sites). Above T_t, as expected, the Mössbauer spectrum of Fe_3O_4 (Fig. 7-26) consists of two superimposed six-line spectra[68] with an intensity ratio of 2 : 1. The Mössbauer parameters of the two spectra at 296 K are as follows:[69] (*a*) $H = +(491.8 \pm 0.5)$ kOe, $\delta = +(0.266 \pm 0.10)$ mm s^{-1} relative to Fe, and $\Delta E_q = \sim 0$; (*b*) $H = -(460.7 \pm 0.5)$ kOe, $\delta = +(0.667 \pm 0.010)$ mm s^{-1} relative to Fe, and $\Delta E_q = \sim 0$.

These observations clearly show that the more intense spectrum is due to Fe^{2+} and Fe^{3+} ions at the B sites. The lines of the B-site spectrum are broadened relative to the less intense A-site spectrum because of electron hopping between the Fe^{3+} and Fe^{2+} ions. In an external magnetic field, the tetrahedral spectrum expands and the octahedral spectrum contracts with increasing applied external field, indicating that the tetrahedral spins are parallel while the octahedral spins are antiparallel to the applied field, giving rise to a difference in the signs of the effective magnetic fields at A and B sites. At 83 K, the spectrum is complex, and the two hyperfine spectra due to Fe^{3+} and Fe^{2+} ions at the B sites and the spectrum due to Fe^{3+} ions at the A sites cannot be completely resolved, indicating that Verwey ordering is by no means complete at this temperature. Each of the observed B-spectrum lines in Fig. 7-26, is an average of the corresponding components of the Fe^{3+} and Fe^{2+} spectra. The broadening of the composite B-spectrum lines due to electron exchange depends on the relaxation time and on the exact position of the magnetic hyperfine-split lines of the two spectra due to Fe^{3+} and Fe^{2+}. From the observed broadening of the B-spectrum lines and the estimated positions of the magnetic hyperfine-split components due to Fe^{3+} and Fe^{2+} ions at the B site, the relaxation time for various lines is found to be 1.1 ± 0.2 ns at room temperature.[69]

The examples cited above clearly show how Mössbauer spectroscopy is effective in examining magnetic transitions in spinels. Rare-earth iron garnets are similarly studied by Mössbauer spectroscopy,[62] where the technique has the added

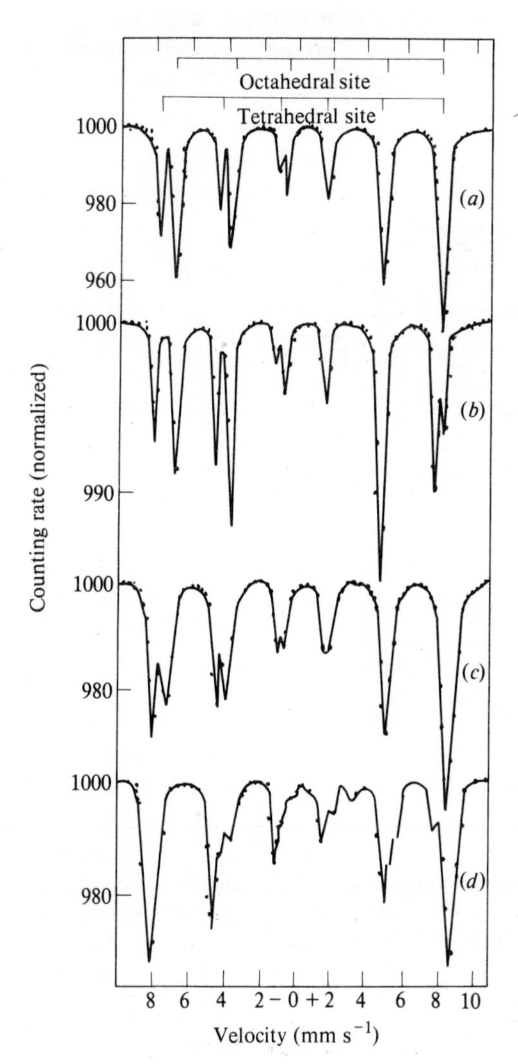

Figure 7-26 Mössbauer spectra of magnetite at 296 K (*a*, *b*), 120 K (*c*) and 83 K (*d*). Spectrum (*b*) shows how the line to the extreme right is resolved in an external magnetic field. The absence of complete resolution below T_t shows that Verwey ordering is incomplete. (*After Kundig et al.*[68])

advantage of providing information on rare-earth–iron exchange interactions if the rare-earth ion is chosen to have Mössbauer nuclei. Magnetic transitions in spinels have been extensively studied and the transition temperatures tabulated by Goodenough[15] and Connolly and Copenhaver.[70] For commercial application, ferrite spinels should have high permeability. The permeability is maximum at the Curie temperature, and it is therefore best if the material has a T_c close to the operational temperature (which is generally room temperature).

7-3 ELECTRICAL PROPERTIES

Solids can be classified on the basis of their electrical properties. If the overlap between orbitals in the valence shells of the constituent atoms is large, bands are formed. Band schemes for different types of solids[71] are schematically shown in Fig. 7-27. If the orbital overlap is very small, the charge carriers are localized

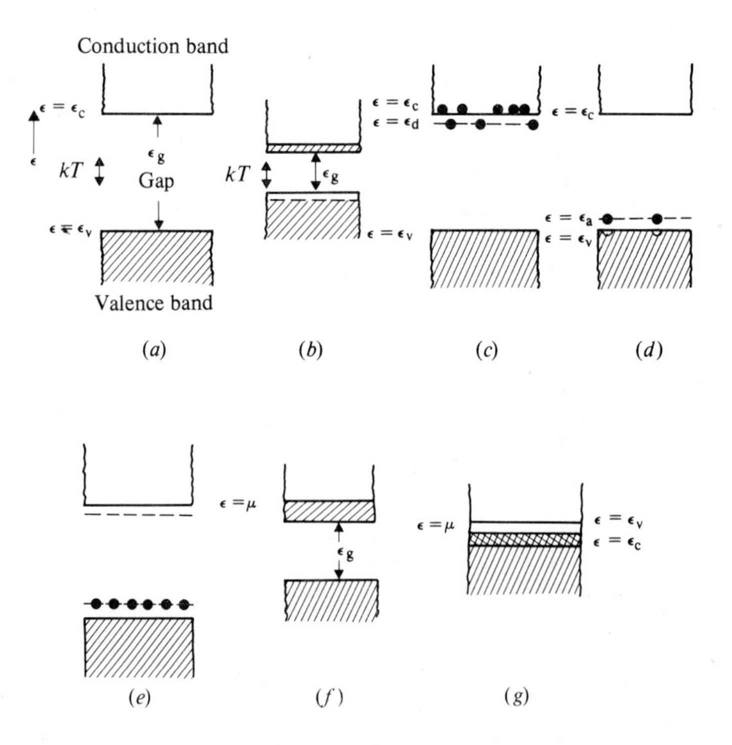

Figure 7-27 Schematic band structures of solids. (*a*) Insulator ($kT \ll \varepsilon_g$); all band states below $\varepsilon = \varepsilon_v$ are occupied and all others are empty. (*b*) Intrinsic semiconductor (kT comparable to ε_g); electrons are thermally promoted from the top of the valence to the bottom of the conduction band. (*c*) and (*d*) Extrinsic semiconductors; impurity levels lie within the gap; $kT \ll \varepsilon_g$, but comparable to $\varepsilon_c - \varepsilon_d$ or $\varepsilon_a - \varepsilon_v$, where ε_d is the ionization energy of the donor impurity (e.g., As in Ge) and ε_a is the ionization energy of the hole due to the acceptor impurity (e.g., Ga in Ge). (*e*) Compensated semiconductor. (*f*) Metal; one band is partially (though extensively) filled with electrons. (*g*) Semimetal; top of the valence band lies above the bottom of the conduction band.

about the atomic centers. A jump of an electron from one atomic site to another can occur if the latter is empty and if the electron acquires the activation energy necessary for diffusive type of motion. Materials where electron transport occurs through such an activated process are called hopping materials or hoppers. There is a third class of narrow-band materials where there is considerable interaction between the charge carriers and the lattice. Here, electrons are neither free nor completely bound. If electronic movement is slightly impeded by weak interactions with the lattice, the interaction is described as a large polaron. Such an interaction causes a small lattice polarization about the electron, and there will be an increase in the apparent effective mass of the electron (relative to the free electron mass). If electron–lattice interaction is strong, we shall have the small-polaron situation involving a strongly deformed lattice about the charge carrier. At low temperatures, small polarons show band-like behavior. With increase in temperature, the band narrows down to the localized limit (as in hoppers).

Besides the different kinds of electronic materials discussed above, there is an important class of materials which show reversible transitions from semiconducting state to metallic state. Such transitions were first discovered by Morin[72] in some oxides of titanium and vanadium. There has been intense activity in the study of semiconductor–metal transitions in recent years, and several oxides and sulfides are now known to exhibit this phenomenon. These transitions are generally accompanied by structural, magnetic, and other changes in the solids and we shall discuss them at some length in this section. Some of the semiconducting and metallic materials become superconducting at very low temperatures. In Table 7-2 we list examples of oxides and sulfides exhibiting different kinds of electronic properties.

Table 7-2 Examples of different types of inorganic electronic materials

Metals	
3*d*-compounds:	TiO, CrO_2, TiS, CoS_2, CuS_2
4*d*-compounds:	NbO, RuO_2
5*d*-compounds:	ReO_3
Semiconductors	
3*d*-compounds:	NiO, CoO, MnO, FeO, Fe_2O_3, Cr_2O_3
	MnS, MnS_2, FeS_2
*Semiconductor–metal transitions**	
3*d*-compounds:	V_2O_3, VO_2, V_3O_5, V_4O_7, V_6O_{13}
	Ti_2O_3, Ti_3O_5
	NiS, CrS, FeS
4*d*-compounds:	NbO_2
4*f*-compounds:	EuO, SmS, $SmTe$
Superconducting transitions	
TiO, NbO, NbS_2, MoS_2	

* These are thermal transitions in all cases except in the 4*f*-compounds where it is by application of pressure.

The above discussion was restricted to electronic materials. Ionic solids like NaCl and AgCl which are electronic insulators conduct electricity through ionic movements. Vacancies (as in NaCl) and interstitial ions (as in AgCl) provide the means of ionic movement in these solids.

Common Electron Transport Properties

We shall briefly discuss some of the common transport phenomena in solids. In doing so, we shall give the important relations employed to interpret transport properties.

(*a*) Electrical conductivity In an ideal solid, the free carriers subjected to an external electric field are accelerated without any interruption. Lattice vibrations (phonons) and other imperfections in the crystal, however, produce some electrical resistance because of scattering of charge carriers. The drift velocity, $\mathbf{v}_d$, of the charge carriers is given by

$$\mathbf{v}_d = \frac{-e\mathbf{E}\tau}{m} = -u_d\mathbf{E}$$

where $-e\mathbf{E}$ is the electric field, τ the relaxation time, m the mass, and u_d the drift mobility. The conductivity is given by

$$\sigma = \frac{ne^2 l}{mv}$$

where l is the mean free path and v the total velocity. For extrinsic semiconductors where the bands are only slightly filled, the average kinetic energy ($\frac{1}{2}mv^2$) is equal to $\frac{3}{2}kT$, and

$$\sigma = \frac{ne^2 l}{(3mkT)^{1/2}}$$

Applying appropriate statistics and assuming that the main scattering is due to phonons, the above equation becomes

$$\sigma = \frac{ne^2 l}{(9\pi mkT/8)^{1/2}}$$

For metals, this equation reduces to

$$\sigma = \left(\frac{8\pi}{3n}\right)^{1/3}\left(\frac{ne^2 l}{m}\right)$$

In the case of semiconductors doped with donors and acceptors, the following equation is applicable in the low-temperature region ($kT \ll \varepsilon_g$):

$$\sigma = \frac{4\sqrt{2g_n(N_d - N_a)}}{3h^{3/2}}\left[le^2(2\pi m_n kT)^{1/4}\, e^{-\varepsilon_d/2kT}\right]$$

Here, g_n is the statistical weight factor, and N_d and N_a are the number of donors and acceptors per unit volume. According to the above equation, $\sigma \sim \exp(-\varepsilon_d/2kT)$, since $T^{1/4}$ has little effect. A plot for $\ln \sigma$ against $1/T$ should yield a straight line with a slope proportional to ε_d. In the high-temperature limit ($kT \approx \varepsilon_g$),

$$\sigma = 2eu_p(b+1)[2\pi(m_n m_p)^{1/2}kT/h^2]^{3/2}\, e^{-\varepsilon_g/kT}$$

where $b = u_n/u_p$ and u stands for mobility. Since the pre-exponential factor is not very sensitive to temperature, a plot of $\ln \sigma$ versus $1/T$ should yield a straight line with a slope proportional to ε_g. In the intermediate temperature region, the extrinsic region gradually goes over to the intrinsic region and the conductivity varies with T, as u_n does (exhaustion region):

$$\sigma = (N_d - N_a)beu_p = (N_d - N_a)eu_n$$

In hoppers, the conductivity follows the diffusion law,

$$\sigma = \frac{e^2 a_n D}{kT}$$

where a_n is the activity of the charge carrier and D the diffusion coefficient. After suitable substitution, the above equation reduces to

$$\sigma = K\left[\frac{\theta(1-\theta)e^2 v^{\pm}}{kT}\right] e^{-\Delta G^{\pm}/kT}$$

where K is a collection of constants, θ is the fraction of occupied sites, $v^{\pm}$ the pre-exponential factor in the rate process, and $\Delta G^{\pm}$ the free energy of activation for hopping. If the concentration of charge carriers is constant (as for a fixed composition, e.g., Pr_6O_{11} or Fe_3O_4), $\log(\sigma T)$ is proportional to $1/T$, and the slope gives the activation energy for conduction. If $\theta = 0$ or unity, $\sigma \to 0$ and the material becomes an insulator (as for "stoichiometric" composition). If $\theta = \frac{1}{2}$, σ will be a maximum.

In ionic crystals, the conductivity is due mainly to the migration of vacancies or interstitials. In the $\log \sigma T$ versus $1/T$ plots of alkali halides where vacancy migration is the predominant mechanism, three nearly linear regions are generally seen: (i) the intrinsic region between ~700 K and the melting point governed by the formation of Schottky defects and migration of cation and anion vacancies, the latter near the melting point; (ii) the extrinsic region between ~550 and ~700 K due to migration of cation vacancies; and (iii) the association region between ~400 and ~550 K representing association of impurities with oppositely charged vacancies and cation vacancy migration. From the slopes of the linear regions, energies associated with various processes can be readily estimated. Thus, $E_I = E_m^c + E_s/2$, $E_{II} = E_m^c$, and $E_{III} = E_m^c + E_a/2$, where E_s is the energy of formation of a Schottky pair, E_m^c is the cation migration energy, and E_a is the association energy between the impurity and an oppositely charged vacancy. Unlike in alkali halides, in silver halides interstitial cation migration is the dominant mechanism of conduction.

Electrical conductivity of solids is generally measured with two- or four-probe methods. The four-probe method is preferable, since the two-probe method suffers from uncertainties due to contact resistance and grain boundary effects. Single crystals are ideal for measurement of conductivity, although pressed pellets with the four-probe method do give reasonable results in ceramic materials.

(*b*) Thermoelectric power The thermoelectric effect is due to the gradient in the electrochemical potential caused by a temperature gradient in a conducting material. The Seebeck coefficient, α, defined as $(\Delta V/\Delta T)$ as $\Delta T \to 0$ where ΔV is the emf, is a very useful quantity and is related to the entropy transported per particle ($\alpha = -S^*/e$). In extrinsic semiconductors, the Seebeck coefficient for electrons is given by

$$\alpha_{\mathrm{n}} = -\frac{k}{e}[2 - \mu_{\mathrm{c}}/kT]$$

For holes, the corresponding expression is

$$\alpha_{\mathrm{p}} = +\frac{k}{e}[2 - \mu_{v}/kT]$$

We see that the sign of α is positive for hole conduction and negative for electron conduction. For metals,

$$\alpha = \frac{\pi^2}{3}\left(\frac{k^2 T}{e}\right)\left(\frac{1}{\mu_0}\right)$$

and α increases with T, unlike in the case of semiconductors. For hoppers, α is given by

$$\alpha = -\frac{k}{e}\left[\ln\left(\frac{1-\theta}{\theta}\right) + \frac{S_T^*}{k}\right]$$

α is large and negative for $\theta = 0$ and large and positive for $\theta = 1$. α changes sign as θ varies from 0 to 1. Further, α is roughly independent of T. Measurement of α can be carried out on single crystals or ceramic samples.

(*c*) Hall effect The Hall coefficient R_{H} is given by the expression

$$R_{\mathrm{H}} = \frac{A}{Zen}$$

where Zen gives the charge carrier density (with the appropriate sign for the charge carriers) and A is a constant depending on whether the material is a semiconductor or a metal. If both σ and R_{H} are known, then the product

$$\sigma R_{\mathrm{H}} = neu_{\mathrm{d}}(A/ne) = Au_{\mathrm{d}}$$

is a measure of the drift mobility.

(*d*) Other transport properties The thermal conductivity of semiconductors is described by the Wiedemann–Franz law,

$$\kappa_e = 2\left[\frac{k^2}{e^2}T\right]\sigma$$

For metals, the proper expression would be

$$\kappa_e = \frac{\pi^2}{3}\left[\frac{k^2}{e^2}T\right]\sigma$$

Since κ_e is proportional to σ, in hoppers κ_e is generally small due to their low electronic conductivity. The Ettingshausen effect and the Righi–Leduc effect are other important techniques employed in characterizing electrical properties of solids.

Theoretical Models

(*a*) Band model As mentioned earlier, there are two limiting descriptions of the atomic outer electrons in solids: the band theory, and the localized-electron theory or ligand-field theory. When there is appreciable overlap between the outer electron orbitals of atoms, the band theory of Bloch and Wilson[73] would be applicable. Where both the size and the electronegativity of the anion and the cation are considerably different, as in the case of the transition metal oxides, the outer *s* and *p*-orbitals form a filled valence band and an empty conduction band separated by a large energy gap (~5 to 10 eV in oxides). The only states that are in the vicinity of the Fermi level would be those in the *d*-band. The *d*-band would be narrow (compared to that in metals) if the metal ions are farther apart.

Let us consider the monoxides of 3*d* transition metals. The oxides TiO to NiO are all cubic with the rock salt structure (see Fig. 7-4*d*). The octahedral crystal field of the anions O^{2-} in these oxides splits the fivefold-degenerate 3*d* band into a lower threefold-degenerate (t_{2g}) sub-band and a twofold-degenerate (e_g) upper band. Although the crystal field splitting is large, a real gap in the density of states will occur only if the bandwidth is of the order of the splitting or smaller. Since the 3*d* band is sufficiently narrow, we would expect an energy gap to exist. In TiO and NbO, there are two and three *d*-electrons respectively and the lower t_{2g} sub-band is only partially filled. From the Bloch–Wilson theory of metals, we know that materials whose bands are either completely filled or completely empty are usually insulators, while materials with partially filled bands should be metallic. Thus we expect TiO and NbO to be metals, as indeed found experimentally. Chromium monoxide, CrO, is unknown; the next 3*d* oxide, MnO, has five *d*-electrons and the *d*-band is still not completely filled. Contrary to expectations, this oxide is not metallic. Stoichiometric MnO is one of the best insulators known, and it is antiferromagnetic; MnO continues to have very low conductivity even up to very high temperatures. According to this model, only FeO with six *d*-electrons (with completely filled lower *d* sub-band) should be an insulator or semiconductor while CoO and NiO should both be metals. Experimentally it is known that the last two oxides are antiferromagnetic semiconductors.

Let us now consider a series of sesquioxides of $3d$ transition metals. Kleiner[74] has shown by a symmetry analysis that the sesquioxides of corundum structure with 1, 3, 5, 7, and 9 d-electrons per cation can, in principle, be insulators; the electrical properties of Ti_2O_3 ($3d^1$), Cr_2O_3 ($3d^3$) and Fe_2O_3 ($3d^5$) do conform to this prediction of the band model; Ti_2O_3 shows metallic conductivity above ~500 K. Also, according to this model, V_2O_3 ($3d^2$), Mn_2O_3 ($3d^4$) and Co_2O_3 ($3d^6$), if they existed with corundum symmetry, would most likely be metallic. In reality, however, only V_2O_3 occurs in the corundum structure (above ~150 K) and this phase of V_2O_3 is metallic.

Invoking the antiferromagnetic nature of some of the oxides, it is possible to account for their insulating behavior at $T = 0$. The magnetic order leads to a doubling of the size of the primitive cell and consequently an exchange splitting of all the bands. This may be valid for NiO and MnO but not for CoO, and to explain the insulating behavior of this last oxide we have to assume that the spontaneous crystallographic distortion to a low symmetry at low temperatures (below the Néel temperature, T_N) introduces an energy gap. However, the finite temperature behavior is not explained, since the compounds should show metallic conductivity at temperatures higher than T_N (NiO, MnO, and CoO are semiconducting at all temperatures). Elementary band theory does not account even for the qualitative features of the electrical properties of oxides which behave as insulators or semiconductors. The reason for this failure is the neglect of electron correlations inherent in the one-electron approach. As pointed out earlier, insulating ground-state behavior at absolute zero can be predicted from band theory by invoking either crystal distortions or antiferromagnetism for the particular material. Band theory, modified by considering electron correlations and electron–phonon interactions, would also predict low-temperature insulating behavior of some of these oxides. The only cases where simple band-structure models give right answers are in the case of highly conducting oxides like TiO. The status of our understanding of oxides and sulfides exhibiting semiconductor–metal transitions has been in a constant state flux, as discussed later.

(*b*) Localized model The localized model or the ligand-field approach is essentially the same as the Heitler–London approach for the hydrogen molecule, and assumes that the crystal consists of an assembly of fixed and independent ions at their lattice positions and that the overlap of the electronic orbitals is very small. When the cation–cation orbital overlap is small, the two important factors that favor the localized behavior of d-electrons are (i) intraatomic exchange or Hund's-rule splitting of different spin states (discussed by Goodenough[15,75] in connection with the transition metal oxide compounds), and (ii) electron–phonon interactions leading to Landau trapping.[76] This will increase the relaxation time of a charge carrier from about 10^{-15} s in an ordinary metal to times of the order of the lattice frequency in polar crystals (~10^{-12} s).

This model has the immediate advantage that it predicts the ground state to be an insulator. At finite temperatures, however, electron–phonon and electron–electron interactions become important especially when the bands are narrow, just as in the case of the *d*-bands. Much work has been carried out on the effect of electron–phonon interactions on the transport properties of oxide materials.[77] The strength of the electron–phonon interaction can be estimated from Frohlich's coupling constant. If the interaction is sufficiently large, electrons will move through the lattice along with the associated polarization; the mobility will be very low and the problem can be treated in the formalism of the classical diffusion theory. Electrical conductivity in these polaron models occurs when, in the course of a thermal fluctuation, a site with a self-trapped electron attains a configuration equivalent to a neighboring unoccupied site, and electron transfer can take place between these two sites. In the presence of an electric field this can be looked at as a preferential diffusion of electrons through the crystal, and a net current results. Such uncorrelated "hopping" of polarons is most favorably encountered in compounds having the same cation in two or more different valence states (e.g., Fe_3O_4, PrO_x, TbO_x).

(*c*) Goodenough's approach The approach of Goodenough to explain properties of transition metal oxides and related materials is essentially based on principles of chemical bonding. With empirically derived criteria for the overlap of cation–cation and cation–anion–cation orbitals as determined by the crystal structures, Goodenough[15,28,29,75] has attempted to provide a unified understanding of the magnetic and electrical properties of a variety of inorganic materials including the simple oxides of transition metals, mixed oxides of perovskite, spinel, and bronze structures and metal sulfides. Goodenough's approach is qualitative but appeals to chemical intuition. Since the model can describe the gross features of many properties of metal oxides and related materials, we shall examine this model at some length.

Goodenough considers the cation–cation and cation–anion–cation interactions in transition metal compounds to be of importance in describing the behavior of electrons, whether they are localized or collective; the property of the Fermi surface distinguishes between these two extrema of behavior.

The Pauli exclusion principle, which prevents any two electrons of the same system from having identical quantum numbers, forces Fermi statistics on the collective electron gas of a partially filled band. This introduces a discontinuity (at the Fermi energy at $T = 0$ K) in electron population versus energy; this population discontinuity is called the Fermi surface. Since electrons that are localized at different atomic positions are distinguishable, the Pauli exclusion principle applies only within each atom and there is no Fermi surface. Any physical property that depends on the existence of a Fermi surface can distinguish collective electrons from localized electrons. Unfortunately, many Fermi-surface-dependent properties such as superconductivity, de Haas–van Alphen effect, and cyclotron resonance are suppressed if the bands are narrow. Useful criteria for the characterization of materials with narrow d-bands are optical reflectance and spontaneous crystallographic distortions (to a lower symmetry at the collective-electron–localized-electron transition).

Let us start with the localized model for the d-electrons in transition metal oxides and see how ligand-field (LF) theory breaks down, depending on the overlap of orbitals, before we attain the band model. According to LF theory, if the transition metal ion is octahedrally coordinated by anions, the five d-orbitals of the metal ion are split into a fourfold-degenerate (including spin) group of e_g symmetry which is directed toward near-neighbor cations (see Figs. 7-4d and 7-18). The orbitals of e_g symmetry are orthogonal to the anionic p_π-orbitals and are therefore modified by covalent mixing with the anionic s and p-orbitals. Orbitals of t_{2g} symmetry, on the other hand, are orthogonal to the anionic s and p-orbitals and are only modified by covalent mixing with the cationic orbitals and the anionic p_π-orbitals. If λ_σ, λ_π represent the covalent mixing parameters and f_e and f_t the atomic orbitals of e_g and t_{2g} symmetry respectively, then the respective wave functions become

$$\Psi_{\mathrm{c}} = N_\sigma(f_e + \lambda_\sigma \phi_\sigma)$$

$$\Psi_{\mathrm{t}} = N_\pi(f_t + \lambda_\pi \phi_\pi + \lambda_{\mathrm{c}} \phi_{\mathrm{c}})$$

where N_σ, N_π are the normalization constants. Here, ϕ_σ, ϕ_π, and ϕ_{c} contain the anionic or near-neighbor cationic s and p-orbitals that are mixed through covalence.

The orbitals in the above equation satisfy the general crystal hamiltonian which consists of terms due to one-ion energies, the many-atom energies being treated as a small perturbation. However, the perturbation energy increases sensitively with the overlap integral and at some critical overlap integral, Δ_{c}, there is a sharp breakdown of the perturbation expression on which the LF theory rests. Thus, whether the d-electrons are localized or collective depends on the magnitude of the overlap or the overlap integrals for d-orbitals on neighboring cations. Four overlap integrals must then be considered:

$$\Delta_{\mathrm{cc}} = |(\Psi_{t1}, \Psi_{t2})| = N_\pi^2[(f_{t1}, f_{t2}) + \lambda_{\mathrm{c}}(\phi_{\mathrm{c}1}, \phi_{\mathrm{c}2})]$$

$$\Delta_{\mathrm{cac}}^\sigma = |(\Psi_{e1}, \Psi_{e3})| = N_\sigma^2 \lambda_\sigma^2$$

$$\Delta_{\mathrm{cac}}^\pi = |(\Psi_{t1}, \Psi_{t3})| = N_\pi^2[\lambda_\pi^2 + \lambda_{\mathrm{c}}^2 + 2\lambda_\pi(f_t, \phi_\pi) + 2\lambda_{\mathrm{c}}(f_t, \phi_{\mathrm{c}})]$$

$$\Delta_{\mathrm{cac}}^{\pi\sigma} = |(\Psi_{t1}, \Psi_{e2})| = N_\pi N_\sigma[\lambda_\pi \lambda_{\mathrm{c}} + \lambda_\sigma \lambda_{\mathrm{c}}(\phi_\sigma, \phi_{\mathrm{c}})]$$

The first of these represents a cation overlap integral, to be distinguished from the last three, which represent cation–anion–cation overlap integrals.

Since $\Delta_{\mathrm{cac}}^\pi < \Delta_{\mathrm{cac}}^{\pi\sigma} < \Delta_{\mathrm{cac}}^\sigma$, the following classification of transition metal compounds can be made: (i) Compounds where LF theory is applicable have $\Delta_{\mathrm{cac}}^\pi < \Delta_{\mathrm{cac}}^\sigma < \Delta_{\mathrm{c}}$ and $\Delta_{\mathrm{cc}} < \Delta_{\mathrm{c}}'$. (ii) Primarily ionic compounds have $\Delta_{\mathrm{cac}}^\pi < \Delta_{\mathrm{c}} < \Delta_{\mathrm{cac}}^\sigma$ and $\Delta_{\mathrm{cc}} > \Delta_{\mathrm{c}}'$. Here, each d-electron is shared collectively by the array of like cations and the collective-electron energy band is referred to as the cation sublattice d-band (class 1 metallic compounds). (iii) Class 2a metallic compounds have

$\Delta_{cac}^{\pi} < \Delta_c < \Delta_{cac}^{\sigma}$ and $\Delta_{cc} < \Delta_c'$. (iv) Class 2*b* metallic compounds have $\Delta_c < \Delta_{cac}^{\pi} < \Delta_{cac}^{\sigma}$ and $\Delta_{cc} < \Delta_c'$. (v) Metallic compounds that are simultaneously class 1 and class 2 have $\Delta_c < \Delta_{cac}^{\pi} < \Delta_{cac}^{\sigma}$ and $\Delta_{cc} > \Delta_c'$. This classification is helpful where the outer *s* and *p*-bands are split into a filled valence and an empty conduction band, as in oxides. In compounds having a valence band that overlaps the *d*-bands, metallic conductivity is also due to partially filled *s* and *p*-bands.

Since the overlap integral Δ_{cc} is sensitive to the interatomic separation R, we may define a critical cation–cation separation R_c, such that $\Delta_{cc} < \Delta_c'$ if $R > R_c$ and $\Delta_{cc} > \Delta_c'$ if $R < R_c$, neglecting for the present the cation–anion–cation interactions. By a consideration of the physical properties of 3*d* oxides, Goodenough has arrived at the following semiempirical expression for R_c:

$$R_{c(\text{oxides})}^{3d} = 3.20 - 0.05m - 0.03(Z - Z_{\text{Ti}}) - 0.04S_i(S_i + 1)\ \text{Å}$$

where m is the formal charge on the cation and Z its atomic number, and $S_i(\neq 0)$ is the net atomic spin for localized *d*-electrons of α or β spin. Since the radial extension of the 4*d* and 5*d*-orbitals is larger than that of 3*d*-orbitals, it follows that

$$R_c^{5d} > R_c^{4d} > R_c^{3d}$$

Goodenough also defines the critical covalent-mixing parameter and arrives at the following conclusions: (*a*) λ increases with m; (*b*) for a given m, the minimum occurs where S is a maximum; and (*c*) $\Delta_{cac}^{\pi} < \Delta_{cac}^{\sigma}$. Goodenough has also shown that Δ_c and R_c are sharply defined so that localized and band descriptions correspond to two different electronic phases. Some aspects of Goodenough's approach were discussed earlier (see Sec. 7-2).

Mott Transitions

Wigner[78] first introduced the idea of electron–electron interactions and suggested that at low densities a free electron gas should "crystallize" to a nonconductive state. Mott[79] suggested that an insulating state can be obtained in materials where all the *d*-bands in the vicinity of the Fermi level are extremely narrow. If the total reduction in kinetic energy does not overcome the total increase in the potential energy due to the additional Coulomb repulsion between electrons in the ionized states of a partially filled band, then the ground state of the system should be nonconducting. In his later papers, Mott[80] has proposed that if an electron is removed from the vicinity of one atom and placed on another atom in the above type of insulator, the free hole and the free electron would attract each other by a Coulomb interaction and form a bound state or "exciton," allowing neither hole nor electron to participate in electrical conduction. However, if many carriers are present, an electron and a hole will attract via a screened Coulomb interaction with a screening constant. At higher values of the screening constant, the interaction becomes too weak to have bound-state solutions, and a sharp

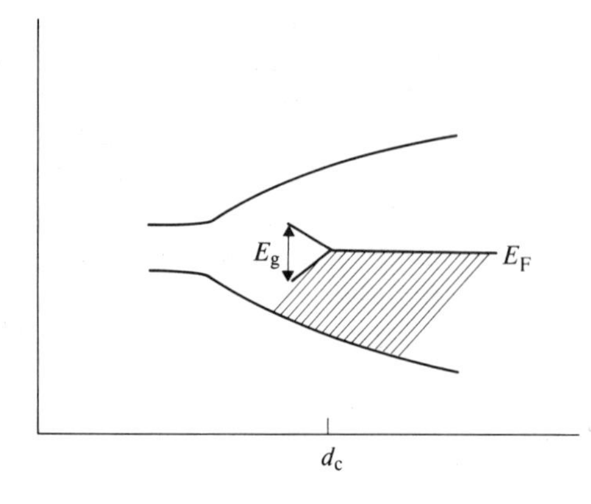

Figure 7-28 Plot of energy vs lattice parameter showing band gap opening up at d_c in the Hubbard model.

transition can result from a state with no free carriers to one with a large number of carriers. According to Mott, this transition should happen at a critical lattice constant and does not necessarily imply a phase transition since the change need be sharp only at $T = 0$ K. Such insulator-to-metal transitions are referred to as Mott transitions.

According to Mott's theory, an insulator-to-metal transition in a solid may be found on application of pressure as the lattice parameter passes through the critical value. Real crystals will have only a limited range of lattice constants that can be varied by application of superpressures. Such a transition has not yet been observed in NiO even when subjected to 500 kbar. Where crystal symmetry changes accompany the electrical transition, it is difficult to verify the original predictions of Mott. We are therefore limited to donors or acceptors in semiconductors, and Mott's equation for the critical concentration, $n_c^{1/3} \sim 0.2a^{-1}$ (a is the lattice constant), has been verified in doped germanium and indium antimonide. A Mott transition was suggested to occur in Cr-doped V_2O_3 and pure V_2O_3 at high temperatures.[81] These results are subject to some doubt;[82,83] further, the high-temperature phase above the transition is not metallic and there appears to be no critical point.

Mott's theory has been put on a more quantitative basis by Hubbard.[84] However, Hubbard has calculated the results only for an s-band and has shown that an insulating ground state is obtained and the energy gap vanishes at a critical lattice parameter (Fig. 7-28). The Mott–Hubbard theory can explain the observed transport properties in d-band materials in a semiquantitative manner. The model predicts a splitting of the narrow $3d$-bands into still narrower bands, thus accounting for the insulating ground state.

Semiconductor–Metal Transitions in V_2O_3, VO_2, and Ti_2O_3

Semiconductor–metal transitions have been found in a number of oxides, sulfides, and other materials in recent years. The subject has been reviewed by many authors,[3,6,28,83,85,86] and Mott[87] has recently written a monograph on it.

The first transitions discovered by Morin[72] were in V_2O_3, VO_2, and Ti_2O_3, and these three oxides have formed the subject-matter of much of the discussion. The theoretical models for semiconductor–metal transitions are also largely based on the transitions in these three oxides since they provide three distinct types of cases. V_2O_3 undergoes a first-order transition (monoclinic–corundum) with a ten-million-fold jump in conductivity accompanied by a magnetic (antiferromagnetic–paramagnetic) transition. VO_2 undergoes a first-order transition (monoclinic–rutile) with a ten-thousand-fold jump in conductivity, but there is no magnetic ordering in the low-temperature phase. Ti_2O_3 undergoes a second-order transition (no change in crystal symmetry) with a hundred-fold jump in conductivity, and there is no magnetic ordering in the low-temperature phase. Even without much knowledge of theory, one would indeed expect maximum change in conductivity in V_2O_3 and least in Ti_2O_3 considering the changes in crystal symmetry and magnetic properties. In Fig. 7-29, features of the insulator–metal transitions in the three oxides are summarized for purpose of comparison. We shall now examine these systems at some length.

At room temperature, V_2O_3 has the corundum structure with rhombohedral symmetry. There is a unique *c*-axis perpendicular to the basal plane which contains three identical crystal axes. Near 150 K, a phase transition occurs to the monoclinic structure involving a slight tilting of the hexagonal *c*-axis of the rhombohedral phase. The transition is accompanied by discontinuous changes in the c/a ratio (Fig. 7-30) and the unit cell volume (increase by about 1.4 percent). There is also a high-temperature anomaly in V_2O_3 around 500 K where there appears to be no change in the crystal parameters, although a DTA transition is found at 430 K. Neutron diffraction and Mössbauer studies on V_2O_3 have confirmed the presence of antiferromagnetic ordering in the low-temperature monoclinic phase. The antiferromagnetic axis lies in a plane parallel to the *c*-axis (in the hexagonal cell) and perpendicular to one of the *a*-axes, and makes an angle of about 71° to the *c*-axis in this plane; the V moments are ferromagnetically coupled in monoclinic (010) or hexagonal (110) layers, with a reversal between adjacent layers. The ordered moment is 1.2 μ_B per V atom. Neutron diffraction, neutron scattering, Mössbauer spectroscopy, and magnetic susceptibility studies indicate that the antiferromagnetic ordering in V_2O_3 disappears at the transition point (see Figs. 7-11 and 7-12). The high-temperature anomaly is associated with a discontinuity in the χ_M, but the substance remains paramagnetic throughout the temperature range 150 to 1000 K.

Associated with the phase transitions in V_2O_3, there occur dramatic changes in the electrical properties. At room temperature, V_2O_3 is a fairly good metal (with the purest samples showing resistivities of the order of 10^{-3} ohm-cm and a positive temperature coefficient of ρ). When the temperature is decreased to 150 K (crystallographic transition point), it undergoes a transition from the metallic state to an insulating state with an accompanying increase in resistivity by about seven orders of magnitude. The characteristic metallic resistivity in V_2O_3 shows an anomaly in the high-temperature region as well. Both the *c*-axis and basal plane resistivities show a rapid increase with temperature in the region near 525 K, but

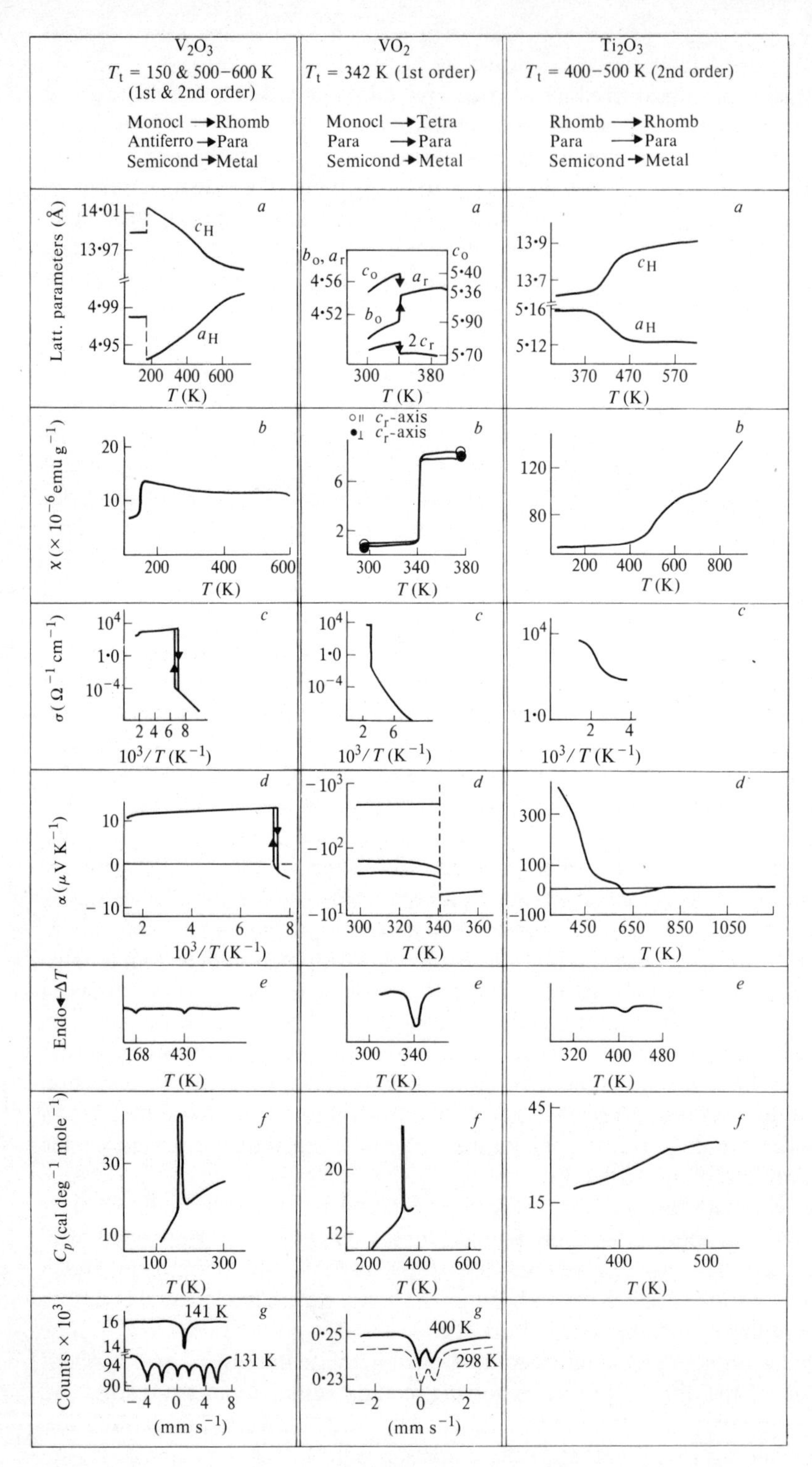

Figure 7-29 Semiconductor–metal transitions in VO_2, V_2O_3, and Ti_2O_3. (*After Rao and Subba Rao.*[3])

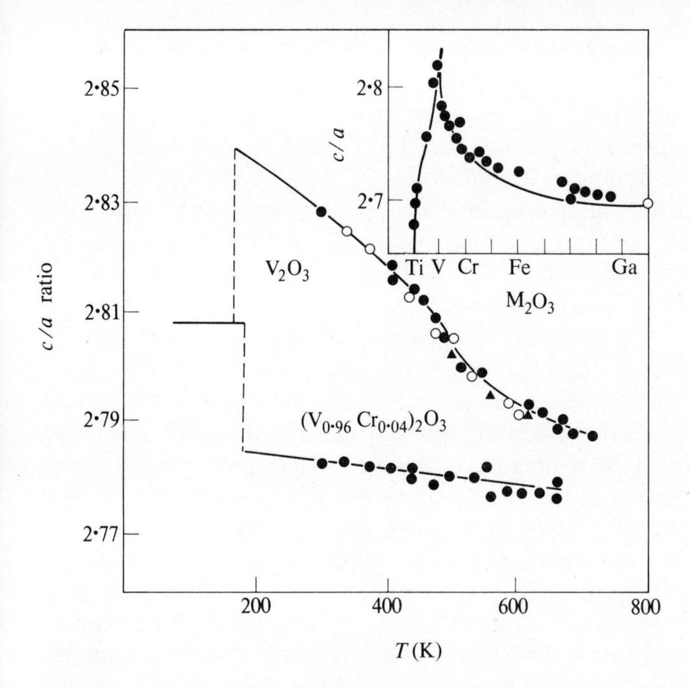

Figure 7-30 Variation of c/a ratio of V_2O_3 with temperature. (*After McWhan et al.*[81]) At the transition temperature we see a drastic change in the c/a ratio. Chromium substitution markedly affects the c/a ratio. In the insert, the variation of c/a ratio in various sesquioxides of corundum structure is shown. The ratio is anomalously high in V_2O_3 (high-temperature corundum phase) and low in Ti_2O_3.

keep monotonically increasing up to 800 K. Discontinuity in α is noted at the low-temperature transition in V_2O_3. Above 150 K, α is positive and small, and below this temperature it changes sign and becomes very small. R_H is negative in the entire range of temperature studied (7–800 K) and does not indicate any anomaly; α does not indicate an anomaly at the high-temperature transition of V_2O_3.

λ-type anomalies are noted in the heat capacities at the low and high-temperature transitions in V_2O_3; DTA studies indicate endothermic peaks corresponding to the transitions. Anomalous behavior of V_2O_3 in the region of the transition point has been noted in the measurements made by a variety of techniques like NMR spectroscopy, positron annihilation, UHF ($\sim$10 GHz) dielectric constant, optical spectroscopy and x-ray photoelectron spectroscopy.

The transition temperature decreases with pressure ($\sim$4 K kbar^{-1}). Application of pressures greater than 25 kbar suppresses the transition completely, and V_2O_3 remains metallic and Pauli-paramagnetic down to 2.2 K without indication of any long-range magnetic order.

All the available data seem to establish that the low-temperature transition in pure V_2O_3 is of first order and that the high temperature one is of second order. The low-temperature transition is sharp and marked by hysteresis. The properties of the metallic state of V_2O_3 are highly anomalous and change rapidly with pressure in the direction of making it more metallic. It therefore appears that pure V_2O_3 is near a critical region and that the application of negative pressure would induce a transition; doping with chromium has an empirical correspondence with the negative pressure, and indeed it is found that a metal-to-insulator transition occurs with Cr-doping in this material.

Since both the resistivity anomalies in V_2O_3 are accompanied by anomalies in thermal expansion, it would appear that they may both be metal–insulator transitions of the type envisioned by Mott. The basis for the idea that the V_2O_3 transitions are Mott-type transitions is contained in the recent work of McWhan and coworkers.[81] These workers have examined the resistivity and the lattice distortion of V_2O_3 as a function of pressure, temperature, and chromium and titanium doping. Three types of phases have been suggested to be present in V_2O_3: the metallic (M), the insulating (I), and antiferromagnetic insulating (AF) phases. Depending on the temperature, pressure, and dopant concentration, all the three phases and the transitions between any two ($M \rightleftharpoons I$; $M \rightleftharpoons AF$; $AF \rightleftharpoons I$) can be realized experimentally. At room temperature and atmospheric pressure, pure V_2O_3 is situated in the metallic phase. As the temperature is lowered, the undoped material passes through the M–AF phase surface at ~ 160 K. Conversely, as the temperature is raised, pure V_2O_3 appears to pass through the extension of the M–I phase boundary at 550 K. However, the M–I phase boundary terminates at a critical point, so that the high-temperature transition in pure V_2O_3 reflects critical behavior. The phase transition is no longer a well-defined, abrupt, first-order transition, but is a gradual change from metallic to insulating behavior. When a small percentage of Cr ions is substituted for vanadium in V_2O_3, a definite first-order phase transition between the metallic and insulating phases exists, with the transition temperature rapidly decreasing as a function of chromium doping. At a critical concentration (~ 3 percent), the $M \rightarrow I$ and $M \rightarrow AF$ transition temperatures are equal (~ 160 K). For Cr dopings greater than 3 percent, an intermediate metallic state does not exist and the only observed transition is a direct $I \rightarrow AF$ transition (at atmospheric pressure). Similarly, at a given temperature (say, 298 K) and Cr concentration (say 4 percent), the $I \rightarrow M$ transition can take place with the application of pressure and without the intervening AF phase. Doping with increasing amounts of Ti has the empirical correspondence to the application of pressure (3.6 kbar atom percent^{-1}), and the system tends to become more and more metallic; at about 7 atom percent Ti, both the transitions in V_2O_3 are suppressed and the system is metallic in the entire range of temperatures, as is the case in pure V_2O_3 above 25 kbar pressure. As mentioned earlier, recent studies of Honig and coworkers[82] throw some doubt[83] on the otherwise consistent picture provided by McWhan et al.

VO_2 is monoclinic at room temperature and transforms to a tetragonal (rutile) structure at 340 K. The transition is of the first order and is accompanied by hysteresis effects and changes in latent heat (Fig. 7-1) and volume. Magnetic susceptibility, Mössbauer, and NMR studies have failed to show any evidence of long-range magnetic ordering in VO_2 in the temperature range 1.7 to 400 K; however, a jump in χ is noted at T_t (Fig. 7-8), and χ is almost temperature-independent both above and below T_t. The electrical characteristics of VO_2 change from those of a semiconductor to those of a metal at T_t, with a large drop in resistivity (by a factor of $\sim 10^5$ for pure and single crystalline material). The Seebeck coefficient and Hall effect also show anomalies at T_t.

Some workers have found evidence for the existence of an intermediate triclinic phase of VO_2 in the range 325 to 340 K by means of NMR, DTA, and x-ray diffraction studies. The temperature range of stability of this intermediate phase may be vanishingly small for pure VO_2, but impurities like Al, Fe, Cr, and Mo appear to be effective in the stabilization of this phase by way of Magneli defects. Recent studies[88,89] show that, with as little as 0.1 percent Cr or Al, a second monoclinic phase M_2 is found below 340 K besides the insulating monoclinic phase M_1. At intermediate temperatures, a triclinic structure appears. The high-temperature metallic phase above 340 K is always rutile.

The effect of pressure on the VO_2 transition has been examined; T_t increases linearly with pressure at a rate of $0.082 \pm 0.005°$ k bar^{-1}. The activation energy in the semiconducting phase decreases linearly with pressure, typically at a rate of 1–2 mV kbar^{-1}. Assuming intrinsic behavior below T_t for VO_2, this indicates that the carrier concentration increases with pressure, but no metallic conduction is encountered up to pressures of ~ 300 kbar at 300 K.

The effect of various impurities on the temperature and nature of the transition in VO_2 has been investigated extensively in the literature. Many elements like Ti, Nb, Mo, Tc, Ta, W, and Re form complete solid solutions with VO_2 and at appreciable concentrations stabilize the high-temperature rutile form of VO_2 at room temperature; the T_t of VO_2 is lowered appreciably and the nature of the transition (at not-too-high impurity concentrations) is changed from that of a semiconductor-to-metal to that of a semiconductor-to-semiconductor. The same effect is produced by the addition of ions like Fe, Co, and Ni, but Al, Cr, and Ge raise the T_t appreciably.

Ti_2O_3 has a narrow range of homogeneity ($x = 1.49$–1.51 in TiO_x) and has the rhombohedral crystal structure at room temperature; there is a change in lattice parameters in the temperature range 400–500 K with the c/a ratio increasing. There is, however, no change in the crystal symmetry. Magnetic susceptibility does not show any significant anomaly in the range 400 to 550 K. Recent neutron diffraction studies by Moon et al. have clearly confirmed the absence of antiferromagnetism in Ti_2O_3 below 400 K. A specific heat anomaly has been reported in Ti_2O_3 in the range 450 to 600 K.

In the range 100 to 300 K, Ti_2O_3 behaves as an intrinsic semiconductor with a band gap of 0.03–0.05 eV (depending on the sample), with the drop in ρ beginning at ~ 400 K and extending up to 470 K. The drop in ρ in the 400 to 470 K range is about a hundredfold. The resistivity of Ti_2O_3 goes through a shallow minimum at 800 K and rises again with further increase in temperature. Hall data below 273 K indicated the charge carriers to be positively charged and with high mobilities. The Seebeck coefficient of pure Ti_2O_3 is positive at ordinary temperatures and drops to smaller values in going through the transition region. The gradual decrease in ρ and α in the region of the transition, the broad nature of the anomalies in χ, heat capacity and DTA measurements indicate that Ti_2O_3 is a relatively wide band material and that the semiconductor-to-metal transition is of a higher order. Since the absence of antiferromagnetism is definitely established in this material, a plausible mechanism appears to be that of band broadening or shifting brought about by the increase in c/a ratio in the vicinity of 400 to 470 K. Accordingly, pressure has negligible effect on the T_t of the Ti_2O_3 transition.

Ti_2O_3 forms solid solutions with V_2O_3 throughout the composition range, but the solid solutions so formed are not ideal and do not obey Vegard's law. The interesting observation is that at $x \sim 0.1$ in $(Ti_{1-x}V_x)_2O_3$ the values of a, c, and α are the same as the corresponding values for pure Ti_2O_3 after it undergoes the electrical transition; the c parameter of Ti_2O_3 is increased by ~ 3 percent by the incorporation of ~ 20 percent V_2O_3, while the corresponding a parameter contracts by ~ 1.5 percent. This strongly lends support to the idea that strong metal–metal bonding across the octahedral edges takes place in Ti_2O_3. Resistivity measurements on $(Ti_{1-x}V_x)_2O_3$ show that, for $0 \leq x \leq 0.04$, ρ undergoes a change in almost the same temperature range as undoped Ti_2O_3; samples with high x are metallic at room temperature and exhibit no transition.

Theoretical models Several models have been proposed to explain the relatively abrupt disappearance of the energy gap at a temperature leading to the semi-donductor-to-metal transition. We shall briefly consider the features of the various models without delving into details.

We might consider whether a Mott transition can be realized in practice by varying temperature. As Mott himself pointed out, the idea of a critical lattice parameter for conduction makes a temperature-induced transition a rare accident. Also, it seems unlikely that such a high energy state would be reached at ordinary temperatures $T < T_m$ (where T_m is the melting point), unless the material accidentally crystallizes with a lattice constant only slightly greater than the critical value. For this reason an ideal Mott transition has not yet been realized experimentally. Similarly, for reasons discussed by Adler,[90] it is highly unlikely for a Hubbard model to exhibit a semiconductor-to-metal transition with variation of temperature.

The simplest model that can be conceived for the semiconductor-to-metal transition is one involving the overlap of the filled valence and the empty conduction bands. As the temperature is increased we may assume that the forbidden energy gap of the intrinsic semiconductor decreases and finally vanishes at a finite temperature, thus leading to metallic conductivity. There is one difficulty with this approach. The gradual decrease of the gap should produce only gradual changes rather than the sharp changes as observed experimentally in some oxides. However, if there is a first-order phase change without the accompanying crystal symmetry change, we may argue for a sharp change in conductivity. The only case where there is a gradual change in resistivity is in Ti_2O_3. A band-crossing or band broadening would be applicable to this system, as suggested by van Zandt, Honig, and Goodenough.

Halperin and Rice[91] have pointed out that if the exciton binding energy is larger than the magnitude of the band gap, the band overlap produces a large change in the conductivity since, in the immediate vicinity of the transition, conditions are satisfied for a Bose condensation of excitons. Halperin and Rice have also noted that, depending on the extent of electron–phonon interaction, the ground state before the transition should be either antiferromagnetic or of a lower crystal symmetry. On the basis of their pressure experiments, McWhan and Rice[92] have argued for the presence of exciton states in V_2O_3, which shows a sharp semiconductor-to-metal transition at $\sim$150 K.

Slater's original assumption[93] of the insulating ground state for materials because of the doubling of the periodicity of the lattice due to antiferromagnetism can be extended to see if a temperature-dependent energy gap may disappear at the transition temperature. This approach has great appeal when the transition temperature corresponds also to the Néel point. However, the main difficulty is that the theory predicts it to be valid only for an exactly half-filled band. Further, no examples are known in which a crystalline distortion is not also associated with a change from an antiferromagnetic to a paramagnetic state.

Adler and Brooks[94] have presented a model for a semiconductor in which the energy gap arises either from a crystalline distortion or from antiferromagnetism. They have shown that half-filled narrow-band materials can lower their ground state energy by a spontaneous crystalline distortion to a lower symmetry provided that the energy gap introduced is of the same order as the bandwidth. Thus, we can think of bonding and antibonding states separated by the energy gap; clearly thermal excitation across the gap (with increasing temperature) decreases the magnitude of the gap, since the excited electron in the antibonding level can no longer contribute to the distortion. This reduction will further lead to increased excitation, and the result is a catastrophic decrease of the gap to zero at a given temperature, leading to the semiconductor-to-metal transition. Wide-band materials will lower their energy by ordering antiferromagnetically, and calculations of Adler and Brooks show that the transition will be first-order (accompanied by latent heat change, hysteresis, etc.) in the case of crystal distortion, but can be second-order if the gap is due to antiferromagnetism. The theory of Adler and Brooks is a band generalization of the Jahn–Teller effect, and the physical objections that can be raised against the theory are that they regard the antiferromagnetic instability and the lattice instability as two separate instabilities and neglect entirely the effects of electron–hole Coulomb interaction on the lattice stability. Secondly, the agreement of theory with the experimental results[95] on V_2O_3 seems to be superfluous, because there are large uncertainties in the determination of the optical energy gap. Further, some of the interpretations are based on pressure experiments of Feinleib and Paul[96] which were only conducted in the low-pressure range. High-pressure studies[92] on V_2O_3 are not in good agreement with the above theory. The discrepancy between the observed and predicted jumps in the magnitude of electrical conductivity in V_2O_3 was originally interpreted as due either to a large correlation effect or to self-trapping of carriers in the semiconducting state. It was later argued that the discrepancy may arise from a combined effect of the crystal structure change and the disappearance of the antiferromagnetic order.

Mott[97] has pointed out that the very high effective mass ($\sim 50m_0$) of charge carriers in the high-temperature phase of V_2O_3 is not consistent with metallic behavior. The high effective mass implies a narrow band (and low mobility), and this phase should in fact be on the insulator side of the transition point.

Finally, one of the important results of the theory of Adler and Brooks is that, in the narrow band limit, the ratio of the energy gap in the insulating state to the transition temperature, E_g/kT_0, should be constant under the application of external agents such as pressure. Now, if the transition remains first-order even if $T_0 \to 0$, the ratio E_g/kT_0 will diverge to infinity as $T_0 \to 0$. This ratio must therefore vary rapidly as a function of the lattice parameter. This conclusion is in apparent disagreement with the earlier prediction. Hanamura[98] has extended the Adler–Brooks theory to take into account the electron–lattice interaction on the lattice instability and the screening effects of the dipolar interactions due to free carriers, and applied it to transitions in vanadium oxides.

Mott[97] has postulated that the high-temperature metallic phase (at least in vanadium oxides) can be considered as a nondegenerate gas of small polarons. The polaron coupling constant is large and the binding energy of a polaron is more than half the Mott–Hubbard correlation energy gap arising from Coulomb interaction. At low temperatures the polarons form a degenerate gas with weak Coulomb interaction and condense in a way not yet understood. According to this model, we may expect magnetic ordering or superconductivity (because of large electron–phonon interaction) in the metallic phase, but these effects have not been noticed down to ~ 2 K in V_2O_3. The importance of electron–phonon interactions has been stressed by Hyland,[99] who has reviewed some of the theoretical models and the implications of the insulating ground state.

Felicov and Kimball[100] have proposed a model which is basically different from the Mott transition or the excitonic insulator transition. This theory is based on a change in occupation numbers of electronic states which remain themselves essentially unchanged in their character. Felicov and Kimball assume the existence of both localized (ionic) and band (Bloch) states, and deduce that the electron–hole interaction is responsible for the anomalous temperature dependence of the number of conduction electrons. They have shown that for interactions larger than a critical value, the first-order semiconductor-to-metal transition occurs. Bari[101] has reviewed the various models and has suggested another electron correlation model, the spinless Fermion model. He has also discussed the role of soft phonons in the crystalline distortion model.

Goodenough has applied his chemical bond approach to explain the observed semiconductor-to-metal and ferroelectric transitions in transition metal compounds. Goodenough[102] explains the semiconductor-to-metal transitions in titanium and vanadium oxides by assuming that in the high-temperature (high-symmetry) phases these oxides have $\Delta^{\pi}_{\text{cac}} < \Delta_{\text{c}}$ and $\Delta_{\text{cc}} > \Delta'_{\text{c}}$, so that they belong to class 1 metallic compounds in which cation sublattice d-bands exist and metallic behavior is noted with a well-defined Fermi surface. As the temperature is lowered, however, the band breaks up into pairs of atoms that are bonded by homopolar bonds in which the electrons are trapped, and a change to lower crystal symmetry (and semiconducting phase) occurs to produce a filled band separated from an empty band by a finite energy gap. Goodenough[103] has also pointed out the relevance of the temperature variation of the c/a ratio to the mechanism of the transitions in Ti_2O_3 and V_2O_3. Obviously the c/a ratio in turn reflects the nature of metal–metal interaction in these compounds.

A characteristic feature of the distortions accompanying the semiconductor-to-metal transitions is a displacement of the cations from the centers of symmetry of their anion interstices toward one or more near-neighbor cations. In ferroelectric transitions (as holds for class 2 metallic compounds like $BaTiO_3$ with narrow crystalline d-bands), however, the distortions will be accompanied by the displacements of the cations toward near-neighbor anions. The narrower the bands, the greater will be the distortions. Further, the presence of electrons in the antibonding empty band either reduces or suppresses completely the transition temperature.

If a semiconductor-to-metal transition were to occur in a class 2 metallic oxide, this may be manifested as a simple disproportionation into two valence states of the ions or a change in the number of molecules per unit cell. It is possible that in some class 2 oxides, the distortion may be accompanied by competitive semiconductor-to-metal or ferroelectric–paraelectric transitions. It should be noted that the Goodenough model of semiconductor-to-metal transitions is in principle a simple extension of Mott's critical lattice parameter criterion.

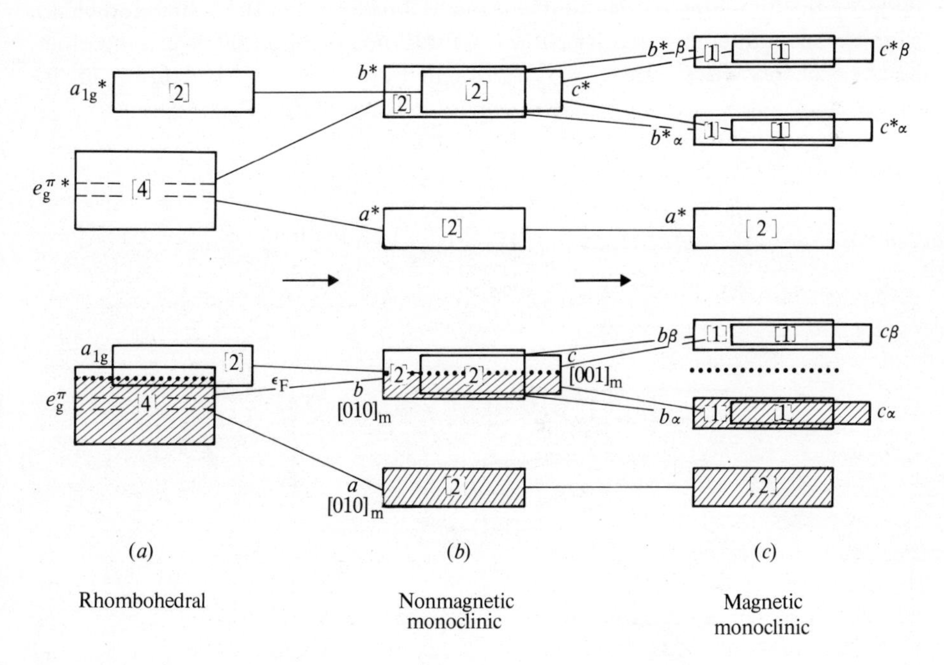

Figure 7-31 Schematic band structure of V_2O_3, following Goodenough.

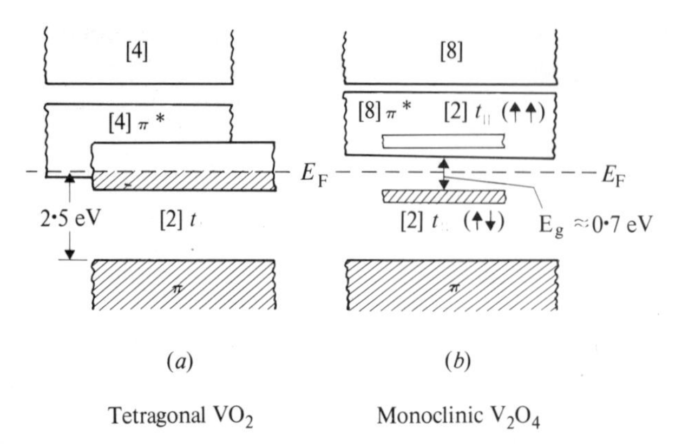

Figure 7-32 Schematic band structure of VO_2, following Goodenough.

The above discussion serves to illustrate how a complete understanding of the nature of semiconductor–metal transitions is still lacking. We close the discussion of the transitions in V_2O_3, VO_2, and Ti_2O_3 by giving schematic band structures of these materials following Goodenough (Figs. 7-31, 7-32, and 7-33). Such diagrams are useful in visualizing the phenomena.

Transitions in Other Systems

Some of the titanium oxides of the general formula Ti_nO_{2n-1} are known to exhibit semiconductor–metal transitions.[3] With the exception of Ti_3O_5, the other members of this series up to $n = 9$ are Magneli phases (shear structures). Ti_3O_5

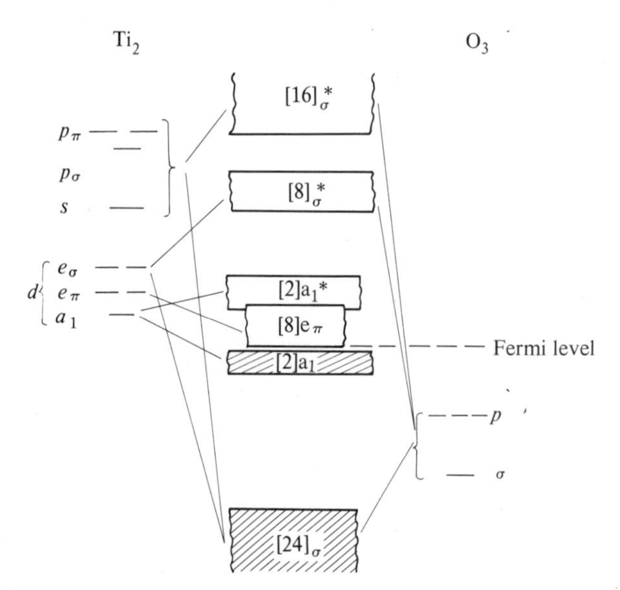

Figure 7-33 Schematic band structure of Ti_2O_3, following Goodenough.

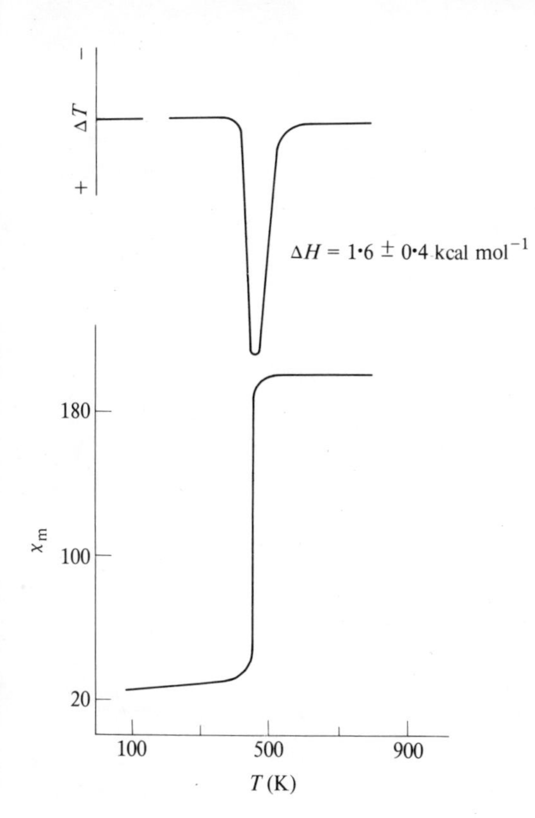

Figure 7-34 Magnetic susceptibility anomaly in Ti_3O_5. (*After Keys and Mulay.*[104]) DTA peak (indicating a first-order transition) is also shown. (*After Rao et al.*[105])

shows a first-order (monoclinic-distorted orthorhombic) transition around 460 K accompanied by susceptibility and resistivity anomalies (Fig. 7-34).[104,105] There appears to be no magnetic ordering in the low-temperature phase of Ti_3O_5. Ti_4O_7 shows two transitions at 125 and 153 K, the latter being associated with resistivity and susceptibility anomalies and the former with structural changes.[106] Ti_5O_9 and Ti_6O_{11} also exhibit semiconductor–metal transitions. Among the vanadium oxides of the general formula V_nO_{2n-1}, the members with $n = 4, 5, 6$, and 8 show semiconductor–metal transitions at T_t ($\Delta H \sim 150$ cal mol^{-1}) and antiferromagnetic ordering below T_N ($T_N < T_t$). These transitions are fairly well characterized.[3,107]

The semiconductor–metal transition in NbO_2 at 1070 K has been fairly well characterized.[108] The structural change is from a distorted rutile structure to the rutile structure and the resistivity change is about tenfold. There is no magnetic ordering in the low-temperature phase. The importance of *c*-axis Nb–Nb pairing and vibration-mode softening was indicated by these studies. Recent neutron scattering studies[109] show soft-mode excitation from above the transition to the distorted structure in which Nb ion pairs are along the *c*-axis. Substitution of V for Nb suppresses the NbO_2 transition. Marked changes in the Nb 4*d*-band in the x-ray photoelectron spectrum accompany the transition[110] (see Fig. 7-35).

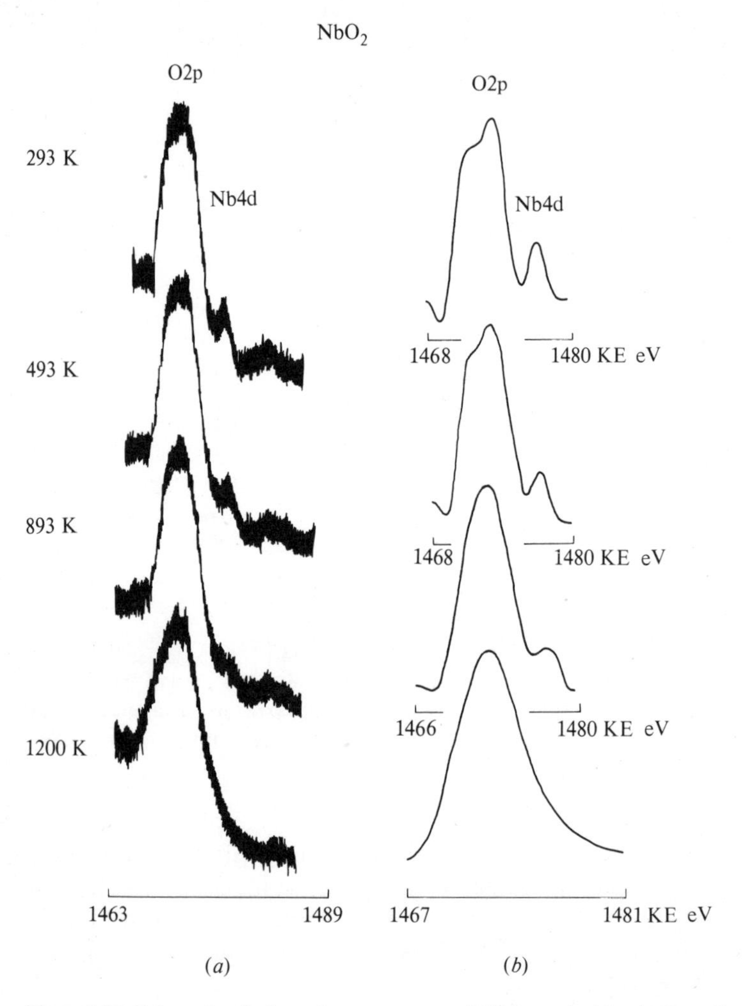

Figure 7-35 Valence band photoelectron spectra of NbO_2 excited by AlK_α radiation: (*a*) raw spectra, (*b*) deconvoluted spectra. (*After Thornton, Orchard, and Rao.*[110])

The *d*-band progressively shifts toward the O2*p*-band with increase in temperature.

Magnetic properties and transitions of Fe_3O_4 were discussed earlier in this chapter. The conductivity anomaly in Fe_3O_4 at the Verwey transition temperature (Fig. 7-25) does not strictly correspond to a semiconductor–metal transition since the high-temperature phase is not truly metallic.[3,90]

Many metal sulfides and other chalcogenides exhibit semiconductor–metal transitions.[6] Thus, NiS shows a magnetic susceptibility anomaly (see Fig. 7-3) and a conductivity anomaly[111] by a factor of about forty at 264 K ($T_t = T_N$); the T_t is sensitive to stoichiometry. The transition is first-order ($\Delta V = 1.9$ percent).

The transition appears to be from an itinerant band antiferromagnet to a delocalized d-band metal without moments rather than from an antiferromagnet with local moments to a delocalized metal.[83] Briggs et al.[112] have determined the low-lying parts of the phonon and magnon spectra of NiS by neutron inelastic scattering at various temperatures, and their results are summarized in Fig. 7-36. CrS undergoes a structural transition (monoclinic–NiAs) around 600 K accompanied by a semiconductor–metal transition.[6,90] The semiconductor–metal transition in FeS was mentioned in the earlier section along with the magnetic transitions (see Fig. 7-16).

SmSe, SmTe, and YbTe undergo continuous semiconductor-metal transitions on application of pressure; however, SmS shows a discontinuous transition at 6.5 kbar at room temperature.[113] In these transitions, electrons from $4f$ levels of the rare earth are promoted to the conduction band. Chemically speaking, the transition involves an $Sm^{2+} \rightarrow Sm^{3+}$-type oxidation reaction. There is no structural change in these transitions, the structure remaining as NaCl type. The transition in SmS is accompanied by ~16 percent change in volume. This ΔV can be brought about by substitution of P in SmS; about 12 percent P gives rise to the same ΔV as 6.5 kbar ($a(Sm^{2+}S) = 5.97$ Å; $a(Sm^{3+}S) = 5.64$ Å). Substitution of Gd for Sm in SmS also causes a marked decrease in the unit cell volume. If a crystal of $Sm_{1-x}Gd_xS$ ($0.16 \leq x \leq 0.22$) is cooled, an explosive first-order electronic transition is observed, due to a sudden expansion in unit cell volume.[114] EuO shows a pressure induced $4f \rightarrow 5d$ first-order transition at 300 kbar at room temperature[115] (transformation to CsCl structure is at 400 kbar).

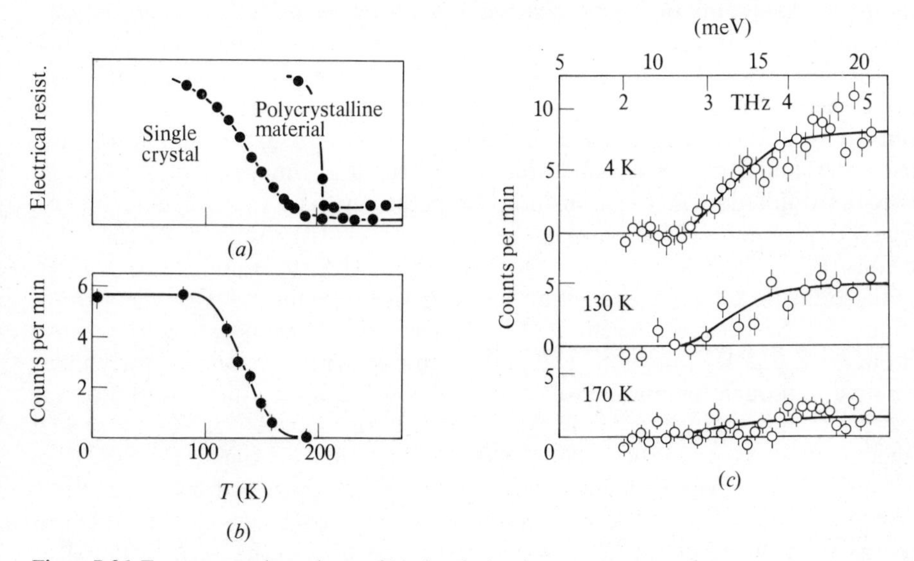

Figure 7-36 Temperature dependence of (a) electrical resistance, (b) peak counting rate for the magnon (in neutron spectra), for a sample of NiS. In (c), the magnon intensity is shown as a function of energy at $q = 0$. Notice that above a gap energy of 13 meV, the antiferromagnon makes its appearance and that the gap varies little with temperature. (*After Briggs et al.*[112])

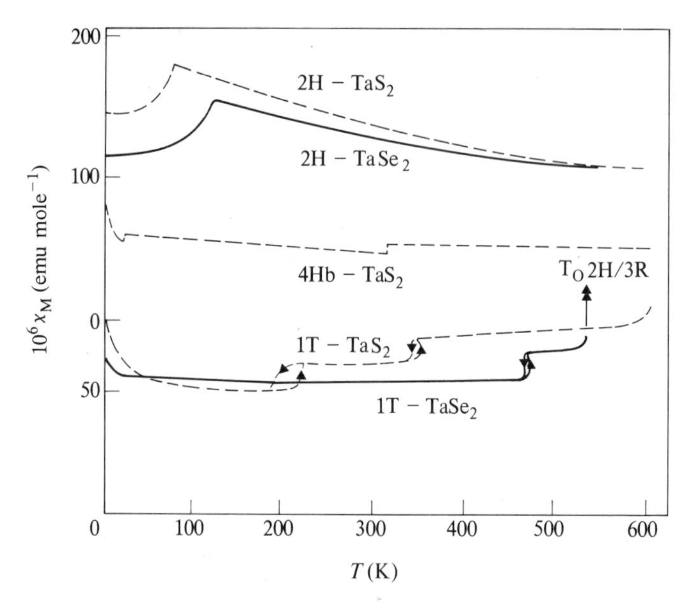

Figure 7-37 Magnetic susceptibility data on tantalum dichalcogenides. (*After Wilson et al.*[116])

Tantalum disulfide, TaS_2, and related chalcogenides like $TaSe_2$ and $NbSe_2$ exist in different polytypic forms like 1T, 2H, 4H, 3R, 6R, and so on.[6,116] These materials show certain anomalous properties which are interesting. According to our understanding of the band structures of such materials, they should have been metallic, but only the magnetic susceptibility data of 2H-TaS_2 show this expected behavior (Fig. 7-37). 1T and 4Hb forms of TaS_2 exhibit anomalously low susceptibilities and, in addition, these polytypes undergo intrapolytypic transitions: 1T, 352 K and 200 K (both first-order); 4H*b*, 315 K and 20 K (both first-order) and 2H, 80 K (second-order). No structural changes could be noticed by x-ray diffraction at the transition temperatures. The marked difference in behavior of 1T and 2H forms can be seen from the resistivity data in the transition regions (Fig. 7-38). The metallic condition of the 2H form is not greatly affected by the transition, but the transition in 1T is like a semiconductor–metal transition. The Seebeck coefficient of 1T changes sign from negative to positive through the 352 K transition. The Hall coefficient shows a break but remains negative. Although the number of carriers above 352 K was high, resistivity was also high; apparently there was extensive scattering above 352 K. These and other anomalous properties, along with the fact that all the transitions were endothermic, had to be explained. Recent studies employing electron diffraction[116] have shown that the anomalous behavior of these chalcogenides can be explained by invoking charge-density waves (first proposed by Overhauser[117]) and their concomitant periodic structural distortions.

Electron diffraction studies show that the anomalous behavior of these $4d^1/5d^1$ dichalcogenides includes the adoption of a superlattice, the size of which is related to the pattern of satellite spots and diffuse scattering found above the phase transitions.[116] The observed periodicities of charge density wave (CDW) states are related to the theoretical form of the Fermi surfaces. The CDWs in 1T and 4H*b* forms are at first incommensurate with the lattice and produce gaps in the density of states at the Fermi level. The room-temperature superlattice in 1T-$TaSe_2$, for example, is obtained when the CDWs rotate in such a way as to become commensurate. At the first-order transition, the Fermi surface energy gap increases beyond that due to the incommensurate CDWs. The charge density (in the CDW) can be treated as an order parameter (in Landau theory) to understand the phase transitions.[118] CDWs are being found in many other systems, such as vanadium sulfide, NbO_2, and so on.

In addition to the several examples of transitions in electronic properties

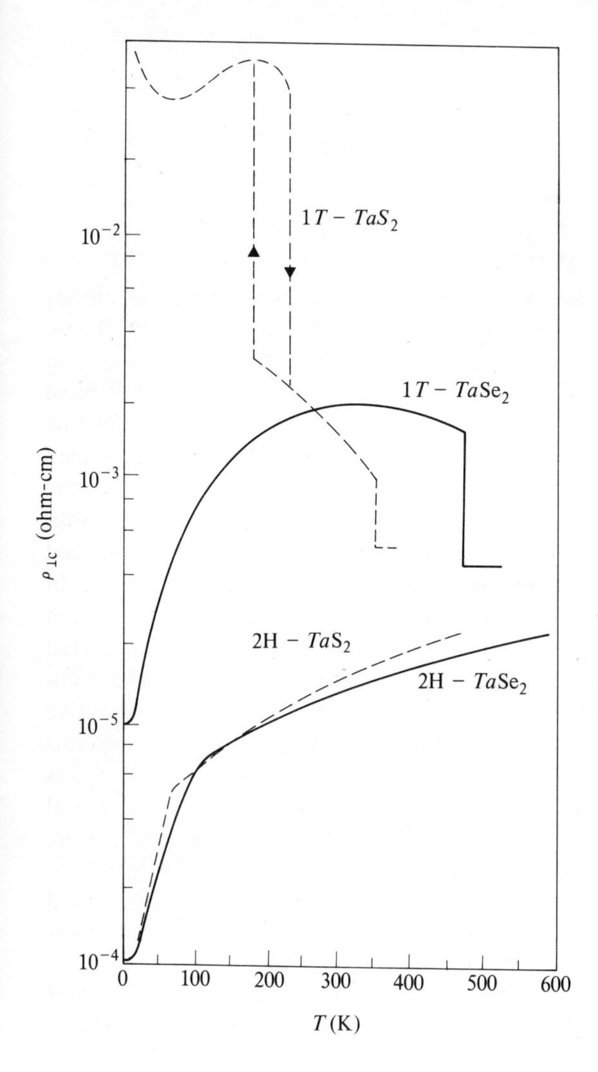

Figure 7-38 Resistivity ($\perp c$) data on tantalum dichalcogenides. (*After Wilson et al.*[116])

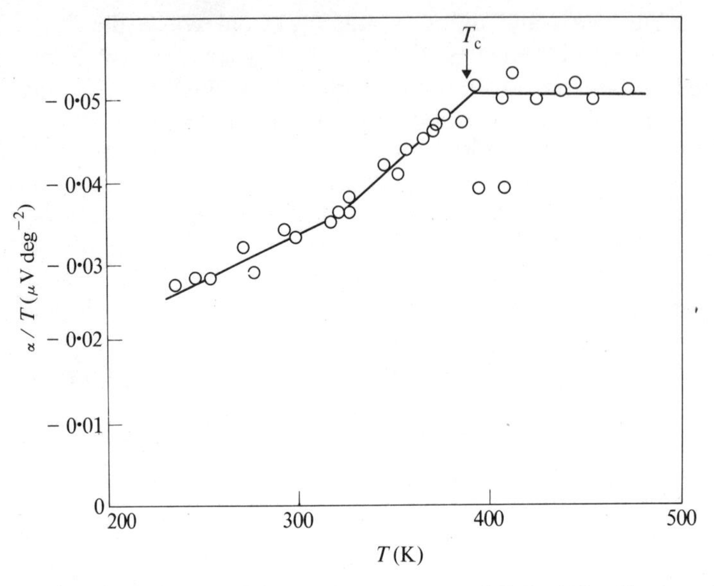

Figure 7-39 Seebeck coefficient–temperature curve of CrO_2. (*After Chapin et al.*[119])

discussed hitherto, there are many other instances where electrical properties of materials show changes at the phase-transition temperatures. Thus, C–A transformations of rare-earth sesquioxides are accompanied by breaks in the resistivity–temperature curves. CrO_2, which is a ferromagnetic metal, shows a break in the Seebeck coefficient–temperature curve[119] at T_c (Fig. 7-39), α being constant at $T > T_c$; at $T < T_c$, α increases with T because of the increase in

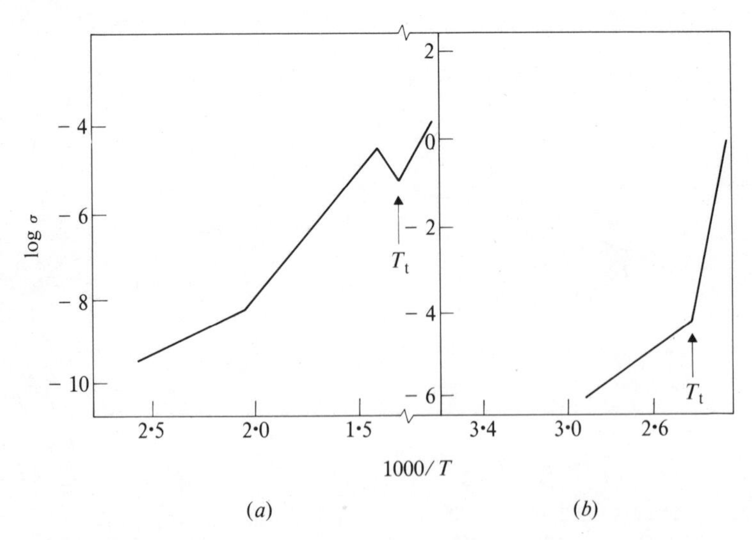

Figure 7-40 Phase transition of (*a*) CsCl (from CsCl structure to NaCl structure) and (*b*) AgI as shown by ionic conductivity data. (*From the laboratory of C. N. R. Rao.*)

spin disorder. Ionic solids like CsCl, AgI, NH_4Cl, etc., show breaks in ionic conductivity–temperature curves at the phase-transition temperatures (Fig. 7-40).

Localized $\rightleftharpoons$ Collective Electron Transitions in Rare-Earth Cobaltites

In $LaCoO_3$ and other rare-earth cobaltites (which have distorted perovskite structures), the Co^{3+} ions are in a diamagnetic low-spin state ($t_{2g}^6e_g^0$) at low temperatures.[23,120–123] With increase in temperature, the low-spin ions transform to the high-spin state ($t_{2g}^4e_g^2$) up to a proportion. Then the two spin states order themselves on unique sites in $LaCoO_3$, giving rise to a lowering of symmetry from $R\bar{3}c$ to $R\bar{3}$; the susceptibility curves show plateau regions due to such ordering (Fig. 7-41) and DTA curves show small endothermic peaks due to ordering. Apart from these spin-state transitions, the rare-earth cobaltites show large endothermic transitions ($\Delta H \geq 1$ kcal mol^{-1}) at high temperatures, T_t (1210 K in $LaCoO_3$), which appear to be entirely electronic in origin. Since there is no structural change (no change in configurational entropy) in the cobaltites at the transition temperature and the Debye–Waller factor actually drops at T_t (negative

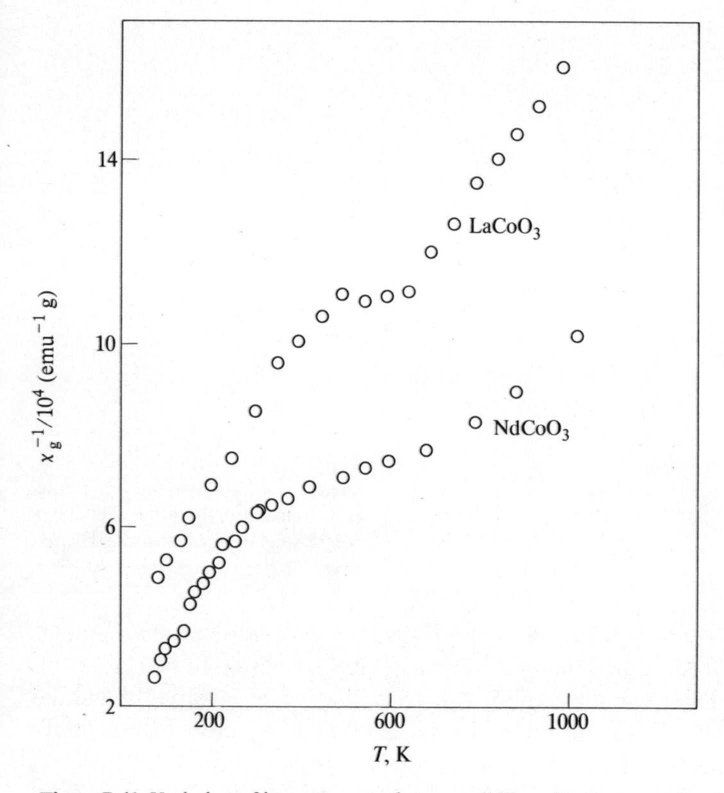

Figure 7-41 Variation of inverse magnetic susceptibility of $LaCoO_3$ and $NdCoO_3$ with temperature. Notice the plateau region. (*After Rajoria et al.*[112])

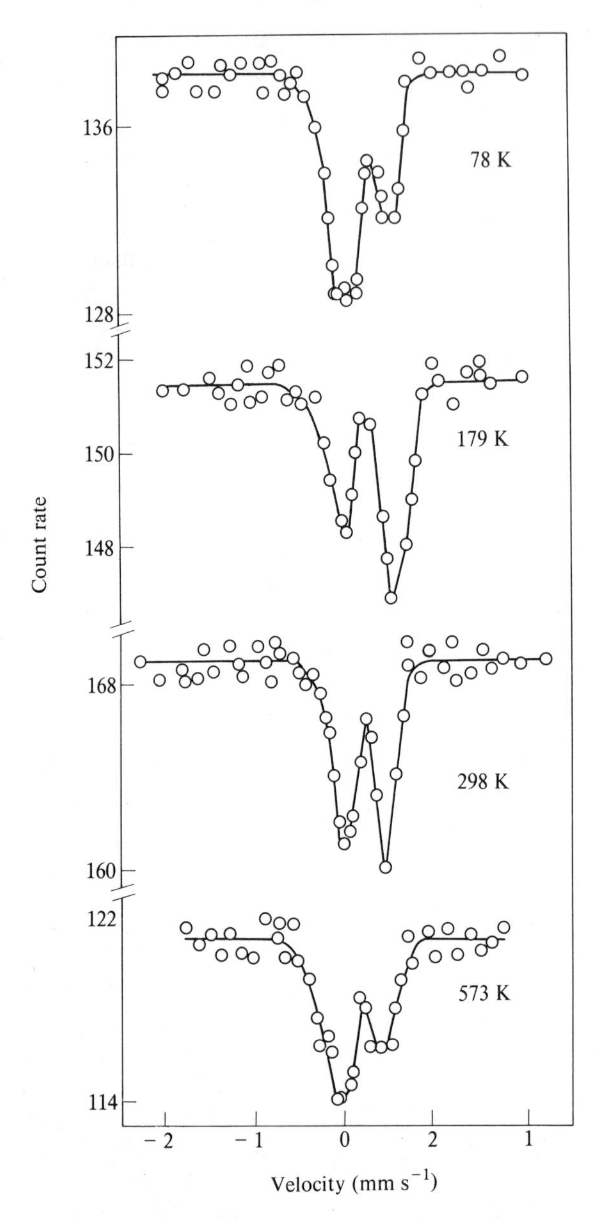

Figure 7-42 Typical Mössbauer spectra of neodymium cobaltite (Co^{57}) matched against $K_4Fe(CN)_6$-$3H_2O$ single crystal absorber. (*After Rao.*[121])

vibrational ΔS), the entropy change in the transition is deemed to arise almost entirely from *d*-electrons. Goodenough[23] considers this transition to be due to the transformation of localized *d*-electrons (e_g) to collective electrons (σ^* bands) thereby indicating that the localized (or ligand field) and collective (band) limits of *d*-electrons are distinct thermodynamic states.

Detailed studies employing Mössbauer spectroscopy (Fig. 7-42) and electron transport measurements[23,120–123] have shown that at high temperatures (above

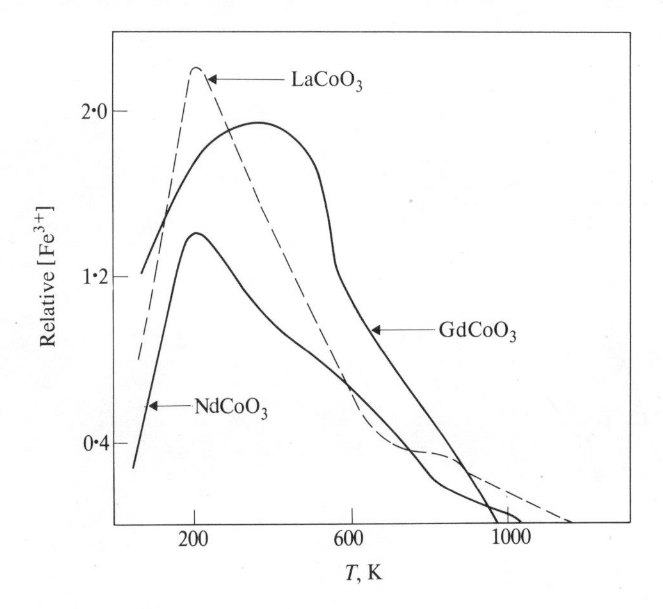

Figure 7-43 Temperature variation of the relative proportion of $Fe^{3+}(Co^{3+})$ in rare earth cobaltites (found by Mössbauer spectroscopy). Note that $[Fe^{3+}]$ becomes zero close to the localized ⇌ collective electron transition temperature. (*After Rao.*[121])

the ordering transitions, ~400 K in $LaCoO_3$), there is electron transfer from high-spin Co^{3+} ions to the low-spin ions producing Co^{4+}, Co^{2+}, and other charge-transfer states until at T_t there are no high-spin ions left (Fig. 7-43). Such charge transfer provides the mechanism of electron transport at high temperatures. With increase in temperature there is increase in Co–O overlap as well. Above T_t, $LaCoO_3$ shows metallic resistivity and a very low Seebeck coefficient (Fig. 7-44). Some of the cobaltites do not show metal-like variation of resistivity with temperature (above T_t), but there is no doubt that the electrons are itinerant at these temperatures. Continuous variation of electrical conductivity across T_t is superficially surprising even though the first-order transition involves a discontinuous change in electronic entropy. However, since the mobile electrons move with equal probability over all the cobalt sites as $T \rightarrow T_t$, there need be no discontinuity across T_t in the number of charge carriers. Similarly, the charge-carrier mobility is not discontinuous across T_t. This situation is indeed unusual for a first-order transition and is very much unlike the semiconductor–metal transitions in oxides discussed earlier. While Mössbauer spectroscopy, specifically the Lamb–Mössbauer factor, is an excellent probe to study such electronic and spin-state transitions (Fig. 7-45), photoelectron spectroscopy[124] directly provides the nature of changes occurring in the valence band (Fig. 7-46).

Substitution of Sr^{2+} for La^{3+} in $LaCoO_3$ brings about remarkable changes in electrical and magnetic properties.[59,60,120,121] In $La_{1-x}Sr_xCoO_3$, if $x > 0.125$, the paramagnetic Curie temperature becomes positive and at low temperatures

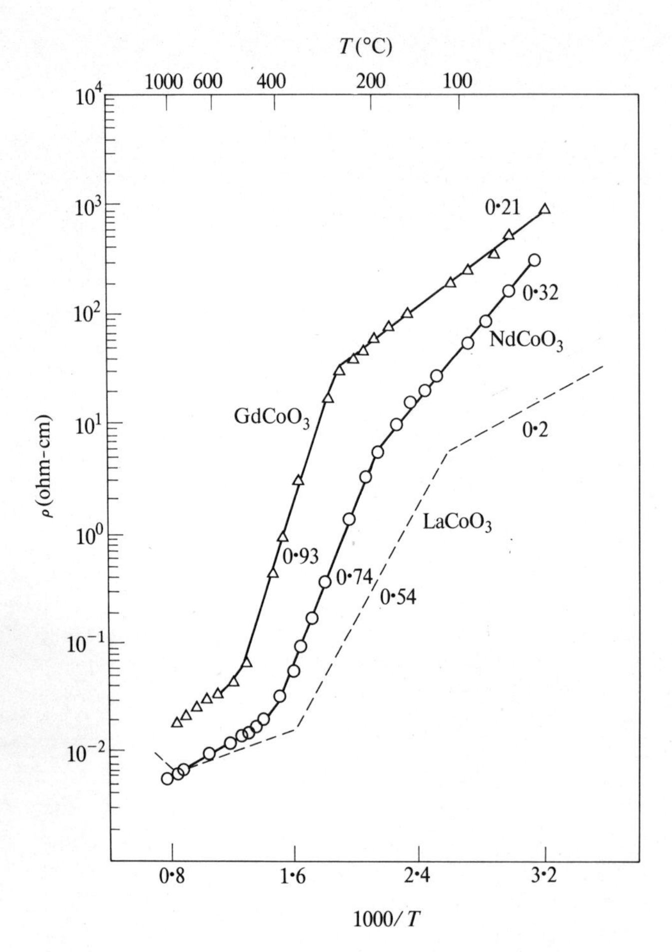

Figure 7-44 Variation of logarithm of electrical resistivity with $1/T$ for $LaCoO_3$, $NdCoO_3$, and $GdCoO_3$. E_a values are given against the curves. (*After Rao.*[121])

ferromagnetism is observed. Electron transport properties and photoelectron spectra[124] show that the electrons become itinerant when $x > 0.125$. Mössbauer spectra at room temperature show that when $x > 0.125$, electrons hop very fast, giving rise to a time-averaged electronic configuration, while the low-temperature spectra show evidence for ferromagnetism. The proportion of ferromagnetism increases with x, and at $x = 0.5$ the material is almost entirely ferromagnetic ($T_c \sim 232$ K) as well as metallic with a brown bronze lustre. The localized$\rightleftharpoons$ collective electron transition found in $LaCoO_3$ is seen in $La_{1-x}Sr_xCoO_3$ up to $x \sim 0.3$. This fact, along with the observation that there is always coexistence of paramagnetism and ferromagnetism in compositions with $x < 0.5$, indicates that these materials are "chemically or electronically inhomogeneous" (although crystallographically they are single phase substances). In other words, in the same crystallographic phase, both localized and collective electron regimes seem to

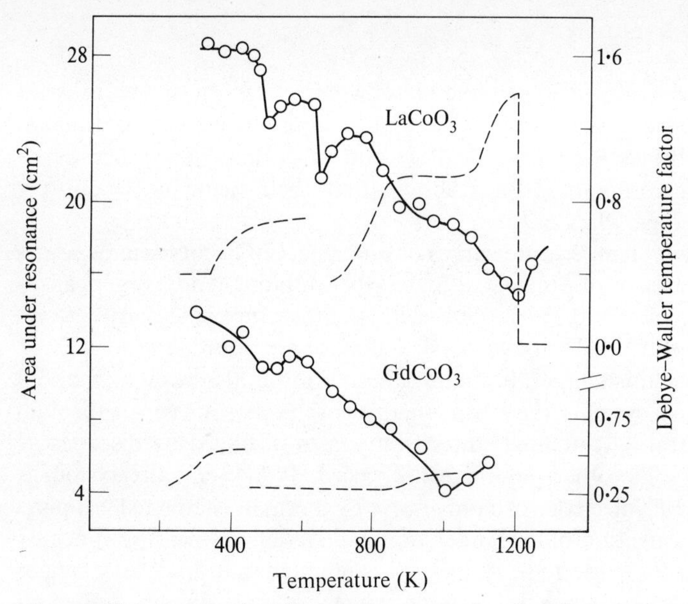

Figure 7-45 Area under the Mössbauer resonance (Lamb–Mössbauer factor) plotted vs temperature. For purpose of comparison, Debye–Waller factors are also shown (dotted lines). The transitions at 1210 and 1000 K in $LaCoO_3$ and $GdCoO_3$ respectively are due to the localized ⇌ collective electron transitions, the transitions at lower temperatures being due to spin-state ordering. (*After Rajoria et al.*[122])

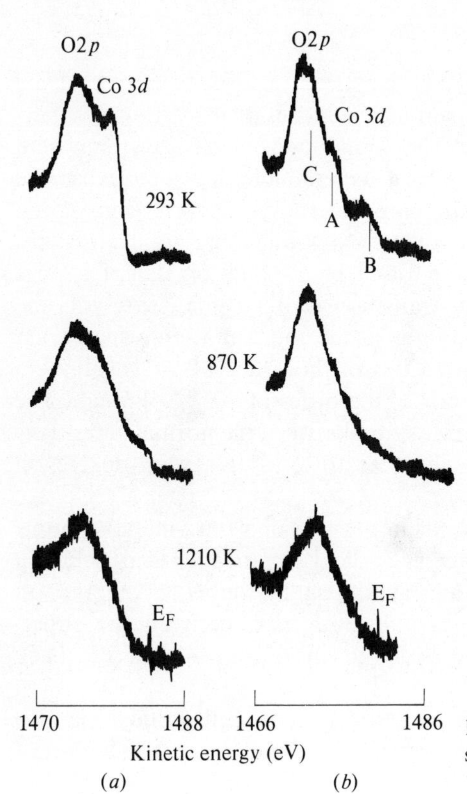

Figure 7-46 Valence bands in $A1K_\alpha$ photoelectron spectrum of (*a*) $LaCoO_3$ and (*b*) $YCoO_3$. (*After Thornton et al.*[124])

coexist in these mixed oxides. The metallic phase when $x = 0.5$, however, appears well-ordered (with alternate Sr^{2+} and La^{3+} ions), as found by electron diffraction studies.[125] Recent studies (of C. N. R. Rao and coworkers) on other Sr^{2+}-substituted $LnCoO_3$ compounds have shown that their behavior is entirely analogous to that of $La_{1-x}Sr_xCoO_3$.

Electrical resistivity–temperature curves of $Ln_{1-x}Sr_xCoO_3$ compounds somewhat resemble the behavior of disordered materials exhibiting Anderson localization.[126,127] Thus, when x is 0.05 or 0.1 the low-temperature resistivity follows the $1/T^{1/4}$ law of Mott[87,128]; above a particular temperature, the usual $1/T$ behavior is noticed. At this temperature limit, thermopower also shows a marked change in slope. In such systems, the Fermi energy of the electrons passes through a mobility edge separating extended states from states localized by disorder as the composition (or some other parameter) is varied. If $E_F > E_c$, the system is "metallic," but if $E_F < E_c$, electrons can only move by thermally activated hopping. The metal insulator transition of the Anderson type (Anderson transition) occurs when E_F and E_c can be made to vary in such a manner that $E_F - E_c$ changes sign. In the regime where there is variable-range hopping due to Anderson localization, resistivity exhibits the $1/T^{1/4}$ behavior. Mott and coworkers[129] have recently discussed the available experimental evidence for Anderson transitions in a variety of systems.

Superconducting Transitions

Although a discussion of this topic may not be strictly within the scope of the book, it would be worthwhile to briefly summarize general properties of superconductors in view of references made to superconducting transitions elsewhere in the text. The most distinctive property of a superconducting material is the near-total loss of resistance at a critical temperature T_c characteristic of the material. Figure 7-47*a* shows schematically two possible types of transitions. The sharp discontinuity is similar to that found in a single crystal of a pure element or an annealed alloy. The broad transition (broken line) represents the transition found in materials that are inhomogeneous and contain unusual strain distributions. Superconductors have resistivities of the order of 10^{-23} ohm-cm compared to the lowest resistivity in metals of the order of 10^{-13} ohm-cm. The temperature interval ΔT_c, over which the transition between the normal and superconductive states takes place, may be as little as 10^{-4} K or several degrees in width, depending upon the material.

A superconducting material below T_c (as in the case of a pure metal) exhibits perfect diamagnetism and excludes a magnetic field up to a critical field H_c, whereupon it reverts to the normal state, as shown in the H–T diagram in Fig. 7-47*b*. The difference in entropy near absolute zero between the superconducting and normal states relates directly to the electronic specific heat, γ; $(S_S–S_N)_{T \to 0} = -\gamma T$.

The large current-carrying capability of Nb_3Sn and similar alloys has led to an extensive study of the physical properties of these alloys. Such high-field

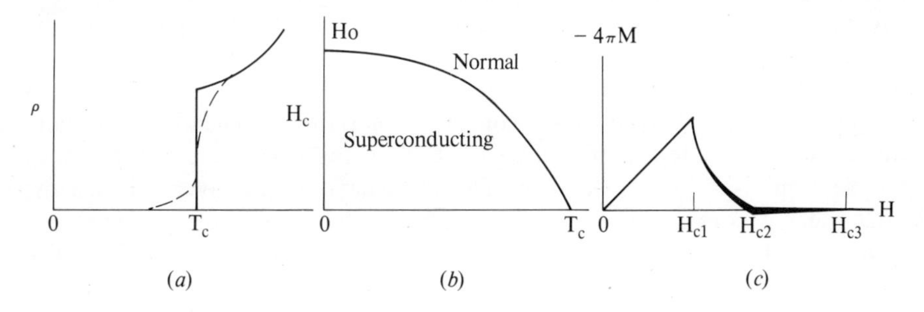

Figure 7-47 Properties of superconductors: (*a*) resistivity–temperature curves of pure (solid line) and impure (or imperfect) (broken line) materials, (*b*) magnetic field–temperature curve for a 'soft' (Type I) superconductor, (*c*) magnetization curve for a 'hard' (Type II) superconductor.

superconductors (Type II) pass from the perfect diamagnetic state (at low magnetic fields) to a mixed state and finally to a sheathed state before attaining the normal resistive state of the metal. The magnetization of a typical high-field superconductor is shown in Fig. 7-47*c*. The magnetic field values separating the four stages are shown as H_{c1}, H_{c2}, and H_{c3}.

The superconducting state below H_{c1} is diamagnetic, as in the case of pure metals which are of the "soft" (Type I) superconductor type. Between H_{c1} and H_{c2} a "mixed superconducting state" is found in which fluxons (a minimal unit of magnetic flux) create lines of normal superconductors in a superconducting matrix. The volume of the normal state is proportional to $-4\pi m$ in the "mixed state" region. At H_{c2} the fluxon density becomes so great as to drive the interior volume of the superconducting material completely normal. Between H_{c2} and H_{c3} the superconductor has a sheath of current-carrying superconductive material at the body surface, and above H_{c3} the normal state exists. High-field superconducting phenomena depend on specimen configuration. For example Hg, which is a Type I superconductor, has an entirely different magnetization behavior (in high magnetic fields) when enclosed in fine filamentary tunnels in vycor glass. A great majority of superconducting materials are of Type II. Most of the elements in pure form and a small number of stoichiometric and annealed compounds are of Type I.

Attempts to evolve criteria for superconductivity in elements, alloys, and other materials are being made continually. A useful empirical criterion is that due to Matthias. According to Matthias, alloys with average numbers of valence electrons per atom on the low sides of valence 5 and valance 7 are likely to have high T_c. The validity of this empirical rule is substantiated by the study of compounds possessing A15 structure.

Some semiconducting compounds become superconducting after or during the application of high pressure. Thus the high-pressure phases of silicon and germanium are superconducting in the dense phases. In general, it appears that all metals become superconducting even though T_c may be close to 0 K.

Crystal structures of known superconductors have provided a basis for discovering new ones, typical examples being the large number of superconducting A15 compounds. Laves phases and α-Mn structures similarly show a tendency to be superconducting. It is to be noted, however, that crystal structure has a minor influence on T_c. The important consideration is that the electronic structure is such as to give rise to a high density of states at the Fermi level. Correlations of the electronic specific heat and the Debye θs have essentially confirmed the BCS (Bardeen–Cooper–Schrieffer) theory within certain groups of materials.

An interesting class of materials are the layered chalcogenides like TaS_2 and NbS_2. The superconducting transition temperatures of these materials are enhanced substantially by intercalating organic molecules (like pyridine) and metal atoms.

It is somewhat disappointing that there has been no real breakthrough in the discovery of superconducting materials with high critical temperatures (>20 K). The question that always looms in the background is whether there is a limit to the superconducting critical temperature somewhere around 25 K. We do not know whether there are yet undiscovered materials with high values of T_c. The technical desirability of finding superconductors with high T_c is obvious.

Peierls Transition in One-dimensional Systems

It was predicted sometime ago by Little[130] that one-dimensional systems such as long-chain linear molecules with easily polarizable side-chains could exhibit high temperature superconductivity. There has been considerable effort in examining crystals in which electron motion is essentially in one dimension. However, all the quasi-one-dimensional crystals so far studied exhibit insulating behavior at low temperatures. This behavior is by no means unexpected. Peierls[131] had pointed out as early as 1955 that a one-dimensional metal should undergo lattice distortions with a wavenumber equal to twice the Fermi momentum. Furthermore, even Coulomb interaction between electrons gives rise to insulating behavior at low temperatures (Mott transition). Presence of disorder would also tend to prevent a one-dimensional system from being metallic at low temperatures.

Two typical systems with high, anisotropic conductivity have been investigated intensely. These are the mixed-valence planar complex, $K_2Pt(CN)_4Br_{0.3} \cdot 3H_2O$ (KCP),[132] and the charge transfer salt between tetrathiafulvalene (TTF) and tetracyanoquinodimethane (TCNQ).[133] Electrical conductivity data of these two compounds[132,134] are given in Fig. 7-48. In both these compounds, the quasi-one-dimensional structure is substantiated by all the physical phenomena of interest. The main interest in these systems is the one-dimensional motion of electrons.

It is difficult to do justice to the vast amount of fine experimental work reported on KCP and TTF–TCNQ in the recent literature.[135] It would suffice to point out that structural data, magnetic susceptibility, phonon spectrum, and the rest of the available information point to the existence of a Peierls transition in KCP; Peierls instability in KCP is associated with the appearance of giant Kohn anomaly. In the case of TTF–TCNQ, the existence of a true Peierls

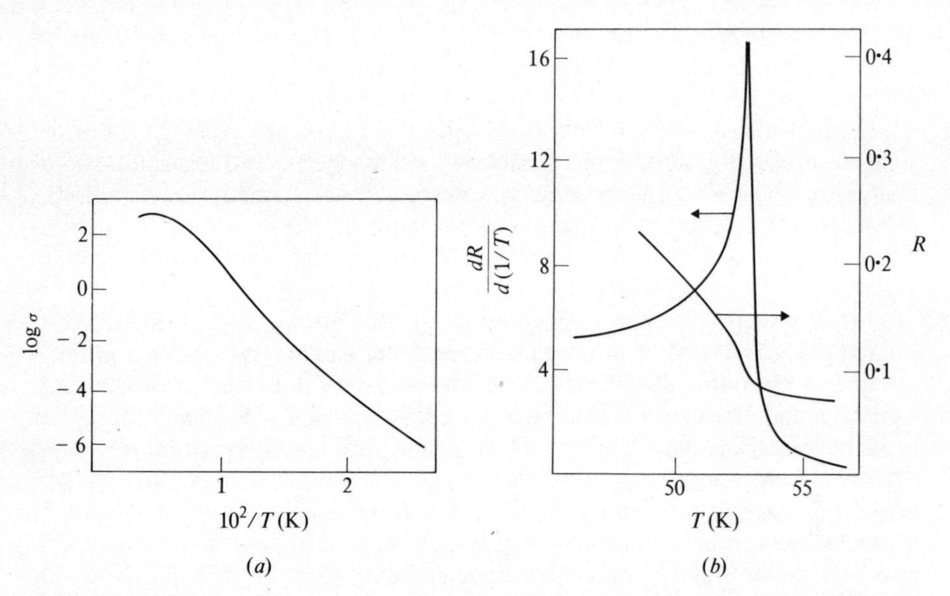

Figure 7-48 (*a*) Conductivity data on KCP. (*After Berenblyum et al. al.*[132]) (*b*) Resistance–temperature plot and $dR/d(1/T)$–temperature plot for TTF–TCNQ. (*After Horn and Rimai.*[134]) Note the second-order transition indicated in the plot of the derivative of resistance.

transition is not as clearly established.[135] Lattice disorder would affect Peierls transitions markedly. Another important aspect to be considered is the existence of paraconductivity up to the Peierls transition in a system like TTF–TCNQ. Peierls transitions in KCP and TTF–TCNQ have been recently reviewed by Bulaevskii,[135] and the reader is referred to this review and the original literature cited there for a detailed study of this interesting phenomenon. In order to obtain organic superconducting materials, it appears that one has to decrease the one-dimensional nature of metallic systems and eliminate Peierls instability. Increased interaction between conduction electrons and intramolecular vibrations could indeed give rise to high T_c values in favorable instances.

7-4 COOPERATIVE JAHN–TELLER EFFECT

According to the Jahn–Teller theorem, if the ground state of an ion in a crystal is orbitally degenerate, with no other perturbation present, the crystal will distort to one of lower symmetry in order to remove the degeneracy. Examples of crystals undergoing tetragonal distortion due to the presence of Jahn–Teller ions like Mn^{3+} and Cu^{2+} were given in Sec. 7-2. Jahn–Teller distortion is observed only if the orbital angular momentum is quenched by ligand fields. The distortion preserves the center of gravity of the e_g level of the cation, and hence the ion can obtain equal stabilization through distortion to tetragonal symmetry with $c/a > 1$ or < 1. The system could resonate between two stable configurations unless one of them is preferred for some reason. This happens if there is coupling between vibrational modes and low-frequency electronic motion, and the effect is then referred to as the dynamic Jahn–Teller effect. The cooperative Jahn–Teller effect (CJTE) is a phase transition driven by the interaction between the electronic states of one of the ions in the crystal and the phonons. The transition can be first- or second-order, and in either case there will be symmetry-lowering lattice distortion and splitting of electronic levels. Since the crystal distortion requires cooperative distortions around the Jahn–Teller ion, the concentration of Jahn–Teller ions must be quite large for such transitions.

Many spinels containing transition metal ions are known to exhibit CJTE. Englman[136] has described properties of such systems in his book. Recent progress in our understanding of CJTE is due to the discovery of a number of rare-earth vanadates and arsenates of zircon structure which show CJTE. Being transparent to visible radiation, these zircons make possible optical and spectroscopic studies of energy levels. Since transitions in these solids occur at low temperatures (10 K or lower), heat capacity anomalies and spectral properties can be studied adequately. Measurements of elastic constants employing ultrasonic and other techniques have also contributed significantly to our understanding of CJTE. If CJTE is accompanied by a second-order transition, then the soft mode would be an elastic excitation mode (strain mode). Variation of the appropriate elastic constant with temperature directly provides information on the strength of coupling of the electronic states to the strain mode. The use of ultrasonic experiments in the study of phase transitions has been reviewed by Rehwald.[137] CJTE has been reviewed extensively by Gehring and Gehring,[138] and we shall briefly examine some aspects of this interesting phenomenon.

Background Information

Jahn–Teller effects may be considered to be corrections to the Born–Oppenheimer approximation, and the JT contribution to the hamiltonian can be written as AQS^2, where A is a measure of the strength of coupling, Q the nuclear coordinate, and S an electronic operator. If we include the elastic energy, $\frac{1}{2}m\omega^2Q^2$, the potential energy exhibits two minima where $E_{\mathrm{JT}} = A^2/2m\omega^2$ at $Q = \pm Q_0$ where $A_0 = A/m\omega^2$. JT interaction does not alter the symmetry or degeneracies. There are four possible values of Q for a given value of energy, and if the value of A is changed, the values of Q and range of energies also change. If experimental observations are made in a short time, the presence of a distortion should be noticeable. An average of a number of observations would indicate a lowering of symmetry. This would be the situation in the static JT effect.

Dynamic JT effects can arise from thermal fluctuations. If $\hbar\omega \ll E_{\mathrm{JT}}$, then at low temperatures $kT \ll E_{\mathrm{JT}}$, and the system will be situated at the bottom of the potential well (static case). At higher T, $kT \gtrsim E_{\mathrm{JT}}$, and thermally induced fluctuations from one potential well to another can occur (dynamic case). A more important case of the dynamic JT effect occurs when $\hbar\omega \gtrsim E_{\mathrm{JT}}$. In this situation, even at the lowest temperature, there will be no stabilization of one distortion.

Another cause of dynamic JT effects occurs when electronic states are coupled to doubly degenerate lattice modes. Here the energy would depend on two linearly independent normal modes in the form $(Q_1^2 + Q_2^2)^{1/2}$, and there would be no local minima in the potential energy surface.

Since the mechanism of the JT effect involves interactions between ligand displacements (and hence the JT ions) due to the elastic properties of the lattice, an entire crystal can become unstable with respect to distortion if the concentration of JT ions is large. Phase transitions resulting from such interactions can result in a parallel or some other alignment of all the distortions. Since an isolated JT ion drives a local distortion, there would be some JT stabilization energy for an assembly of ions, and this would not make any contribution to the cooperative effect. One has to subtract this self-energy from the total energy to evaluate the cooperative effect.

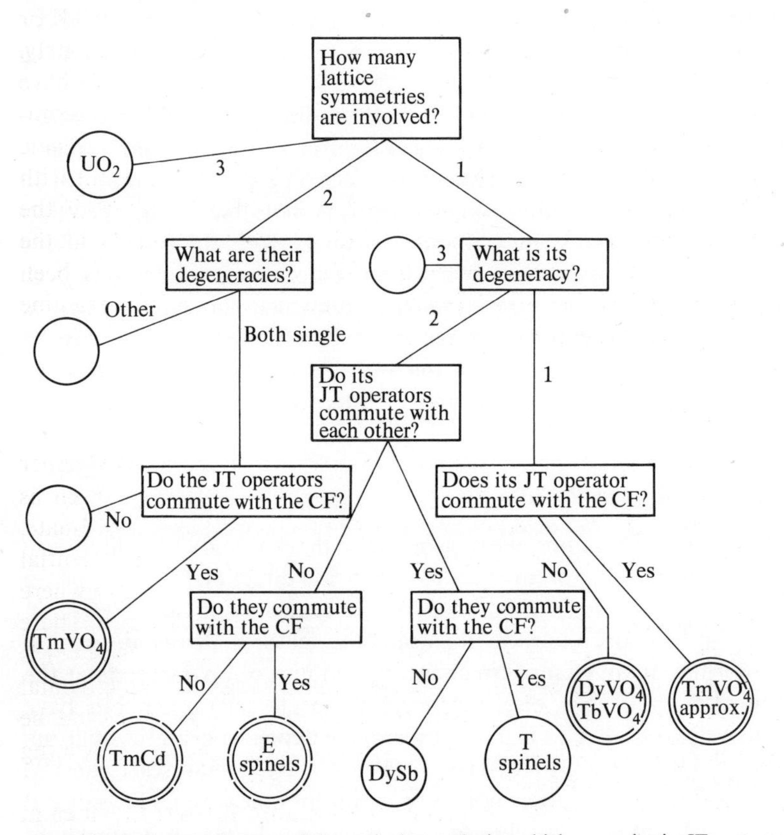

Figure 7-49 Various degrees of theoretical complexity which can arise in JT systems. (*After Gehring and Gehring.*[138]) The simplest theories correspond to answers on the right. The materials in the circles are those for which the particular theory has been used. A single circle indicates a first-order transition and a double circle indicates a second-order transition. A single circle plus a broken circle indicates a transition which is first-order because of the existence of anharmonic forces. CF stands for crystal field.

Most of the experimental results on CJTE can be explained on the basis of molecular field theory. This is because the interaction between the electron strain and elastic strain is fairly long-range. Employing simple molecular field theory, expressions have been derived for the order parameter, transverse susceptibility, vibron states, specific heat, and elastic constants. A detailed discussion of the theory and its applications may be found in the excellent review by Gehring and Gehring.[138] In Fig. 7-49 various possible situations of varying complexities that can arise in JT systems are presented schematically.

As mentioned earlier, rare-earth zircons are ideal cases for the study of CJTE. In $TmVO_4$, at high temperatures, the lowest electronic state of Tm^{3+} ion is an E doublet. (In Kramers ions there can be no true JT effect.) A pseudo-JT effect occurs if there is accidental or near degeneracy. $DyVO_4$ is such an example where two Kramers doublets are separated by 9 cm^{-1}; another example is $TbVO_4$. The rather unusual features of the low-lying electronic states of rare-earth zircons have been discussed by Pytte and Stevens[139] and Elliott et al.[140] Phonon modes and elastic constants of these materials are discussed in the review by Gehring and Gehring.[138]

Other compounds which exhibit CJTE are the cubic spinels, AB_2O_4, where A and B are both transition metal ions. The JT effect can arise from either A or B site ions or both simultaneously. The lowest electronic state can be a doublet (E spinel) or a triplet (T spinel). Since the electrons responsible for the JT effect are on the outside of the ions, they interact strongly with the lattice, giving rise to structural phase transitions at fairly high temperatures. This should be contrasted with the behavior of rare-earth zircons, which show transitions at very low temperatures. Rare-earth pnictides (of NaCl structure) show first-order phase transitions involving magnetic ordering and structural distortions. In these systems there is an interplay of magnetic and JT interactions.

Experimental Methods and Results

We shall briefly indicate the nature of experimental data reported in the literature on systems undergoing CJTE. Specific heat data provide direct evidence for phase transitions arising from CJTE. In Fig. 7-50, specific heat data of Cooke et al.[141] on $DyVO_4$ and $TmVO_4$ are given to illustrate the features. X-ray diffraction directly gives information on changes in structure and unit cell parameters at the transition. Optical methods (e.g., birefringence) and spectroscopic methods have been used extensively to study CJTE. The temperature dependence of the splitting of the E_g phonon mode in $DyVO_4$ and $TbVO_4$ (as found by Raman scattering[140]) is shown in Fig. 7-51. Raman scattering is very useful for studying CJTE, since it provides energies of zone-center phonons as well as vibrons in transparent materials. Lattice parameters of $TbVO_4$ are also shown in Fig. 7-51.[142] The distortion in this second-order transition is only 2 percent (compared to $\sim$8 percent in the first-order transition of $CuCr_2O_4$). In Fig. 7-52, the temperature dependence of the ground-state splitting of $TmVO_4$ is shown,[143] along with the theoretical curve from molecular field theory. Ultrasonic and Brillouin scattering methods have been used to measure the temperature variation of elastic constants. Such measurements directly provide information on the coupling of JT ions to the crystal lattice. Figure 7-53 shows the presence of a soft strain mode in $DyVO_4$, as indicated by the temperature dependence of the elastic constant.[144] Neutron scattering has not been as successful in the study of CJTE because scattering by electronic states is very weak. One case of a second-order JT transition studied by this technique

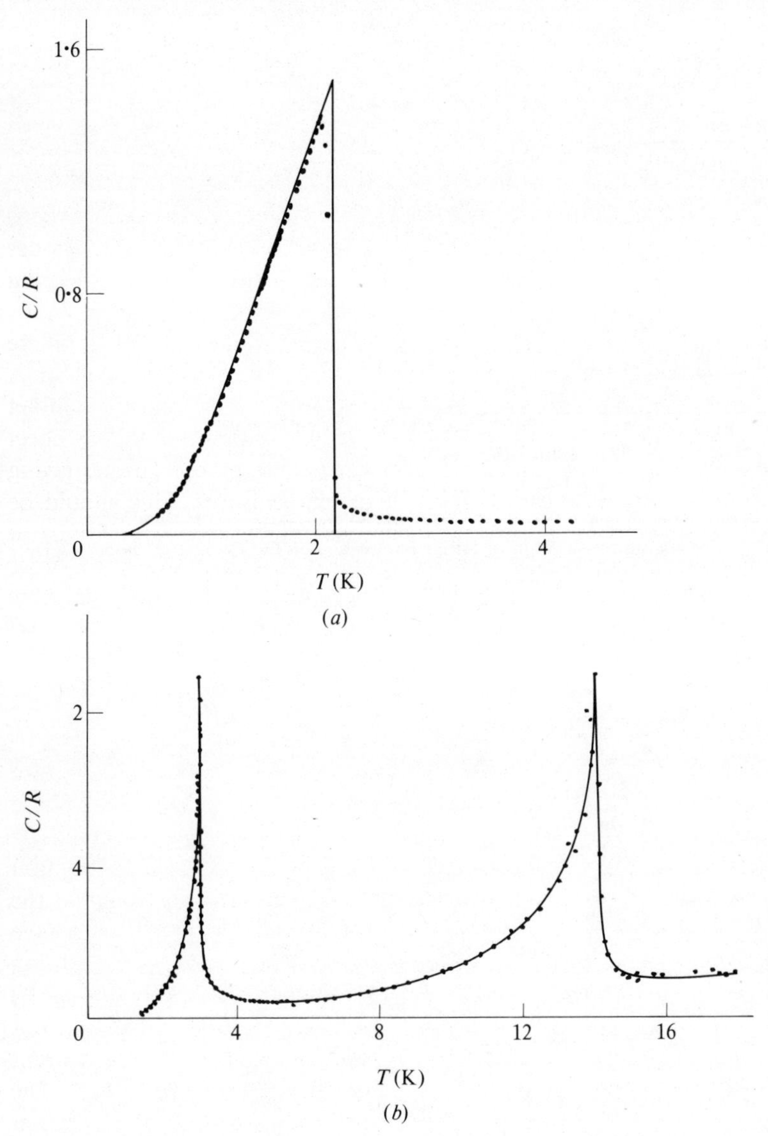

Figure 7-50 Specific heat of (*a*) $TmVO_4$, showing λ anomaly associated with the JT transition, and (*b*) $DyVO_4$, showing λ anomalies associated with a magnetic transition at 3 K and JT transition at 14 K (*After Cooke et al.*[141])

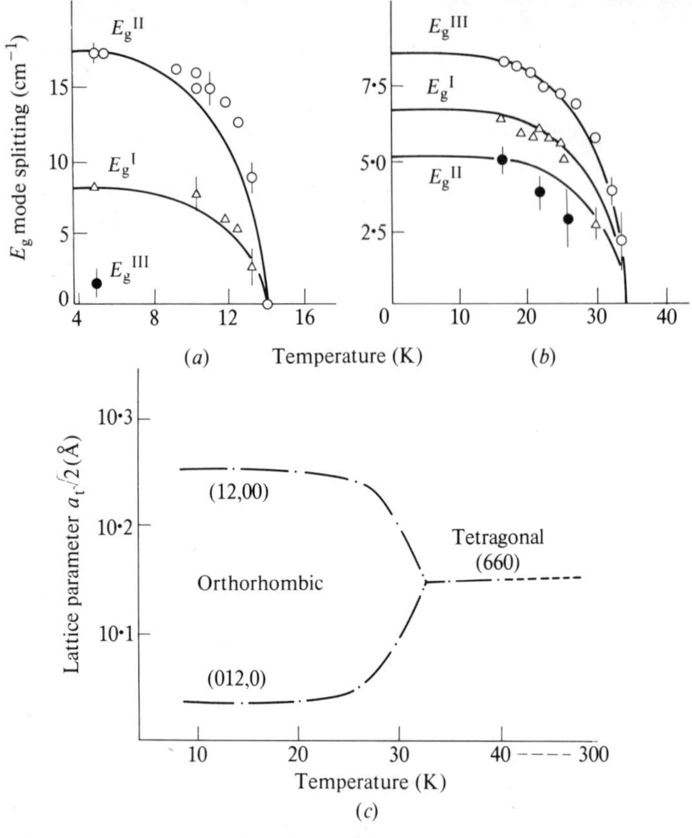

Figure 7-51 Temperature dependence of the splitting of the E_g phonon mode: (*a*) $DyVO_4$, (*b*) $TbVO_4$. (*After Elliott et al.*[140]) Temperature variation of lattice parameters of $TbVO_4$ is also shown. (*After Will et al.*[142])

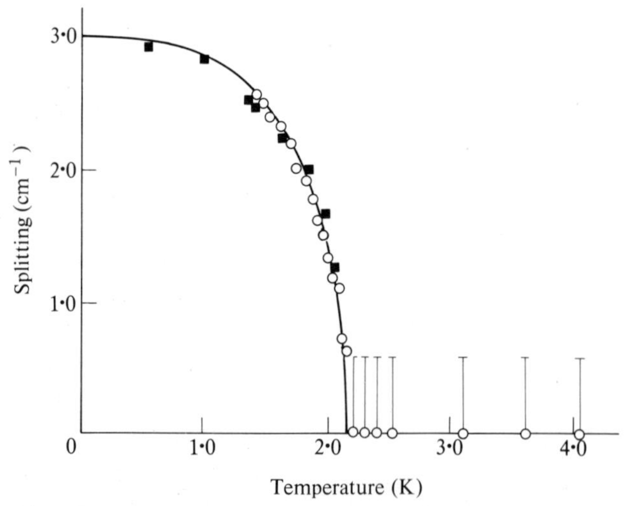

Figure 7-52 Temperature dependence of the ground-state splitting in $TmVO_4$ from magnetic measurements (squares) and optical absorption (circles). The line is from molecular field theory. (*After Becker et al.*[143])

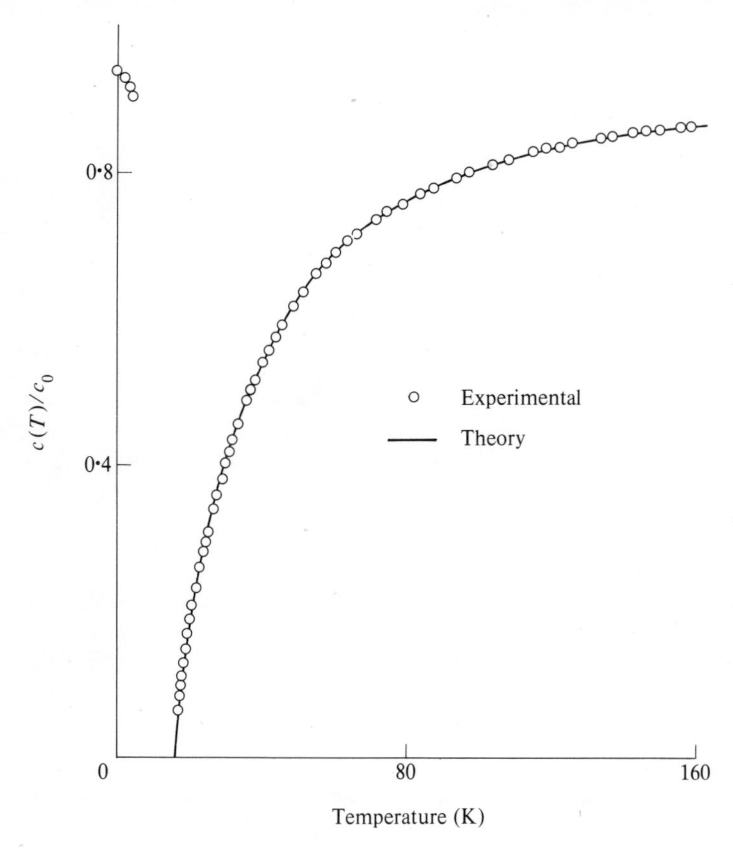

Figure 7-53 Elastic constant of $DyVO_4$ as a function of temperature. (*After Melcher and Scott.*[144])

is that of $PrAlO_3$ by Birgeneau et al.[145] Applications of uniaxial stress and magnetic field have been most useful in studying CJTE, since these effects convert the crystal to a single domain. Mössbauer spectroscopy is ideally suited for examining distortions accompanying CJTE, and some results were discussed earlier in Sec. 7-2 (see for example $FeCr_2O_4$).

Gehring and Gehring[138] have listed a number of CJTE materials along with literature references. There is no doubt that there will be continued activity in studying this interesting phenomenon in a number of systems. Before closing this section, we shall briefly examine the transitions of $PrAlO_3$ which are quite fascinating. $PrAlO_3$ undergoes three phase transitions, starting from the high-temperature cubic perovskite structure through trigonal and orthorhombic phases to a tetragonal structure at $T = 0$ K. These transitions can be understood in terms of rotations of the AlO_6 octahedra coupled to the electronic levels of the Pr^{3+} ion through electron–phonon interaction.[146] The orthorhombic–monoclinic transition (second-order) at 151 K is driven by the coupling of the lowest-lying exciton to phonons;[145] the first-order trigonal–orthorhombic transition at 205 K is also similarly due to electron–phonon interaction. For such systems, order

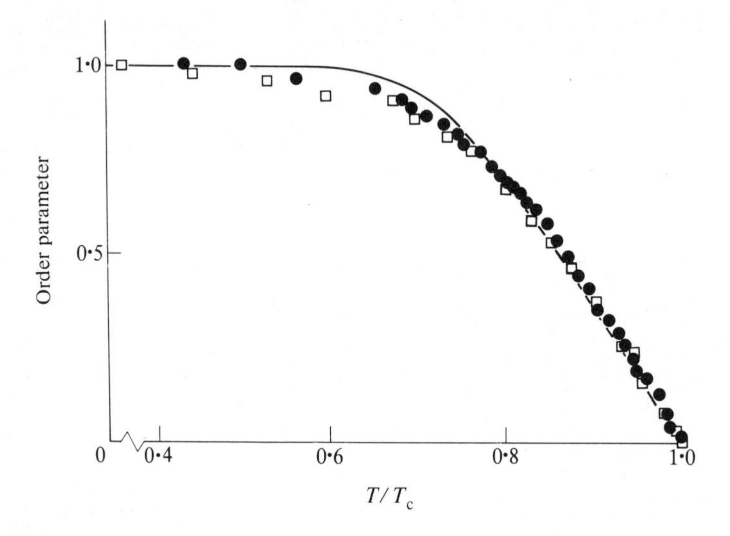

Figure 7-54 Comparison of the different-order parameters for the 151 K second-order transition in $PrAlO_3$. (*After Sturge et al.*[148]) The full line is the smooth curve through the internal displacement order parameter ($\cos^2 2\phi$ from ESR). Closed circles represent the electronic order parameter (from optical studies) and squares represent the reduced macroscopic strain from elastic neutron scattering.

parameters can be derived from the splitting of the electronic levels, the macroscopic strain, and the appropriate internal displacements, and all these order parameters should in principle show the same temperature dependence.[147] All the above three order parameters have been derived for the second-order transition of $PrAlO_3$ at 151 K: electron splitting from optical absorption, fluorescence, and electronic Raman spectroscopy, internal displacements by ESR spectroscopy, and macroscopic strain by neutron scattering. The three order parameters have been compared[148] and found to show fairly good agreement (Fig. 7-54). The order parameters also follow the $(T_c - T)^{1/2}$ behavior within 0.2° of T_c.

7-5 DIELECTRIC PROPERTIES

The dielectric properties of a material are governed by the response of the material to an applied electric field at the electronic, atomic, molecular, and macroscopic levels. Polarization and dielectric loss in materials are phenomena of interest, and these are generally studied as a function of frequency. According to Maxwell's equations,

$$D = \varepsilon E$$

where D is the dielectric displacement, E the electric field strength, and ε is the dielectric constant of the medium; ε is equal to the product $\varepsilon_v\varepsilon_r$, where ε_r is the dielectric constant relative to vacuum and ε_v is the dielectric constant of vacuum. Applying an electric field to a material causes a displacement of electric charges, creating or reorienting the dipoles in the material. This property, called polarization, P, is given by

$$P = \varepsilon_v(\varepsilon_r - 1)E = \varepsilon_v \chi_e E$$

where χ_e is the electric susceptibility. P can be expressed in terms of the elementary dipole moments, p, as $P = Np$ where N is the number of dipoles per unit volume and $p = \alpha E$ where α is the polarizability. The total polarization of a multiphase material containing permanent dipoles will have electronic, ionic, orientational, and interfacial (space charge) contributions:

$$P = P_e + P_i + P_O + P_s$$

In a single-phase material the last term, due to interfacial polarization, P_s, will be absent, and P will be given by,

$$P = P_e + P_i + P_O = P_e + P_i + (Np^2E/3kT)$$

A dipole in a crystal experiences not only the external field E but also the field due to the polarization medium around it. The effective field (local field), E^1, is given by

$$E^1 = E + \frac{P}{3\varepsilon_v} = \left(\frac{\varepsilon_r + 2}{3}\right)E$$

so that the polarizability for unit volume is related to the relative dielectric constant of the material, ε_r, by the expression

$$\frac{N\alpha}{3\varepsilon_v} = \frac{\varepsilon_r - 1}{\varepsilon_r + 2}$$

In terms of molar polarization, π, the above equation becomes

$$\pi = \frac{N_O\alpha}{3\varepsilon_v} = \frac{\varepsilon_r - 1}{\varepsilon_r + 2}\left(\frac{M}{\rho}\right)(m^3)$$

where $N_O = NM/\rho$ = Avogadro number per kg mole, and ρ is the density in kg m^{-3}. This equation is the well-known Clausius–Mosotti equation.

When a time-dependent electric field is applied to a dielectric material, $D = \varepsilon^* E$, where $\varepsilon^* = \varepsilon' - i\varepsilon''$; here, ε' and ε'' are the real and imaginary parts of the dielectric constant. The time-lag between the response and the stimulus is given by a phase angle δ such that, for small values of δ,

$$\tan \delta = \frac{\varepsilon''}{\varepsilon'}$$

The time-dependence of ε'' and ε' are characterized by the relaxation time, τ, which follows an Arrhenius-type equation, $\tau = \tau_0 \exp(\Delta E/kT)$. In terms of frequency and time,

$$\varepsilon' = \varepsilon_\infty + \frac{\varepsilon_s - \varepsilon_\infty}{1 + \omega^2\tau^2}$$

$$\varepsilon'' = \frac{\omega\tau(\varepsilon_s - \varepsilon_\infty)}{1 + \omega^2\tau^2}$$

and

$$\tan\delta = \frac{\omega\tau(\varepsilon_s - \varepsilon_\infty)}{\varepsilon_\infty\omega^2\tau^2 + \varepsilon_s}$$

Here, ε_s and ε_∞ are the static (low-frequency) and optical (high-frequency) dielectric constants respectively.

From the relations given earlier, we obtain

$$P = \frac{N\alpha E}{1 - (N\alpha/3\varepsilon_v)}$$

The susceptibility is therefore given by

$$\chi_e = \frac{P}{\varepsilon_v E} = \frac{N\alpha/\varepsilon_v}{1 - (N\alpha/3\varepsilon_v)} = \varepsilon_r - 1$$

We see that when $N\alpha/3\varepsilon_v = 1$, both polarization and susceptibility go to infinity. At a critical temperature, T_c, called the Curie temperature, the randomizing effect of temperature is balanced by the orienting effect of the internal field. Under such conditions χ_e is given by

$$\chi_e = \varepsilon_r - 1 = \frac{3T_c}{T - T_c}$$

This equation, called the Curie–Weiss law, is similar to the one described under ferromagnetism earlier in the chapter. Below T_c, the internal field increases the polarization and *vice versa*, and the material becomes spontaneously polarized or ferroelectric. Above T_c, dipole directions are randomized because of thermal agitation and the material is paraelectric, while below T_c dipoles exhibit parallel alignment. The Curie–Weiss law is generally written in the form

$$\varepsilon = \varepsilon_\infty + \frac{C}{T - T_c}$$

where the Curie constant, C, is given by $Np^2/3\varepsilon_v k$. In Fig. 7-55, a plot of $1/\varepsilon$ against temperature is given for $BaTiO_3$. The plot yields a value of 1.5×10^5 K for C and 393 K for T_c.

An important explanation of ferroelectricity in $BaTiO_3$ and other materials is based on the lattice-dynamical theory of Cochran[149] and Anderson.[150] Here, a transverse optical mode which varies with temperature as $\omega_T^2 \propto (T - T_c)$ is

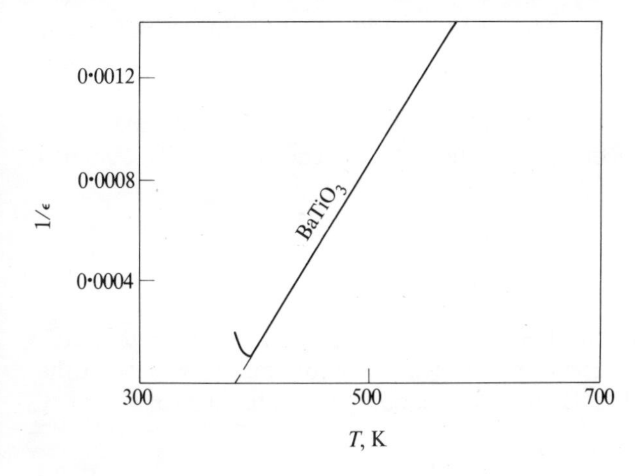

Figure 7-55 Variation of $1/\varepsilon$ of $BaTiO_3$ with temperature.

identified. When $T \rightarrow T_c$, $\omega_T \rightarrow 0$ and $\varepsilon \rightarrow \varepsilon_\infty$ (since $\varepsilon \propto 1/\omega^2$), giving rise to the paraelectric–ferroelectric transition. The existence of such soft modes has been verified in several materials by neutron scattering and Raman spectroscopy (Chap. 6), and further discussion will follow later in this section.

If the internal field gives rise to an antiparallel alignment of dipoles in adjacent unit cells (instead of parallel alignment, as in ferroelectrics), the material is said to be antiferroelectric. Above a critical temperature, an antiferroelectric become paraelectric. While in ferroelectric transitions there is condensation of a soft mode at the Brillouin zone center, in antiferroelectric phase transitions (where the unit cell size increases) soft-mode condensation is at the zone boundary. In both cases, the order parameter is related to the static part of the normal coordinate of the corresponding soft mode. In the simple model of antiferroelectricity, one normally considers the two sublattice polarizations to be equal to each other (and there is only one order parameter). Kittel[151] has developed a model with two collinear sublattice polarizations as thermodynamic variables, and this general model can, in principle, describe ferroelectrics and ferrielectrics as well as antiferroelectrics.

Thermodynamics of Ferroelectric Transitions

We shall briefly discuss the thermodynamics of ferroelectric transitions in the light of Landau's theory of structural phase transitions (see Chap. 2). According to Landau's theory,[152] a ferroelectric transition can be described in terms of an order parameter whose appearance at T_c breaks the symmetry of the paraelectric phase. The order parameter vanishes above T_c and is nonzero below T_c. The order parameter measures the degree of long-range order of dipoles (in order–disorder transitions) or degree of displacement of certain ionic groups (in displacive transitions). The order parameter in ferroelectric transitions is the spontaneous polarization; in antiferroelectric transitions it is the sublattice polarization. Landau's theory was applied to ferroelectrics by Devonshire.[153]

Following Landau, the expression for free energy density is given by

$$g(T, P) = g_0(T) + \tfrac{1}{2}a(T)P^2 + \tfrac{1}{4}b(T)P^4 + \tfrac{1}{6}c(T)P^6 + \cdots$$

where P is the spontaneous polarization along the ferroelectric axis. The equilibrium value of spontaneous polarization, P_0, at temperature T is obtained by minimizing g:

$$\left(\frac{\partial g}{\partial P}\right)_{P=P_0} = 0$$

Thus, $P_0[a(T) + b(T)P_0^2 + c(T)P_0^4] = 0$. One of the solutions of this equation is $P_0 = 0$, applicable to the paraelectric phase. The other solution, $P_0 \neq 0$, is for the ferroelectric phase. The stable solution corresponding to a minimum in g is

$$\left(\frac{\partial^2 g}{\partial P^2}\right)_{P_0} > 0$$

Since $(\partial g/\partial P) = E$, the stability condition is equivalent to $\chi^{-1} > 0$.

Taking the second derivative of $g(T, P)$, we obtain

$$\chi^{-1} = a(T) + 3b(T)P_0^2 + 5c(T)P_0^4 > 0$$

For the paraelectric phase ($P_0 = 0$), the above equation becomes

$$\chi^{-1} = a(T) > 0$$

Near the stability limit T_0, $a(T) \approx a'(T - T_0)$, and $a' = (\partial A/\partial T)_{T=T_0} > 0$. This gives rise to the Curie–Weiss law of dielectric susceptibility of the paraelectric phase,

$$\chi_T = \frac{C}{T - T_0}$$

where $C = 1/a'$ and $T > T_0$. Since $b(T)$ and $c(T)$ would only vary slightly with temperature around the transition temperature, we may treat them as constants:

$$b(T) = b(T_c) = b \qquad \text{and} \qquad c(T) = c(T_c) = c$$

Here, c can be taken as positive, while b can be positive or negative.

A phase transition will be of the second order if $b > 0$, and first-order if $b < 0$. The order parameter will be a continuous function of T in a second-order transition and a discontinuous function in a first-order transition. The case when $b = 0$ corresponds to a "critical" transition; fluctuation in the neighborhood would be very large in such a case ($a = b = 0$ and $T = T_0$), since the free energy would be sixth-order in P. If $b \neq 0$, the increase in free energy is fourth-order in P when $a = 0$, $T = T_0$. Equilibrium properties of ferroelectrics and antiferroelectrics have been discussed in detail by Fatuzzo and Merz[154] as well as Blinc and Zeks.[155]

In the ferroelectrics discussed so far, the order parameter was the spontaneous polarization, and anomalies in dielectric properties were due to increased correlation in the fluctuations of order parameters at T_c. Such ferroelectrics are considered to be proper ferroelectrics. There are ferroelectrics where the order parameter is not the spontaneous polarization. Because of coupling between these two quantities, they exhibit a nonvanishing order parameter accompanied by spontaneous polarization at T_c. These ferroelectrics are called improper ferroelectrics. Two classes of improper ferroelectrics can be visualized: (1) where P and the order parameter have different symmetry properties (e.g., $Gd_2(MoO_4)_3$), and (2) where the two have the same symmetry (e.g., KH_2PO_4). Thermodynamic properties of these two cases have been reviewed by Blinc and Zeks,[155] who have also discussed dynamic properties of ferroelectrics at length.

Symmetry and Phase Transitions

Landau[152] was the first to apply group theory to thermodynamics. Following Landau, we shall examine the relation between the high-temperature and low-temperature symmetry of crystals undergoing ferro- or antiferroelectric transitions. We shall also look at the symmetry of the soft modes driving such transitions. The discussion will be concerned with second-order transitions where the order parameter changes continuously, but the symmetry of the system changes discontinuously causing the appearance or disappearance of certain symmetry elements (unlike the case of first-order transitions, where there is no relation between the symmetries of the high and low-temperature phases).

Let $\rho_0(x, y, z)$ represent the density function which determines the different positions of atoms in a crystal above T_c. Let the symmetry of the crystal be determined by the set G_0 of all coordinate transformations. On cooling below T_c, certain symmetry elements disappear, resulting in a lower symmetry of the crystal. The new density function $\rho(x, y, z)$ is given by

$$\rho(x, y, z) = \rho_0(x, y, z) + \delta\rho(x, y, z)$$

where $\delta\rho(x, y, z)$ is the small change caused by the lowering of symmetry. The symmetry group of ρ (say, G_1) is the same as that of $\delta\rho$ and cannot contain elements of symmetry not present in G_0. Thus G_1 should be a subgroup of G_0. We can expand $\delta\rho$ in terms of functions $\phi_i^{(n)}(x, y, z)$ which form the bases of the n irreducible representations of G_0:

$$\delta\rho = \sum_i \sum_n C_i^{(n)} \phi_i^{(n)}$$

Since a transition at a temperature would arise from changes in symmetry corresponding to a single irreducible representation of the high-temperature group G_0, we can rewrite the summation as

$$\delta\rho(x, y, z) = \sum_i C_i \phi_i(x, y, z)$$

If we find the irreducible representation of the space groups and examine their properties, we shall have determined the possible symmetry changes in a second-order transition. Each basis function of an irreducible representation of a space group is characterized by the **k** vectors in the reciprocal lattice as follows:

$$\phi_i(x, y, z) = U_{i,\mathbf{k}}(x, y, z)\, e^{i\mathbf{k}r}$$

Only a small number of representations would be relevant to any particular situation such as the ferroelectric–paraelectric transition. In the transitions of proper ferroelectrics, the unit cell size does not change and soft mode condensation is at the zone center, $\mathbf{k} = (0, 0, 0)$; thus one has only to find the irreducible representations of the crystalline point group. The values of $C_i^{(n)}$ can be determined from thermodynamic considerations. Since the crystal has the symmetry ρ_0 at the transition (T_c), all $C_i^{(n)}$ must vanish at this point. That is, at $T = T_c$, $\rho = \rho_0$ or $\delta\rho = 0$. Since the transition is second-order, $\delta\rho$ should vanish gradually and the coefficients C_i should get smaller as the transition is approached. The free-energy density can be expanded in terms of power of C_i and T_c in the following manner:

$$\eta^2 = \sum_i C_i^2 \qquad \text{and} \qquad C_i = \eta\gamma_i$$

where η is the order parameter, γ is the symmetry parameter, and $\sum_i \gamma_i^2 = 1$. Thus, each term in the expansion would contain only scalar invariant combinations of C_i of the corresponding order. (Note that free energy has to be independent of the choice of the coordinate system.) We can now write the expression for g as

$$g = g_0 + g_1 = g_0 + a\eta f^{(1)} + A\eta^2 f^{(2)} + B\eta^3 f^{(3)} + C\eta^4 f^{(4)} + \cdots$$

The coefficients a, A, B, etc., are all temperature-dependent, and $f^{(l)}$ is a homogeneous function of order l in the coefficients γ_i. Only those $f^{(l)}$ functions which are scalar invariants under all operations of G_0 can occur. Furthermore, $f^{(1)} = 0$ (since first-order invariants come in only for identity representation) and $f^{(2)} = 1$.

Stability conditions are obtained by

$$\frac{\partial g}{\partial \eta} = 0 \qquad \text{and} \qquad \frac{\partial^2 g}{\partial \eta^2} > 0$$

That is, $\eta = 0$ is stable if $A > 0$, and $\eta \neq 0$ is stable if $A < 0$. The state of minimum free energy will correspond to a nonzero η and $\delta\rho$. A transition from high symmetry (G_0) to lower symmetry (G_1) occurs at $A = 0$; if the crystal should be stable for $A = 0$ and $\eta = 0$, g has to increase for both positive and negative changes of η. This can happen only if the third-order terms in the free-energy density expression are zero (or $f^{(3)} = 0$ by symmetry).

The symmetry conditions for a second-order transition may be summarized as follows: (1) the symmetry group of one state (G_1) is a subgroup of that of the other state (G_0); (2) the change in crystal transformation should correspond to a single irreducible representation of G_0 (but not the identity representation); and (3) free energy expansion in terms of the order parameter cannot have third-order terms. We should note that, despite satisfying all the above three conditions, if $C < 0$, the transition will be of the first order. The second-order terms do not contain γ_i and are determined by minimizing fourth and higher-order terms. The symmetry parameters found in this manner determine the symmetry of the two temperature phases of the crystal. The γ_i coefficients along with the appearance of a nonzero order parameter η breaks the symmetry of the high-temperature phase. Thus we have

$$A > 0{:}\ T > T_c, \qquad \rho = \rho_0, \qquad g_{\min} = g_0 \qquad \text{and} \qquad G = G_0$$

$$A < 0{:}\ T < T_c, \qquad \rho = \rho_0 + \delta\rho, \qquad g_{\min} = g_0 + g_{1,\min}, \qquad G = G_1$$

In the case of ferroelectric transitions of $BaTiO_3$ (the high-temperature paraelectric phase is the cubic perovskite), three possible solutions have been worked out, giving rise to tetragonal ($P \parallel [100]$ axis), orthorhombic ($P \parallel [110]$ axis), and rhombohedral ($P \parallel [111]$ axis) phases.[156]

In addition to the three necessary and sufficient conditions for the occurrence of a second-order transition mentioned earlier, Lifshitz[157] has derived a fourth condition which essentially states that the unit cell of a crystal below T_c is a simple multiple of the original cell. This condition is useful in discussing antiferroelectrics and improper ferroelectrics.

Since Landau-type analysis can be somewhat complex, a simpler alternative approach is often employed to find out compatible groups G_0 and G_1 in ferroelectric and antiferroelectric transitions. This approach, often referred to as the Curie principle,[158] states that the symmetry group of the low-temperature ordered phase G_1 contains all the symmetry elements of the high-temperature phase G_0 and the group $G_{\inf}$ of the order parameter which appears below T_c. Thus G_1 is a subgroup of G_0 formed by the intersection of G_0 and $G_{\inf}$. By varying the direction of the symmetry elements of $G_{\inf}$ with respect to the symmetry elements of G_0, all possible ferro- and antiferroelectric subgroups for a paraelectric group can be found. The possible ferroelectric or antiferroelectric point groups which can result from the 32 paraelectric point groups (for various directions of the spontaneous polarization) have been worked out.[155]

Since the eigenvector of the soft mode is the order parameter of ferro- and antiferroelectric transitions, the structure of the ordered phase below T_c would be the superposition of the frozen-in soft-mode displacements and the structure of the high-temperature disordered phase. The symmetry of the soft mode involved in a transition can therefore be worked out. The reader is referred to the book by Blinc and Zeks[155] for detailed information on symmetries of soft modes.

Ferroelectric Materials

Of the 32 crystal classes, 11 are centrosymmetric while 21 are noncentrosymmetric. Of the 21 noncentrosymmetric classes, 20 are piezoelectric, exhibiting electric polarity when subjected to stress. Ten of the 20 piezoelectric classes possess a unique polar axis and are pyroelectric (showing change in polarization with temperature). Pyroelectrics whose polarity can be reversed by application of

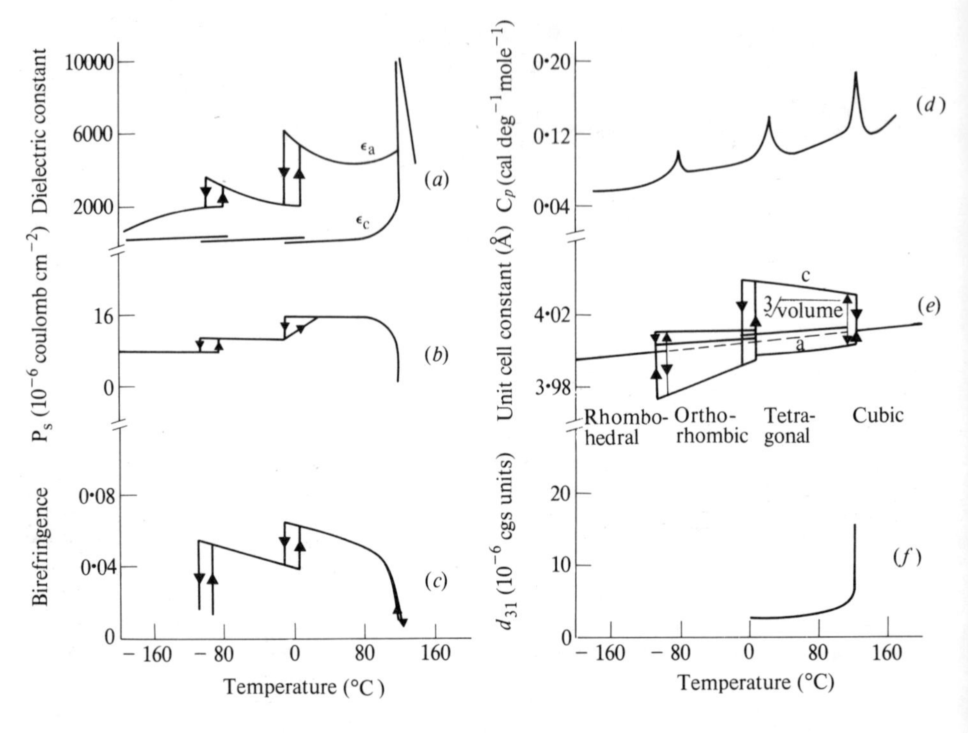

Figure 7-56 Transformations in $BaTiO_3$ accompanied by changes in (*a*) dielectric constant, (*b*) spontaneous polarization, (*c*) birefringence coefficient, (*d*) heat capacity, (*e*) lattice dimensions, and (*f*) piezoelectric coefficient. Experimental points are not shown.

electric fields are ferroelectric. Thus all ferroelectric materials are also piezoelectric, although the reverse is not true. Various types of ferroelectric materials have been discovered and characterized and the subject has been reviewed extensively in the literature.[159,166] We shall first examine the results of studies on $BaTiO_3$ and related materials to understand typical characteristics of ferroelectric materials.

Barium titanate, which crystallizes in the perovskite structure, has cubic symmetry above 393 K, with Ba^{2+} in the body center and TiO_6 octahedra in the corners. It undergoes a transformation to a tetragonal structure at 393 K, to an orthorhombic structure at 278 K, and to a rhombohedral structure at 183 K (Fig. 7-56). Relative to the cubic phase, elongation occurs along one of the edges ([100] direction) in the tetragonal phase, along one of the face diagonals ([110] direction) in the orthorhombic phase, and along one of the body diagonals ([111] direction) in the rhombohedral phase. The Ti^{4+} ion moves in these directions as the crystal is cooled from the cubic phase. The ionic positions in the cubic and tetragonal forms are shown in Fig. 7-57, along with the possible orientations of the polar axis in the three ferroelectric phases. Besides the dielectric constant and polarization, various other physical properties like heat capacity,

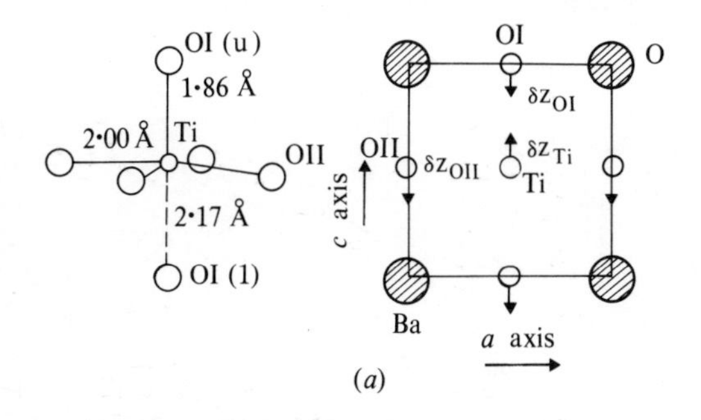

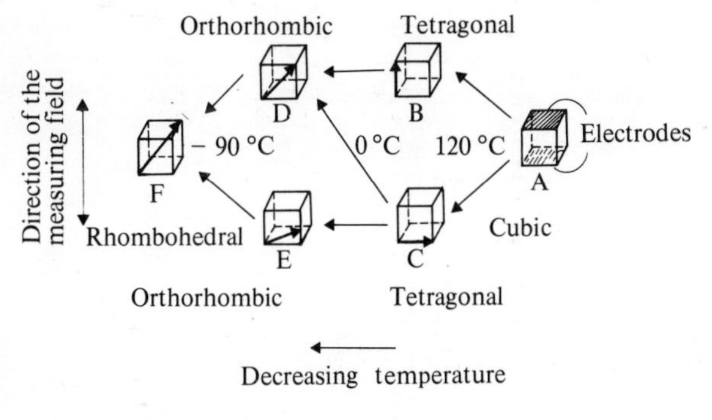

Figure 7-57 (*a*) Distortion of TiO_6 octahedron in tetragonal $BaTiO_3$ and schematic projection on (010). (*b*) Possible orientations of the polar axis when an electric field is applied along the pseudo-cubic [001] direction of $BaTiO_3$. Polar axes are shown by arrows inside each cube.

birefringence, and thermal expansion coefficient show anomalous changes at the three phase transformations (Figs. 7-56 and 7-58). The plot of $1/\varepsilon$ against T showing Curie–Weiss-law behavior above 393 K is shown in Fig. 7-55.

The polarization of a ferroelectric material varies nonlinearly with the applied electric field. The P–E behavior is characterized by a hysteresis loop similar to the B–H behavior of ferromagnetic materials. Observation of the hysteresis loop is the best evidence for the existence of ferroelectricity in a material. The hysteresis loop has its origin in the rearrangement of domains under the influence of an applied electric field. Generally the domains are randomly distributed, giving a net zero polarization. Under an applied field or mechanical stress, favorably oriented domains grow at the expense of the less favorably oriented domains until a single domain configuration is obtained. The domain structure itself is related to the crystallography of the ferroelectric phase with respect to the para-electric phase. Thus, in the tetragonal phase of $BaTiO_3$, adjacent domains may have their polar axes making angles of 90° or 180°.

The importance of soft modes in relation to ferroelectricity was discussed in Chap. 6 (and also earlier in this section), where the cases of $BaTiO_3$ and $SrTiO_3$ were specifically mentioned. Studies of the Mössbauer spectra of Co^{57}-doped $BaTiO_3$ (Fig. 7-59) and Sn^{119}-doped $PbTiO_3$ have shown that the Lamb–Mössbauer factor[161b] undergoes anomalous change at T_c. This change is obviously related to the temperature-dependent optic mode. As pointed out in Chap. 6,

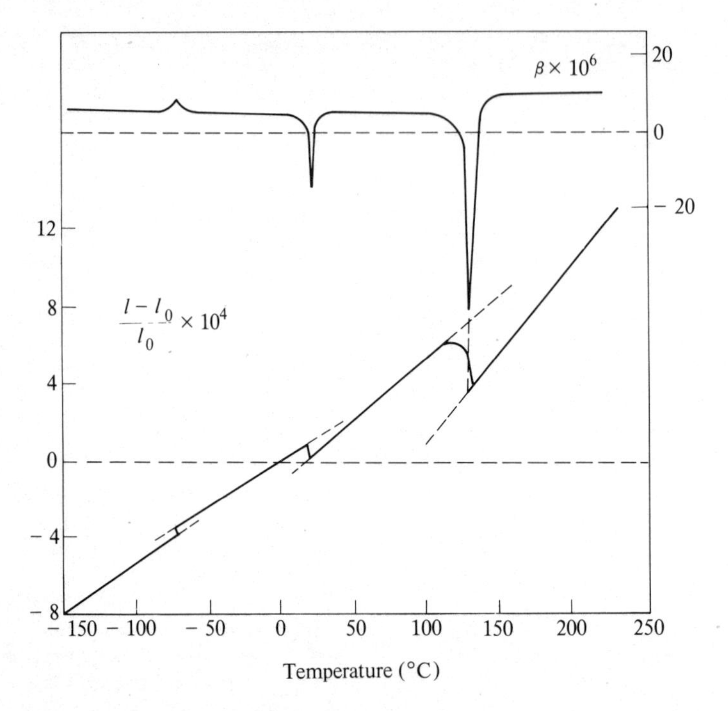

Figure 7-58 Coefficient of linear thermal expansion of ceramic $BaTiO_3$ and fractional length change, $\Delta l/l$, as functions of temperature. Experimental points are not shown. (*After Shirane and Takeda.*[161a])

neutron scattering and Raman spectroscopy are by far the most powerful tools for studying soft modes. Raman spectra show clear evidence of phase transitions, the cubic phase generally giving second-order spectra. Temperature-dependence of the various modes gives information on their relative contributions. In Fig. 7-60 we have shown the Raman spectra[162] of $PbTiO_3$ and $KNbO_3$ to illustrate these aspects. Soft modes in ferroelectrics have been extensively reviewed by Blinc and Zeks.[155]

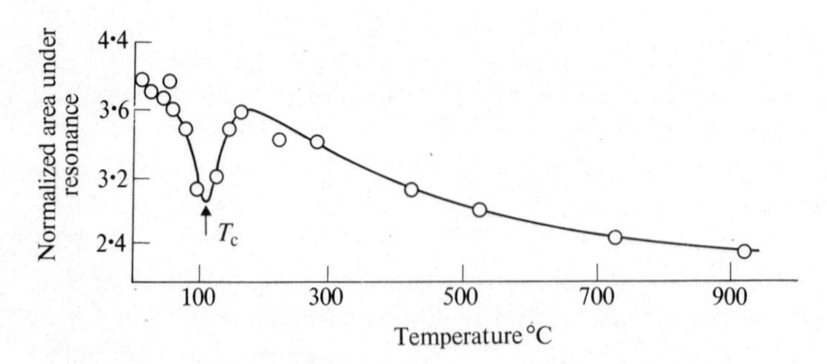

Figure 7-59 Variation of the area under the Mössbauer resonance in Fe^{57}: $BaTiO_3$ as a function of temperature. (*After Bhide and Multhani.*[161b])

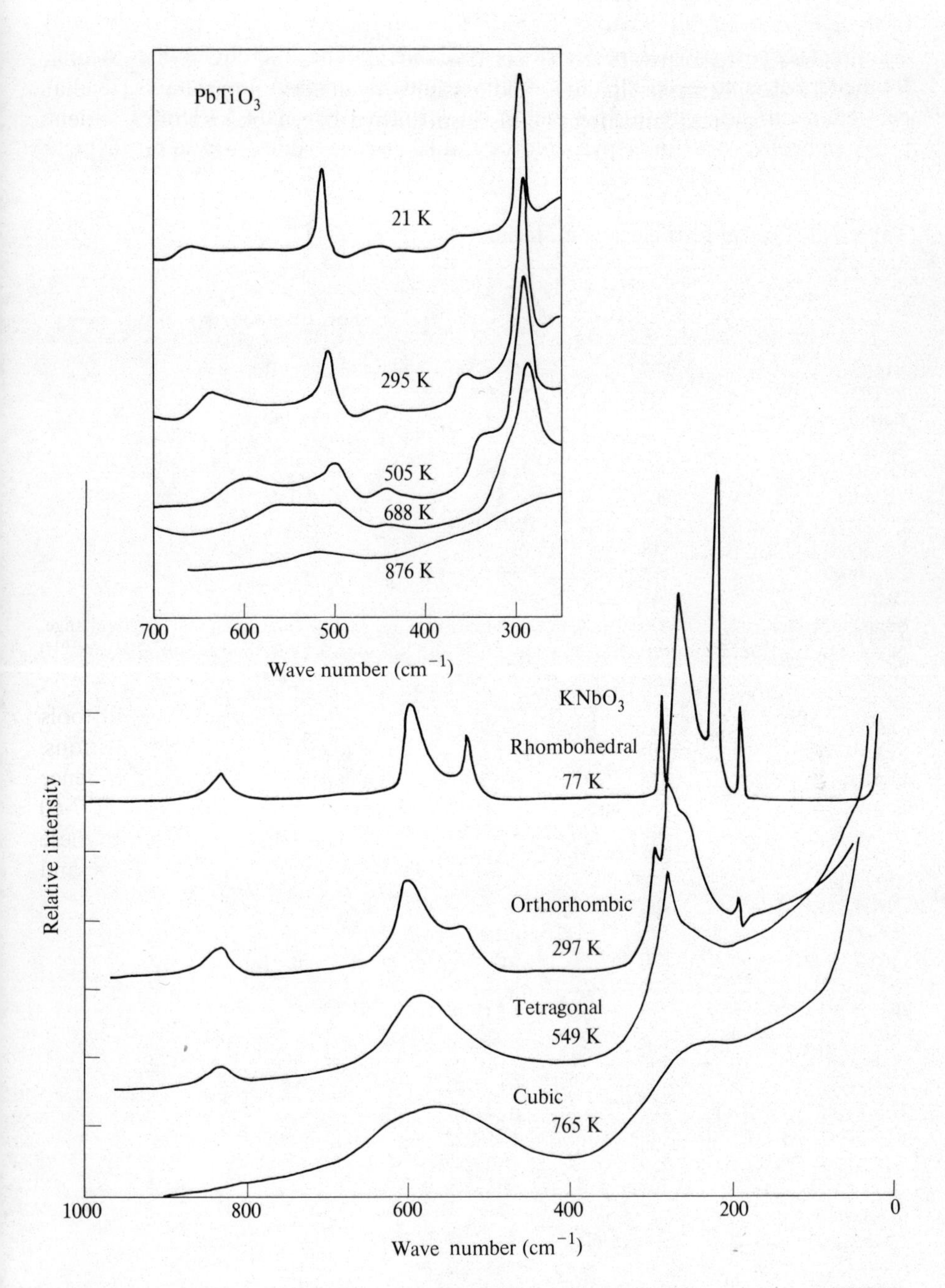

Figure 7-60 Raman spectra of $KNbO_3$ ($T_c \approx 710$ K) in four phases. In the insert, spectra of $PbTiO_3$ ($T_c \approx 760$ K) at different temperatures are shown. (*After Perry and Tornberg.*[162])

Besides $BaTiO_3$ and related perovskites, a large number of compounds belonging to different families have been found to exhibit ferroelectricity. Many of these have been fully characterized in terms of the various properties,[160] and a complete list of known ferroelectrics is available.[159] The different families include Rochelle salt, simple halides, potassium cyanides, ammonium sulfates, fluoroberyllates, nitrates, nitrites, potassium dihydrogen phosphates, selenites, alums, tungsten bronze structures, pyrochlores and layer-type oxides, and so on. Typical

Table 7-3 Typical ferroelectric materials

	T_c (K)	P_s (T, K) (10^{-6} C cm^{-2})	Other transitions (K)
$BaTiO_3$	393	26.0 (296)	183, 278, 1713
$PbTiO_3$	763	> 50 (296)	173?
$KNbO_3$	73	12.0 (73)	627, 835, 913
WO_3	233	—	290, 603, 1013, 1183, 1503
$LiNbO_3$	1483	71 (296)	—
$YbMnO_3$	993	5.6	—
$PbTa_2O_6$	533	10.0 (298)	—
$LiKSr_4Nb_{10}O_{30}$	418	28	—
$Cd_2Nb_2O_7$	185	6.0 (88)	85
$Bi_4Ti_3O_{12}$	948	> 30	—
$Sm_2(MoO_4)_3$	470	0.24 (323)	—
$Ni_3B_7O_{13}Cl$	610	—	—
HCl	98	1.2 (83)	120
DCl	105	—	—
SbSI	293	25 (273)	—
FeS	410	0.7	200, 600
$NaNO_2$	436	8 (373)	168, 438
KNO_3	397, 383	6.3 (394)	—
KH_2PO_4	123	4.75 (96)	—
KD_2PO_4	213	4.83 (180)	—
RbH_2PO_4	147	5.6 (90)	—
$(NH_4)_2SO_4$	224	0.62 (221)	—
K_2SeO_4	93	0.065 (80)	130
$(NH_4)_2HSO_4$	270, 154	0.8 (155)	—
$(ND_4)_2DSO_4$	262, 158	—	—
$(NH_4)_2BeF_4$	176	0.2 (163)	—
$(ND_4)_2BeF_4$	179	—	—
$NaH_3(SeO_3)_2$	194	—	111
$RbHSO_4$	258	0.65 (103)	—
$NH_4Fe(SO_4)_2 . 12H_2O$	88	0.40 (86)	—
$K_4Fe(CN)_6 . 3H_2O$	248.5	1.45 (223)	—
$K_4Fe(CN)_6 . 3D_2O$	255	1.50 (233)	—
$NaKC_4H_4O_6 . 4H_2O$ (Rochelle Salt)	297, 255	0.25 (278)	—
$NaKC_4D_4O_6 . 4D_2O$	308, 251	0.35 (279)	—
$Ca_2B_6O_{11} . 5H_2O$	266	0.65 (203)	—
$BaMgF_4$	none	7.7	—

members of these families are listed along with the ferroelectric Curie temperatures and P_s values in Table 7-3. All these materials, with the exception of ammonium bisulfates, thiourea, and Rochelle salt, exhibit ferroelectricity from 0 K up to T_c. Hydrogen-containing ferroelectrics like Rochelle salt and KH_2PO_4 (KDP) exhibit deuterium isotope effects with T_c increasing on deuteration, the only exceptions being alums and ammonium sulfate. KDP has perhaps the simplest system of hydrogen bonds, and we shall examine its ferroelectric transition in some detail.

The hydrogen bonds in KDP have essentially two directions perpendicular to each other (Fig. 7-61). KDP may be the simplest case of a phase transition of mixed displacive and order–disorder character with one transition triggering the other. It is ferroelectric below 122 K and paraelectric above this temperature. The classification of the transition as a mixed one is based on the following features: (i) The structural change from $Fdd2$ (C_{2v}^{19}) symmetry in the ferroelectric phase to $I\bar{4}2d$ (D_{2d}^{12}) in the paraelectric phase is due to displacements of the K and P ions relative to each other along the c-axis and from a rearrangement of protons. The displacements of heavy ions remove the dielectric polarization. In the ferroelectric phase, the protons are situated asymmetrically with respect to the neighboring oxygens, but ordered throughout the crystal (Fig. 7-61). In the paraelectric phase, the protons appear to have two equilibrium sites along the hydrogen bonds or to be positioned in the centers between the oxygens with a thermal amplitude elongated in the bond direction. (ii) The total entropy change in the transition ($0.422R$) can be understood with the assumption that in the paraelectric phase the protons are distributed on to two sites with the conditions that one

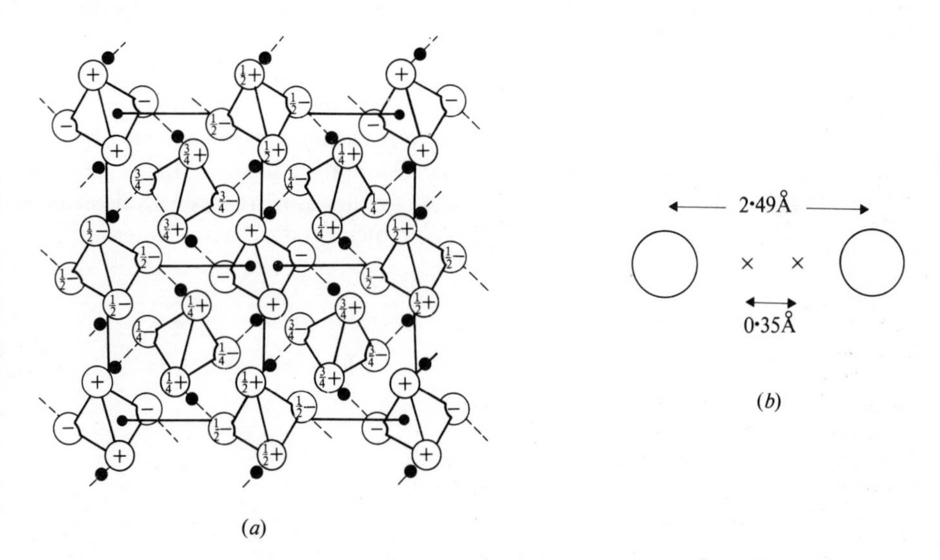

Figure 7-61 (*a*) A view on to the *a–b* plane of KDP in the ferroelectric phase. Rectangles represent oxygen tetrahedra. The P ions in the centres of tetrahedra and the K ions along the *c*-axis are not shown. Hydrogen is denoted by the full dark circles. (*b*) Equilibrium sites (X) between oxygens in the paraelectric phase.

proton is found within each bond and that only two of the four hydrogen-bonded protons around a PO_4 tetrahedron are on sites close to the tetrahedron. (iii) Upon deuteration, T_c shifts from 122 K to 213 K. This large deuterium isotope effect can be understood if the distribution of the protons on the two sites is assumed to be dynamical and due to a tunnelling motion. NMR and other studies support this assumption. NMR measurements have provided valuable information on the proton motion and dynamics of the crystal lattice, and the results have been reviewed by Blinc[163] as well as Gupta and Vijayaraghavan.[164] NMR studies also show the presence of a soft mode that governs the ferroelectric behavior.

It appears that the mechanism of the transition in KDP involves heavy ion displacements triggered by the order–disorder transition in the proton system and this transition then being affected by the ion displacements. If the protons fluctuate between two sites and only two protons are allowed close to a PO_4 group, strong correlations in the fluctuations of neighboring protons are to be expected. One would also expect transitions between the two sites to be coupled to the dynamics of the heavy ion lattice such that the trapping of the protons at the ordered sites may give rise to the shift of the heavy ion positions. Two models have been suggested with regard to the correlations in the proton tunnelling transition, a tunnelling mode model[149,165] and a short-range correlation model.[166] Besides the tunnelling mode (symmetry B_2) there would be three other modes, since there are four hydrogen bonds per unit cell. With regard to the coupling to the heavy ion lattice, a model involving the coupling of the tunnelling mode to ion displacements such that it becomes a part of the optical B_2 lattice mode has been proposed.[149,167] By this coupling, the mode decomposes into two, ω_+ and ω_-; ω_- becomes soft for long wavelengths as T_c is approached. The essential atomic displacements in this soft mode are shown in Fig. 7-62.

There is considerable evidence for a mode of coupled tunnelling and ion displacements. A zone-center soft mode has been found in KD_2PO_4 by neutron spectroscopy,[168] and this mode corresponds to the atomic displacements discussed earlier. A soft mode of B_2 symmetry has been found[169] in the Raman spectrum of KH_2PO_4. A second B_2 optical mode whose frequency increases with decreasing temperature has also been identified.[170] A predicted piezoelectric interaction of

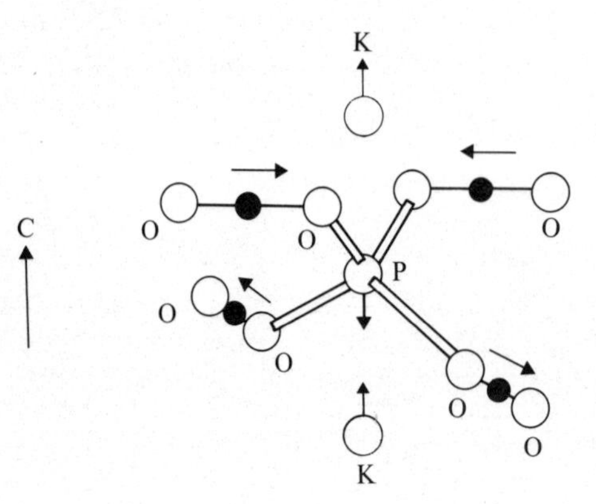

Figure 7-62 Displacements of protons and the K and P ions in the soft mode. The displacements are directed towards the equilibrium positions in the ferroelectric phase.

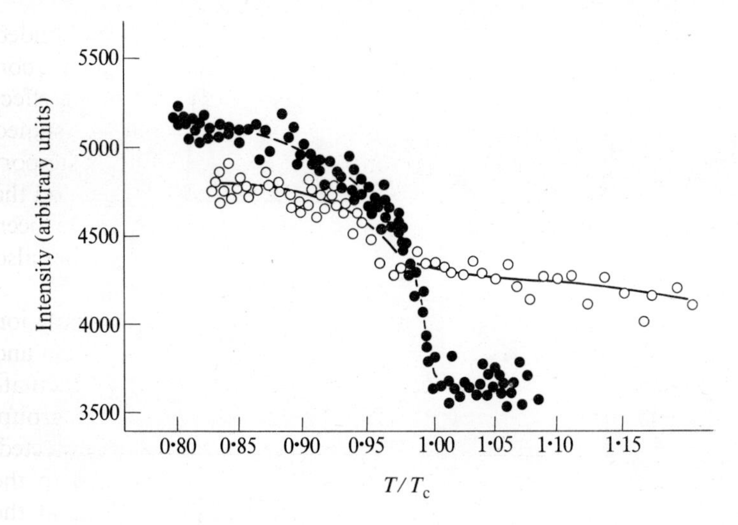

Figure 7-63 Intensity of elastic, incoherent neutron scattering in KDP as a function of temperature ($134\ K \geq T \geq 97.5\ K$). (*After Arsik-Eskinja et al.*[172])

the soft mode with a transverse acoustic mode, causing the transition to occur at a temperature slightly higher than T_c of the soft mode, has been observed by Brillouin scattering.[171] Studies of incoherent neutron scattering[172] (Fig. 7-63) show how, in going from the paraelectric to the ferroelectric phase, the time-averaged density of the individual proton varies from an elongation in the direction of the hydrogen bond to an elongation in the crystallographic c-axis, nearly perpendicular to the hydrogen bonds. The anomalous elongation in the bond direction is due to tunnelling between two equilibrium sites. Coherent scattering studies on KDP indicate a soft mode similar to that in KD_2PO_4, except that the c-component of the proton motion appears to be in phase with K rather than P ions. A comparison between the temperature variation of the soft-mode frequency and of the proton cloud as well as some observations on the effect of an external electric field indicate that the tunnelling lattice-mode coupling model does not entirely explain the mechanism of the transition.

Before closing our discussion of ferroelectric materials, we shall point out the unusual transition found in KNO_3. KNO_3 at room temperature (phase II) has the aragonite structure with D_{2h}^{16} space group and four molecules per unit cell. On heating, KNO_3 (II) transforms around 130°C to structure I closely related to the calcite structure (D_{3d}^{6}) containing two molecules per unit cell. Phase I persists on cooling down to 125°C. On cooling further, a new phase III is found in the range 398–375 K (see Chap. 2). It is this metastable phase III (probable space group C_{3v}^{5}) with one molecule per unit cell that is associated with ferroelectricity.

Ferroelectricity in KNO_3 is due to the ordering of permanent dipoles; the permanent dipole in the paraelectric phase is believed to be due to the displacement of the nitrate ion from the center of the unit cell. The amplitude of this oscillation is 0.4 Å along the c-axis. If we consider instead that the structure is a disordered

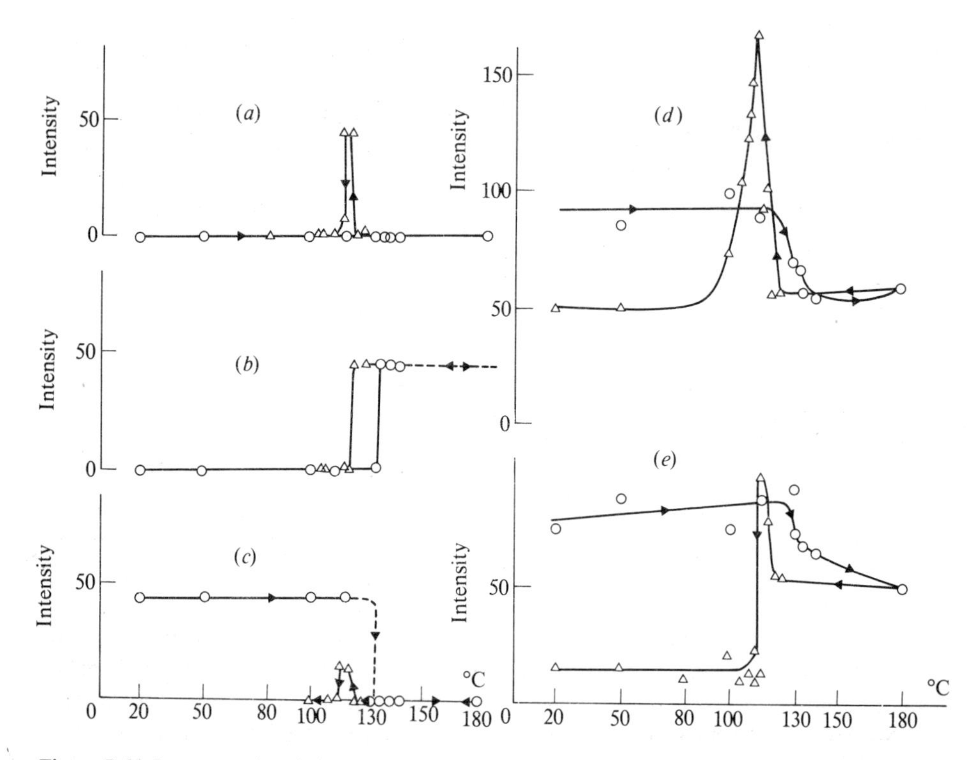

Figure 7-64 Raman study of the phase transitions in KNO_3. Open circles represent data while heating and triangles while cooling. (*After Balkanski et al.*[175]) (*a*) 1352 cm^{-1}, (*b*) 1428 cm^{-1}, (*c*) 1348 cm^{-1}, (*d*) 1054 cm^{-1}, and (*e*) 714 cm^{-1}.

array of nitrate ions displaced from the center of the unit cell, the calculated dipole moment per unit cell is very close to the value of spontaneous polarization in KNO_3. A double potential along the *c*-axis is considered to be a good model for explaining the NO_3^- ion displacement. A statistical theory based on this model and on the assumption of a lattice-dependent internal field explains the origin of the electrostriction effect and observed anomalies at the ferroelectric transition. Infrared and Raman spectroscopy have been employed by a number of workers to study the phase transitions of KNO_3. Thus, the NO_3^- internal vibration frequencies at 720,830 and 1055 cm^{-1} in the infrared spectrum are shifted at the transitions; temperature-dependence is also shown by the lattice vibrations.[173,174] Detailed studies of Raman spectra have been reported by Balkanski and co-workers,[175,176] who have carried out normal vibration analysis of all the three phases of KNO_3 and found close correspondence between normal modes of different phases. They also report a complete KNO_3 phase transition cycle in Raman scattering (Fig. 7-64). On heating, all the ionic and rotational modes in phase II vanish abruptly at 403 K, suggesting that the transition II → I is rather sudden. A notable and continuous broadening of the rotational mode at 83 cm^{-1}

is also observed near T_t. The spectra seem to confirm a C_{3v}^5 space group for the ferroelectric phase (III).

Between 398 and 373 K, on cooling, the spectra suggest that the limits between phase III and II may be less precise. The III → II phase transition probably occurs more gradually than the other phase transition. A broad band around 120 cm^{-1} whose half-width varies with temperature is also seen in the ferroelectric phase. At higher pressures, phase III seems to be more stable, although the lattice dynamical behavior of the II–III transition is similar to that at atmospheric pressure.

Antiferroelectric Materials

These materials show superstructure in the antipolar phase as well as a dielectric constant anomaly and changes in other physical properties at the phase transition (T_c) from the antiferroelectric to the paraelectric phase. Antiferroelectric materials, however, do not show the P–E hysteresis loop. Since the energy difference between antiferroelectric and ferroelectric states is rather small, application of a large electric field, mechanical stress, or compositional variation can induce antiferroelectric materials to become ferroelectric. A typical antiferroelectric material is $PbZrO_3$, which has the perovskite structure. Other examples are $NaNbO_3$, $CsPbCl_3$, $BiFeO_3$, $PbCo_{0.5}W_{0.5}O_3$, $NH_4H_2PO_4$, and $Cu(HCOO)_2 . 4H_2O$. All the known antiferroelectric materials have been tabulated in the literature.[159] Soft modes are also associated with antiferroelectric–paraelectric transitions, as mentioned earlier in this section.

Paired Properties

In recent years, a large number of materials exhibiting other interesting properties besides ferroelectricity have been reported. Such materials have been tabulated and discussed in the literature.[159,177] Typical paired properties with examples are listed below:

Ferroelectric–ferroelastic	$Gd_2(MoO_4)_3$, $KNbO_3$, $BaCoF_4$
Ferroelectric–antiferromagnetic	$YMnO_3$, $HoMnO_3$, $BaCoF_4$, FeS
Ferroelectric–ferromagnetic	$Fe_3B_7O_{13}Cl$, $Bi_9Ti_3Fe_3O_{27}$
Antiferroelectric–antiferromagnetic	$BiFeO_3$, $Cu(HCOO)_2 . 4H_2O$
Ferroelectric–semiconducting	FeS, reduced $SrTiO_3$, and $KTaO_3$, $YMnO_3$
Ferroelectric–superconducting	$SrTiO_3$, GeTe, V_3Si

It is obvious that, depending on the temperature and other conditions, one can have paired properties with materials in the paraelectric or paramagnetic phase as well. Paired properties of the kind shown above have important technological implications.

REFERENCES

1. C. N. R. Rao and K. J. Rao, "Progress in Solid State Chemistry," vol. 4, Pergamon Press, Oxford, 1967; see also C. N. R. Rao, in "Modern Aspects of Solid State Chemistry," ed. C. N. R. Rao, Plenum Press, New York, 1970.
2. C. N. R. Rao and M. Natarajan, "Crystal Structure Transformations in Binary Halides," *NSRDS–NBS Monograph* 41, National Bureau of Standards, Washington, D.C., 1972.
3. C. N. R. Rao and G. V. Subba Rao, "Transition Metal Oxides: Crystal Chemistry, Phase Transitions and Related Aspects," *NSRDS–NBS Monograph* 49, National Bureau of Standards, Washington, D.C., 1974.
4. C. N. R. Rao, B. Prakash, and M. Natarajan, "Crystal Structure Transformations in Inorganic Nitrites, Nitrates and Carbonates," *NSRDS–NBS Monograph* 53, National Bureau of Standards, Washington, D.C., 1975.
5. C. N. R. Rao and B. Prakash, "Crystal Structure Transformations in Inorganic Sulfates, Chromates, Phosphates and Perchlorates," *NSRDS–NBS Monograph* 56, National Bureau of Standards, Washington, D.C., 1975.
6. C. N. R. Rao and K. P. R. Pisharody, "Transition Metal Sulfides," "Progress in Solid State Chemistry," vol. 10, Pergamon Press, Oxford, 1975.
7. J. B. Goodenough and J. M. Longo, "Crystallographic and Magnetic Properties of Perovskite and Perovskite Related Compounds," *Landolt–Börnstein, New Series, Group III*, vol. 4*a*, Springer-Verlag, Berlin, 1970.
8. A. R. Ubbelohde, in "Reactivity in Solids," ed. J. H. de Boer, Elsevier, Amsterdam, 1961.
9. S. W. Kennedy, *J. Appl. Cryst.*, **6,** 293, 1973; *J. Materials Sci.*, **9,** 2053, 1974, and references cited therein.
10. H. M. Rietveld, *J. Appl. Cryst.*, **2,** 65, 1969.
11. K. J. Rao and C. N. R. Rao, *J. Materials Sci.*, **1,** 238, 1966; see also M. Natarajan, A. R. Das, and C. N. R. Rao, *Trans. Faraday Soc.*, **65,** 3081, 1969.
12. C. N. Berglund and H. J. Guggenheim, *Phys. Rev.*, **185,** 1022, 1969.
13. (*a*) C. N. R. Rao, M. Natarajan, G. V. Subba Rao, and R. E. Loehman, *J. Phys. Chem. Solids*, **32,** 1147, 1971; (*b*) G. V. Chandrashekhar, H. L. C. Barros, and J. M. Honig, *Mat. Res. Bull.*, **8,** 367, 1973.
14. J. G. Allpress and J. V. Sanders, *J. Appl. Cryst.*, **6,** 165, 1973.
15. J. B. Goodenough, "Magnetism and the Chemical Bond," John Wiley, New York, 1963.
16. D. H. Martin, "Magnetism in Solids," MIT Press, Cambridge, Mass., 1967.
17. N. Menyuk, in "Modern Aspects of Solid State Chemistry," ed. C. N. R. Rao, Plenum Press, New York, 1970.
18. P. Weiss, *J. Phys.*, **6,** 667, 1907; L. Néel, *Ann. Phys. (Paris)*, **3,** 137, 1948.
19. E. Barthelemy, O. Gorochov, and H. McKinzie, *Mat. Res. Bull.*, **8,** 1401, 1973.
20. W. J. L. Bugers, G. Dowling, J. Sakurai, and R. A. Cowley, "Neutron Inelastic Scattering," *Proceedings of IAEA Symposium, Copenhagen*, 1968, vol. 2, 126.
21. D. S. McClure, in "Excitons, Magnons and Phonons in Molecular Crystals," ed. A. B. Zahlan, Cambridge University Press, London, 1968; see also P. Day et al., *Phys. Rev. Lett.*, **30,** 19, 1973; *Chem. Phys. Lett.*, **19,** 529, 1973.
22. S. P. S. Porto, in "Light Scattering Spectra of Solids," ed. G. B. Wright, Springer Verlag, New York, 1969.
23. P. M. Raccah and J. B. Goodenough, *Phys. Rev.*, **155,** 932, 1967; see also V. G. Bhide, D. S. Rajoria, G. Rama Rao, and C. N. R. Rao, *Phys. Rev.*, **B6,** 1021, 1972.
24. J. Chenavas, J. C. Joubert, and M. Marezio, *Solid State Comm.*, **9,** 1057, 1971.
25. P. W. Anderson, in *Solid State Physics*, vol. 14, ed. F. Seitz and D. Turnbull, Academic Press, New York, 1963.
26. J. Kanamori, *J. Phys. Chem. Solids*, **10,** 87, 1959.
27. J. B. Goodenough, *J. Phys. Chem. Solids*, **30,** 261, 1969.
28. J. B. Goodenough, "Progress in Solid State Chemistry," vol. 5, Pergamon Press, Oxford, 1971.
29. J. B. Goodenough, in "Solid State Chemistry," ed. C. N. R. Rao, Marcel Dekker, New York, 1974.

30. M. D. Banus and T. B. Reed, in "The Chemistry of Extended Defects in Non-Metallic Solids," North-Holland, Amsterdam, 1970.
31. P. F. Bongers, quoted in Ref. 15.
32. See detailed references listed in Ref. 6.
33. D. R. Huffmann and R. L. Wild, *Phys. Rev.*, **148,** 526, 1966.
34. W. S. Carter and K. W. H. Stevens, *Proc. Phys. Soc.*, **B69,** 1006, 1956; **76,** 969, 1960.
35. L. Corliss, N. Elliott, and J. Hastings, *Phys. Rev.*, **104,** 924, 1956.
36. W. Rudorff, G. Walter, and J. Stadler, *Z. Anorg. u Allgem. Chem.*, **297,** 1, 1958.
37. S. Foner, *Phys. Rev.*, **107,** 683, 1957; *J. Phys. Radium*, **20,** 336, 1959.
38. F. M. Johnson and A. H. Nethercot, Jr., *Phys. Rev.*, **104,** 847, 1956; **114,** 705, 1959.
39. S. Foner, *J. Appl. Phys. Supp.*, **32,** 635, 1961.
40. I. E. Dzialoshinsky, *J. Expt. Theoret. Phys. (USSR)*, **33,** 807, 1957.
41. F. J. Morin, *Phys. Rev.*, **78,** 819, 1950.
42. D. J. Robbins and P. Day, *Chem. Phys. Lett.*, **19,** 529, 1973.
43. P. H. Carr and S. Foner, *J. Appl. Phys. Suppl.*, **31,** 344S, 1960.
44. T. Shinjo and K. Kosuge, *J. Phys. Soc. Japan*, **21,** 2622, 1966.
45. K. Dwight, R. W. German, N. Menyuk, and A. Wold, *J. Appl. Phys.*, **33,** suppl. 3, 1341, 1962.
46. B. van Laar, *Phys. Rev.*, **156,** 654, 1967.
47. K. Dwight, N. Menyuk, and J. A. Kafalas, *Phys. Rev.*, **B2,** 3630, 1970.
48. T. J. A. Popma, C. Haas, and B. van Laar, *J. Phys. Chem. Solids*, **32,** 581, 1971.
49. H. F. Franzen, D. M. Strachen, and R. G. Barnes, *J. Solid State Chem.*, **7,** 374, 1973.
50. J. P. Delamaire, H. Le Brusq, and F. Marion, *C. R. Acad. Sci.*, **C272,** 2144, 1971.
51. F. Grønvold, H. Heraldsen, B. Pedersen, and T. Tufte, *Rec. Chim. Min.*, **6,** 215, 1969.
52. A. B. DeVries and C. Haas, *J. Phys. Chem. Solids*, **34,** 651, 1973.
53. E. Hirahara and M. Murakami, *J. Phys. Chem. Solids*, **7,** 281, 1958; *J. Phys. Soc. Japan*, **13,** 1407, 1958.
54. C. B. Van den Berg, *Ferroelectrics*, **4,** 117, 1972.
55. E. F. Bertaut, *Acta Cryst.*, **6,** 557, 1953.
56. J. B. Goodenough, *Phys. Rev.*, **164,** 785, 1967; *J. Appl. Phys.*, **39,** 403, 1968.
57. N. Menyuk, K. Dwight, J. A. Kafalas, and J. B. Goodenough, *J. Appl. Phys.*, **40,** 1324, 1969.
58. J. B. MacChesney, H. J. Williams, J. F. Potter, and R. C. Sherwood, *Phys. Rev.*, **164,** 779, 1967.
59. P. M. Raccah and J. B. Goodenough, *J. Appl. Phys.*, **39,** 1209, 1968.
60. V. G. Bhide, D. S. Rajoria, V. G. Jadhao, G. R. Rao, and C. N. R. Rao, *Phys. Rev.*, **12B,** 2832, 1975.
61. D. H. Saunderson, C. G. Windsor, G. A. Briggs, M. T. Evans, and E. A. Hutchison, "Neutron Inelastic Scattering," *Proceedings of the Grenoble Symposium, IAEA*, 1972, p. 639, and references cited therein.
62. H. B. Mathur, in "Solid State Chemistry," ed. C. N. R. Rao, Marcel Dekker, New York, 1974, and references cited therein.
63. D. G. Wickham and W. J. Croft, *J. Phys. Chem. Solids*, **7,** 351, 1958.
64. P. A. Miles, W. B. Westphal, and A. von Hippel, *Rev. Mod. Phys.*, **29,** 279, 1957.
65. E. J. W. Verwey and coworkers, *J. Chem. Phys.*, **15,** 174, 181, 1947.
66. T. Riste and L. Tenzer, *J. Phys. Chem. Solids*, **19,** 117, 1961.
67. M. T. Evans, E. Warming, and G. L. Squires, "Neutron Inelastic Scattering," *Proceedings of the Grenoble Symposium, IAEA*, 1972, p. 649.
68. W. Kundig, H. Bommel, G. Constabaris, and R. H. Lindquist, *Phys. Rev.*, **142,** 327, 1966.
69. W. Kundig and R. S. Hargrove, *Solid State Comm.*, **7,** 223, 1969.
70. T. F. Connolly and E. D. Copenhaver, *ORNL-RMIC-7* (Rev. 2), Materials Information Center, Oak Ridge National Laboratory, 1970.
71. J. M. Honig, in "Modern Aspects of Solid State Chemistry," ed. C. N. R. Rao, Plenum Press, New York, 1970.
72. F. J. Morin, *Phys. Rev. Lett.*, **3,** 34, 1959.
73. A. Wilson, "Theory of Metals," Cambridge University Press, London, 1954.
74. W. H. Kleiner, *MIT Lincoln Laboratory, Solid State Research Report 3*, 1967.

75. J. B. Goodenough, *Czech. J. Phys.*, **17B,** 304, 1967.
76. R. W. Gurney and N. F. Mott, *Proc. Phys. Soc.*, **49A,** 32, 1937.
77. J. Appel, *Solid State Phys.*, **21,** 193, 1968.
78. E. P. Wigner, *Trans. Faraday Soc.*, **34,** 678, 1938.
79. N. F. Mott, *Proc. Phys. Soc.*, **62A,** 416, 1949.
80. N. F. Mott, *Canad. J. Phys.*, **34,** 1356, 1956; *Nuovo Cimento,* **7,** 312, 1958; *Phil. Mag.*, **6,** 287, 1961; *Adv. Phys.*, **16,** 49, 1967.
81. D. B. McWhan and J. P. Remeika, *Phys. Rev.*, **B2,** 3734, 1970, and other papers by McWhan and others in the same volume.
82. J. M. Honig, G. V. Chandrashekhar, and A. P. B. Sinha, *Phys. Rev. Lett.*, **32,** 13, 1974; *Phys. Lett.*, **47A,** 185, 1974.
83. B. K. Chakravarty, *J. Solid State Chem.*, **12,** 376, 1975.
84. J. Hubbard, *Proc. Roy. Soc.*, **A276,** 238, 1963; **A277,** 237, 1964; **A281,** 401, 1964; **A285,** 542, 1965 and **A296,** 100, 1966.
85. C. N. R. Rao and G. V. Subba Rao, *Physica stat. solidi,* **1a,** 597, 1970.
86. Articles in *Rev. Mod. Phys.*, **40,** 673, 1968.
87. N. F. Mott, "Metal Insulator Transitions," Taylor & Francis, London, 1974.
88. G. Villeneue and M. Drillon, quoted in Ref. 83.
89. M. Marezio, D. B. McWhan, J. P. Remeika, and P. D. Dernier, *Phys. Rev.*, **B5,** 2541, 1972.
90. D. Adler, *Rev. Mod. Phys.*, **40,** 714, 1968.
91. B. I. Halperin and T. M. Rice, *Solid State Phys.*, **21,** 115, 1968.
92. D. B. McWhan and T. M. Rice, *Phys. Rev. Lett.*, **22,** 887, 1969.
93. J. C. Slater, *Phys. Rev.*, **82,** 538, 1951.
94. D. Adler and H. Brooks, *Phys. Rev.*, **155,** 826, 1967.
95. D. Adler, J. Feinleib, H. Brooks, and W. Paul, *Phys. Rev.*, **155,** 851, 1967.
96. J. Feinleib and W. Paul, *Phys. Rev.*, **155,** 841, 1967.
97. N. F. Mott, *Rev. Mod. Phys.*, **40,** 677, 1968.
98. E. Hanamura, *Rev. Mod. Phys.*, **40,** 744, 1968.
99. G. J. Hyland, *J. Solid State Chem.*, **2,** 318, 1970.
100. L. M. Felicov and J. C. Kimball, *Phys. Rev. Lett.*, **22,** 997, 1969.
101. R. A. Bari, *J. Solid State Chem.*, **12,** 383, 1975.
102. J. B. Goodenough, *Mat. Res. Bull.*, **2,** 37, 165, 1967.
103. J. B. Goodenough, *Proc. of 10th Intern. Conf. on Phys. of Semiconductors, Cambridge, Mass.*, 1970.
104. L. K. Keys and L. N. Mulay, *Phys. Rev.*, **154,** 453, 1967.
105. C. N. R. Rao, S. Ramdas, R. E. Lochman, and J. M. Honig, *J. Solid State Chem.*, **3,** 83, 1971.
106. M. Marezio, *J. Solid State Chem.*, **6,** 213, 1973.
107. S. Kachi, K. Kosuge, and H. Okinaka, *J. Solid State Chem.*, **6,** 258, 1973.
108. C. N. R. Rao, G. R. Rao, and G. V. S. Rao, *J. Solid State Chem.*, **6,** 340, 1973; see also A. K. Cheetam and C. N. R. Rao, *Acta Cryst.*, **B32,** 1579, 1976.
109. S. M. Shapiro, J. D. Axe, G. Shirane, and P. Raccah, *Solid State Comm.*, **15,** 377, 1974.
110. G. Thornton, A. F. Orchard, and C. N. R. Rao, *Phys. Lett.*, **54A,** 235, 1975.
111. J. T. Sparks and T. Komoto, *Rev. Mod. Phys.*, **40,** 752, 1968.
112. G. A. Briggs, C. Duffill, M. T. Hutchings, R. D. Lowde, N. S. Satyamurthy, D. H. Saunderson, M. W. Stringfellow, W. B. Waeber, and C. G. Windsor, "Neutron Inelastic Scattering," *Proceedings of the Grenoble Symposium, IAEA*, 1972, p. 669.
113. A. Jayaraman, V. Narayanamurti, E. Bucher, and R. G. Maines, *Phys. Rev. Lett.*, **25,** 368, 1970; see also *Phys. Rev. Lett.*, **25,** 430, 1970; A. Chatterjee, A. K. Singh, A. Jayaraman, and E. Bucher, *Phys. Rev. Lett.*, **27,** 1571, 1971.
114. A. Jayaraman, E. Bucher, P. D. Dernier, and L. D. Longinotti, *Phys. Rev. Lett.*, **31,** 700, 1973.
115. A. Jayaraman, *Phys. Rev. Lett.*, **29,** 1674, 1972.
116. J. A. Wilson, F. J. Disalvo, and S. Mahajan, *Adv. Phys.*, **24,** 117, 1974.
117. A. W. Overhauser, *Phys. Rev.*, **B3,** 3173, 1971; **167,** 691, 1968.
118. W. L. McMilan, *Phys. Rev.*, **12,** 1187, 1197, 1975.
119. D. S. Chapin, J. A. Kafalas, and J. M. Honig, *J. Phys. Chem.*, **69,** 1402, 1965.

120. C. N. R. Rao and V. G. Bhide, *Proc. of the 19th Conference on Magnetism and Magnetic Materials, Boston*, American Institute of Physics, 1974.
121. C. N. R. Rao, *J. Indian Chem. Soc.*, **51,** 979, 1974.
122. D. S. Rajoria, V. G. Bhide, G. R. Rao, and C. N. R. Rao, *J. Chem. Soc. Faraday II*, **70,** 512, 1974; see also *Phys. Rev.*, **B8,** 5028, 1973.
123. V. G. Jadhao, R. M. Singru, G. N. Rao, D. Bahadur, and C. N. R. Rao, *J. Phys. Chem. Solids*, **37,** 113, 1975; see also *J. Chem. Soc., Faraday II*, **71,** 1885, 1975.
124. G. Thornton, A. F. Orchard, and C. N. R. Rao, *J. Phys. C.*, **9,** 1991, 1976.
125. P. L. Gai and C. N. R. Rao, *Mat. Res. Bull.*, **10,** 787, 1975.
126. P. W. Anderson, *Phys. Rev.*, **109,** 1492, 1958.
127. C. N. R. Rao, V. G. Bhide, and N. F. Mott, *Phil. Mag.*, **32,** 1277, 1975.
128. N. F. Mott, *Adv. Phys.*, **21,** 816, 1972.
129. N. F. Mott, M. Pepper, S. Pollitt, R. H. Wallis, and C. J. Adkins, *Proc. Roy. Soc.*, **A345,** 169, 1975.
130. W. A. Little, *Phys. Rev.*, **134,** 1416, 1964.
131. R. E. Peierls, "Quantum Theory of Solids," Clarendon Press, Oxford, 1955.
132. A. S. Berenblyum, L. I. Buravov, M. L. Khidekel, I. F. Shchegolev, and E. B. Yakinov, *Zh. Eksper. Teor. Fiz. Pisma*, **13,** 619, 1971.
133. L. B. Coleman, M. J. Cohen, D. J. Sandman, F. G. Yamagishi, A. F. Garito, and A. J. Heeger, *Solid State Comm.*, **12,** 1125, 1973.
134. P. M. Horn and D. Rimai, *Phys. Rev. Lett.*, **36,** 809, 1976.
135. L. N. Bulaevskii, *Usp. Fiz. Nauk SSR*, **115,** 263, 1975.
136. R. Englman, "The Jahn–Teller Effect in Molecules and Crystals," John Wiley, London, 1972.
137. W. Rehwald, *Adv. Phys.*, **22,** 721, 1973.
138. G. A. Gehring and K. A. Gehring, *Repts. on Progr. in Phys.*, **38,** 1, 1975.
139. E. Pytte and K. W. H. Stevens, *Phys. Rev. Lett.*, **27,** 862, 1971.
140. R. J. Elliott, R. T. Harley, W. Hayes, and S. R. P. Smith, *Proc. Roy. Soc.*, **A328,** 217, 1972.
141. A. H. Cooke, D. M. Martin, and M. R. Wells, *Solid State Comm.*, **9,** 519, 1971; A. H. Cooke, S. J. Swithenby, and M. R. Wells, *Solid State Comm.*, **10,** 265, 1972.
142. G. Will, H. Gobel, C. F. Sampson, and J. B. Forsyth, *Phys. Lett.*, **38A,** 207, 1972.
143. P. J. Becker, M. J. M. Leask, and R. N. Tyte, *J. Phys. C.*, **5,** 2027, 1972.
144. R. L. Melchur and B. A. Scott, *Phys. Rev. Lett.*, **28,** 67, 1972.
145. R. J. Birgeneau, J. K. Kjems, G. Shirane, and L. G. Van Uitert, *Phys. Rev.*, **B10,** 2512, 1974.
146. R. T. Harley, W. Hayes, A. M. Perry, and S. R. P. Smith, *J. Phys. C.*, **6,** 2382, 1973.
147. J. Feder and E. Pytte, *Phys. Rev.*, **B8,** 3978, 1973.
148. M. D. Sturge, E. Cohen, L. G. Van Uitert, and R. P. van Stapele, *Phys. Rev.*, **B11,** 4768, 1975.
149. W. Cochran, *Adv. Phys.*, **9,** 387, 1960; **10,** 401, 1961; **18,** 157, 1969.
150. P. W. Anderson, "Fizika dielektrikov," ed. G. I. Skanavi, Akad Nauk SSR, Moscow, 1959.
151. C. Kittel, *Phys. Rev.*, **82,** 729, 1951.
152. L. D. Landau, "Collected Papers of L. D. Landau," ed. D. ter Haar, Gordon and Breach, New York, 1954; see also L. D. Landau and E. M. Lifshitz, "Statistical Physics," Pergamon Press, Oxford, 1958.
153. A. F. Devonshire, *Phil. Mag.*, **40,** 1040, 1949; **42,** 1065, 1951.
154. F. Fatuzzo and W. J. Merz, "Ferroelectricity," John Wiley, New York, 1967.
155. R. Blinc and B. Zeks, "Soft Modes in Ferroelectrics and Antiferroelectrics," North-Holland, Amsterdam, 1974.
156. C. Haas, *Phys. Rev.*, **140,** 863, 1940.
157. E. M. Lifshitz, *Zh. eksp. teor fiz.*, **11,** 255, 269, 1941.
158. I. S. Zheludev and A. L. Shuvalov, *Kristallographia*, **1,** 681, 1956; see also A. S. Sonin and I. S. Zheludev, **4,** 487, 1959.
159. E. C. Subbarao, in "Solid State Chemistry," ed. C. N. R. Rao, Marcel Dekker, New York, 1974.
160. F. Jona and G. Shirane, "Ferroelectric Crystals," Pergamon Press, Oxford, 1962.
161. (*a*) G. Shirane and A. Takeda, *J. Phys. Soc. Japan*, **7,** 1, 1952; (*b*) V. G. Bhide and M. S. Multhani, *Phys. Rev.*, **139,** 1983, 1965.

162. C. H. Perry and N. E. Tornberg, in "Light Scattering Spectra of Solids," ed. G. B. Wright, Springer Verlag, New York, 1969.
163. R. Blinc, in "Advances in Magnetic Resonance," vol. 3, ed. J. S. Waugh, Academic Press, New York, 1968.
164. L. C. Gupta and R. Vijayaraghavan, in "Solid State Chemistry," ed. C. N. R. Rao, Marcel Dekker, New York, 1974.
165. M. Tokunaga, *Progr. Theor. Phys. Osaka*, **36,** 857, 1966.
166. J. Villain and S. Aubry, *Phys. stat. solidi*, **33,** 337, 1969.
167. K. Kobayashi, *J. Phys. Soc. Japan*, **24,** 497, 1968.
168. J. Skalyo, Jr., B. C. Frazer, and G. Shirane, *Phys. Rev*., **B1,** 278, 1970.
169. I. P. Kaminow and T. C. Damen, *Phys. Rev. Lett*., **20,** 1105, 1968.
170. J. P. Coignac and H. Poulet, *J. Phys*., **32,** 679, 1971.
171. E. M. Brody and H. Z. Cummins, *Phys. Rev. Lett*., **21,** 1263, 1968.
172. M. Arsic-Eskinja, H. Grimm, and H. Stiller, "Neutron Inelastic Scattering," *IAEA Symposium*, Grenoble, 1972, p. 825.
173. R. K. Khanna, J. Lingschied, and J. C. Decius, *Spectrochim. Acta*, **20,** 1109, 1964.
174. A. A. Shultin and S. V. Karpov, *J. Phys. Chem. Solids*, **30,** 1981, 1969.
175. M. Balkanski, M. K. Teng, and M. Nusimovici, *Phys. Rev*., **176,** 1098, 1968; also in "Light Scattering Spectra of Solids," ed. G. B. Wright, Springer Verlag, New York, 1969.
176. M. K. Teng, M. Balkanski, and J. F. Mourey, *Solid State Comm*., **9,** 465, 1971.
177. H. Schmid, in "Magnetoelectric Interaction Phenomena in Crystals," ed. A. J. Freeman and H. Schmid, Gordon and Breach, New York, 1975.

INDEX